Encyclopedia of Sex and Gender

Encyclopedia of Sex and Gender

VOLUME 1

a–c

Fedwa Malti-Douglas
EDITOR IN CHIEF

MACMILLAN REFERENCE USA
A part of Gale, Cengage Learning

GALE
CENGAGE Learning

Detroit • New York • San Francisco • New Haven, Conn • Waterville, Maine • London

GALE
CENGAGE Learning™

Encyclopedia of Sex and Gender

Fedwa Malti-Douglas, Editor in Chief

For more information, contact
Macmillan Reference USA
A part of Gale, Cengage Learning
27500 Drake Rd.
Farmington Hills, MI 48331-3535
Or you can visit our Internet site at
gale.cengage.com

LIBRARY OF CONGRESS CATALOGING-IN-PUBLICATION DATA

Encyclopedia of sex and gender / Fedwa Malti-Douglas, editor in chief.
p. cm
Includes bibliographical references and index.
ISBN 978-0-02-865960-2 (set hardcover) – ISBN 978-0-02-865961-9 (v. 1 hardcover) — ISBN 978-0-02-865962-6 (v. 2 hardcover) — ISBN 978-0-02-865963-3 (v. 3 hardcover) – ISBN 978-0-02-865964-0 (v. 4 hardcover
1. Sex–Encyclopedias. 2. Sex–Cross-cultural studies. I. Malti-Douglas, Fedwa.
HQ16.E52 2008
306.703–dc22

2007020796

0-02-865960-0 (set)
0-02-865961-9 (v. 1)
0-02-865962-7 (v. 2)
0-02-865963-5 (v. 3)
0-02-865964-3 (v. 4)
This title is also available as an e-book.
ISBN 978-0-02-866115-5, 0-02-866115-X
Contact your Gale representative for ordering information.

Printed in the United States of America
2 3 4 5 6 7 14 13 12 11 10 09 08

Editorial Board

Editorial and Production Staff

PROJECT EDITOR

Deirdre S. Blanchfield

CONTRIBUTING EDITORS

Monica M. Hubbard
Jennifer York Stock

EDITORIAL TECHNICAL SUPPORT

Mark Drouillard
Mike Weaver

MANUSCRIPT EDITORS

Kari Bethel
Judith Clinebell
Laurie J. Edwards
Jessica Hornik Evans
William Kaufman
Sharon R. Gunton
Jen Hirt
Elizabeth Inserra
Christine Kelley
Eric Linderman
Eric Lowenkron
Raymond Lukens
David E. Salamie
Eleanor Stanford
Marie L. Thompson
John Yohalem

PROOFREADER

John Krol

INDEXER

Laurie Andriot

PRODUCT DESIGN

Pamela A.E. Galbreath

IMAGING

Lezlie Light

GRAPHIC ART

GGS Information Services

RIGHTS ACQUISITION MANAGEMENT

Leitha Etheridge-Sims

COMPOSITION

Evi Abou-El-Seoud
Mary Beth Trimper

MANUFACTURING

Drew Kalasky

DIRECTOR, NEW PRODUCT DEVELOPMENT

Hélène Potter

PUBLISHER

Jay Flynn

Contents

Preface

Although the vast amount of media attention devoted to sex may make it seem more important than ever, in some ways sex is actually less important today than ever before. In the developed world, there has been a trend away from the wide-open spaces of agrarian settings and toward overcrowded cities, which means that most couples no longer have an urgent need to reproduce to provide offspring to take care of them when they get older. With fewer fields to till, infant mortality reduced, and improved health care allowing people to work for many more years, having a large number of children is no longer the standard method of retirement planning. So although at one time the ability to limit pregnancies would have had catastrophic results, today's birth rates reflect this new reality, be it voluntarily as in Europe, or involuntarily as in China. And now, with artificial insemination, we don't even need the sex act to make babies. So if we humans were ever to lose the ability to have sex at some point in the future (heaven forbid!), these new technologies would allow our kind to continue to inhabit the earth for as long as the earth was inhabitable.

But whereas sex has lost its importance in its primary sense, it has grown in importance in another, keeping people together as couples, leading to its current state where we humans are having more sex than ever before. I don't need a study to prove that because one reason for this increase is simply the fact that we're living longer, and so each of us is having more sex than did past generations over the course of our longer lifetimes. But the added leisure time in our modern societies also frees us to put more focus on sex, so while the sex act has been decoupled somewhat from its original purpose, it remains very much at the center of our daily lives.

Many of these changes have taken place over generations, but there have been significant changes with regard to sex that have occurred in only the past half century or so. I'll even take some credit for one or two of those. One significant change is that so many more women know now that they should be enjoying sex rather than just putting up with it in order to have a family. In my lectures, I often make reference to a Victorian mother who, when telling her about-to-be-married daughter about the birds and bees, would say, "Lie back and think of England." But while those dark ages continue for too many women, millions of others have made the transition to being sexually fulfilled by acquiring the knowledge needed to have orgasms, and the independence to demand them from their partners. So the pleasure that comes from engaging in sexual relations, which has historically been more important for one gender than the other, can be shared now by both men and women equally. And one could say that this happened just in time, because as the reproductive role of sex lessens, its role in keeping parents together has become more important.

It has always been important for children to have two parents for their survival, but historically, children were given adult roles much earlier than they are today. In order to support a child through the college years, parents must find ways of cementing their relationship over a much longer period of time. And sex is an important part of the glue that keeps partners together. That is not to say that many divorced couples do not send their children to college, but it becomes much more of a financial burden if the funds have to come from two separate households. So as the reproductive aspects of sex have been sinking in importance, it is the pleasurable aspects for both males and females that have been rising to the top. This is especially true in societies where women have increasingly been able to support themselves. When women were financially dependent on their partners, they had less leverage when it came to asking for sexual satisfaction. But now that women can survive when living alone, the sexual aspects of a marriage, for both partners, play a more important role in their combined desire to remain a functioning couple.

This encyclopedia is not only about the sexual act, but also about gender, which traditionally stood for males and females but these days may be open to further interpretations, as sexual orientation may not necessarily follow one path linked to the physical attributes of male and female.

Just as sex has changed in its importance over the last half century, so has gender. Not that long ago everyone's place in the world was determined, to some degree, by their gender. Every year that goes by, that becomes less and less true, and so conversely, as with sex, knowing about gender becomes more and more important. If all the old assumptions are wrong, then we all have a duty to learn about the new possibilities. And to do that, you need as up-to-date a road map as you can find, and that is exactly what you will find inside these many pages.

When I first went on the radio and used words like *penis* and *vagina*, people were shocked. Today there is hardly a word in the English language that would shock anyone. And yet so many people, young and old, have shocking lacunae in their knowledge of sex and gender. I want to commend Macmillan and Fedwa Malti-Douglas for putting this magnificent set of volumes together, and I hope that the result will be that when it comes out, that gap in knowledge will become somewhat smaller.

Dr. Ruth Westheimer
September 2007

Introduction

NEED FOR THE ENCYCLOPEDIA

No issues are more debated today than those that swirl around the subjects of sex and gender; in debates that often seem to generate more heat than light. In this area of rapid social change, and equally rapid progress in scientific knowledge and understanding, the necessity of a comprehensive encyclopedia of sex and gender is overwhelming. The need is critical for a reference work that covers in detail the territory from biology to culture (by way of the social sciences and the humanities), that examines our swiftly changing present in the light of new understandings of our past, and one that places all these debates in a global perspective.

"Sex" and "gender." Two words that can have a powerful effect, whether taken separately or together, on those who encounter them. They, and the discussions around them, may be anathema to some. These subjects may be taboo for others. There are still many who, under the guise of a defense of traditional mores, believe that by shutting their eyes and ears (while loudly opening their mouths) they can stop the results of centuries of social evolution. To those who think that sex, in all its variety, is a subject best not talked about (lest talking lead to action), the *Encyclopedia of Sex and Gender* stands as a challenge. Closets are not healthy places; and where there are problems, as there are in all aspects of human life, they are best confronted in the open, not buried behind walls of ignorance and denial. Fortunately, the voices of censorship are losing their power as a swiftly growing segment of the population embraces knowledge of sex and gender, seeing in this knowledge a mode of liberation and a recognition that the topics treated under the rubrics of sex and gender have been central to all world cultures from the beginning of time. Perhaps had the snake in the Garden of Eden not tempted Eve, she might not have tempted Adam to eat of the fruit of the tree of knowledge. Once that door was opened, it could not be closed. Whatever else it may imply, this ancient story transmits two basic truths: the relation of sex and knowledge, and the fact that we cannot go back.

Now, in the first decade of the twenty-first century, it seems timely and appropriate to produce an *Encyclopedia of Sex and Gender*. It has been over half a century since the publication of Dr. Alfred Kinsey's groundbreaking and controversial studies of sexuality in the human male and the human female. Much ink has been spilled over what constitutes sex and sexuality. And it seems that we, as human animals, have barely begun to imagine the ramifications of the still unfolding area of sex. Our human emotions are being put to the test by the rapidly expanding areas of technology. *Can We Fall in Love with a Machine?* was the title of a multi-media exhibit at the Wood Street Galleries in Pittsburgh in 2006.

SCOPE AND CONTENTS: WHAT IS SEX AND GENDER?

Our task is not made easier by the fact that the word "gender" (especially as distinguished from sex) has a distinct relationship to the English language. In French, for example, when one wishes to express the idea of masculine and feminine social roles, one is thrown back on the word for sex. A similar situation pertains with Arabic. All this is because gender, as it is used in this encyclopedia, is a recent construct in English. The English term "gender" used to refer to a linguistic category of masculine and feminine. But grammatical gender in English can be misleading, explaining why the jump from grammar to human behavior is easier in English than in other languages. English grammatical gender encourages the blurring of boundaries. For, in English we have natural or biological gender. Nouns with a male or female sex (e.g., he, she, mother, father, ewe, ram) carry the appropriate grammatical gender. Nouns deemed sexless (e.g., table, cloud) are neuter. Grammatical gender carries sexual information. Not so in other languages. In most, grammatical gender is merely a division of nouns into categories. While a few terms may have been pulled towards biological sex (e.g., *le père, la mère*), the overwhelming majority of nouns is classified according to morphology, not content. A famous example is that the German term for a young woman, Fräulein, is grammatically neuter not feminine. Did Americans who developed the new thinking about gender merely exploit the resources of their language or did the particularities of their language influence the creation of their categories?

As will become clear from this encyclopedia, gender is a crucial term for the way in which societies organize sexual categories, sexual roles, sexual behavior, sexual identification, and so on. Gender Studies has appeared as an avatar, or more correctly an evolution, from Women's Studies. That is, a disciplinary area still practiced today (and as such a major intellectual force in this encyclopedia) and has traditionally concentrated on women's history, the status, image, and role of women in various societies, cultural forms, etc. Gender Studies is more englobing and its paradigms are at the same time more flexible and more complex than those traditionally associated with the discipline of Women's Studies. To take but one example: scholars and scientists have become aware that even biology (not to speak of society) is not so simply dichotomous as we used to think it was, i.e. the male sex with its attendant chromosomes or the female sex, also with its attendant chromosomes. Science has broadened our universe, at the same time as it has complicated it. Now we must include a category of intersex, in which human chromosomes are not identical to those of the male and female of the species but rather represent a mixture of the two. Intersex individuals are not fertile, and therefore cannot propagate themselves. But they can live normal sexual lives, with some phenotypically females free of the menses that plague women for a large part of their existence.

Science, biology, and technology have also permitted something that might well have been surprising to nineteenth and early twentieth scientists and physicians. Even Sigmund Freud, the father of psychoanalysis, might raise his eyebrows at bodily transformations that have become part and parcel of our gendered universe. When Donald McCloskey, a prominent economist, decided to change his sexual identity through surgery and hormonal treatments from male to female, in other words to become what we today consider a transsexual individual, his family had him arrested for insanity. Today, Donald lives happily as Deirdre and retains her position as a prominent social scientist.

It is younger generations of individuals, those in their teens and twenties, who have led the revolution to change sexual mores, at the same time transforming gender into a much more elastic category. A masculine young woman, already sporting short hair and dressed in blue jeans, may one day decide to no longer play what was left of the female role that society had assigned to her, and instead adopt the identity of a male with a simple first-name change. I experienced this personally in my office and had to constantly apologize to the male when

I called him by his previous female name. He laughed it off, adding that everyone gets him confused.

Gender confusion. This is not identical to hermaphroditism, in which a person possesses some combination of male and female genitalia and secondary sexual characteristics. Hermaphrodites have existed for as long as humans have. It is simply that in earlier centuries medicine, lacking the combination we possess today of biological and technological means, relegated the unusual physical types to their own categories. The great French historian, Michel Foucault, who has done so much to make us rethink our ideas about sexuality, isolated and popularized the account of a young French hermaphrodite, whose story has even become a film.

The unusual (and the perverse) have always been part and parcel of our ideas on sex and gender. Prominent authors like Jean Genet and artists like Andy Warhol played on the edges of that world. And let us not forget Sado-Masochism, named after the famous Marquis de Sade and the physician Sacher-Masoch. And while many have traditionally combined the exotic with the sexually forbidden, today's world with its lightning-fast modes of communication and transportation can easily move a pedophile from California to East Asia where he can fulfill his fantasies at a far lower cost and less danger than in his home country. What is sometimes referred to today as "sex tourism" is an enormous industry, part of the new globalized face of the far older commercialization of sex.

Yet, even the term "sex" is not without its ambiguities. To start with, it has two basic meanings. Sex is biological: the divisions of individuals in a species into two distinct groups such that one from each group must come together and exchange genetic material to create the next generation. Sexual reproduction is an elegant and creative way of multiplying the genetic variation needed for evolution. It is no surprise, therefore, that with the exception of benighted creatures at the lowest rungs of the evolutionary ladder, sex makes the world go around. The sexes, therefore, are biological categories dividing most animals, humans included.

But sex is also an act or acts, specifically those necessary to accomplish sexual reproduction. Again, not so simple. Many human cultures have classified as sexual, acts which of themselves do not lead to reproduction. The fact that some of these acts may have been characterized as more or less proper, shameful, or even unnatural does not change their assimilation to sexual practices. A recent American scandal makes a fine example. For the purposes of Paula Jones's suit against President William Jefferson Clinton, the court adopted the so-called Jones definition of sexual acts, a definition that included lots of non-procreative activities. President Clinton tried to evade the charge of perjury by claiming that what he indulged in with Monica Lewinsky did not constitute sex according to the Jones definition. Few found his explanation credible. But there was a sense to his more general argument that he had not had sex with Monica Lewinsky if one did not include fellatio (in which by everyone's definition the couple engaged) as constituting having sex. Sexual acts, both narrowly and broadly construed, are a major focus of this encyclopedia.

The first definition of sex, that which creates the biological categories of male and female, stands in a paradigmatic relationship with gender. That is, these concepts can replace one another and are, indeed, often confused. After all, do they not both refer to males and females, the masculine and feminine? If sex refers to the biological basis of this distinction, gender refers to the innumerable cultural traits that have grown up around the original biological reality, and which historically have varied from place to place, culture to culture, and epoch to epoch. Perhaps the main reason for developing the concept of gender was to create an analytical distance from biology, often mistakenly called "nature" (it is a mistake because culture is natural for human beings). The space between biological sex, on the one hand, and gender, on the other, has cut the idea of gender loose from the original dichotomy of male and female. The degree to which gender roles or gendered behavior are social constructs and the degree to which they reflect biological realities or predispositions remains highly controversial and the subject of ongoing debate and research.

To say that gender partakes of cultural constructs means that it operates within the symbolic realm. Religions are among our most potent definers of the symbolic order. They are also labelers and regulators of behavior. Should it be a surprise then that debates about gender (which combines symbolism and action) are so often cast in religious terms? Accordingly, also, religious doctrines, religious texts and figures, play a large role in the *Encyclopedia of Sex and Gender*.

WHY NOW? OR HOW WE CAME TO THIS POINT

Why this sudden concern with sex and gender? Is it just the unhealthy obsession of a society too rich and bored? Our debates about sex and gender do not come out of nowhere. They reflect the culmination of a series of converging technological, economic, social, and intellectual movements. The most basic background lies in demography, specifically what has commonly been called the demographic transition. Generalizing broadly, through most of human history, high birth rates were met by high death rates. Women had many children, the majority of whom died in the first three years of life (and many women died in childbirth). Population was stagnant or grew only slowly. Beginning in the eighteenth-century in Europe, due largely to improved agriculture and transportation, this situation changed, more children survived, and with a high birth rate and low death rate, population shot up dramatically. Finally, in the third phase, women stopped having so many children and, with low birth rate matching a low death rate, populations began to stabilize. Most of the globe is now in this third phase. This has had two fundamental consequences, one on sex and the other on gender roles. With low fertility, birth control is common and sex is no longer tied as closely to reproduction. The separation of sex from reproduction has recently increased with new reproductive technologies like in vitro fertilization. Lower birth rates also mean that women no longer spend most of their existences bearing and nurturing young children. Hence, they can do more things with their lives and, hence, the movements for women's emancipation from traditional gender-defined roles.

The attack on traditional gender roles was strengthened by the related process of the industrial revolution. Industrialism, which replaces human and animal power with inanimate sources of energy, decreases the importance of physical strength in economic activity. The greater physical strength of males, a traditional support of gender differentiation, has become less and less important.

The new more flexible relations between sex, reproduction, and gender have become strikingly visible in contemporary America. The daughter of the otherwise quite conservative Vice-President of the United States announced the happy event of her impending motherhood. Except that she was having this child in the context of her on-going lesbian relationship with her partner. The source of the sperm and its physical trajectory were discretely kept private.

Clearly, the case of Vice-President Cheney's daughter reflects a host of changes in social attitudes. The first of these, in time, and perhaps also in logic, is a reevaluation of the status of women. By the end of the eighteenth century, daring social thinkers were beginning to argue that the winds of emancipation and equality blowing across the Atlantic world should extend to women. Two major women's demands (developed throughout the two succeeding centuries) were: 1) political equality, especially the suffrage, and 2) access to most traditionally male forms of employment. Women's suffrage is now a given in all the world's democracies; and the last barrier, access to the highest political offices, is crumbling.

Women have always worked, both inside and outside the home. What they sought in the nineteenth and increasingly in the twentieth centuries was access beyond traditional women's work. World Wars I and II, with the men folk in arms and the need for economic mobilization for total war, brought women many new job opportunities. Rosie the Riveter may have been sent home when the fighting finished, but she was not forgotten. Middle- and upper-class women struggled to enter the professions from which an increasingly antiquated idea of women's intellectual capacity still too-often barred them.

Like other emancipatory movements, that for women spawned a doctrine which was an explanation of its history, a justification of its claims, and an elaboration of its hopes: feminism. As with similar political-intellectual systems, feminism has adapted to changing times, taken on new ambitions (from sexual freedom to ecology), and developed divergent and sometimes conflicting schools. Yet, even for those who decry them, the fundamental conceptions of feminism have become an integral part of all our thinking on matters relating to sex and gender. In the process, feminism has also linked to topics that intersect with gender, like racism, militarism, and attitudes to the body.

To the growing numbers of women in the knowledge-production-and-transmission-business, aka the professoriate, it was obvious that traditional curricula tended to ignore half the human race, that is, women. From this perceived lack, Women's Studies was born. Women's Studies works to restore women's place in history, economics, literature, and the arts. This academic field has shone a bright light not only on the activities of women but also on the image of women and the conceptions of women held by the dominant patriarchal society.

One of the things that Women's Studies scholars and feminists swiftly discovered (both through their research and the resistance they encountered in their professional careers) was that roles for and attitudes to women were inextricably tied to attitudes to masculinity vs. femininity (that is, gender) and to sexuality and the body. It would not be possible to liberate women, many began to feel, without also liberating attitudes to sexuality and the body. In the process, Women's Studies has given birth to Gender Studies.

Liberating sex involves understanding it, and is tributary to the modern scientific field of sexology, from Krafft-Ebing to Kinsey and their successors. The psychoanalysis of Sigmund Freud, because of its emphasis on the primacy of the sexual drive, has also contributed mightily to the recognition and exploration of the role of sexuality in modern life. Between the sexual revolution of the 1970s and the renewed push associated with second-wave feminism, other groups oppressed by the traditional patriarchal order of sex and gender also demanded dignity and equality. The HIV-AIDS epidemic helped force male homosexuality out of the closet and contributed to the main-streaming of gay culture. Other sexual minorities followed suit: lesbians, bisexuals, transvestites, intersex individuals, transgendered individuals, etc. As the law struggles to catch up, we deal with the gay marriage debate. Again, it is the family of Vice-President Cheney that best manifests the contemporary American paradox. Not only is his daughter in a same-sex relationship but his wife included a lesbian love scene in a novel. Yet Cheney belongs to an administration that says it wants a constitutional amendment prohibiting the recognition of gay marriage. The best index that an idea is gaining ground is the number of individuals who vociferously object to it. Same-sex marriage, in one form or another, is being incorporated into a growing number of legal systems outside the United States. The trio of sex, marriage, and reproduction (always more inseparable in the symbolic realm than in actual practice) is dissolving. New forms and new connections are replacing it.

As we reevaluate our attitudes, we become aware of their mutability and we look back through our own traditions to see how they have changed and how they have evolved. Was the Ancient World a paradise of homosexuality or did the Greeks and Romans follow rules that are foreign both to our Judeo-Christian heritage and to our most liberated aspirations? Was original Christianity patriarchal? If it was, does it need to remain so? This debate has probably advanced farthest in Christianity and Judaism but it has penetrated, to a greater or lesser degree, into other religious traditions. All this is part of sex and gender.

TIME AND SPACE: THE PARAMETERS OF THE ENCYCLOPEDIA

Since we reproduce sexually and organize our cultures through gender, it is hard to imagine an aspect of human life that is not in some way touched by sex and gender. To the challenge of this inherent breadth, the editors of this encyclopedia have added two others. The first concerns time. The *Encyclopedia of Sex and Gender* recognizes that our attitudes to sex and gender, our practices, were not born yesterday. The examination of our past not only helps us understand our present, it also shows us that even our own traditions often contained more variety than we dared to imagine.

The second challenge is space, or in human terms, the enormous variety of cultures across the globe. Since the *Encyclopedia of Sex and Gender* is written in English and is being published within contemporary Western culture (to which it seeks to make a contribution), it is only natural that the greatest attention be directed to Western culture, its history, and its current controversies. Yet, a reference work limited to the West would give a seriously truncated vision of sex and gender. Globalization is drawing the world swiftly together. The West itself has historically and continues in the present to borrow from other cultures, as it is itself a major player in the emerging world systems of sex and gender. Hence, while the West receives more space than its percentage of the world population would presently allow, the *Encyclopedia of Sex and Gender* will also serve as a reference guide to non-Western cultures.

These challenges of time and space guided the selection of the editorial team. The associate editors were chosen first of all for their expertise in sex and gender and their distinction and maturity as scholars, writers, and teachers. Beyond this, each editor was chosen for broader expertise in time, space and discipline. Jamsheed Choksy combines both the Middle East and South Asia with a chronological spread from the ancient world to the present. Judith Roof brings together the more traditional with the digital arts as well as biology and the law. Francesca Canadé Sautman ranges from the Middle Ages to the present and adds Africa to Europe. To better cover the civilizations of the Far East, we added two consultants, Liana Hong Zhou and Sumie Jones, with expertise in China and Japan. Together this editorial team chose many other scholars, scientists, and practitioners who composed the articles.

AUDIENCE AND ORGANIZATION

Today the audience for an *Encyclopedia of Sex and Gender* must go beyond the scholars, teachers, and students whom one would expect and for which its scientific expertise is a requisite. The encyclopedia is also designed to be a tool for people who are not experts in or students of sex and gender. With all the changes and debates going on about proper roles and forms of sexuality, with all the rapid evolution in our ideas of gender-appropriate behavior (indeed of what constitutes gender) there is a great need among members of the educated general public for a reliable dispassionate guide to the minefields of sex and gender. In preparing the *Encyclopedia* we have been as mindful of this larger public as well as the more scholastic one. But knowledge is more than a practical necessity. It is also a form of personal growth and of entertainment. The *Encyclopedia of Sex and Gender* is also directed to educated general readers interested in learning more about areas that affect their lives.

The *Encyclopedia* serves its audiences through a combination of articles that range from several thousand to several hundred words in length. This range of length permits us to present both extended essays on topics of general interest (from sports to sexuality or the history of art) and shorter pieces that explain specialized terms or illuminate particular practices. Entries are also devoted to personalities, though only dead ones, in keeping with a wise Macmillan policy. Individuals have been chosen not for their general importance (this is not a biographical dictionary), but for their contributions (whether by their work, their theories or their example) to the evolution of sex and gender. Figures chosen range from Sappho to Sade, from Foruq Farrokhzad to D.H. Lawrence, from Peter-Paul Rubens to Frida Kahlo. There are 239 black and white illustrations that supplement the articles with works of art, portraits of historical figures and representations of social or political activities.

Controversy is inherent in many of the topics treated in the encyclopedia, from homosexuality and Christianity, to bondage, pornography and pedophilia. Entries explore theories linking hot button issues like sexuality, race, and violence. The editorial board asked its contributors only to distinguish between theory or opinion and accepted knowledge, and, where appropriate to note differing points of view. With the assistance of the staff of Macmillan, the editorial board has worked with the authors to create a sufficient consistency of style and presentation. Yet, these are signed articles for whose contents the authors take responsibility. The editorial board has not wished to blanch out completely the personality of the authors or the originality of their contributions. Points of view are held in balance, but they survive. To do otherwise would be to give a misleading view of the state of knowledge on sex and gender. If there is an underlying assumption it is in favor of openness, to subjects as well as opinions.

To make the *Encyclopedia* accessible to expert and general reader alike, the entries are organized in alphabetical order. As sex and gender affect each other, so do many of the entries in the *Encyclopedia of Sex and Gender* raise issues treated in other entries. We hope that the reader will explore the interconnections between topics. The list of related entries can be a guide. But it cannot cover all connections. Here, we direct readers to the index. Another form of interconnections (or of browsing) can be achieved with the help of the list of entries by topics.

In the last analysis, all writing, like all art, is selection. There will be some whose thirst for knowledge may not be slaked. But I can only hope that the bibliographies following each article will help the reader to go further. This encyclopedia is meant to open the gates of knowledge, to create pathways to new areas of inquiry. Sex and gender are exciting topics, in every sense of the word. We hope the reader will find the *Encyclopedia of Sex and Gender* not only useful and illuminating but entertaining as well.

ACKNOWLEDGMENTS

I would be remiss if I did not begin by thanking the Vice-President of the American Council of Learned Societies, Steve Wheatley, as the person responsible for my being Editor-in-Chief of the *Encyclopedia of Sex and Gender*. At an annual meeting of the ACLS, he pointed me out to Nathalie Duval as the one to undertake such an encyclopedia. Nathalie and I met and discussed the project, about which I was very excited. My first task was to choose Associate Editors, and I have never regretted the choice I made. Jamsheed Choksy, Judith Roof, and Francesca Canadé Sautman have consistently displayed not just the expertise for which I chose them but also the wisdom and patience necessary for the myriad decisions, negotiations, and compromises involved in a multi-year, multi-volume, collective project. A dinner in New York brought us together with Nathalie Duval and Monica Hubbard. Nathalie Duval and Monica Hubbard were invaluable catalysts as the editors shared ideas and goals for the encyclopedia, a task that led to the compilation of topics. That meeting was followed by several get-togethers with Nathalie Duval in New York during which we honed the items and areas to be included. At one such meeting, Nathalie and I decided to add consultants for China and Japan. There could not have been more ideal candidates for those positions than Sumie Jones, an expert on Japanese sexuality, and Liana Zhou, the Director of the Library at the Kinsey Institute for the Study of Sexuality and Reproduction at Indiana University, Bloomington. It seemed fitting that such an encyclopedia should emanate from the university in which Dr. Alfred Kinsey, one of the world's leading sexologists, had courageously undertaken his research on sexuality in the human male and female. My gratitude also goes to the Museum of Sex in New York, where I met curators who enriched the encyclopedia through their insights and contacts.

The dauntless energy of the Associate Editors and Consultants, when combined with the patience and guidance of Deirdre Blanchfield at Thomson Gale, drove the project forward. Hélène Potter was always there as a guiding light, arranging a meeting with the prominent Dr. Ruth Westheimer at which Dr. Ruth generously agreed to pen a Preface for the encyclopedia. It was when Jennifer Stock actually sent me the illustrations for the four volumes that the encyclopedia became alive. Without the endless energy and support of all these individuals, this encyclopedia would not exist. I cannot express in words the depth of my gratitude to them. In Bloomington, my Research Assistant, Whitney Jones Olson, proved to be a pillar of strength. A poet and writer, she was sensitive to the nuances and meanings of the articles I myself wrote.

As the months and years passed, my own intellectual world was greatly broadened as I read the entries included in the four volumes. It is to the authors of these entries that I also express my sincere appreciation. Their patience with sometimes having to edit and reedit their contributions was exemplary. Like a guardian angel, Allen Douglas helped keep me focused during moments of uncertainty and frustration. He, along with my feline companions—those who saw the beginning of the project and those who witnessed its completion—contributed an emotional support without which I would not have been able to see the encyclopedia to fruition.

Fedwa Malti-Douglas
Editor in Chief

List of Articles

C

Contributors

Margaret Abraham
Professor
Sociology Department
Hofstra University
INFANTICIDE

Evelyne Accad
Professor Emerita
University of Illinois, Lebanese
American University
VIOLENCE

Rita Cano Alcalá
Professor
Scripps College
MALINCHE

Dennis W. Allen
Professor
English Department
West Virginia University
CIRCUIT PARTY
DADDY
PHYSICAL CULTURE

Sophia Andres
Professor
University of Texas of the Permian
Basin
PRE-RAPHAELISM/SYMBOLISM

Steven Angelides
Doctor
School of Political and Social Inquiry
Monash University, Australia
BISEXUALITY

Diane Apostolos-Cappadona
Professor
Prince Alwaleed Bin Talal Center for
Muslim-Christian Understanding
Georgetown University
ART
NUDE IN VISUAL ARTS

Margot Badran
Doctor
Alwaleed ibn Talal Center for
Muslim-Christian Understanding
Georgetown University
EGYPTIAN FEMINIST UNION

Matthew Bagger
Professor
Brown University
MYSTICISM

Hamid Bahri
Doctor
Adjunct Assistant Professor
The City College of New York
BATHS, PUBLIC: II. MUSLIM MIDDLE EAST
DAUGHTER OF THE NILE UNION
MUSIC, WOMEN IN MUSLIM AFRICA

Cynthia M. Baker
Professor
Religious Studies Department
Santa Clara University
HAIR
VEILING

David P. Barash
Professor
Psychology Department
University of Washington
MONOGAMY

Christine Bard
Professor
Université d'Angers, France
SUFFRAGE

Halbert Barton
Doctor
Associate Professor of Anthropology,
Department of Sociology-
Anthropology
Long Island University
SALSA

Judith R. Baskin
Professor
Knight Professor of Humanities
University of Oregon
BIBLE, OLD TESTAMENT OR TANAKH

Roberta Malee Bassett
Doctor
Center for Higher Education
Management and Policy at
Southampton (CHEMPaS)
University of Southampton, England
EDUCATION: III. INTERNATIONAL ISSUES

Margaret Pabst Battin
Professor
Department of Philosophy and
Division of Medical Ethics and
Humanities

University of Utah
CONTRACEPTION: V. POLICIES AND EFFECTS

Juan Battle
Professor
Department of Sociology
The Graduate School, The City University of New York
FAMILY, ALTERNATIVE

Tina Beattie
Doctor
Reader in Christian Studies
Roehampton University, England
IMMACULATE CONCEPTION
MARY, MOTHER OF JESUS

Lois Beck
Doctor
Anthropology Department
Washington University, Saint Louis
NOMADISM

Hazel Glenn Beh
Professor
Associate Dean for Academic Affairs
William S. Richardson School of Law
SEXUAL EDUCATION

Jennifer Lyon Bell
Blue Artichoke Films
PENTHOUSE
PRODUCTION CODE (HAYS CODE)

Sandra Bell
Professor
Anthropology Department
University of Durham, The Netherlands
ABSTINENCE

Tovah Bender
University of Minnesota, Twin Cities
MIDDLE AGES

Edith Joyce Benkov
San Diego State University
BOSWELL, JOHN
DAMIAN, PETER
FABLIAUX
JOAN OF ARC
LESBIANISM
PASSING (WOMAN)
TRIBADISM, HISTORICAL

Kathleen Biddick
Professor
History Department
Temple University
DESIRE, AS HISTORICAL CATEGORY

Michael R. Bieber
Doctor
Houston-Galveston Psychoanalytic Institute
ADOLESCENT SEXUALITY
EROTIC TRANSFERENCE
INFANTILE SEXUALITY
NARCISSISM
PUBERTY

Julia Biery
English Department
Sharon High School
BIG BAD WOLF

Erika Bourguignon
Professor Emerita
Anthropology Department
Ohio State University
POSSESSION

Anthony P. Browne
Doctor
Africana & Puerto Rican/Latino Studies Department
Hunter College, The City University of New York
FAMILY, ALTERNATIVE

Rachel M. Brownstein
Professor
English Department
Brooklyn College and The Graduate School and University Center, The City University of New York
WOLLSTONECRAFT, MARY

Marjo Buitelaar
Doctor
Anthropology of Muslim Societies
University of Groningen, The Netherlands
WIDOWS AND WIDOWERS

Vern L. Bullough
Distinguished Professor Emeritus
State University of New York
GALEN
HIPPOCRATES

Israel Burshatin
Professor
Levin Professor of Spanish and Comparative Literature
Haverford College
ELENO
INQUISITION, SPANISH

Joseph Cady
Doctor
New York University School of Medicine
MIGNONS

Clay Calvert
Professor
College of Communications
Pennsylvania State University
CENSORSHIP
VOYEURISM

María M. Carrión
Professor
Department of Spanish and Portuguese
Emory University
DON JUAN

Gary P. Cestaro
Professor
DePaul University
FILM, GENDER AND EROTICISM: IV. LESBIAN, GAY, AND QUEER FILM

John Champagne
Doctor
School of Humanities and Social Sciences
Penn State Erie, The Behrend College
GAY
GENDER IDENTITY

Michael A. Chaney
Professor
Dartmouth College
SUPERHEROES

Tina Chanter
Professor
Philosophy Department
DePaul University
PHILOSOPHY, FEMINIST

Christopher Key Chapple
Doctor
Doshi Professor of Indic and Comparative Theology
Loyola Marymount University
JAINISM

Susannah Mary Chewning
Associate Professor of English
Union County College
BINGEN, HILDEGARD OF

Margaret H. Childs
Professor
East Asian Languages and Cultures
University of Kansas
JAPAN: IV. COURTLY LOVE

Carol E.B. Choksy
Doctor
School of Library and Information Science

Indiana University, Bloomington
BUNDLING
ESPIONAGE

Jamsheed K. Choksy
Professor
Indiana University, Bloomington
MANICHAEISM
MITHRAISM
ZOROASTRIANISM

Beverly Lyon Clark
Professor
English Department
Wheaton College
BIG BAD WOLF

Cindy Dell Clark
Professor
Pennsylvania State University
CHILDCARE

Robert L.A. Clark
Doctor
Department of Modern Languages
Kansas State University
CONDUCT BOOKS
KISS, PRE-MODERN
LE ROMAN DE SILENCE
MANLINESS
SIN CONTRA NATURAM

Cheryl Clarke
Dean
Rutgers University, New Brunswick Campus
BLACK ARTS MOVEMENT

Jeffrey Jerome Cohen
Professor
English Department
George Washington University
ANIMALS, SEXUAL SYMBOLISM OF

Diana Conchado
Professor
Hunter College, The City University of New York
CANON, REVISING THE

David B. Cook
Professor
Rice University
MARTYRDOM

Emma Crandall
Doctor
English and Women's Studies Departments
University of Michigan, Ann Arbor
BULLDAGGER
DRAG KINGS
ELLIS, HENRY HAVELOCK
FROTTAGE
FURRIES
GENDER CONFUSION
LESBIAN, CONTEMPORARY: I. OVERVIEW
LESBIAN, CONTEMPORARY: II. POST 1950
LESBIAN, CONTEMPORARY: III. STATUS
MANLY (MASCULINE) WOMAN
SEX RESEARCH
SEXOLOGY
SHEPARD, MATTHEW WAYNE
TILL, EMMETT LOUIS
TRANSSEXUAL F TO M

Jenny Daggers
Doctor
Liverpool Hope University, England
PROTESTANTISM

Shamita Das Dasgupta
Manavi, Inc.
FEMINISM: II. ASIAN

Olga M. Davidson
Doctor
Wellesley College
LOVE POETRY

Craig Davis
Doctor
Director, Civil Society Division
International Research and Exchanges Board (IREX)
DEMOGRAPHY: III. MIDDLE EAST AND NORTH AFRICA
HONOR CRIMES
LABOR AND WORKFORCE IN AFRICA, ASIA, AND THE MIDDLE EAST

Robbie Davis-Floyd
Doctor
Anthropology Department
University of Texas Austin
BIRTH

Victor de Munck
Professor
Anthropology Department
State University of New York and New Paltz
CHASTITY

L. Anne Delgado
Professor
Indiana Unviersity, Bloomington
VAMPIRES

Furjen Deng
Professor
Sociology Department
Sam Houston State University
CANCER, BREAST

Marilynn Desmond
Professor
English and Comparative Literature Departments
Binghamton University
HELOISE AND ABELARD
PIZAN, CHRISTINE DE

Giuseppe C. Di Scipio
Professor
Hunter College and The Graduate School and University Center, The City University of New York
AQUINAS, THOMAS
BEATRICE
BOCCACCIO, GIOVANNI
CATHOLICISM
COURTLY LOVE, WESTERN
DANTE ALIGHIERI
EROS, CUPID
GENTILESCHI, ARTEMISIA
JUVENAL
MARY MAGDALENE
PAUL (SAINT)
SAINTS, MALE AND FEMALE
SONG OF SONGS
SUSANNA AT HER BATH

Maribel Dietz
Professor
History Department
Louisiana State University
PILGRIMAGES: II. CHRISTIANITY

Mario DiGangi
Professor
Lehman College and The Graduate School and University Center, The City University of New York
SHAKESPEARE, WILLIAM

Wendy Doniger
Professor
Divinity School
University of Chicago
KAMA AND THE KAMA SUTRA

Elsa Dorlin
Professor
Philosophy Department
University of Panthéon-Sorbonne, France
ALLEGORY
SADE, MARQUIS DE

Allen Douglas
Professor
West European Studies Department
Indiana University, Bloomington

ANCIENT GREECE
DEMOGRAPHY: I. AMERICA AND EUROPE
FASCISM
GOUGES, OLYMPE DE
REICH, WILHELM
TERRORISM

Marymay Downing
Professor
Institute of Women's Studies
University of Ottawa, Canada
INCEST

Alice D. Dreger
Professor
Medical Humanities and Bioethics Program
Feinberg School of Medicine, Northwestern University
INTERSEX

Donna J. Drucker
History Department
Indiana University, Bloomington
CHINA: III. EROTIC ART
FOOT BINDING
ONE-CHILD ONE-FAMILY POLICY
SEX MUSEUMS, CHINESE

Terry Morehead Dworkin
Dean, Office for Women's Affairs
Indiana University, Bloomington
HARASSMENT, SEXUAL

Konrad Eisenbichler
Professor
Renaissance Studies Programme
Victoria College, University of Toronto, Canada
CODPIECE
ONE-SEX THEORY

Garrett P.J. Epp
Professor
English and Film Studies
University of Alberta, Canada
CHRIST

Dionne Espinoza
Professor
Department of Chicano Studies & Director of the Center for the Study of Genders and Sexualities
California State University, Los Angeles
CHICANA MOVEMENT

Laurie L. Essig
Professor
Sociology/Anthropology Department
Middlebury College
BURLESQUE

Paolo Fasoli
Department of Romance Languages
Hunter College and The Graduate School and University Center, The City University of New York
CATHERINE THE GREAT
MEDUSA
OVID
POLITICAL SATIRE
ROMEO AND JULIET
SEX MANUALS, ANCIENT WORLD

Priscilla Ferguson
Professor
Sociology Department
Columbia University
FOOD

Ellison Banks Findly
Professor
Religion Department, Asian Studies Program
Trinity College
PATTINI
SEX MANUALS, INDIA
YONI WORSHIP

C. Tabor Fisher
Professor
Philosophy Department
Le Moyne College
SPACE, PUBLIC AND PRIVATE

Cornelia Butler Flora
Professor
Sociology Department
Iowa State University
FOTONOVELAS

Lee Fontanella
Professor
Independent Scholar
BATHS, PUBLIC: I. GRECO-ROMAN
PLAT LYNES, GEORGE

Melissa Fore
English Department
Michigan State University
HATE CRIMES
KEPT
MISCEGENATION
STRANGE FRUIT

Miriam Forman-Brunell
Professor
History Department
University of Missouri-Kansas City
TOYS

Peter Forster
Professor
DePaul University
STAR-CROSSED LOVERS

Neil Forsyth
Professor
University of Lausanne, Switzerland
ADAM AND EVE

Johanna Frank
Professor
English Department
University of Windsor, Canada
SWITCHHITTER

Susan Schuller Friedman
Doctor
Center for Professional Development
ELDERLY, SEX AMONG

Ellen Lorraine Friedrich
Doctor
Department of Modern and Classical Languages
Valdosta State University
ROMANCE OF THE ROSE

Lynda Garland
Professor
School of Classics, History and Religion
University of New England, Australia
BYZANTIUM

Barbara Geller
Professor
Religion Department
Wellesley College
PILGRIMAGES: V. JUDAISM

Silvia Gherardi
Professor
Department of Sociology and Social Research
University of Trento, Italy
SYMBOLISM

Jennifer A. Glancy
Professor
Religious Studies Department
Le Moyne College
SALOME

Ellen Goldberg
Professor
Religious Studies Department
Queen's University, Canada
YOGA

Deirdre Good
Professor
General Theological Seminary
BIBLE, NEW TESTAMENT

Marco Gottardo
Department of Religion
Columbia University
PILGRIMAGES: I. BUDDHISM

Benjamin Graber
Doctor
Independent Scholar
BRAIN

Fritz Graf
Professor
Department of Greek and Latin
The Ohio State University
ARTEMIS DIANA

Cynthia A. Graham
Doctor
Oxford Doctoral Course in Clinical Psychology
University of Oxford, The Kinsey Institute for Research in Sex, Gender, & Reproduction
NECROPHILIA

Clara Greed
Doctor
School of Planning and Architecture
University of the West of England
Bristol, England
TOILETS, PUBLIC

Helen Gremillion
Professor
Department of Gender Studies
Indiana University, Bloomington
EATING DISORDERS

Carol Groneman
Professor
John Jay College of Criminal Justice and the Graduate Center of the City University of New York
NYMPHOMANIA

Sara Gross
MUSIC

Ellen Gruenbaum
Professor
Anthropology Department
California State University, Fresno
FEMALE GENITAL MUTILATION

Noah D. Guynn
Professor
University of California, Davis
ALAN OF LILLE

Adele J. Haft
Professor
Classical and Oriental Studies Department
Hunter College, The City University of New York
OEDIPUS, MYTH OF
TROJAN WOMEN

Rosemary Drage Hale
Dean
Dean, Faculty of Humanities, Brock University
St. Catharines, Ontario, Canada
MONASTICISM
SHAʿRAWI, HUDA

Kira Hall
Professor
Departments of Linguistics and Anthropology
University of Colorado
X (RATED)

Marcus Desmond Harmon
Musicology Department
University of California, Los Angeles
MUSIC VIDEOS
ROCK AND ROLL

Jennifer Hart
Religious Studies Department
Indiana University, Bloomington
BOGOMILS AND CATHARS
GNOSTICISM
HOKHMA
INITIATION
ORACLES
SOPHIA

Joy L. Hart
Professor
Communication Department
University of Louisville
CANCER, PROSTATE
SYPHILIS

Heidi Hartmann
Doctor
Institute for Women's Policy Research
WELFARE

Nichole Harvey
School of Nursing, Midwifery, and Nutrition
James Cook University, Australia
WET NURSES

Jane Hathaway
Professor
History Department
Ohio State University
HAREMS

Sîan Hawthorne
Doctor
SOAS
University of London, England
FEMINISM: IV. WESTERN
RELIGION, STUDY OF

Kelly E. Hayes
Professor
Department of Religious Studies
Indiana University-Purdue University-Indianapolis
BODY MODIFICATIONS

Ronald Hendel
Professor
Norma and Sam Dabby Professor of Hebrew Bible and Jewish Studies
University of California, Berkeley
ISRAELITE SOCIETY

Scott Herring
Professor
English Department
Indiana University, Bloomington
CRUISING

Brandon J. Hill
Department of Gender Studies,
Indiana University, Bloomington
The Kinsey Institute for Research in Sex, Gender, and Reproduction
SEX MANUALS, OLD AND MODERN WEST
TRANSGENDER
TRANSSEXUAL M TO F

Ruth Hoberman
Professor
English Department
Eastern Illinois University
RENAULT, MARY

Ingeborg Hoesterey
Professor
Germanic Studies and Comparative Literature
Indiana University, Bloomington
DIETRICH, MARLENE

Brian D. Holcomb
English Department
Michigan State University
AVUNCULAR
BACKROOM
BUTTOCKS
COMING OUT
COPROPHILIA
DIVINE

DRAG QUEENS
EFFEMINACY
EROTICISM, URETHRAL
G.I. JOE
GARLAND, JUDY
IMPOTENCY
LADYBOYS (KATHOEYS)
LIBERACE
LITTLE RED RIDING HOOD
MALE
MAPPLETHORPE, ROBERT
MEN'S MOVEMENT
MONROE, MARILYN
ONANISM
QUEEN
QUEENS
RENT BOY
SATYRIASIS
SCATOLOGY
SODOMY
TRANNIE WHORE
WET DREAMS
WHITMAN, WALT
YMCA/YWCA

Ana Holguin
PhD Candidate
PEDOPHILIA
SADISM
SEXUAL OBJECTS

Susan Tower Hollis
Doctor
Empire State College, State University of New York
ISIS

Gail Holst-Warhaft
Professor
Institute for European Studies
Cornell University
DEATH

renée c. hoogland
Professor
Cultural Sexuality Studies/American Studies
Radboud University Nijmegen, The Netherlands
BODY, THEORIES OF
GENDER, THEORIES OF
LITERATURE: V. LESBIAN, CREATIVE
QUEER

Desmond Hosford
Ph.D. Program in French
The Graduate School and University Center, The City University of New York
MARIE ANTOINETTE
OPERA
ROYALTY

Jaime Hovey
Independent Scholar
CAMP
DAUGHTERS OF BILITIS
DILDO
DYKE
ESSENTIALISM
FEMME
FOPS
GENDER DYSPHORIA
HOMOPHOBIA
INTIMACY
KISS, MODERN
KRAFFT-EBING, RICHARD
LUBRICANT
MASTURBATION
MELANCHOLIA AND SEX
NOSE
PERVERSITY, POLYMORPHOUS
SEX AIDS
SEX SYMBOL
SEXUAL IDENTITY
SEXUAL INVERSION
SEXUAL PERVERSION
SEXUAL PRACTICES
SEXUAL SUBCULTURES
SEXUALITY
STEIN, GERTRUDE AND ALICE B. TOKLAS
STORY OF O
THIRD SEX
TONGUE
TRANSVESTISM
TRIBADISM, MODERN
WILDE, OSCAR
WOOLF, VIRGINIA

Julia Huang
Professor
Anthropology Department
Yale University
NOMADISM

Wen Huang
CHINA: IV. EROTIC LITERATURE

Clarke Hudson
Department of Religious Studies
Indiana University, Bloomington
DAOISM (TAOISM)

Gregory S. Hutcheson
Professor
Department of Classical and Modern Languages
University of Louisville
NEFANDUM

Habiba Ibrahim
Professor
University of Washington
AFROCENTRISM
SCOTTSBORO CASE

Masako Ishii-Kuntz
Professor
Sociology Department
University of California, Riverside
MOTHERHOOD

Madeleine Jeay
Professor
French Department
McMaster University, Canada
FOLKLORE
MARRIAGE BED, RITUALS OF
VETULA, OLD WHORE

Carole Joffe
Professor
Sociology Department
University of California, Davis
ABORTION, MEDICAL ISSUES

Dawn Johnsen
Professor
Indiana University School of Law, Bloomington
ABORTION, LEGAL AND POLITICAL ISSUES

Colin R. Johnson
Doctor
Gender Studies Department
Indiana University, Bloomington
DANDYISM
DATING
METROSEXUALS

Drew Jones
Professor
Queens College
City University of New York
GENET, JEAN

Malcolm Jones
Doctor
University of Sheffield, England
OBSCENE

Sumie Jones
Professor
Indiana University, Bloomington
JAPAN: II. EROTIC LITERATURE

Whitney Jones Olson
Professor
Indiana University, Bloomington
CANNIBALISM
VAMPIRISM

Scott Juengel
Professor
Michigan State University
FANNY HILL

Jeremy C. Justus
Professor
English Department
West Virginia University
DRUGS, RECREATIONAL
PEEP SHOWS
PENIS EXTENDERS
PERSONALS
SEX SHOP
THROAT
TOP/BOTTOM

Loren Y. Kajikawa
Department of Musicology
University of California, Los Angeles
BLUES

Sylvie Kandé
Professor
History and Philosophy/English Departments
State University of New York, Old Westbury
AFRICA: I. HISTORY
AFRICA: II. POLITICAL AND CULTURAL AGENDAS
AFRICA: III. ART AND LITERATURE
BAKER, JOSÉPHINE
BEATRICE OF THE KONGO
DAHOMEY, WOMEN WARRIORS/WIVES OF THE KING

Melinda Kanner
Doctor
The University of Houston, Downtown
PENANCE
POSSESSION
SODOM AND GOMORRAH

Ahmad Karimi-Hakkak
Professor
Director of the Center for Persian Studies
University of Maryland
FARROKHZAD, FORUQ

Claire E. Katz
Professor
Texas A&M University
PHILOSOPHY

Alison Keith
Professor
University of Toronto, Canada
SEX AND EMPIRE

Erick Kelemen
Doctor
University of Kentucky, Lexington
ADULTERY
ASEXUALITY
LUST

Helen King
Professor
Classics Department
University of Reading, England
MEDICINE, ANCIENT

Rebecca Kippen
Doctor
Demography Department
The Australian National University
DEMOGRAPHY: II. AUSTRALIA

Sunita Kishor
Doctor
Macro International, Inc.
Calverton, Maryland
DEMOGRAPHY: IV. ASIA

Anna Kłosowska
Professor
French and Italian Department
Miami University
HOMOAFFECTIVITY, CONCEPT

Jennifer Wright Knust
Professor
School of Theology
Boston University
PORNEIA

Ekaterina Korobtseva
Doctor
Wadham College, University of Oxford, England
JAPAN: VII. FAMILY ROLES

Susan Koslow
Professor Emeritus
Art History Department
Brooklyn College and The Graduate School and University Center, The City University of New York
RUBENS, PETER PAUL

Steven F. Kruger
Professor
English Department
Queens College and The Graduate Center, City University of New York
CAMILLE, MICHAEL
CHAUCER, GEOFFREY
CLOSETS
DREAMS AND EROTICISM, DREAM BOOKS
FOUCAULT, MICHEL
JUDAISM, GENDER AND QUEERING
OTHER, CONSTRUCTING THE
QUEERING, QUEER THEORY, AND EARLY MODERN CULTURE

Julia Lamber
Professor
School of Law
Indiana University, Bloomington
EMPLOYMENT DISCRIMINATION
FAMILY LEAVE ACT

Siobhan Lambert-Hurley
Doctor
School of Arts and Humanities
Nottingham Trent University, England
PILGRIMAGES: IV. ISLAM

Julie Langford-Johnson
Professor
History Department
University of South Florida
ANCIENT ROME

Maureen Lauder
Professor
English Department
Michigan State University
AIDS AND HIV: I. OVERVIEW
AIDS AND HIV: II. HISTORY
AIDS AND HIV: III. EFFECTS ON POPULATION
AIDS AND HIV: IV. TREATMENTS AND PREVENTION
AIDS AND HIV: V. SOCIAL AND POLITICAL RESPONSES
AROUSAL
BONDAGE AND DISCIPLINE
BOYS, CONSTRUCTION OF
CALL GIRL
CASTRATI
CASTRATION
DATE RAPE DRUGS
DOMINATION
ESQUIRE
FOREPLAY
GIRLS, CONSTRUCTION OF
HETEROSEXUALITY
LOLITA
PEDERASTY
SEX INDUSTRY
TATTOOING
VENUS DE MILO
VIRGINITY
WATERSPORTS

Lori Hope Lefkovitz
Doctor
Reconstructionist Rabbinical College
PRAYER

John A. Lent
Professor
International Journal of Comic Art
BETTY BOOP
COMICS CODE
COMICS/COMIC STRIPS
EROTIC/ADULT COMICS
WONDER WOMAN

Arthur S. Leonard
Professor
New York Law School
DOMESTIC PARTNERSHIP

Leora Lev
Professor
Bridgewater State College
PIN-UPS

Carole Levin
Professor
History Department
University of Nebraska, Lincoln
ELIZABETH I

Daniel Little
Doctor
University of Michigan-Dearborn
COMMUNISM AND MARXISM

C. Scott Littleton
Professor of Anthropology, Emeritus
Occidental College
SHINTOISM

Rosemary Lloyd
Professor
Indiana University, Bloomington
SAND, GEORGE

Kathryn Lofton
Professor
Indiana University, Bloomington
FUNDAMENTALISM

Heather Love
Professor
University of Pennsylvania
BUTCH/FEMME

Andrew P. Lyons
Professor
Department of Anthropology
Wilfrid Laurier University, Canada
CIRCUMCISION, MALE

Harriet D. Lyons
Professor
Department of Anthropology
University of Waterloo, Canada
CIRCUMCISION, MALE

Xiaonian Ma
Professor
Tsing Hua University
Yu Quan Hospital, China
VAN GULIK, ROBERT

Ed Madden
Doctor
English Department
University of South Carolina
RAFFALOVITCH, MARC-ANDRE

Sabina Magliocco
Professor
Department of Anthropology
California State University, Northridge
WITCHCRAFT

Jennifer Maher
Professor
Gender Studies Department
Indiana University, Bloomington
WOMEN'S STUDIES

Fedwa Malti-Douglas
Professor
Indiana University, Bloomington
ARABIAN NIGHTS
HUSTLER
ISLAM
KAHLO, FRIDA
LEWINSKY AFFAIR
PLAYBOY
SEX MANUALS, ISLAM
TERRORISM
VARGAS, ALBERTO
WARHOL, ANDY

Susan Maneck
Professor
History Department
Jackson State University
BAHA'I FAITH

Susan Marine
Boston College Lynch School of Education
EDUCATION: I. GENDER IN AMERICA
EDUCATION: II. GLBT ISSUES

Sophie Maríñez
The Graduate School and University Center, The City University of New York
HERMAPHRODITES

Claudia Marquis
Doctor
English Department
University of Auckland, New Zealand
BEHN, APHRA
RENAISSANCE

Joss Marsh
Professor
English Department
Indiana University, Bloomington
VAMPIRES

Ana M. Martínez Alemán
Professor
Lynch School of Education
Boston College
EDUCATION: I. GENDER IN AMERICA

Victor H. Matthews
Doctor
Missouri State University
JOSEPH STORY, THE

Mary McAlpin
Professor
University of Tennessee
ENLIGHTENMENT

Kimberly McBride
Doctor
TRANSGENDER
TRANSSEXUAL M TO F

Sally McConnell-Ginet
Professor
Department of Linguistics
Cornell University
LANGUAGE

Maureen McDonnell
Doctor
English Department
Eastern Connecticut State University
ADVERTISING
FEMALE

Keren R. McGinity
Professor
Brown University
HISTORY AND HISTORIOGRAPHY, MODERN

Susan McGury
Professor
DePaul University
STAR-CROSSED LOVERS

Elizabeth McMahon
Fashion Institute of Technology
CLOTHING

Peter Metcalf
Professor
Department of Anthropology
University of Virginia
FUNERARY CUSTOMS, NON-WESTERN
FUNERARY CUSTOMS, WESTERN

Gwendolyn Mikell
Doctor
Georgetown University
FEMINISM: I. AFRICAN (SUB-SAHARAN)

Valentine Moghadam
Doctor
Sociology and Women's Studies

Purdue University
FAMILY
FEMINISM: III. MIDDLE EASTERN

Patricia Monaghan
Doctor
DePaul University
LEGENDS AND MYTHS

William Monter
Professor
History Department
Northwestern University (Emeritus)
WITCH TRIALS, EUROPE

Brenda L. Moore
Professor
Sociology Department
University at Buffalo, State University of New York
MILITARY

Vera B. Moreen
Doctor
Independent Scholar
ESTHER

Jacqueline Murray
Professor
Department of History
University of Guelph, Canada
BUGGER, BUGGERY
CANON LAW

Guity Nashat
Professor
University of Illinois at Chicago
KHADIJA

Jenifer Neils
Professor
Case Western Reserve University
ATHENA

Jule A. Nelson
Doctor
Global Development and Environmental Institute
Tufts University
ECONOMICS

Vivien Ng
Professor
University at Albany, State University of New York
SEX, RACE, AND POWER: AN INTERSECTIONAL STUDY

Bertrade Ngo-Ngijol Banoum
Professor
Women's Studies Program
Lehman College and The Graduate School and University Center, The City University of New York
DEMOGRAPHY: V. AFRICA
UMOJA
WOMEN'S HUMAN RIGHTS

Justus Nieland
Professor
English Department
Michigan State University
HIMES, CHESTER

Amy Nolan
Professor
Department of English and Modern Languages
Wartburg College
BODY IMAGE
CHASTITY BELT
FRIGIDITY
HITE REPORT
MISTRESS
NUDIST CAMPS

Raymond J. Noonan
Doctor
Fashion Institute of Technology of the State University of New York
SURROGATES, SEXUAL

Lance Norman
Professor
Michigan State University
MALE BONDING
MASCULINITY: I. OVERVIEW
MASCULINITY: II. ATTRIBUTES AND FUNCTIONS
MASCULINITY: III. CONTEMPORARY THEORIES
MASCULINITY: IV. IN MEDIA AND CULTURE
MEN'S STUDIES

Vivian-Lee Nyitray
Religious Studies Department
University of California, Riverside
CONFUCIANISM
YIN AND YANG

Maura O'Neill
Doctor
Chaffey College
CELIBACY

David O. Ogungbile
Professor
Department of Religious Studies
Obafemi Awolowo University, Nigeria
AFRICA: IV. RELIGIONS

Jordan Paper
Professor Emeritus
York University, Canada
MENARCHE, CULTURAL AND SPIRITUAL MEANINGS

Michelle Parke
English Department
Michigan State University
DOMESTIC VIOLENCE
GENDER ROLES: IV. FEMINIST AND GAY/LESBIAN PERSPECTIVES
HOMOSEXUALITY, CONTEMPORARY: I. OVERVIEW
HOMOSEXUALITY, CONTEMPORARY: II. HISTORY
HOMOSEXUALITY, CONTEMPORARY: III. CULTURAL FUNCTIONS
HOMOSEXUALITY, CONTEMPORARY: IV. ISSUES
MADWOMAN IN THE ATTIC
MENOPAUSE
PLANNED PARENTHOOD
RAPE
SEXUAL REVOLUTION

Sylvia A. Parsons
Professor
Foreign Languages and Literatures Department
Louisiana State University
AMAZONS

Jacqueline Z. Pastis
Doctor
Religion Department
La Salle University
CHRISTIANITY, EARLY AND MEDIEVAL

Laurie Patton
Professor
Religion Department
Emory University
HINDUISM

Karen Pechilis
Professor
Religion Department
Drew University
GODDESS WORSHIP
GODDESSES, EARTH
GODDESSES, MOTHER

Stephan Pennington
University of California, Los Angeles
PRESLEY, ELVIS

Rosa Alvarez Perez
Doctor
Literary and Cultural Studies Department

Bryant University
JEWISH TRADITION, GENDER AND WOMEN
JEWISH WOMEN'S LEAGUE
JUDAISM
JUDITH
RABELAIS, FRANÇOIS

Jean Eldred Pickering
Professor
California State University, Fresno
NATIONALISM

Vinciane Pirenne-Delforge
Doctor
Fonds National de la Recherche Scientifique
University of Liège, Belgium
APHRODITE

Wioleta Polinska
Professor
Religious Studies Department
North Central College
CREATION STORIES
TIAMAT

Karin M. Polit
Doctor
Department of Anthropology, South Asia Institute
University of Heidelberg, Germany
PILGRIMAGES: III. HINDUISM

Cherise A. Pollard
Professor
Department of English
West Chester University of Pennsylvania
LORDE, AUDRE

Barbara Postema
Michigan State University
CHAT ROOM
GENDER ROLES: III. CONTEMPORARY UNDERSTANDING
INTERNET
SEXUAL ABUSE

Frank Prerost
Professor
Department of Behavioral Medicine
Midwestern University
GUILT

Gerald A. Press
Professor
Hunter College and The Graduate School and University Center, The City University of New York
PLATO

Jason Prior
Doctor
Research Fellow, Faculty of Design, Architecture and Building
University of Technology, Sydney, Australia
BATHS, PUBLIC: III. WEST, MIDDLE AGES—PRESENT

Helmut Puff
Doctor
University of Michigan
HOMOSEXUALITY, MALE, HISTORY OF
SODOMY, REPRESSION OF

Tison Pugh
English Department
University of Central Florida
MARBOD OF RENNES
MARRIAGE, SPIRITUAL

Kristina Banister Quynn
Michigan State University
COITUS
GENDER ROLES: II. HISTORY
MENARCHE, PHYSIOLOGY AND PSYCHOLOGY
SEX ROLES

Charlotte Radler
Doctor
Theological Studies Department
Loyola Marymount University
HONOR AND SHAME
POLITICS

Ellie Ragland
Professor
English Department
University of Missouri, Columbia
CHILDHOOD SEXUALITY
LACAN, JACQUES
PSYCHIATRY

Rachel Raimist
Department of Gender, Women and Sexuality Studies
University of Minnesota
RAP MUSIC

Christine R. Rainey
Independent Scholar
CONTRACEPTION: I. OVERVIEW
CONTRACEPTION: II. BELIEFS AND MYTHS
CONTRACEPTION: III. METHODS
ERECTILE TISSUE
ERECTION
FAP

Rubina Ramji
Doctor
Cape Breton University, Canada
ANTHROPOLOGY

Holly Elizabeth Ransom
San Diego State University
BRANTÔME
CARLINI, BENEDETTA
KING HENRY III OF FRANCE

Robert F. Reid-Pharr
Professor
English and American Studies
The Graduate School and University Center, The City University of New York
BALDWIN, JAMES

Daniella Reinhard
Doctor
The American University of Paris, France
MATRIARCHY

Alice Ristroph
Professor
University of Utah, S.J. Quinney College of Law
PRISON, DETENTION AND CORRECTIONAL INSTITUTIONS

Massimo Riva
Professor of Italian Studies and Modern Culture and Media
Brown University
CASANOVA

Judith Roof
Professor
Department of English
Michigan State University
ANORGASMIC
ARTISTS, WOMEN
AUTOMOBILES
BEAUVOIR, SIMONE DE
BIOLOGY
BONAPARTE, MARIE
COLETTE, SIDONIE-GABRIELLE
EJACULATION
EROGENOUS ZONES
EROTIC ART
EROTIC PHOTOGRAPHY
FATHERHOOD
FILM, GENDER AND EROTICISM: II. ART AND AUTEUR CINEMA
FORNICATION
FREUD, SIGMUND
GAZE
GENDER ROLES: I. OVERVIEW
GENDER STUDIES
GENETICS AND GENDER

GENITALIA, AS APOTROPAIC
GIGOLO
G-SPOT
GYPSY ROSE LEE
HOMOSEXUALITY, DEFINED
JAZZ
KINSEY, ALFRED
LADY CHATTERLEY'S LOVER
LADY MACBETH
LAWRENCE, D. H.
LESBOS
LIBIDO
LITERATURE: I. OVERVIEW
LITERATURE: II. THE STUDY OF
LITERATURE: III. POPULAR
MAKING OUT
MATRILINEALITY
MEDIA
MÉNAGE À TROIS
MILLER, HENRY
MUCOUS MEMBRANES
NEUTER
NIN, ANAÏS
ORAL SEX
ORGY
PASOLINI, PIER PAOLO
PATRILINEALITY
PENETRATION
PHONE SEX
PORNOGRAPHY
PRIVACY
PSYCHOANALYSIS
REPRODUCTION (PROCREATION)
SEDUCTION
SEX
SEX CRIMES
SEX MUSEUMS
SEXUAL INSTINCT
SEXUAL ORIENTATION
SEXUAL TENSION
SNUFF FILMS
SODOMY LAWS
SVENGALI
TIRESIAS
URANIANS
UTERUS
VAGINA
WEST, MAE
WOMEN WRITERS, EMERGENCE

Christine Rose
Doctor
Independent Scholar
PLEASURE

Jennifer Rose
Doctor
School of Religion
Claremont Graduate University
ANAHITA
JEH
KALI
MENSTRUATION
ZENOBIA

Christopher Nigel Ross
Reverend
United American Catholic Church
Virginia Beach, Virginia
HOMOSEXUALITY IN THE CHRISTIAN CHURCH

Joyce Rothschild
Professor
School of Public and International Affairs
Virginia Tech
HIERARCHY

Leyla Rouhi
Professor
Romance Languages Department
Williams College
CELESTINA
DULCINEA

Anya Peterson Royce
Professor
Chancellor's Professor of Anthropology
Indiana University, Bloomington
DANCE

Francesca T. Royster
Doctor
Associate Professor, English Department
DePaul University
BLAXPLOITATION FILMS

Rosemary Radford Ruether
Professor
Claremont Graduate University
CHRISTIANITY, REFORMATION TO MODERN
PATRIARCHY

Nerina Rustomji
Professor
St. John's University
HOURI

Chris Ryan
Professor
Department of Tourism and Hospitality Management
The University of Waikato, Australia
SEX TOURISM

Regina Salmi
English Department
Michigan State University
ARTIFICIAL INSEMINATION

James M. Saslow
Professor
Queens College and The Graduate Center, City University of New York
CARAVAGGIO, MICHELANGELO MERISI DA
CELLINI, BENVENUTO
GANYMEDE
MICHELANGELO

Francesca Canadé Sautman
Professor
Hunter College and The Graduate Center of the City University of New York
ANDROGYNY
BEARD
BIJOUX INDISCRETS
BOSCH, HIERONYMUS
CANON, REVISING THE
FAIRY TALES
FILM, GENDER AND EROTICISM: III. CULT AND MARGINAL CINEMA
HERRENFRAGE
LESBIAN-LIKE
MARGINALIA IN MEDIEVAL MANUSCRIPTS
MERMAID
PLANTS, SEXUAL SYMBOLISM OF
QUEEN OF SHEBA, MYTH OF
QUEENS, POWER AND SEXUALITY
ROUGH MUSIC
SAME-SEX LOVE AND SEX, TERMINOLOGY
SPORTS
SUFFRAGE
TEMPTATION OF SAINT-ANTHONY (IMAGE)
VERNIOLLE, ARNAUD DE

Diane Saylor
CLITORIS
CONTRACEPTION: IV. RELATION TO SEXUAL PRACTICES AND GENDER ROLES
FERTILITY
GENITALS, FEMALE
GENITALS, MALE
HORMONES: I. OVERVIEW
HORMONES: II. SEX HORMONES
HORMONES: III. HORMONAL DISEASES
HYSTERECTOMY
INFERTILITY
PERFORMANCE ENHANCERS
PREGNANCY
REPRODUCTIVE TECHNOLOGIES
SEXUALLY TRANSMITTED DISEASES
STERILIZATION

Larry Scanlon
Associate Professor of English
Rutgers University
BURCHARD OF WORMS

Peter R. Schmidt
Professor
Anthropology Department
University of Florida
IRON, GENDERED SYMBOLISM

Celia E. Schultz
Professor
Classics Department
Yale University
GYNAECEUM
VENUS
VESTAL VIRGIN

Howard Schwartz
Professor
University of Missouri-St. Louis
LILITH
SHEKHINAH, GOD'S BRIDE

Timon Screech
Professor
School of Oriental and African Studies
University of London, England
JAPAN: III. EROTIC ART

Sayida Self
Doctor
Anthropology Department
The Graduate School and University Center, The City University of New York
SLAVERY

Susan Starr Sered
Doctor
Suffolk University
FOLK BELIEFS AND RITUALS
FOLK HEALERS AND HEALING

Russell Shuttleworth
Doctor
Visiting Lecturer
Faculty of Health Sciences, The University of Sydney
DISABILITY, FETISHIZATION OF
DISABILITY, SEX AND

Juha Sihvola
Professor
University of Helsinki, Collegium for Advanced Studies, Finland
ARISTOTLE

Kemal Silay
Professor
Indiana University, Bloomington
COMPUTERS

Walter Simons
Professor
History Department
Dartmouth College
BEGUINES

Nikky-Guninder Kaur Singh
Professor
Colby College
SIKHISM

Michael Skafidas
Professor
Comparative Literature
The City University of New York
FASHION SYSTEM

D. Skara
Doctor
University of Zadar, Croatia
BODY, DEPICTIONS AND METAPHORS

Jamie Skerski
Professor
College of St. Catherine
SCOUTS, BOY AND GIRL

Elisa J. Sobo
Associate Professor
Department of Anthropology
San Diego State University
ABSTINENCE

Patricia Sokolski
Humanities Department
LaGuardia Community College
MAIDEN

Susan L. Solomon
Comparative Literature Department
Brown University
ROSIE THE RIVETER
WAR

Claire Sponsler
Professor
University of Iowa
HOMOEROTICISM, FEMALE/MALE, CONCEPT

Richard Stites
Professor of History, School of Foreign Service
Georgetown University
KOLLONTAI, ALEXANDRA

Beverly J. Stoeltje
Professor
Anthropology Department
Indiana University, Bloomington
BEAUTY PAGEANTS

Gaylyn Studlar
Professor
Screen Arts and Cultures Department
University of Michigan, Ann Arbor
SACHER-MASOCH, LEOPOLD VON
SADOMASOCHISM

Barbara Tedlock
Doctor
Distinguished Professor of Anthropology
State University of New York, Buffalo
MAYA

Joan Templeton
Professor
English Department
Long Island University, Brooklyn Campus
IBSEN, HENRIK

Polly Thistlethwaite
Professor
The Graduate School and University Center Library, City University of New York
STONEWALL

Jessika L. Thomas
Doctor
West Virginia University
PENIS

Julie L. Thomas
Doctor
Gender Studies Department
Indiana University, Bloomington
BARBIE
FAMILY PLANNING
MAIL-ORDER BRIDES
SANGER, MARGARET

Faye E. Thompson
Doctor
School of Nursing, Midwifery, and Nutrition
James Cook University, Australia
MIDWIVES

Shaun Tougher
Doctor
Cardiff School of History and Archaeology
Cardiff University, England
EUNUCHS

Lan Tran
Independent Scholar
ART, DRAMA/PERFORMANCE

Weipin Tsai
Doctor
CHINA: V. WOMEN'S ROLES IN MODERN

Joyce Tyldesley
Doctor
CLEOPATRA
EGYPT, PHARAONIC
NEFERTITI

Ruth Vanita
Professor
Liberal Studies Program
University of Montana
FRIENDSHIPS, PASSIONATE
HALL, RADCLYFFE
SAPPHO

Michelle Veenstra
English Department
Michigan State University
AFTERGLOW
BLOOD
DWARVES AND GIANTS
EXHIBITIONISM
FLIRTING
GENDER STEREOTYPE
KINKY
MOTORCYCLES AND MOTORCYCLE CULTURES
PETTING
PIERCINGS
PREDATOR, SEXUAL
SATISFACTION
SEXUAL FANTASY
SLANG, SEXUAL
SWINGING
TOMBOY
TRAFFICKING OF WOMEN
WHORE

Sherry M. Velasco
Professor
Spanish and Portuguese Department
University of Southern California, Los Angeles
CATALINA DE ERAUSO

Shane Vogel
Professor
Department of English
Indiana University
HARLEM RENAISSANCE

Michelle Voss Roberts
Doctor
Department of Religious Studies
Rhodes College
LOVE, DEVOTIONAL AND EROTIC

Caroline Vout
Doctor
Faculty of Classics and Christ's College, University of Cambridge, England
GRECO-ROMAN ART

Robert Walser
Musicology Department
University of California, Los Angeles
BLUES
MUSIC
MUSIC VIDEOS
PRESLEY, ELVIS
ROCK AND ROLL

Diane Watt
Professor
English Department
University of Wales, Aberystwyth, England
IDE AND OLIVE

Ronald Weitzer
Professor
George Washington University
PROSTITUTION

Joan Goodnick Westenholz
Professor
Bible Lands Museum Jerusalem, Israel
INANNA-ISHTAR

Ruth Westheimer
Doctor
Princeton University
Yale University
PREFACE
SEXUAL LITERACY

Joshua Wickerham
School of International Relations and Pacific Studies
University of California, San Diego
CHINA: I. PRE-MODERN
CHINA: II. MODERN
ZHANG, JINGSHENG

Melissa M. Wilcox
Professor
Whitman College
NEW RELIGIONS, WOMEN'S ROLES IN

Patrick Williams
Professor
Nottingham Trent University, England
COLONIALISM

Christine Wilson
Professor
English Department
Michigan State University
ECOFEMINISM

Elizabeth Wilson
Professor
Miami University of Ohio
MARRIAGE

Michael Winkelman
Professor
School of Human Evolution and Social Change
Arizona State University
PRIESTHOODS, PRIESTS, AND PRIESTESSES
SHAMANISM

Gregory Woods
Professor
School of Arts and Humanities
Nottingham Trent University, England
LITERATURE: IV. GAY, CREATIVE

Neguin Yavari
Professor
History and Humanities
The New School
'A'ISHA
FATIMA
JINN

Carina Yervasi
Professor
Swarthmore College
FILM, GENDER AND EROTICISM: I. HISTORY

Serinity Young
Doctor
Anthropology Department
American Museum of Natural History
BUDDHISM
COURTESANS
HIJRĀS
MAGIC
TANTRA

Liana Zhou
The Kinsey Institute
Indiana University, Bloomington
CHINA: II. MODERN
JAPAN: I. MODERN
JAPAN: V. WOMEN'S LITERATURE IN MODERN
JAPAN: VI. WOMEN'S ROLES IN MODERN
SEX MANUALS, CHINA
SEX MANUALS, JAPAN

Harriet Zurndorfer
Professor
Leiden University, The Netherlands
CONCUBINAGE

Lynda Zwinger
Professor
English Department
University of Arizona
MISSIONARY POSITION
ORGASM
SPINSTER

Thematic Outline

The following classification of articles arranged thematically gives an overview of the variety of entries and the breadth of subjects treated in the encyclopedia. Along with the index and the alphabetic arrangement of the encyclopedia, the thematic outline should aid in the location of topics. It is our hope that it will do more, that it will direct the reader to articles that may not have been the object of a search, and that it will facilitate a kind of browsing that invites the reader to discover new articles, new topics, related, perhaps tangentially, to those originally sought.

1. BODY AND BODY PARTS

2. BODY ART

3. BODY MODIFICATION

4. BIOLOGY OF SEX

G-Spot
Hormones: I. Overview
Hormones: II. Sex Hormones
Hormones: III. Hormonal Diseases
Male
Mucous Membranes
Penis
Uterus
Vagina

5. CIVILIZATIONS AND CULTURES (GENERAL)

Allegory
Death
Dreams and Eroticism, Dream Books
Drugs, Recreational
Eating Disorders
Education: III. International Issues
Funerary Customs: I. Non-Western
Labor and Workforce in Africa, Asia, and the Middle East
  Feminism: II. Asian
Language
Magic
Sports
Symbolism
  Animals, Sexual Symbolism of
  Plants, Sexual Symbolism of

6. CIVILIZATIONS AND CULTURES (SPECIFIC)

AFRICA

Africa: I. History
Africa: II. Political and Cultural Agendas
Africa: III. Art and Literature
Africa: IV. Religions
Afrocentrism
Beatrice of the Kongo
Dahomey, Women Warriors/Wives of the King
Demography: V. Africa
Egypt, Pharaonic
Feminism: I. African (Sub-Saharan)
Iron, Gendered Symbolism
Music, Women in Muslim Africa
Nefertiti
Umoja

ANCIENT GREECE (HELLENIC AND HELLENISTIC)

Amazons
Ancient Greece
Aphrodite
Aristotle
Artemis Diana
Athena
Cleopatra
Eros, Cupid
Ganymede
Gynaeceum
Hippocrates
Lesbos
Medusa
Oedipus, Myth of
Plato
Sappho
Tiresias
Trojan Women

ANCIENT ROME AND BYZANTIUM

Ancient Rome
Byzantium
Galen
Juvenal
Ovid
Venus
Vestal Virgin
Zenobia

CHINA

China: I. Pre-Modern
China: II. Modern
China: III. Erotic Art
China: IV. Erotic Literature
China: V. Women's Roles in Modern
Demography: IV. Asia
Foot Binding
Sex Manuals, China
Sex Museums, Chinese
Van Gulik, Robert
Zhang, Jingsheng

GRECO-ROMAN

Baths, Public: I. Greco-Roman
Greco-Roman Art
Medicine, Ancient
Sex Manuals, Ancient World

INDIA

Kama and the Kama Sutra
Sex Manuals, India

ISLAMIC CIVILIZATION

Arabian Nights
Baths, Public: II. Muslim Middle East
Demography: III. Middle East and North Africa
Farrokhzad, Foruq
Feminism: III. Middle Eastern

JAPAN

Demography: IV. Asia
Japan: I. Modern
Japan: II. Erotic Literature
Japan: III. Erotic Art
Japan: IV. Courtly Love
Japan: V. Women's Literature in Modern
Japan: VI. Women's Roles in Modern
Japan: VII. Family Roles
Sex Manuals, Japan

MESO-AMERICA

Maya

WESTERN CIVILIZATION

Camp
Conduct Books
Demography: I. America and Europe
Demography: II. Australia
Don Juan
Eleno
Enlightenment
Funerary Customs: II. Western
Heloise and Abelard
King Henry III of France
Marginalia in Medieval Manuscripts
Middle Ages
Mignons
Raffalovitch, Marc-Andre
Renaissance
Rosie the Riveter
Scouts, Boy and Girl
Sexual Revolution
Slang, Sexual
Svengali
Welfare
YMCA/YWCA

7. COMMERCE AND CRIME

Call Girl
Concubinage
Courtesans
Date Rape Drugs
Gigolo
Harassment, Sexual
Kept
Mistress
Predator, Sexual
Prostitution
Rape
Rent Boy
Sex Crimes
Sex Industry
Sex Museums
Sex Shop
Sex Tourism
Sexual Abuse
Trafficking of Women
Trannie Whore
Vetula, Old Whore
Whore

8. DANCE AND PERFORMANCE

Baker, Joséphine
Beauty Pageants
Burlesque
Circus, Fair and Street Performance
Dance
Gypsy Rose Lee
Peep Shows

9. DIGITAL AND MASS MEDIA

Advertising
Chat Room
Computers
Internet
Personals

10. DISEASES

AIDS and HIV: I. Overview
AIDS and HIV: II. History
AIDS and HIV: III. Effects on Population
AIDS and HIV: IV. Treatments and Prevention
AIDS and HIV: V. Social and Political Responses
Cancer, Breast
Cancer, Prostate
Sexually Transmitted Diseases
Syphilis

11. FILM

Betty Boop
Blaxploitation Films
Dietrich, Marlene
Divine
Film, Gender and Eroticism: I. History of
Film, Gender and Eroticism: II. Art and Auteur Cinema
Film, Gender and Eroticism: III. Cult and Marginal Cinema
Film, Gender and Eroticism: IV. Lesbian, Gay, and Queer Film
Garland, Judy
Monroe, Marilyn
Pasolini, Pier Paolo
Production Code (Hays Code)
Sex Symbol
Snuff Films
West, Mae
X-Rated

12. FOLK AND POPULAR CULTURE

Big Bad Wolf
Fairy Tales
Folk Beliefs and Rituals
Folk Healers and Healing
Folklore
Food
Legends and Myths
Little Red Riding Hood
Mermaid
Vampires

13. GENDER ROLES

Boys, Construction of
Dandyism
Education: I. Gender in America
Education: II. GLBT Issues
Effeminacy
Fops
Gender Confusion
Gender Dysphoria
Gender Identity
Gender Roles: I. Overview
Gender Roles: II. History
Gender Roles: III. Contemporary Understanding
Gender Roles: IV. Feminist and Gay/Lesbian Perspectives
Gender Stereotype
Gender, Theories of
Girls, Construction of
Maiden
Male Bonding
Manliness
Manly (Masculine) Woman
Masculinity: I. Overview
Masculinity: II. Attributes and Functions
Masculinity: III. Contemporary Theories
Masculinity: IV. In Media and Culture
Men's Movement
Metrosexuals
Neuter
Passing (Woman)
Physical Culture
Spinster
Tomboy
Transgender

14. HIGH ART

Art
Art, Drama/Performance
Artists, Women
Black Arts Movement
Bosch, Hieronymus
Caravaggio, Michelangelo Merisi da
Cellini, Benvenuto
Erotic Art
Gentileschi, Artemisia
Kahlo, Frida
Michelangelo
Nude in Visual Arts
Pre-Raphaelism/Symbolism
Rubens, Peter Paul
Susanna at Her Bath
Venus de Milo
Warhol, Andy

15. LITERATURE, AUTHORS

Alan of Lille
Baldwin, James
Bingen, Hildegard of
Boccaccio, Giovanni
Brantôme
Casanova
Catalina de Erauso
Chaucer, Geoffrey
Colette, Sidonie-Gabrielle
Dante Alighieri
Genet, Jean
Hall, Radclyffe
Himes, Chester
Ibsen, Henrik
Lawrence, D. H.
Lorde, Audre
Marbod of Rennes
Miller, Henry
Nin, Anaïs
Pizan, Christine de
Rabelais, François
Renault, Mary
Sacher-Masoch, Leopold von
Sade, Marquis de
Sand, George
Shakespeare, William
Stein, Gertrude and Alice B. Toklas
Whitman, Walt
Wilde, Oscar
Woolf, Virginia

16. LITERATURE, GENERAL

Courtly Love, Western
Harlem Renaissance
Literature: I. Overview
Literature: II. The Study of
Literature: III. Popular
Literature: IV. Gay, Creative
Literature: V. Lesbian, Creative
Love Poetry
Women Writers, Emergence

17. LITERATURE, GENRES, TITLES, AND CHARACTERS

Beatrice
Celestina
Dulcinea
Fabliaux
Fanny Hill
Ide and Olive
Lady Chatterley's Lover
Lady MacBeth
Le Roman de Silence
Lolita
Romance of the Rose
Romeo and Juliet
Star-Crossed Lovers
Story of O

18. MAGAZINES AND PIN-UPS

Esquire
Hustler
Penthouse
Pin-Ups
Playboy
Vargas, Alberto

19. MARRIAGE AND FAMILY

Adultery
Avuncular
Chastity
Domestic Partnership
Family
Family, Alternative
Family Leave Act
Fatherhood
Fornication
Honor and Shame
Honor Crimes
Incest
Mail-Order Brides
Marriage
Matriarchy
Matrilineality
Miscegenation
Monogamy
Motherhood
Patriarchy
Patrilineality
Rough Music
Virginity
Widows and Widowers

20. MEDIA, PERFORMANCE, AND THE ARTS (GENERAL)

Censorship
Media
Obscene
Pornography

21. MUSIC

Blues
Jazz
Liberace
Music
Music Videos
Opera
Presley, Elvis
Rap Music
Rock and Roll
Salsa

22. OBJECTS

Barbie
Clothing
Codpiece
Fashion System
G.I. Joe
Toys

23. PHOTOGRAPHY AND COMICS

Comics Code
Comics/Comic Strips
Erotic/Adult Comics
Erotic Photography
Fotonovelas
Mapplethorpe, Robert
Plat Lynes, George
Superheroes
Wonder Woman

24. POLITICS

Beauvoir, Simone de
Behn, Aphra
Bonaparte, Marie
Catherine the Great
Chicana Movement
Colonialism
Communism and Marxism
Domestic Violence
Ecofeminism
Elizabeth I
Employment Discrimination
Espionage
Essentialism
Fascism
Feminism IV. Western
Gouges, Olympe de
Hate Crimes
Hierarchy
Kollontai, Alexandra
Lewinsky Affair
Malinche
Marie Antoinette
Military
Nationalism
Political Satire
Politics
Prison, Detention and Correctional Institutions
Queens
Queens, Power and Sexuality
Royalty
Scottsboro case
Sex and Empire
Sex, Race and Power, Theories of
Shepard, Matthew Wayne
Slavery
Stonewall
Strange Fruit
Suffrage
Terrorism
Till, Emmett Louis
Violence
War
Wollstonecraft, Mary
Women's Human Rights

25. RELIGION (GENERAL)

Adam and Eve
Celibacy
Creation Stories
Fundamentalism
Initiation
Joseph Story, The
Love, Devotional and Erotic
Marriage, Spiritual
Martyrdom
Monasticism
Mysticism
Oracles
Prayer
Priesthoods, Priests, and Priestesses
Queen of Sheba, Myth of
Religion, Study of
Saints, Male and Female

26. RELIGIOUS TRADITIONS

BIBLE

Bible, New Testament
Bible, Old Testament or Tanakh
Esther
Judith
Porneia
Sodom and Gomorrah
Song of Songs

BUDDHISM

Buddhism
Pattini
Pilgrimages: I. Buddhism
Pilgrimages: V. Judaism

CHRISTIANITY

Aquinas, Thomas
Beguines
Burchard of Worms
Canon Law
Carlini, Benedetta
Catholicism
Christ
Christianity, Early and Medieval
Christianity, Reformation to Modern
Damian, Peter
Homosexuality in the Christian Church
Immaculate Conception
Inquisition, Spanish
Joan of Arc
Mary Magdalene
Mary, Mother of Jesus
Paul (Saint)
Penance
Pilgrimages: II. Christianity
Protestantism
Salome
Sophia
Temptation of Saint-Anthony (image)
Verniolle, Arnaud de
Witch Trials, Europe
Witchcraft

HINDUISM

Hijrās
Hinduism
Kali
Ladyboys (Kathoeys)
Pilgrimages: III. Hinduism

Hermaphrodites
Heterosexuality
Homoaffectivity, Concept
Homoeroticism, Female/Male, Concept
Homophobia
Homosexuality, Defined
Homosexuality, Contemporary: I. Overview
Homosexuality, Contemporary: II. History
Homosexuality, Contemporary: III. Cultural Functions
Homosexuality, Contemporary: IV. Issues
Homosexuality, Male, History of
Infantile Sexuality
Intersex
Lesbian, Contemporary: I. Overview
Lesbian, Contemporary: II. Post 1950
Lesbian, Contemporary: III. Status
Lesbianism
Lesbian-Like
Nefandum
One-Sex Theory
Pederasty
Pedophilia
Puberty
Queen
Queer
Same-Sex Love and Sex, Terminology
Sex Roles
Sexual Identity
Sexual Inversion
Sexual Orientation
Sexual Perversion
Sexuality
Sin contra naturam
Sodomy
Sodomy Laws
Sodomy, Repression of
Switchhitter
Third Sex
Transsexual F to M
Transsexual M to F
Tribadism, Historical
Tribadism, Modern
Uranians

32. SPACES AND PLACES

Automobiles
Backroom
Baths, Public: III. West, Middle Ages—Present
Motorcycles and Motorcycle Cultures
Nudist Camps
Privacy
Space, Public and Private
Toilets, Public

33. SYSTEMS OF KNOWLEDGE

Anthropology
Boswell, John
Camille, Michael
Canon, Revising the
Desire, as Historical Category
Economics
Ellis, Henry Havelock
Erotic Transference
Foucault, Michel
Freud, Sigmund
Gender Studies
Guilt
Herrenfrage
History and Historiography, Modern
Hite Report
Kinsey, Alfred
Krafft-Ebing, Richard
Lacan, Jacques
Libido
Literature: II. The Study of
Lust
Mad Woman in the Attic
Melancholia and Sex
Men's Studies
Narcissism
Nymphomania
Other, Constructing the
Perversity, Polymorphous
Philosophy
Philosophy, Feminist
Pleasure
Psychiatry
Psychoanalysis
Queering, Queer Theory, and Early Modern Culture
Reich, Wilhelm
Sadism
Sadomasochism
Satisfaction
Sex Research
Sexology
Sexual Education
Sexual Fantasy
Sexual Instinct
Sexual Literacy
Sexual Objects
Surrogates, Sexual
Women's Studies

A

ABORTION, LEGAL AND POLITICAL ISSUES

Beginning with its 1973 decision in *Roe* v. *Wade*, the U.S. Supreme Court in large measure has defined the contours of the debate over the status of abortion. That landmark decision struck down a 1854 Texas law that criminalized abortion except when necessary to save the woman's life. The Court, by a seven-to-two margin, held that the Texas law violated a woman's fundamental right to decide whether to continue a pregnancy free of governmental interference before the point of fetal viability (i.e., the capacity to live if born). On the same day the Court also struck down a more "modern" 1968 Georgia abortion law that prohibited most abortions but lifted criminal penalties in limited circumstances.

THE COURT DECISIONS

Although the Court ruled that the Constitution places substantial aspects of reproductive liberty beyond the reach of government, abortion continues to play a prominent role in electoral and legislative politics. Literally hundreds of abortion restrictions have been litigated in state and federal courts. *Roe* has inspired mass celebrations, marches, and protests. Some abortion opponents have resorted to violence and even murder. Abortion politics also has affected a range of other issues, from pregnancy prevention policies at home and abroad to scientific research involving stem cells.

Of course, the legal, political, and social ferment and the practice of abortion did not begin with *Roe*. *Roe* cannot be viewed apart from the preceding decades of activism, controversy, and change over not only abortion but also contraception and, more broadly, the status of women. At the time of *Roe* the Court was just beginning to recognize the right of women to constitutional protection from sex discrimination and social and political movements were beginning to lessen barriers to women's equality.

In light of the nascent state of sex equality, it is not surprising that the Court premised *Roe* on the fundamental right to privacy found in the guarantee of liberty in the Fifth and Fourteenth amendments rather than in the constitutional guarantee of equal protection (which the Court soon afterward interpreted to protect against sex discrimination). The *Roe* Court built upon earlier decisions in which it held unconstitutional state laws that criminalized the use of contraception (*Griswold* v. *Connecticut* in 1965) or ordered forcible sterilization as punishment for certain felonies (*Skinner* v. *Oklahoma* in 1942). The Court rejected the argument that the Constitution protects a right to life from the moment a sperm fertilizes an egg or that the government may prohibit abortion to protect the embryo or fetus in the first stages of pregnancy. Instead, the Court declared the right of women throughout the United States to decide when and whether to have children, free from the risks illegal abortions posed to their health, future fertility, and lives.

THE POLITICAL EFFECTS

The political effect of *Roe* was to energize opponents of legal abortion while reassuring most supporters that the courts would protect reproductive liberty. Until 1989 the courts invalidated most governmental efforts to restrict abortion, with the notable exceptions of restrictions on public funding and mandatory parental notice and consent laws. Within a decade the two major political parties had divided on abortion (though some individuals break

Bork Testifies at Confirmation Hearing. *Supreme Court nominee Robert Bork testifies at his confirmation hearing in 1987. Bork was not confirmed, in large part because of his oppostion to abortion.* CNP/GETTY IMAGES.

with their parties on this issue), with the Democratic Party supporting *Roe* and the Republican Party calling for its overruling and the appointment of federal judges specifically to accomplish that end.

In the 1980s President Reagan replaced three of the seven justices in the *Roe* majority. The issue of reproductive liberty and privacy proved extremely consequential in the last of Reagan's Supreme Court appointments, as prochoice Americans began to realize that *Roe* was at risk. Reagan first nominated Robert Bork, but the Senate narrowly refused to confirm him, in significant part because of his opposition to any judicially protected right to reproductive liberty, including the right of married couples to use contraception protected in *Griswold* v. *Connecticut.* Since Bork's rejection abortion has remained a contested issue in Supreme Court appointments. Nominees routinely attempt to avoid disclosing their views on *Roe* while communicating support for the Court's decision in *Griswold.*

By 1992 President George Herbert Walker Bush had made two more Republican appointments to the Supreme Court. Prochoice Americans became more engaged in activism and politics as the Court seemed to be on the verge of overruling *Roe.* The Court surprised all sides in *Planned Parenthood* v. *Casey* by reaffirming, five to four, a narrowed version of *Roe.* (If Bork had been confirmed, he almost certainly would have cast the fifth vote needed to overrule *Roe.*) The *Casey* Court announced that it would continue to invalidate the most onerous abortion restrictions, including husband notification requirements and outright bans. However, the Court no longer would protect a "fundamental right" to reproductive choice and, under a far less protective "undue burden" standard, would uphold many more governmental restrictions.

State legislatures responded to *Casey* by substantially increasing antiabortion legislation. Congress also became more involved in restricting abortion, contrary to many abortion opponents' pre-*Casey* position that abortion regulation is the prerogative of state governments. Public opinion polls over the years show majority support for choice and *Roe,* but the degree of support varies significantly with the way the question is phrased. Elected officials typically are far more antichoice than are their constituents.

At the outset of the twenty-first century *Casey* remained the prevailing law and the Court by a narrow margin continued to provide some level of meaningful protection. Genuine reproductive choice, though, has been precarious and, for a growing number of women, nonexistent. Abortion services are less available in the United States than at any time since *Roe*, and antichoice organizations openly pursue an incremental strategy to create "abortion-free" states, including legal restrictions that the courts now uphold, diminished abortion training in medical schools, and harassment and violence directed at abortion providers at home and at work. As in the years before *Roe*, the women who suffer most from legal and practical obstacles to safe abortion services are those who live hundreds of miles from the nearest provider and lack the resources and ability to travel.

BIBLIOGRAPHY

Balkin, Jack M., ed. 2005. *What* Roe v. Wade *Should Have Said: The Nation's Top Legal Experts Rewrite America's Most Controversial Decision*. New York: New York University Press.

Garrow, David J. 1998. *Liberty and Sexuality: The Right to Privacy and the Making of* Roe v. Wade. Berkeley: University of California Press. (Orig. pub. 1994.)

Ginsburg, Ruth Bader. 1985. "Some Thoughts on Autonomy and Equality in Relation to *Roe v. Wade*." *North Carolina Law Review* 63(2): 375–386.

Griswold v. *Connecticut*, 381 U.S. 479 (1965).

Planned Parenthood v. *Casey*, 505 U.S. 833 (1992).

Roe v. *Wade*, 410 U.S. 113 (1973).

Siegel, Reva B. 1992. "Reasoning from the Body: A Historical Perspective on Abortion Regulation and Questions of Equal Protection." *Stanford Law Review* 44: 261–381.

Dawn Johnsen

ABORTION, MEDICAL ISSUES

Scholars have shown that for every society for which some recorded history exists, there is evidence of abortion. Indeed after an exhaustive review of materials from three hundred fifty ancient and pre-industrial societies, the anthropologist George Devereux (1954) concluded, "There is every indication that abortion is an absolutely universal phenomenon, and that it is impossible even to construct an imaginary social system in which no women would ever feel at least compelled to abort" (p. 98). One of the earliest known medical texts, attributed to the Chinese Emperor Shen Nung (2737–2696 BCE), refers to mercury as a substance that will "cause abortion." The Ebers Papyrus of Egypt (1550–1500 BCE) contains several prescriptions for abortion, including one that combined acacia leaves and the plant colocynth, both of which have been shown in laboratory tests to have certain anti-fertility properties.

In both classical Greece and Rome, abortion was apparently widely practiced and highly visible. Most abortions were attempted through herbal preparations, but archaeological evidence indicates that in the Greco-Roman era, there were several types of vaginal specula, as well as an apparatus designed to irrigate the intrauterine cavity. Specific instruction in abortion through instrumentation is found in the writings of the tenth century Persian physician Al-Rasi (Joffe 1999).

MODERN METHODS OF ABORTION

Despite this striking record of early understandings of abortion techniques, this knowledge appeared to be willfully forgotten as abortion became increasingly controversial. For the next several centuries the medical profession, for the most part, ignored abortion, with the procedure being offered by some physicians only to a select few patients, while other women attempted self-abortions or received them from the hands of nonphysicians with varying skill levels. It was not until the mid-nineteenth century that the medical profession began to rediscover and refine what had been known to practitioners centuries earlier (Joffe 1999).

Dilation and Curettage (D&C) and Vacuum Aspiration

In 1842, the modern curette (from the French verb, *curer*, "to cleanse") was adapted for use in the uterus, and dilators (for opening the cervix) were developed by the German physician Alfred Hegar in the 1870s. *Dilatation and curettage*, or, as it is commonly known, "D&C," became the leading form of abortion as practiced by physicians.

The D&C method of performing first trimester abortions eventually was replaced in most of the developed world by the *vacuum suction machine*, also known as the vacuum *aspiration method*. This method is greatly preferred by practitioners because it replaces the "sharp curettage" of the D&C and causes less blood loss and injury. In the developing world, however, because of a lack of training opportunities and equipment, vacuum aspiration has been slower to replace the D&C method.

Early Abortion Methods: Medication Abortion and Manual Vacuum Aspiration Several important advances in abortion technology took place toward the end of the twentieth century, developments which both allow abortions to be delivered earlier in pregnancy than conventional vacuum aspiration, and in the case of women in the developing world, more accessibly. The first was the discovery of *mifepristone* (formerly known as "RU-486" or the "abortion pill"), by a team of French scientists led by Etienne Baulieu. This pill, when taken with another medication, *misoprostol*, is highly effective in terminating abortions for up to eight or nine weeks. Because administration of this form of abortion does not require specialized surgical training, it can be dispensed by a wider variety of providers, and in a greater range of medical settings than aspiration abortion. Since its introduction in France in 1988, tens of millions of women worldwide have had mifepristone abortions.

Another form of medication abortion is use of the drug *methotrexate* in combination with misoprostol. Methotrexate is a drug that is primarily used in cancer treatment and for several other purposes. Although most abortion providers prefer mifepristone because of its faster action and higher success rate, methotrexate is also effective for terminating ectopic pregnancies, while mifepristone is not.

The use of misoprostol (the second drug in the mifeptristone regime) alone is an additional form of medication abortion that is seeing increasing usage, particularly in the developing world where abortion remains illegal. Known primarily by its most common trade name, Cytotec, this is an ulcer medication that can be bought over the counter in many areas; in women who are pregnant, the drug causes the uterus to contract and begin a miscarriage. Gynuity Health Projects, a non-governmental organization specializing in reproductive health, has taken the lead in disseminating guidelines on the most effective use of misoprostol alone (Gynuity Health Projects 2007).

Finally, the late 1990s saw the reintroduction into abortion providing circles of the *MVA*, or *Manual Vacuum Aspirator*. This handheld device can be used very early in pregnancy, as soon as a pregnancy is confirmed (while conventional vacuum aspiration is typically not performed until about six or seven weeks after a missed period). Another advantage, pertinent to the developing world, is that the MVA is not dependent on a source of electricity.

Later Abortions The major form of second trimester abortion as practiced in the United States and parts of Europe is a procedure called *dilatation and evacuation* (*D&E*). This procedure is often a two-day process. *Laminaria*, a seaweed preparation, or a similar manufactured preparation, is inserted into the woman's cervix to help it dilate. A substance, *digoxin*, is used by many physicians to cause fetal demise, and then the fetus is surgically removed. A rarely used variation of the D&E is "*intact dilatation and extraction*" in which the fetus is removed intact, after partial (passage through the birth canal) vaginal delivery. Intact D&Es (sensationalized by abortion opponents in the United States as "partial birth abortions") accounts for less than one percent of all abortions performed in the United States (Finer and Henshaw 2003) and are typically performed to preserve the pregnant woman's health.

RISKS OF ABORTION

When performed by trained providers, abortion is one of the safest of all medical procedures. After the legalization of abortion in the United States in 1973, the risk of death associated with abortion fell to less than 0.6 per 100,000 procedures, leading the Council of Scientific Affairs of the American Medical Association to conclude that the risk of death from abortion was less than one tenth as large as the risk from dying in childbirth (Council on Scientific Affairs, AMA 1992).

Of the approximately seven hundred thousand mifepristone abortions that have taken place in the United States since 2000, there have been only four deaths associated with a rare *C. Sordellii* infection, and one from an additional infection, leading to an approximate mortality rate of 1/140,000 total infection deaths. The *C. Sordellii* infections continue to puzzle researchers and have been associated with other reproductive events as well, including births and miscarriages, and it is unclear as of this writing whether mifepristone or misoprostal had any role in causing these deaths (Winikoff 2006).

For those women in the developing world, however, who do not have access to safe abortion, the situation is very different. The World Health Organization estimates that some sixty-eight thousand women die each year from unsafe abortions and many thousands more are severely injured (Ahman and Shah 2004).

BIBLIOGRAPHY

Ahman, Elisabeth, and Iqbal Shah. 2004. *Unsafe Abortion: Global and Regional Estimates of the Incidence of Unsafe Abortion in 2000.* 4th edition. Geneva: World Health Organization.

Council on Scientific Affairs, American Medical Association, 1992. "Induced Termination of Pregnancy Before and After *Roe v Wade.*" *Journal of the American Medical Association*, 268 (22): 3231–3239.

Devereux, George. 1954. "A Typological Study of Abortion in 350 Primitive, Ancient and Pre-industrial Societies." In *Therapeutic Abortion: Medical, Psychiatric, Anthropological, and Religious Considerations*, ed. H. Rosen. New York: Julian Press.

Finer, L., and S. Henshaw. 2003. "Abortion Incidence in the United States in 2000." *Perspectives on Sexual and Reproductive Health* 35(1): 6–15.

Gynuity Health Projects. 2007. Instructions for Use of Misoprostal in Women's Health. Available from http://www.gynuity.org.

Joffe, C. 1999. "Abortion in Historical Perspective." In *A Clinician's Guide to Medical and Surgical Abortion*, ed. M. Paul, E. Lichtenberg, L. Borgatta, D. Grimes, and P. Stubblefield. New York: Churchill Livingstone.

Winikoff, B. 2006. "*Clostridium Sordellii* Infection in Medical Abortion." *Clinical Infectious Diseases* 43: 1447–1448.

Carole Joffe

ABSTINENCE

Across times and cultures, individuals and groups of sexually mature people have been culturally defined and socially positioned as celibates on the basis of temporary or long-term abstinence from certain types of sex. This abstinence may vary in relation to *volition* (it can be elected or imposed) and *temporality* (it can be temporary or permanent), but it always is related to the sociocultural significance of the body and its sexuality (Sobo and Bell 2001).

ECONOMIES OF ABSTINENCE

Although people of any age or sexual orientation can be abstinent, in the United States and European culture "abstinence" typically refers to the specifically *heterosexual* activities of biologically mature persons. This is due partly to the relationship between sex and reproduction, which is embedded in a political economy of kinship.

Kinship systems often require absolute celibacy in certain categories of persons to preserve symbolic capital (e.g., honor and purity) that is essential for the status of the family as a whole. Requiring female virginity before marriage is an example. The relationship among the symbolic value of virginity, regulation of reproduction, and the flow of material resources explains why most societies that impose sexual abstinence on adolescent girls prescribe a dowry system. A girl is not only a potential wife but an heiress who is expected to attract a good mate. Abstinence prevents the girl from becoming pregnant with an inappropriate suitor who will be able to press claims on her, her child, her future children, and her dowry (Schlegel 2001).

Along these lines, prosperous families in medieval Europe gained if females retired to convents after being widowed. Allowing a widow to enter a convent and make a vow of abstinence entailed a "small immediate loss to her husband's lineage but a large gain in resources in the long run by preventing remarriage and the possibility of conflict of interest between her former husband's kin" (Hager 1992, p. 392).

Abstinence can benefit kin directly by allowing them to reproduce. In bio-evolutionary theory this is called "inclusive fitness." In humans, mechanisms of kin recognition can be manipulated to this end. Forms of institutionalized celibacy such as monasticism use this tactic by introducing metaphorical kin terms (e.g., brother) and using visual cues such as uniforms and hairstyles to encourage what evolutionary biologists call "false phenotypic matches," meaning they "look the same" or as if they were immediately related. This can motivate adherence to vows of abstinence (Qirko 2001).

PERSONAL AND SOCIAL IDENTITY

Abstinence does not only benefit others. It assists individuals in achieving personal and culturally recommended goals and thus is a potent ingredient in identity construction. This is clear in contexts in which sexuality is associated with a discourse of purity and pollution, for example, in cases in which "each sex is a danger to the other through contact with sexual fluids" (Douglas 1966, p. 3). Avoiding such contact helps one maintain purity and thus reinforces one's social standing and sense of self.

Additionally, when people subscribe to a hydraulic model of sexual energy, in which forces not expressed in one way will be expressed in another, they may practice abstinence to save energy for other identity-related pursuits. For example, self-help literature that promotes the "biomoral" benefits of male celibacy (*brahamcarya*) in northern India, such as increased wisdom, stamina, and personal power, has a wide circulation (Alter 1997). Other examples connecting abstinence to identity formation include the Vatican's claim that permanent celibacy confers spiritual gifts that are important to the priestliness of the clergy.

CHARISMA AND CONTROL

Control of sexual energy commonly is regarded as an important technique for the generation and maintenance of socially beneficial shamanic or spiritual powers. As a result of her abstinence, a celibate spinster (*celibe*) in rural Mexico may ignore everyday female behavioral imperatives and occupy special ceremonial roles that provide "a link between the communal ritual of adult males and the familial ritual of adult females" (Arnold 1978, p. 53).

Interpretations of celibacy often involve speculation about its effect on the disposition of celibate persons or institutions. Celibacy often is construed as a source of charismatic authority. For example, Max Weber notes that "the permanent abstinence of charismatic priests and religious virtuosi derives primarily from the view that chastity, as a highly extraordinary type of behavior, is a symptom of charismatic qualities and a source of valuable ecstatic abilities" (Weber 1978, p. 603).

Weber describes two fundamental positions that promote celibacy as an instrument of salvation. The first is "mystical flight from the world" (p. 603). The other is asceticism, which represents sex as inimical to "rational, ascetic alertness, self control and the planning of life" (p. 604). The two perspectives often are combined, operating simultaneously to generate hostility towards sexual conduct and related social intermingling.

COMMENTARY AND CRITIQUE

Abstinent individuals and groups often comment on the nature of social life and what it means to be human. For example, celibacy (and concomitant communal living) in Shaker communities indicated a complex critique of asymmetrical property relations and related gender inequalities in the surrounding context of emergent capitalism (Collins 2001).

Those who propagate the biomoral value of *brahamcarya* in northern India also engage in a critique of modernity. They believe that "postcolonial India is enslaved by its 'freedom' to develop and Westernize;

enslaved not so much to sex itself—although certainly that—as to the idea that power is a function of potency, and virility the coefficient of modernization" (Alter 1994, p. 57). Modern *brahamcarya* represents an attempt to diffuse the celibate ideal throughout the body politic, whereas Shaker and other forms of celibacy in the United States in the nineteenth century were practiced more often by people who opted out of the body politic.

COMPLEX CONFIGURATIONS

Celibacy always is enacted as part of a complex configuration of ongoing negotiations regarding socio-cultural values, in which stakes are claimed and positions recalculated as events unfold. Out of those negotiations come patterned gains and losses. The religious celibate forswears sex but gains sacred status and/or economic support while helping his or her community. The Balkan "sworn virgin" relinquishes her female gender to become a man, gaining access to resources for her family and access to traditionally male occupations with higher social status (Gremaux 1994). In these ways sexual abstinence can be managed and even manipulated as a channel for cultural creativity and innovation as well as self-advancement.

Those who are abstinent often attempt to remove themselves from the larger social world, alter that world in an active fashion, or critique it passively. Thus, abstinence entails much more than personal sexual inaction. It can improve or alter one's personal status and perpetuate or change one's society. It also can further one's own and one's family's social, material, symbolic, spiritual, and genetic fortunes.

SEE ALSO *Celibacy; Chastity; Virginity.*

BIBLIOGRAPHY

Alter, Joseph S. 1994. "Celibacy, Sexuality, and the Transformation of Gender into Nationalism in North India." *Journal of Asian Studies* 54(1): 45–66.

Alter, Joseph S. 1997. "Seminal Truth: A Modern Science of Male Celibacy in North India." *Medical Anthropology Quarterly* 11(3): 275–298.

Arnold, Marigene. 1978. "Celibes, Mothers and Church Cockroaches." In *Women in Ritual and Symbolic Roles*, ed. Judith Hoch Smith and Anita Spring. New York: Plenum.

Collins, Peter. 2001. "Virgins in the Spirit: The Celibacy of Shakers." In *Celibacy, Culture, and Society: The Anthropology of Sexual Abstinence*, ed. Elisa J. Sobo and Sandra Bell. Madison: University of Wisconsin Press.

Douglas, Mary. 1966. *Purity and Danger: An Analysis of Concepts of Pollution and Taboo.* London: Routledge & Kegan Paul.

Gremaux, René. 1994. "Woman Becomes Man in the Balkans." In *Third Sex, Third Gender: Beyond Sexual Dimorphism in Culture and History*, ed. Gilbert Herdt. New York: Zone Books.

Hager, Barbara. 1992. "Get Thee to a Nunnery: Female Religious Claustration in Medieval Europe." *Ethnology and Sociobiology* 13: 385–407.

Qirko, Hector N. 2001. "The Maintenance and Reinforcement of Celibacy in Institutional Settings." In *Celibacy, Culture, and Society: The Anthropology of Sexual Abstinence*, ed. Elisa J. Sobo and Sandra Bell. Madison: University of Wisconsin Press.

Schlegel, Alice. 2001. "The Chaste Adolescent." In *Celibacy, Culture, and Society: The Anthropology of Sexual Abstinence*, ed. Elisa J. Sobo and Sandra Bell. Madison: University of Wisconsin Press.

Sobo, Elisa J., and Sandra Bell, eds. 2001. *Celibacy, Culture, and Society: The Anthropology of Sexual Abstinence.* Madison: University of Wisconsin Press.

Weber, Max. 1978. *Economy and Society: An Outline of Interpretive Sociology*, ed. Guenther Roth and Claus Wittich. Berkeley: University of California Press. (Orig. pub. 1914.)

Elisa J. Sobo
Sandra Bell

ADAM AND EVE

Two different creation stories are told in the first three chapters of Genesis, with the break coming at Chapter 2:4b. The two stories come from quite different sources such that they use two different expressions for God: *Elohim* and *Yahweh Elohim.* In English Bibles those terms usually are translated "God" and "the Lord God." Scholars refer to the supposed author of the first story as *P*, for "the Priestly writer," who wrote in approximately 500 to 400 BCE, and the second often is known as *J*, or the Yahwist, from his title for God (spelled with a *J* in German). His narrative is much older, perhaps from the tenth or ninth century BCE.

THE P VERSION AND THE J VERSION

In *P*'s version the creation of humankind (*'adam*) comes on the sixth day as the climax of a series of acts: "male and female he created them." Thus, man and woman are created simultaneously and together receive the command to "be fruitful and multiply," to subdue and have dominion over the earth.

In the *J* story everything begins again, but this time there is no orderly progress over six days of divine activity. God makes man (*'adam* again) from the dust of the ground (*'adamah*, the first of several puns in this part of the story) and breathes into his nostrils the breath of life. Then God plants a garden eastward in Eden and puts the man there. God then makes all the trees grow, including the tree of life and the tree of the knowledge of good and evil. He explains that the man may eat from every tree except the last one, for "in the day you eat of it you shall surely die." Only then does God say, "It is not good that the man should be alone; I will make him a helper as a partner" (2.18). Even so, the reader is made to wait while God first forms all the animals and birds and brings them to the man to name them. Then the story continues: "but for the man was not found a helper as his partner. So the Lord God caused a deep sleep to fall upon the man, and he slept; then he took one of his ribs and closed up its place with flesh. And the rib that the Lord God had taken from the man he made into a woman and brought her to the man." Then the man says a little poem: "This at last is bone of my bones and flesh of my flesh; this one shall be called Woman, for out of Man this one was taken." (The word for *woman*, *'ishshah*, also involves a play on the word for *man* in 2:23b, *'ish*, a pun that also works in English.) Therefore, says the narrator, "a man leaves his father and mother and clings to his wife, and they become one flesh. And the man and the woman were both naked, and were not ashamed."

The differences between the two stories are striking. In the first story language is generative: God speaks, and something comes into being. In contrast, in the second language is used for naming and ordering the world, and it is the man who is given that task. Indeed the focus of the Yahwist's version is on man's work, whereas the point of interest in the first story is Elohim, God. The most notorious difference is the creation of woman. In the first story God creates man and woman at the same time, but in the second God first makes man and then seems to search for a mate among the animals to which the man gives names before making another creature from the man's rib. Most commentators see a contradiction between a story in which man and woman are equal from the beginning and one in which the woman is almost an afterthought, created simply as a helper for the man, and is inferior to him. Indeed, she apparently is given her title *Woman* as a kind of further act of naming by the man.

The focus on humankind becomes even clearer as the story continues in Chapter 3 with the story of the serpent and his address to the woman. The woman explains that God has forbidden the eating of the tree in the middle of the garden or they will die. However, the serpent persuades her to eat, saying, "You will not die; for God knows that when you eat of it, your eyes will be opened and you will be like God, knowing good and evil." Thus, "the woman saw that the tree was good for food, and that it was a delight to the eyes, and that the tree was to be desired to make one wise," and she took and ate and gave also to her husband. "Then the eyes of both were opened, and they knew that they were naked." God then curses the serpent and makes him go on his belly in the future. He punishes the woman by increasing the pain of childbearing and by saying that her husband shall rule over her. He punishes the man by cursing the ground for his sake and telling him that "by the sweat of your face you shall eat bread until you return to the ground, for out of it you were taken; you are dust and to dust you shall return." At this point—and only now—"the man named his wife Eve (*hawwa*), because she was the mother of all living [*hay*]." Finally God points out that "the man has become like one of us, knowing good and evil." Thus, so that the man cannot put out his hand for the tree of life as well and so live forever, God expels him from the garden of Eden.

SCHOLARLY AND THEOLOGICAL INTERPRETATIONS

Every detail of the story has been analyzed by generations of scholars and theologians. The word *'adam* is eventually used without the article as a proper name only in the next chapter, at 4.25: "Adam knew his wife again, and she bore a son." Until that point it means "the man" or indeed "humankind," as in *P*'s creation story. Eve is named only in 3:20, after what came to be known as "the Fall" (because of overlapping with the fall of angels from heaven), and as in the word for her husband, a pun or wordplay is involved. These playful usages are characteristic of the Yahwist: He even plays with the word for *naked*, *'arummim*, in 2:25 in that in the first verse of the next chapter he calls the serpent crafty (*'arum*).

Does this mean that the story itself, with its magic trees and hesitant jealous God, is not serious in its original context? Is the talking snake who tells Eve the truth about the tree and God's warning (as God admits in 3:22) a kind of trickster, a figure common in the myths of many other cultures? After all, this story fills a slot familiar from many other cultures: It narrates the origin of death and incidentally explains why people wear clothes.

Oddly enough, there is no further reference to the story in the whole of the Jewish scriptures. However, most subsequent commentators took the Eden story very seriously. For Philo of Alexandria (c. 20 BCE–50 CE) it was an allegorical warning of what can happen when the rational mind (Adam) allows itself to be overcome by the pleasures (the serpent) of the senses (Eve). In the Apocryphal and Pseudepigraphical literature (200 BCE to 200 CE), the serpent came to be thought of as a form of Satan, and there was a good deal of speculation about the nature of the human sin: The desire for sex, for knowledge, or for sexual knowledge begins to appear as an explanation, but as to whether it was primarily Adam's or Eve's responsibility there were various opinions.

In I Enoch 98:4 neither Adam nor Eve are culpable (it is simply "people" who invented sin), and in 4 Ezra it was Adam's "evil heart," a common rabbinic concept, that was responsible. However, as time went on and especially in the later literature of Judaism, the Talmud and Midrash (200–600 CE), there was an attempt to shape women's lives by retelling Eve's story, usually by putting the blame on her. Already in *Sirach* (Ecclesiastes, 180 BCE) 25:24 it is said, "From a woman sin had its beginning and because of her we all die," although Eve is not named, and the reference may be more general, including the many bad women listed in the accompanying verses. Indeed, this may refer to the story of the seduction of the angels by the daughters of men, a myth mentioned briefly in Genesis 6:1–4 and given much fuller development in the various books of Enoch.

But there was a wide range of interpretive opinion even in the rabbinic tradition as scholars tried to cope with the apparent contradiction between the two creation stories: Was there an original androgyne or hermaphrodite, did God change his mind, were there two different Eves? In some cases Eve copulates with the serpent or with the evil angelic presence (Satanail in 2 Enoch 31:3–6) usually known as Sammael (who replaces or acts through the serpent) and gives birth to Cain (*Targum Pseudo-Jonathan* on Genesis 4:1, 5:3, *Pirke de Rabbi Eliezer*, chapters 21–22; *Questions of Bartholemew* 4:58–59, a Christian apocryphal gospel that echoes the Jewish stories). This idea also occurs in the teachings of Mani, which eventually gave rise to Manichaeism (Ibn al-Nadīm, *Fihrist*, 58:11–61:13), but for the most part the serpent is simply "more skilled in evil than all the beasts of the field."

EVE IN THE NEW TESTAMENT

In the Christian New Testament the negative view of Eve is enormously influential. In 1 Timothy, one of the pseudo-Pauline pastoral epistles, Paul is made to write that women should not teach or have authority over a man and should even be silent during worship: "For Adam was formed first, then Eve; and Adam was not deceived, but the woman was deceived and became a transgressor. Yet she will be saved through childbearing" (1 Timothy 2:13–15). Such texts defined the subordinate role of women and still are cited in discussions about women serving as priests or bishops.

Yet the authority of women was clearly a major issue in the early Church, and those who opposed the orthodox, who generally are referred to as Gnostic, sometimes used the figure of Eve in a different way. Thus, in the *Secret Gospel or Apocryphon of John*, Eve represents the higher power that emerged from Adam as he slept, urging him to awaken to spiritual enlightenment. But from the end of the second century CE, when Irenaeus and others were denouncing such heretical ideas and establishing a sacred canon, orthodoxy was defining the path that much of subsequent Christianity would follow. A key text was 1 Corinthians 11.7, in which Paul says that women should cover their heads when praying or prophesying but not men, "since he is the image and glory of God, but woman is the glory of man. Indeed man was not made from woman, but woman from man." The reference to the hierarchy of Genesis 2 is clear. Paul announced (Romans 5:12–17) that Christ was a second Adam and thus put the Genesis myth at the center of the story of fall and redemption that Christianity learned to tell. It was left to followers such as Justin to add the parallel relationship of Eve to Mary, and soon it was commonplace to see Mary's virginity as the compensation for Eve's sexuality. Interpretations often turn on ideas of sexual morality. Whereas Clement saw God's blessing on marriage and procreation in Paradise, the ascetic Jerome insisted that God's plan was for Adam and Eve to stay virgin: They were united in marriage only after the Fall and their shameful exile from "the Paradise of virginity" (Letter 22, 18).

The misogyny of the Church Fathers can be illustrated by a passage from Tertullian, who wrote "On the Apparel of Women" in about 202 CE and recommends (I:1) that women "affect meanness of appearance, walking about as Eve mourning and repentant, in order that by every garb of penitence she might the more fully expiate that which she derives from Eve—the ignominy, I mean, of the first sin, and the odium attaching to her as the cause of human perdition.... You are the devil's gateway."

Not all the Fathers were quite so definite. Thus, John Chrysostom invokes both the original equality implied by Genesis 1:27 and the subordinate status of Eve in the Yahwist's story. He has his "loving God" say to Eve, "In the beginning I created you equal in esteem to your husband, and my intention was that you would share with him as an equal ... but you abused your equality of status. Hence I subject you to your husband, and he will be your master" (*Homily* 17). Augustine also admits the original equality but spends most of his energy reflecting on the purpose of creating a woman—to have children (*De Genesi Ad Litteram* 9:5, 401 CE)—or on the doings of Eve and the serpent. Like most commentators he worries about Paul's refusal of the image of God to her in 1 Corinthians 11:7, where she is instead the glory of man. Perhaps she had not yet received the gift of the knowledge of God but was supposed to receive it gradually from her husband. Thus, she jumped the gun. Adam, however, ate the fruit not through lust for his wife, which he still could control, but because "he did not wish to make her unhappy, fearing she would waste away without his support" (11.42.59).

This generous attitude to Adam did not last, and soon Augustine came to identify Adam's deed as the "original sin" from which all people have suffered ever since, which befouled the world. He thought he found that idea in the text of Paul's letter to the Romans 5:12 about Adam "in whom all have sinned." Paul's Greek text simply connects the origin of death with the fact that Adam had sinned, but in the Latin Vulgate translation it became the foundational text for a new and immensely influential doctrine: the transmission of Adam's corrupt seed to all his descendants.

INTERPRETATIONS IN THE MIDDLE AGES

There was considerable resistance to this view of the story throughout the Middle Ages. One example is the Latin poem *Carmen de Deo* by Dracontius, from the end of the fifth century CE, in which the author describes Eve as she stands before Adam "naked like a nymph of the sea." The two are commanded to live in *honesta voluptas* (honest pleasure). The writer is very clearly adapting the tradition of pagan Latin poetry, both Lucretius and Ovid, to the Christian topic. Throughout the tradition of representing the first humans there is an oscillation between adapting and rejecting the pagan world. In Augustine, and thus more often in the medieval period, it is rejected, but Augustine did allow for the possibility of sexual intercourse in Paradise.

Islamic Interpretations After 600 CE Islam enters the picture as a distinct religious tradition. Adam is mentioned in several Suras of the Qur'an. Although Eve is not named, she is referred to as Adam's mate or wife. Her creation is not mentioned, and she is not made responsible for the primary act of disobedience. But two of the learned traditions (*hadith*) contend that God created Eve (Hawwa in Arabic) as a source of "rest" for Adam (which the Qur'an itself says about all spouses) and emphasize her culpability by saying that Adam at first refused to eat the fruit of the forbidden tree (al-Tabari on Q.2.35 and 36, written in the 800s). In the Qur'an (Surahs 2 and 15 especially) the reason for Iblis or Shaitan to tempt her to disobedience is jealousy of Adam because the angels are told to prostrate themselves before him. This story is found first in the Adam literature that developed in Jewish and Christian circles, for example, in the text known by its Latin title as *Vita Adae et Evae* (it exists in many other languages and variants, including Armenian and Greek), and it is one sign among many that early Islam made considerable use of noncanonical Jewish and Christian stories. The Islamic serpent has four legs in some versions, "as if it were a camel," an idea that reappears in the medieval Jewish *Pirke de Rabbi Eliezer*, in which the angel Sammael mounts and rides it, an unusual way of explaining how fallen angel and snake both could be present in the story (Chapter 13, c. 700–800s). In other versions, both Islamic and Jewish, Eve's punishment is to bleed every month, "just as you have made this tree to bleed." Again, as in some medieval Jewish versions, Eve's method of seduction is to get Adam drunk, the forbidden fruit being a grape.

Jewish Interpretations It is in the medieval period that within the Jewish tradition the rabbinic idea of Adam's two wives, which comes from interpretation of the two successive creation stories in Genesis, develops the figure of Lilith as a separate first wife. But whereas God earlier had removed the first Eve because Adam was disgusted by her, now (e.g., in *The Alphabet of Ben Sira*, c. 800s–900s) Lilith leaves of her own accord, refusing to lie below Adam on the grounds that they are equal. In several legends Lilith lives on and becomes a general threat to men or to newborn babies, in alliance with demons. That idea was contested by many rabbis but remained popular.

Medieval Christians officially lived their faith in the light of Augustine's misogyny. When Aquinas added a dash of Aristotle, man was understood as the "form" and woman as the "matter" of sexual reproduction. If all went well, a baby was male, but if something went wrong, such as a south wind blowing, a misbegotten or defective male, that is, a female, would result (Aquinas, *Summa Theologiae* 13, Qu. Ia, 92, 99).

Female mystics often took a notably different view. Hildegard of Bingen, for example (1098–1179), argued that woman's association with the body tied her more closely to the Incarnation. Eve was the mother of humanity ("all living" in Genesis), and Mary the mother of God incarnate: It was woman who gave humankind the chance to participate in the divine image. Christine de Pizan (1365–c. 1430) complained about clerics who indoctrinated schoolboys with stories of Adam and other men supposedly deceived by women. Instead, Eve innocently accepted the serpent's words as true and guilelessly shared the news with Adam ("Letter of the God of Love," 260–280, 604–616, 1399). In the Anglo-Norman play *Mystère d'Adam* (1150–1200) Eve thinks the fruit will give them great wisdom and charges Adam with cowardice when he refuses to eat; he then agrees. In some English medieval mystery plays Eve is under the impression that the visitor, an actor dressed in a snake costume and walking upright, is actually a messenger from heaven, and so she says to Adam: "A ffayr Aungell thus seyd me tylle / To Ete that appel take nevyr no drede" (*Ludus Coventriae* 11 238–239, 1450). The fruit had by then become an apple because of a Latin pun: *Malum* means "evil" (with a short *a*) and "apple" (with a long *a*). The expression *Adam's apple* originates in the popular idea that the fruit stuck in his throat as he ate.

This partially sympathetic view contrasts with that of the *Malleus Malleficarum* [Hammer of witches] (1496), a work by two Dominican inquisitors that encouraged two centuries of persecution of witches on grounds such as that "there was a defect in the formation of the first woman, since she was formed from a bent rib." That work collects much misogynist lore. It even describes the word *Femina* as coming from *Fe* and *Minus*, "she of lesser faith." Adam "was tempted by Eve, not the devil, so she is more bitter than death," it says, citing Revelations 6:8 (Part I, Qu. 6,

Adam and Eve by Lucas Cranach the Elder. *Adam and Eve eating the forbidden fruit.* THE ART ARCHIVE/NATIONAL MUSEUM OF PRAGUE/DAGLI ORTI.

ed Montague Summers, pp. 42–45). By contrast, in a Latin play by the Renaissance humanist Hugo Grotius, *Adamus Exul* (1601), Eve is faced with a choice between bearing a race of captives or a race of free men, and she acts in the name of freedom.

PROTESTANT INTERPRETATIONS

The leading figures of the Protestant Reformation took the Augustinian idea of original sin very seriously. The Fall had devastated all human life. In abolishing monasticism, Martin Luther insisted that patriarchal marriage was the necessary result of the Fall. Once equal partner to the man, woman was obliged through Eve's sin to subject herself to her husband. For Jean Calvin, "Thou shalt desire nothing but what thy husband wishes" (*Commentaries on the First Book of Moses Called Genesis* Vol. 1, p. 172, on 3:16). Calvin had a complex understanding of the text of Genesis, which he read in the light of the New Testament passages, largely Pauline, that mention it. Thus, on the one hand, "Adam was not deceived but the woman" (1 Timothy 2.14), and so it was his wife's allure, not Satan's, that persuaded Adam. Thus, he was not present when the serpent tempted Eve (a matter about which the text of Genesis 3:6 leaves some doubt because "she gave also unto her husband with her"). On the other hand, Paul says at Romans 5:12 that "sin came not by the woman but by Adam himself" (*Commentaries* on Genesis 3:6): "No excuse was left to him who had obeyed his wife rather than God" (on 3:17).

These paradoxes are explored thoroughly in the most influential literary treatment of the story, Milton's *Paradise Lost*, in which it is Adam who is made to bear the larger part of the blame because he falls "not deceived/ But fondly overcome with female charm" (IX 999). Most of the more overtly misogynist statements are put into Adam's mouth in his misery after the Fall, for example, when he aligns Eve with the serpent (like much of the tradition): "Out of my sight, thou serpent!" (X 867). Although some readers find a more specifically Miltonic misogyny in statements such as "He for God only, she for God in him" (IV 299) and in the explicit statement that she was made for subjection even if "required with gentle sway" (IV 308), others see those statements as the ways in which Milton honestly faced the implications of the story (especially in view of the Pauline interpretations) and of Western misogyny and thus explained Eve's sin on the grounds of her feeling of inferiority: As she says while debating whether to give Adam the fruit, "for inferior, who is free?" (IX 825). Milton balances the egalitarian and hierarchical readings of Genesis. Adam had asked God for an equal and thought of Eve as "the last and best/ Of all God's works" (IX 896–897). Yet he is reproved explicitly for having been so moved by passion that he listened to his wife, whom he should have ruled.

An enormous variety of views about the Genesis story can be found amid the revolutionary fervor of early modern England in which Milton participated, and thence in American tradition. It had implications for ideas of government, gender, and class. Was Adam like a modern peasant, or was he far above later people in the heights of his intellect? Was Eve responsible for the lack of political rights among her daughters, modern women? Should contemporary society try to re-create the original state of Adam as patriarchal head of the family or as "borne free"? Even gardening manuals could hark after the original state of innocence and the holiness of digging.

The story was potentially subversive as soon as anyone began to question it seriously. Genesis 3:22 states: "Behold the man is become as one of us to know good and evil." If God were not being ironic here, as many, such as Luther, were forced to argue, he admits the force and truth of the serpent's discourse. The fruit did indeed contain real wisdom. So why was it banned? It is a short step from this question to the Socinian Stephen Nye's position that the God represented by this story, who banishes Adam and Eve from the garden in case they should eat from the tree of life also, has "the *just* Character of *an Almighty Devil.* For if the Devil had Supream Power, what worse could he do?"

One justification that frequently has been offered for the ban on the fruit is that Adam and Eve were still like children, not ready for the knowledge contained in the fruit, especially if it was sexual knowledge (their lack of shame at their nakedness supported that reading). This doctrine is common in the Jewish tradition and in the Eastern (later the Orthodox) Church and was espoused especially by Irenaeus in the West. Augustine had rejected that view because it makes the temptation (in his view Satanic) unfair. Calvin followed Augustine and denounced the French Libertines for seeking "to return to that innocent state which Adam enjoyed before he sinned ... and like a child let himself be led by his natural sense." And yet an originally mature, adult Adam raises the problem of how he fell at all. Augustine had great difficulty with this in light of his exalted conception of Adam and Eve and eventually insisted on an inherent weakness of the will before the act of eating. His followers did not find the problem any easier to solve. No wonder Edward Gibbon in *The Decline and Fall of the Roman Empire* could describe the Western church's adoption of Augustine's views as conducted "with public applause and secret reluctance."

Thinkers who were under Paracelsan influence thought of the forbidden tree as an aphrodisiac. Or was it a kind of magic "smart drug," genuinely enlightening, as God admits, but overwhelming for human beings who were not properly prepared or adult? Other, even more radical trends began to be heard in this period. An example is the Quaker Margaret Fell, author of *Women's Speaking* (1666), who rejected the hierarchical model and encouraged women to speak up in meetings. The seed promised to Eve's descendants in Genesis 3:15, understood as Christ, more than compensated for the transgression, and the Church is spoken of as a woman. Anyone who denies all this is "of the Seed of the Serpent, wherein lodges the enmity." Moreover, "Christ in the Male and in the Female is one."

INTERPRETATIONS IN THE UNITED STATES

In the United States the Quaker influence was even stronger, and Sarah Grimké and her sister, former slave owners who converted to Quakerism, became prominent spokeswomen both for the abolitionist movement and for women's rights. In her *Letters on the Equality of the Sexes and the Condition of Woman* (1838) Sarah Grimké denounced the hierarchical reading of Genesis and argued ingeniously that the so-called curse of Yahweh to Eve was not a command but a prophecy: "Thou wilt be subject unto thy husband, and he will rule over thee." Unfortunately, she thought, Hebrew does not differentiate *shall* from *will* as does English. The translators saw only through the medium of a perverted judgment. What the words actually mean is that "the consequence of the fall was an immediate struggle for dominion, and Jehovah foretold which would gain the ascendancy." It is time to right that wrong, since Adam and Eve "fell from innocence and consequently from happiness, *but not from equality.*"

Other American sects, such as the Shakers, went so far as to argue from Genesis 1:26–27 that there is truly "a Heavenly Divine Mother as there is a Heavenly Divine Father" (Frederick W. Evans, *Autobiography of a Shaker*, 1888, p. 199). Mary Baker Eddy, the founder of Christian Science, went further. The true creation account was that in Genesis 1, whereas the contradictory version in Genesis 2–3 was simply an allegory of error. They could not both be true, and she picked out in particular the mist that arises in Genesis 2:6 and Adam's sleep in 21–22 as signs of the error of giving predominance to the world of matter (circa 1875). Soon one among many of the spoof versions of the tale was written, Mark Twain's *The Diaries of Adam and Eve* (1892–1893), in which the first extract from Adam's diary begins: "This new creature with the long hair is a good deal in the way. It is always hanging around and following me about. I don't like this; I am not used to company. I wish it would stay with the other animals."

CONTEMPORARY INTERPRETATIONS

In the twentieth and twenty-first centuries, especially in the United States, the story has continued to be a focus for debate, almost always political. Some conservative thinkers, whether Jewish, Christian, or Muslim, have defended the hierarchical views implied by the text and insisted on the so-called household code of the New Testament, but under the inspiration of the feminist movement there have been new ways of reading the story.

In 1972 Phyllis Trible read a paper to the Andover Newton Theological Seminary in which she argued that God created an androgyne that became male only when God separated out the female parts for Eve. Genesis 3:16 did not sanction male supremacy but condemned it. The myth places under judgment the patriarchal culture from which it comes. Judith Plaskow, a Jewish scholar, wrote an essay called "The Coming of Lilith" in which she told a new story, in the mode of *midrash*, of Adam's first wife as a woman so aware of her own value that she refused to become Adam's servant. Adam then asked for a new and more docile partner, but eventually Eve escaped and joined Lilith, returning to Eden with plans to make it new. Within Islam there have also been some stirrings in these new directions, as in the work of Riffat Hassan, a Pakistani woman living in the United States who argues that in the Qur'an "both men and women were made in the same manner, of the same substance, at the same time." The radical Egyptian feminist Nawal El Saadawi used ambiguities in the Adam and Eve story as part of her attack on traditional gender roles. Such reinterpretations remain marginal, however, and the most important recent trends in Muslim countries have seen the strengthening of traditional patriarchal understandings of the religion.

SEE ALSO *Creation Stories.*

BIBLIOGRAPHY

Alter, Robert. 1981. *The Art of Biblical Narrative.* New York: Basic Books.

Brenner, Athalya, and Fokkelien van Dijk-Hemmes, eds. 1993. *On Gendering Texts: Female and Male Voices in the Hebrew Bible.* Leiden and New York: Brill.

Evans, Frederick W. 1888. *Autobiography of a Shaker.* New York: American News Co.

Evans. J. M. 1968. Paradise Lost *and the Genesis Tradition.* Oxford, UK: Clarendon.

Kvam, Kirsten E.; Linda S. Schearing; and Valarie H. Ziegler, eds. 1999. *Eve and Adam: Jewish, Christian, and Muslim Readings on Genesis and Gender.* Bloomington: Indiana University Press.

Luttikhuizen, Gerard P., ed. 2000. *The Creation of Man and Woman: Interpretations of the Biblical Narratives in Jewish and Christian Traditions.* Leiden, Netherlands: Brill.

Malti-Douglas, Fedwa. 1995. *Men, Women, and God(s): Nawal El Saadawi and Arab Feminist Poetics.* Berkeley: University of California Press.

Pagels, Elaine. 1988. *Adam, Eve and the Serpent.* New York: Random House.

Stratton, Beverly J. 1995. *Out Of Eden: Reading, Rhetoric and Ideology in Genesis 2–3.* Sheffield, UK: Sheffield Academic Press.

Neil Forsyth

ADOLESCENCE

SEE *Adolescent Sexuality.*

ADOLESCENT SEXUALITY

Prepuberty and puberty refer to the physiological, anatomical, and hormonal changes in sexual maturation. Puberty begins with menarche in girls and the first ejaculation in boys, and marks the beginning of adolescence, a complex psychological and developmental process that spans the years roughly from eleven to twenty (Tyson and Tyson 1990, p. 62). Three transformations occur in adolescence: There is disengagement from the infantile ties to the parents; there is the discovery of orgasm and sexual desire directed away from the parents; and there is a primary identification with one of the parents as an adult. In Freudian theory, for heterosexuals the primary identification would be with the same sexed parent, for homosexuals the primary identification is the opposite sexed parent. These transformations begin with the onset of adolescence, which many writers agree is a recapitulation of infancy. Infantile sexuality, repressed during latency, is revived in adolescence with the reappearance of Oedipal conflicts: the threat of attraction to the opposite sexed parent, and the wish for the disappearance or death of the same sexed parent.

In the United States, largely through the work of Peter Blos and Margaret Mahler, adolescence is viewed as the culmination of a process of maturation. The process of mourning becomes important. Anna Freud drew attention to the similarity of adolescence, with its emotional disappointments, and a period of mourning. The adolescent's sexual feelings must detach from the parents and focus on new objects, and this results in mourning for infantile wishes. The new objects, or individuals, are pursued for narcissistic and grandiose fantasies that characterize this development stage. The most specific change in adolescence is managing the dual tasks of integrating a genitally mature body in society and also becoming autonomous. The work of becoming autonomous challenges the narcissistic attitude of the adolescent and reveals the internal world of the young adult and exposes the secure and insecure attachments of his or her character. It also challenges the adolescent's ego to take control of functions that have until then been the responsibility of the parents.

The development that occurs in adolescence has a form and conclusion conditioned by the culture and family to which it belongs. The culture and family are capable of interfering with this process. The parents of adolescents are often in the midst of their own midlife problems and this can add confusion between the adolescent and the parents. Also, the adolescent's actualization of some of the parents' own unresolved conflicts can add more confusion and dissension to this period and contribute to the adolescent feeling misunderstood.

External reality becomes a mediator for the adolescent, capable of reinforcing or weakening the structures of the psychic apparatus. The task for the adolescent is to separate from infantile objects and wishes, and resume identification with narcissistically acceptable objects. Mediator figures include parents, teachers, friends, ideologies, and religions. They can provide for the adolescent a temporary support or identification as they develop a self-image that is truly his or her own.

Sigmund Freud rooted gender in the discovery of genital differences, but research has suggested that gender development is influenced by many factors and there is not a single route to adult gender identity. Many writers have come to agree that individuals unconsciously make both heterosexual and homosexual attachments, with any person's outcome just one of a wide continuum of possibilities. The idea is that individuals are not simply homosexual or heterosexual, but some unique mixture. One's gender identity is a developmental outcome that results from individual differences, the influences of culture and family, as well as fantasy, conflict, defenses, regression, and making and breaking relationships internally and externally while trying to maintain a stable self.

There was a paradigm shift in the study of gender identity over the last few decades of the twentieth century. Historically, gender identity was considered binary: One was either homosexual or heterosexual, and culture encouraged conformity to this view. Psychoanalytic feminism began documenting the pathogenic processes and effects of psychological conformity to the cultural gender binary (Bassin 2000, Layton 2000, Stimmel 2000). This more recent approach argues that gender identity is not just absorbed from one's culture, but individuals engage the influence of cultural proscription and talk back. Gender not only acts on and against one, but it is also available to the individual to use for his or her own aims. Gender identity is best understood as a social category and psychic identity position that is a compromise formation held in the tension between the pressures of conformity and compliance, on one hand, and the individual's continuous project of self-creation and self-protection on the other (Person, Cooper, and Gabbard 2005, p. 102).

Gender identity has moved from dualism to multiplicity. Gender is both fluid and embodied, not unified. As Ethel Spector Person (1999, p. 314) has written, "Against what appears to be a dichotomously, categorical expression of gender, there exists in each person a complicated, multi-layered interplay of fantasies and identifications, some feminine, some masculine. … In essence, conscious and unconscious diversity co-exist." The diversity of gender identity is seen in the early twenty-first century in adolescent behavior: It is acceptable, even popular, to talk about oneself as bisexual, or even to resist the imperatives in this label, and refuse to claim one position on the gender identity continuum.

SEE ALSO *Puberty.*

BIBLIOGRAPHY

Bassin, D. 2000. "On the Problem(s) with Keeping Difference(s) Where They Belong." *Studies in Gender and Sexuality* 1(1): 69.

Layton, L.B. 2000. "The Psychopolitics of Bisexuality." *Studies in Gender and Sexuality* 1 (1): 41–61.

Person, Ethel Spector. 1999. *The Sexual Century*. New Haven, CT: Yale University Press.

Person, Ethel Spector; Arnold M. Cooper; and Glen O. Gabbard, eds. 2005. *The American Psychiatric Publishing Textbook of Psychoanalysis*. Washington, DC: American Psychiatric Publishing.

Stimmel, B. 2000. "The Baby with the Bath Water." *Studies in Gender and Sexuality* 1(1): 79–85.

Tyson, Phyllis, and Robert L. Tyson. 1990. *Psychoanalytic Theories of Development: An Integration*. New Haven, CT: Yale University Press.

Michael Bieber

ADULTERY

Adultery is a nearly universal concern. It is defined by Judaic, Christian, and Muslim formulations, and in legal codes deriving from Roman law. Known colloquially as *cheating* or *infidelity*, adultery is more complex than simple faithlessness and is not to be confused with *fornication*, or sex between two unmarried people. In its simplest definition, adultery occurs when a married person has sex with someone other than his or her spouse. Marriage is requisite, on the one hand, for an action to be called adultery. On the other hand, the cheating couple also must not be married to one another; otherwise the situation is not adultery but *bigamy* or *polygamy*, even in jurisdictions where such is proscribed. It is sometimes the case that spouses agree beforehand that one or both spouses will seek sexual pleasure outside their marriages, a situation that has been called *open marriage*. Regardless of the level of consent or of participation by the offended spouse, most legal and religious authorities still consider such activity to be adulterous.

Simple definitions aside, whether a particular act can be called adultery depends very much on historical, legal, and cultural contexts. That is, what qualifies as adultery in one jurisdiction would not in another, or even in the same jurisdiction in another era. In some definitions, both "cheating" partners are adulterers if either of them is married, and each is to be treated similarly. In practice, one partner—usually the woman—is often punished more severely than the other. In many definitions, a married man commits adultery only if he has sex with a married woman not his wife; if the man's paramour is not married, neither is an adulterer. Under the same definitions, a married woman commits adultery when she has sex outside her marriage, regardless of the marital status of her partner. The primary variable in this diversity of definitions historically would seem to be the status of women. The more repressive the code or culture, the more likely it is that there will be a double standard regarding men and women in adulterous relationships, to the point that in some jurisdictions a woman can be guilty of adultery even if she did not consent to having sex.

The legal principle of property underlies many secular definitions of adultery, in the sense that the marriage bond is one in which one partner has rights to another (or, in some formulations, each has rights to the other), so that infidelity amounts to a kind of larceny. What are these rights? Under a dynastic model of marriage, what seems to be at stake is a man's right to legitimate heirs—that is, to sons and daughters of his own engendering, which adultery throws into question. Under more companionate models, the right would seem to be to exclusive enjoyment. It is rarer, though not unknown, for adultery to be considered a crime against the state so that the state might take action, regardless of the desires of the offended spouse or spouses. The logic behind such a position is that marriage is a foundational social relationship, so that individual acts of adultery undermine the society as a whole. Such is the logic behind the United States military's prosecutions of adultery. The Uniform Code of Military Justice, the code under which service people are tried in courts martial, does not specifically mention adultery. Rather, when an adultery case is brought, it falls under what is called the "General Article," which proscribes all conduct "to the prejudice of good order and discipline" and all conduct "of a nature to bring discredit" to the armed forces.

JUDAISM AND CHRISTIANITY

In the Judeo-Christian tradition, adultery is proscribed in the sixth or seventh *mitzvah* or commandment of the Decalogue (Exodus 20), what is colloquially called the Ten Commandments (sixth or seventh because different religions and denominations group the commandments differently). Perhaps the most notorious adulterer in the Hebrew scriptures is also one of the most revered kings, David, whose adulterous affair with Bathsheba and the punishments he received for it are prominently narrated in 1 Samuel. The prohibition against adultery (and incest) is one of the three strongest in Talmudic thinking, the others being those against murder and against idolatry, such that a person is enjoined from committing adultery even to save his own life. In Deuteronomy (chapters 20 and 22), the punishment for an adulterous couple is death, in order to purge the impurity brought on the community by such sin—"so shalt thou put away evil from Israel" (Deuteronomy 22:22, King James Version).

But Rabbinic law by the time of Roman occupation became decidedly averse to the death penalty, so that the condemned adulteress was only sent away and prohibited from rejoining either her husband or her paramour. Even under this new leniency, however, adultery remained a violation of God's ordained social order, and a husband was required to divorce his adulterous spouse, even if inclined to forgive her. In Deuteronomy, adultery depends entirely on the woman's marital status, occurring when a man has sex with a married woman or even a woman who is betrothed but not yet married. If the woman is not married or betrothed, it is not adultery, even if the man is already married. Similarly, if she is a slave, she is not guilty because Rabbinic law assumes she is not free to act as she might. The story of Tamar in Genesis illustrates the complications that could arise from these definitions in combination with other laws, in this case the requirement in Deuteronomy that a widow must marry her husband's brother in order to continue her husband's line. Tamar is the widow of Er and of his brother, Onan. Her father-in-law, Judah, keeps her from his remaining son, Shelah, so she disguises herself as a prostitute and has sex with unwitting Judah. When Tamar becomes pregnant, Judah threatens her with execution for adultery, since she is technically betrothed to Shelah. Tamar exposes Judah as the father, and in so doing exposes his injustice in keeping Shelah from her, thus saving her life. As early as 70 CE, Rabbi Yochanan ben Zakkai saw the injustice of these double standards during a proliferation of adultery, so he abolished the ordeal (involving the drinking of a bitter liquid in a public ceremony) that was supposed to test the guilt or innocence of the accused woman.

In some ways Jesus's teachings about adultery are more strict than the Deuteronomic tradition out of which they arise, expanding the question of adultery beyond physical acts to include desires and intentions: "Ye have heard that it was said by them of old time, Thou shalt not commit adultery: But I say unto you, That whosoever looketh on a woman to lust after her hath committed adultery with her already in his heart" (Matt. 5:27–28). In effect, the commandment against coveting a neighbor's wife is subsumed under that against adultery. Jesus also adds (Matt. 5:32) that any divorce, except on grounds of infidelity, will cause a woman to commit adultery when she remarries, a position that is much stricter than the Jewish laws. Moreover, Jesus expands the definition of adultery to include any married man who has sex outside of marriage. It is no surprise, therefore, that early Christian thinking held the marriage bond to be of such importance—elevated to the point that it replicates the bond between God and the Church—that any adulterous act wounds the bond between God and man (see, for instance, Ephesians 5:22–32). And yet, for all this strictness, Jesus also seems to be in accord with the Rabbinic thought of the period, so that in the famous *Pericope Adulterae*, or story of the woman taken in adultery, Jesus does not sentence the woman to death but drives off her accusers with the question of their own sinfulness and frees her with an admonition to cease sinning (usually found at John 7:53–8:11).

Roman Catholic doctrine toward adultery derives from Jesus's teachings and from early Christianity's writings about marriage and adultery, and develops over the course of the Middle Ages. Because Catholic doctrine defines various stages and degrees of marriage, what constitutes adultery can be complicated. Unlike Jewish law, engagement to be married is not sufficient to make sexual intercourse with someone other than the fiancé adulterous. But if a couple agrees to marry, then has intercourse, they are sufficiently married in the eyes of the Church for any other sexual relations to be adulterous. Similarly, *matrimonium ratum* (which occurs when a couple has gone through the marriage ceremony but has not yet had intercourse in order to consummate the marriage) is also sufficient to make any other sexual relations adulterous.

While Jewish law allows divorce for virtually any reason and in fact has required it following adultery, Catholic doctrine never permits or recognizes *divortium plenum*, or absolute divorce, for marriages sanctified by the Catholic Church. This doctrine is based upon Jesus's rejection of divorce in Mark 10:9–12 and similar passages: "What therefore God hath joined together, let not man put asunder. . . . Whosoever shall put away his wife, and marry another, committeth adultery against her. And if a woman shall put away her husband, and be married to another, she committeth adultery." It may be remarked that the similar passage from Matthew (mentioned above) seems to contain an exception, that divorce is permitted if the spouse is adulterous, but Catholic doctrine rejects the possibility that the passages conflict with one another and that Jesus allowed absolute divorce in this limited circumstance. Catholic doctrine will allow in the case of adultery a *divortium imperfectum*, or a limited divorce, in which the marriage bond remains indissoluble though the couple lives apart from one another. Furthermore, canon law (see below) requires that the offended party seek redress within six months of discovering the infidelity, or else he or she is assumed to have condoned or forgiven the transgression and cannot take action. Nevertheless, in practice in such cases, the Catholic Church has often been known to grant annulments, declaring that a true marriage not only does not exist but never occurred in the first place, which, though doctrinally different from divorce, has the effect of allowing the couple to remarry elsewhere.

Just as doctrines about marriage complicate Catholic definitions of adultery, so too do doctrines about sexual acts. Under Catholic teaching, adultery requires intercourse, so that some sexual behavior between a married person and another married person may not amount to adultery, no matter how sinful the behavior may be. Similarly, according to some theologians, some sexual acts, such as sodomy, are adulterous even when the partners are married to one another.

ISLAMIC LAW

While the several varieties of Islamic law, or *sharia*, practiced in some Muslim countries differ in some particulars, the prohibition against adultery is shared by all and derives from the Qu'ran and from *hadith*, or traditions concerning the practices of the Prophet Muhammad. Though the Qu'ran does not quote the Decalogue, it does refer to it and seems to draw upon its tradition. Adultery is considered one of the most serious offenses, known as the *Hadd* offenses, because they are specified as offenses in the Qu'ran, another of which is the false accusation of adultery. Perhaps because the accusation is so serious, there are restrictions on it. The punishment for adultery is traditionally *rajm*, death by stoning, but this punishment is based only upon hadith, as the Qu'ran makes no mention of it. The seriousness of the crime necessitates under sharia a high standard of evidence, such as a voluntary confession or four reliable male eyewitnesses to the same act of penetration. In most schools of sharia, pregnancy is too circumstantial to be admitted as reliable evidence, but when it is admitted, most schools accept a counter-claim of rape as enough to free the woman from charges.

The variety of sharia followed in some Nigerian provinces, namely *Maliki*, is alone among the sharia schools to require some proof of rape to admit the counter-claim. A few high-profile cases of adultery brought before the sharia courts in some regions of Nigeria after 1999 generated worldwide debate about sharia's treatment of women. The Taliban regime in Afghanistan was widely decried for its radical interpretation of sharia. Under the Taliban, it was enough for a woman to be found in the company of a man who was neither her husband nor a near relation to be found guilty and to be executed. Although the Taliban were forced from power in 2001, as late as 2005 an Afghani woman, Bibi Amena, was executed by her family and community for having been found in the company of a man not her husband. The man reportedly received forty lashes. Iran has executed scores of men and women for adultery since the Islamic Republic came to power there in 1979. Most Islamic countries have laws against adultery on the books (as do many countries in Europe and North America) but make the burden of proof so high as

Death Sentence. *This Nigerian Woman was sentenced to death by stoning for adutlery in Nigeria in 2002.* © REUTERS/CORBIS.

to be very nearly impossible to result in executions. Some regions substitute jail terms, such as Dubai in the United Arab Emirates, where the maximum term in an adultery conviction is eighteen months. In most cases, imputations of adultery, or any other doubts thrown on a woman's honor, are handled extra-legally. Execution of the offending females (as in so-called honor crimes) by a family member is still common in many countries.

ROMAN LAW AND ITS SUCCESSORS

At least since the time of Augustus (63 BCE–14 CE), Roman law treated adultery as a criminal action, and required adulterers to be exiled. Adultery under this definition depends entirely on the woman's marital status. A wife commits adultery when she has sex with any man other than her husband. If the woman is not married, it is not adultery, though there may well be penalties for her actions. A man's marital status is not part of the question. According to Augustus's laws, known as the Julian marriage laws, a father is justified in killing his adulterous daughter, and a husband justified in killing his wife's paramour. Regardless of the husband's willingness to forgive, Roman law required him to prosecute within a certain time frame, and required the couple's divorce. These laws did not prove popular, and Augustus himself was forced to exile his own daughter, Julia, for her adulterous acts only fourteen years after enacting his marriage laws. Later emperors softened and even ignored the laws. They are important, however, in that in the form of sixth-century Byzantine emperor Justinian's *Corpus Juris Civilis*, they help form the basis of canon law, which began to take its current form in twelfth-century western Europe. It may be interesting to note that adultery under Justinian's code did not apply if the husband was not offended by his wife's infidelity, such as when he prostitutes her. Such is not the case in canon law. As the laws of the Catholic Church courts, canon law had jurisdiction over many offenses—including adultery—anywhere Roman Catholicism held sway, including England, where canon law continued to evolve after the English Reformation. Even though English Protestantism held that marriage is not a sacrament, English canon law did not permit divorce, even for adultery, for many years. As the English church lost power in judicial matters, adultery began to be a secular court concern, and in 1857 England established a court specifically to take divorce out of the hands of the church. Under the laws of that time, husbands could obtain a divorce for simple adultery, but women were required to prove cruelty or desertion in addition.

The Napoleonic Code is a civil code promulgated by Napoleon I in 1804, forming the basis for the laws of many European countries besides France, and is an influence in the laws of Louisiana, New Mexico, and Puerto Rico. The Napoleonic Code derives from earlier French law, Roman law, and Justinian's *Corpus Juris Civilis*, but borrowed also from the laws of other nations. Again, it is not a criminal code, but is concerned largely with determining matters of property; as such, it concerns itself with adultery insofar as questions of marriage and divorce matter help determine the status of property and the determination of inheritance. Adultery, under the Napoleonic code, covers extramarital sex on the part of either the husband or the wife, but as a cause for action in divorce applies unequally, giving more restrictions to women at virtually every turn. Either husband or wife may sue for divorce on account of adultery, but the wife can divorce her husband only if he brings into their home his adulterous partner, called a *concubine* in the Code. Again, if a divorce should be granted because of adultery, the adulterous spouse—whether male or female—is prohibited from ever marrying his or her adulterous partner; but the Code adds that, should the wife be the adulteress, she may also be sent to a correctional facility for a three-month to two-year period. Children conceived through adultery are illegitimate under the Code, restricting their claims to inherit. But the Code does not permit accusations of adultery in an effort to disinherit a certain child, unless it can be proven that the legal father was absent from his wife during the period spanning from three hundred to one hundred and eighty days prior to the birth of the child. Napoleon's regime is also responsible for a penal code promulgated in 1810, which allows a man to kill his wife and her lover if he catches them in the act of adultery. No similar allowance is made for an offended woman.

CONCLUSION

Adultery would appear to be an unending human worry. In 2000, for instance, China revised a twenty-year-old marriage law in an effort to reduce adulterous activity, which many sensed to be on the rise. Keeping concubines was supposedly common in pre-communist China and seems to have reemerged after the economic reforms of the 1980s, but Chinese officials believe that adultery is contrary to proper socialist thought. Given that these reforms coincided with religious reform movements against rising adultery rates in Muslim and Christian cultures as well, one might wonder if adultery is not the constant and a culture's attitudes toward it the variable instead.

SEE ALSO *Marriage.*

BIBLIOGRAPHY

"China Tackles Adultery." 2000. *BBC News* (March 11). Available from http://news.bbc.co.uk/1/hi/world/asia-pacific/674015.stm.

Collins, R. F. 2003. "Adultery (in the Bible)." *New Catholic Encyclopedia.* 2nd edition. Detroit: Gale.

"Nigeria: Shelled by the Sharia." 2002. *Newsweek* (Atlantic Edition) 139.4 (January 28).

Rahman, Fazlur. 2005. "Islam: An Overview." In *Encyclopedia of Religion.* 2nd edition, ed. Lindsay Jones. Detroit: Macmillan Reference.

Stone, Lawrence. 1977. *The Family, Sex, and Marriage in England, 1500–1800.* New York: Harper and Row.

U.N. Office for the Coordination of Humanitarian Affairs. 2005. "Afghanistan: Woman Executed for Adultery." Available from http://www.irinnews.org/report.asp?ReportID=46914.

United States. 2004. "Uniform Code of Military Justice." Title 10 U.S. Code, Sec. 934, Art. 134. Available from http://www.au.af.mil/au/awc/awcgate/ucmj.htm.

Erick Kelemen

ADVERTISING

Advertising, a form of communication between a paying sponsor and an identified audience (Dunn and Barban 1986), has become ubiquitous. Advertising's financial impact is significant: In 2004 within the United States alone, $263.77 billion was spent on advertising (Coen 2006). However, focusing exclusively on advertising's economic impact means that one overlooks the significant cultural power that advertising wields. Corporations, consumers, and other agencies have begun examining the phenomenon with more complexity to measure the degree of social and political influence of advertising. They note the limitations of seeing advertising only as a paid communication designed to sell products or services to an identified audience, acknowledging that many factors—including the advertised messages and their visual elements, contexts, and viewers—shape the meaning of the advertisement. More importantly, they argue that focusing on the economic role of advertising omits the degree to which other messages and values are being, if not *sold*, at least circulated within society. With growing attentiveness to the values that are associated with advertising (along with consumerism and marketing), many have critiqued the pervasiveness of advertising, its increasingly specific targeting of populations, and the cultural values associated with particular products. Since the 1960s, as advertising became a larger part of consumer culture, a number of questions emerged from a variety of disciplines. How are various identities—such as gender, sexuality, age, and race—portrayed in advertising? How do companies reinforce or challenge social identities? What values and perspectives are being advertised along with specific products?

MARGINALIZATION OF NON-DOMINANT GROUPS

There is a relationship between how people are represented in advertising and the perceived societal role of those groups. Women, people of color, older citizens, and other non-dominant groups (including gay, lesbian, bisexual, and transgendered [GLBT] audiences) have traditionally played a marginal role in the creation of advertising. These groups have historically held little control over their representation, let alone the values and messages that advertising portrays about them. As a result, advertising can convey notions about the perceived values of a group that might not correspond with the actual desires and experiences of the group itself. In addition, although advertisers frequently organize their audiences by various identity factors (e.g., gender, sexuality, age, race, class, and religion), they do not always research those audiences. Consequently, advertisers may not be aware of products and services that might benefit that population. Indeed, they might choose to market products with known health risks (e.g., fast food, tobacco, and alcohol) to particular groups, such as people of color (Dates and Barlow 1990) or women (*Deadly Persuasion* 2003). Given the ways in which portrayals of non-dominant groups have often been misogynist, racist, and homophobic, such patterns can create social discord (Kellner 1995).

Certainly, other media traffic in these images; however, advertising helps defray the cost of most media to consumers, so *all* media must consider the dominant images within advertisements. Most media outlets are directly supported by advertisers; in 1990, it was estimated that general audience magazines received 50 percent of their revenues from advertisers, whereas newspapers collected seventy-five percent from advertisers, and broadcasters relied almost exclusively on advertising income (Herman 1990). It is not surprising, perhaps, that the information presented in media outlets can be affected by the interests of their financial supporters (i.e., advertisers). It becomes increasingly difficult for individuals to overlook the influence of advertising when trying to determine their own relationship to society, let alone that of other groups when "neutral" media can be influenced by advertisers. Advertising, then, is a central promoter of values within public discourse, providing "perhaps the most dynamic and sensuous representations of cultural values in the world" (Lears 1994).

REINFORCEMENT OF GENDER NORMS

Advertising can reinforce particular gender norms; advertisements directed at women, for instance, often valorize nurturing and supportive roles. Such depictions, which confine women to the domestic sphere, persist despite the fact that by the 1980s, only ten percent of families included a wife and mother whose sole job was taking care of her children while her husband worked (Levitan, Belous, and Gallo 1988). Other stereotypical feminine or misogynist behaviors are portrayed as representative of all women, including women as naggers, nymphomaniacs, mentally incompetent, animalistic, and as bodies (rather than as humans). In contrast, men are typically featured as dominant, heroic, and/or competent subjects (rather than objects). Male voices are more likely to be featured in voiceovers, reinforcing the notion that authority is masculine. Such representations, then, reinforce norms of men as being linked primarily with the public sphere, whereas women are associated with the private sphere. The few exceptions seem incapable of challenging gendered norms.

In the late 1980s, images began surfacing that featured men as foolish (particularly when juxtaposed with items traditionally thought as feminine, such as those related to food preparation) or as fathers. Yet men are infrequently depicted as caregivers in advertisements. When they do appear as parents, they and the children usually participate in conventionally masculine activities. Such images suggest that men can assume a nurturing role, which has been socially defined as feminine, but they are rarely portrayed in additional feminine modes. For example, in 1999, Kaufman pointed out that men are "never shown caring for girls," suggesting that such choices might be read as excessively effeminate.

OBJECTIFICATION OF WOMEN

When women are represented in advertising—a public domain—they are frequently depicted as objects, rather than as subjects. This objectification of women, and their bodies, can be better understood when one considers the "gaze," which controls and fetishizes the female body (Mulvey 1975). Mulvey's work offers a productive point of origins for many scholars, including John Berger, who highlights the gendered dynamics of this concept: "Men act; women appear. Men look at women. Women watch themselves being looked at. Thus she turns herself into an object—and most particularly an object of vision—a sight" (Berger 1977). Rather than being an active subject with agency, women are presented as passive or decorative objects, who rarely interact with the products being sold (Sheehan 2003): This passivity is part of a larger cultural message being sold along with the product. These objectifying gazes have acquired moralistic dimensions: What is beautiful is considered self-evidently good (Wolszon 1998). Objectification is presented as a desirable goal that can be accomplished *if* one buys the appropriate products and services. Although advertisers have expanded their portrayal of who can benefit from these products and services—businesswomen, women of color, women of various ages—the demand on consumers to be sexually appealing is still a central theme of many advertisements (Kilbourne 2003).

It has become commonplace that "sex sells" when advertising strategies are discussed. However, the degree to which this maxim might be true has sparked debates and research. In one such study, female subjects on magazine covers had their heads emphasized only four percent of the time (the ratio for men is 900% more); their torsos and bodies (along with their heads) comprise the remaining shots (Lambaise and Reichert 2006). Feminist critique has focused on the high frequency of nearly or completely nude female bodies in advertisements as well as the visual dismemberment of those bodies. Feminists and others have critiqued the disturbing trend of using extremely young girls as sexual objects in ads (Kilbourne 2003, 2000). Such patterns reinforce the objectification of women, presenting it as a normal social phenomenon.

INFLUENCE ON STANDARDS OF BEAUTY

Others have rightly noted that consumers may view the highly artificial portrayal of female beauty (models typically have a lower body weight than the average consumer, are styled by many people, and may have their images digitally touched up in the editing room) as a documentary of female beauty rather than as a highly stylized fiction. Some researchers have found that there is little, if any, proof that an attractive model or spokesperson prompts consumer spending decisions (Cabellero, Lumpkin, and Madden 1989). And yet, these appeals to beauty continue to be pitched at women and girls rather than at men: such appeals appeared in fifty-six percent of television commercials that ran during teenage girls' preferred television shows; in contrast, such appeals appeared in only three percent of television advertisements aimed at men during viewing hours where they were the major audience (Signorelli 1997). Naomi Woolf has maintained that this "beauty myth" is a means of prescribing behavior to women (investing one's time and financial resources to portray youth and naïveté) and not appearance (1992). This distinction focuses on the appeal of beauty as a social control: As images of beauty continually shift, insecure consumers may perpetually justify their purchases of products and services. By endlessly manipulating and redefining beauty, advertising and corporate profits are secured.

OBJECTIFICATION OF MEN

Some researchers see insecurity as the motivating force behind the abundance of overtly muscular or conspicuously athletic men in advertising (Klein 1993). These representations masculinize the values, products, and services that appear in the media. Granted, these masculine images differ from norms of female models—male models are encouraged to exhibit physically strong and intimidating bodies whereas female models are encouraged to be excessively thin—but these images speak to the ways in which men, too, can be objectified in the media. As advertisers began foregrounding the bodies of male models, consumers (women and men) were invited to become voyeurs of male bodies. While sexual objectification of women remains a long-standing phenomenon, consumers have begun to witness an increase in the sexual objectification of men. Mulvey's concept of the "gaze" has been revived with this acknowledgement that men might also be eroticized—and disempowered—as objects of desire (Mulvey 1975, Schroeder and Zwick 1999). When paired, women and men are often positioned to foreground the competition, power, and domination between the two (Goffman 1979). Such domination is often eroticized (hooks 1997).

Calvin Klein Underwear Advertisement. *The Calvin Klein ads are known for their use of sex appeal and controversy.* © BETTMANN/CORBIS.

FUNCTION RANKING AND VIOLENCE

While a model's appearance is scrutinized by advertisers and researchers, other elements of the image matter as well: clothing, activity, facial expression (or lack thereof), setting, other objects, postures, sex of the people portrayed, and other attributes of identity (e.g., race, class, and age). Researchers contend that the action of models within advertising can underscore the power differential between groups. Erving Goffman defines this phenomenon as "function ranking," the relative passivity of female models when male models are present, a pattern that he sees as supporting male dominance; Ellen Seiter finds a similar pattern when analyzing advertising images of black children observing their more active white playmates, which subtly hints at white supremacy (Goffman 1979, Seiter 1995). This passivity becomes even more troubling when advertisers accentuate this power differential so that violence becomes part of the message.

Violence in advertising may include linguistic aggression (using specific language, such as "bitch"), may highlight fear (by featuring models in perilous situations), and may even feature models posed as corpses. Typically, violence is presented as erotic or fashionable with male models as the aggressive party. Given that in the United States one in four women experiences domestic violence and that one in five women and one in thirty-three men have experienced an attempted or completed rape (Tjaden 2000, Rennison 2001), this strategy exploits and glamorizes what is a painful reality for many survivors. Some consumers have negatively responded to these portrayals of sexual objectification and of violence through boycotts, complaints, and media awareness campaigns. Such campaigns include Joan Kilbourne's "Killing Us Softly" video series, the work of the activist organization Guerilla Girls, and the long-running "No Comment" section of *Ms. Magazine*, which includes objectionable ads and the company's contact information on its penultimate page. These negative responses—particularly those that affect the public image of the company or the financial future of a given product—have affected an industry leery of alienating consumers (Twitchell 1996).

MARKETING TO TARGET GROUPS

This negotiation of sexuality—given its commercial appeal—becomes increasingly coded upon consideration of advertising images that are constructed to be appealing to both heterosexual and homosexual audiences. Brumbaugh and Grier's concept of "encoding" describes the phenomenon in which

> marketers draw on knowledge of the selected segment to create advertising that carries a certain intended meaning for that segment. Markets 'encode' the meaning through the use of cues such as culturally similar actors, shared cultural symbols, appropriate media placement, and preferred language or vernacular. The marketer's hope is that the cues will be 'decoded' by viewers in the target segment to yield the intended meaning that encourages favorable evaluates of the product and firm.
>
> *(Brumbaugh and Grier 1999)*

These coded messages allow advertisers to access a larger market of consumers: gay and lesbian audiences are meant to interpret these ads as representing their culture(s) and experiences, subcultural codes that are presumably not legible to heterosexual consumers (Clark 1996). When this strategy works, advertisers can market to the GLBT community without necessarily acknowledging their intent or the existence of the GLBT community.

Additional strategies have emerged to maintain coded ambiguity for GLBT audiences. Ads with "androgynous marketing" deploy "a multifaceted eroticism that includes homoeroticism," including the use of beautiful models of the same sex without presenting their relationship as non-platonic (Soldow 2006). Another strategy that relies on ambiguity is that of "gay window" advertising, which portrays same-sex couples or groups in ads where heterosexual couples might have traditionally appeared (Stabiner 1982). Companies advertise their products in less ambiguous ways when the ads are placed in media that are planned for and used primarily by GLBT people, such as *Instinct*, *Out*, *The Advocate*, and the cable network LOGO. Advertisers might specifically place ads in gay-friendly media despite past policies of discrimination against GLBT employees. For instance, the Adolph Coors Company placed an ad in *Instinct* in 2000, presenting an attractive image to a community that had previously boycotted Coors for its homophobic company policies in the 1970s. Some images are marketed to both GLBT and heterosexual audiences; however, many have critiqued these strategies.

Some lesbians have contended that objectifying women, as that ad does, fails to become more palatable just because women's desires are acknowledged. They realize that this pattern of portrayal is lucrative, especially in mainstream presses where "lesbian" images cater to male heterosexual viewers. In addition, they note that the financial incentives of presenting homoeroticism in a positive light do not mandate that those representations are personally salient or empowering (Clark 1996). In fact, they can be quite exploitative (Williamson 1986).

Yet companies continue to recognize the financial benefits of broadening their consumer base and have responded accordingly. It has been estimated that corporations within the United States spend about $232 million annually in gay media and in sponsoring gay-specific events (Commercial Closet Association 2007). Advertising in gay media has grown significantly: for example, print ad revenues quadrupled between 1994 and 2007, and there was a 241.9 percent jump in ads with "gay-specific" content between 2003 and 2004 (Commercial Closet Association 2007). Despite the ways in which these groups (and people of color) may be marginalized, advertisers remain aware that these groups have spending power. This research area remains quite undeveloped (O'Guinn, Allen, and Semenik 1998).

DISCRIMINATION IN ADVERTISING

Despite their considerable consumer power, the representations of older adults—and the effects of those representations on consumers—deserve further scrutiny as well. Ageism affects advertising: Consumers' disrespect for or dread about aging are assumed in ads that advertise products designed to restore or resurrect one's youth. For female consumers, physical signs of age that are thought to negatively impact beauty (such as weight gain and facial wrinkles) are presented as terrors that can be avoided. Presenting particular bodies as "too old" reinforces discrimination against older citizens. Certain publications that target these populations, including media presented by the AARP (American Association of Retired Persons), have articulated their criteria for disapproval of such images and insist that advertisers recognize the diversity and dignity of older people (Wood 1989).

Such recognition of human dignity would also alter the representation of people of color. Historically, there has been a pattern of racist and demeaning images, typically in marketing to white audiences, when people of color are included—if they are at all. The rise of the post–civil rights era alerted marketers to the financial gains in addressing African-American audiences. However, racist images persist, such as ads which depict people of color as primitive or as a subservient class. The 1980s marked an increase in advertising companies deliberately seeking out people of color, particularly African-Americans. Researchers have noted that white consumers do not object to having African-Americans in such ads; however, the fact that researchers felt compelled to notice this tacit approval indicates the power differential between these groups (Gren 1999). Some advertisers use different methods to reach people of color than they do for mainstream audiences; in addition, some agencies have begun to specialize in marketing products and services for those populations (Cortese 2004).

CONSUMER BEHAVIOR AS A SOCIAL SCIENCE

Consumers have responded in various ways to advertisers' efforts. Some attempt to distance themselves from the consumerism that these ads foster (Dominquez and Robin 1999). In contrast, some people deliberately seek out advertising as a form of entertainment (including television channels devoted to advertising), often in venues where commercials are seen as more noteworthy than the purported entertainment event: The Super Bowl may be the most notorious example.

Advertisers are understandably interested in what consumers find compelling. Brand images create "a set of associations linked to the brand that consumers hold in memory" (Keller 1993); typically, the strongest ads have held consistent images for two or three decades or longer (Aaker 1991). Other agencies are also interested in the impact of advertising. Public service ads promote programs or values thought to be for the public good. The government is also aware that certain products can cause direct and indirect risks. Sometimes product advertisements are regulated; for instance, tobacco companies must display health warnings in their advertisements. The government is also involved in investigating the process by which goods are marketed; indeed, one of the Federal Trade Commissions tasks is the monitoring of deceptive, and therefore illegal, advertising.

The growth in media corporations and new technologies has furthered the impact and pervasiveness of advertising. Advertising can appear in major mediums: print (e.g., magazines, newspapers), communication networks (including television, Internet, radio), public space (such as billboards), and electronic arenas. In the early 2000s, researchers became increasingly interested in how word of mouth might entice would-be consumers (Rosen 2002). Historically, advances in media have been followed by an increase in advertising. Radio, for instance, debuted without advertising in 1920 and subsequently adopted sponsorship programs and other advertising campaigns in the 1940s and 1950s. The success of such advertising was so impressive that the study of consumer behavior became defined as a social science after World War II (Woods 1995). To learn more about the marketing itself, continued attention to advertising's audience, visual components, copy, and consumer response help the public learn how to decipher the product—and our culture.

SEE ALSO *Media.*

BIBLIOGRAPHY

Aaker, David. A. 1991. *Managing Brand Equity: Capitalizing on the Value of a Brand Name.* New York: Free Press.

Baehr, Helen, and Ann Gray, eds. 2002. *Turning It On: A Reader in Women & Media.* London: Oxford University Press.

Barthel, Diane. 1989. *Putting on Appearances: Gender and Advertising.* Philadelphia: Temple University Press.

Berger, John. 1977. *Ways of Seeing.* New York: Penguin.

Brumbaugh, Anne, and Sonya Grier. 1999. "Noticing Cultural Differences: Ad Meanings Created by Target and Non-Target Markets." *Journal of Advertising* 28(Spring): 79–93.

Caballero, Lumpkin & Madden. 1989. See Lin, Carolyn A. "Use of Sex Appeals in Prime-Time Television Commercials." *Sex Roles: A Journal of Research* 38(5-6): 461–475.

Carter, Cynthia, and Linda Steiner, eds. 2003. *Critical Readings: Media and Gender.* Columbus, OH: Open University Press.

Clark, Danae. 1996. "Commodity Lesbianism." *Camera Obscura* 25(6): 181–210.

Coen. (2006, February 27). Coen's Spending Totals. Available from http://adage.com/datacenter/article.php?article_id=48629.

Commercial Closet Association. Available from http://www2.commercialcloset.org/cgi-bin/iowa/index.html.

Cortese, Anthony Joseph Paul. 2004. *Provocateur: Images of Women and Minorities in Advertising.* 2nd edition. Lanham, MD: Rowman and Littlefield Publishers.

Cronin, Anne M. 2000. *Advertising and Consumer Citizenship*: Gender, Images, and Rights. New York: Routledge.

Cross, Mary, ed. 1996. *Advertising and Culture: Theoretical Perspectives.* Westport, CT: Praeger.

Culley, James D., and Rex Bennett. 1976. "Selling Women, Selling Blacks." *Journal of Communication* 26:160–74.

Dates, Jannette, and William Barlow, eds. 1990. *Split Image.* Washington, DC: Howard University Press.

Davis, Simone Weil. 2000. *Living Up to the Ads: Gender Fictions of the 1920s.* Durham, NC: Duke University Press.

Deadly Persuasion: The Advertising of Alcohol and Tobacco. 2003. Produced and directed by Sut Jhally. Media Education Foundation.

Dines, Gail, and Jean M. (McMahon) Humez, eds. 2002. *Gender, Race, and Class in Media: A Text-Reader.* 2nd edition. Thousand Oaks, CA: Sage Publications.

Dominguez, Joe, and Vicki Robin. 1999. *Your Money or Your Life: Transforming Your Relationship with Money and Achieving Financial Independence.* New York: Penguin.

Douglas, Susan J. 1995 [1994]. *Where the Girls Are: Growing Up Female with the Mass Media.* New York: Three Rivers Press.

Dunn, S. Watson, and Barban, Arnold M. 1986. *Advertising: Its Role in Modern Marketing.* 6th edition. Chicago: Dryden Press.

Faludi, Susan. 1991. *Backlash: The Undeclared War against American Women.* New York: Crown.

Fowles, Jib. 1996. *Advertising and Popular Culture.* Thousand Oaks, CA: Sage Publications.

Frith, Katherine Toland, ed. 1998. *Undressing the Ad: Reading Culture in Advertising.* New York: Peter Lange Publishing.

Gauntlett, David. 2002. *Media, Gender and Identity.* New York: Routledge.

Goffman, Erving. 1979. *Gender Advertisements.* Cambridge: Harvard University Press.

Gren, Corliss. 1999. "Ethnic Evaluations of Advertising: Interaction Effects of Strength of Ethnic Identification, Media Placement, and Degree of Racial Composition." *Journal of Advertising* 28(1): 49–50 .

Hambleton, Ronald. 1987. *The Branding of America.* Dublin, NH: Yankee Books.

Herman, Edward. 1990. "Media in the U.S. Political Economy." In *Questioning the Media: A Critical Introduction*, ed. John Downing, Ali Mohammadi, and Annabelle Sreberny-Mohammadi. Newbury Park, CA: Sage.

Hicks, Gary R. 2003. "Media at the Margins: Homoerotic Appeals to the Gay and Lesbian Community." In *Sex in Advertising: Perspectives on the Erotic Appeal*, ed. Tom Reichert and Jacqueline Lambaise. Mahwah, NJ: Lawrence Erlbaum Associates.

hooks, bell. 1997. bell hooks: *Cultural Criticism and Transformation.* Northampton, MA: Media Education Foundation.

Kaufman, Gayle. September 1999. "The Portrayal of Men's Family Roles in Television Commercials." *Sex Roles: A Journal of Research* 41: 439–458.

Keller, K. L. 1993. "Conceptualizing, Measuring, and Managing Consumer-based Brand Equity." *Journal of Marketing* 57: 1–22.

Kellner, Douglas.1995. *Media Culture: Cultural Studies, Identity, and Politics between the Modern and the Postmodern.* London: Routledge.

Kilbourne, Jean. 2003. *Deadly Persuasion: The Advertising of Alcohol and Tobacco.* Northampton, MA: Media Education Foundation.

Kilbourne, Jean, and Mary Pipher. 2000. *Can't Buy My Love: How Advertising Changes the Way We Think and Feel.* New York: Free Press.

Klein, Alan M. 1993. *Little Big Men: Bodybuilding Subculture and Gender Construction.* Albany: State University of New York Press.

Klein, Naomi. 2003. *No Logo: Brands, Globalization, and Resistance.* Northampton, MA: Media Education Foundation.

Lambaise, Jacqueline, and Tom Reichert. 2006 "Sex and the Marketing of Contemporary Consumer Magazines: How Men's Magazines Sexualized their Covers to Compete with Maxim." In *Sex in Consumer Culture: The Erotic Content of Media and Marketing*, ed. Tom Reichert and Jacqueline Lambaise. Mahwah, NJ: Lawrence Erlbaum Associates.

Lears, T. J. Jackson. 1994. *Fables of Abundance: A Cultural History of Advertising in America.* New York: Basic Books.

Leiss, William; Stephen Kline; and Sut Jhally. 2005. *Social Communication in Advertising: Consumption in the Mediated Marketplace.* 3rd edition. Revised by Jacqueline Botterill. New York: Routledge.

Levitan, Sar A.; Richard S. Belous; and Frank Gallo. 1988. *What's Happening to the American Family?: Tensions, Hopes, Realities.* Baltimore, MD: Johns Hopkins University Press.

Manca, Luigi, and Alessandra Manca, eds. 1995. *Gender & Utopia in Advertising: A Critical Reader.* New York: Syracuse University Press.

Messaris, Paul. 1994. *Visual "Literacy": Image, Mind, and Reality.* Cambridge: Westview Press.

Messaris, Paul. 1996. *Visual Persuasion: The Role of Images in Advertising.* Cambridge, MA: Westview Press Thousand Oaks, CA: Sage Publications.

Mulvey, Laura. 1975. "Visual Pleasure and Narrative Cinema." *Screen* 16(3): 6–18.

Nixon, Sean. *Advertising Cultures: Gender, Commerce, Creativity.* Thousand Oaks, CA: Sage Publications.

O'Guinn, Thomas C.; Chris T. Allen; and Richard J. 1998. *Advertising.* Cincinnati, OH: South-Western College Publishing.

Quart, Alissa. 2003. *Branded: The Buying and Selling of Teenagers.* Cambridge, MA: Perseus.

Reichert, Tom, and Jacqueline Lambaise, eds. 2003. *Sex in Advertising: Perspectives on the Erotic Appeal.* Mahwah, NJ: Lawrence Erlbaum Publishers.

Reichert, Tom, and Jacqueline Lambaise, eds. 2006. *Sex in Consumer Culture: The Erotic Content of Media and Marketing.* Mahwah, NJ: Lawrence Erlbaum Associates.

Rennison, Callie Marie. October 2001. "Intimate Partner Violence and Age of Victim, 1993-1999." Rockville, MD: United States Department of Justice, Bureau of Justice Statistics.

Rosen, Emanuel. 2002. *The Anatomy of Buzz: How to Create Word of Mouth Marketing.* New York: Currency.

Scanlon, Jennifer. 1995. *Inarticulate Longings: The Ladies' Home Journal, Gender, and the Promises of Consumer Culture.* New York: Routledge.

Schor, Juliet B. 1999. *The Overspent American: Why We Want What We Don't Need.* New York: HarperPerennial.

Schroeder, J. E., and D. Zwick. 1999 October. "The gaze, the male body, and advertising: A visual analysis." Paper presented at the meeting of the Association for Consumer Research, Columbus, Ohio. Cited by Stern, Barbara.

Seiter, Ellen. 1995. "Different Children, Different Dreams: Racial Representation in Advertising." In *Gender, Race, and Class in Media*, ed. Gail Dines and Jean M. Humez. Thousand Oaks, CA: Sage.

Sheehan, Kim Bartel. 2003. *Controversies in Contemporary Advertising.* Thousand Oaks, CA: Sage Publications.

Shields, Vickie Rutledge and Dawn Heinecken. 2002. *Measuring Up: How Advertising Affects Self-Image.* Philadelphia: University of Pennsylvania Press.

Signorelli, Nancy. April 1997. "A Content Analysis: Reflections of Girls in the Media: A Study of Television Shows and Commercials, Movies, Music Videos, and Teen Magazine Articles and Ads." Washington, DC: Kaiser Family Foundation and Children Now.

Slim Hopes: Advertising and the Obsession with Thinness. Produced and directed by Sut Jhally. Media Education Foundation.

Soldow, Gary. 2006. "Homoeroticism in Advertising: Something for Everyone with Androgyny." In *Sex in Consumer Culture: The Erotic Content of Media and Marketing*, ed. Tom Reichert and Jacqueline Lambaise. Mahwah, NJ: Lawrence Erlbaum Associates.

Stabiner, Karen. 1982. "Tapping the Homosexual Market." *New York Times Magazine*, sec. 6, p. 34, May 2.

Stanford, Cheraine. 2000. "Advertising in Black and White: How and Why Perceptions of Difference Shape Magazine Advertising." *Eruditio Online* 20(1)

Stern, Barbara B. 2003. "Masculinism(s) and the Male Image: What Does it Mean to Be a Man?" In *Sex in Advertising: Perspectives on the Erotic Appeal*, ed. Tom Reichert and Jacqueline Lambaise. Mahwah, New Jersey: Lawrence Erlbaum Associates.

Tjaden, Patricia, and Nancy Thoennes. 2000. "Extent, Nature, and Consequences of Intimate Partner Violence." National Institute of Justice and the Centers for Disease Control and Prevention.

Twitchell, James B. 1996. *Adcult USA: The Triumph of Advertising in American Culture.* New York: Columbia University Press.

Williamson, Judith. 1986. "Woman Is an Island: Feminity and Colonization." In *Studies in Entertainment: Critical Approaches to Mass Culture.* ed. Tania Modleski. Bloomington: Indiana University Press.

Williamson, Judith. 1994. *Decoding Advertisements: Ideology and Meaning in Advertising.* London: Marion Boyars.

Wirthlin Worldwide. March 1999. *Buying Influences: Consider the Source.* Reston, VA: Author.

Wolf, Naomi. 1992. *The Beauty Myth: How Images of Beauty Are Used against Women.* New York: Anchor Books, Doubleday.

Wolszon, L. R. 1998. "Women's Body Image Theory and Research." *American Behavioral Scientist.* 41.4: 542–557.

Wood, Robert. Winter 1989. "Attacking Ageism in Advertising." *Media and Values* 45(Winter 89).

Woods, Gail Baker. 1995. *Advertising and Marketing to the New Majority.* Belmont, CA: Wadsworth Publishing.

Mary McDonnell

AFRICA

This entry contains the following:

I. HISTORY

The gendering of African studies constitutes one of the most significant epistemological breakthroughs in the last decades of the twentieth century. From the African Eve to the first African female elected president, women have indeed assumed a pivotal role in shaping African history, and, in turn, major historical episodes such as colonization and decolonization have considerably affected their status. Moreover, as African cultures have so far rested on the notions that at birth individuals are endowed with both a male and a female principle, and that the genders complement one another, women have been perceived as invaluable direct or symbolic participants in all domains of society.

The significance of African women's contributions has, however, often been played down by the combined forces of patriarchy and racism. African women who have internalized these repressive ideologies have often promoted practices detrimental to their health and freedom, such as clitoridectomy or arranged marriages, and have become the carriers of the heaviest loads in terms of production and reproduction, in exchange for a few counter-privileges, most notably in the spiritual realm. This awareness has encouraged new generations of African women to commit to change and self-representation, for both the preservation of their interests and the increased well-being of their continent as a whole.

PREHISTORY TO COLONIAL TIMES

The specific challenges attached to reconstituting African history—namely the preference shared by a number of African societies for an oral mode of memorization; the deleterious effect of climate, wars and poverty on existing documents; and the weight of a widely diffused corpus of texts and images that grossly distorted African realities—are compounded, when it comes to writing a history of women in precolonial times, with historiographical lacunae resulting from the gender-blind approach characteristic of both the humanities and social sciences, well into the 1990s. The relative disinterest for women as historical agents stems also from the nationalist climate in the midst of which African history gained recognition as a discipline: Emphasis was put on decolonizing knowledge, rather than on checking it for gender biases. New scholarship is actively working, not only at filling the gaps, but ultimately at gendering the disciplines.

"Pre-her-story" According to genetic studies conducted in the mid-1980s, the most recent common matrilineal ancestor of humans alive today lived 150,000 years ago in East Africa. Through mitochondrial DNA—that is, organelles passed from mothers to offspring—scientists have reconstituted an unbroken line of daughters back to the so-called mitochondrial or African Eve. The ancillary idea that "Eve" is older than "Adam" similarly is related to some African myths of origin that ultimately "link human life directly with God through woman," according to the theologian John Mbiti. For instance, according to the Akposso people from Togo, God (Uwolowu), in his process of creation, first made a woman and bore with her the first child. For the Ibibio people of Nigeria, God is the mother-divinity called Eka Abassi. A Fon myth from Benin refers to Mawu, the supreme god, as the male or female offspring of a primordial mother, Nana Buluku.

Women could arguably be credited also with the Neolithic Revolution that occurred possibly as early as 16,000 BCE in the Nile Valley. The invention of agriculture and the attendant process of sedentarization could be an extension of the previous task of plant gathering, probably undertaken by women who thus gained extensive knowledge about vegetation growth and reproduction (Laberge 2001). Several myths of origin corroborate this hypothesis: During a drought, Kipsigi women would have found a grass seed that had germinated in elephant dung. After tasting it, they planted more, enabling a stronger Kipsigi community to control the region located in what is today Kenya (Pala and Ly 1979). Indeed, from ancient times until the first decades of the twentieth century, agriculture in Africa remained the preserve of women, who developed a "hoe culture" everywhere except in the Sahel region (Baumann 1928).

Women in Ancient Egypt and Roman Africa (3000 BCE–sixth century BCE) Ancient Egyptian civilization, born out of the demographic concentration around the Nile that accompanied the Sahara's desertification (9000–3000 BCE), most likely granted women a unique form of gender equality, attested to by both Egyptian and foreign sources. Though made "ladies of the house" by marriage, women moved freely in and out of the public sphere without a veil. They could also theoretically serve in any professional position, from field hands to high priests. Documents show them steering cargo ships and holding scribal palettes as well—an indication that the female elite was literate. In the Old Kingdom, fifth to sixth dynasties, Peseshet, the first female physician in world history, headed a department of female colleagues, while Nebet was one of the two women who held the title of vizier, judge, and magistrate.

Endowed with full legal and economic rights, Egyptian women could independently manage property, sue in court, and enter into any type of contract. Though rarely pharaohs themselves, women, as carriers of the royal line, conferred authority to the rulers by marriage or filiation. The pharaoh himself had to rule in accordance with the principles of cosmic harmony symbolized by a female deity, Maat (Lumpkin 1984). Some royal women imposed themselves through their political or military genius. Queen Ahhotep (sixteenth dynasty, c. 1560–1530 BCE) received the highest military decoration, the Order of the Fly, for her campaigns against the Hyksos. Queen Hatshepsut (eighteenth dynasty, r. 1503–1482 BCE) was so revered for her campaigns against Nubia that her son ordered the obliteration of her images. Nefertiti (eighteenth dynasty, fourteenth century BCE) ruled as co-regent with her husband, Akhenaton (also known as Amenhotep IV), and led a religious revolution. Arsinoë II (c. 316–270 BCE) was deified in her lifetime. Cleopatra (r. 51–30 BCE), the last great ruler of the Ptolemaic era, committed suicide after a brilliant political career.

The names of women such as Perpetua and Monica remain attached to the history of early Christianity in Roman Africa. After a first mission was established in Alexandria in the first century CE, Christianity spread westward into Berber North Africa. One of the first North African Christian martyrs was Perpetua, a young mother born in Carthago who left a diary detailing her reasons for seeking martyrdom in 203. Monica, the mother of Aurelius Augustinus (354–430), also known as St. Augustine of Hippo, one of the founding fathers of Roman Christianity, was the main agent of his conversion. She accompanied her son, then a Manichaean, to Italy and begged Bishop Ambrose to mentor him. She died on their way back to Africa, shortly after his baptism in 387.

Women and Islam (seventh century CE–) The spread of Islam into African societies from the seventh century on had an ambivalent effect on the status of women. Critical of the African premium placed on fecundity over chastity, Muslim visitors or African converts often sought to dismantle the existing local religions. They consequently undermined women's spiritual powers, while introducing limited reforms in their favor, such as the restriction of polygyny to four wives and the abolition of female circumcision in Timbuktu (Iliffe 2007). In its efforts to impose patrilineal rules of succession, Islam encountered resistance, as illustrated by the war waged by Kahina, a female Christian or Jewish leader of the matrilineal Berbers. After wrestling Carthage from Arab control, Kahina decided on an ill-fated scorched-earth policy, and she was eventually defeated in 702.

The literacy Islam brought to sub-Saharan Africa led, from the twelfth century on, to the opening of libraries to house Islamic texts, as well as learning centers for the African production of knowledge in various disciplines, from religion to prosody and from astronomy to the political sciences. Among the estimated one million manuscripts written in Timbuktu and its vicinity, a sizable number were either copied or written by women (Haidara, 1.3). Men of weight such as Sheikh Usman dan Fodio (1754–1817), sultan of the Sokoto califate and prominent Islamic scholar, condemned women's illiteracy in writing. His daughter, Nana Asma'u (1793–1864), a scholar and poet, launched the Yan Taru movement for African female intellectuals who made the hajj, the Muslim pilgrimage to Mecca.

Women and Slavery Valued workers, African women have been massively sold on the domestic (African), transatlantic, and Oriental markets. In fact, the majority of slaves in sub-Saharan Africa were women (Robertson and Klein 1983). Often kidnapped, as related in chapter two of Olaudah Equiano's autobiography (first published in 1789), women and girls were also pawned for debt repayment, as was the Nigerian novelist Buchi Emecheta's mother at the dawn of the twentieth century. Female slaves were particularly appreciated as wives or concubines because paternity rights were granted to their husbands/owners without dowry, and divorce was unattainable. In the first decades of the twentieth century, when domestic slavery was abolished by both British and French colonial administrations, concubines of elite men were often strategically ordered by the courts to remain in forced marriages. In dynastic societies, such as Dahomey (present-day Benin), female slaves played pivotal roles at the court. Twice barred from dynastic claims, they formed the king's personal guard as well as a pool of potential wives. The queen mother (symbolic "double" of the king rather than his biological mother) was usually a foreigner and a slave. In a few postcolonial African nations, such as Mauritania and the Sudan, enslavement of both women and men is still practiced on occasion.

Famous for their agricultural skills, women represented 35 percent of the human cargoes in the transatlantic slave trade. They were kept on the slave ship's deck to prevent them from inciting men to revolt, and to provide sexual gratification to the crew. One of these women who experienced the Middle Passage was Phillis Wheatley: Born in Africa around 1753, she became the first African American writer to be published. Conversely, some entrepreneurial women were beneficiaries of the transatlantic slave trade, such as the Euro-African *signaras* (ladies) from Senegambia in the seventeenth and eighteenth centuries (Brooks 1976).

The Oriental slave trade—which has never been officially abolished—deported a majority of the African women who were marched toward the East Coast or to Middle Eastern countries, where they served mostly as domestics and concubines. To illustrate the hardships inflicted upon women and children by Swahili or Arab merchants, French missionaries published the archetypal story of Swema, a Yao girl who was sold in 1865, buried alive in Zanzibar, and eventually rescued (Robertson and Klein 1983).

Women as Leaders Conversely, examples of African women exerting direct political leadership abound, although their power depended on seniority, motherhood, and wealth. Semi-historical figures, such as Amina of Hausaland, credited to have extended fifteenth-, sixteenth-, or seventeenth-century Kano through military conquest, or Abla Pokou, the eighteenth-century founding mother of the Baule who sacrificed her infant to save her people, coexist with women leaders who distinguished themselves in the anticolonial struggle. Nzinga (c. 1581–1663) waged a quasi-lifelong war against the Portuguese who came to Angola in search of minerals and slaves. Dressed as a man, she is rumored to have kept a harem of young men performing as her "wives." Yaa Asantewa (c. 1840–1921), queen mother of one of the Ashanti states in Ghana, organized a massive rebellion against the protectorate imposed by the British in 1896. Her capture apparently required two thousand troops. Nehanda (c. 1863–1898), medium and leader of the Shona, fought against Cecil Rhodes's colonization of what is now Zimbabwe, and was hanged (Sweetman 1984). One of the lesser-known women fighters, Sarraounia of the Azna, who fought the French commanders Paul Voulet and Julien Chanoine in 1899, is the eponymous character in a 1986 film directed by Med Hondo and based on Abdoulaye Mamani's 1980 novel.

Women and Re/production Until colonization, African women's main tasks consisted of the production of subsistence food, reproduction, and trade between economically complementary regions. State formation (and the husband's class), rules of descent, and religious and sometimes environmental contexts influenced the condition of women (Coquery-Vidrovitch 1994). But given women's dominance in the main economic sector—agriculture—their rights over land and cattle were generally protected (Pala and Ly 1979). Even if the cattle belonged to the male head of the family, women often received a few heads, and had access to a piece of land, which ensured at least their partial economic autonomy.

With a maximal fecundity ratio (one child every three years), African women have also held a "uterine power," as it were. Matriarchy was arguably the first state of human societies and the notion of descent through women still characterizes the "southern cradle" of the world, according to the historian Cheikh Anta Diop (1978). Indeed, a matriarchal belt skirts Central Africa; matriarchal clusters exist in Ghana and Senegambia, and residual matriarchal aspects, such as the notion of uterine kinship and the naming of the child after the mother, still have wide currency in early-twenty-first-century Africa. For instance, according to the Kikuyu myth of creation, Gikuyu and Moombi gave birth to nine daughters, after whom each of the nine main Kikuyu clans of the Moombi nation was named. For a long time, the all-powerful Moombi women practiced polyandry. Moombi men, having impregnated women, overthrew them, but could not, however, alter the clans' female names, which have lasted in Kenya into the twenty-first century. Moreover, the social importance of the female procreative function has generated specific institutions, such as "woman-to-woman marriage," by which an heirless woman could acquire rights over another woman's childbearing capacity (though not over her sexuality).

The dowry, while granting paternity rights to the husband, entitled a woman to her kin's help in times of crisis. Married women could request divorce, though in patriarchal communities they would lose their children to the father's family. In rural polygamous settings, the senior wife often had the upper hand in choosing a cowife to share her domestic and field work. Others examples of women's resourcefulness in reducing their oppression and labor included the circulation of children and the organization of "tontines" (French *tontine* was the equivalent of English "esusu" or "osusu," which became *susu* in Caribbean, where the institution survives; hence also known as "e/o susu"), that is, rotating associations for collective labor or money savings toward the completion of individual projects.

Women gained extra income and status through local and long-distance trade, and wealthy "market queens" in cities such as Onitsha, Lomé, or Accra (today named "Mama Benz" or "Nana Benz" after their chauffeured cars) have also acquired political influence. In 1850, for instance, Freetown women traders convinced the colonial authorities to build a new market, and, similarly, in 1977 market women obtained from the Guinean Marxist leader Sékou Touré the right to self-manage their market, as well as the legalization of private small trade (Coquery-Vidrovitch 1994).

Women's esoteric knowledge entitled them to major functions in nonmonotheistic religions. Involved in divination and witchcraft, women were often associated with rainmaking. For instance, Mujaji (Modjadji), the queen and rainmaker of the Lovedu, commands such respect that both Shaka (c. 1787–1828), the Zulu king, and Nelson Mandela (b. 1918), the South African political leader, invoked endorsement from the Mujaji of their respective eras. In addition, membership in female secret associations (such as the Sande or Bundu, a Mende initiation society in Sierra Leone) gave women a voice in communal decision-making processes.

Conclusion The condition of African women in precolonial times, still insufficiently understood, remains at the core of an intense debate. Some scholars, such as Niara Sudarkasa (1996), have strived to demonstrate that "female" and "male" were clusters of statuses for which gender was one of the defining characteristics. Therefore, the normative gender stratification of the early twenty-first century did not exist in precolonial Africa, and women's participation in economic, political, religious, and artistic matters was deemed indispensable to the life of their societies. Others, such as Catherine Coquery-Vidrovitch (1994), insist that women were trained from a young age, and often through harsh rituals, to submit to male power: Defined by the three Ss—silence, sacrifice, and service—they remained, though with notable exceptions, legal minors throughout their lives. From this vantage point, the glorification of their reproductive role appears to have been a mere compensation for the disregard they met in their productive functions. A clearer picture of the female condition in precolonial Africa would indeed require in-depth research on the plural and complex networks women simultaneously belonged to—an arrangement that was probably geared to offset some of the social handicaps they experienced in both patriarchal and matriarchal communities.

COLONIAL PERIOD

Colonization (1880s–1960s) affected African women in contradictory ways. To a large extent, they lost control of their own world, and their consulting role in the external affairs previously handled by men all but disappeared. Redirected toward cash crop production, they were also subjected to forced labor on plantations, taken as hostages to pressure men into meeting production quotas, recruited to perform sexual services, and sent to concentration camps (see the films by Jean-Marie Teno, *Le malentendu colonial* [The colonial misunderstanding 2004]; and Peter Bate, *Congo: White King, Red Rubber, Black Death* [2003]). Unaware of the system of parallel chieftancies, colonizers suppressed women's autonomous organizations, in possible connivance with African patriarchs. New laws made the husband the head of the household and imposed his name onto his wife. The dowry (*lobola*) calculated in cash came to signify a new commodification of gender relations (Mama 1996). Moreover, voting rights were granted to women much later in the colonies than in the metropole (Goerg 1997).

If a handful of women benefited from colonization, such as Madame Yoko, who served as paramount chief of the Kpaa-Mende of Sierra Leone from 1878 to 1908, the majority vigorously expressed discontent. In 1929 the attempt to impose taxation on women in Nigeria resulted in the Igbo Women's War, with ten thousand rural women demonstrating against their diminishing political rights. During the Franco-Algerian War (1954–1962), an estimated ten thousand Algerian women worked for the National Liberation Front (FLN), and one out of five arrests or killings involved a woman. Despite later controversies, Winnie Mandela, the "Mother of the Nation," remains the symbol of South African women's intrepid resistance against Apartheid. In all their conflicts with the colonial (and later the postcolonial) state, women have resorted to original strategies, such as sit-ins and invasions of officers' private space, derisive songs, and even nudity to signify social breakdown—the latter tactic used again in 1990 to condemn violence in Côte d'Ivoire.

Yet, the colonial and postcolonial city has undeniably granted women more autonomy, allowing them to take on new social identities. Escaping rural constraints, women have found in Nairobi, Kampala, or Lagos new sources of income, in the area of services and commerce (including prostitution), enabling them to achieve home ownership, finance their children's studies, and sometimes travel abroad. They have become a vital part of the informal economic sector, outside of state control. Far from their kin, they have managed to negotiate transethnic or caste-blind marriages, and have sometimes established polyandric fiefs (Gondola 1997).

Similarly, the spread of Christianity, first by the Portuguese in the coastal areas as early as the fifteenth century, and then by European and American missionaries in the nineteenth century, resulted in both limiting and expanding African women's freedom. As civilization was presented to Africans as coterminal with Christianity, a number of cultural changes related to spirituality, matriarchal regime, and clothing were imposed by missionaries as religiously mandated. Although, as a result of this, women lost their spiritual powers, as well as the economic and personal independence that made divorce, for instance, an easy and common procedure, they seized a number of emancipatory opportunities offered by the new religion—namely, monogamy, deferral of marriage until adulthood, and access to literacy, education, and employment. Consequently, most early Christians in Africa were women: According to the historian John Iliffe (1995), they represented 80 percent of Anglican communicants in Abeokuta in 1878.

Women who found inspiration in the Biblical message but suffered racial or gender discrimination within the church often founded or joined African Independent Churches (AICs). Inaugurated in the Kongo with the Antonine movement spearheaded by Kimpa Vita (Beatriz of the Kongo) in the early eighteenth century, a tradition of female-headed independent churches developed in nineteenth- and twentieth-century Africa and was often fed by conflicts that arose from the colonial situation. The new converts wished either to Africanize the clergy or to Africanize Christianity itself. The issue of female circumcision, for instance, led thousands of Christians in Kenya in the 1920s and 1930s to leave Protestant churches to found their own (Labode 1999). Cynthia Hoehler-Fatton (1999) argues that women's participation in the AICs illustrates Africa's ability to reconcile the old and the new. The recurrence of founding mothers for these churches rested on the precolonial concept of female mediumship, and indeed the new religion often managed to incorporate elements of the local cults and spirit-possession practices. For instance, in the Luo Roho movement of western Kenya, a body of female soldiers (*askeche*) protected congregations, in line with a local tradition of women possessed by the spirit of slain warriors. Some of the most famous female heads of the AICs include Christianah Abiodun (Nigeria), Grace Tani (Ghana), Marie Lalou (Cote d'Ivoire), Mai Chaza (Zimbabwe), Alice Lenshina (Northern Rhodesia [present-day Zambia]), and Gaudencia Aoko (Kenya) (pp. 430–431).

Ultimately, men confiscated leadership in the AICs, and Christian conversions barely affected polygyny. Christianity, to some extent, presented itself as a foil for Islam, enabling it to construct itself as an anticolonial religion in nationalist eras. Yet, Christianity has grown to become one of the two major African religions, practiced in the early twenty-first century by close to 150 million women on the continent.

THE EARLY-TWENTY-FIRST-CENTURY SITUATION

A Food and Agriculture Organization of the United Nations survey of nine African countries in 1996 revealed that women assume 70 percent of the agricultural activities and 100 percent of the food processing (Manuh 1998). They are also responsible for procuring 80 percent of water and fuel supplies. Consequently, they bear the brunt of Africa's increasingly limited access to natural resources, technology costs, obsolete customary laws, and economic migrations, which leave them in charge of men's former tasks. In Cameroon and Nigeria for instance, women have replaced cultivating yams (formerly handled by men) with cultivating the less time-consuming but less nutritious cassava.

The "feminization of poverty" results from a combination of factors: Globalization and its attendant constraints—prices established at the center, adjustment programs imposed by the International Monetary Fund and the World Bank, corporations' initiatives such as genetic seed sterilization or large-scale fishing—play an important role in the development of this phenomenon. Illiteracy primarily affects girls, who are often taken from school for domestic chores or early marriages, and accounts in part for the scarcity of elected women officials. For instance, among the Togolese people over fifteen years of age, 60 percent of women as compared to 27 percent of men are illiterate (UNFPA 2000). In 2006 for the first time in African history, a woman was elected president, and this event took place in Liberia. In her inaugural address, Ellen Johnson-Sirleaf pledged a "fundamental break" with decades of military and political violence in her country.

Multiple forms of violence are visited upon African women. In 2003 African nations agreed in Maputo, Mozambique, to end female genital mutilation, forced marriages, and punitive widowhood rituals. Yet the World Health Organization estimates that 40 percent of African women undergo some form of "body marking," such as lip and neck elongation, ablation of the uvula, or forced feeding (Coquery-Vidrovitch 1994). With new forms of war that primarily target civilians, women are killed, raped, or enslaved in disproportionate numbers throughout the African continent. Wangari Mathai, the Kenyan woman activist recipient of the 2004 Nobel Peace Prize—the first African woman to receive this award—is convinced that there is an environmental root to wars. Her Green Belt movement, founded in 1977, has employed eighty thousand women to plant 15 million trees and combat government-sponsored deforestation. Moreover, women have become the main victims of the AIDS crisis that feeds, in the African context, on poverty, wars, displacements, illiteracy, and sexual violence. Its epicenter is in South Africa, and disenfranchised urban women between the ages of fifteen and twenty-four are particularly at risk. In spite of clear progress made in Central Africa, gender equality is ultimately the cure for the pandemic.

Regardless of patriarchal, colonial, or postcolonial repression, masses of women merchants and peasants, as well as some elite women, have fought over the years to transform their condition. Though a history of African feminism (which Gwendolyn Mikell [1994] describes as heterosexual, pro-natal, and concerned with survival) remains to be written, several women who have theorized their militant practices for gender equality stand out, including Adelaide Casely-Hayford (1868–1960, Sierra Leone), Aoua Kéita (1912–1980, Mali), Nawal El Saadawi (b. 1931, Egypt), Molara Ogundipe-Leslie (b. 1949, Nigeria), and Filomina Chioma Steady (Sierra Leone).

SEE ALSO *AIDS and HIV: I. Overview; Anthropology; Creation Stories; Daughter of the Nile Union; Economics; Employment Discrimination; Female Genital Mutilation; Feminism: I. African (Sub-Saharan); Folk Healers and Healing; Folklore; Gender Studies; Harems; Honor and Shame; Honor Crimes; Initiation; Menstruation; Nomadism; Rape; Sex Roles; Slavery; Veiling; Violence; Virginity; Women's Human Rights.*

BIBLIOGRAPHY

Baumann, Hermann. 1928. "The Division of Work According to Sex in African Hoe Culture." *Africa* 1(3): 289–319.

Brooks, George E., Jr. 1976. "The Signares of Saint-Louis and Gorée: Women Entrepreneurs in Eighteenth-Century Senegal." In *Women in Africa: Studies in Social and Economic Change*, ed. Nancy J. Hafkin and Edna G. Bay. Stanford, CA: Stanford University Press.

Coquery-Vidrovitch, Catherine. 1994. *Les Africaines: Histoire des femmes d'Afrique noire du XIXè au XXè siècle* [The Africans: An History of Women of Sub-Saharan Africa, 19th-20th century]. Paris: Editions Desjonquères.

Diop, Cheikh Anta. 1978. *The Cultural Unity of Black Africa: The Domains of Patriarchy and of Matriarchy in Classical Antiquity*. Chicago: Third World Press.

Emecheta, Buchi. 1977. *The Slave Girl: A Novel*. New York: Braziller.

Equiano, Olaudah. 1996. *Equiano's Travels*, abridged and ed. Paul Edwards. Oxford, UK: Heinemann. (Orig. pub. 1789.)

Goerg, Odile. 1997. "Femmes africaines et politique: Les colonisées au féminin en Afrique occidentale" [African Women and Politics: Colonized Women in West Africa]. *Clio* 6: 105–125.

Gondola, Ch. Didier. 1997. "Unies pour le meilleur et pour le pire: Femmes africaines et villes coloniales; Une histoire du métissage" [United in Good and Bad Times: African Women and Colonial Cities. An History of Hybridization]. *Clio* 6: 87–104.

Haidara, Abdul Kader. "Lumière sur les plus importantes bibliothèques à Tombouctou" [Insights on the Most Important Libraries in Timbuktu]. Available from http://www.ebad.ucad.sn/sites_heberges/manifestations/colloque_BN_2003/Akha%C3%AFdara.htm.

Hoehler-Fatton, Cynthia. 1999. "Christianity: Independent and Charismatic Churches in Africa." In *Africana: The Encyclopedia of the African and African American Experience*, ed. Kwame Anthony Appiah and Henry Louis Gates. New York: Basic Civitas Books.

Iliffe, John. 2007. *Africans: The History of a Continent.* 2nd edition. Cambridge, UK: Cambridge University Press.

Laberge, Claude. 2001. "La deuxième révolution agricole: Notre déf." [The Second Agricultural Revolution: Our Challenge]. *L'Agora*, 48 (Summer). Available from http://agora.qc.ca/magazine/agora.nsf/Index/Agora.

Labode, Modupe. 1999. "Christianity, African: An Overview." In *Africana: The Encyclopedia of the African and African American Experience*, ed. Kwame Anthony Appiah and Henry Louis Gates. New York: Basic Civitas Books.

Lumpkin, Beatrice. 1984. "Hypatia and Women's Rights in Ancient Egypt." In *Black Women in Antiquity*, ed. Ivan Van Sertima. New Brunswick, NJ: Transaction Books.

Mama, Amina. 1996. "Women's Studies and Studies of Women in Africa during the 1990s." CODESRIA Working Paper Series, no. 5. Dakar, Senegal: Council for the Development of Social Science Research in Africa (CODESRIA).

Mamani, Abdoulaye. 1980. *Sarraounia: Le drame de la reine magicienne* [The Tragedy of Queen-Magician Sarraounia]. Paris: L'Harmattan.

Manuh, Takyiwaa. 1998. "Women in Africa's development." *Africa Recovery Online, a Publication of the United Nations* 11. Available from http://www.un.org/ecosocdev/geninfo/afrec/bpaper/maineng.htm.

Mbiti, John. 1988. "Flowers in the Garden: The Role of Women in African Religion," *Cahiers des Religions Africaines* 22: 69-82.

Mikell, Gwendolyn, ed. 1997. *African Feminism: The Politics of Survival in Sub-Saharan Africa.* Philadelphia: University of Pennsylvania Press.

Pala, Achola O., and Madina Ly. 1979. *La femme africaine dans la société précoloniale* [African Women in Pre-colonial Societies]. Paris: UNESCO.

Robertson, Claire C., and Martin A. Klein, eds. 1983. *Women and Slavery in Africa.* Madison: University of Wisconsin Press.

Sudarkasa, Niara. 1996. "The 'Status of Women' in Indigenous African Societies." In *Women in Africa and the African Diaspora: A Reader*, ed. Rosalyn Terborg-Penn and Andrea Benton Rushing. 2nd edition. Washington, DC: Howard University Press.

Sweetman, David. 1984. *Women Leaders in African History.* London: Heinemann.

United Nations Population Fund (UNFPA). 2000. *State of World Population, 2000: People, Poverty, and Possibilities.* New York: Author.

Sylvie Kandé

II. POLITICAL AND CULTURAL AGENDAS

From antiquity to the middle of the twentieth century, the European and North American production of knowledge on Africa distorted the image of that continent and its peoples by silencing or overpowering African voices. That situation resulted from what philosopher V. Y. Mudimbe has termed the "epistemological ethnocentrism" of the West (Mudimbe 1988, p. 15). Moreover, although a distinct European identity emerged in the fifteenth century from the colonial conquest of new lands and the concomitant invention of race and otherness, the birth of Africa as a self-defining cultural entity has been the product of the deportation of 12 million to 20 million Africans to Europe and the Americas over four centuries. Consequently, it was in the diaspora rather than on the continent itself and in the midst of suffering that a collective African identity first coalesced. Ironically, although Africa has been feminized in its relationship with Europe and North America, the African subject in discourses by Africans and non-Africans alike generally has been presumed to be male.

THE NAMING OF AFRICA

The process by which the African continent was named and mapped reflects the nature of European and Asian involvement in that region. Referred to as Ethiopia in both the Bible and Greek historical literature, the Africa known in antiquity encompassed the land west of Egypt (Libya) and the land east and south of Egypt up to contemporary Chad (Ethiopia). After the Romans invaded the African shores of the Mediterranean, they renamed their colonies, possibly after a local population, the Afers. The adoption of the Roman name *Africa* in its Arabicized form *Ifriqiya* by the Muslim armies that marched through the Sahara from the seventh century on inscribed that project in the same colonial tradition. Similarly, from the fifteenth century on the name *Africa* came to be applied to the various coastal locations *discovered* by Portuguese navigators and eventually to the land mass defined by Bartolomeu Diaz's (1457–1500) 1488 circumnavigation of South Africa.

However, it was the sixteenth-century German cartographer Mercator (1512–1594) who imposed a still insufficiently challenged image of Africa. Compressing the southern hemisphere to a third of the world map, the Mercator projection gives Africa a rounded, somewhat *passive* form that must have echoed the notion of femininity in the chauvinistic world of the Renaissance, as emblematized by Vesalius and Durer's voyeuristic dissections of the female body (Brotton 2002). Later African allegories also often associated animals or monsters and a black woman, the Other, who "in [her] abnormal differences, specifies the identity of the Same" (Mudimbe 1988, p. 12).

EARLY IMAGES AND CHARACTERIZATIONS

For classics scholar Frank Snowden, Jr., Greek historians' terminological decision to call Ethiopians (*burnt faces*) both non-Egyptian Africans and Indians exemplifies the Greeks' exoticist yet nonracialist vision of the world, whereas Mudimbe sees a tradition of locating Africans in a "geography of monstruosity" (1994, p. 78), emerging in Herodotus (484–425 BCE) resurfacing in Pliny (23–79 CE), and redeployed in nineteenth-century European and North American anthropologists' writings (1988, p. 71). The institution of slavery contributed to social discrimination against Africans in the Arab world, regardless of the lack of racial prejudice in the Koran and despite the literary, musical, religious, and military contributions of Africans to Muslim societies. The descriptions of Sudanese empires left by Arab scholars such as Al-Fazari (eighth century), Al-Bakri (eleventh century), and Ibn Battuta (fourteenth century), though colored by their interest in gold and conversion, constitute invaluable sources for the reconstitution of medieval African history. Al-Bakri, for instance, alludes to the matriarchal organization at the court of Ghana, to men with shaved beards and women with shaved heads, and to the king's *female* adornments (Shillington 2005).

Until the High Middle Ages Africa in the European imagination was associated with fabulous places, such as the kingdom of Prester John, a legendary Christian priest-king identified as the Abyssinian ruler, or larger-than-life figures, such as Mansa Musa (1312–1327), the emperor of Mali, who was represented holding a gold nugget by Abraham Cresques (d. 1387) in his 1375 world map. Spectacular embassies from Senegambia, the Kongo, and Ethiopia created long-lasting impressions and led to both more realistic portrayals of Africans and the introduction of the new convention of the dark-skinned Magus in the nativity scene (Northup 2002).

SLAVERY AND COLONIALISM

The massive transportation of enslaved Africans to the Americas required new narratives and new images. As Eric Williams (1994) argues, economic motives caused slavery, which in turn caused racism. As Africa became a reservoir of free laborers, Africans became Ham's offspring cursed by Noah, a race defined by the excesses of local climate and devoid of intellectual abilities and human feelings. Many of the most important modern thinkers subscribed to those notions, from Voltaire (1694–1778) to Hegel (1770–1831).

Colonialism reinforced the previous stereotypes. In the overarching European and North American dualism that subordinates nature to culture, the colonized subject was assimilated to nature and subtly feminized, sparing experts the need to compare African women's precolonial and colonial conditions. For instance, the system of dual chieftaincy in Nigeria, with both a female leader and a male leader, was ignored in gender-blind studies and destroyed by British indirect rule, which supported male leadership only. Though gender is a central element in any analysis of kinship, linguistics, division of labor, use of space, memory, and religion, African women were both caricatured and neglected in anthropological studies.

The case of Saartjie Baartman (1789–1815), the *Hottentot Venus*, is the attempt by scientific racism to locate sites of bestiality on the African female body. Brought from southern Africa to Europe in 1810, Baartman was exhibited in zoos and shows for her prominent buttocks and offered money by the French anatomist Georges Cuvier (1769–1832) to have her *Hottentot apron* examined. Her skeleton, genital parts, and brain were dissected after her death and preserved in the Musée de l'Homme in Paris until 1974 and were not returned to South Africa until 2002 (Bancel and Blanchard 2004).

Even after the 1920s anthropologists who participated in the deconstruction of the hegemonic notion of civilization and practiced participant observation in African societies paid less attention to women than photographers did. These photographic images show, however, ahistorical women, or "metaphors for a continent willing to be possessed and penetrated by the white man" (Boetsch and Savarese 1999, p. 130), that speak primarily of colonial desires. The French anthropologist Denise Paulme wrote in the 1985 introduction to *Women of Tropical Africa* (1960) that she "regretted most not to have previously worked with women. The image [she] brought back was that of a male world" (Héritier, p. 7). This first ethnological work dedicated to African women has been criticized for being a celebration of heroines intended to counter the colonial discourse that had portrayed African women as enslaved to an indigenous patriarchal order, and to illustrate the feasibility of the political and economic equality that the second wave of European and North American feminists demanded for themselves (Becker 2005).

AFRICANISM AND FEMINISM

Africanism, or knowledge about Africa, constituted itself in the mid-1950s through a fusion of anthropology and other disciplines (Mudimbe 1994). The field of Africanist gender studies has been dominated by anthropologists and historians since its inception in the 1960s and 1970s, though literary critics have contributed their expertise and creativity (Becker 2005). Both fields have been challenged to decolonize knowledge before and after independence.

After another shift from the mid-1970s to the late 1980s with the return of the African-woman-as-victim paradigm, more recent feminist scholarship has deconstructed woman as a unitary category and begun examining the previously unquestioned gender roles of men. Although black feminists such as Oyeronke Oyewumi (2004) and Niara Sudarkasa (b. 1938) have questioned the existence of gender in precolonial times, it may seem that women's condition as that of a "missing person[s] whose structure of difference produces the hybridity of race and sexuality in the postcolonial discourse" (Bhabha 1994, p. 53) has not been used sufficiently to theorize women's negotiations of gender roles and tensions between *traditions* and modernities, both at home and in situations of migration. However, the brand of African feminism delineated in the 1980s by Filomina Steady (1996), who advocated a rehabilitation of precolonial gender dynamics, sisterhood, and a bigendered fight against racism, has been challenged by social scientists such as Mamphela Ramphele (b. 1947). Stating that "men do not hold the monopoly over the potential to dominate," she suggests that viable intervention strategies should take in consideration "the various social hierarchies that shape and are shaped by gender" (Olukoshi and Nyamnjoh 2006, p. 2).

PAN-AFRICANISM

The idea of a common African/black identity results from the collective experience of the Middle Passage that turned various slave ports on the African coast and their adjacent hinterlands into a "Motherland" and the European ideological justification for that operation—race—into a factor in unity and even a political agenda. The term *diaspora*, which was borrowed from Jewish history to account for the scattering of Africans throughout the world, rests on the notion of a lost original wholeness. Indeed, the dream of returning to the *womb*, clandestinely carried into the hole of the slave ship by the *naked migrants* (in W. W. Glissant's [1992] terms), provided an alternative to the stereotype of a quintessentially hostile African environment. It has assigned the aspirations of slaves and their descendants to another spiritual or political order. The afterlife, for instance, entailed a recrossing of the ocean *back home* to Guinea, a metonymy of the continent as a whole; that myth also gave several layers of meaning to the recurrent references to boats and the Promised Land in spirituals. Similarly, early diasporic *nations*, from Maroon communities to the Haitian Republic, can be interpreted as enclaves in which institutions and social life mimicked an African model (Kandé 1998).

Not surprisingly, it was from Haiti, a Caribbean island under attack for its early political independence and its African cultural retentions, that there came an immediate refutation of Gobineau's thesis on the inequality of races. Though Anténor Firmin's book *De l'Egalité des races humaines* (1885) was not engaged with in French intellectual circles (Magloire-Danton 2005), its existence and arguments constitute a landmark in the history of the pan-African movement.

Pan-Africanism is a movement born in the diaspora that proclaims the centrality of Africa and acknowledges the bond created by a common experience of enslavement, colonialism, and racism among all people of African descent. Not surprisingly, a 1389 Chinese map and the 1402 Korean *Kangnido* anticipated the first accurate European map of southern Africa (1502), as the exchanges between China and the eastern coast of Africa that began as early as the second century BCE intensified between the eight and the fifteenth centuries CE and works toward the liberation of the *Motherland*. Pan-Africanism, which ideologically brought together black internationalists as diverse as E. W. Blyden (1832–1912), Marcus Garvey (1887–1940), Adelaide Casely Hayford (1868–1960), Tovalou-Quenum, C. L. R. James (1901–1989), and Malcolm X (1925–1965), has a cultural wing represented by the Francophone Négritude movement of the 1930s to the 1960s led by Léopold Sédar Senghor (1906–2001), Aimé Césaire (b. 1913), and Léon Gontran Damas (1912–1978). The writings of those scholars were aimed specifically at the rehabilitation of the African past.

Kwame Nkrumah (1909–1972), the first president of Ghana, made pan-Africanism a state ideology, insisting on the necessity for Africans to reconcile themselves to their triple heritage: precolonial, Euro-Christian, and Muslim. He also pointed out that "the degree of a country's revolutionary awareness may be measured by the political maturity of its women" (Nkrumah 1969, p. 131). Another pan-Africanist head of state, Thomas Sankara (1949–1987), took steps to draw attention to the plight of women in Burkina Faso, condemning female circumcision and polygamy and establishing a market day for men.

THE CONTEMPORARY SITUATION

The competition to (re)imagine Africa has become fiercer than ever. Superpowers and transnational companies have become interested in African mineral resources—diamonds, uranium, and oil—fostering political instability in regions of their production. Furthermore, troubled or impoverished nations sometimes are chosen to receive factories that exploit cheap local labor for international brands or to become dumping grounds for nuclear waste. Meanwhile, the major interest of tourists remains observing the fauna and flora in natural reserves such as the Chewore in Zimbabwe and the W park in Niger.

International public expectations about Africa are conditioned by stereotypes that are propagated widely by the mass media. Those stereotypes undermine the credibility of African endeavors to establish viable civil societies that can compete in international markets and in the intellectual realm, confining African contributions to the visual and performing arts. Many of those stereotypes have found an additional outlet in an Afro-pessimist discourse according to which AIDS will depopulate Africa, the high fecundity rate responsible for famine and emigration, and male polygamy is the rule.

Although the African continent has paid the heaviest toll in the AIDS pandemic, positive results have been obtained, most notably in Uganda but also in Senegal, thanks to an array of strategies, including grassroots work. Noreen Koleba, the female head of TASO (The AIDS Support Organization) in Uganda, emblematizes the African fight against AIDS.

Although Africa still has the world's highest African fecundity ratio with six children per woman in sixteen of its countries, those figures have to be understood in a historical perspective. The second largest continent, Africa accounted for 14 percent of the world population in 1700 and only 6 percent in 1900. The fecundity ratio must be reevaluated in light of the mortality ratio and an average life expectancy of forty-eight years, and the African mortality ratio (9.6% compared with 0.7% in developed countries). Even with a number of megalopoles, the African continent is underpopulated. Birth rates, in decline since the 1990s, were expected to decrease significantly in the first decades of the twenty-first century, and the concomitant aging of the population in the absence of social coverage is the most significant threat that looms over Africa.

Well rooted in rural and urban African societies, the institution of polygamy is limited and declining. Polygamous husbands have on average 2 to 2.5 wives. Flourishing in precolonial rural settings in the absence of land ownership, polygamy has become costly for city dwellers and thus has become a status symbol. It is also often the result of first arranged marriages with relatives. Challenges to the traditional meaning attached to marriage and gender relations and to elder brothers' ability to control their siblings' unions, coupled with a rise in the matrimonial age for educated girls, have been eroding the institution slowly (Courade 2006).

The ability of scholars of Africa to diffuse alternative views is a key factor in epistemological change. Much of the early work was done by the Egyptologist Cheikh Anta Diop (1974), who succeeded in reinserting Egypt on the African map and proving its ties to other sub-Saharan cultures. The deciphering of the *libraries in the sand* in the vicinity of Timbuktu represents the next crucial step. Tens of thousands of manuscripts redacted in African languages but written in Arabic script and covering subjects from astronomy to poetry are being exhumed. Some of them were produced at the time of the European invention of the printing press and have the potential to change the global understanding of African intellectual history.

BIBLIOGRAPHY

Becker, Heike. 2005. "Review of Andrea Corwall, ed." *Readings in Gender in Africa*." H–SAfrica. Bloomington: Indiana University Press.

Bancel, Nicolas, Pascal Blanchard, et al. 2004. *Zoos humains: Au temps des exhibitions humaines*. Paris: Découverte.

Bhabha, Homi. 1994. *Location of Culture*. London and New York: Routledge.

Boetsh, Gilles, and Eric Savarese. 1999. "Le corps de l'Africaine: Erotisation et inversion." *Cahiers d'Etudes Africaine* 153: 5–12

Brotton, Jerry. 2002. *The Renaissance Bazaar: From the Silk Road to Michelangelo*. Oxford and New York: Oxford University Press.

Courade, Georges. 2006. *L'Afrique des idées recues*. Paris: Belin.

Diop, Cheikh Anta. 1974. *The African Origin of Civilization: Myth or Reality*, trans. Mercer Cook. New York: L. Hill Books.

Glissant, Edouard. 1992. *Caribbean Discourse: Selected Essays*, trans. Jean-Michael Dash. Charlottesville: University Press of Virginia.

Heritier, Francoise. 1999. "Denise Paulme-Schaeffner (1909-1998) ou l'histoire d'une volonté" *Cahiers d'Etudes Africaines* XXXIX (1) 153: 5–12.

Kandé, Sylvie. 1998. *Terres, urbanisme et architecture "créoles" en Sierra Leone XVIIIe–XIXe siècles*. Paris: L'Harmattan.

Magloire-Danton, Gérarde. 2005. "Anténor Firmin and Jean Price-Mars: Revolution, Memory, Humanism." *Small Axe* 9(2): 150–172.

Mudimbe, V. Y. 1988. *The Invention of Africa: Gnosis, Philosophy, and the Order of Knowledge*. Bloomington: Indiana University Press.

Mudimbe, V. Y. 1994. *The Idea of Africa*. Bloomington: Indiana University Press.

Nkrumah, Kwame. 1969. *Axioms of Kwame Nkrumah: Freedom Fighters' Edition*. New York: International Publishers.

Northrup, David. 2002. *Africa's Discovery of Europe, 1450–1850*. New York: Oxford University Press.

Olukoshi, Abedayo, and Francis B. Nyamnjoh. 2006. "The African Woman." *CODESRIA Bulletin* 1/2: 1–2.

Oyewumi, Oyeronke. 2004. "Conceptualizing Gender: Eurocentric Foundations of Feminist Concepts and the Challenge of African Epistemologies." *JENda* 2(1): 1–8.

Paulme, Denise, ed. 1960. *Femmes d'Afrique noire*. Paris: Mouton.

Shillington, Kevin. 2005. *History of Africa*. Oxford: Macmillan Education.

Steady, Filomina. 1996. "African Feminism: A Worldwide Perspective." In *Women in Africa and the African Diaspora*, eds. Rosalyn Terborg-Penn and Andrea Benton Rushing. Washington, DC: Howard University Press.

Williams, Eric. 1994. *Capitalism and Slavery*. Chapel Hill: University of North Carolina Press.

Sylvie Kandé

III. ART AND LITERATURE

African arts are an ancient component of world heritage. The discovery of 77,000-year-old artifacts—including chunks of ochre engraved with geometric patterns—in the Blombos cave of South Africa reveals that creative and symbolic thinking associated with behavioral modernity first appeared in Africa. It had previously been assumed that rock paintings, which depict with significant regional and chromic variations, humans, animals and *therianthropes* (semihuman, semianimal creatures), were Africa's oldest form of art.

African arts is, however, a deceptive label that privileges visual arts (and sculpture more specifically) over architecture, textiles, body adornment, performing arts, or literature. Indeed, for the European and North American public, wooden masks have become emblematic of African art—although museification has generally deprived these objects of their dramatic function. Additionally, the notion of African arts often still refers to sub-Saharan artistic production, regardless of the region's crucial ties with North Africa and Ancient Egypt. Indeed, cultural historian Amadou Hampate Ba (1900 or 1901–1991) was able to identify evidence of such interactions in rock paintings representing proto-Fulani ceremonies at the prehistoric site of Tassili-n-Ajjer. Ancient Egypt clearly shares with the rest of Africa a number of aesthetic conventions. For instance, African carvers from Egypt and beyond routinely emphasize rulers' smooth facial features to symbolize the well-being of the land, and adorn them—even some female rulers—with the beard of wisdom. Implicit in the notion of African arts is also the culturally irrelevant distinction between fine arts and popular crafts, challenged by the exquisite treatment of an array of ordinary objects, from the Dogon heddle pulleys and the Kasai *velours*, to the Zulu spoons and Ashanti combs. This distinction has devalued women's artistic activities, with the exception of the famous Ndebele house painting tradition that South African painter Esther Mahlangu (b. 1935) has reinterpreted.

The belated, though enthusiastic, reception African arts elicited in early twentieth-century Europe ultimately opened a thorough questioning of the universal nature of European and North American aesthetic conventions and categories. African arts not only provided European and North American artists with new aesthetic solutions, but also gave anticolonial African intellectuals tangible evidence of an African philosophy needed to prepare for decolonization.

In modern Africa, whereas the local production of arts and crafts is generally strained by the importation of European and North American commodities and tourists' demands for affordable exotica that have replaced African patronage, a growing number of artists are attempting to redefine their role as either culture brokers or unaligned talents and as economic agents on the transnational art market. Appropriating media, techniques, and vocabulary, both from the contemporary European and North American art scene and from precolonial African aesthetic traditions, those artists have created bold fusions, or *métissages*. Women artists, in particular have been daring in crossing aesthetic and social boundaries.

Contemporary African art demonstrates an acute awareness of international events, global crises, and their local implications, studied by intensely committed artists whose gaze may nevertheless seem distanced, cruel, or sarcastic. Whereas power figures (*nkissi*) are locally being created in response to the AIDS pandemic, Congolese painter Cheri Samba (b. 1956) depicts its urban daily reality in a cartoon-like way; Kofi Setordji (b. 1957) (Ghana) created a monument to the 800,000 victims of the 1994 genocide in Rwanda, and painter Sylvia Katende (b. 1961) (Uganda) engages her audiences on politicofeminist themes, such as sustainable development.

African arts are infinitely diverse and resist totalizing aesthetic definitions. Indeed, the paradoxical absence of a signifier for art in African languages suggests a thorough dissemination of artistic creativity throughout all aspects of individual and collective life. African arts transcend binary oppositions, such as religious versus secular, high art versus crafts, and culture versus nature. Indeed, spiritually charged masks or statues are also utilitarian objects in the context of rituals ensuring social balance: Akuaba dolls, for instance, before transiting to shrines, are carried and nursed by Ashanti women seeking fertility. Moreover, the same category of objects, for instance, staffs or stools, may have several competing functions, both material and symbolic.

By and large, criteria of aesthetic achievement in African arts include inventiveness within an established tradition, a combination of abstraction with naturalism, repetition and contrast, and gender complementarity. A dance performance is evaluated in terms of both its faithful execution of known (and clearly gendered) steps and its sense of individual improvisation and self-celebration. Similarly, the fame of the headrests from the nineteenth-century Kinkondja workshop (Congo) results from their conformity with but also their divergence from

Luba conventions—apparent in the cascading treatment of the hair. Furthermore, on sculptures, naturalistic features (face, sex, hairdo, or scarifications) routinely coexist with enlarged body parts or emphatic volumes: prominent heads suggest inner vision and rounded breasts, fertility. Protrusions highlight the role of the face's orifices as contact zones between human and divine realms. Ubiquitous patterns account for both symmetry and movement in sculptures, for textiles' geometric designs, and for polyrhythm in musical compositions that corresponds to polycentrism in dances: Each part of the body, responding to a selected rhythm, moves in isolation from yet in coherence with the others.

The notion of gender complementarity permeates African arts, governing even the type of artistic activity undertaken. In casted societies, griots and griottes can perform oral texts, though the recitation of epics or royal genealogies are generally a male preserve. Blacksmiths can also be wood sculptors and jewelers, whereas their wives specialize in pottery making. Sculptures representing a pair of founding ancestors illustrate the paramount importance of achieving a unified vision of personhood and community through association of genders. The Dogon male associations meeting chambers are supported by posts adorned with female figures in a similar concern for gender balance. The same artifact often unites male and female attributes, as does the Queen of Holo carving that evokes Nzinga, the ideal ruler.

African societies have, with notable exceptions such as ancient Egypt and Ethiopia, chosen orality over writing for textual preservation and communication. An immense and constantly renewed corpus, oral literature encompasses compositions varying from diminutive proverbs to lengthy epics (such as the thirteenth-century Sunjata' epic that relates the foundation of the Mali empire), and several uniquely African genres, such as southern African praise poems (*izibongo*). African oral texts are generally conceived for performance and are accompanied by music and dancing. Memorialists include men and women.

The spread of Islam brought to the northern, western and eastern regions a new script that literate African Muslims used to transcribe oral literature and to create new texts. From the fifteenth century on, Timbuktu was the center of an intense production of manuscripts (some of them authored or copied by women) on a variety of subjects written in Arabic language or script.

Modern literature of Africa written in the colonial or excolonial languages emerged in the first decades of the twentieth century, with the limitations imposed by the colonial order. The Negritude movement, initiated in the 1930s by a group of Francophone writers—chief among them Léopold Sédar Senghor (1906–2001), who eventually would be elected into the French Academy—represents the first attempt to define an autonomous African literary aesthetics. Negritude has been criticized for its allegedly essentialist vision of racial relations and its inability to promote women's poetic expression. After World War II (1939–1945), major authors asserted themselves, such as Chinua Achebe, with his seminal novel, *Things Fall Apart* (1958), and Wole Soyinka (b. 1934), who was granted the Nobel Prize of Literature in 1986. Ngugi Wa Thiongo (b. 1938) has promoted modern African literature written in African languages by publishing some of his novels in the Gikuyu language.

The era of independence is characterized by a proliferation of fictions dealing with the condition of women, authored by Sembene Ousmane (also cited as Ousmane Sembene) (b. 1923) and Mongo Beti (1932–2001), most notably. By the 1970s, pioneering women writers, such as Flora Nwapa (1931–1993), Mariama Ba (1929–1981), and Buchi Emecheta (b. 1944), had transformed the literary landscape by inventing writing modes appropriate to their denunciation of African patriarchy. They paved the way for new generations of women writers, represented by Calixthe Beyala (b. 1961) or Tsitsi Dangaremba (b. 1959), who unequivocally advocate feminism. Though southern African literature focused mainly on Apartheid until the mid-1990s, Bessie Head (1937–1986) and Miriam Tlali (b. 1936) have forcefully evoked women' struggles. North African literature has been no less prolific, with a mix of Francophone writers such as Kateb Yacine (1929–1989) and Assia Djebar (b. 1936) (a member of the French Academy since 2006) and others who publish in both Arabic and English, such as Naguib Mahfuz (1911–2006), winner of the Nobel Prize of Literature in 1988. Egyptian writer Nawal el Saadawi (b. 1931) is well known for her courageous stands on women's issues, circumcision and prostitution especially.

Contemporary African arts are thriving, as illustrated by the biennales held in Dakar, Senegal, and Johannesburg, South Africa, and by the canonization of African literature both in Europe and North America and in Africa. Contemporary artists and writers have made their mark by paying tribute to past generations, all the while breaking a number of taboos. These include the prohibition for both noncasted people and women to engage in certain artistic activities. Salif Keita (b. 1949), a descendant of the Malinke ruling family, transgressed this rule by becoming an internationally famous musician, and Ousmane Sembene provocatively defined the African writer as a griot. In the same spirit, Doudou Ndiaye Rose (b. 1928) has produced a band of drummers, exclusively composed of women.

Artists have further complexified the notion of African arts by multiplying the forms, medium, and materials of their expression. A strong tradition of modern painting has developed in the Congo, whereas photography, with Seydou Keita (1921–2001), and cinema, with Souleymane Cisse (b. 1940), Safi Faye (b. 1943) and Flora M'Mbugu-Schelling, have acquired a well-deserved transnational fame. Instead of limiting themselves to perishable materials, artists work also in cement, aluminum, plastic, or recycled objects. Although new sources of patronage—banks, government offices, churches, or foreign foundations—have recently surfaced, few African artists can live off their artistic output.

In troubled postcolonial times, African writers and artists share concerns about the definition of their identity. Whereas many remain committed to the future of their continent of origin, a sizable number assert their right to be recognized solely for the quality of their works.

BIBLIOGRAPHY

Achebe, Chinua. 1958. *Things Fall Apart.* London: Heinemann.

Appiah, Anthony. 1992. "The Postcolonial and the Postmodern" *In My Father's House: Africa in the Philosophy of Culture.* New York: Oxford University Press.

Blier, S. P. 1999. "African Art and Architecture," *Africana*, ed. Kwame Anthony Appiah and Henry Louis Gates, Jr. New York: Basic Civitas Books.

Leiris, M. 1996. "La crise nègre dans le monde occidental" *Miroir de l'Afrique*. Paris: Gallimard, pp. 1125–1159.

Musée du quai Branly. 2000. "Sculptures Luba." *Sculptures. Afrique, Asie, Oceanie, Amériques.* Paris: Seuil.

Steiner, Christopher. 1994. *African Art in Transit.* Cambridge, UK: Cambridge University Press.

Timeline of Art History—Africa. Metropolitan Museum of Art. Available from http://www.metmuseum.org/toah/hm/04/af/hm04af.htm.

Vansina, Jan. 1984. *Art History in Africa.* London: Longman.

Visona´, Monica Blackman, et al. 2001. *A History of Art in Africa.* New York: Harry N. Abrams.

Wilford, J. N. 2001. "Artifacts in Africa Suggest an Earlier Modern Human." *New York Times*, December 2, sec. 1A, p. 1.

Zahan, D. 1980. *Antilopes du Soleil: Arts et rites agraires d'Afrique noire.* Vienna: A. Schlend.

Zimmer, William 1999. "Art: Layers of Complexity in a Show of African Objects." *New York Times*, December 12.

Sylvie Kandé

IV. RELIGIONS

African indigenous religions have certain similar structures that are visible among the many diverse peoples of Africa, showing the interlinking relationships among the human, spiritual, and natural entities. Mythic narratives and ritual performances express and articulate, linguistically and symbolically, the gendered relationship and categorization within the African universe. Historian of religion Ninian Smart's (2006) presentation of the seven dimensions of religious phenomena is quite revealing of the components and structures of African indigenous thought. While mythic and ritual dimensions are crucial to indigenous religious expression, other aspects such as ethics, experience, social doctrines, images, and symbols are constructed and created from myths and rituals. The seven dimensions assist in understanding the nature and structure of African indigenous religions.

MYTHS, THE COSMOS, AND SPIRITUAL BEINGS

Like most other indigenous peoples, Africans have a variety of myths through which they define and express their existence in the cosmos. Most hold that many spiritual beings exist, with a supreme being at the apex. Deities who express the nature, character, and power of the Supreme Being are both male and female.

Supreme Beings African communities have different names expressed in indigenous languages, which are descriptive of their perception of the Supreme Being. Most communities in Africa hold that the Supreme Being is male, largely due to the patriarchal nature of these communities. Some supreme beings are, however, either female or androgynous (both male and female). The Ashanti of Ghana, for instance, speak of Nyame as the great Mother who gives life to all, while the Ewe-speaking peoples of Ghana believe that Nana-Buluku, the Ancient Deity, is androgynous. The variations in the conception, description, and portrayal of supreme beings as male, female, or androgynous in most cases are due to the social structures and patterns of the different communities and localities. However, the roles of the supreme beings are both masculine and feminine.

The basic African conception envisions the Supreme Being as the originator of all existence. In all cases the Supreme Being possesses attributes such as omnipotence, omniscience, omnipresence, transcendence, immanence, and benevolence.

Deities The deities (or divinities) are lesser spiritual beings that function in different capacities and manifest certain aspects and characters of the Supreme Being. These deities are capable of manifesting as human beings and natural phenomena. In fact, myths hold that some of the deities existed at different times both as human beings and natural phenomena. This notion supports the view that the deities exhibit both positive and negative human characteristics. The deities serve as intermediaries between the Supreme Being and human beings as well as other nonhuman entities. Human beings, who express the reality of the deities in ritual performances, present interlinking connections among the spiritual beings, the natural phenomena, and other unseen entities that populate the universe. The relationships of the human beings to both the Supreme Being and divinities are described in anthropological terms in some cases as fathers, mothers, and friends.

The Supreme Being in most mythic narrative created and continues to maintain the universe through the assistance and in collaboration with male and female deities. For instance, the male and female twins of Amma, the Dogon Supreme Being, were the progenitors of the human race. Among the Akan of Ghana (West Africa), Nyame created Okane, the first man, and Kyeiwaa, the first woman. The Mende myth of creation tells of Ngewo, who, after creating the earth and all things in it, made a man and woman to populate the universe. The Yoruba present a fascinating myth of creation and maintenance of the universe that includes male and female deities called *òrìsà*. After creating the *òrìsà*, Olódùmarè, the Supreme Being, delegates responsibility for the universe to his principal *òrìsà*, among whom are Obàtáálá, Òrúnmìlà, Ògún (males), and Òsun (female). Another prominent female deity who participates in the maintenance of the universe is Obà, a river deity. While the complementarity of the male and female deities is intrinsic and strong, Yoruba cosmology also teaches that female deities possess and exercise spiritual powers that could submerge those of their male counterparts.

Most African deities continue to function through the natural phenomena they embody, such as rain, wind, forest, and river. Some deities manifest as entities of the terrestrial universe, including the sun, moon, and stars. The male-female relationship makes vitality and productivity possible.

Most water deities serve as agents of human procreation and productivity. The deities have a role in fertility through ritual processes, thus sustaining the human community. Osun, Oya, and Yemoja, goddesses, exemplify this belief among the Yoruba and African Disapora.

Deities associated with the sky and rain are male, and fertilize the deities associated with the earth. According to the Edo of eastern Nigeria, Chukwu created Igwe, or Amadioha, the Sky deity, and Ala, the Earth deity; Igwe took the form of rain to fertilize Ala, his wife. Most male deities exhibit anger and hot-bloodedness, whereas female deities are gentle and cool. Examples of male-female complementary deities include Gua and Bosomtwe of the Akan (Ghana); Sango and Osun of the Yoruba (Nigeria); and Amadioha and Ala of the Igbo (Nigeria). Human beings explore and exploit their own complementary roles in procreation and productivity by participating in ritual practices.

RITES AND RITUAL PRACTICE

Ritual practice provides a context for the meeting of the spiritual, humans, and the natural world. In the spirit-nature-human relationship, the human body serves as the focal point for, and the center of, the connection through words, recited, uttered, and sung in ritual activities. Rivers and lakes symbolize female deities whereas hills and mountains perform that function for male deities. Natural elements such as iron and stone also represent male deities. The shrine of any particular deity often houses the emblems and symbols of deities of other sexes. Explanations for this are that, in ritual practices, (a) the male-female principle operates in the sense of primordial existence, which has continual relevance; and (b) male and female deities collaborate in ritual observances that are employed for human well-being and ordering of the universe. Moreover, symbols and emblems have practical utility in ritual practice. Participants believe that words used in the rituals possess creative and spiritual power.

Ritual prescriptions follow the male-female principle in response to primordial dictate. Worshipers offer deities ritual meals, specific to each deity and either offered up directly or consumed by humans as an indirect offering. Some meals are forbidden for particular deities. In most cases, prescriptions and taboos are dictated by the sex of the deity. Meals including liquids, such as the blood of hen and she-goat and water, which are characterized by coolness and softness, are appropriate for female deities, while rougher materials are prescribed for male deities. Shrines display the prescribed rituals. Worshipers sometimes place the meals of female deities at the shrines of male deities in an attempt to assuage the fury and that the latter show toward human beings.

Ritual provides a renewal, reinvigoration, revitalization, rejuvenation, and rebirth of spaces and times through the agency of human beings. Ritual activities based on mythic narratives often dictate, order, and empower processes of commitment and objectification.

RITES OF PASSAGE

Societies support rites of passage, otherwise called rites of transition, to transit its members from one stage of life to another. The first phase of transition includes naming and circumcision for boys and girls. In indigenous African religious communities, the girl children were circumcised on the seventh day after birth, the boy children on the ninth day. The next phase is puberty. The rites of transition for the female at this phase coincide with marriage rites and are usually performed when a girl's breasts begin to mature or at the onset of menstruation. The rites include food taboos and training in domestic responsibilities. A male adolescent may request the rites or the community may call for them based on the child's physical growth. Such rituals can involve symbolic death, which may in fact be fatal, and shaving the initiates' heads. Rites of passage involve seclusion for both males and females.

Marriage rites, usually communal and protracted, involve the extended families of the marriage partners. The rite culminates in an elaborate ceremony of gift-giving and merriment. The two families become one, staying intact through times of joy and sorrow.

Burial rites are the most elaborate in terms of significance, symbolism, and performance. Male burial rites are more important as a social event. The reasons for this are obvious: African societies are patriarchal and the social structure places men in positions of power. Men's burial rites are relatively longer than those of women. Women, however, are required to observe a long period of mourning for deceased husbands. They remain indoors and dress in dark clothing. Women shave their heads during this period in some cultures. Some societies forced a young widow to become the spouse of another member of the man's family, but this is no longer enforced.

RELIGIOUS SPECIALISTS

Religious specialists are priests and priestesses who consult the deities on behalf of individuals and communities. They serve male and female deities, that is, gods and goddesses. Chief priests and priestesses give instructions, prescribe rituals, and, where required, divine signs and omens. Ritual specialists also direct and participate prominently at annual and occasional indigenous festivals.

The most common categories of religious specialists, in addition to priests and priestesses, are mediums, diviners, herbalists, and witch-doctors. Their roles, however, are fluid and confusing. Whereas priests and priestesses have specific duties and full commitment to the shrines of their personal or community deities, diviners serve in a general capacity as mediums for the clients who consult them in times of distress and uncertainty. Priesthood may be assumed or ascribed through spirit possession, selection by the family through divine consultation, or training by senior ritual specialists. A religious specialist may assume several roles.

African priestesses participate prominently in festivals and ritual practices with specific and defined functions and roles. Their psychic abilities display in such activities as drumming, clapping, singing, and ecstatic movement, and they are skilled in extemporaneous singing and recitation of praise-poetry. Priests however exhibit spirituality more often through meditative actions. Though both perform divination, priests speak at length during the process. In some cases different instruments are used by priests and priestesses.

Sorcerers and witches constitute a unique spiritualist category. They are spiritual agents whom many African communities view as diabolical agents of terror. Sorcerers, predominantly male, are believed to possess the characteristics of good and evil, whereas witches, predominantly female, are believed to be essentially and inherently evil. Witchcraft, embodied in the image of old, ugly, haggard women who take the form of animals such as cats, lizards, and cockroaches, is a source of terror in some communities. Sorcerers and witches are indispensable in the scheme of ritual performance because priests and priestesses solicit their support and cooperation.

Priests and priestesses often collaborate in ritual performances, particularly with regard to healing. Different taboos exist for priests and priestess. Empowerment of priests and priestesses follows different patterns and ritual prescriptions.

Some African religious specialists reenact a community's pact with the deity instrumental in founding it. Priests and priestesses jointly engage in the renewal of shrines and other sacred places. Festival dramas, whether hegemonic, that is, marking the foundation of towns, or celebratory, commemorating other important events or persons, are done in the spirit of civil religiosity, where everybody who claims to belong to the community by origin, or lives in the community, regardless of their religious persuasions, is expected to participate.

During festival performances, ritual spiritualists wear costumes representing sex or gender roles. Notwithstanding their sexes, they often wear costumes of the deities that they serve and to which they are committed. In West Africa, performers at Gelede and Osun festivals put on female headdresses. Male Sango priests plait their hair in female patterns. These activities probably have primordial origins.

Other materials used in ritual practices and festivals are gender-ascribed, reflecting statuses and roles. A good example is the drum: Some drums are male, others female. Use of some drums is restricted by sex or deity.

CONTEMPORARY DEVELOPMENTS

Contemporary studies in African indigenous religions reveal the hidden resources in African sacred oral texts, contained in chants, corpus, songs, symbols, and proverbs. Researchers are moving away from colonial influences and early biased studies and views of African religions.

Early-twenty-first-century scholars recognize Islam and Christianity as African religions. Pentecostal and evangelical sects in Africa have done much to encourage women to refute the negative image of them imposed by early Christian missionaries. Islam has also made advances in gender issues. Women now establish and lead Muslim societies and movements.

BIBLIOGRAPHY

Adegbola, E. A. A., ed. 1998. *Traditional Religion in West Africa.* Ibadan, Nigeria: Sefer.

Awolalu, J. Omosade, and P. Adelumo Dopamu. 1979. *West African Traditional Religion.* Ibadan, Nigeria: Onibonoje Press.

Blakely, Thomas D.; Walter E. A. van Beek; and Denis Thomson, eds. 1994. *Africa: Experience and Expression.* London: James Currey; Portsmouth, NH: Heinemann.

Clarke, Peter B., ed. 1998. *New Trends and Developments in African Religions.* Westport, CT: Greenwood Press.

Gennep, Arnold van. 1960. *The Rites of* Passage, trans. Monika B. Vizedom and Gabrielle L. Caffe. Chicago: University of Chicago Press.

Idowu, E. Bolaji. 1973. *African Traditional Religion: A Definition.* Maryknoll, NY: Orbis.

Mbiti, John S. 1991. "Flowers in the Garden: The Role of Women in African Religion." In *African Traditional Religions in Contemporary Society*, ed. Jacob K. Olupona. New York: International Religious Foundation.

Mol, Hans. 1977. *Identity and the Sacred: A Sketch for a New Social Scientific Theory of Religion.* New York: Harper and Row.

Moore, Henrietta L; Todd Sanders; and Bwire Kaare, eds. 1999. *Those Who Play with Fire: Gender, Fertility and Transformation in East and Southern Africa.* New Brunswick, NJ: Athlone Press.

Murphy, Joseph M., and Mei-Mei Sanford, eds. 2001. *Osun Across the Waters: A Yoruba Goddess in Africa and the Americas.* Bloomington: Indiana University Press.

Olajubu, Oyeronke. 2003. *Women in the Yoruba Religious Sphere.* Albany: State University of New York Press.

Olupona, Jacob K., ed.. 2000. *African Spirituality: Forms, Meanings and Expressions.* New York: Crossroad Publishing.

Parrinder, Edward Geoffrey. 1974. *African Traditional Religion.* London: Sheldon Press

Ray, Benjamin C. 1976. *African Religions: Symbol, Ritual and Community.* Englewood Cliffs, NJ: Prentice Hall.

Smart, Ninian. 2000. *Worldviews: Crosscultural Explorations of Human Beliefs.* Upper Saddle River, NJ: Prentice Hall.

David O. Ogungbile

AFROCENTRICISM

Afrocentricism, or Afrocentricity, is a theoretical and philosophical stance that places pan-African experience at the center of African-descendent people's lives. This stance challenges a dominantly Eurocentric view of civilization, which centralizes European cultural standards and white racial identity. In many parts of the world, people of African descent share a common history of displacement and oppression, as a result of contact with European colonialists and enslavers. This history of colonialism and slavery, as Afrocentrists point out, has allowed Europeans to dominate ways of thinking, and deprived African-descendent people of the freedom to control their own lives. Afrocentrists argue that European dominance required the devaluing of African cultural legacies and perspectives. Afrocentricism, therefore, is an approach to liberating people of African descent from a history of Eurocentric oppression, and to affirming the value of African humanity for African people.

In the United States, Afrocentricism stems back to black nationalist movements of the 1960s and 1970s. As the civil rights movement, which gained momentum in the 1950s and early 1960s, seemed to yield slow advances in the battle for equal rights, black nationalists perceived a more radical approach to continuing the struggle. They actively confronted racism while affirming the value of a black "consciousness," derived from a communal black experience, black cultural aesthetics, and a politics of racial unity and cultural recognition. "Black Power" exemplified an empowerment that was all encompassing—politically, culturally, and spiritually—and referred to a common vision for the community of African Americans.

Afrocentricity, a term defined by Molefi Kete Asante in the early 1980s, continued to develop as an interpretive paradigm within Black Studies departments in academia throughout the 1980s and 1990s. Critics, however, have argued that, by implicating a collective identity that is fundamentally "African," the theory either reduces or discounts the actual diversity of pan-African experience. A tendency in this regard is to either subordinate or ignore gender and sexuality in favor of racial concerns. This tendency does not allow for a thorough investigation of how race is experienced in differing ways across gender lines, nor how pan-African gender issues are related to power within Eurocentric societies. It also does not account for how power dynamics work between African-descendant men and women themselves, irrespective of a white, outsider presence.

One Afrocentric view maintains that, within African cultures, gender relations are cooperative rather than oppositional. Manhood and womanhood are "complementary," making up a reciprocal, non-hierarchical process of definition. Schools of feminism, in this view, all belong to a European perspective that is not only inadequate for addressing the particular realities of African-descendant women, but ignorant of these realities. As early Western feminist thought privileged the conditions of white women, without attending to the ways in which gender is experienced in differing ways across racial lines, "feminism" continues to imply the subordination of African-descendant women, to both European norms generally and to white femininity.

In the United States during the 1970s, emergent modes of black feminism challenged the limited scope of dominant feminist politics that largely ignored many class, racial, and sexual realities of women's lives. Audre Lorde, a black, lesbian feminist poet, created an intellectual and political space for publicly exploring the complexity of her multiple modes of identity. Having taught herself about African history and understanding Africa as her distant homeland, Lorde incorporated an Afrocentric sensibility to her vision of liberation. Such a worldview enabled a politics that was both African and women-centered.

As theorist Patricia Hill Collins has argued, an Afrocentric viewpoint that, at its most extreme, restricts feminine civic involvement and sexuality also neglects the interests of African-descendant women. Attentiveness to the complexities of gender and sexuality elaborates on the Afrocentric impulse to expand, rather than limit, available perspectives of the world.

SEE ALSO *Africa: I. History; Nationalism.*

BIBLIOGRAPHY

Asante, Molefi Kete. 1998. *The Afrocentric Idea*, revised and expanded edition. Philadelphia: Temple University Press.

Collins, Patricia Hill. 1998. *Fighting Words: Black Women and the Search for Justice.* Minneapolis: University of Minnesota Press.

De Veaux, Alexis. *Warrior Poet: A Biography of Audre Lorde.* New York: W.W. Norton & Company, 2004.

Mazama, Ama. 2001. "The Afrocentric Paradigm: Contours and Definitions." *Journal of Black Studies* 31(4): 387–405.

Nnaemeka, Obioma, ed. 1998. *Sisterhood, Feminisms and Power: From Africa to the Diaspora.* Trenton, NJ: Africa World Press, Inc.

Habiba Ibrahim

AFTERGLOW

Afterglow can be defined as a blissful period of mental and physical relaxation after orgasm during which a person enjoys the rush of endorphins produced by sexual climax. As a result of the increased flow of blood, people may physically appear to glow, with flushed cheeks and skin. Afterglow is seen as a time of heightened emotional and psychological sensitivity during which the body is no longer open to further physical stimulation. Accounts include ecstatic feelings such as loss of self, intense connection with one's partner or surroundings, and timelessness. For this reason, practitioners of Tantric sex, who see intercourse as a spiritual and thoughtful union instead of a goal-oriented process, describe afterglow as one of the means through which enlightened sex can lead to a higher mental state.

Afterglow generally is considered the final step in the sexual response cycle defined in physiological studies of human sexuality. First explained in the studies of William Masters and Virginia Johnson (1966 and 1970), these stages are arousal or excitement, plateau, orgasm, and resolution. Afterglow thus often is grouped with resolution, the phase of the sexual act marked by the return to an unaroused state in which blood pressure, heart rate, and breathing decrease and blood leaves the genital area. Generally, the more intense the orgasm, the more intense the experience of afterglow. Afterglow also has been termed *afterplay*, the end partner to foreplay.

Although men and women enjoy afterglow similarly, physical and cultural distinctions are attached to this postcoital period. Physically, men enter a state called the *refractory period* after orgasm and ejaculation that limits their ability to become sexually aroused for a period ranging from five minutes to twenty-four hours or more. Women do not have the equivalent reaction and may remain open to continued sexual activity, potentially achieving multiple orgasms. Anecdotally, men are more likely to fall asleep during this period, whereas women are more likely to remain awake despite the intense relaxation they experience. Women thus may be more likely to see afterglow as conscious quality time with the partner. In support of this distinction, some researchers (Hardy 1981, Taylor 2002) have argued that women's attachment to afterglow is a result of maternal, nurturing instincts originally directed toward infants. In terms of survival, the female who keeps her sexual partner close to her after coitus protects both herself, her potential unborn children, and her existing offspring from physical danger. It is therefore in her best interest to continue being kind and physically attentive so the male will not leave too quickly.

Despite these gendered distinctions, cultural associations of afterglow show more commonality than difference. One association is *pillow talk*, or intimate conversation between partners that occurs in bed, often after sex. In addition, people enjoying afterglow stereotypically smoke cigarettes, since the rush of nicotine adds to the natural endorphin rush of orgasm. Thus, when films show couples smoking cigarettes in bed, this scene often stands in for the sex act, as the film may cut from foreplay to afterglow, leaving the audience to fill in the gaps. (Despite this common association, cigarettes have become less prevalent in American media in the wake of a 1999 federal lawsuit against tobacco companies.) In light of this function, the significance of afterglow as the final stage of sex often is emphasized in fictional narratives that, more than lived experience, rely on closure.

SEE ALSO *Coitus.*

BIBLIOGRAPHY

Hardy, Sarah Blaffer. 1981. *The Woman That Never Evolved.* Cambridge, MA: Harvard University Press.

Masters, William H., and Johnson, Virginia E. 1966. *Human Sexual Response.* Boston: Little, Brown.

Pearsall, Paul. 1987. *Super Marital Sex: Loving for Life.* Garden City, NY: Doubleday.

Taylor, Shelley E. 2002. *The Tending Instinct: How Nurturing is Essential to Who We are and How We Live.* New York: Times Books.

Michelle Veenestra

AIDS AND HIV

This entry contains the following:

I. OVERVIEW

AIDS (acquired immunodeficiency syndrome) presents as a variety of diseases and illnesses, all of which result from infection by the human immunodeficiency virus (HIV). HIV attacks the human immune system, weakening the response of the body to infection and disease and rendering a patient susceptible to various illnesses. HIV causes few symptoms, and an infected person may appear and feel healthy for years after contracting the virus. Once the virus has weakened the immune system sufficiently, the disease progresses to full-blown AIDS, which is marked by a variety of illnesses from which the patient has increasing difficulty in recovering. Death from AIDS results from the effects of secondary illnesses.

HIV/AIDS is believed to have arisen in western and central Africa in the mid-twentieth century. The virus is transmitted through bodily fluids such as blood, semen, and vaginal secretions. It is communicated primarily through sexual contact but also can be transmitted from mother to child (prenatally, during delivery, or during breast-feeding), through the sharing of contaminated needles by intravenous drug users, through the use of infected blood in medical procedures, and by other means of blood contamination (needle punctures, contamination of open wounds, etc.).

HIV is a retrovirus capable of rapid mutation that produces a latent infection that develops over a long period. To infect a human, HIV must attach to specific host cells known as CD4 cells, which are responsible for regulating the immune system. Once it has occupied a host cell, the virus copies the DNA of the cell, rendering it invisible to the body's defense system. The virus replicates itself within the cells, producing numerous virus particles that bud from the surface of the cell, destroying the cell and moving on to attach to another CD4 cell. For several weeks or months after initial infection the patient is highly infectious, although HIV testing will not reveal the patient's positive status. After this initial period, which is known as the window period, the virus incubates, destroying many CD4 cells but being fended off by the immune system. Some two million CD4 cells are destroyed each day by some ten billion newly produced virus particles. The incubation period for HIV is quite long, averaging around ten years. Once the balance between CD4 cells and virus particles shifts in favor of HIV, however, symptoms begin to appear.

In the United States the diagnosis of AIDS is tied to CD4 counts as well as to secondary symptoms. When an HIV-positive individual's CD4 counts falls below 200 (a healthy person's count appears to range from 500 to 1,600) or when that person is determined to have any one of twenty-six opportunistic infections, a diagnosis of AIDS is made. In less developed or poorer countries, however, means for testing CD4 counts are often unavailable or prohibitively expensive. In such cases doctors rely on clinical examination of the patient to make the diagnosis. Certain infections, including tuberculosis and meningitis, are particularly common in HIV-positive individuals.

SEE ALSO *Sexually Transmitted Diseases.*

BIBLIOGRAPHY

Barnett, Tony, and Alan Whiteside. 2006. *AIDS in the Twenty-First Century: Disease and Globalization.* 2nd edition. New York: Palgrave Macmillan.

Maureen Lauder

II. HISTORY

AIDS (acquired immunodeficiency syndrome) appears to have originated in Africa at some time in the twentieth century. The human immunodeficiency virus (HIV) is assumed to be a variant of a simian immunodeficiency virus (SIV) that became capable of crossing the species barrier. It is unclear how that crossover first occurred, although scholars have posited contamination in the slaughter of bush meat or contamination of an oral polio vaccine cultured on chimpanzee kidneys that was administered widely in parts of Africa. In either case it appears that HIV and AIDS were present in the human population long before they were recognized.

Scholars have identified isolated deaths in European countries as early as the 1950s that now appear to be the result of AIDS and HIV, and analysis in the 1980s of blood samples originally drawn from African subjects in 1959 turned up one sample contaminated by HIV. It is possible that isolated individuals or communities experienced AIDS outbreaks earlier in the century, but political and social upheaval in Africa after World War II, coupled with widespread vaccination campaigns in regions that often could not afford to use disposable needles, provided an environment in which HIV was readily transmissible.

AIDS first came to public attention in the United States in 1979 and 1980, when doctors in New York and Los Angeles began noticing an increased incidence of fatalities resulting from extremely rare and normally benign diseases. In Los Angeles doctors were seeing multiple cases of a deadly form of pneumonia caused by *Pneumocystis carinii*, a generally harmless and extremely common protozoan that rarely induces illness and almost never causes death. In New York physicians were also seeing *Pneumocystis carinii* pneumonia as well as cases of Kaposi's sarcoma, an extremely rare and benign skin cancer that normally afflicted (though seldom killed) elderly men of Jewish and Mediterranean origin. In New York, however, Kaposi's sarcoma suddenly was making fairly young men extremely ill and, often coupled with other opportunistic infections, leading to rapid deterioration and death. All those early cases of AIDS involved homosexual men.

The gay rights movement of the 1970s had been invested in the importance of sexual freedom. If mainstream America deemed gay sexuality distasteful and shameful, there seemed no better way to confront and overturn those prejudices than by celebrating gay sex. In the early 1970s sexual promiscuity not only was accepted but was considered politically and socially desirable, a means of forging a new kind of community that resisted heteronormative ideals of partnership, family, and sexual practice.

By the late 1970s bathhouses designed expressly to facilitate fast, anonymous sex were a common feature of gay life in some urban centers, notably New York and San Francisco. The first victims of AIDS had in common frequent bathhouse attendance and a promiscuous lifestyle that included lifetime sexual contacts that numbered in the thousands and sometimes in the tens of thousands. Because of their numerous sexual partners, those early victims were an ideal vector for the disease, and because of the long incubation period that preceded the symptoms, HIV was well established in urban centers in the United States before anyone knew it existed. By the time people became aware of it, gay men in other areas of the country—men who were not part of the San Francisco or New York gay scenes but who may have slept with someone who was or once had been—had been infected.

In the second half of 1981 reports began to surface of AIDS infections in the heterosexual population. Drug addicts who used intravenous drugs became sick in noticeable numbers, infant children of drug addicts fell ill shortly after birth, and hemophiliacs and those who had received blood transfusions started to develop symptoms. Intense political pressure surrounding the disease, however, stymied the attempts of doctors, health officials, and activists to mobilize a defense. Many doctors and health officials were reluctant to accept evidence that the epidemic was not limited to the homosexual population, and the testing of blood donors for HIV was instituted much too late to stem the progression of the disease.

The gay press often considered claims of the prevalence and severity of the disease to be hysterical, overly alarmist, and indicative of widespread homophobia, whereas the mainstream press largely refused to touch an issue that involved primarily gay sexuality. Only when evidence that AIDS could strike heterosexuals became overwhelming did the major news organs begin to run stories about HIV and AIDS, and even then there were relatively few compared with earlier, much smaller epidemics. The Reagan administration provided little leadership or research funding, and the response of the National Institutes of Health (NIH) was slow and was accompanied by inadequate funding. Ultimately, AIDS research and prevention in the first decade after the emergence of the disease were driven by local groups and individual doctors, activists, health officials, and politicians, usually with insufficient resources and funding. Thus, by the time the U.S. government gave HIV and AIDS substantive attention, the virus was well entrenched and spreading rapidly in U.S. society and throughout the world.

BIBLIOGRAPHY

Barnett, Tony, and Alan Whiteside. 2006. *AIDS in the Twenty-First Century: Disease and Globalization*. 2nd edition. New York: Palgrave Macmillan.

Hooper, Edward. 1999. *The River: A Journey to the Source of HIV and AIDS*. Boston: Little, Brown.

Shilts, Randy. 1988. *And the Band Played On: Politics, People, and the AIDS Epidemic*. New York: St. Martin's.

Maureen Lauder

III. EFFECTS ON POPULATION

In most countries human immunodeficiency virus (HIV) infection initially spreads primarily through a group of core transmitters who are at particular risk. Sex between men may have a transmission rate as high as one in ten, depending on sexual practices. Transmission rates among intravenous drug users are high because a contaminated needle can introduce HIV directly into the bloodstream. Sex workers also have an elevated risk of contracting and transmitting HIV. HIV/AIDS (acquired immunodeficiency syndrome) often establishes itself in those high-risk groups before moving into the general population. As the mode of transmission shifts from sex between men and the sharing of needles by intravenous drug users, the rate of HIV diagnosis among women often increases dramatically, leading to greater numbers of children being born with HIV or orphaned by AIDS. HIV is most likely to be a generalized epidemic in poorer countries, which may lack the infrastructure, money, and political stability for effective wide-scale treatment and prevention.

THE UNITED STATES

In the United States HIV/AIDS first became widespread among populations of homosexual men, which suffered widespread fatalities in the early years of the epidemic. As a result AIDS long was considered a "gay" disease, and there is still a lingering perception that AIDS victims are most likely to be homosexual men. In later years, however, the nature of the epidemic changed noticeably. More than 50 percent of new HIV diagnoses have been among African Americans, and some three-quarters of women diagnosed with HIV are African American. The wide availability of antiretroviral therapy has led to a substantial decrease in AIDS deaths; African Americans, however, have substantially lower survival rates than does the white population. In 2002 the death rate of African Americans with AIDS was twice that of whites.

AFRICA

Sub-Saharan Africa bears a disproportionate burden from the AIDS epidemic; it is home to about 10 percent of world population but contains 60 percent of HIV cases worldwide. In Africa the epidemic is widespread and generalized, with most transmission occurring through heterosexual sex.

Widespread poverty, lack of infrastructure, inconsistent or ineffective prevention programs, expensive or unavailable treatment, and social and political upheaval have contributed to the spread of infection in many countries in that region. As a result the areas hardest hit by HIV/AIDS are often the least able to respond effectively. Because AIDS is most likely to kill people in the prime of life, local and national productivity has been affected seriously. Households with one or more AIDS victims often are strained by the loss of income and the need to provide care and treatment to the afflicted member; young children and the elderly often end up shouldering much of the burden. Local communities also are strained by AIDS deaths because extended families and elderly grandparents with limited resources often take in children orphaned by AIDS.

EASTERN EUROPE AND ASIA

In many countries in Eastern Europe and Asia, HIV infections have been on the rise. The Ukraine experienced a tremendous upsurge in HIV diagnoses after 2000, with a significant incidence in women and the heterosexual population. Russia also has seen an increase in HIV cases, apparently linked to widespread intravenous drug use in its population. In several other countries in Eastern Europe, AIDS is spreading rapidly through intravenous drug users. The epidemic is expected to become more generalized as drug users begin transmitting the virus to their partners.

In many East Asian countries most new infections are transmitted by sex workers, who often cannot insist on condom use. In Thailand, however, a government mandate requiring universal condom use among sex workers has slowed the advance of HIV/AIDS dramatically. Because of the sheer size of many Asian nations, the raw number of HIV-infected individuals in that region is expected by some to overtake that of sub-Saharan Africa.

WOMEN

As HIV infection becomes increasingly generalized in a population, women tend to be affected disproportionately. Of the estimated 39.4 million HIV cases worldwide at the end of 2004, some 17.6 million were women. Almost 75 percent of those women lived in sub-Saharan Africa, where women accounted for 57 percent of HIV infections. Among young women in that region, the gap between male and female infections has been even more striking: It has been estimated that some thirty-six women between the ages of fifteen and twenty-four are infected for every ten men in the same age group.

The increased infection rates among women may be in part biological—evidence suggests that it may be easier for men to transmit HIV to women than vice versa—but it is often also a reflection of the relative status and power of women in a society. Researchers in sub-Saharan Africa, for example, have noted that HIV transmission among women is accelerated in societies in which large numbers of women are not in a position to refuse sex or to insist on

Mozambique Women Discuss Sex and AIDS. *A group of rural women discuss sexual relations and AIDS transmisssion in their community in Maputo, Mozambique.* © GIDEON MENDEL/CORBIS.

safe sex, for example, when they are physically or economically dependent on a male head of household's earnings, gifts from a lover, or earnings from prostitution. In countries stricken by warfare increases in the number of rapes also help spread infection. In societies in which the economic and social status of women has risen, researchers have found that transmission rates tend to drop.

CHILDREN

As of the end of 2004 some 2.2 million children were infected with HIV. Although many children are infected by their mothers, several countries have seen a marked increase in early sexual activity among children, making that population more vulnerable to HIV infection. Additionally, some children are infected in the course of sexual molestation and abuse by adults. In addition to those directly infected by HIV, millions of children worldwide have been orphaned by AIDS. It appears that some 11 million children or more are AIDS orphans; that number was projected to more than triple by 2020.

Societies that have large numbers of orphans are also those which have few institutional structures to help care for them. In sub-Saharan Africa, which is home to some 12 percent of orphans worldwide, extended families traditionally have shouldered the burden of caring for the children of deceased relatives, often straining already tight resources. Members of families that have taken in orphans are more likely to be malnourished and their children and foster children are more likely to be stunted. Orphans often have increased responsibilities at home, are less likely to attend school, and are more likely to do poorly when they do attend. Lack of resources to care for orphaned children probably will affect a region or nation over the long term as malnourished and uneducated children grow into an unskilled adult population with a variety of health problems.

BIBLIOGRAPHY

Barnett, Tony, and Alan Whitehead. 2006. *AIDS in the Twenty-First Century: Disease and Globalization*. 2nd edition. New York: Palgrave Macmillan.

Maureen Lauder

IV. TREATMENTS AND PREVENTION

Treatment and prevention measures for human immunodeficiency syndrome (AIDS) vary widely from country to country and region to region. The availability of treatment for human immunodeficiency virus (HIV) infection and AIDS is highly variable and largely dependent on national wealth and medical infrastructure. Prevention programs also differ greatly between countries, and in places where the epidemic has been stemmed, that often has been the result of a number of complex and interrelated factors rather than a single prevention strategy.

TREATMENT

In wealthy societies with a strong medical infrastructure and widespread public or private health insurance coverage, treatment of HIV/AIDS often begins shortly after a patient is diagnosed with HIV. In the early stages of the infection, when HIV is present but CD4 counts are high, it is recommended that individuals engage in generally healthy practices: eating well, avoiding exposure to other diseases or infections, and refraining from behaviors, such as smoking, that might weaken the body's immune response. As the CD4 count begins to drop, doctors may begin prophylactic treatment designed to prevent common opportunistic infections. In later stages of the disease antiretroviral (ARV) drug therapy is instituted.

A number of antiretroviral drugs may be used singly or in combination. Single-drug therapy is the least expensive but tends to provoke rapid mutation of the virus. Dual therapy is cheaper than triple therapy but works more slowly and may not be as effective over the long term. Triple therapy is considered a HAART (highly active antiretroviral therapy) regimen, which means that it is capable of reducing the viral load in a significant number of people and remains effective for many years. Triple therapy is able to reduce viral loads quickly to almost undetectable levels. Early HAART treatment reduces the risk of bodily damage during extended periods of high viral load but leaves few options if the patient later develops resistance to the drugs. As a result some doctors choose to begin with single-drug therapy and gradually increase the treatment level.

The cost of antiretroviral drugs is substantial and for many people and nations prohibitive. In wealthier nations AIDS drug therapy can range from $10,000 to $20,000 per patient per year or even more. Political pressure and competition from generics have resulted in substantially lower drug costs in many underdeveloped countries; some ARV triple-drug therapies are available for less than $200 per year. In most instances, however, those prices are still prohibitive for residents of many countries; researchers have estimated that drug costs have to be lowered by at least two-thirds. Moreover, drug therapy requires regular consultations and follow-up visits as well as routine testing of CD4 levels and often tests for drug resistance.

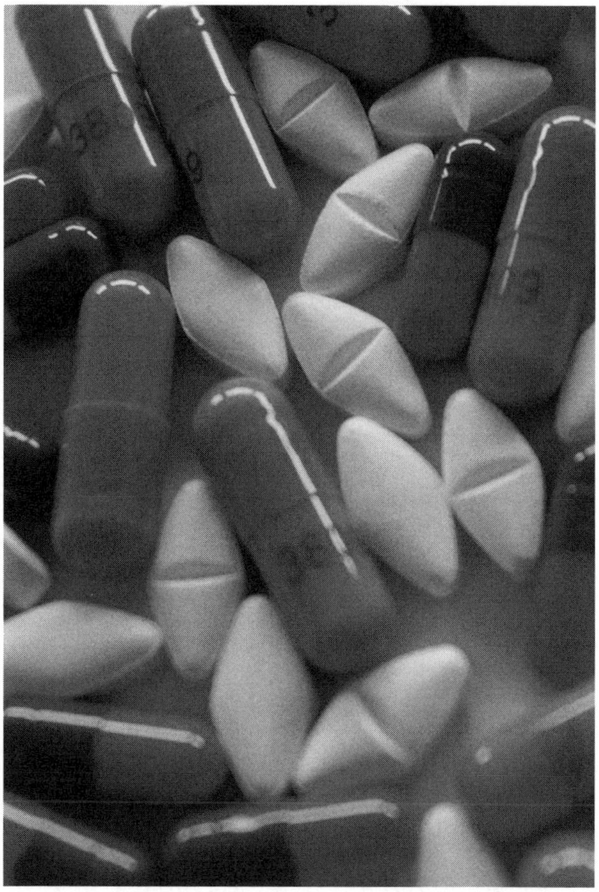

Anti-retroviral Drugs. *Anti-retroviral drugs Stuvudine, Lamivudine, and Stocrin. These medications supress the replication of HIV by blocking the enzymes HIV uses to replicate itself.* © KRISTA KENNELL/CORBIS.

In many developing countries such care is often inaccessible, unavailable, or unaffordable. Poverty tends to make adherence to a drug regimen difficult, and when adherence drops too low, viral resistance develops. ARV drugs provided without adequate funding and support thus may increase mutation and drug resistance in HIV strands. Additionally, patients in poorer regions are far more likely to have secondary infections before ARV treatment begins; treatment for secondary conditions such as tuberculosis and meningitis is often unavailable or unaffordable.

PREVENTION

AIDS prevention programs take two primary tacks: biomedical intervention and behavioral modification.

Recommended biomedical interventions include securing the safety of blood and blood products, usually through the screening of donors; treating other sexually transmitted diseases that may increase the risk of HIV infection; and treating HIV-infected pregnant women with ARVs to reduce the risk of transmission to their children. A number of researchers are working to develop an AIDS vaccine, though that task is complicated by the rapid mutation of the virus and appears to be a number of years off. Another possible biomedical intervention would be the development of a microbicide—an agent capable of killing bacteria and viruses—that could be applied vaginally before sexual activity. Microbicides might have an advantage over condoms because they would allow women to assert greater control over their sexual safety, but their development has been given relatively little attention.

Behavioral intervention is used to modify the behaviors and practices of people to reduce the likelihood of transmission. Most behavioral interventions follow the ABC model: *a*bstain, *b*e faithful, use *c*ondoms. Prevention programs thus encourage people to wait longer to become sexually active, have fewer partners, and use condoms if they have multiple partners.

The success of those programs has been highly variable. In societies in which resistance to or embarrassment about discussing sexual matters is common, it is difficult to improve knowledge and change attitudes on a wide scale and even more difficult to affect behavior substantially. Condoms are often unavailable or too expensive, and even in places where their use is fairly common, it appears to be highly inconsistent. Moreover, in extremely poor regions where expectations for future standards of living are low there may be little incentive to avoid AIDS. Although those populations may have sufficient knowledge about HIV/AIDS and its transmission, daily concern about finding enough to eat may override any impetus to change a behavior that has only long-term consequences.

Many countries have contained the spread of HIV by altering behaviors and through a biomedical response early in the course of the epidemic. Countries that moved quickly to institute screening of their blood supplies shut down a major vector by which HIV moves from a group of core transmitters to the general population. Targeting core transmitters for particular kinds of interventions also has been successful when done early enough. Gay men in the United States, for example, shifted their behaviors rapidly in the first decade of the epidemic, moving from a culture of free love and promiscuity to one that valued safe sexual practice. Needle exchange programs in several countries have reduced transmission between intravenous drug users significantly, and the Thai government reduced transmission rates by mandating condom use among sex workers.

Countries with fewer resources and more generalized epidemics typically have had more difficulties. Uganda is one of the few that have made great strides; many people credit that success to that nation's multilateral, open response to the issue. The government and its leader instituted conversations on multiple levels and among various agencies, sparking a nationwide awareness of and response to the problem. In Uganda first sexual contact among young people has been delayed, and couples are more likely to be in a monogamous relationship. The example of Uganda has demonstrated that behavioral interventions can work, but that success has been fairly unusual among developing countries.

BIBLIOGRAPHY

Barnett, Tony, and Alan Whiteside. 2006. *Aids in the Twenty-First Century: Disease and Globalization*. 2nd edition. New York: Palgrave Macmillan.

Green, Edward C. 2003. *Rethinking AIDS Prevention: Learning from Successes in Developing Countries*. Westport, CT: Praeger.

Usdin, Shereen. 2003. *The No-Nonsense Guide to HIV/AIDS*. London: Verso.

Maureen Lauder

V. SOCIAL AND POLITICAL RESPONSES

AIDS research, drug development, and treatment and prevention strategies have been advanced, shaped, and sometimes stymied by a complex interaction among social responses, political activism, governmental policy, business interests, and artistic and cultural interventions.

GOVERNMENT POLICY

In the United States the early governmental response to the AIDS crisis is considered by many people to have been deplorable. Despite quick action on the part of the Centers for Disease Control (CDC) to determine the causes and modes of transmission of AIDS, its investigations were crippled by underfunding and inadequate staffing. The National Institutes of Health (NIH) moved at what many considered a maddeningly slow pace in opening up the grant process for funding AIDS research, and most early federal funding was forced on the Department of Health and Human Services by congressional appropriations bills. The Reagan administration was silent on the question of AIDS; Reagan did not give a speech on AIDS until 1987, six years after the CDC began work on tracking and controlling the epidemic and after more than twenty thousand Americans had died of the disease.

Although federal funding increased dramatically, it was often too little too late. Moreover, AIDS prevention and education programs were hampered by guidelines written by and resistance from right-wing members of Congress and the administration. Many public health officials had argued for the importance of large-scale HIV testing, but when the federal government began to move toward the articulation of a national prevention policy, discussions often were stymied by right-wing insistence on mandatory testing coupled with a refusal to agree to anonymous testing or guarantee nondiscrimination toward those who tested positive. Moreover, the administration was deeply resistant to AIDS prevention programs that provided education on safe sex. Believing that such programs advocated promiscuity and homosexual behaviors, the Reagan administration advocated prevention programs that emphasized abstinence and moral behavior.

In 1987 Congress passed legislation banning federal funding for educational materials that indirectly or directly promoted homosexual activity. As late as 1988 most federal AIDS policy came from Congress, which continued to push through ever-larger spending bills and challenge the lack of direction provided by the nation's health agencies.

The 1990s saw increased federal involvement in and funding of the AIDS crisis, including the Ryan White CARE (Comprehensive AIDS Resources Emergency) Act, which provided federal funds for organizations providing community-based treatment. Steps were taken to prevent discrimination against HIV-positive individuals, and a federal court struck down the 1988 restrictions on AIDS educational materials. In 1993 the Clinton administration established the White House Office of National AIDS Policy, which was designed to provide federal leadership and guidance in the national response to AIDS, and in 1999 it established the LIFE (Leadership and Investment in Fighting an Epidemic) initiative to address the global AIDS epidemic. Funding for AIDS research, treatment, and education—both nationally and globally—increased throughout the 1990s, and by 2000 both Congress and the Clinton administration had earmarked significant funding for the HIV response and had created a number of agencies and commissions to help develop and implement future AIDS policies.

In 2003 President Bush announced the President's Emergency Plan for AIDS Relief (PEPFAR), a five-year, $15 billion plan to fight AIDS globally. Although Bush was credited for making AIDS a significant part of his foreign policy, his administration was criticized for endorsing abstinence-only prevention programs. One-third of PEPFAR funding was reserved for agencies promoting abstinence programs. In 2004 new CDC regulations, which had to be followed by any organization receiving federal money for HIV prevention programs, required that educational materials include information on the lack of effectiveness of condom use and prohibit sexually suggestive content; in 1993 the CDC had issued a statement with the NIH and the U.S. Food and Drug Administration (FDA) declaring that condom use was highly effective in curtailing HIV transmission.

After 2000 the United Nations and the World Health Organization took the lead in organizing global treatment and prevention programs. Such undertakings, however, were underfunded and often fell short of their goals.

POLITICAL ACTIVISM

In the face of lackluster U.S. government leadership in the AIDS epidemic, members of the gay community, particularly in urban centers that had been hard hit by HIV, became active participants in the political, medical, and social processes by which research funding was generated and treatment and prevention methods were developed. In the early 1980s much of that effort was at a local level: Gay leaders and activists raised funds, recruited help from local politicians, and set up community treatment centers that pooled resources for and information about treating AIDS patients.

In mid-1980s, frustrated by the slow pace of AIDS research and the inaccessibility of effective treatment methods—particularly drug therapies—to many AIDS patients, gay activists and their supporters began to organize in greater numbers. In 1985 Project Inform was created to provide treatment information and advocacy to members of the San Francisco community, and amfAR (American Foundation for AIDS Research) was organized to fund and promote AIDS research and prevention. In 1986 the *AIDS Treatment News* was founded as a clearinghouse for new information about experimental and standard treatments. Project Inform and *AIDS Treatment News* were crucial to the dissemination of new and emerging medical information to AIDS patients and their caregivers and helped create a community with substantial medical and clinical knowledge. The technical expertise of AIDS advocacy groups was a key factor in their intervention in the development, pricing, and accessibility of drug treatments.

In 1987 members of the gay and lesbian community in New York formed ACT UP, the AIDS Coalition to Unleash Power, as a mechanism for forcing change in the social and political response to AIDS. Insisting on the importance of access to clinical trials for people with AIDS, ACT UP and other organizations took aim at the slow drug approval process and restrictive guidelines for clinical trials followed by the FDA. In the late 1980s and early 1990s ACT UP staged demonstrations in a

ACT UP Protest. *An ACT UP demonstration against the high price of AIDS drugs.* AP IMAGES.

variety of venues, including on Wall Street to protest the exorbitant price of the new antiviral drug AZT (azidothymidine), at the post office on the day tax returns were due to gain increased media coverage and raise awareness of the AIDS crisis, at St. Patrick's Cathedral to protest the stand of the Catholic Church on contraceptive use, and at the offices of the Hearst Corporation, whose publication *Cosmopolitan* in 1988 had published an article suggesting that women were not at risk of AIDS transmission during heterosexual sex.

As the nature of the AIDS epidemic changed in the 1990s, so too did the kind of activism it inspired. As activism, advocacy, and the availability of antiretroviral drugs and triple therapy began paying off in the form of a decreased death rate among the most severely affected population, homosexual men, the center of political and social activism shifted to other groups that were experiencing increased infection rates. As a result of the increased prevalence of HIV among African-Americans, activist groups became more likely to focus on improving education, treatment, and access to drugs and clinical trials among minority and low-income groups.

The growing dimensions of the AIDS crisis in developing nations, particularly in sub-Saharan Africa, engendered an increased emphasis on global aspects of AIDS treatment and prevention. Some organizations, such as Health GAP (Global Access Project), formed in 1999, and the Global AIDS Alliance, founded in 2001, were created specifically to deal with AIDS on a global level and generally advocated full funding of the United Nations' Global Fund to Fight AIDS, TB, and Malaria; debt cancellation for third-world nations; better trade policies; improved accessed to treatment; and the development of more effective prevention mechanisms. Such groups often formed coalitions with global trade activists, public health organizations, and domestic AIDS organizations, including ACT UP.

DRUG DEVELOPMENT

The activism of the gay community and the technological savvy of many of its organizations were instrumental in reforming the FDA's approval process and policies on clinical trials. Doctors, AIDS patients, and supporters in the 1980s had regarded the long and slow approval process of the FDA, which averaged eight years in the early 1980s, with increasing frustration. The few drug treatments that were available were limited to clinical trials, in which scientific principles demanded double-blind studies in which half the participants in a trial were given placebos. Additionally, policies designed to protect trial participants severely limited the eligibility of many AIDS patients. Because of the rapid progression of the disease, many doctors and patients felt that the only hope lay in access to experimental drugs. AIDS activist organizations became increasingly vocal about the need to speed both drug development and the approval process, and networks of activists, scientists, doctors, and AIDS patients began to work through alternative channels, exchanging drugs, expertise, and anecdotal evidence about new treatment possibilities.

Activists vocally challenged drug companies and scientists to explore new therapies and means of testing and distributing them while applying increased pressure on the FDA to take charge of the response to the epidemic. Agitation against the FDA sparked congressional hearings in 1987. In 1988, when the FDA commissioner announced that only two drugs could be approved before 1991, networks of AIDS activist amassed enough information to challenge that assertion. A protest at the FDA headquarters by twelve hundred demonstrators received extensive media coverage and initiated a substantial loosening of FDA regulations, including approval of the importation of unapproved drugs for those with life-threatening illnesses.

From the beginning drug prices were exceedingly high and generated a great deal of concern among activists, which was exacerbated by secrecy surrounding development costs. The first antiviral drug to be approved by the FDA, Zidovudine (AZT), cost between $8,000 and $10,000 per patient per year, a price that seemed exorbitant to many, particularly in light of the fact that AZT originally had been developed as a cancer therapy with federal funding. Activists protested against the drug's maker, Burroughs-Wellcome, on Wall Street, and the company was lobbied by a large coalition of activists and legislators. In response, the company reduced its pricing by 20 percent.

Drug companies were criticized for inflating prices and restricting the access of poorer countries to cheaper generic drugs. International pressure and global health initiatives led to significantly decreased drug pricing and wider access to drug therapy in developing nations, though most researchers continued to believe that the price of drugs was far too high to allow widespread access in poorer countries.

SOCIAL AND CULTURAL REACTIONS

In the first half of the 1980s, while AIDS was ravishing homosexual men, the rest of the population of the United States took little note. The desire to believe that AIDS was a gay disease was strong and resulted in minimal media coverage of AIDS outside the gay community. In 1985, however, when Rock Hudson's diagnosis of AIDS became public, the nation was electrified. Almost overnight AIDS became a widespread point of concern for gay and straight populations alike. The illness of Ryan White, a young boy who had been infected with HIV as an infant, generated further mainstream public concern.

HIV and AIDS engendered a great deal of artistic and cultural output after that time. In 1985 *An Early Frost* represented the first major network broadcast of a film dealing with AIDS. That film was followed by a number of mainstream films and television movies that dealt with AIDS and HIV, including *Parting Glances* (1986), *The Ryan White Story* (1986), *Longtime Companion* (1990), and *Philadelphia* (1993). A 1989 Bob Huff mockumentary, *Rockville Is Burning*, chronicled AIDS activism, and in the 1990s a number of playwrights wrote plays that later were turned into general-release and cable films, including *Love! Valour! Compassion!* by Terrance McNally, *Jeffrey* by Paul Rudnick, and *Angels in America* by Tony Kushner. Randy Shilts's *And the Band Played On* (1988), which depicted the early years of the AIDS epidemic, became an HBO movie in 1993. In 1996 the musical *Rent* broke barriers by featuring the controversial subjects of AIDS and sexuality on Broadway.

In 2003 Daniel Bort premiered a short film called *Bugchaser* at the Austin Gay and Lesbian Film Festival; the short appeared with a documentary by Louise Hogarth titled *The Gift*. Both films concerned a practice known as bugchasing, in which gay men attempt to contract HIV from HIV-positive men. The phenomenon appears to be quite rare, though it has generated some mainstream attention. Psychological reasons for bugchasing may involve survivor's guilt, a belief that sharing the virus creates intimacy, the excitement generated by the danger of infection, and a general relief of anxiety at having one's HIV status definitively established.

BIBLIOGRAPHY

"AIDS Policy Timeline." 2005. Now: Politics and Economy. PBS. Available from http://www.pbs.org/now/science/aidstimeline.html.

AIDS Treatment News. 2006. Available from http://www.aidsnews.org.

Arno, Peter S., and Karyn L. Feiden. 1992. *Against the Odds: The Story of AIDS Drug Development, Politics, and Profits*. New York: HarperCollins.

Farber, Celia. 2006. *Serious Adverse Events: An Uncensored History of AIDS*. Hoboken, NJ: Melville House.

Shilts, Randy. 1988. *And the Band Played On: Politics, People, and the AIDS Epidemic*. New York: Penguin.

Treichler, Paula A. 1999. *How to Have Theory in an Epidemic: Cultural Chronicles of AIDS*. Durham, NC: Duke University Press.

Maureen Lauder

'A'ISHA
614–678

'A'isha, who was born in Mecca, was the beautiful and beloved third wife of the Prophet Muhammad and the daughter of Abu Bakr (reigned 632–634), the first caliph of Islam and one of Muhammad's closest companions. The conflicting representations of 'A'isha in medieval Islamic sources have occupied the imagination of Muslims and especially feminist Islamic scholars in the contemporary period.

Apart from her youth—her marriage was consummated in 623 or 624—and elevated position among the Prophet's wives, 'A'isha was pivotal to an incremental demarcation of gender relations in the fledgling Islamic community of Medina. Shortly after her marriage revelations stipulating the veiling and segregation of the Prophet's wives were received. Other verses stipulated that Muhammad's wives were not to remarry after and labeled them "mothers of the believers." Veiling and seclusion soon emerged as standard practice for Muslim women in general. However, the elevated status and separate legal obligations of the Prophet's wives did not prevent Muslim scholars from appropriating them as exemplars to be emulated by the rest of the community's female believers.

THE LIFE

Controversy always accompanied the narrative of 'A'isha's life. In 627, returning with the Prophet from an expedition, she accidentally was separated from the caravan at the last station before Medina. She was found eventually and escorted back to Medina by a young man, a situation that provided grounds for rumors and innuendo. She was vindicated by a revelation, *sura* 24:11, exonerating her and rebuking those who slandered her. Some of the references to her in medieval mystical literature describe the unbreakable bond of love and affection between the Prophet and 'A'isha and the sublimating impact of that love on her, for example, in a moving anecdote in Book I of Rumi's *Mathnawi*.

Widowed at age eighteen and childless, 'A'isha devoted her influence and energy to the political cause of her father and his allies. According to medieval accounts, 'A'isha masterminded an alliance with several of the Prophet's best known companions in opposition to 'Ali's ascension to the caliphate in 656. 'Ali bin Abu Talib (reigned 656–651), Muhammad's cousin and son-in-law, was the first male convert to Islam, the fourth caliph, and the first imam of the Shi'is. Known as the *fitna*, the failed uprising against 'Ali was condemned almost universally by Muslims across the centuries and is firmly entrenched in 'A'isha's historical legacy. Her participation and leadership are marked in the title of the battle, which is known as the Day of the Camel because 'A'isha sat in her litter atop a camel and observed the progress of the war at first hand. That battle marked the genesis of the first permanent split between Sunnis and Shi'is in Muhammad's community, a rift that has defined Muslim politics and theology for the last fourteen hundred years.

CRITICISM AND INTERPRETATION OF THE LIFE

The role of 'A'isha in fostering strife and division was a favorite theme of Muslim political theorists, especially those who wrote treatises on governance. The main result of the Day of the Camel was to caution rulers against proximity and consultation with women. A frequently invoked anecdote is in the *Siyar al-muluk* [The conduct of kings] of Nizam al-Mulk (d. 1092), which celebrated the vizier Saljuq. Nizam al-Mulk invokes her name to remark on the lack of religiosity of the Shi'is in their willingness to curse 'A'isha for her role in the Battle of the Camel. In a longer anecdote Nizam al-Mulk relates how Muhammad was sick and had to find a substitute to lead the communal prayers. 'A'isha favored 'Umar (the second caliph, reigned 634–644), and the Prophet wanted her father, Abu Bakr. She insisted several times, and with his head lying in her breast, he turned and asked one of the men present to ensure that Abu Bakr was called upon, following the adage that the advice given by women should be reversed because the exact opposite of their suggestions is invariably the right choice. The controversial legacy of

'A'isha is complicated further by her almost universally recognized authority as an important transmitter of the deeds and dicta of the Prophet. Retiring to Mecca after 'Ali's victory, 'A'isha is said to have related more than a thousand traditions from the Prophet, although only about three hundred survive in the canonical *hadith* collections of scholars Muslim (d. 875) and Bukhari (d. 870). 'A'isha's recollections, if not her advice, remained trustworthy.

'A'isha's role as the nemesis of Fatima (d. 633), Muhammad's daughter and the only one of his offspring to outlive her parents, adds another dimension. 'A'isha's physical attributes and recollection in detail of the consummation of her marriage as recorded in the medieval sources and the revelation of a Qur'anic verse condemning slander and gossip that was occasioned by accusations of adultery brought against her conjure a notion of womanhood that, although reminiscent of the popular medieval wiles of women literature, is fraught with playfulness, manipulation, conspiracy, and eagerness to wield influence beyond the confines of the home; this stands in direct contrast with the ideals of piety and probity associated with religious demeanor and ethos.

After the succession dispute that followed the death of Muhammad, with one side advocating for her husband and the other championing the cause of her father, the antithetical representations of Fatima and 'A'isha have come to define Islamic rhetorical language on women. The allegorical association of those two women with Eve and Mary, respectively, were not lost on Muslim thinkers. The insistence of the medieval Sunni exegetes on perhaps exaggerating the centrality of 'A'isha to the growing body of prophetic lore, for example, should be read in juxtaposition to accusations of laxity and adultery raised with equal intensity by Shi'i scholars. The religiosity of 'A'isha is crafted along the lines of her special relationship with Muhammad as his favorite wife, the only one in whose presence the Prophet received revelation and prayed and in whose arms he died. This is meaningful only when contrasted with Fatima's piety, which is centered on chastity, austerity, filial loyalty, fidelity, and exemplary motherhood. 'A'isha, who was legitimated through *hadith* (a play on tradition), the cornerstone of Muhammad's *sunna* (practice) as transmitted by his trusted companions, is the paradigmatic Sunni foil to the emblems of prophetic legacy in Shi'i Islam, which is expressed through the primordial connection of Fatima to Muhammad's progeny: her children, the imams.

These complicated, nuanced, and multivalent representations show that the casting of women in a negative light and their use as symbols of temptation against the dictates of reason and prudence is as old as literary records of human civilization. Those representations were spread among so many different cultures and across such long stretches of history that they have become practically bereft of any analytical value for the explanation of historical and social developments, among which the unequal status of women is a common denominator.

MODERN CONTROVERSIES

In the second half of the twentieth century, with the Islamization of political discourse across the Muslim world, the activism associated with 'A'isha's political undertakings was taken by some Islamic feminists as validating a certain rereading of the Qur'an. Their endeavors have been undermined by their failure to provide a context for their readings of the qur'anic text. 'A'isha's political activism is not lauded in the primary sources and certainly is never read to imply women's empowerment.

The controversies surrounding the historical persona of 'A'isha were revived in the 1980s, when a Sunni Anglo-Indian novelist, Salman Rushdie, became the target of Muslim anger after publishing a fictional account of the Prophet's life, *The Satanic Verses*, in which he dealt extensively with the travesties of Muhammad's spouse, belittling the source of revelation that had exonerated the historical 'A'isha many centuries earlier. It was the Shi'i leader of Iran, Ayatollah Khomeini, who declared Rushdie an apostate because of his novel and rendered permissible the shedding of his blood.

SEE ALSO *Islam.*

BIBLIOGRAPHY

Ahmed, Leila. 1992. *Women and Gender in Islam: Historical Roots of a Modern Debate.* New Haven, CT: Yale University Press.

Ibn Sa'd, Muhammad. 1997. *The Women of Medina*, trans. 'A'isha Bewley. London: Ta-Ha.

Morsy, Magali. 1989. *Les femmes du Prophète.* Paris: Mercure de France.

Spellberg, D. A. 1994. *Politics, Gender and the Islamic Past: The Legacy of 'A'isha bint Abi Bakr.* New York: Columbia University Press.

Yavari, Neguin. 2004. "Polysemous Texts and Reductionist Readings: Women and Heresy in the *Siyar al-muluk*," In *Views from the Edge: Essays in Honor of Richard W. Bulliet*, ed. Neguin Yavari, Lawrence G. Potter, and Jean-Marie Ran Oppenheim. New York: Columbia University Press.

Neguin Yavari

ALAN OF LILLE
c.1128–1203

The theologian, preacher, and poet Alan of Lille, who it is thought was born in the Flemish city of Lille, was one of the major thinkers associated with the School of Chartres. Alan was the author of many influential works of speculative, theoretical, and practical theology, including one of the earliest dictionaries of scriptural terminology, a systematic exposition of *The Rules of Theology*, an *Art of Preaching*, and a tract defending the Catholic faith against heretics, Jews, and "Mohammedans." He is best known, however, for his works of allegorical poetry: *The Plaint of Nature* (1168–1170) and *Anticlaudianus* (1182–1183). Those works enthralled later vernacular writers, including Jean de Meun, Dante, and Chaucer. Alan died at the Abbey of Cîteaux in France.

SEX AND GENDER

Alan's theories of sex and gender are elaborated most fully in *The Plaint of Nature*. Although it is a work of imaginative literature, the *Plaint* is also a compendium of contemporary knowledge about the natural world, the liberal arts, and poetics. Its primary concern, however, is sexual deviance, specifically the vices Alan understands as *contra naturam* (against nature).

The poem opens with an elegy in which the poet laments the fact that men openly flout Nature's decrees. Nature personified soon appears, wearing a dress and diadem adorned with flora, fauna, the elements, and the celestial bodies. The poet, suddenly stricken with delirium, is revived by Nature, who reveals her identity ("the deputy of God" and man's "foster-mother") (p. 117) and the purpose of her visit (to reprove man for his vices). She declares that "all things by the law of their origin are held subject to my laws" and "obey my edicts as a general rule" (p. 131). Man, however, "denature[s] the natural things of nature" (p. 131) through his monstrous desires. Nature explains that if desire is bridled by reason, it will not lead to vice but instead will allow for the lawful propagation of species. However, when desire is allowed to escape rational control, it degenerates morals and alienates man from his Creator.

As God's vicar, Nature is concerned particularly with denouncing the crimes of effeminacy and male homosexuality, though she also provides a standard catalogue of all vices, including many nonsexual ones. To fight the army of the Vices, she calls forth the Virtues and her consort Genius, who will lead the charge. Genius is a tutelary figure linked to procreation (*genius,* from *gignere,* "to beget") and also a priest armed with a "pastoral staff" (p. 206) and the "punitive rod of excommunication" (p. 208). Adhering closely to the Catholic rite of excommunication, Genius pronounces an anathema in which he calls for all those who violate the laws of Nature to be "set apart from the harmonious council of the things of Nature" (p. 220).

CRITICAL REACTION

Although a number of scholars have argued that the question of sexual sin is incidental in the *Plaint,* there is considerable evidence to suggest that medieval readers felt otherwise. Several manuscripts of the *Plaint* have a colophon that reads "Let the profane sodomite perish," possibly suggesting an ad hominem attack on homosexuals. The Dominican theologian Robert Holcot praised the *Plaint* as a particularly effective tool in the campaign against sodomy, "the most unspeakable vice." Walter de Burgh added three verses on sodomy, including an ad hominem attack on an enemy, to another poem attributed to Alan and explained that his verses were inspired by "the plaint of Nature against a sodomite prelate." Finally, though the evidence is circumstantial, scholars have speculated that Alan's *Plaint* may have influenced the Third Lateran Council (1179), which prohibited the "sin against nature" for the first time. Alan is known to have attended the council, and there are remarkable similarities between Genius's anathema and Canon 11 of the Third Lateran, which calls for laymen accused of unnatural crimes to be excommunicated.

The moral value of the *Plaint* is complicated, however, by its tendency toward rhetorical excess and ambiguity. Although many of the moral teachings in the *Plaint* are rigorously orthodox, those teachings often are formulated in language that is morally uncertain. The poet describes Nature as a "mirror for mortals" and a "light-bearer for the world" (p. 128), yet Nature admits that she is incapable of comprehending ultimate truths. Indeed, like many of his contemporaries, Alan was ambivalent about the natural world as a moral guide. As Mark Jordan (1997) argues, the "*Plaint of Nature* is not only a complaint against sexual sins, it is a complaint against Nature's failure to speak satisfactorily about those sins" (Jordan 1997, p. 87). Similarly, although Genius embodies the righteous authority of the priesthood, he too is not above suspicion. At the end of the *Plaint,* Genius appears holding a pen and writing alternately with his right hand and his left. The right hand produces *orthography* (actual species perpetuated through lawful intercourse), and the left produces *pseudography* (shadowy, perverse images that lack substantial being). These writings are received either by Truth (a dutiful, chastely conceived daughter) or by

Falsehood (a misshapen, misbegotten hag who disfigures Genius's script). Thus, even orthography can be turned to falsehood, since it is liable to misappropriation. Alexandre Leupin (1989) argues that Alan ultimately leaves the reader to imagine that all writing "originate[s] in the left hand, the hand sinfully brimming with phantasmal images" (p. 78).

A "queer" reading of the *Plaint* reveals that many of the metaphors the poet and Nature employ are so ambiguous as to compromise the moral integrity of the text as a whole. For example, in his opening elegy the poet laments the fact that emasculated men have failed to harvest the "crop" of women's kisses from their willing lips, yet the metaphor takes on a life of its own: "Why do so many kisses lie fallow on maidens' lips while no one wishes to harvest a crop of them? If these kisses were but once planted on me, they would grow honey-sweet with moisture, and grown honey-sweet, they would form a honeycomb in my mouth" (p. 71). As Jordan observes, "Kissing takes two, and the kisses lying on virgins' lips are the kisses of their otherwise preoccupied male lovers" (Jordan 1997, p. 73). One may wonder, then, "whose kisses ... our narrator mean[s] to harvest," men's or women's. Moreover, it would appear that "the effect of harvesting the kisses is to impregnate not the maidens, but the narrator himself. In him they grow into honeycomb" (Jordan 1997, p. 73). The narrator emasculates himself even as he denounces the monstrous Venus who unmans man; metaphorically, he contravenes nature by imagining male parturition.

AMBIGUITY AND IDEOLOGY

Are these ambiguities intentional or unintentional? More importantly, do they compromise the ideological effectiveness of the *Plaint*? Françoise Hudry (1995) believes, on the basis of a set of personal letters she attributes to Alan of Lille, that early on in his life Alan was accused of unnatural crimes and was compelled to do penance at a remote abbey in Wearmouth, England. Hudry hypothesizes that Alan wrote the *Plaint* while there and that the moral zeal of the text is a reaction to his castigation. Although Hudry does not say so, this would explain the recurrence of homoerotic themes in a text that deplores homosexuality. Alan's repressed desires return in the very text that is meant as an act of contrition.

There is, however, another way of approaching this problem without resorting to biographical speculation. Larry Scanlon (1995) argues that the ideological value of Nature and Genius lies precisely in their semantic and moral indeterminacy. If these allegories are not wholly reliable as sources of moral truth, their ambiguity requires a compensatory gesture: not sexual renunciation but a new form of pleasure linked to penitential discipline. If the *Plaint* demonstrates how even the most orthodox moral language can lapse into immorality, it also provides a model for reinvesting libidinal desire in the punitive practices of the Church. Genius's anathema does not force the libido into quiescence; instead, it demonstrates how the castigation of sexual sins can be an ideologically useful form of pleasure. In short, the ambiguities of Alan's allegory thus work to sustain rather than diminish the authority of the clergy to regulate sexual morality.

SEE ALSO *Allegory; Catholicism; Christianity, Early and Medieval.*

BIBLIOGRAPHY

Alan of Lille. 1980. *The Plaint of Nature,* trans. James J. Sheridan. Toronto: Pontifical Institute of Mediaeval Studies.

Burgwinkle, William E. 2004. *Sodomy, Masculinity, and Law in Medieval Literature: France and England, 1050–1230.* Cambridge, UK, and New York: Cambridge University Press.

Guynn, Noah D. 2007. *Allegory and Sexual Ethics in the High Middle Ages.* New York: Palgrave Macmillan.

Hudry, Françoise. 1995. "Introduction," in Alain de Lille, *Règles de théologie,* trans. Hudry. Paris: Cerf.

Jordan, Mark D. 1997. *The Invention of Sodomy in Christian Theology.* Chicago: University of Chicago Press.

Leupin, Alexandre. 1989. *Barbarolexis: Medieval Writing and Sexuality,* trans. Kate M. Cooper. Cambridge, MA: Harvard University Press.

Scanlon, Larry. 1995. "Unspeakable Pleasures: Alain de Lille, Sexual Regulation and the Priesthood of Genius," *Romanic Review* 86(2): 213–242.

Solére, Jean-Luc; Anca Vasiliu; and Alain Galonnier, eds. 2005. *Alain de Lille, le Docteur Universel: Philosophie, théologie et littérature au XIIe siécle.* Turnhout, Belgium: Brepols.

Noah D. Guynn

ALBIGENSIANS

SEE *Bogomils and Cathars.*

ALLEGORY

The word *allegory* comes from the Greek *allègoreïn,* which literally means "to talk differently." An allegory is a transfer of meaning. Most often, it consists of an image that develops within a coherent narrative context, referring systematically—often metaphorically—to a referential universe of a different nature (e.g., abstract, philosophical, or moral). As a figure of speech, it is commonly distinguished from a metaphor or a comparison by the number of its elements. Because an allegory is characterized by the systematically maintained coexistence of a double meaning, literal and symbolic, literal and figurative, it is a complex figurative system whose interpretation is difficult. An allegory is thus always at risk of remaining enigmatic or undecipherable. However, its obscure character, its sometimes sinuous or elliptical logic, also gives it its strength and permanence: an allegory is always rich with meaning, versatile, polysemic.

LINGUISTIC CONCEPTUAL MODES

Resorting to a *personifying* allegory has often been a defense against this possible confusion or incomprehension. Personifying involves ascribing human traits, feelings, and behaviors to inanimate beings or abstractions. The readability of the personifying allegory thus prevents misinterpretations: virtues (e.g., Justice, Temperance, Charity), passions (e.g., Envy, Vengeance, Glory, Vanity), fortune or time (e.g., Death, Old Age as well as seasons or months), nations, the temperaments of ancient and modern medical anthropology (e.g., Sanguine, Phlegmatic, Irascible, Melancholic), the five senses, the liberal arts (e.g., Grammar, Rhetoric, Dialectic, Arithmetic, Geometry, Astronomy, Music), fine arts and their Muses, and other categories are easily depicted.

All these allegories are predominantly feminine, as if this gender facilitates comprehension of the figure of speech. Several explanations can be offered for this feminization of the allegory. From antiquity, poets have personified all these beings of reason, these abstract notions, these techniques, these eminently human feelings and desires, so as to transform them into divinities of flesh and blood, animated characters, or the familiar figures of the Greek mythology best known from the writings of Homer in *Iliad* or the *Odyssey*. One of the first explanations given concerning allegory's gender is that the gender of the word, notion, or concept determined the gender of the personification: Because numerous terms were grammatically feminine in ancient (and some modern) languages, they were depicted as feminine. This philological explanation, although perhaps less than satisfying, is nonetheless heuristically sound. In her *Cité des Dames*, Christine de Pisan places real women by taking seriously the grammatical gender of allegorical figures of political, philosophical, scientific, or artistic authority. Through direct usage of allegorical personification, she reduced the figurative to the literal, the symbolic to the domestic. She thus transcribed her feminine characters into reality. She gave them a historical and proclamatory density, as shown by the positions she took in her *Querelle de la Rose* (Quilligan 1991). Women *are* not authority, women *have* authority. However, in doing so, Christine de Pisan purely and simply sacrificed allegory.

Angus Fletcher defines allegory as a technique to encode a text: Allegory says one thing and means another (Fletcher 1982). The feminine gender of personifications and other allegorical figures thus necessarily refers to something else: it appears to show itself, to unveil itself, but it always has to fade away to serve a coded, hidden meaning. The gendered incarnation of allegory may be defined as a "power transfer game": The feminine body of the allegorical figure serves a world that is in fact dominated by men. One then better understands why, during the seventeenth century—the century of the allegory—Madeleine de Scudéry (1607–1701) chose the cartographical allegory to represent relationships between the sexes. This kind of cartographical allegory had been present since ancient times and was commonly used by Christian thinkers. It allowed the representation of complex relationships as well as the visualization of metaphysical, moral, social, and political values as they related to one another; by definition, a map has coordinates and is thus symbolically hierarchical, whereas benefiting from a panoptical and thus immediately inclusive acquisition mode. The seventeenth century saw the development of what is called "gallant geography," first in the Parisian salons, then in England. *La Carte du Tendre (Map of Tenderness)*, conceived by Madeleine de Scudéry and expanded by François Chauveau (1613–1676) in his engravings illustrating Scudéry's poetry, certainly is the most famous of these productions (Reitinger 1999). In this representation of the meanderings of the heart, feelings are likened to so many rivers, mountains, lakes, seas, forests, boroughs, or towns. This de-gendering of allegory allowed courtesans to reinvent the norms of gallant friendship. Given that love's passions and virtues were no longer fixed allegorically in female or male characters, they could be truly incarnated by women and men meeting freely: thus testifying to the strength of the societal trend that was critical of inequality between the sexes, which developed during the classical age.

SHIFTING HISTORICAL SENSES OF A TROPE

At the end of the eighteenth century, allegory became one of the favorite forms of expression of political power. In Europe, as in America, a profusion of female allegorical characters arose in the texts of neoclassicism and, later on, romanticism. Just when new nations were born and old nations called for their own "regeneration," allegory contributed to the great fabric of founding narratives. Allegory then becomes "a kind of physiognomy of history" (De Baecque 1994, p. 112). During the nineteenth century, for example, the painter Eugène Delacroix (1798–1863) gave France a human face with his *La Liberté Conduisant le Peuple* (Freedom Leading the People). The allegorical female characters of modern nations almost systematically contradict dominant norms of femininity. The characters *Marianne, Britannia,* and *Germania* are inspired by the warrior goddess Athena: These secularized guardian divinities; these female armed authorities (the bayonet of the French republic, the trident of *Britannia,* and the sword of *Germania*) appeared just when the separation between the public sphere and the private sphere—to which most women were assigned—was confirmed. But more fundamentally, just when the modern, exclusively male citizen thought of himself as a free Subject, liberated from any material and social determination, masculinity could no longer be an efficient signifier, because it was confounded with the neutral, the undetermined, and the universal. The allegorical character could consequently be only female, because its gender is by definition a matter of determination and concrete characterization. Only the feminine can thus signify the most abstract notions, embody a concept, and give it meaning and reality (e.g., Freedom, Independence).

However, as soon as nations were transformed into colonial empires, the allegory not only served to represent national values, it also became a real discursive and political matrix (Dorlin 2006). The allegorical femininity of the nation was entirely confounded with motherhood: she simultaneously generated and represented her people. The metaphor thus acquired a performative dimension: The nation was represented as an agricultural divinity. *Marianne* was, for example, represented as the maternal, nurturing, and white goddess Ceres, whereas the colonies and other overseas possessions were represented as both *hyper-eroticized* and *grotesque* bodies. The indigenous, hyper-eroticized, almost systematically naked bodies represented a wildness to be civilized, an eternal childhood of peoples allegedly devoid of history, as well as the erotic object par excellence, on which the colonizers' desire could licitly focus. Just when European nationalisms arose at the end of the nineteenth century and allegorical female characters repeatedly represented an excessive and virilized motherhood, those colonized incarnated all sexual fantasies. This allegory was made of all sexual desires: The exoticism of the colonies was the signifier of sexuality. These colonized bodies became grotesque as they were outrageously racialized through the animalization of gender: Men represented an animal-like virility far from the predominant civilized masculinity. Allegory is crafty, however, because this racialization—in the literal sense of the word—of colonized nations expressed the racialization of the colonizing nations; "the continent," in the words of Césaire (1955), "proceeds to savagery."

BIBLIOGRAPHY

Césaire, Aimé. 2001 (1955). *Discourse on Colonialism.* New York: Monthly Review Press.

De Baecque, Antoine. 1994. "The Allegorical Image of France, 1750–1800: A Political Crisis of Representation." *Representations.* 47: 111–143.

Dorlin, Elsa. 2006. *La Matrice de la Race: Généalogie Sexuelle et Coloniale de la Nation Française* [The Racial Matrix: Sexual and Colonial Genealogy of the French Nation]. Paris: La Découverte.

Fletcher, Angus. 1982 (1967). *Allegory: The Theory of a Symbolic Mode.* Ithaca, NY: Cornell University Press.

Quilligan, Maureen. 1991. *The Allegory of Female Authority: Christine de Pizan's Cité des Dames* [The Ladies' City]. Ithaca, NY: Cornell University Press.

Reitinger, Franz. 1999. "Mapping Relationships: Allegory, Gender and the Cartographical Image in Eighteenth Century France and England." *Imago Mundi* 51: 106–130.

Elsa Dorlin

ALPHA MALE

SEE *Male.*

AMAZONS

In Greek literature and art, the Amazons are a tribe of women, said to be descended from the god Ares and living on the geographical margins of the Greek world, near the river Thermodon or, alternatively, in Libya. Their primary activity is fighting, and their social organization reverses patriarchal norms. First mentioned in the *Iliad,* they play a part in the legends surrounding Achilles, Hercules, and Theseus. As a collective enemy to Athens, they offer in the classical period a foil for Athenian self-definition. Herodotus and later anthropological writers develop an account of their customs, and some writers record contact between the Amazons and Alexander the Great. Literary and anthropological strands of Amazon lore survived into the Middle Ages and beyond. Scholarly debate over the Amazons remains a testing ground for issues of gender and culture in classical studies. While scholars have attempted to find a historical basis for the Amazons, even casting them as reflections of an original matriarchy, scholarship at the turn of the twenty-first century tends to agnosticism on the historical basis of the myth and focus on its cultural deployment as

Amazons Fighting. *Two Amazons fighting a Greek soldier.* THE ART ARCHIVE/BIBLIOTHEQUE DECORATIFS PARIS/DAGLI ORTI.

a reflection of the self-definition of patriarchal Greek culture through a fascination with or repudiation of its opposite Other.

Amazons are mentioned in the *Iliad* as women "equivalent to men," with whom male heroes have military encounters. In the *Iliad* these encounters are in the poem's past (Priam's youth, the inset story of Bellerophon), reflecting already a tendency both to integrate the Amazons into the lives of various heroes and to posit them as long ago and far away. The existence of an Amazon tomb outside Troy is an early literary glimpse of the attribution to Amazons the origins of tombs and cities scattered through the Greek world.

The fullest early account of Achilles' fight with an Amazon is lost: the *Aethiopis*, an installment of the post-Homeric epic cycle (7–6th century BCE), told the story of Penthesilea, the Amazon queen who came in on the Trojan side of the Trojan War after the death of Hector. Achilles defeats Penthesilea and later kills the Greek Thersites for suggesting that Achilles had been sexually attracted to her for mocking Achilles. The (probably) third-century CE Quintus of Smyrna develops this episode (*Posthomerica*, Book 1).

The role of the Amazons in the legends of Hercules and later Theseus reflects the ambivalent status of the female warrior in the mythic tradition. One of the tasks of Hercules is to steal the girdle of the queen of the Amazons; this involves a military encounter (Euripides, *Hercules Furens* ln. 408–411 and *Heraclidae* ln. 217; Apollonius Rhodius, *Argonautica* ln. 2.966–969; the legend is better attested in visual art than in early literature). To the function of Amazons as male-equivalent opponents for the hero is added the ambiguity of their femininity, for the stealing of the girdle, an emblem of the loss of virginity, figures the violence of Hercules's Amazon encounter as rape rather than warfare. In the Theseus legend this is explicit, as Theseus rapes and carries off the Amazon queen Hippolyta, with a twofold effect: The Amazons invade Attica to recover their queen and are defeated by the Athenians; and the Amazon concubine/wife bears Theseus a son, Hippolytus, whose rejection of marriage may reflect his Amazon heritage. (Theseus's Amazon encounter is told in another lost source, the *Theseid*; among extant sources, see Plutarch's *Life of Theseus*.) Both the individual combats of Achilles, Hercules, and Theseus with Amazons and pitched battles involving Amazons are frequent subjects in Greek art. Athenian propaganda, both verbal and visual, links the Amazon invaders of Attica to the Persian invaders of Greece.

The myth of an all-female society of Amazons generated anthropological literature that posited a female-dominated society that must nonetheless have negotiated a relationship with men to secure its propagation. Herodotus (4.110–117) recounts an initially hostile encounter between Amazons and Scythian men that leads to marriage and the formation of a new people, the Sauromatians. The Amazons, resisting integration into patriarchal society, insist on keeping their military customs. According to the first-century BCE historian Diodorus Siculus, Amazon society includes men, but men are subordinated and allotted the "female" tasks of child care and household management (3.53.1–3). Another arrangement appears in the work of the geographer Strabo, who declares that the Amazons live by themselves, but have set encounters with a people called the Gargarians for purposes of conception (11.5.1–2). A common anthropological datum is that Amazons cauterize the left breast in order to wield the bow and javelin; they are also sometimes said to kill or mutilate male children. Thus an exclusively or dominantly female society is defined by violence visited on both male and female bodies. Yet the portrait that emerges from the anthropological accounts is of a constructively functional society, capable of civilized negotiation from a position of strength.

Several authors (Diodorus Siculus, Justin, Quintus Curtius Rufus) record Alexander the Great's encounter with the Amazon queen Thalestris, who strikes a bargain whereby she preserves her independence and has an opportunity to conceive Alexander's child, though ancient opinion on the incident remained skeptical (see the works of Arrian and Plutarch). The negotiation of childbearing reflects the anthropological interest in the propagation of Amazon society; it also allows the male-equivalent Amazons of the mythical tradition a fully functional sexuality and an encounter with a male hero that features neither doomed combat nor rape.

In the Middle Ages Amazons continued to provide a venue for thinking about gender construction and essentialism within culture. The encyclopedist Isidore of Seville (560–636) cites two traditional etymologies of "Amazon." One, derived from "without breast," emphasizes the constructed and sacrificial aspects of the femininity-wounding experiment in the autonomous femininity that the Amazons represent; the other, derived from "living together," stresses instead the communal completeness of an all-female society. Two literary treatments of the Amazon from the twelfth century consider similar dichotomies. Joseph of Exeter in his Troy epic the *Ylias* makes Penthesilea's *aristeia* (her display of prowess in a series of combats) and death a showcase for gender in epic. While allowing her opponent to mock her for shaming Mars by wielding male weapons, the narrator shares with the reader anthropological data that accounts for Penthesilea's nature while bypassing gender: the cold climate she comes from, the reader is told, makes her hardy and warlike. At the moment of her death, however, the poet borrows from Virgil and Ovid to reassert Penthesilea's biologically embodied and culturally coded femininity. Pierced through the nipple like Virgil's Camilla, she gathers her garments around her as she falls in a gesture borrowed from Ovid's sacrificed Polyxena. Another twelfth-century epic, Walter of Châtillon's *Alexandreis*—adapting Quintus Curtius Rufus's account of Alexander's encounter with Thalestris, and playing on themes of concealment and display, appearance and reality—transfers the gaze at least temporarily from Alexander to the Amazon Other, and suggests that the mutilation to which Amazons subject their bodies marks a positive cultural reconfiguration of the imposed lack of femininity.

SEE ALSO *Ancient Greece*.

BIBLIOGRAPHY

Bachofen, Johann Jakob. 1948. *Das Mutterrecht*. Basel: Schwabe.

Blok, Josine H. 1995. *The Early Amazons: Modern and Ancient Perspectives on a Persistent Myth*. New York: Brill.

von Bothmer, Dietrich. 1957. *Amazons in Greek Art*. Oxford, UK: Clarendon.

duBois, Page. 1982. *Centaurs and Amazons: Women and the Pre-History of the Great Chain of Being*. Ann Arbor: University of Michigan Press.

Townsend, D. 1995. "Sex and the Single Amazon in Twelfth-Century Latin Epic." *University of Toronto Quarterly* 64: 255–273.

Tyrrell, William Blake. 1984. *Amazons: A Study in Athenian Mythmaking*. Baltimore, MD: Johns Hopkins University Press.

Sylvia A. Parsons

ANAHITA

Anahita is one of the most popular *yazatas* (beings worthy of worship) in the Zoroastrian religion. A Zoroastrian hymn highlights her function as intimately concerned with the wellbeing of the community, women in particular. In this hymn, Anahita is referred to as Aredvi Sura Anahita, meaning "moist, strong, undefiled." These three attributes assert her identity as a powerful, but chaste, water divinity.

The Crowning of Narses by the Goddess Anahita. © GIANNI DAGLI ORTI/CORBIS.

The Zoroastrian hymn in honor of Anahita is usually called the *Aban Yasht* (Hymn to the waters). It describes the *yazata* as increasing water-channels, herds, fields, possessions, and land. Anahita is identified as a mythical world river, which flows from Mt. Hukairya into the Vourukasha Sea, and is the source of all the waters. In this role, she has been compared with the Vedic Sarasvati.

The *Yasht* praises Anahita as bestowing fertility: She "purifies the seed of all males, and purifies the womb of all females for giving birth," and "makes childbirth easy for all females and makes [their] milk flow at the proper time" (*Yasht* 5.2). Even in the twenty-first century, girls hoping to marry and pregnant women invoke Anahita's beneficent action. Women in the Parsi (Indian Zoroastrian) community recite certain verses of the hymn, which form the prayer known as the *Aban Niyayesh*, to ensure a smooth delivery and the birth of a healthy child.

Anahita is also referred to in the hymn as a warrior for justice, who steers a chariot pulled by four horses, protecting Iran and vanquishing its foes. She bestows chariots and arms, as well as household goods, to worshippers; brings victory to warriors in battle; and the destruction of all enemies, both mortal and demonic. Artaxerxes II (r. 404–358 BCE) was the first Achaemenid monarch to invoke Anahita, in his royal inscriptions at Susa. The hymn describes Aredvi Sura Anahita "in the form of a beautiful maiden, very strong, fair of form, high-bodiced, erect, of noble birth" (*Yt.* 5.64). In keeping with her association with water, she wears beaver skins (Yt. 5.129). As a celestial being, she also has a golden mantle, and jewelry consisting of golden earrings, necklace, and an eight-sided crown with a hundred stars, adorned with ribbons (*Yt.* 5.127f).

Such physical descriptions, alongside the reports of Greek historians, suggest that from early times statues were used in her worship, although to date none have been found. From the Achaemenid period onward, devotion to Anahita seems to have involved an element of syncretism. The Babylonian priest scribe Berossus records that Artaxerxes II was the first Persian king to erect statues of *Aphrodite Anaitis.* Anaitis is the Greek rendition of Anahita, and seems to derive from a western Iranian name for the goddess of the planet Venus (Anahiti, the Pure One). The Persian word for Venus—Nahid—echoes this connection, and remains a popular Iranian girl's name. The Greeks identified Anahita with several goddesses from their own pantheon—sometimes Aphrodite or Athena, but most frequently Artemis, due to her association with purity. According to Plutarch, the "Persian Diana" was chief of all the gods adored by the "barbarians beyond the Euphrates" (*Lucullus*, 24).

Anahita is also identified with other goddesses of western Asia, such as Ishtar, Inanna, and Nana. Both Nana and Anahita were widely worshipped in Iran and Armenia, and both goddesses have characteristics that may derive from the Magna Mater cult of the region, particularly that relating to Phrygian goddess Cybele. Classical sources refer to several temples dedicated to Anahita, under a Persian priesthood, both in Persia proper and elsewhere in western Asia. The Greek historian Strabo claims that Anahita was the most popular of the Persian divinities worshipped by the Armenians, and numerous shrines to Anahit are attested there.

Anahita was revered as the protective yazata of the Sasanian dynasty (224–651 CE), the last Persian Zoroastrian monarchy. Coins from the reign of Bahram II (r. 276–293 CE) apparently depict Anahita handing the regnal diadem to the king. Although the Sasanian capital was at Ctesiphon, the dynastic temple, dedicated to Anahita, was at Estakhr in Pars. There the Sasanian monarchs were crowned. External texts describe how the Sasanians hung the heads of their enemies against the temple walls, thus acknowledging Anahita's guardianship.

The title of "Lady" bestowed upon Anahita in Middle Persian inscriptions and Armenian texts probably derives from Sumerian Inanna, meaning "Lady of Heaven." Sogdian texts from Panjikent also refer to "Nana the Lady." The modern Persian *banu* (the Lady) is used of Anahita in later Zoroastrian texts, and also in the name of a shrine in Iran, where Anahita was apparently worshipped. Banu-Pars (Lady of Pars) shrine in Yazd is set above a river, below a spring of water, and remains a holy place for Iranian Zoroastrians. Other shrines continue this tradition of venerating Anahita in the form of her natural icon, water, including a "spring of Anahit" on the slopes of Mt. Ararat, where the water is believed to cure barrenness and to protect crops from locusts.

Most contemporary Zoroastrians are familiar with the offering made on the day dedicated to the waters, the eighth day of the tenth month. In India on this day, Parsis offer flowers and dar-ni-pori (a sweetened lentil mixture in pastry) to the waters, after reciting a prayer by the sea or a river. Although men also observe the festival, the ritual is particularly associated with women, perhaps because of the belief that the source and sustenance of all the waters is the *yazata* Aredvi Sura Anahita.

SEE ALSO *Aphrodite; Venus; Zoroastrianism.*

BIBLIOGRAPHY

Boyce, Mary. 1967. "Bibi Shahrbanu and the Lady of Pars." *Bulletin of the School of Oriental and African Studies* 30: 30–44.

Choksy, Jamsheed K. 2002. *Evil, Good, and Gender: Facets of the Feminine in Zorastrian Religious History.* New York: Peter Lang.

Choksy, Jamsheed K., and Firoze M. Kotwal. 2005. "Praise and Piety: Niyāyišns and Yašts in the History of Zorastrian Praxis." *Bulletin of the School of Oriental and African Studies* 68: 215–252.

Russell, James R. 1987. *Zoroastrianism in Armenia.* Cambridge, MA: Harvard University and National Association for Armenian Studies and Research.

Jenny Rose

ANATH

SEE *Religion, Study of.*

ANCIENT GREECE

Since at least the Renaissance (1350–1600), European—and subsequently North American—society has looked to ancient Greece as a cultural model in the arts and philosophy and, increasingly in modern times, as the birthplace of democracy. In the twentieth century helenophilia was balanced by a negative judgment of the Greeks' treatment of women. One of the paradoxes that emerge from such evaluations is that the status of women was relatively better in the less democratic Greek polities. Ancient Greek misogyny may have been congenial to those who opposed women's rights in modern Europe, but the system for the regulation of sex and gender was quite different in the ancient world from that which developed in medieval and modern Europe. For example, women's status might have been reflected most visibly in the right, like that of Greek men, to exercise in the nude.

MYTH AND MATRIARCHY

The earliest versions of the origins of the Greek gods, as preserved by Hesiod (c. 700 BCE), seem to show the replacement of ruling maternal deities by male gods. Some scholars, echoing the general theory of primitive matriarchy and noting the prominence of female figurines in early archaeological remains, have suggested that a Bronze Age (3200–1200 BCE) matriarchal culture was overthrown by Greek-speaking patriarchal invaders. That theory has been questioned by those who note that myths of primitive matriarchy may be simple justifications of patriarchal control; also, the worship of the female form is compatible with male power. The classical Greek pantheon is controlled by the patriarchal Zeus (feuding with his wife Hera) but also includes goddesses, though many of them, such as the spear-carrying Athena, were known for their masculine qualities. The Olympian myths even include the idea of male parthenogenesis, as in the case of Athena, born from the head of Zeus. Although the world evoked in the Homeric epics featured colorful women with strong personalities, it reflected a heroic culture with unabashed male dominance in virtually all spheres. Women were under the authority of their fathers and husbands and were held to sexual fidelity. Men, especially those in the upper classes, could have all the slaves or concubines they could afford along with their legitimate spouses.

CLASSICAL MORES

During the archaic and classical periods, roughly from 800 to 323 BCE, Greeks organized themselves around the institution of the *polis*, or independent city-state. The most important social distinctions were between citizens (only males), other freeborn individuals (male or female), and slaves of both sexes. Political power was reserved for citizens, though the wives and daughters of citizens had certain protections not enjoyed by other free women. Sexual relations were covered by the fourth-century claim: "We have mistresses for our enjoyment, concubines to serve our persons, and wives for the bearing of legitimate offspring" (quoted in Pomeroy 1995, p. 8). That ideal, of course, was available only to those with resources and leaves out the same-sex liaisons available to men.

The low status of women, even the wives of citizens, had results that are familiar from examinations of other patriarchal societies. The need to provide dowries for daughters and the occasional desire to limit population led to female infanticide being considerably more common than male. Women also had shorter life spans, perhaps because they regularly were fed less. One result was a sexual imbalance in the population that was exacerbated by the deaths of men in war. For men alternative satisfaction could be found in homosexual relations or with prostitutes. According to Sarah Pomeroy (1995), many prostitutes originally were abandoned female infants (abandonment was the normal mode of infanticide), thus closing the circle and restoring a sexual balance.

The wife of an Athenian citizen was expected to be modest in attire, leave the house as little as possible (chiefly for participation in female religious cults), and be sexually faithful. The husband could, in addition to his wife, keep slaves or concubines, visit male or female prostitutes, and avail himself of the company of the educated female companions called *hetairai*. The husband also controlled a couple's joint property as long as the marriage lasted, and the wife could not enter into contracts in her own name. Of course, those ideals could not always be maintained in practice, especially by people of more modest means, and citizens' wives apparently visited with neighbor women.

Women of undemocratic Sparta had more freedom. They were allowed and even expected to exercise regularly and in the nude, and their rations were equal to those of men. Those factors and a system of trial marriages to see if a couple was fertile were aspects of the recognition of the role of healthy mothers in the creation of a new generation of warriors. As a general rule and within the limits of their conceptions of the proper roles of men and women, the leaders of Greek cities were willing to tinker with the rules governing marriage to promote the demographic interests of the polis.

SEXUAL POLITICS

The purpose of marriage was the provision of legitimate offspring and thus the continuation of the *oikos*, the jointly economic and familial unit headed by the male. Children belonged to the male, who kept them after divorce, partly because it was believed that the woman contributed no genetic material to the fetus. She was only an empty vessel, on the analogy of a plowed field. It was recognized, however, that women enjoyed sexual intercourse, and it was recommended that a man have relations with his wife at least three times a month to maintain harmony in the household. Divorce was fairly easy to arrange and apparently was common. This general idea of female passivity had other effects. A man caught in the act of adultery could be killed by the aggrieved husband (though this right was regulated) or could be held for ransom or turned over to a court for prosecution. The woman, however, largely escaped punishment. Her husband was obliged to divorce her and she could not make certain ritual sacrifices, but she could and often did remarry. This is in sharp contrast to the practice of other ancient societies, such as those in the Near East, which condemned adulterous women to death.

According to David Cohen (1991) the Greeks did not have a word for an adulterous woman, as if she were merely the passive recipient of the immoral act.

There is a general perception that ancient Greece was a kind of paradise of homoeroticism or at least that shame applied only to the passive partner. Although Greek theory and practice were far from Judeo-Christian homophobia, that conclusion must include certain nuances. Xenophon (c. 427–355 BCE) noted that some Greek cities condemned *pederasty* and others explicitly permitted it. According to Plato the laws of Athens were contradictory (Cohen 1991). Further, as was noted by Cohen, the absence of statutory prohibition did not necessarily indicate that an act was blameless, only that it was not felt to disturb the public order.

In Athens sexual use of a boy with or without consent or payment was considered a crime as well as bringing dishonor to the boy. Although ancient sex manuals sometimes speak as if boys and young women were virtually interchangeable as sex objects for the male, and although there is evidence that many males used other males as sex partners when women were not available, for example, on military campaigns, there is abundant evidence that ancient Greek society noted a difference between men more drawn to boys and men more drawn to girls. The first group was seen to be smaller and less estimable. Indeed, literary sources show powerful examples of heterosexual attraction in a society that often erected barriers to its fulfillment to protect the purity of patriarchal descent. Plato's famous defense of love between men applied specifically to a less carnal relationship.

Female homoeroticism received far less social attention. The case of the poetess Sappho of Lesbos (c. 630 or c. 612–c. 570 BCE) may testify as much to the greater freedom of the women of that island (similar to the greater freedom of the women of Sparta) as to an exclusive homoerotic orientation. There is also evidence of women using dildos.

PHILOSOPHY AND LITERATURE

Ancient Greece, especially Athens in the classical period, has been influential through its literature and philosophy. In the case of literature this extends throughout European and North American civilization; in the case of philosophy through the Islamic civilization also. The plays of Sophocles (495–406 BCE) and Euripides (c. 480–406) are famous for the strength and individuality of their female characters, who often are thought to belie the image of the oppressed, marginalized Greek woman. Those portrayals can be seen as reflections on an earlier heroic age when most of the plays take place or as tensions embodied in Greek social practice. The philosopher Aristotle argued that women lack the higher mental faculties of men. Plato, his teacher, held that women are the equals of men in all matters that do not depend on physical strength. It is telling that it has taken two and a half millennia for the position of Plato to achieve an incomplete victory over that of Aristotle. Plato, in many ways the more adventurous thinker on gender matters, also imagined a utopian community in which women could accede to high office, though not full equality, and in which the economic–sexual family unit would be abolished.

HELLENISTIC GREECE (323—30 BCE)

The conquests of Alexander the Great and the later struggles between his generals destroyed the independence of the Greek city-states and subordinated them to territorial empires. They also scattered new Greek cities throughout the non-Greek Near East. That development seems to have improved the opportunities, both political and economic, of women. Some Hellenistic queens, among whom Cleopatra was the most famous, exercised direct political power. Other women became wealthy and were able to buy political rights previously unavailable to members of their sex. As the status of citizen grew to carry less power, it became available to more people. Concomitant with the breakdown of the polis system as a source of relative female emancipation was exposure to other cultures, some of which, such as the ancient Egyptians, were more open to public participation by women than had been the ideal in classical Greece.

Greek sculpture during its classical periods had tended to pair the idealized male nude with the chastely draped female figure. By the time of the Hellenistic age, however, nude and beautiful Aphrodites competed with erotic females for the gaze of the spectator.

BIBLIOGRAPHY

Cohen, David. 1991. *Law, Sexuality, and Society: The Enforcement of Morals in Classical Athens.* Cambridge, UK: Cambridge University Press.

Pomeroy, Sarah B. 1995. *Goddesses, Whores, Wives, and Slaves: Women in Classical Antiquity.* New York: Schocken.

Stanton, Donna C., ed. 1992. *Discourses of Sexuality from Aristotle to AIDS.* Ann Arbor: University of Michigan Press.

Allen Douglas

ANCIENT ROME

The sexual activities of the Romans and their bawdy depictions in art and literature have for centuries embarrassed scholars who studied Roman society. In fact, the subject of sex was so little explored that it was only in the late 1970s that scholars attempted to define precisely the "naughty" words that had been so scrupulously avoided by the nineteenth-century compilers of the Greek and Latin lexicons. Before the 1970s, when scholars discussed sexual attitudes and practices at all, they did so by unproblematically equating modern conceptions of sexuality to ancient ones. Michel Foucault's 1979 claim that sexuality is constructed and therefore specific to a particular time and place caused scholars to question whether their basic assumptions concerning sexuality and, by extension, gender roles were accurate or useful in understanding the Romans. Since Foucault, a flood of scholarship has explored the constructed nature of Roman sexuality and gender through examinations of literary and material culture. At the same time, however, other scholars found sexual behaviors among the Romans that looked similar to modern ones, especially in reference to modern homosexuality, which led them to take an essentialist stance. John Boswell was chief among those who asserted that sexuality was a stable enough category to justify its study through the centuries (1980). Most scholars now walk a line between the two schools by rejecting the modern homosexuality/heterosexuality dichotomy in favor of an active/passive paradigm in which Roman male citizens exerted their political and social dominance over their partners by playing the active, penetrating role in sexual acts. These same scholars make a nod to the essentialists by acknowledging that while sexuality seems to be constructed, the biological desire for a particular sex is not.

LITERARY EVIDENCE FOR ROMAN SEXUAL PRACTICES AND ATTITUDES

The active/passive paradigm is most clearly seen in evidence from literary sources composed almost exclusively by and for elite Roman citizens. These legal and medical texts, and poetry and public political discourse, display attitudes toward sexual practices that varied considerably based upon the political and social status of the participants. In general, a Roman male citizen could penetrate anyone under his power of a lower social or political status without incurring societal disapproval. This category included slaves, freedmen, foreigners, and prostitutes of both sexes. In this context, the sex of the penetrated partner was not nearly as important as his or her social standing. Indeed, literary sources from as early as the third century BCE attach no stigma to a male desiring to penetrate another male be he a boy or fully grown man. So long as the Roman male citizen was the penetrator, he need not worry about a perceived lost of masculinity regardless of the sex of his partner.

Sexual access to Roman citizens was more complicated. Citizens of both sexes were born with *pudicitia*, a state of inviolability which was destroyed if he or she were sexually penetrated in any orifice. A man was expected to maintain *pudicitia* throughout his life and indeed this seems to have been a necessary quality if the man wished to become prominent in politics; a woman could maintain her *pudicitia* so long as she was penetrated only by her husband and only vaginally. The *pudicitia* of an individual was considered a familial possession since *stuprum,* the term for the violation of *pudicitia,* endangered legitimate inheritance in the case of unmarried women and in the case of boys and men, the quality of masculinity so necessary for political life. *Stuprum* was punished by the *paterfamilias,* the guardian of the violated party, and punishments could entail the rape or even death of the offender. Roman male citizens who submitted to penetration in any orifice and at any age were mocked as effeminate and sometimes socially shunned as being polluted. The mere accusation of a young man submitting to or desiring *stuprum* could prevent him from a successful political or military career. Though boys were seen as sexual objects, they were off-limits unless they were of a lower social and political class than the penetrator, and in this the Romans differ from the Greeks and their institutionalized pedophilia.

According to literary sources, female Roman citizens were ideally to limit their sexual experiences to their husbands. Even within marriage, sexual practices were socially prescribed. Though sources suggest that it was unmanly for a male to concern himself with the pleasure of his partner, a woman's orgasm was thought by medical writers either to aid in or be essential for conception. It therefore seems likely that social prescriptions were sometimes disregarded for practical reasons. Yet even when a husband turned his attention to his wife's pleasure, certain practices were still frowned upon: because the mouth was a revered part of the body, fellatio and cunnilingus were thought to be unworthy of a citizen.

In reality, women may well have had sexual relations outside their marriages. Certain social conditions may have facilitated such relationships. In the first centuries BCE and CE, women could achieve a degree of financial independence that was unheard of in the ancient world. The traditional form of marriage, which placed the bride financially and legally under the control of her husband and his family, was increasingly displaced by the *sine manu* form that allowed her to stay under the control of her own father or a guardian. The *sine manu* arrangement gave the bride financial leverage and helped to balance an essentially unbalanced power relationship (girls could be married as early as twelve while men often waited until their thirties to marry). Under the emperor Augustus, elite Roman women who produced three children, common Roman or Italian women who produced four, and provincial women who produced five were legally allowed to manage their own finances. Some scholars believe that this financial independence allowed for greater sexual freedom. It was also under Augustus that marriage legislation was enacted, forcing men to divorce adulterous wives and forbidding others from marrying these women.

There is little evidence either in literature or in art for sexual encounters between females and modern notions of lesbians; that is, women whose identities are shaped by their sexual preference for women seem to be without Roman parallel. The Greek poetess Sappho and her love of women was well known by Roman authors, though the practice named after her homeland, lesbianism, had little to do with sex between women. Instead, lesbianism was another term for fellatio. When literary sources do mention women having sex with other women, cunnilingus is less prominent than tribadism, in which dildos were employed to please their partners.

Finally, it was common for slaves and some freeborn women to work as prostitutes or pimps. Prostitution was a legalized and socially accepted institution and was even taxed under the emperor Vespasian. Sources attach no stigma to men visiting prostitutes of either sex unless they became emotionally attached to the prostitute or visited too often. On the other hand, prostitutes were marked out from other women by their costume: They were to wear togas, curiously, the garment usually worn only by Roman male citizens. Freeborn prostitutes were seen as social pariahs and under the Empire, elite classes were forbidden to marry them.

FAMILY PLANNING

The regulation of birth was a regular topic of discussion in medical treatises and poetry. Medical writers were more concerned with methods to aid in conception than prevent it, but the Romans practiced multiple forms of birth control including exposure, barrier methods and chemical treatments. Exposure occurred when, for whatever reason, the father refused to acknowledge a child as his own. Shortly after birth, the baby would then be placed in a trash heap outside the city where she or he would either die of exposure or be rescued and raised as a slave. Predictably, exposure earned the fiery censure of early Christians.

Women were the chief practitioners of other types of birth control. Barrier methods consisted of a wad of wool soaked in olive oil and placed at the mouth of the cervix. Some medical writers prescribed sponges soaked in vinegar or cedar resin used in the same fashion. Chemical treatments came from plants and were ingested or used as pessaries: Silphium, a stalky plant that grew only on the shores of Cyrene, was thought to be particularly effective and by the Imperial period was worth its weight in silver. Queen Anne's Lace seeds were ingested the day after sexual intercourse and seem to have served as an early abortificant.

MATERIAL EVIDENCE FOR ROMAN SEXUAL ATTITUDES AND PRACTICES

Evidence from art and material culture presents a far broader range of sexual attitudes and practices than those found in literature, perhaps because material culture addressed a more diverse audience. No more than ten percent of Roman society might be expected to read literature, but art touched society from the grandest to the humblest in both public and private spheres. The quality of Roman art reflects the social standing of its owners; pieces depicting sexual themes range from life-size marble statues to modest clay lamps. Placed in plain view and without embarrassment, wall paintings, statuary, tableware and lamps depict examples of the very acts that literature labeled unworthy of Roman citizens. For example, the famous silver Warren Cup and various high priced cameos present seemingly sympathetic depictions of male homoerotic acts, apparently between men of equal ages and political status, just the sort of arrangement so frowned upon in literature. Likewise, cunnilingus and fellatio are prominently displayed in public and private contexts. Depictions on clay lamps boast sexual orgies consisting of three or even four participants at a time. Images of erect phalluses and the god Priapus, a guardian god whose primary feature is a two-foot-long phallus, were ubiquitous, appearing in such diverse contexts as the entrances to wealthy homes, on street pavers, or shrines painted on the exteriors of house walls. Public bathhouses were often decorated with comic depictions, such as black men, apparently slaves, who sported enormous erect phalluses.

Who created these works, under whose commission and who were the intended audiences are questions currently occupying art historians. Since the 1990s scholars have taken some important steps in unraveling these issues, but there are considerable difficulties in studying sexual life through material culture. Because of the moral scruples of the excavators and collectors, a substantial amount of evidence was destroyed or removed from its context, an act that makes interpretation far more difficult. Early excavators of Pompeii, for example, tore "obscene" images from walls, wrenched statuary from gardens, and thrust moveable objects with sexual themes into secret collections. Until recently, these were kept under lock and key, safely away from the eyes of the impressionable.

Art historians are busily engaged in recontextualizing this art, and their findings have underlined conclusions of

Foucault as well as those of Boswell. That is, some art celebrates love between men seemingly of equal ages and classes; the media of this art testifies to an upper class context in which homosexual men were mocked. In this, Boswell's thesis that homosexuality is a useful category of analysis, finds some merit. Yet one need not look far to find depictions that underline the specificity of Roman notions of sexuality. For instance, the Suburban baths at Pompeii feature wall paintings depicting a number of sexual encounters frowned upon in literature. But these seem to be mnemonic devices for remembering where one put one's toga, or by the interpretation of another scholar, in order to cause bathers to laugh and thus avert the evil eye. Likewise the bronze flying phalluses with dangling bells, mosaics of black men sporting enormous phalluses, and images of Priapus are thought to defuse the power of the evil eye by laughter.

GENDER IN LITERARY SOURCES

Though the demand that a Roman male citizen penetrate rather than be penetrated was clearly an important part in achieving masculinity, it seems to have been only one of several requirements. Early Roman literature points to a definition of *virtus*, rather weakly translated as "masculinity," which seems to mean aggressive courage in military engagements. The late third century BCE and the infusion of Hellenistic culture and philosophy into Rome saw the broadening of this concept to include a number of other traits involving the physical and emotional control of oneself and others. By the second century BCE, martial *virtus* took on a component of restraint, especially in reference to ruling others by keeping the peace in the provinces or at home, or by controlling others through the medium of rhetoric and oratory. Control of one's own body was also a high priority since it allowed others to judge visibly the *virtus* of a man. Thus literary sources dwell upon cultural codes such as the length of one's tunic and sleeves (the shorter, the manlier), the ability to withstand cold and hunger, and the careful balance struck between grooming the body and effeminately preening. Men who did not control themselves and others were often depicted as effeminate and occasionally accused of playing the passive role in sexual encounters with other men. Curiously, it was these same men, *cneidi* or *pathici*, who were accused of blatant and uncontrolled adultery, that is, of violating the *pudicitia* of married women. These adulterers were not seen as hypermasculine for their ability to seduce married women; rather they were considered effeminate because they were unable to control their passions.

The expanded meanings of *virtus* sometimes extended to descriptions of women as well as men. In the Republican period there are only a handful of instances when this quality is ascribed to women, and it most often means courage. Under the Empire, however, funerary inscriptions attribute *virtus* to non-noble women. In these cases, the word seems to indicate the later ethical qualities of the word, especially in terms of restraint. Literary references seem to indicate that women could share masculine qualities with men, but the line between a woman being admirable for such qualities and being presumptuous for stepping out of line was indeed a fine one that could be portrayed positively by friends or negatively by enemies.

In general, the Romans constructed their world in such a way that elite women were expected to stay at home and care for their homes and families. As funerary inscriptions attest, lower class women could and did practice professions, very often those of their husbands. Though the dominant rhetoric envisioned women's intellectual ability or moral fortitude as weaker than men's and thus not fit for political life, the Romans seemed also to recognize that individual women in extraordinary circumstances could carry themselves well in public life. Thus, a fitting closure to this entry seems a selection from the *Laudatio Turiae*, a funeral inscription for a first-century BCE woman erected by her husband:

> You became an orphan suddenly before the day of our wedding, when both your parents were murdered together in the solitude of the countryside. It was mainly due to your efforts that the death of your parents was not left unavenged... So strenuously did you perform your filial duty by your insistent demands and your pursuit of justice that I could not have done more if I had been present... How you reacted to this, with what presence of mind you offered resistance, I know full well, although I was absent. ... You have innumerable other merits in common with all married women who care for their good name. It is your very own virtues that I am asserting, and very few women have encountered comparable circumstances to make them endure such sufferings and perform such deeds. Providentially Fate has made such hard tests rare for women.

Not only does this inscription underline that some Roman women could navigate through the dangers of dominant gender definitions which marginalized them, it also hints at very real dangers women faced in everyday life: seeing to family businesses, managing finances and raising children alone while men were at war, surviving the dangers of childbirth, and seeing to their own personal safety.

BIBLIOGRAPHY

Adams, J. N. 1990. *The Latin Sexual Vocabulary*. Baltimore, MD: Johns Hopkins University Press.

Boswell, John. 1980. *Christianity, Social Tolerance, and Homosexuality: Gay People in Western Europe from the Beginning of the Christian Era to the Fourteenth Century*. Chicago, London: University of Chicago Press.

Cantarella, Eva. 1987. *Pandora's Daughters: The Role and Status of Women in Greek and Roman Antiquity*. Baltimore, MD: Johns Hopkins University Press.

Clarke, John R. 1998. *Looking at Lovemaking: Constructions of Sexuality in Roman Art, 100 B.C.-A.D. 250*. Berkeley: University of California Press.

Clarke, John R. 2003. *Roman Sex, 100 B.C.-A.D. 250*. New York: Harry N. Abrams.

Corbeill, A. 1996. *Controlling Laughter: Political Humor in the Late Roman Republic*. Princeton, NJ: Princeton University Press.

Dixon, S. 2001. *Reading Roman Women: Sources, Genres and Real Life*. London: Duckworth.

Fantham, E. 1994. *Women in the Classical World: Image and Text*. New York: Oxford University Press.

Flemming, R. 2000. *Medicine and the Making of Roman Women: Gender, Nature, and Authority from Celsus to Galen*. Oxford and New York: Oxford University Press.

Foucault, M. 1978. *The History of Sexuality*, trans. Robert Hurley. New York: Pantheon Books.

Gardner, J. 1986. *Women in Roman Law and Society*. Bloomington: Indiana University Press.

Hemelrijk, Emily Ann. 1999. *Matrona Docta: Educated Women in the Roman élite from Cornelia to Julia Domna*. London and New York, Routledge.

Henderson, J. 1975. *The Maculate Muse: Obscene Language in Attic Comedy*. New Haven, CT: Yale University Press.

Joshel, S. R., and S. Murnaghan. 1998. *Women and Slaves in Greco-Roman Culture: Differential Equations*. London and New York: Routledge.

Lefkowitz, M. R., and M. B. Fant. 1982. *Women's Life in Greece and Rome*. Baltimore, MD: Johns Hopkins University Press.

McDonnell, M. A. 2006. *Roman Manliness: Virtus and the Roman Republic*. Cambridge, UK and New York: Cambridge University Press.

McManus, Barbara F. 1997. *Classics & Feminism: Gendering the Classics*. New York and London: Twayne Publishers and Prentice Hall International.

Pomeroy, S. B. 1975. *Goddesses, Whores, Wives, and Slaves: Women in Classical Antiquity*. New York: Schocken Books.

Richlin, Amy. 1983. *The Garden of Priapus: Sexuality and Aggression in Roman Humor*. New Haven, CT: Yale University Press.

Riddle, J. M. 1992. *Contraception and Abortion from the Ancient World to the Renaissance*. Cambridge, MA: Harvard University Press.

Setälä, P. 2002. *Women, Wealth and Power in the Roman Empire*. Rome: Institutum Romanum Finlandiae.

Williams, Craig A. 1999. *Roman Homosexuality: Ideologies of Masculinity in Classical Antiquity*. Oxford and New York: Oxford University Press.

Younger, John G. 2005. *Sex in the Ancient World from A to Z*. London and New York: Routledge.

Julie Langford-Johnson

ANDROGYNY

Androgyny is the combination or blurring in one being (not necessarily limited to the human) of certain identifiable sex-differentiated traits. The androgyne may display both male and female characteristics at once, but often remains overall so sexually ambiguous that these traits blend into each other and sexual identification is impossible. Androgyny is found in art and in religion, and is constructed in various ways in social life and culture. The distinction between these realms is drastic, as the incorporation of androgyny in the representation and imagination of divine figures in a given culture by no means guarantees that gender-ambiguous appearance or behavior among humans will be acceptable. Ambiguity, indifferentiation, mixture, fluctuation, and uncertainty are fundamental features of the androgyne, whose body, unlike the hermaphrodite's, need not permanently display symmetrical and opposite sexual organs. True androgyny is thus neither hermaphroditism proper, nor can it be rendered by the juxtaposition of essentialist sexual principles, nor represented by the sexual conjoining of male and female. Such conflations have, nevertheless, been the norm in much discussion of androgyny (Zolla 1981).

ANDROGYNY AND RELIGION

The incorporation of androgyny in religious representations and mystical practices is most evident in Hinduism and Buddhism, as well as in religious systems such as that of the Lakota, in the United States, or the Dogon, in Mali. In such systems, the essence of the godhead is precisely the ability to manifest its divinity through transformation and the abolition of the laws of nature, by eschewing physical limitations inherent to human beings, and by incarnating the wholeness of being and the world. Such is the case with the Hindu god and Ŝiva—who-becomes-mother (Ŝiva Mātṛbhūteśvara) and the Buddhas Avalokiteśvara (who becomes the Lady of Mercy) and Ŝakyamuni (Zolla 1981). Many Egyptian gods were androgynous at least at times: the goddesses Isis, the Moon, and Neith, and the god Yama (Krappe 1945). Androgynous deities of the ancient Greek world are connected to either the moon or the planet Venus who takes the form of two stars, worshipped as double Iŝtar, a bearded morning warrior goddess, or Iŝtar of Akkad, the masculine Iŝtar (*ziqarat*), and the evening goddess of love Iŝtar of Erech, equivalent to Aphrodite Ourania; Dionysos seems to have been androgynous before being effeminate and was a former moon god, while Aphrodite of Cyprus is bearded and both female and male.

The Western view of androgyny is informed by Plato's (c. 428–348 BCE) *Symposium*, in which the original human beings made of two bodies are, because of their

Figure Called Ardhanarisvara in Sanskrit. *This eleventh century stature of the androgynous forms of Shiva and Parvati shows the duality of the godhead as well as the interdependence of man and woman.* AP IMAGES.

rebelliousness, cleft in half by an angry Zeus's thunderbolt. From then on, the two halves search for each other and seek to be reunited through love and sexual union! While this foundational myth includes different sexual combinations of bodies, the separation of the male-female one, originally an androgynous figure, signals the disappearance of androgyny in a punitive context and its permanent replacement by a binary separation of the sexes, now propelled towards a ritual and obligatory practice of heterosexual sex. The Western tradition privileged this sexual binary to the exclusion of same-sex possibilities; thus in French Renaissance texts, such as Rabelais'(c. 1483–1553) work, the term *androgyne à deux dos* (androgyne with two backs) references Plato's myth to designate the sexual coupling of a man and woman, and inscribes androgyny normatively within language.

A clear demarcation between the sexes is prescribed by the Bible in such texts as Deuteronomy, which inveighs strongly against any mixture of distinct natural substances or entities. Gnostic movements contemporary with early Christianity have, on the other hand, freely incorporated variations on androgyny in their mystical texts, such as *The Apocryphon of John* whose teachings were known by or before 185 CE and in which Christ appears as Father, Mother, and Son all in one (Nag Hammadi, 104-105). In the *Gospel of the Egyptians* a Gnostic work preserved in Coptic and claiming Seth as its author, from an "ageless, unproclaimable Father," proceed the androgynous Father, the Son, crown of Silence, and the Mother, "ineffable," and endowed with the power of autogenesis (Nag Hammadi 1988, p. 209). Christian devotional movements have also made way for many forms of androgynous ambiguity (Cloke 1995; Davis 2001, 2002; Kitchen 1998; Minghelli 1996; and others). Passing as male, whether a temporary state or reversed at death, is extolled for women saints, who thus protect their virtue. Further, historians of medieval Christianity such as Newman and Bynum have suggested that there was an implied, veiled, androgyny of divinity in the person of Christ as incarnated God, who becomes Christ-the Mother or Christ as tender, nurturing being, inflected towards the feminine (Newman 1995; Bynum 1982). Caroline Walker Bynum has defined the move towards the feminization of Jesus and the mystical expression of God as Mother as initiated by some of the leading male theologians in the twelfth century and later amplified by the anchoress Julian of Norwich (1342–c.1416). Bynum points out the ambivalence of some of the most male-centered authors, such as Anselm of Canterbury, who sways between objecting "... to calling God 'mother' because male is superior to female and because the father contributes more to the child than the mother in the process of reproduction..." (Bynum 1982, p. 113) but, in other texts, compares Jesus and Paul to mothers. Christian attitudes towards androgyny in devotional texts remain ambivalent, because of the danger to the doctrinal gender order posed by equalizing male and female. As Shawn Krahmer puts it in a study of the virilization of women in Bernard of Clairvaux's (1090–1153) commentary on the Bride, this image of the Bride "... startles, challenges, and inspires precisely because of the tensions that remain in the reader's mind between the normally negative connotations of the feminine and the positive connotations of virility that are paradoxically also associated with a feminine figure ..." (Krahmer 2000, p. 321). Thus in many cultures the devaluation of the feminine and of women has been a durable obstacle to a total fusion of male and female through androgyny, a quandary too easily ignored by those who seek to normalize the androgyne (Zolla 1981). In alchemy as well, some symbols are completely androgynous—for instance the Rebis, or personification of cosmic wisdom, with a male and female head, one red and one white wing as represented in the sixteenth-century German manuscript of the *Splendor Solis* by Solomon Trismosin (reproduced in Zolla, p. 61)—while others involve the calcification of the material female dross to attain the superior male element.

ANDROGYNY IN LITERATURE

Literature has treated the ambiguities of androgyny with varying degrees of suspicion. The greater value of the male being and masculinity is underscored in several narratives of Ovid's (43 BCE–c.17 CE) *Metamorphoses*. In the story of the nymph Salmacis and Hermaphroditus, the latter's excessive beauty incurs an ill fate. When he dives naked into the waters, the nymph Samalcis is blinded with lust, jumps in after him, naked as well, and fastens her lips to his, clinging to his body with hers. In the end, with "...weakened members and a girlish voice," he is made one with her "so two became nor boy nor girl/neither yet both within a single body" (Book IV, 121–122). Of Atalanta, the brave huntress who joins the chase of the wild boar with Meleager, it is said that "her lovely face seemed boyish for a virgin/and yet was far too girlish for a boy." Meleager is smitten by her courage and ambiguous beauty, but, when he honors her over the others, all ends badly with the murder of his uncles and his own death (Book VIII, 224–225). The girl Iphis, brought up as a boy, is married to Ianthe and laments the womanly state that, in her view, will not allow her sexual concourse with her bride, until her mother calls upon Isis to transform Iphis into a man (Book IX, 265–269); a story that was taken up again in medieval literature.

In medieval texts such as the fabliau and some romances, androgyny was cast in a negative light through such tropes as the *beardless youth* and the female *virago*. Yet other texts, such as the Thirteenth-Century *Ide and Olive* and *Roman de Silence* efficaciously displaced the category through cross-dressing and narrative devices that required the suspension of disbelief. In these texts, maidens are disguised or brought up as knights and seen as credibly male until the disclosure of their *natural* sex or their full sexual transformation (Sautman 2001).

Literature has availed itself of a claimed relationship to the divine through inspiration and of its privileged negotiation of the symbolic to represent the androgyne positively even when society condemns it. Artists and poets can praise the androgyne as an inspired, superior, divinely-infused creative being while, applied in the social arena, the term may remain hostile. Thus the limits of androgyny at both extremes were evoked by the nineteenth-century poet Theodore de Banville: The woman with a beard, he wrote, was caged like a beast, with a sad, resigned expression on her face, while the artist Rosa Bonheur, who dressed as a man to paint daily but posed in portraits in austere female clothing, was the apex of androgynous achievement. The French author Francis Carco's 1914 novel *Jesus La Caille* stresses the sexual power exercised on both men and women by the androgynous street urchin. Several Works of modern literature seize upon the allegorical and gender-breaking potential of androgyny, ranging from Honoré de Balzac's *Seraphita* (1835), to Rachilde's *Monsieur Venus* (1884), Robert Musil's *The Man without Qualities* (1930–1943), and to Virginia Woolf's *Orlando* (1928), where androgyny rejoins shape-shifting. A more recent work, Jeanette Winterson's *Written on the Body* (1993), imbeds androgyny in writing itself through devices such as the elimination of gender-defining pronouns.

MODERN PERSPECTIVES ON ANDROGYNY IN POPULAR CULTURE

Resistance to androgyny's denaturalizing effect was evident in European medical and criminological discourse of the nineteenth and early twentieth centuries. Experts in those equated androgyny with underdevelopment, degeneracy and sexual confusion, men with physical female traits (gynécomastie), women with male traits (*masculisme*), and the promiscuity and violence attributed to lower-class women. Androgynes and hermaphrodites were frequently lumped together in discussions of deviance, labeled 'inverts' and were most bothersome when they did not simply hide in laboratories or circus cages. The hermaphrodite who attempted to live as an integral part of the community attracted distinct hostility, or could not adapt easily to another sex. This was the case for example with Herculine Barbin (1838-1868). Known also under the name Alexina, she was declared a girl at birth, lived twenty-two years as a woman, trained as a schoolteacher, and then was reassigned as male, her birth certificate being legally rectified in 1860 to designate her as a man with the name of Abel. However, Abel found it too difficult to live with this new identity and eventually committed suicide (Foucault 1978). Yet androgyny could be highly marketable as well, as shown by the life of Madame Delait, the bearded lady of the Vosges in the early 1900s. Married, she lived fully integrated in her community and was a local celebrity, producing postcards of herself for sale, in which images played with gender interchangeability and with emphasized gender-conformist traits. Her corpulence, physical posture, and language were completely masculine when she posed as a man, but as a woman, she juxtaposed delicate feminine clothing with her startling dark beard (Nohain and Caradec 1969). In the late nineteenth century, androgyny was feared as a social disrupter and *unnatural, mannish* women were suspected of being lesbians (Sautman 1996).

Since the twentieth century, in European and North American cultures, society has had a more positive view of androgyny. It is often associated with the culture of desire in the lesbian and gay male world. In lesbian cultures in particular, androgyny has acquired a high valuation as a strong expression of beauty, erotic pull, and physical self-assuredness against masculinist canons of body appearance. The androgyne is a specific identity category within the spectrum of lesbian gender identifications, distinct from butch and passing. Even when not physically evident and complete, androgyny remains a dynamic category of the performative and of lesbian consciousness in response to which many lesbians shape their own identity. While identity categories and their political messages shift over time within lesbian communities, androgyny has remained a durable category of bodily identity and personhood.

Mainstream heterosexual culture is not impervious to the attraction of the androgyne, cultivated in the public eye especially through the self-fashioned persona of popular music stars. David Bowie, Boy George, and Michael Jackson garnered solid followings by combining lyrics, musical style, and stage performance with a carefully crafted androgynous appearance that created the spectacle of illusion and ambiguity at the safe distance of the stage. Boy George has combined this cultivated ambiguity with the acknowledgment of different sexual identity, and come out as a gay man. K. D. Lang, a lesbian performer with a clearly androgynous appearance, has also effectuated a successful crossover into mainstream culture. However unlike the male performers mentioned above, it is Lang's voice, not her androgynous appearance that appealed first to the mainstream, although it is certainly a strong factor with a lesbian audience. This subtle difference speaks to the different ways the androgyny of men and women continues to be perceived today and to the higher value placed on the feminized male over the virile female.

Commercial film has tapped into the androgyne's erotic power of attraction, but has also carefully contained it by returning androgynous performance to normative safety, for instance in the very popular *Shakespeare in Love* (1998). The sexual aura of androgyny permeates the screen temporarily, but normativity is reaffirmed offscreen, a function filled by television shows, tabloids and "people"-oriented publications. Thus publicly heterosexual actors provide a social safety net by playing queer roles that queer actors cannot comfortably perform, and by reminding audiences of the fictional and transitional nature of their performance of androgyny. The presence of androgynous women on screen can remain a scripted negative type simply recognizable as a lesbian (*A Rage in Harlem* [1991]), or revert to heterosexuality to further complicate sexual and identity tensions (Bridget Fonda in *Single White Female* [1992]). The deeper signification of androgyny for women remains largely the purview of lesbian cinema (*Go Fish* [1994]). While male androgyny is frequently seen as a locus of sexual fulfillment, it is hardly any more acceptable to mainstream audiences. One film that successfully made that crossover is Neil Jordan's *The Crying Game* (1992), with its compelling portrayal of a young transvestite who, reverting to his "natural" garb and body styling becomes deeply androgynous. It is however to be noted that what made that film so effective was in part its incorporation of matters of race and contemporary politics into the representation of sexual androgyny.

Androgyny, thus, is not only an ambiguous body appearance, but also an ambiguous function in a variety of societies where it can be at once rejected and embraced. It can be incorporated or appropriated by an extremely conventional, normative, discourse of sex and gender that, in the end, reasserts binaries and the primacy of the male (Zolla 1981). It can also be ascribed intrinsic value, and, viewed not as a temporary state or heterosexual teaser; it can challenge essentialist views of sex and gender and their binary gender scripts. Embraced in this form, and allowed to flourish, it refutes the precept that gender—and sex—are natural, unequivocal and thus inescapable.

SEE ALSO *Beard; Butch/Femme; Film, Gender and Eroticism: IV. Lesbian, Gay, and Queer Film; Hermaphrodites; Ide and Olive.*

BIBLIOGRAPHY

Banville, Theodore Faullain de. 1970. *Les Camées parisiens* [Parisian cameos]. Genève: Slatkine Reprints. (Orig. pub. 1866.)

Bynum, Caroline Walker. 1982. *Jesus as Mother: Studies in the Spirituality of the High Middle Ages.* Berkeley: University of California Press.

Cloke, Gillian. 1995. *This Female Man of God: Women and Spiritual Power in the Patristic Age*, A.D. 350-450. London: Routledge.

Davis, Stephen J. 2001. *The Cult of St. Thecla: A Tradition of Women's Piety in Late Antiquity.* Oxford: Oxford University Press.

Davis, Stephen J. 2002. "Crossed Texts, Crossed Sex: Intertextuality and Gender in Early Christian Legends of Holy Women Disguised as Men." *Journal of Early Christian Studies* 10.1: 1–36.

Foucault, Michel, ed. 1978. *Herculine Barbin, dite Alexina B.* Paris : Gallimard.

Kitchen, John.1998. *Saints' Lives and the Rhetoric of Gender: Male and Female in Merovingian Hagiography.* New York: Oxford University Press.

Krahmer, Shawn M. 2000. "The Virile Bride of Bernard of Clairvaux." *Church History* 69(2): 304–327.

Krappe, Alexander H. 1945. "The Bearded Venus." *Folklore* 56(4): 325–335.

Minghelli, Marina. 1996. *Santa Marina la travestita* [Saint Marina the transvestite]. Palermo: Sellerio.

Newman, Barbara. 1995. *From Virile Woman to WomanChrist: Studies in Medieval Religion and Literature*. Philadelphia: University of Pennsylvania Press.

Nohain, Jean, and François Caradec.1969. *La Vie exemplaire de la femme à barbe: Clémentine Delait 1865–1939* [The exemplary life of the bearded woman: Clementine Delait 1865-1939]. Paris: La Jeune Parque.

Ovid. 1958. *Metamorphoses: A Complete New Version*, trans. and ed. Horace Gregory. New York: Viking Press.

Plato. 1983. *Lysis; Symposium; Gorgias*, trans. W.R. M. Lamb. Cambridge: Harvard University Press.

Robinson, James W. 1978; 1988. General ed. *The Nag Hammadi Library*. San Francisco: Harper and Row/Leiden: E.J. Brill.

Sautman, Francesca Canadé. 1996. "Invisible Women: Lesbian Working Class Culture in France, 1880–1930." *Homosexuality in Modern France*, ed. Jeffrey Merrick and Bryan T. Ragan, Jr. New York: Oxford University Press.

Sautman, Francesca Canadé. 2001. "What Can They Possibly Do Together: Queer Epic Performance in *Yde et Olive* and *Tristan de Nanteuil*." In *Same-Sex Love and Desire Among Women in the Middle Ages*, ed. Francesca Canadé Sauman and Pamela Sheingorn.

Winterson, Jeanette. 1993. *Written on the Body*. New York: Alfred Knopf.

Woolf, Virginia. 1993. *Orlando*. New York: QPBC. (Orig. pub. 1928.)

Zolla, Elémire. 1981. *The Androgyne: Reconciliation of Male and Female*. New York: Crossroad.

Francesca Canadé Sautman

ANIMALS, SEXUAL SYMBOLISM OF

Humans have always shared their world with other animals, both feral and domesticated. As predator, prey, and companion, animals have served a variety of purposes: source of food, provider of clothing, assistant in hunting and herding, source of spectacle and amusement, and docile laborer. Some of the earliest human attempts at representational art center on beasts, which are portrayed in cave paintings in vigorous hunt scenes. Every culture has its favored animals, fauna that seem suspended between the human and the diabolical or divine: Egyptian cats, jackals, and beetles; the biblical Leviathan; Cretan bulls; Hindu cows, monkeys, and elephants; early Christian fish and lambs; American Indian buffalo and deer; and Inuit whales and seals.

The animals that haunt the imagination most are what might be called intimate aliens: undeniably familiar but intransigently strange. Even if they seem vaguely anthropomorphic, such beasts remain inhuman, residents of a liminal or in-between state that only increases their allure. This combination of intimacy and otherness typically is found in animals that have been given a sexual charge in specific cultures. Although certain creatures, such as snakes, have a seemingly universal aura of lasciviousness, whether a particular animal will be employed as a sexual sign is culturally specific and depends greatly on the animals that populate a particular geography. This expanse is as imaginative as it is physical: Dragons and unicorns can coexist in such spaces with dogs, horses, serpents, and hares.

As erotic figures animals have an ancient and enduring history, from Stone Age artwork to contemporary Internet sites devoted to zoophilia, zoomorphism, and furries (fans of anthropomorphic animals in contemporary media). During the Bronze Age (1800–500 BCE), for example, unknown residents of what is now the northern Bohuslän district of Sweden carved illustrations of men, women, and fauna into the local rocks. Many of those figures seem to be engaged in fertility rites. One scene depicts a man with an enormous phallus copulating with a cow, a union of human and animal that probably was motivated by a desire to ensure a productive year. Roughly contemporary carvings in Italy depict one man engaged in coitus with a donkey and another attempting to mate with an elk.

Representations of humans sexually conjoined with animals make cultural sense in pastoral societies in which survival depends on the increase and multiplication of flocks. The mutual dependence of human and herd is underscored by mutual ardor and life-giving union. Depictions of bestiality also can be found among peoples whose way of life was mainly agrarian, because the sexuality of plowing oxen was intimately related on a symbolic level with the sexuality of the farmer guiding them and the fecundity of the fields. In both cases the erotic charge of the animal is in some ways utilitarian, motivated by the human desire to exert control over an unpredictable world.

However, cultural use value and attempts at asserting human dominion over nature cannot be the whole story. Because they combine haunting similarity with perturbing difference and proximity with otherness, animals have long been the vehicles through which humans explore their own identities. Through the beast, humans fantasize of new possibilities and enact forbidden desires. Thus, it is not surprising that one of the most ancient functions of the animal is as an erotic symbol. In ways both positive and negative humans have always realized that amatory desire is, like other bodily drives, a passion *Homo sapiens* shares with other animals.

Leda and the Swan. *This nineteenth-century painting depicts the seduction of Leda by Zeus, who takes the form of a swan.* PAUL PROSPER TILLIER/FINE ART PHOTOGRAPHIC/GETTY IMAGES.

ANIMAL IMAGERY IN THE CLASSICAL WORLD

The rooster was a familiar ancient Greek erotic symbol, forming the animal counterpart to the god Priapus. A bronze Corinthian mirror illustrates Eros grasping the bird in front of his crotch, and there are numerous vase paintings on which the active lover in a homosexual tryst holds a cock, the symbol of his victory in love over his partner. Classical myth depicts many unions of mortals with animals, though in most cases the beast turns out to be a god in disguise. Zeus impersonates a swan fleeing an eagle to be admitted into Leda's protective embrace. He has his way with her, and their union produces twin progeny. Zeus seduces the maiden Europa while shaped like a bull. In punishment for her husband's offense of admiring a beautiful white bull too much to sacrifice it to Poseidon, Queen Pasiphae of Crete is made to fall in love with the animal. Their amorous conjoining is enabled by a special device fashioned by the inventor Daedalus, and the son of their union is the Minotaur. This creature forever suspended between the human and the bestial embodies the animal as erotic symbol, for no beast can symbolize human sexuality or activate human desire until it has been partially (but *only* partially) anthropomorphized.

Writers in ancient Greece and Rome exhibited what seems to be a timeless male penchant to speak of the penis as if it has an existence and personality distinct from the body to which it is attached. The male member was described variously as a snake, a lizard, or a bird that follows its own inclinations (Adams 1982). Of these three animals the snake has the most cross-cultural currency as a phallic symbol, probably by reason of analogy. Animal doppelgangers of the vagina in classical sources appear less frequently, though *porcus* (the piglet) apparently was used in Roman nurseries (Adams 1982). The psychoanalyst Sigmund Freud (1856–1939) described the snake-headed Medusa as a representation of the female genitals, but it is unclear if Greek and Roman mythographers saw the same fearful image there. Although Medusa heads are familiar icons on Greek vases and in Roman mosaics and although the writhing serpents that form her tresses have an undeniable sexual charge to their undulations, what is significant about the Medusa in classical literature and art is her stunning beauty, her animal-enabled allure. This attractiveness does not seem different from what remains in the mortal love objects of the gods once the goddesses have transfigured them out of human shape. Io, formerly a priestess of Hera adored by Zeus and later a snow-white heifer, is radiant in either form.

ANIMAL IMAGERY IN THE MIDDLE AGES

The playful connections between genitals and animals found in classical sources have a medieval analogue in the fabliaux, short stories with sexual or scatological themes. Sex organs are described with animal epithets such as "ferret" and "horsy" for the penis and "little hare" for the vagina. Fabliaux are unusual among extant medieval texts for their frank celebration of the erotic.

Building on a vocabulary developed by the Church Fathers, authors in the Middle Ages more typically employed animals to underscore the necessity of human mastery over the flesh. Thus in the *Life of Saint Anthony*, a desert-dwelling hermit who has renounced sexual relations is haunted in his solitude by his lust. In his visions this return of sexual desire takes the form sometimes of women and sometimes of beasts, making clear another enduring twinning: The female body frequently is coded as more animalistic than the male. In Saint Jerome's *Life of Saint Hilarion* (late fourth century), when the aspiring ascetic is tormented by the onset of puberty, he beats his body into submission. Hilarion describes his flesh as an ass in need of brutal domestication, articulating a logic that will hold true in much medieval thinking about beasts: Animals are carnal and lascivious and do not hesitate to act on their lusts; humans are affected by the same desires, but what sets humans—especially the holiest humans—apart is their ability to triumph over their animal-like bodies. Medieval rhetoric linked sexuality to bestiality so often that the connection between lust and animals was commonplace.

A compendium of allegory and lore called the *Physiologus* was among the most influential texts on animals to have been bequeathed to the Middle Ages. Composed originally in Greek, perhaps at Alexandria, this widely extant text was circulated by the end of the fourth century. Its entries combine science and folklore deriving from Egyptian, Roman, Greek, Jewish, and Indian sources. Early translations of the book into Ethiopian, Syrian, Armenian, and Latin survive; later versions include Old English, Old High German, Icelandic, Flemish, Russian, and Provençal (*Physiologus*, preface). The work remained popular in Europe through the early modern period.

The appeal of the *Physiologus* lay in part in its transformation of animals and natural phenomena into biblical truths. The owl, for example, represented the Jews, whose refusal to see the light of Christ's truth doomed them to perpetual night. The Phoenix, reborn from his own ashes, was a type for Jesus, who similarly returned from the dead. Several of the animals described in the *Physiologus* are noted for their sexual habits. The female viper, for example, is said to possess a human form from the face to the navel and a crocodile's body thereafter. Because she does not possess genitals, the viper must have oral sex with her partner (which, it is mentioned, has a male's face as well as—one is led to assume—a penis). After drinking the semen of her lover, she castrates and kills him. Because she has no vagina, however, the young vipers engendered through this mating must rip their way through her belly, ending her life. The entry concludes by describing the viper as a figure for the Jews, who cannot think symbolically but only in literal terms. Jews practice circumcision on their flesh, for example, rather than seeing this ritual of covenant with God as an act to be undertaken only spiritually (that is, metaphorically). The viper thereby assists in articulating Christian identity by distinguishing it from the Judaism from which it emerged.

The weasel also is said to copulate orally, though she gives birth through her ears (right for boys, left for girls). Weasels, it is pointed out, are a symbol of those who allow wicked sayings to enter their minds and engender sin. The beautiful unicorn cannot be captured by hunters, but if a chaste maiden offers her lap, he is happy to lay his head there; lest the image become suggestive, the reader is told immediately that the unicorn is Christ, the virgin is Mary, and there is (by implication) nothing sexual about this strange equine's ardor for placing his long horn in maidenly laps.

The *Physiologus*, like much early Christian writing, stresses the value of chastity and the dangers of desire. One of its animals is notable for its complete absence of amorous feeling. The elephant and his wife symbolize Adam and Eve, who before the snake led them into temptation never desired each other and had no knowledge of coitus. Elephants, *Physiologus* asserts, mate only out of necessity and even then would not be able to copulate without the use of the aphrodisiac mandrake root. Elephants thus are the purest of animals and an inspiration to abstinence.

It is hard not to wonder whether the eroticism of animals such as vipers, weasels, and unicorns can be displaced so easily through allegorization. Surely one of the appeals of the *Physiologus* is its narration of fellatio, hermaphroditism, and homosexuality among beasts even as it transforms those stories into tidy Christian morals.

Thus, the fascinating story of the hyena is repeated almost obsessively in most medieval bestiaries. A creature of two natures, this desert-dwelling animal sometimes acts the part of a male and sometimes that of a female. According to Clement of Alexandria (died c. 215) and many later writers, the lewd hyena possesses the sexual organs of both sexes and employs them promiscuously (Boswell 1980). The hyena may simply, as the Latin *Physiologus* asserts, be a figure for the inconstant Jews, who once worshipped the true God but have turned away. Perhaps the double-gendered beast is simply a representation of the synagogue, metaphorically an unclean animal. However, perhaps the hyena as an erotic animal grants something not otherwise available within circumscriptive systems of allegory and abnegation: a figure through which can be dreamed potentialities and desires that otherwise are not easy to express.

Sexuality brings humans outside themselves; it is the surrender to a loss of individuality. Animals as erotic symbols in the Middle Ages often represent the anxieties that accompany such potential loss, but they also convey a certain inventiveness, a certain promise of possibilities beyond the limits of the merely human.

The twelfth-century writer Marie de France knew this liberating potential of the animal. In a narrative poem she called *Yonec,* the heroine is imprisoned for seven lonely years by an elderly husband whom she cannot love. After she has declared wistfully that she wishes that the world depicted in romances were true, a regal hawk flutters into her room and transforms itself into a knight. The hawk was considered an aristocratic bird, as revered as the warhorse and the greyhound; it makes a perfect animal counterpart to the lady's new love, mixing hints of danger (it is, after all, a raptor) and desire (the bird is meant to be adored; the use of spikes by the lady's husband to kill the hawk is the ultimate proof of his exclusion from the story's erotic world).

The ethnographer and apologist for the English invasion of Ireland, Gerald of Wales, another twelfth-century author, employed animals as sexual symbols in a way that bears little resemblance to the aesthetic pleasure attached to the hawk in *Yonec*. Eager to depict the Irish as a degenerate people in need of English civilization, Gerald wrote that bestiality was their favorite vice. The sin was practiced most often, he asserted in the *History and Topography of Ireland*, against cattle. This was particularly insulting because the Irish were a society that reckoned wealth and status not according to money as in England but according to the number of cows a person owned. Gerald sexualizes this bond between the Irish and their culturally revered beasts, insisting that through coitus with their livestock the Irish had engendered numerous man-animal hybrids, Hibernian Minotaurs. A cleric who had much at stake in maintaining the supremacy of a celibate identity, Gerald also wrote of a woman who had sex with a lion and another who lay with a goat. So great was his distaste for the subject that he illustrated the bestial encounters in prurient detail. The goat and the lion serve as sexual symbols for Gerald, but rejected ones; in both cases, so do the women, as well as the Irish. All are part of a world denied to him, a world he defined himself against, and therefore a world to be denounced as never having been desirable anyway.

THE IMPLICATIONS OF ANIMAL IMAGERY

Rock carvings of couplings with oxen, queer Greek roosters, Pasiphae's longing for the white bull, Gerald's fantasies about Irish sexual practices, and King Kong's love for a beautiful visitor to his lonely island all have this in common: When an animal serves as an erotic symbol, it erodes the boundary between species, sometimes through joyful commingling, sometimes accompanied by horror mixed with fascination. As intimate aliens, animals embody a very human ambivalence. Because the encounter with the erotic is an encounter with the other, interspecies ardor reminds people of the inhuman within and the human without. Animals as sexual symbols suggest the insufficiency of using other animals as creatures to define humanity against and the inability of humans to control completely the meanings of the animal world. By bringing people out of their proper, individualized identities, by bringing embodiment to its limit, they offer a glimpse of a less anthropocentric and thus more unpredictable world.

SEE ALSO *Ancient Greece; Ancient Rome; Erotic Art; Fabliaux; Folklore; Mermaid.*

BIBLIOGRAPHY

Adams, J. N. 1982. *The Latin Sexual Vocabulary*. Baltimore, MD: Johns Hopkins University Press.

Baker, Steve. 2001. *Picturing the Beast: Animals, Identity, and Representation*. Chicago: University of Illinois Press.

Boswell, John. 1980. *Christianity, Social Tolerance, and Homosexuality: Gay People in Western Europe from the Beginning of the Christian Era to the Fourteenth Century*. Chicago and London: University of Chicago Press.

Creager, Angela N. H., and William Chester Jordan, eds. 2002. *The Animal-Human Boundary: Historical Perspectives*. Rochester, NY: University of Rochester Press.

Dekkers, Midas. 1994. *Dearest Pet: On Bestiality*, trans. Paul Vincent. London and New York: Verso.

Hassig, Debra. 1995. *Medieval Bestiaries: Text, Image, Ideology*. Cambridge, UK, and New York: Cambridge University Press.

Physiologus. 1979. Trans. Michael J. Curley. Austin: University of Texas Press.

Salisbury, Joyce E. 1994. *The Beast Within: Animals in the Middle Ages*. New York: Routledge.

Wolfe, Cary. 2003. *Animal Rites: American Culture, the Discourse of Species, and Posthumanist Theory*. Chicago: University of Chicago Press.

Jeffrey Jerome Cohen

ANOREXIA

SEE *Eating Disorders.*

ANORGASMIC

The term *anorgasmic* (experiencing *anorgasmia*) refers to a condition in which individuals do not achieve orgasm during sexual intercourse. Also known as orgasmic disorder, orgasmic inhibition, orgasmic dysfunction, inhibited sexual excitement, and delayed ejaculation, anorgasmia occurs more commonly in women than in men. Anorgasmia has both physical and psychological causes. It is treated primarily by means of therapy and counseling.

Women may be affected by one of four categories of anorgasmia. *Primary anorgasmia* is a condition in which an individual has never experienced an orgasm. Although women with this condition may enjoy the sexual excitement produced by kissing, touching, hugging, and other forms of foreplay, they do not achieve climax. If a woman enjoys sexual intercourse, her lack of an orgasm may make her frustrated or irritable and she may suffer pelvic pain.

It is not always clear why an individual has primary anorgasmia. Some women are medically unable to climax because they have been victims of genital mutilation in which the clitoris has been removed or the opening of the vagina has been restricted. They may suffer genital pain (*dyspareunia*), may have scarring from an injury, or may have nerve damage. Often, however, the causes of primary anorgasmia are psychological or cultural. Individuals may be ignorant about sexuality. They may be inhibited by familial or cultural attitudes or may have performance anxiety. They may have had a traumatic sexual experience that makes sexual activity unpleasant or emotionally and physically difficult. They may have unskilled partners who have no understanding of female sexuality, have difficulty maintaining an erection, or ejaculate prematurely. These women simply may not like the person with whom they are having sex.

Secondary anorgasmia occurs when women who experienced orgasms previously lose the ability to have them. This may be caused by the chemical, hormonal, and emotional effects of substance abuse, alcoholism, medications, illness, or menopause. It also may be a psychological response to sexual trauma such as rape.

Situational anorgasmia is the inability to have orgasms in some situations. This term refers to normal variations in sexual response. For example, a woman or a man may achieve climax only with some partners or in some situations. *Random anorgasmia* occurs when individuals sometimes fail to achieve orgasm.

Males also experience these forms of anorgasmia. They may be unable to achieve orgasm because nerve damage inhibits ejaculation or because they cannot achieve an erection. They may have hormonal imbalances or suffer the effects of substance abuse. They may hold cultural attitudes that prevent them from participating fully in sexual activity or encourage them to "hold back."

Therapy for anorgasmia includes treatment for physical causes when possible but primarily focuses on sex therapies, education, and counseling. Sex therapies involve helping couples focus on sensations, encouraging women and men to discover how their bodies respond by encouraging masturbation or mutual exploration. Counseling helps identify the ideas and emotions that prevent participation and release. Education provides an alternative range of practices and conditions that may help partners find a more satisfying sexual experience.

SEE ALSO *Female Genital Mutilation; Frigidity; Orgasm.*

BIBLIOGRAPHY

Boston Women's Health Book Collective. 2005. *Our Bodies, Ourselves: A New Edition for a New Era.* New York: Simon & Schuster.

Wincze, John P., and Michael P. Carey. 2001. *Sexual Dysfunction: A Guide for Assessment and Treatment.* 2nd edition. New York: Guilford Press.

Judith Roof

ANTHROPOLOGY

Anthropology, a social science discipline, explores the multifaceted dimensions of human civilizations and is central to the modern way of understanding sex and gender in contemporary societies. During the nineteenth century, anthropology began to emerge as a separate academic discipline. By the mid-nineteenth century, social evolutionists argued that societies had evolved from the simple to the complex and from the chaotic to the orderly. Progress in society was desired, so simpler societies were seen as inferior. The most well-known evolutionary scheme used by social evolutionists, such as Edward Burnett Tylor (1832–1917), Herbert Spencer (1820–1903), and Lewis Henry Morgan (1818–1881), classified and ranked societies according to whether they existed in a primitive state or whether they had become civilized over time by virtue of the survival of the fittest. The evolutionary explanation was invoked to rationalize women's exclusion from the public realm and their subordinate position to men in Western society. Biological necessities rendered women physically and intellectually inferior to men. Male dominance was seen to have evolutionary origins grounded in the biological differences between the sexes.

EARLY-TWENTIETH-CENTURY ANTHROPOLOGY

By the beginning of the twentieth century, social evolutionary explanations of human social organization were replaced by the functionalist orientation, a leading school of thought in British anthropology. The functionalist orientation, espoused by Émile Durkheim (1858–1917), Bronisław Malinowski (1884–1942), and Alfred Reginald Radcliffe-Brown (1881–1955), viewed a society as a bounded whole with all of its practices and institutions working together harmoniously to fulfill individual needs or to sustain the society, and to ensure its continued existence over time. Although this approach to studying human behavior differed from social evolutionism, arguments about gender roles had not significantly changed. Edward E. Evans-Pritchard (1902–1973), a leading British functionalist, saw the differences between men and women to be based on "deep biological and psychological factors" (1965, p. 55). Anthropologists who used the functionalist point of view assumed that both women's exclusion from the public realm and male dominance were natural and necessary.

EARLY PIONEERS IN THE ANTHROPOLOGY OF WOMEN

American anthropology, when it established itself as a primary field of academic study, heavily emphasized culture instead of society. Therefore the two best known female anthropologists in the early twentieth century, Margaret Mead (1901–1978) and Ruth Benedict (1887–1948), focused on culture and personality. They both wrote about the cross-cultural malleability of "natural" sex roles. Theoretical movements from the 1920s through to the 1960s ignored or naturalized sexual difference.

The early twentieth century brought about a rejection of generalizing theories such as social evolutionism and a desire for more critical systematic examination. Mead and Benedict, early pioneers in American anthropology, made significant contributions to the cross-cultural study of gender by using sophisticated ethnography and rigorous methodology. Mead was one of the first to discredit unsophisticated claims about the biological causes of sex differences with ethnographies, such as *Coming of Age in Samoa* (1928), about adolescent girls. She argued that individuals are born with the potential to develop whatever gender role society dictates. Mead and Benedict wrote about the cross-cultural malleability of "natural" sex roles. It was during this period of anthropological study up to the 1930s when cultural studies assumed that male dominance was natural and ignored sexual differences. Anthropologists such as Mead, Elizabeth Fernea, Susan Carol Rogers, and Annette Weiner claimed that the women being studied often enjoyed a higher status within their culture than was originally recorded, sometimes even higher than that of Western women. Mead's ethnography titled *Sex and Temperament in Three Primitive Societies* (1935) claimed that women in the Chambri tribe of Papua New Guinea were dominant with no specific effects on their society. This book became a cornerstone for the women's liberation movement. These figure's works, however, were not considered central to anthropology until feminist anthropologists of the 1970s established gender as pivotal to anthropological concerns.

Beginning in the 1950s an increasing part of academic literature and public discourse began using the term *gender* for the self-identified masculinity or femininity of a person. John Money first used the term in this context in 1955. In the late 1960s, the theory that the division of labor was based on sex/gender was put forward. Sherwood Washburn and Chet Lancaster (1968) advanced the "man-the-hunter" model of human evolution, stating that biology, psychology, and customs were what separated humans from apes. This model was used to explain gender roles, a biased model presuming that behaviors exclusive to men resulted in the evolution of all that is considered uniquely human. Sally Slocum (1975) seriously critiqued this model as problematic in its assumptions that emphasized hunting as the prime motivator in human evolution. The works of feminist archeologists such as Margaret Conkey and Janet Spector (1984) and Joan Gero (1985) have furthered Slocum's pioneering work by calling into question the traditional assumptions about prehistoric gender roles and pointing to the complexities involved in reconstructing gender relations in past societies.

Second-wave feminist Simone de Beauvoir (1908–1986), in *The Second Sex* (1949), argued that woman is the essential "other" to the male "self": "woman is made, not born," which both reinforces and reflects male power. Her social constructionism helped create the sex/gender dichotomy. Betty Friedan (1921–2006), in her best-selling book *The Feminine Mystique* (1963), was influential in igniting many women's awareness of inequality through the societal definitions of gender roles that restricted women to the home. Over the next few decades, North American society was questioned in terms of its assumptions about the biological differences between men and women that limited women's prospects. The discipline of anthropology, which had traditionally ignored the importance of gender, began to recognize its negligence regarding women in traditional social science investigations.

THE RISE OF FEMINIST ANTHROPOLOGY

When insights about gender roles and inequality arose in the 1970s, the discipline of "feminist anthropology" was born.

The term gender as a category of analysis was introduced. Feminist research had demonstrated that what were then called sexual roles varied widely across cultures and therefore challenged the essentialist pronouncement that biology is destiny. Behaviors could not be reduced simply to the inevitable natural and universal fact of sex differences. Gender analysis transcends biological reductionism by interpreting the relationships between men and women as cultural constructs that result from imposing social, cultural, and psychological meanings on biological sexual identities. As a consequence it became necessary to distinguish between "gender" as a symbolic creation; "sex," which refers to the biological fact of being male or female; and "sexuality," which concerns sexual preferences and behavior. But the development of gender theory has not led to an agreement on the concept of gender itself. Although gender stands for socially defined relationships between men and women, its political meaning and implications are not always clear.

The early phase of feminist anthropology produced a wide range of studies that concentrated on identifying the position and status of women cross-culturally. By looking at how traditional anthropology viewed women, feminist anthropologists uncovered a wide range of variation in gender roles, in the values placed on activities performed by men and women, and in men's and women's access to important societal resources. As a result, they were able to expose biases in earlier anthropological studies and expose how male-centered perspectives had helped create a distorted depiction. Feminist anthropologists not only corrected ethnographic records but also questioned biological determinist accounts of gender. They argued that variation in the roles and status of men and women uncovered by their studies suggested that gender might not be determined by biology. As a result, assumptions about gender differences that underpinned women's inequality in their own society began to be questioned.

Feminist anthropologists write about the variation in gender roles to symbolize their concerns with both sexes and the culturally and temporally changeable relationships of gender roles between men and women. Gender can be understood as the meanings that a particular society gives to the physical or biological traits that differentiate males from females. These meanings provide the individuals of a society with views about how to act, what to believe, and how to make sense of their experiences. Feminist anthropology has made important contributions to assessing the validity of the notions about the inherent differences between men and women that prevail in the United States and other Western societies. Because gender constructs are cultural understandings of physical differences, they are open to alteration.

Although the focus of gender as a cultural construct had begun, there was little agreement among feminist anthropologists as to the best way to conceptualize and understand gender roles and inequality. By 1974 a new school of thought emerged, put forward by Nancy Chodorow, Sherry B. Ortner, Michelle Zimbalist Rosaldo, and Louise Lamphere, which held that gender was constructed by social and cultural factors. Ortner argued that the subordination of women was based on cultural ideologies and symbols. Rosaldo researched the notion that women frequently participate in behavior that limit them, and therefore, one must look at the overall system. Rayna R. Reiter (1975) found that at least some of the time the sexes were treated equally in primitive cultures that were free of Western bias, and that the universal subordination of women was not necessarily a social structure. She concluded that the gender asymmetry that does exist in many societies is caused by differences in power, class, and production. In 1975 Betty Freidl founded another school of thought known as comparative analysis. Freidl argued that women's roles changed to adapt to changes in the technology within society such as agriculture and industry as well as to specializations in the labor force.

Jane Fishburne Collier and Sylvia Junko Yanagisako (1987) expanded Rosaldo's work by analyzing gender forming through hierarchy. Henrietta L. Moore (1988) attempted to compose a theoretical understanding of previous work done in anthropology. Moore outlined three types of male bias that flawed previous anthropological research and theory: the bias inherent in the anthropologist's own beliefs, the bias inherent in the culture being studied, and the bias brought about by the anthropologist's tendency to theorize from Western standards. Anthropologists often take for granted that the asymmetrical relationships of men and women in other cultures are similar to the hierarchical nature of gender relations in Western society. Thus male biases cause the anthropologist to overlook important social structures in which women play a role. Moore asserts that feminist anthropology has made an outstanding contribution to anthropology by developing theories relating to gender identity and the cultural construction of gender.

THE EMERGENCE OF THE ANTHROPOLOGY OF GENDER

The early feminist approach to the anthropological study of women, concerned with the revision of Western cultural assumptions, was put aside by certain women who considered it exclusionary because they did not feel that the category of *woman* represented them. The issue of race is subsumed within the argument of gender difference. The new phase of feminist anthropology focuses on gender and culture, but also places gender in relation to the historical and material circumstances in which gender, race, ethnicity, class, religion, and socioeconomic status interconnect and interact on a daily basis. The anthropological study of gender challenges the earlier arguments of biological essentialism and surpasses it by analyzing the ways cultures construct differences between women and men.

This new anthropological approach includes critiques regarding white middle-class feminism by women of color and lesbians, who began focusing on social inequalities. The anthropological publication *This Bridge Called My Back* (first published in 1981), has demanded that feminist anthropologists reevaluate the ways in which First World women have unselfconsciously constructed a cultural other in their images of "Third World" or "minority" women. It underscored the importance of creating new alliances among women that would acknowledge differences of race, class, sexual orientation, educational privilege, religion, and nationality. This new approach recognizes the inextricable relationship of culture to politics, economics, and history. Roger N. Lancaster and Micaela di Leonardo (1997) argue that sexuality and gender are intimately connected to the social construction of race and political economy. This reexamination has led feminist anthropologists to uncover the fact that ethnography is itself deeply gendered and situated within relations of power and subordination. It has raised the question of who has the right to write culture (portraying people through the process of cultural representation, which has now become contestable) for whom. It was also during this time that men, within what became known as the "anthropology of men," began to look at the term *man* in a similar manner as feminists had been evaluating *woman*.

The anthropological study of gender has become much more sophisticated and diversified since the 1970s with the development of gender studies, expanding to include such theoretical orientations as postmodernism, poststructuralism, and postcolonialism. di Leonardo's edited work *Gender at the Crossroads of Knowledge* (1991) investigates gender and power in terms of how relations of production and reproduction are organized in a society and programmed into cultural categories. She states that some feminist scholars have a tendency to define feminist theory as a totality in literary poststructuralist terms, which in turn ignores all of material, social life and leaves out of the equation any means for justifying a feminist-theoretical stance. Although feminist anthropology has itself been critiqued for mirroring the andocentric bias derived from male ethnographers studying men, the field has attempted to address the issue by focusing more broadly on the issue of gender and moving away from an exclusive "anthropology of women."

Research in the "anthropology of gender" in the United States has put an emphasis on the body. Peggy Reeves Sanday (1990) looked at power relationships through rape and argued that the relationship between the sexes had to be explored in terms of conflict and tension, which are at the heart of daily life in many societies. Emily Martin (1997), in a somewhat separate manner, investigated physical science's stereotypes in both its research and its discourse to illustrate how women's biological processes were considered less worthy than those of men. Contemporary research goes beyond including the female voice—it analyzes current and pressing issues such as gender divisions in the labor force, child care, reproductive rights and technologies, pornography, the politics of family values, identity politics, violence and aggression, female genital modification, and motherhood, to name just a few.

Cultures are no longer bounded entities, and cultural entities cannot be mapped onto geographical territories without problems ensuing. Because of globalization and growing relationships between societies, the anthropology of gender's concerns with diversity and difference will continue to steadily develop in the next few decades. As Lancaster and di Leonardo so eloquently express it, "feminism, gay studies, race research, and historical political economy, working together on global materials, enable us to unfasten the intellectual straitjackets binding us as we rethink carnal knowledge, as we work to embody liberatory meanings for all humanity" (1991, p. 7).

BIBLIOGRAPHY

Ardener, Shirley, ed. 1975. *Perceiving Women*. London: Malaby Press.

Bonvillain, Nancy. 2001. *Women and Men: Cultural Constructs of Gender*. 3rd edition. New Jersey: Prentice Hall.

Collier, Jane Fishburne, and Sylvia Junko Yanagisako, eds. 1987. *Gender and Kinship: Essays toward a Unified Analysis*. Stanford, CA: Stanford University Press.

Conkey, Margaret, and Janet Spector. 1984. "Archaeology and the Study of Gender." *Advances in Archaeological Method and Theory* 7: 1–38.

di Leonardo, Micaela, ed. 1991. *Gender at the Crossroads of Knowledge: Feminist Anthropology in the Postmodern Era*. Berkeley: University of California Press.

Evans-Pritchard, E. E. 1965. *The Position of Women in Primitive Societies, and Other Essays in Social Anthropology*. New York: Free Press.

Gero, Joan. 1985. "Socio-politics and the Woman-at-Home Ideology." *American Antiquity* 50(2): 342–350.

Hirschon, Renée, ed. 1983. *Women and Property—Women as Property*. New York: St. Martin's Press.

Lamphere, Louise; Helena Ragoné; and Patricia Zavella, eds. 1997. *Situated Lives: Gender and Culture in Everyday Life*. New York: Routledge.

Lancaster, Roger N., and Micaela di Leonardo, eds. 1997. *The Gender/Sexuality Reader: Culture, History, Political Economy*. New York: Routledge.

Leacock, Eleanor. 1978. "Women's Status in Egalitarian Society: Implications for Social Evolution." *Current Anthropology* 19(2): 247–275.

MacCormack, Carol P., and Marilyn Strathern, eds. 1980. *Nature, Culture, and Gender*. Cambridge, UK: Cambridge University Press.

Martin, Emily. 1997. "The Egg and the Sperm: How Science Has Constructed a Romance Based on Stereotypical Male-Female Roles." In *Situated Lives: Gender and Culture in Everyday Life*, ed. Louise Lamphere, Helena Ragoné, and Patricia Zavella. New York: Routledge.

Mascia-Lees, Frances E., and Nancy Johnson Black. 2000. *Gender and Anthropology*. Prospect Heights, IL: Waveland Press, INC.

Mead, Margaret. 1949. *Male and Female: A Study of the Sexes in a Changing World*. New York: Morrow.

Moore, Henrietta L. 1988. *Feminism and Anthropology*. Cambridge, UK: Polity Press.

Moraga, Cherríe, and Gloria Anzaldúa, eds. 2001. *This Bridge Called My Back: Writings by Radical Women of Color*. 3rd edition. Berkeley: Third Woman Press.

Ortner, Sherry B., and Harriet Whitehead, eds. 1981. *Sexual Meanings: The Cultural Construction of Gender and Sexuality*. Cambridge, UK: Cambridge University Press.

Reiter, Rayna R., ed. 1975. *Toward an Anthropology of Women*. New York: Monthly Review Press.

Rosaldo, Michelle Zimbalist, and Louise Lamphere, eds. 1974. *Woman, Culture, and Society*. Stanford, CA: Stanford University Press.

Sanday, Peggy Reeves. 1990. *Fraternity Gang Rape: Sex, Brotherhood, and Privilege on Campus*. New York City: New York University Press.

Sanday, Peggy Reeves, and Ruth Gallagher Goodenough, eds. 1990. *Beyond the Second Sex: New Directions in the Anthropology of Gender*. Philadelphia: University of Pennsylvania Press.

Slocum, Sally. 1975. "Woman the Gatherer: Male Bias in Anthropology." In *Toward an Anthropology of Women*, ed. Rayna R. Reiter. New York: Monthly Review Press.

Strathern, Marilyn. 1987. "An Awkward Relationship: The Case of Feminism and Anthropology." *Signs* 12(2): 276–292.

Tylor, Edward Burnett. 1871. *Primitive Culture: Researches into the Development of Mythology, Philosophy, Religion, Language, Art, and Custom*. 2 vols. London: J. Murray.

Washburn, Sherwood, and Chet Lancaster. 1968. "The Evolution of Hunting." In *Man the Hunter*, ed. Richard B. Lee and Irven DeVore. Chicago: Aldine Press.

Rubina Ramji

ANTI-GAY VIOLENCE

SEE *Homophobia.*

APHRODITE

The Greek goddess Aphrodite calls to mind ideas of sex, love, pleasure, and beauty. In the Greek language her name has generated the expression *ta aphrodisia*. The semantic field of this word points to what is called "sexuality"—that is, the set practices and imagery associated with sex. Aphrodite is the only Greek divinity whose name generates a word that designates her sphere of intervention. Two fields have to be investigated to understand this divine representation of sexuality: Greek literature carrying myths on the one hand and Greek cult practice on the other.

The first important myth with Aphrodite is the Hesiodic tradition of her birth. According to the *Theogony* (conventionally dated from the early seventh century BCE), the first creatures emerging in the cosmos are the physical entities: earth (Gaia), sky (Uranus), mountains, and so on. Amongst these cosmic gods appears also Eros, whose name in Greek means more or less "Love," the sexual impulse that promotes union and reproduction. Aphrodite emerges as the first anthropomorphic goddess from the genitals of the sky god, Uranus, severed by his son Cronos and thrown into the sea god, Pontos. The poet explains the name "Aphrodite" by the marine and seminal foam (*aphros*) from which she grows. At this moment Eros becomes the goddess's powerful agent. Her sphere of honor and of intervention in the human world will be "virgins' whisperings, smiles, deceits, pleasure and sexual relationship." The deep ambivalence of sexuality, expressed as "works of Aphrodite," is rooted in the description of her sudden epiphany, a subtle mixture of desire and violence, tension and appeasement (*Theogony*, 188–206).

In Homer's *Iliad* (conventionally dated from the eighth century BCE), Aphrodite is the daughter of Zeus and Dione, and concerned with the "works of marriage" or "works of sex," according to the translation chosen for the Greek word *gamos* (*Iliad* 5, 429). Aphrodite's genealogy is not the same as in the *Theogony*, but her sphere of intervention remains unchanged: the sexuality legitimated by society (with marriage), as well as its destructive aspect (the rape of Helen by Paris, presented as a reward offered by Aphrodite, is the core of the Trojan war narrated by the Homeric *Iliad*). This ambivalence is exemplified by many other Greek texts, mainly in the classical Athenian tragedies of the fifth century BCE, which illustrate how necessary it is to submit to sexual union and to what extent the goddess's anger can be disastrous to the human, male or female, refusing this destiny. The young Hippolytus, son of Theseus and an Amazon, despises sexual union and marriage, just as do the fifty daughters of Danaos, the Danaides. Hippolytus must die, and the Danaides must each kill her husband

Marble Aphrodite Statue. THE ART ARCHIVE/ ARCHAEOLOGICAL MUSEUM RHODES/DAGLI ORTI.

during the wedding night (forty-nine do). On the Athenian stage, the contempt of sexuality breeds an outburst of violence and fury. This tradition intersects the theme of submission to sexuality with that of the production of children to assure the survival of the community. As goddess of sexuality, Aphrodite's field of manifestation includes fecundity and fertility in close connection, but it would be inadequate to interpret the Greek Aphrodite only as a "mother-goddess" or a "fertility-goddess." From Sappho to Lucretius, poetry celebrates the power of love, the impact of beauty, the force of desire and its violence, closely connecting them with Aphrodite's sphere.

The common thread that runs through the cult worship of Aphrodite in the Greek cities is her patronage of the sphere of sexuality, in all its complexity. Thus in many cities, girls about to be married sacrificed to Aphrodite so that their first sexual experience might be propitious. Boys, too, may have worshiped her, but the evidence is not so well attested. Widows prayed to the goddess for another marriage. But sexuality is much broader than marriage; Aphrodite protected all forms of sexual union: in or outside marriage, heterosexual or homosexual, with concubines, courtesans, or prostitutes. The city of Corinth was particularly known for the beauty and luxurious living of its courtesans, who revered the local Aphrodite. It is unlikely, however, that her sanctuary on Acrocorinth was the location of an institutionalized form of what is generally called "sacred prostitution" a strictly modern term that associates prostitution with sanctuaries: Girls or women dedicated to a goddess, temporarily or for life, would have sold their bodies inside the sacred place at the financial advantage of the temple. This practice is not documented in ancient Greece. This term amalgamates the Greek practice of manumission of slaves by consecration to a god and some doubtful evidence of prostitution inside sanctuaries in Mesopotamia.

The field of sexuality for the Greeks includes *charis*, "grace" and "charm." As soon as young people become full of active *charis*, Aphrodite is present. In mythology, Harmony is daughter of Aphrodite and Ares, "Love" and "War." Such symbolic associations encompass the goddess's associations with civic harmony, concord, and order. Since the fifth century BCE at least, magistrates honored her in their official capacity at the end of service. Two interpretations, which are not incompatible, have been proposed: on the one hand, these officials thank the goddess for the harmonious performance of their duties; on the other hand, these *aphrodisia* mark the return from duty to the pleasures of private life and the release of tension. This "civic" aspect of Aphrodite's sphere is an extension of her patronage of sexuality: Her powerful ability to rouse up the vital impulse, to unite beings and to mingle their bodies, is connected with social cohesion. Aphrodite is often called Aphrodite Pandemos ("she of all the people"), a qualification that declares the goddess responsible for political concord and civic inclusiveness.

Plato in his *Symposium* (180d–e) opposes Aphrodite Pandemos with Aphrodite Urania ("celestial Aphrodite"). They represent, respectively, vulgar heterosexual love and spiritual love between males. This philosophical fantasy became very popular in antiquity, but it contradicts the evidence for both cults. *Pandemos* does not mean "vulgar love" in the cult (even if comic poets associate the cult's foundation and funds received from public brothels), and the Athenian cult of Urania is deeply rooted in heterosexual love and marriage. On the island of Cos, Aphrodite was worshipped as Pandamos (Doric form of *Pandemos*), just like in Athens, but also as Pontia, "she of the sea." Both aspects are reflected in the worshippers' quality and obligations. All women who marry on the island—citizen women, illegitimate women, and metics (free non-citizens)—have to offer a sacrifice to the goddess within a year: a good summary of sexual and inclusive divine functionality. On the other hand, sea-traders also have to honor the goddess, "she of the sea." Such an association with the sea is widely attested in the Mediterranean by epithets like *Euploia* ("she who gives good sailing") or *Limenia* ("she of the shore"). One way to explain this refers to the peculiar birth of the goddess from the sea foam. Another refers to her general power to provoke but also to calm and to dissolve disorder, be it human or natural.

Another prerogative of the goddess is the martial dimension that characterizes some of her cults. In myth and cult, her relationship with Ares is well attested. A priori, the goddess has little concern for such matters. Once more, one has to engage with the notion of "sexuality": In literature, the martial imagery is used to describe the sexual union itself and the tremendous impulse that it provokes in human beings. Inversely, sexual imagery is used in epic descriptions of the battlefield. Sexuality is an ambiguous force, and Aphrodite's connections with war belong to this ambivalence.

A last prerogative is the connection with the black earth when the goddess is worshiped as *Melainis*, "the black one." One way of interpreting the name is to refer to the blackness of night and the nocturnal sexuality. However the web of mythical imagery comes to support and makes another interpretation possible: Fertilizing moisture and the growth of vegetation are conceived on the model of the sexual union between the sky and the earth. Aphrodite's patronage of vital humors fits well in this context.

The desiring impulse is the very image of life and of its drive, creative and potentially destructive. This impulse and its fulfillment in sexual union constitute the frame on which mythical discourse and cultic performances are woven, the imagery of myths and cults concerned with Aphrodite and her *aphrodisia* are woven. The myths and cults of Aphrodite are closely connected to this imagery.

SEE ALSO *Anahita; Inanna-Ishtar; Venus.*

BIBLIOGRAPHY

Budin, Stephanie Lynn. 2003. *The Origin of Aphrodite*. Bethesda, MD: CDL Press.

Calame, Claude. 1999. *The Poetics of Eros in Ancient Greece*, trans. Janet Lloyd. Princeton, NJ: Princeton University Press.

Delivorrias, Angelos. 1984. "Aphrodite." Vol 2 of *Lexicon Iconographicum Mythologiae Classicae*. Zürich.

Dillon, Matthew. 2002. *Girls and Women in Classical Greek Religion*. London: Routledge.

Farnell, Lewis Richard. 1896–1909. *The Cults of the Greek States*. Vol 2. Oxford, UK: Clarendon.

Friedrich, Paul. 1978. *The Meaning of Aphrodite*. Chicago: University of Chicago Press.

Graf, Fritz. 1995. "Aphrodite." In *Dictionary of Deities and Demons in the Bible*. Leiden: 118-125.

Halperin, David M.; John J. Winkler; and Froma I. Zeitlin, eds. 1990. *Before Sexuality: The Construction of Erotic Experience in the Ancient Greek World*. Princeton, NJ: Princeton University Press.

Parker, Robert. 2002. "The Cult of Aphrodite Pandamos and Pontia at Cos." In *Kykeon: Studies in Honour of H.S. Versnel*, ed. H.F.J. Horstmanshoff, et al. Leiden: Brill.

Pirenne-Delforge, Vinciane. 1994. *Kernos Supplément 4: L'Aphrodite grecque: Contribution à l'étude de ses cultes et de sa personnalité dans le panthéon archaïque et classique*. Liège: Centre international d'étude de la religion grecque antique.

Pirenne-Delforge, Vinciane. 2006. "'Something to do with Aphrodite': *Ta aphrodisia* and the Sacred." In *Blackwell Companion to Greek Religion*, ed. D. Ogden. London: Blackwell.

Pironti, Gabriella. 2005. "Entre ciel et guerre: Figures d'Aphrodite en Grèce ancienne." PhD diss., École Pratique des Hautes Études.

Rudhardt, Jean. 1986. *Le rôle d'Eros et d'Aphrodite dans les cosmogonies grecques*. Paris: Presses Universitaires de France.

Winkler, John J. 1990. *The Constraints of Desire. The Anthropology of Sex and Gender in Ancient Greece*. New York: Routledge.

Vinciane Pirenne-Delforge

AQUINAS, THOMAS
c. 1225–1274

Thomas Aquinas, born in Roccasecca, near the Abbey of Monte Cassino, Italy, is considered the most eminent Catholic philosopher and theologian of the Middle Ages. Aquinas provided a comprehensive analysis of philosophy and theology, drawing from Greek and Roman philosophers (Plato, Aristotle, Cicero, the Stoics) as well as from the Christian Fathers, especially Augustine, Peter Lombard, and Albert the Great, who was his teacher. A "Doctor of the Church" who was canonized on July 18, 1323, he was declared in 1567 "Doctor Angelicus" (Angelic Doctor) by Pope Pius V. Thomas was born of an ancient family, descending from Frederick I through his father and from the Norman dynasty of Hauteville through his mother. Thomas's sister Maria became an abbess and played an important role in his canonization. From age five, Thomas was educated at the Benedictine monastery of Monte Cassino. He died in Naples on March 7, 1274.

EDUCATION AND WRITINGS

Thomas entered the newly founded prestigious University of Naples in 1239, where he excelled in the study of the liberal arts curriculum (the trivium and quadrivium) and philosophy under the tutelage of Peter of Ireland and Peter Martini. He joined the Dominican order in 1243 against his family's opposition and spent the rest of his life studying, teaching, and writing for that order. He studied from 1245 to 1248 in Paris and from 1248 to 1252 in Cologne with Albert the Great, who was his most important intellectual influence. Thomas returned to Italy in 1259, teaching and writing in major centers of the Catholic Church and university centers of the Dominican order. He died en route to the Council of Lyon, in which he was to play a major theological role, at the invitation of Pope Gregory X. Some, including Dante and the chronicler Giovanni Villani, believed that Thomas was poisoned at the behest of Charles of Anjou. Charles feared that Thomas would denounce his political misdeeds.

Aquinas wrote Latin hymns, included in "Liturgy on the Corpus Christi," such as *Pange Lingua* [Sing o tongue the glorious mystery] and *Adoro devote, latens veritas* [Thee I adore, secret truth], as well as more than sixty treatises, including *The Commentary on the Sentences of Peter Lombard*, reflecting his years in Paris (1252–1256) and including a treatment on the soul and the state of souls after death, and the *Summa Contra Gentiles* [Treatise against the Gentiles] (1259–1264), a comprehensive treatment of non-Christian doctrines in light of the principles of the Christian faith that was directed at nonbelievers. The *Summa* also addresses the ultimate felicity of humanity, affirming that "all human affairs serve the contemplation of truth" (*Summa*, III, 37). *Summa Theologica* [Treatise on theology] was begun in 1266 and left unfinished at his death. It is a summation or synthesis of Aristotelianism as incorporated into Christian theology that is now called Thomism.

Aquinas concentrated on the exposition of reason and faith in their respective operational spheres to provide understanding and intelligibility in terms of the self, God, and the world. He considered the nature of all things in 512 questions, or 2,658 articles. Selected works of Aristotle, translated from Greek and Arabic in the twelfth and thirteenth centuries, such as the *Nicomachean Ethics*. the *Metaphysics*, *Physics*, *Politics*, and *De anima* [On the soul], have been incorporated into Christian thought as an intellectual synthesis of the Christian truth.

The *Summae* are considered the basis of Catholic teaching on topics such as war and peace, sedition, unbelievers, justice, homicide, theft, usury, virginity, types of lechery, unnatural vices, abortion, and contraception. Aquinas clearly affirms the prohibition against abortion; he does not believe, however, that the human fetus has a soul until some time after conception. Some commentators therefore think that Aquinas would not have considered an abortion in the first stage of pregnancy to be murder (Sigmund 1988, "Injustice"). For Aquinas, sensuality does not belong to the sphere of knowledge but to

Thomas Aquinas. **NEW YORK PUBLIC LIBRARY PICTURE COLLECTION.**

that of the appetite, and original sin is equal in all, as libido is equal in all: "The libido which is said to transmit original sin to the child is not inordinate sexual desire actually experienced" (Sigmund 1988, 1a2ae, 82, 4). Baptism can take away its guilt but not its concupiscence, which remains present in human conception (*Summa Theologica*, vol. 26, pp. 128–132).

In the treatises on law Aquinas discusses moral obligation inherent in the laws under which humankind lives: Those laws are either just or unjust, and they are as binding in conscience as the eternal laws from which they derive ("Law and Political Theory" (Sigmund, 1a, 2ae, 95, 2). His fundamental principle is that the source of obligation is rooted in God's mind and infused into the minds of humans. The three laws—eternal, natural, and human—are united into one and are specified progressively, but they all derive ultimately from eternal law.

AQUINAS ON MARRIAGE AND SEXUALITY

Aquinas's teachings on women and marriage still have great influence in the Catholic Church. He believed that woman is defective and intellectually inferior and was subject to man from the beginning: "Such is the subjection in which woman is by nature subordinate to man, because the power of natural discernment is by nature subordinate to man, because the power of rational discernment is by nature stronger in man" (Sigmund 1a, 92, 1).

An exception to this is the Virgin Mary, to whom he dedicates much of the third part of the *Summa* (vol. 51, *Our Lady*). Her sanctification took place before her birth but only after the infusion of her soul (animation). Christ had no sinful flesh because the Holy Spirit cleansed Mary of all sin, including the original sin. Moreover, Aquinas affirms that there never was a true consummated marriage between Mary and Joseph. Thus, Mary did not transmit the original sin, and her purification was necessary as the vessel of God: "This anterior purification of the blessed Virgin was not required to prevent the transmission of original sin, but because it was proper that the mother of God should shine with the greatest purity. Nothing is worthy to receive God unless it be a spotless vessel, according to the text, holiness, O Lord, becomes thy house" (Aquinas 1a, 2ae. 81, 5).

Because she was the "mother of God," Mary was bestowed with the greatest grace, dignity, and worth ever given to any creature except Christ. Aquinas treats Mary extensively in both *Summae*, in the *Commentary on the Sentences of Peter Lombard*, and in *Expositions on the Gospels of Matthew and John*. However, in his view Mary can be understood only in relation to Christ, and he identifies the major points of her cult as her sanctification, her virginity, her bethrothment, the Annunciation, and the Conception. He concludes that "the blessed Virgin never sinned, mortally or venially" (Aquinas 3a, 28, 4), and when she learned that it was pleasing to God, she consecrated her virginity to Him.

SEE ALSO *Catholicism.*

BIBLIOGRAPHY

WORKS BY

Thomas Aquinas. 1955 (1259–1264). *Summa Contra Gentiles* [Summa against the Gentiles], ed. and trans. A. C. Pegis et al. Garden City, NY: Doubleday.

Thomas Aquinas. 1965 (1266–1274). *Summa Theologica*, Blackfriars edition. New York and London: McGraw-Hill.

WORKS ABOUT

Gilson, Etienne. 1948. *The Philosophy of St. Thomas Aquinas*, trans. Edward Bullough. New York: Dorset Press.

Sigmund, Paul E., ed. and trans. 1988. *St. Thomas Aquinas on Politics and Ethics: A New Translation, Backgrounds, Interpretations*. New York and London: Norton and Company.

Weisheipl, James A. 1974. A. *Friar Thomas D'Aquino: His Life, Thought, and Work*. New York: Doubleday.

Giuseppe Di Scipio

ARABIAN NIGHTS

The work known in the Europe and North America as *The Arabian Nights* is the translation of an Arabic original, *Alf Layla wa-Layla* [The thousand and one nights, or The thousand nights and a night]. This classic of Arabic literature has stirred the imagination of European and North American authors and artists, turning the *Nights* into an unparalleled work in world literature and culture. Replete with danger; murder; tales of sex, love, and treachery; and supernatural beings able to cross continents, the text of the *Nights* has inspired European and North American artists (e.g., Marc Chagall [1887–1985]), composers (e.g., Rimsky-Korsakov [1844–1908]), novelists (e.g., John Barth [b. 1930]), and short-story writers (e.g., Edgar Allan Poe [1809–1849]). As the most influential literary text to come out of the Islamic world, *Nights* has played an enormous role in shaping European and North American attitudes to Middle Eastern Islamic culture.

This is not to speak of the enormous presence of the *Nights* in world cinema. As Robert Irwin points out, "hundreds of *Arabian Nights* films have been made" (Marzolph 2004, p. 22). The most artistically ambitious cinematic adaptation of the *Arabian Nights* is most certainly Pier Paolo Pasolini's *Il fiore delle Mille e una notte* (1974). Pasolini made changes in the structural arrangements of the stories, but his is, of all modern adaptations, probably the only one to have remained faithful to the erotic spirit and omnisexual explicitness of the Arabic original. The animated adventures of *Aladdin*, immortalized by the Disney Studios (1992, and later sequels) have made the *Nights* a major element in contemporary mass culture, not only through the films themselves but also through the aggressive merchandising of children's toys and paraphernalia.

The Arabs themselves have not shied from evoking this part of their heritage. Almost from its origins in the nineteenth century, modern Arabic literature has exploited stories from the *Nights*. Famous stage versions include Tawfiq al-Hakîm's 1934 *Shahrazâd* and Alî Ahmad Bâkathîr's 1953 *Shahrazâd's Secret*. The Egyptian feminist Nawal El Saadawi included a radical revision of the frame story in her highly charged *The Fall of the Imam* (1987). Taken generally modern Arab authors have been more interested in using the *Nights* to explore political and social problems, including the politics of authorship. They have shied away from the sexual focus of so many of the tales.

Despite its frequent use in modern Arabic high culture, the Arabic original was a middlebrow work, normally transmitted orally by professional storytellers in a relatively accessible form of the language (rather than the ornate, sophisticated Arabic of the high cultural Medieval prose works). Ninth-century references exist to a rudimentary form of the text. Over the centuries layers

Shahrazâd and the Sultan. *Illustration of Scheherazade prolonging her life by telling stories to amuse the king.* THE GRANGER COLLECTION, NEW YORK.

and stories were added, enlarging it and embellishing upon it. The earliest layer of the *Nights* is undoubtedly pre-Islamic, with other major additions coming at the time of the Abbasids (c. 750–1250 CE) (with the frequent references to the famous Caliph Harun al-Rashid) and the last major additions came in the time of the Mamluks. (c. 1250–1500 CE)

The translation of the *Nights* into French by Antoine Galland (1704) used manuscripts as well as other stories that the French Orientalist collected. Translations by British Orientalists, such as Sir Richard Burton (1821–1890) and Edward Lane (1801–1876), helped give the *Nights* a place in English literature alongside the one that Galland had created in French.

The frame story of the *Nights* is also the best known and most often retold. It is a story of sex and betrayal. *The Arabian Nights* revolves around the tale of two ruler brothers, Shahriyar and Shahzaman, who are both traumatized by the infidelity of their wives. Seeing his wife in the midst of a sexual act with a slave, Shahriyar goes off on a trip with his brother who has experienced the same trauma. On their voyage the two brothers are, against their will, lured into sexual acts with a young woman. This woman is herself being held prisoner by an *ifrit* who had kidnapped her on her wedding night. The lesson the brothers learn is one of sex as betrayal and coercion. Shahriyar proceeds to have his sexual pleasure with a virgin every night and have her executed in the morning. Shahrazâd enters the scene, winning a verbal duel with her father, the vizier, who attempts in vain to keep her from setting foot in a situation that will leave her another victim of Shahriyar. Her self-imposed task is to drastically alter the behavior of this serial-killer ruler. She brings along her sister Dinarzad (Dunyazad in some versions). Shahrazâd's ruse is to narrate a story every night for the king. But Shahrazâd's stories are never completed at the break of day, thus assuring the continuity of her life, as she will carry on her story cycle the next evening. In this way Shahrazâd is able to keep herself and her sister alive. At the end of the text the reader discovers that the storyteller has borne the king three sons. An elaborate marriage ceremony takes place in which Shahrazâd weds Shahriyar, and her sister, Dinarzad, weds Shahzaman. The sexual disturbance with which the text began has been rectified, with the establishment of the patriarchal couple.

The stories Shahrazâd narrates include adventure, chance, dramatic twists, disguises, and rediscoveries. Probably the most consistent topic, however, is human sexuality, both as love and as lust. The full panoply of sexuality is also on display, including orgies, same-sex relations, and play with the physically deformed. The treatment of sexuality in the *Nights* is strikingly open, even nonjudgmental. When there is a morality present, it is most often one of love, trust, and honesty.

This sexual explicitness is seen as threatening by many in the contemporary Arab world. Between the neo-Puritanism of the Islamists, the heritage of Victorian prudery absorbed under European imperialism, and the shame felt by some secularized Arabs that their culture should be best known by such fanciful tales, the unexpurgated Arabic *Nights* is generally unavailable in the Middle East. The famous nineteenth-century Bulaq edition is censored in its native Egypt and can only be purchased on the black market.

BIBLIOGRAPHY

Aboul-Hussein, Hiam, and Charles Pellat. 1981. *Chéhérazade, Personnage Littéraire*. Algiers: Société Nationale d'Edition et de Diffusion.

Ali, Muhsin Jassim. 1981. *Sheherazade in England: A Study of Nineteenth-Century English Criticism of the Arabian Nights*. Washington, DC: Three Continents Press.

Malti-Douglas, Fedwa. 1991. *Woman's Body, Woman's Word: Gender and Discourse in Arabo-Islamic Writing*. Princeton: Princeton University Press.

Malti-Douglas, Fedwa. 1997. "Shahrazâd Feminist." In *The Thousand and One Nights in Arabic Literature and Society*, ed. Richard G. Hovannisian and Georges Sabagh. Cambridge, MA: Cambridge University Press.

Malti-Douglas, Fedwa. 2004. "Homosociality, Heterosexuality, and Sheherazade." In *The Arabian Nights Encyclopedia*, ed. Ulrich Marzolph and Richard van Leeuwen. Santa Barbara: ABCCLIO.

Marzolph, Ulrich, and Richard van Leeuwen, eds. 2004. *The Arabian Nights Encyclopedia*. Santa Barbara: ABC-CLIO.

Fedwa Malti-Douglas

ARETINO

SEE *Sex Manuals: Old and Modern West.*

ARISTOTLE

384–322 BCE

Aristotle was a philosopher whose concepts, theories, and implicit assumptions have shaped the development of Western intellectual and political culture. His views on sex and gender have been as influential as other aspects of his philosophy. Not only in philosophy but also in law and politics, influential arguments that have been used to support the superiority and authority of men over women can be dated back to Aristotle. The standard view of Aristotle as an archetypal sexist is, however, not the whole truth. There are also more egalitarian elements in his discussion of gender issues that have encouraged feminist interpretations of his ideas.

ARISTOTLE ON SEX AND GENDER

Aristotle explored issues of sex and gender in various contexts. He was interested in the relationship between the metaphysical notion of species and the sexual notions of male and female. He insisted that male and female are contrary attributes that belong to the genus animal as such but do not divide the genus into different species. Aristotle also argued that male and female are differences in each animal species but not in their forms. This implies that whatever differences there are between male and female capacities, for example, in reproduction, they do not belong to the essence of what it is to be a member of certain animal species. Aristotle has a clear tendency to play down the difference between the sexes.

Aristotle's biological works include meticulous studies of reproductive capacity, its physiological preconditions, and the sexual behavior of animals. Aristotle never approached his topics from a purely empirical viewpoint but applied his metaphysical notions to achieve a comprehensive theory of natural philosophy.

Aristotle describes a common reproductive pattern underlying the differences between animal species in their sexual organs and methods of copulation. In Aristotle's view the male and the female in each species have different sexual capacities indicated by differences in their sexual organs, but there is surprisingly little difference between the two sexes in the process they undergo in reproduction.

In Aristotle's biology both males and females transform food by concocting it into blood and then into seed, but this capacity is stronger in males. Males are able to produce semen, whereas females merely have menses, although the female product also is called seed. The quantitative difference turns qualitative when Aristotle assumes that the male is the formal cause and the female is the material cause of generation. Their stronger capacity to concoct makes males capable of giving a form of an animal to seed, whereas females are able only to receive the form and provide the matter for future offspring through the menses.

Aristotle's theory of generation indicates a conviction about the supremacy of the male over the female. Aristotle assumed a hierarchical relationship between form and matter, and so the ascription of the formal role to the male gives support to the idea that the male is the more active, governing, and clearly better sex. The female is called a natural imperfection in the species. Aristotle did not provide any evidence for his evaluation of the male as the stronger sex except the greater natural heat and the corresponding stronger ability to concoct blood in the male. His belief in male supremacy seems to have been more ideological than philosophical.

POLITICAL AND SOCIAL IMPLICATIONS

Aristotle also drew political conclusions from his theory of sex difference. He suggested that men should have permanent authority over women in the household and that women should not hold political offices. The claim for male power is derived solely from the nature of the female deliberative faculty, which Aristotle said is "without authority." He did not see essential moral or intellectual differences between men and women except the inclination of women to weakness of the will, but he still endorsed a strict hierarchical and functional division of gender roles.

The social aspect of human sexual life is a peripheral topic in Aristotle's works; this is surprising in light of his biological interest in sex and the prominent role of affectionate friendship in his ethics. He understood sexual appetite as structurally analogous to eating and drinking. These basic appetites are common to all animals. They are directed to the pleasures of taste and touch and related to the bodily processes of replenishment and dissolution.

In Aristotle's ethics the virtue of moderation is concerned with the control of the basic appetites, which are in themselves natural and not morally reproachable. Aristotle also thought that humans are innately disposed to develop correct forms of desires and emotional responses to bodily pleasures. The basic appetites, however, can generate moral problems because without the influence of reason they are likely to develop in harmful directions. Excessive attention to them is slavish and bestial because they belong to people not as humans but as animals.

Aristotle showed only limited interest in the problems of sexual ethics. His view of marriage was, however, exceptional in his time. Whereas the ancient Greeks typically regarded marriage only as a means to produce legitimate children, Aristotle saw broader prospects for the relationship of husband and wife. Despite the permanent hierarchy in family, the husband's rule over his wife is defined as political and thus is understood as being based on a kind of equality. Family life should aim at activities performed together for the common good as well as for mutual affection and delight. Husband and wife may reach the highest form of friendship, based on virtue, if each partner is good in an appropriate way.

Aristotle's remarks about the violations of marriage are again in accordance with Greek popular morality. Adultery is one of the acts he said is always wrong, but the term he used means violating the rights of other men to their wives and possibly their daughters. Extramarital sex with prostitutes or pederastic lovers is not morally problematic, whereas sleeping with a married woman is always unjust, assuming that the adulterer is aware of the status of his partner. Aristotle did not comment much on same-sex relationships but, again following mainstream attitudes, expressed a negative attitude toward the disposition of some men toward sexual passivity and their tendency to assume the passive role in a homoerotic relationship.

BIBLIOGRAPHY

WORKS BY

Aristotle. 1984. *The Complete Works of Aristotle.* The Revised Oxford Translation, vols. I–II, ed. Jonathan Barnes. Princeton, NJ: Princeton University Press.

WORKS ABOUT

Freeland, Cynthia A. ed. 1998. *Feminist Interpretations of Aristotle.* University Park, PA: Pennsylvania State University Press.

Sihvola, Juha. 2002. "Aristotle on Sex and Love." In *The Sleep of Reason: Erotic Experience and Sexual Ethics in Ancient Greece and Rome*, ed. Martha C. Nussbaum and Juha Sihvola. Chicago: University of Chicago Press.

Juha Sihvola

AROUSAL

Arousal is a state of sexual excitation marked by increased blood flow to the genitals, elevated heart rate, and the tumescence (swelling) of the clitoris and penis. Arousal can be initiated by physical and mental stimuli and is profoundly impacted by individual psychology and cultural conditioning.

PHYSIOLOGY

Also called the excitement phase, arousal is the first stage of the human sexual response cycle developed by William H. Masters and Virginia E. Johnson (1966). Arousal is followed by the plateau stage, in which tensions initiated by arousal are intensified. The third stage, orgasm, involves the sudden release of this tension, and the final resolution stage incorporates the gradual reduction of physiological tension and often includes a period of emotional calm and well-being.

Sexual arousal engenders a variety of physiological responses. Women experience erection of the nipples and, as arousal moves toward the plateau stage, an increase in breast size resulting from vasocongestion, or the swelling of tissues owing to increased blood flow. The heart rate and blood pressure both increase in direct relation to increasing tension. Late in the excitement phase, a female may experience some muscle tension, including expansion of the vaginal wall and tensing of the abdominal muscles. The late excitement phase may also include the sex flush, a red rash that begins on the upper abdomen and spreads quickly to the breasts.

Within the first thirty seconds of arousal, vaginal lubrication appears. The clitoral glans becomes tumescent and vasocongestion increases the diameter of the clitoral shaft, engorges the labia, expands and lengthens the vaginal barrel, and alters the vaginal wall to a darker, purplish color. Expansion and separation of the vaginal walls causes the folded pattern of the vagina to smooth out. Finally, the uterus begins to elevate into the greater pelvis, which lies above and in front of the pelvic brim.

The initial physiological response to sexual stimuli in males is the erection of the penis. Once the penis is fully erect, arousal may continue for only a few moments or for several minutes. When the excitement phase is prolonged, the penis may lose and regain its erection one or more times. Penile erection is often extremely sensitive to the discontinuation and resumption of physical sexual stimulation. The penis is also sensitive to asexual stimuli, which may cause a partial or complete loss of the erection even when physical stimulation is constant.

During arousal, males also experience a thickening of the scrotal covering and an elevation of the scrotal sac and testes. As with females, males experience an increased heart rate and elevated blood pressure when sexually aroused. Men also experience muscle tension, including partial elevation of the testicles and contraction of the abdominal and intercostals muscles (the latter being the muscles that run between the ribs). About 60 percent of men also experience nipple erection, though it is inconsistent and may not appear until the plateau phase.

Though the precise role of the brain in sexual arousal has not been determined, studies have consistently found increased right-brain activity in response to arousal. More complex studies have found that a variety of cortical and subcortical brain regions are implicated in sexual arousal, and some researchers have argued that this demonstrates the complexity of the cognitive, physiological, emotional, and psychological processes involved in sexual arousal.

PSYCHOLOGY

Though Masters and Johnson have been greatly influential in the conceptions of human sexual response, many researchers have taken issue with their exclusive focus on physiological response. Helen Singer Kaplan (1974) modifies their model to a three-stage model that includes desire, excitement, and orgasm. Some find this model more useful in that it allows for a consideration of the psychological effects of desire and motivation on arousal.

Further modifications of sexual response models have suggested distinguishing between spontaneous desire, or libido, and stimulus-driven desire, or arousability. Some researchers find that this distinction allows for an evolutionary explanation of differing modes of male and female desire, wherein men experience a biological drive to successfully disseminate their genetic material whereas female success, which is tied to the rearing of offspring, depends on selecting an appropriate mate, a selection that will be driven by external cues. For some clinicians, this model of sexual response has proved useful in that it allows for the complex mediation between internal and external stimuli that occurs in sexual arousal, as well as for consideration of the physiological, psychological, and relationship factors that affect arousal.

Ultimately, sexual arousal is dictated by an exceedingly complex interaction of psychological, cultural, behavioral, neurological, cognitive, physiological, and interpersonal factors. Though certain kinds of stimulation (of the genitals, for example) seem to be universally interpreted as sexual, whether or not such stimulation is arousing depends on individual and cultural conditioning, as well as situational and relationship factors—all of which are mediated by the central nervous system.

Erotic stimulation in both men and women appears to be largely the result of conditioning in which certain kinds of stimuli become associated with positive sexual outcomes. Though some stimuli are more easily eroticized, studies have demonstrated that people can be quite readily conditioned to respond sexually to neutral objects. Sexual arousal, moreover, is almost always context-dependent; what may carry an erotic charge in one situation does not necessarily in another. Men and women report arousal increases with the sexual explicitness of the stimuli, though men and women are excited by different sexual situations. Men, for example, are more excited by viewing group sex than women, while women report greater arousal in response to films that emphasize the desire and enjoyment of both partners. Sexual fantasy is an important source of arousal for both men and women. Fantasy alone can generate moderately high sexual excitement and a concomitant physiological response; it can moreover serve as mechanism for exerting control over a physiological function often considered involuntary.

Emotional states greatly impact sexual arousal, though the nature of this impact is often complex and little understood. Emotions themselves are multidimensional and can be experienced in varying degrees of intensity. Certain negative emotions, such as guilt or embarrassment, inhibit arousal, while others, such as sadness, do not necessarily. Emotions that themselves invoke a certain physiological arousal, such as anger, often increase sexual arousal, though only to a certain limit. Additionally, the source of the emotion—whether it occurs outside of the sexual situation or arises out of it—changes its relation to sexual arousal. And the valence of certain emotions changes greatly depending on the situation: Anxiety surrounding body image may inhibit sexual arousal, whereas anxiety about getting caught having sex in a public place may be sexually arousing. Finally, there is some evidence that sexual arousal itself may be considered a sort of emotional state, in which persons experience an extremely heightened, positive state of being.

CULTURAL SIGNIFICANCE

Sexual arousal is intimately related to the culture in which it occurs. The particular stimuli that people find arousing are culturally inflected, either by societal taboos or eroticized representations. Edward Shorter (2005), for example, links the newly common practice of deep tongue kissing in the late nineteenth century to kinetoscope depictions of male–female kissing. Shorter finds a similar tendency at work in the eroticization of various body parts, arguing that an earlier emphasis on the face and genitals as the primary sites of sexual attraction was replaced in the twentieth century with an erotic interest in other body parts, including the breasts, nipples, and buttocks. This shift in the erotic charge of particular parts of the body occurs in tandem with the production of art, photography, and pornography that call attention to these areas of the bodies as legitimate stimuli for sexual arousal. Similarly, an increase in experimentation with different sexual techniques, including oral sex, appears to have followed its depiction in popular pornographic works of the period.

The correspondence between erotics and popular culture has been one of the hallmarks of the film industry, which has legimated as much as it has reflected the cultural eroticization of certain kinds of sexual stimulation. Similarly, the sexual liberation movement of the 1960s and 1970s has been consistently linked to the increasing visibility of men's magazines, such as *Playboy*, which valorized alternative forms of sexual expression. Since at least the 1970s, sexual arousal has been an important component of mainstream depictions of sexuality. Sex manuals and men and women's magazines alike emphasize the importance of arousal to sexual expression, often providing detailed instructions for pleasing one's partner. Mainstream films, magazines, romance novels, and soft-core porn often attempt to incite sexual arousal by depicting individuals who are themselves sexually aroused, as marked by parted lips, heavy breathing, and splayed limbs. One effect of this kind of representation is that sexual arousal is constructed as itself sexually arousing.

SEE ALSO *Foreplay.*

BIBLIOGRAPHY

Kaplan, Helen Singer. 1974. *The New Sex Therapy: Active Treatment of Sexual Dysfunctions.* New York: Brunner/Mazel.

Masters, William H., and Virginia E. Johnson. 1966. *Human Sexual Response.* Boston: Little, Brown.

McAnulty, Richard D., and M. Michele Burnette, eds. 2006. *Sex and Sexuality.* Vol. 2: *Sexual Function and Dysfunction.* Westport, CT: Greenwood Press.

Shorter, Edward. 2005. *Written in the Flesh: A History of Desire.* Toronto: University of Toronto Press.

Maureen Lauder

ART

The landmark exhibition *Fémininmasculin, Le Sexe de l'Art* (Femininemasculine, The Sex of Art) presented at the Centre Pompidou, Paris, France, in 1995 attempted to address, through both exhibited works of art and companion catalogue, how twentieth-century art has traversed, transferred, and transformed the issue(s) of sexual difference. The 500 images on display appeared, however, to be divided between the traditional view of the differences between the sexes and an alternate axis that both experimented with and transgressed upon the established biological distinctions between and functions of both men and women. As the exhibition curators sought to clarify what they saw as a series of discrete distinctions between the overtly sexual and the implicitly erotic and the expanding academic boundaries of gender, they offered a new term, *fémininmasculin*, as a solution, especially in terms of art. For them, the issue was not feminine–masculine, sex in art, but rather femininemasculine, the sex of art.

Their point of art historical departure for this new term was the first work in the exhibition *L'Origine du Monde* (The Origin of the World, painted in 1866 by Gustave Courbet (1819–1877). Within his canvas, Courbet depicted only a lower female torso with legs spread open to draw the viewer's eye directly to the exposed genitalia as simultaneously the locus of sexual pleasure and symbolic of fertility and procreation. This new conception of art, then, provides a new way of seeing and interpreting art that presages what would become the twentieth-century preoccupation with discussions, examinations, and debates over the meaning of sex, sexuality, and—ultimately—gender.

Traditionally, art has been understood as performing certain functions, including the pedagogy of manners, social customs, cultural values, and behavior, in addition to beautifying human environs from the domestic to the public. The typical point of entry into seeing or interpreting a work of art is through representational, abstract, or symbolic renderings of the human body. Artists have conferred a variety of forms, shapes, postures, gestures, and costumes upon the human body to conform to the attitudes of different cultures, historical periods, and religious communities. These stylistic and culturally referenced differences allow researchers to see and critique the embedded inscriptions of gender, class, identity, and power in works of art. The reality that body types vary not simply from geographic region to geographic region but also within cultural categories and transmute according to prevailing economic, political, religious, and social attitudes is not lost upon artists, even those dedicated to the depiction of the ideal versus the real.

Analyses of the comparative expressions of mass, weight, and volume coordinate projections of natural versus ideal body types, symbolic patterns of the human body, and nutritional and medical factors that reveal information about sex and gender. One of the significant components in art has been in the social and cultural constructions of gender, that is, what distinguishes the categories of feminine and masculine in modes of behavior, demeanor, dress, and meaning. Biology determines sex, whereas society, from its privileged coordination of culture, economics, politics, and religion, conditions definitions of and attitudes toward gender.

Expressive of a diverse spectrum of cultural attitudes and religious values, artistic renderings of the human body, therefore depictions of sex and gender, has been instrumental in: fertility rites, magic ceremonies, cult objects and rituals, idolatry, natural medicine, social advancement, intellectual achievement, and sacred correspondence. However, an overview of the depiction of male and female forms reveals a dramatic contrast between Asian and European and North American attitudes toward the human, and perhaps thereby toward art, culture, and values. For example, Hindu artists traditionally render voluptuous goddesses and powerful gods engaged in joyful acts of sexual union in contrast to the chaste prayerful postures of asexual male and female saints of Christian art.

ART AS VISUAL COMMUNICATOR AND MIRROR OF SEX AND GENDER

Artistic images provide a venue for understanding cultural perceptions of gender, power, and sex. Universally, human beings convey identity and information through images. The basic human urge to create images is a fundamental form of the communication of ideas, precepts, and concepts. Such expression through and reflection in works of art is premised on the depiction of the human body or anthropomorphic figurations. The transformation of thinking in images into the concrete representation of seeing visions, dreaming dreams, imagining distant lands, recreating ancient the past, and living by memories defines the fundamental nature of art whether categorized individually as painting, sculpture, and, more recently, photography or collectively as fine arts and naive arts. Regardless of the medium art contributes to the shaping of identifiable cultures as the process of visualization translates abstract concepts into visible figures whose major messages, in turn, appeal to and influence viewers.

The symbolic language of the human figures and the ambiance rendered by the landscape, or background, and surrounding objects and attributes, provide a special mode of communication that transcends verbal literacy or formal education and training. Traditionally, even into the twenty-first century images have projected modes of understanding and interpreting gender, sex, race, ethnicity, sexual orientation, and age in a socially appropriate construction of the self. Artistic images, then, question our notions of sex and gender and challenge our concepts of appropriate social behavior and relationships. What late-twentieth-century commentators have characterized as the multivalent character and personalized receptivity of images may have been at the heart of the professional and societal distrust of images—thereby an (over)emphasis on logocentrism in the Europe and North America, especially within the academic disciplines—since the Enlightenment (1600–1800).

Any examination of sex and gender in art, then, is predicated upon two universal notions: first, that the visual is primary historical evidence equitable to written documentation; and second, that the traditionally textually illiterate masses read images. Art is a critical vehicle for the formation, transformation, and dispersal of cultural and societal histories and their analyses. Images evoke authority and reality in the process elsewhere termed *visual analogy*. Images are internalized and identified as one's own by viewers and thereby have profound effects on individual members of a community. Art is critical to the process of socialization by which one enters into the societal and cultural order and signifies oneself as being male or female within that societal construct. Individual notions of gender, then, are affected by societal expectations premised on cultural definitions and redefinitions. Thus, even in art and for artists, sex is determined biologically, whereas gender is societal and cultural.

The contemporary twenty-first-century situation is made more complex by the pluralism of cultural constructions, societal expectations, religious attitudes, and the expanding power of images through technology and globalization. The historical reality is even more damaging in that many works of art—representative, perhaps, of countercultural or alternate religious attitudes—have been destroyed by war and political conflict. Misogyny and patriarchy, as understood in Europe and North America, have played a crucial role in the loss of art, especially images related to the power or authority of women and other marginalized groups. The permanent loss of art—either through the activity of religious iconoclasm or cultural war, or the passivity of natural disasters such as earthquakes or tsunami—account for an irretrievable diminution of both images of marginalized groups, such as women, and of countercultural attitudes. History may be written by the winners; however, cultural interpretations of societal propriety and excellence are clearly inscribed in art. For many contemporary feminist interpreters, the patriarchal basis of European and North American culture has resulted in the elimination, if not simple diminution, of any visual images of marginalized genders in motifs of power and authority.

Artistic images render visible, tangible, and thereby mimicable, societal perceptions of appropriate and inappropriate behavior for both men and women. The recognition that images are gendered—that is, projecting the proper attitudes, gestures, postures, and dress for what is culturally identified as masculine, feminine, androgynous, hermaphroditic, or homosexual—and that the prevalence of gendering through images is formative as well as reflective of cultural attitudes make it impossible to regard images simply as benign expressions or neutral objects. Prior to the scholarly changes in the late 1960s initiated by recognizing the marginalized, analyses and presentations of the power of images have been premised upon the predominant male-oriented hierarchical structure of artistic creativity, knowledge, and scholarship. Those critical studies of images of the marginalized—whether racial, ethnic, or sexual—did not exist prior to the early 1970s.

Earlier examinations of the human body and its meaning in art emphasized descriptions of works in the canon of European and North American art to the neglect, if not negation, of critical analyses of the body with all its racial, ethnic, sexual, cultural, or gendered variations. Critical to both a fair analysis of these earlier texts and of directions for future scholarship is the question of whether or not this interest or preoccupation with the identifying of sex and gender in and through art is a universal human concern or simply a European and North American preoccupation. For example, in most languages outside of English, there is minimal to no linguistic distinction between sex and gender; in addition, there is culturally no distinction between art, life, and religion let alone the modern concepts of sex and gender. However, feminist scholars since the late 1950s, affirmed by the landmark ruling of Judge Ruth Bader Ginzburg (b. 1933) on gender discrimination, have sought to examine the European and North American societal and cultural history of women through gendered lenses.

MODES OF ANALYSES OF SEX AND GENDER IN EUROPEAN AND NORTH AMERICAN ART

Typically, studies of sex and gender in the visual arts have taken one of two fundamental approaches in analyzing and interpreting images: iconographic or iconological. Iconography, or the reading of the signs and symbols, or iconology, the cultural history of the evolution of an image, can be incorporated within either a thematic or chronological frame. Central to both modes of analysis is a series of questions that delineate the communicative nature of art, which is both reflective and formative upon individuals and societies. For example, inquiry into the rationale and identification of the artist led to considerations of the process of artistic creativity and the nature of the aesthetic experience.

Further, the historical reality as to who was permitted to train as an artist was equally dependent upon sex and gender as upon artistic ability. For example, in Europe, even into the seventeenth century, only those women who were the wives or daughters of artists were able to enter into the studio as apprentices. The role of the patron and the collector in both the commissioning and the cultural valuation of art is transformed through history as the realms of gender, race, class, and economics evolve. So, for example, during those periods when women experienced political and economic power, that power was expressed through the subject matter in the art they created, commissioned, or collected. The cultural receptivity to works of art—the how and the why by which individual works are valued, and their influence on a society or a community—is related to the function of art as well as to artistic merit. Additional considerations would include the variations in cultural meaning when art shifts its center from the ecclesiastical or public domains to the domestic sphere as both media and motif are transformed accordingly.

The following examples of studies in sex and gender in European and North American art—first through thematic motifs and second by chronology—provide the methodological skeletons upon which more detailed interpretations and analyses can be structured. The thematic motif can be developed through a variety of patterns, such as the iconography of a specific event such as childbirth or an individual such as a specific monarch or general, whereas the chronological mode can be concentrated within one specific historical period or artistic style, such as the Renaissance (1350–1600), or survey the centuries. The crucial question, however, is whether or not the contemporary consideration of sex and gender was a distinct or discrete element in the creative design, aesthetic appreciation, and cultural evaluation of works of art throughout human history. For example, in his magisterial study, *The Nude: A Study in Ideal Form*, art historian Kenneth Clark (1990) distinguished the physical and symbolic differences between representations of both the naked from the nude and of men from women without direct referencing to sex and gender as overt categories. Rather, Clark's investigation was dependent upon the interdependence of art, culture, life, philosophy, and religion that created an identifiable cultural milieu that either embraced or decried the idea of the nude. His mode of analysis was a journey through a series of motifs that ranged from ideal individuals, that is, Apollo and Venus, to the embodiments of emotions, that is, energy, pathos, and ecstasy.

EXAMPLES OF MOTIFS OF SEX AND GENDER IN EUROPEAN AND NORTH AMERICAN ART

The Power and Authority of the Male Figure Late twentieth-century feminist scholars have asserted that the male figure was normative in the Europe and North America for the cultural definition of power and authority. Thereby, a brief comparison between a male figure and a female figure can serve as one interpretive mode in the consideration of sex and gender in art. Referencing the High Renaissance sculpture of *David* by Michelangelo (1475–1564) as a fine example of the visualization of the classical principles of harmony and order through the male figure, the handsomeness of this masculine form becomes quickened by muscular tensions, especially in David's arms, legs, and torso, and the intimations of respiration in his diaphragm. This sculpted rendition of male energy and movement can be read as expressive of ideal form, kingship and guardianship, and the prevalent social and cultural order. A figure of extraordinary vitality, *David* visually attests to the so-called European principle of the authority of the male figure. Muscular structure, movement (whether internal or external), and the ability to connote emotion through facial expression, gesture, or pose, are among the sculptor's tools in transmitting both the idea and ideal of male authority.

***David.** Sculpture by Michelangelo.* SCALA/ART RESOURCE, NY.

By contrast, Donatello's (1386–1466) early Renaissance sculpture of *Judith and Holofernes* proffers an image of the female hero who, like David, signified democracy and the defense of the city to contemporary Florentines. The initial contrast between the nearly nude Holofernes and the seemingly overdressed Judith can be read as the Christian dialectic of vice and virtue or the Renaissance values of male potency and female humility. Clearly, the two bodies display overt signs of distinguishing the man (broad shoulders, powerful musculature) from woman (peaking breasts, smaller frame). This Judith is not the visualization of any canon of feminine beauty but, rather, a depiction of societal structures and of the female body more as symbol than organic composition. She is carefully positioned astride her drunken victim who rests between her legs.

Any sexual connotations to this composition of a man and a woman must be surrendered to the larger reading of her entire body posture—bent knees, arching body, upraised right arm, and lowered left arm as her hand clasps Holofernes's tendrils while a rider holds the reins. The energy and power signified in the flowing swirls of Judith's garments move in opposition to the arch of her body in the exact fashion that a rider's costume responds to the dynamism propelled by the horse's gait. Donatello's *Judith*, then, mirrors the well-established constructs of authority, power, and sovereignty of the ruler or general who astride his horse commands his army into battle. Thereby, this female hero garners her identity by her masculine posture, gestures, and symbols of power.

Maternity as the Power and Authority of the Female Figure The universal category of maternity connotes the fertilization, conception, and gestation of a child in the female body and the commensurate acts of childbirth, lactation, and nurture to maturity. Whereas a man can act in a maternal fashion by nurturing, emotionally supporting, and gently guiding his child, partner, or friend, biology denies him the female power and authority of pregnancy and motherhood. A survey of artistic images of maternity transcends historical, cultural, and geographic boundaries, revealing its universality through pregnancy, giving birth, lactation, and scenes with a mother and her child.

Sex as biological thereby trumps gender; however, in so doing it confirms that artistic depictions of maternity simultaneously denote more than the iconographic convention of mother and child as found in the Egyptian images of Isis with Horus, medieval renderings of the Madonna and Child, or Mary Cassatt's (1824–1926) nineteenth-century variations of mothers cuddling, nursing, bathing, dressing, or educating their children. Rather, the limitless importance of female fertility, whether culturally or religiously aligned with that of the Earth, and its achievement in the survival of the species is ahistorical and generic. Thus, the reality behind Courbet's title, *L'Origine du Monde* (The Origin of the World), becomes apparent.

SURVEY OF EUROPEAN AND NORTH AMERICAN IMAGES OF SEX AND GENDER

This preliminary survey proffers a series of investigative principles for a chronological model to examine sex and gender in the visual arts. For purposes of clarity this present outline will emphasize the evolution of the female figure in European and North American art. Having their artistic (and religious) origins in fertility figures, women's images appeared as the fulfillment of socially recognized and sanctioned life stages: virgin, wife, mother, and widow. Further, women were depicted in relation to the major elements of the life cycle: birth, puberty, marriage, pregnancy, maternity, and death. Predominately, the female has been depicted as passive—that is, restricted to the domestic setting and engaged in the so-called feminine activities, such as needlework or cooking; by contrast, the male figure was actively engaged outside the realm of hearth and home. The primary visual distinction, then, will be found in the physicality of the male versus the female body, and the secondary visual difference will be in the activities such as familial nurture versus military leadership. These differences will be highlighted through the artistic presentations of the human body and its commensurate gestures, postures, dress, and companion signs and symbols.

Classical art characterizes the female form as a source of maturity, stability, and domesticity. Typically, the female figure was depicted as fully clothed with a thickened waist, small breasts, and wide hips. Those physical characteristics that twenty-first-century viewers would identify as expressive of female sexuality—a narrow waist and voluptuous breasts and hips—were not understood as sites of eros or femininity in the classical world. Evolving from the preclassical models, such as the famed *Venus of Willendorf* (c. 24,000–22,000 BCE) that emphasized the presentation of the female abdomen, genitalia, and thighs as sites of fertility and female energy, classical Greek or Roman presentations of women favored the strength and authority exerted by the almost androgynous—to twenty-first-century viewers—presentations of goddesses such as Hera or Athena and empresses such as Julia or Octavia. Images of even the slender Aphrodite emphasize her abdomen and thighs more than her breasts and waist.

With the establishment of Christianity, depictions of the human body were transformed from the beauty and idealism favored by the classical artists to more symbolic representations in which the reality of the body, regardless of its sexual identification, was suppressed for an emphasis on the theological values of the narrative. Often characterized as asexual stick-like figures, the human body was the locus for symbolic meanings and interpretations, not for sexuality. Therefore, the flattened female body devoid of the classical artistic precepts of mass and volume was a conveyor of the appropriate or inappropriate roles of women in the early Christian world, that is, as humble, chaste, and obedient, as opposed to the seductive charms of Eve and her female descendants. Modes of dress—ranging from the androgynous Greek *chitōn* worn by both men and women, to the eventual Hellenistic interest in the skillful mastery of pleated and flowing drapery—disguised rather than emphasized the sex of the human body. Similarly, the hair—as veiled, uncovered and flowing, or elegantly coiffed—signified the sex and social status of the female figure.

Whereas the societal reality of women as wives, daughters, and courtesans was part of the classical Mediterranean world, it was the early Christian world, especially in the fourth century, that clearly represented the dichotomy of woman as virgin or whore, that is, the good Christian woman following the model of the Virgin Mary or the temptress who was Eve. Church leaders, following the lead of Jerome (347–420), defined appropriate modes of dress even unto hairstyles, cosmetics, and jewelry for the proper Christian woman. The visual distinction here was premised upon the female body as a site of shame or humility that was the locus of wanton sexuality or chaste motherhood.

The transition into the medieval modes of rendering the human body manifested the social and cultural shifts initiated in the fourth century and early Christian art toward a theocentric universe in which God was the origin, locus, and ultimate goal of all creation. The human was merely, as characterized by Augustine (354–430), a player with a clearly defined role in a larger drama of Christian history. Women continued to be interpreted culturally and artistically within the dialectic of the virgin and the whore, and as such, their bodies were artistically rendered as either asexual (almost unto androgyny) or sexually likened to a beast, usually the snake. So, for example, consider the disembodied characteristics of the Madonna as she was carved into cathedral capitols and tympani as opposed to the reptilian characterizations of Eve, as found in the famous image by French sculptor Gislebertus (active 1125–1135) at Autun Cathedral.

As the Middle Ages (476–1350) expanded both in chronological time and geographic regions, a commensurate series of stylistic shifts occurred in the rendering of the human body. As if an accompaniment of the medieval interest in the theology of God's transcendence, cathedral architecture evolved with an emphasis on height—a reaching to the heavens, if you will—and was paralleled in the elongation and thereby slenderizing of the earlier Romanesque figurations of matronly women into the Gothic elegance of shaped postures, which emphasized a more feminine line and softness to the female body. Elongated torsos gently directed the viewer's eye to the swell of the female belly as a sign of fecundity, female sexuality, and male authority. Diminished breasts were bound or hidden by the thick layers of clothing that featured a high waist, tightly fitted sleeves, and voluminous, pleated skirts.

The cultural and social revolution identified as the Renaissance brought new energy and principles of the human body into art. As the transfer into an anthropomorphic, or human-centered, world, the Renaissance has been characterized as being open 360 degrees to all attitudes, ideas, and teachings of the classical world and the more modern sciences, including Aristotelian philosophy, mathematics, and medicine. The commensurate interest in the human led to a retrieval of the classical principles of the body as the site of beauty, balance, and harmony and to the artistic redefining of the body according to the precepts of modern medical knowledge, especially anatomical studies. As a result the female body was refashioned within the purview of the classical nude but with a clear touch of the erotic. Nonetheless, it remained rare to find depictions of women in positions of power and authority, as the fundamental image of woman remained as imperfectly male.

Baroque art, whether created by northern European artists who followed the teachings of the Reformers or southern European artists who stood steadfast with Rome, expanded the dichotomy of the imagery of woman as either alluring temptress or asexual saint. The discovery and refinement of the moveable type printing press allowed for the mass production of prints and engravings, making these modes of artistic imagery easily and financially accessible. The northern European development of the so-called moralizing prints called special attention to the feminine images of vices and virtues. Feminine virtue was characterized by asexual, almost disembodied, presentations of the female figure, with minimal breasts, thickened waists, and other physical attributes almost indistinguishable from what twenty-first-century viewers would categorize as masculine. These women were heavily draped from head to foot and identified by their performance of good deeds or acts of female obedience. Alternatively, feminine vices were orchestrated by either partially or totally naked women whose large, sagging breasts were paralleled by visual emphases on their genitalia as they pursued their often unnatural activities, such as decapitating drunken or sleeping men, riding broomsticks in the sky, or consorting with pigs, horses, or other wild beasts. Southern European artists attempted to expand their iconography of saintly Christian women by reemphasizing the singularity of Mary's virginity and obedience through the visual evolution of new motifs, such as the Immaculate Conception and the Assumption of the Virgin.

As the cultural world turned toward the eighteenth-century evolution to the rococo (1700–1760) and later the Enlightenment, depictions of women in the now dominant modes of secular art were highlighted by a softening of the female form and a sentimentalizing of attitudes toward women, especially as mothers and muses. Artists now rendered delicate feminine forms, either in states of frothy dress or partial undress, characterized by rosy skin tones, pale blond hair coiffed with ringlets and gentle curls, and light, airy garments that highlighted the softened curves of the female form from gently peaking breasts to wispy waists. The reintroduction of the stronger, more stable, matronly forms presaged the expanding social and cultural roles of women during the French and American revolutions.

The nineteenth century was a time of multiple artistic and social revolutions, prophesying the pluralism of the modern art styles of the twentieth century. The rapid succession of art styles—from romanticism to impressionism or from realism to symbolism and abstraction—signified both the speed of steam that powered the industrial revolution and the rapid expansion of economic, political, and religious ideas throughout the expanding geographic reach of the Europe and North America. Such a diversity of artistic styles resulted in a commensurate variety of interpretations of the female figure ranging from the idealized beauty of the romantics to the stunners of the pre-Raphaelites, to the sexuality of the symbolists. Thereby, the female form could be interpreted as a conveyor of societal attitudes and mores more than as a presentation of the individuality of women.

Multiple attitudes toward female beauty, thereby to the visualizing of sex and gender, paralleled the stylistic variations. Without doubt, the artistic imaging of women was influenced by the invention and development of photography, especially as it moved from a technical recording of events or individual portraiture to a recognized art form in the early twentieth century. Almost simultaneous with the advent of photography as it moved from portraiture of women vis-à-vis traditional high-art portraits to artistic interpretations of the female form in the hands of such distinguished photographers as Alfred Stieglitz (1864–1946) to Robert Mapplethorpe (1946–1989) was a transformation in the understanding of the female body in terms of health and medicine. So the wispy waists and overflowing bosom and hips manifested by the whalebone corset gave way first to the American girl and bloomer girl of the late nineteenth century; then to the slender, waif-like flappers of the 1920s emphasized in the designs of Coco Chanel (1883–1971); then to the stability and strength of Rosie the Riveter during World War II (1939–1945); and later to the voluptuous feminine forms of the 1950s highlighted by both the clothes of Christian Dior (1905–1957) and the celebrity of movie stars such as Jane Russell (b. 1921) and Marilyn Monroe (1926–1962).

Modern art, it is often argued, is about the *shock of the new* as characterized by art critic Robert Hughes (b. 1938). One of the fundamental elements of that shock of the new has been the multiple configurations and refigurations of the human body in terms of abstraction and postmodernism. Those bodily elements, most often large or engorged breasts and highlighted female genitalia, were abstracted from the realistic portrayals of the female body and came to characterize both the sex and gender of woman in twentieth-century art, from the sculptures of Constantin Brancusi (1876–1957) to the canvases of Pablo Picasso (1881–1973) and Willem De Kooning (1904–1997). The latter half of the twentieth century was characterized by the raised voices of the marginalized, especially feminist scholars, authors, and artists, who called for the recognition of the female presence in the arts as artist, muse, and subject.

DIRECTIONS FOR THE FUTURE STUDY OF SEX AND GENDER IN ART

Gendered images are more than a mode of sexual identification or socialization into a community; they are a symbolic communication through gestures, postures, dress, attributes, and activities of the common experiences of being human. A comparative or cross-cultural study of sex and gender in art, such as the motif of divine messengers or warriors, reveals the gendered interpretations of being male and female in any given cultural or historical epoch and serves to sharpen perceptions of the historicizing of sex and gender. This is especially significant for European and North American viewers who learn that the scholarly presuppositions in the categorizations and structures of their cultures are not necessarily valid universally or, perhaps, that traditional their concepts of both sex and gender, and the power of images, must be reconsidered.

The diversity of characteristics and roles in which men and women are represented in non-European and non-North American art points to the racial, ethnic, and nutritional diversity of both globalization and the marginalized that is otherwise lost to the art of elite monotheistic and patriarchal cultures of Europe and North America. This is not to propose that non-European and non-North American cultures are not patriarchal in religious, cultural, or social structures but, rather, proposes that sex and gender may be imaged and experienced differently. The potential exploration of these *differences* opens new avenues for investigation and revised formulations for the iconology of sex and gender in art within the expanding parameters of globalization.

BIBLIOGRAPHY

Aldridge, Robert, ed. 2006. *Gay Life and Culture: A World History*. New York: Universe.

Apostolos-Cappadona, Diane. 1998. *Dictionary of Women in Religious Art*. New York: Oxford University Press.

Apostolos-Cappadona, Diane. 1998. "Art." In *Encyclopedia of Women and World Religions*, Vol. 1, ed. Serenity Young. Detroit: Macmillan.

Apostolos-Cappadona, Diane. 2004. "Humanity in the Arts." In *New Dictionary of the History of Ideas*, Vol. 4, ed. Maryanne Cline Horowitz. New York: Scribner's Sons.

Apostolos-Cappadona, Diane. 2005. "Human Body: Human Bodies, Religion, and Art." In *Encyclopedia of Religion*. 2nd edition, ed. Lindsay Jones. Detroit: Macmillan.

Apostolos-Cappadona, Diane, and Lucinda Ebersole, eds. 1995. *Women, Creativity, and the Arts: Critical and Autobiographical Perspectives*. New York: Continuum.

Barasch, Moshe. 1991. *Imago Hominis: Studies in the Language of Art*. Vienna, Austria: IRSA.

Bernadac, Marie-Laure, and Bernard Marcade, eds. 1995. Fémininmasculin, *Le Sexe de l'Art*. Paris: Galimard and Electa.

Bowie, Theodore, and Cornelia V. Christenson, eds. 1970. *Studies in Erotic Art*. New York: Basic Books.

Broude, Norma, and Mary D. Garrard, eds. 1982. *Feminism and Art History: Questioning the Litany*. New York: Harper & Row.

Carson, Fiona, and Claire Pajackowska, eds. 2001. *Feminist Visual Culture*. New York: Routledge.

Chadwick, Whitney. 1996. *Women, Art, and Society*. New York: Thames and Hudson.

Clack, Beverley. 2005. "Human Body: Human Bodies, Religion, and Gender." In *Encyclopedia of Religion*. 2nd edition, ed. Lindsay Jones. Detroit: Macmillan.

Clark, Kenneth. 1990. *The Nude: A Study in Ideal Form*. Princeton, NJ: Princeton University Press.

Feher, Michel; Ramona Naddaff; and Nadia Tazi, eds. 1989. *Fragments for a History of the Human Body*. Cambridge, MA: MIT Press.

Flynn, Tom. 1998. *The Body in 3 Dimensions*. New York: Harry N. Abrams.

Freedberg, David. 1989. *The Power of Images: Studies in the History and Theory of Response*. Chicago: University of Chicago Press.

Lucie-Smith, Edward. 1991. *Sexuality in Western Art*. New York: Thames and Hudson.

Mullins, Edwin. 1985. *The Painted Witch: How Western Artists Have Viewed the Sexuality of Women*. London: Carroll & Graff.

Nelson, Sara M., and Myriam Rosen-Ayalon, eds. 2002. *In Pursuit of Gender: Worldwide Archaeological Approaches*. Walnut Creek, CA: AltaMira Press.

Perry, Gill, ed. *Gender and Art*. 1999. New Haven, CT: Yale University Press.

Saslow, James M. 1999. *Pictures and Passions: A History of Homosexuality in the Visual Arts*. New York: Viking.

Steinberg, Leo. 1996. *The Sexuality of Christ in Renaissance Art and in Modern Oblivion*. Rev. edition. Chicago: University of Chicago Press.

Suleiman, Susan Rubin, ed. 1986. *The Female Body in Western Culture: Contemporary Perspectives*. Cambridge, MA: Harvard University Press.

Diane Apostolos-Cappadona

ART, DRAMA/ PERFORMANCE

The initial appearance of performance in many cultures took the form of public rituals and ceremonies involving dance, speech, masks, costumes, and performers with special roles. With the addition of an audience and a stage, those rituals evolved into the early beginnings of drama, or theater, which often reflected the cultural mores of a society, particularly in relation to gender values, expected behaviors, and traditional roles.

GREECE

In ancient patriarchal societies in which men had all the power, cultural values sometimes were expressed in performances lauding masculinity. Many components of Greek comedy in the fifth century BCE resemble ceremonial phallic rites of that era, which celebrated the phallus as a symbol of creative energy, with choruses that sang and danced as they carried large phallic symbols on poles. Greek tragedies from that period were written by men, were performed by all-male casts, and played to predominantly male audiences. Women generally were depicted as passive and suffering; when written as characters with power, they often were presented as negative and destructive, such as Clytemnestra, Medea, the Gorgons, the Sirens, and the Harpies. In ancient Greek tragedies sexuality is addressed thematically most notably by Sophocles (c. 496–406 BCE) in *Oedipus Rex* (c. 430–425), which deals with incest, and by Aristophanes (c. 446–385 BCE) in *Lysistrata* (411 BCE), in which a sex strike is conducted to end a war.

ROME

In the ancient Roman era theater was male-dominated, with men accounting for the majority of actors. The one format in which females were allowed was mime, which was erotic in nature and was known to involve nudity. For that reason actresses were regarded as being on the same level as prostitutes; both were denied religious rites unless there was a deathbed repentance. However, in the sixth century the mime actress Theodora (c. 500–548) not only made a name for herself as an entertainer but also became the mistress of Justinian (c. 482–565), the heir to the throne of his uncle, the emperor Justin I. Although Justinian wanted to marry Theodora, that was prohibited by an old Roman law that did not allow government officials to marry women of the theater. After successfully petitioning for the law to be repealed, they married in 525. When Justin became emperor of the Eastern Roman Empire, Theodora influenced him to pass laws banning forced prostitution.

INDIA

The association of female performers with prostitutes was not unique to the Romans. In ancient India, where theater also originated with public ritual—in this case temple dances—*nati* dancing girls, though valued for their physical talents, which were thought to please the gods, received little respect even though their performances were given under the authority of temple priests. The ancient epic Sanskrit tale *Ramayana*, which, along with *Mahabharata*, has been the revered source material for many dramatic productions, mentions theatrical dance performances as well as feasts and gatherings with dancing girls for entertainment. Nonetheless, the *Dharmasastras*, or metrical law books, state clearly that if married, dancing girls need not be treated with the respect typically accorded to another man's wife. In *Kama sutra* a dancing girl's position is the lowest among the courtesans.

JAPAN

Another form of dramatic performance that began with dance is Kabuki, which can be traced back to 1603, when Okuni (c. 1572–1613), a female dancer from the Izumo Grand Shrine, started doing public performances on an improvised stage in a Kyoto riverbed. Her Kabuki programs, which were sexually suggestive, cast women in both male and female roles in comic playlets that were interspersed with dances. As the popularity of the programs quickly increased, many imitation Kabuki troupes formed, presenting equally lascivious material so that eventually Kabuki came to be associated with prostitution. In fact, the earliest skits were referred to as *keiseikai*, or "hiring a prostitute," and *chaya asobi*, "playing in a teahouse brothel."

In 1629 the shogun's government decided that the eroticism of Kabuki and its practice of having women play men were immoral and banned women from appearing on stage. Immediately after the period of women's Kabuki came young men's Kabuki, in which young men played all the female roles; those performances attracted raucous audiences clamoring for seductive material. *Yaro hyobanki* (critical guidebooks) rated the young male actors more for their sexual attractiveness than for their acting skills.

When fights broke out at performances over the attentions of the young actors, the shogunate banned young men from the stage in 1652; this gave rise to men's Kabuki the next year. In this form only mature men were allowed to perform, and they did so in a more sophisticated, highly stylized manner. Nevertheless, the shogunate required that the *onnagata*, male actors who specialized in women's roles, shave their heads to render them less sexually desirable and less likely to tempt audiences. As a result the *onnagata*, who typically came from a family of specialists, wore a silk head covering over the shaved forelock that remains a standard part of the costuming.

THE MUSLIM WORLD

In Muslim passion plays from ancient times to the present the dramatic representation of women on stage has been curbed to discourage lustful reactions. Whereas representations of men or masculinity are uninhibited, women are portrayed by men who are discouraged from physically mimicking femininity and instead rely on language or other signifiers; alternatively, they are portrayed by women in a manner that downplays sexual attractiveness.

CHINA

In the Beijing opera, which began in the late eighteenth century, actresses were not banned from the stage, but during feudal times it was considered unfitting for men and women to appear on the same stage. In addition to the male *sheng* roles of the Beijing opera, which are subdivided into old men (*lao sheng*), young men (*xiao sheng*), and warriors (*wu sheng*), men played the female *dan* roles, which are subdivided into the quiet and gentle (*qing yi*), the vivacious and dissolute (*hua dan*), warrior maidens (*wu dan*), and old women (*lao dan*). In fact, the most famous performers, such as Mei Lan Fan (1894–1961), Cheng Yanqiu (1904–1958), Shang Xiaoyun (1900–1976), and Xun Huisheng (1899–1968), have been men known for their portrayals of female roles.

MORALITY AND PROPRIETY ON THE EUROPEAN STAGE

Across cultures the prevalent casting of men in female roles is usually done because of societal morals related to propriety. However, in traditional Kathakali, which originated in Kerala in southern India in the seventeenth century, it was not uncommon for dancing, musical, and ritual performances featuring performers with vividly painted faces and elaborate costumes to last as long as seven or eight hours (an entire night). In light of the stamina and energy required to sustain such a presentation, the casting of young boys in female roles was rooted in practical physical concerns, not solely societal values.

Thematically, concerns involving sexual propriety such as marital infidelity and the unwitting husband, or cuckold, received much comic attention on stage in European drama in the late Middle Ages. Niccolò Machiavelli (1469–1527) in his 1528 satire *The Mandrake* pokes fun at a gullible older husband who agrees to let another man bed his wife for convoluted fertility reasons. John Heywood (c. 1497–1580) in his 1533 play

Johan, Johan shows a henpecked husband as a farcical subject who finally manages to drive off his condescending wife and her lover, a priest, only to continue fretting about what they are doing while away from him. In Italian *commedia dell'arte*, or comedy of professional players, which reached its height in the period 1550–1650, this form of comedic improvisation with stock characters and stock plots frequently used cuckoldry as one of the main plot points to explore the follies of people and love.

In England in the Elizabethan era (1558–1603), when cross-casting young boys in female roles was the norm, William Shakespeare (1564–1616) explored themes of gender identity, mistaken and otherwise, in two plays written around 1600. In *As You Like It*, Rosalind is a girl (who would have been played by a boy) who disguises herself as a boy, Ganymede, who unwittingly attracts the love interest of a woman who believes that Rosalind is male; at the same time Rosalind (as Ganymede) plays the role of a girl in a mock wooing scene with her male love interest, Orlando. In *Twelfth Night, or What You Will* the protagonist, Viola (who also would have been played by a boy), spends the majority of the play disguised as a boy, Cesario, again attracting the unwanted affections of another female, Olivia, while Viola is in love with the Duke, who has accepted her in disguise as a trusted male confidant. Both plays are comedies, and so the mistaken identities ultimately are resolved and end in happy marriages.

Also benefiting from the prevalence of cross-casting were the troupes of young actors, or boy players as they were known. Consisting largely of boys between the ages of eight and twelve with prepubescent voices, the players often were educated in grammar, logic, and rhetoric; they were musically talented, and some spoke Latin. The most accomplished of them included Christopher Beeston (c. 1579–1638), who continued acting well into maturity and parlayed his knowledge of the theater into a career as a theater manager; Nathaniel Field (1587–1620), who was a favorite of the playwright Ben Jonson (1572–1637), penned his own plays, and was a member of the King's Men, the company to which Shakespeare belonged, which often played at the Royal Court; and Edward Kynaston (c. 1640–1712), who was one of the last prominent boy players and a main character in the 2004 film *Stage Beauty*.

During the Restoration period (1660–1700) Charles II reigned with a promiscuous enthusiasm that was reflected in brazenly sexual plays. One of the most notorious was *The Country Wife* (1675) by William Wycherley (c. 1640–1716), in which the protagonist, a licentious womanizer, convinces all the men in town that he is impotent, giving him access to all the married women, whom he proceeds to seduce. Also notable in that era was the introduction of professional actresses into theaters. Many productions took advantage of the novelty of having women on stage by casting them in "breeches roles," or roles in which actresses wore tightly fitting male clothes that outlined their figures and showed off their legs. Those roles were so successful in drawing an audience to the theater that they would be inserted gratuitously in revivals of older plays; among all the plays produced in London between 1660 and 1700, it has been estimated that nearly a quarter included a breeches role. Successful actresses of that era include the witty Nell Gwyn (1650–1687), who overcame illiteracy. She was one of Charles II's mistresses, bore him two sons, and said to her coachmen (who was fighting a man who had called her a whore), "I *am* a whore. Find something else to fight about." Elizabeth Barry (1658–1713) had a talent for tragic performance that is credited with popularizing "she-tragedy." Susanna Moutfort, also known as Susanna Verbruggen (c. 1667–1703), had many breeches roles created especially for her. The sexual liberation of the Restoration period also nurtured the career of Aphra Behn (1640–1689), one of the first successful woman playwrights.

THE MODERN ERA

In contrast to the morally carefree theater of the Restoration period, the modern realist movement in theater that began in the mid-nineteenth century was concerned with depicting brutal social truths; those plays often were met with popular resistance and controversy. When the Norwegian playwright Henrik Ibsen (1828–1906) attempted to stage *A Doll's House* (1879), in which a young wife leaves her husband and two children after realizing that her husband regards her as little more than a doll, some theaters refused to present the play unless the ending was changed. At theaters where Ibsen retained the original ending asserting a woman's right to individuality, critics attacked the work as unrealistic and incendiary, for what woman would dare leave her family in such an irresponsible manner? *A Doll's House*, which many consider the first true feminist play, was banned in England for a time. Despite resistance to his work, Ibsen continued to raise awareness for women's rights in plays such as *Ghosts* (1881), which dealt with venereal disease, incest, illegitimacy, and adultery through a protagonist who has suffered her husband's philandering only to find out that her son, who is dying of syphilis inherited from his father, wants to marry their maid, who is his half sister, a product of the husband's infidelity. This depiction of an individual who is victimized by her dutiful adherence to societal morals was equally difficult for critics and audiences to stomach. However, Ibsen found support among his artistic peers, such as the Irish playwright George Bernard Shaw (1856–1950), who was influenced by Ibsen's example to examine social concerns in his own work.

In *Mrs. Warren's Profession* (1893) Shaw, who spent most of his time in England, frankly portrayed (and condemned) the social circumstances that led women to prostitution. His matter-of-fact characterization of the protagonist as a working-class woman neither young nor beautiful and not enamored of finery or self-indulgence was a distinct departure from popular fallen woman narratives of the nineteenth century, as exemplified by Alexandre Dumas (1824–1895) in *La dame aux camélias* (*Camille*), in which a youthful pretty heroine who is full of love and life, fond of luxury, and financially and emotionally dependent on men faces an inevitable downfall, sacrifices herself for the sake of others, and dies tragically. In contrast, Shaw's title character enters prostitution and becomes an independent, prosperous business owner. This notion was so scandalous that *Mrs. Warren's Profession* was banned in England, and when it was publicly staged at a theater in New York in 1905, the house manager was arrested and warrants were issued for the cast and crew.

As a theatrical performer the American entertainer and playwright Mae West (1893–1980) presented a highly unconventional depiction of prostitution, which she parlayed into great success. In 1926 West staged *Sex*, casting herself as the heroine, a sexually charismatic entertainer and prostitute who is boldly unapologetic about her opportunistic aims. Unlike other Broadway plays of the 1920s featuring prostitutes as women who eventually met with ruin, West's characterization was that of a sassy, empowered female who took the lead in all her sexual relationships. Her sexual aggressiveness was criticized by the *New York Times*, which called *Sex* "crude and inept," and *Variety* described it as "nasty, infantile [and] amateurish." The show, however, was popular with audiences.

On February 9, 1927, after 350 performances, New York policemen raided the show. Along with the producers, the theater owner, and the cast, West was arrested for corrupting morals, sentenced to ten days in jail, and fined $500. She used the ensuing public attention to publicize the wrongs done to her and went on to stage more successful theatrical productions—*The Wicked Age* (1927), *Diamond Lil* (1928), *The Constant Sinner* (1931), and *Catherine Was Great* (1944)—all of which featured her as a prostitute or kept woman who takes wealthy men for lovers, only to cast them aside when a richer one comes along. An outspoken advocate of sex as a basic human rights issue, West was also a proponent of gay and transgender rights. She wrote *The Drag* (c. 1927) about homosexuality; it was banned from Broadway but was a box-office hit in New Jersey.

Geraldine Farrar as Madame Butterfly. *Famous opera singer Geraldine Farrar leans over a stage surrounded by flowers as she assumes her role of the submissive Madame Butterfly.* © CORBIS.

Contemporary theater has witnessed a great deal of identity reclaiming in the realms of sex and gender as well as a continued commitment to social issues. In the 1960s the Saudi Arabian playwright Ali Ahmed Bakthir wrote a play calling for the general education of Arab women. In 1975 the African-American playwright Ntozake Shange (b. 1948) wrote *For Colored Girls Who Have Considered Suicide/When the Rainbow Is Enuf: A Choreopoem*, which explored numerous aspects of black female identity via poetry, dance, and theater. In the same year the Nigerian playwright and Nobel recipient Wole Soyinka (b. 1934) penned *Death and the King's Horsemen*, calling attention to the sacrifices sons must make for their fathers, families, and society. *Care and Control* by Michelene Wandor (b. 1940), the first British play about the rights of lesbian mothers in custody battles, was staged in 1977. Eleven years later David Henry Hwang (b. 1957) reworked the stereotype of the submissive Asian female from Puccini's opera *Madame Butterfly* in *M. Butterfly*, recasting the passive, suicidal Japanese geisha as a cunning Beijing opera diva and spy who, unknown to his European lover and mark, is really a man. The year 1988 saw *The Heidi Chronicles* by Wendy Wasserstein (1950–2006), which reflects the evolution of feminism through the protagonist, Heidi Holland, who was regarded as embodying the new feminine feminist.

In the late 1980s and 1990s gay, lesbian, and bisexual solo performance artists were active in American theater as AIDS awareness and issues of queer rights emerged. In 1989 Michael Kearns (b. 1950), the first openly HIV-positive gay actor in Hollywood, wrote *Initimacies*, an award-winning multicharacter solo performance exploring the personal stories of HIV-positive individuals. The bisexual Japanese-American solo performance artist Denise Uyehara subverted many common Asian female and sexual stereotypes with *Hello (Sex) Kitty: Mad Asian Bitch on Wheels*. The queer solo performance artists Karen Finley (b. 1956), John Fleck (b. 1951), Holly Hughes (b. 1955), and Tim Miller (b. 1958), all recipients of a solo performer fellowship from the National Endowment for the Arts (NEA) in 1990, suddenly had their funding revoked when political pressure groups deemed their sexuality-focused and body-focused work inappropriate for federal funding. The "NEA 4," as they were dubbed by the media, took their case to the Supreme Court, which upheld the NEA's decision on the basis of general standards of decency, thus implying that those artists' work was indecent. The NEA then stopped funding individual artists.

BIBLIOGRAPHY

Anand, Mulk Raj. 1950. *The Indian Theatre*. London: D. Dobson.

Aston, Elaine. 1995. *An Introduction to Feminism and Theatre*. New York: Routledge.

Berthold, Margot. 1991. *The History of World Theater: From the Beginnings to the Baroque*. New York: Continuum.

Bieber, Margarete. 1961. *The History of Greek and Roman Theater*. 2nd edition. Princeton, NJ: Princeton University Press.

Brandon, James R. 1967. *Theatre in Southeast Asia*. Cambridge, MA: Harvard University Press.

Brewer, Mary F. 1999. *Race, Sex, and Gender in Contemporary Women's Theatre: The Construction of "Woman."* Portland, OR: Sussex Academic.

Brockett, Oscar Gross. 1979. *The Theatre: An Introduction*. New York: Holt, Rinehart, and Winston.

Brockett, Oscar Gross. 1987. *History of the Theatre*. Boston: Allyn and Bacon.

Chen, Jack. 1949. *The Chinese Theatre*. London: D. Dobson.

Ernst, Earle. 1974. *The Kabuki Theatre*. Honolulu: University Press of Hawaii.

Flores, Yolanda. 2000. *The Drama of Gender: Feminist Theater by Women of the Americas*. New York: P. Lang.

Freedley, George, and John A. Reeves. 1968. *A History of the Theatre*. 3rd edition. New York: Crown.

Gascoigne, Bambier. 1968. *World Theatre: An Illustrated History*. Boston: Little, Brown.

Hartnoll, Phyllis. 1985. *The Theatre: A Concise History*. New York: Thames and Hudson.

Harrison, Paul Carter; Victor Leo Walker II; and Gus Edwards, eds. 2002. *Black Theatre: Ritual Performance in the African Diaspora*. Philadelphia: Temple University Press.

Hill, Errol G., and James V. Hatch. 2003. *A History of African American Theatre*. Cambridge, UK: Cambridge University Press.

Kirby, Ernest Theodore. 1975. *Ur-Drama: The Origins of Theatre*. New York: New York University Press.

Pullen, Kristen. 2005. *Actresses and Whores: On Stage and in Society*. Cambridge, UK: Cambridge University Press.

Wickham, Glynne. 1985. *A History of the Theatre*. New York: Cambridge University Press.

Zelenak, Michael X. 1998. *Gender and Politics in Greek Tragedy*. Vol. 7 of *Artists and Issues in the Theatre*, ed. August W. Staub. New York: P. Lang.

Lan Tran

ARTEMIS DIANA

The Greek goddess Artemis, the daughter of Zeus and Leto and twin sister of Apollo, was a strict virgin without any male lover and any offspring; she was typically in the company of the nymphs, young women of nubile age. Images represent her as a young woman, often a hunter in short dress and with bow and quiver, sometimes accompanied by a stag. Her counterpart in Roman myth was Diana.

In Greek and, by extension, Roman cult, Artemis had multiple and widely varying functions, most clearly gendered. Their common denominator was her protection of human activities in marginal space and time.

SPACE FUNCTIONS

In space, Artemis oversaw the uncultivated area outside the city and the cultivated land that is the space of transition between individual cities. Here, hunting, traveling, and warfare were the dominant human activities. Artemis protected hunters and presided over their prey, the wild animals; as such, she was closely connected with deer, especially the stag, and acted as "Mistress of Animals," the divine protector of wild animals.

From the Neolithic epoch onward, hunting was an exclusively male occupation, one whose performance excluded any sexual interest or activity: Sexuality belonged to the secluded space of the city and its houses. Several myths tell about the disastrous consequences of disregarding this separation. In the myth of the Calydonian hunt, the female hunter Atalanta provoked the love of Meleager, who forgot the rules of hunting and was subsequently killed by his mother. Whereas this story warns against importing sexuality into the realm of Artemis, the myth of Hippolytus

Marble Statue of Artemis. THE ART ARCHIVE/EPHESUS MUSEUM TURKEY/DAGLI ORTI.

warns against extending Artemis's realm into the city: The young hunter Hippolytus worshiped only Artemis and refused sexuality; Aphrodite, the goddess of erotic love, punished him by making his stepmother Phaedra fall in love with him, which caused his death through his father's curse.

Warfare is closely connected with hunting and as defense of the city's borders with the uncultivated surrounding spaces; Artemis Agrotera ("the Wild One") received regular sacrifices before a battle. In a few cases, the goddess also acted as a protector of cities under siege. At some point in time, she also was identified with Selene, the moon goddess, paralleling her brother Apollo's identification with Helios, the sun god.

SOCIAL FUNCTIONS

A major area of Artemis's concern was the life of adolescent humans of both genders; she presided over this socially all-important transition from childhood to adulthood, to the roles of citizen, husbands, and warriors, and of childbearing wives, respectively. Many relevant cults took place in a sanctuary outside the cultivated area of the city and its fields: This combines spatial and temporal liminality and transition.

With respect to young men, two cults should be singled out. One is the festival of Artemis Tauropolos in Halae Araphenides on the east coast of Attica. During its rites, a young man received a small knife cut in his throat to draw blood, an action meant to incarnate Orestes being sacrificed to the savage Artemis of the Taurians (north shore of the Black Sea). This Artemis had the epithet Tauropolos, literally "steer herder," because the male adolescents were designated as young steers; this meaning, however, got lost early, and later Greeks understood the name as referring to the Taurians (Euripides, *Iphigenia in Tauris*).

The other cult is the annual ritual in the sanctuary of Artemis Orthia in Sparta. In its older form, it was a contest between two groups of young men, one trying to steal cheese from the altar, the other fiercely defending the altar. Later, it was turned into the annual flogging of young men, until they bled. The priestess of Artemis carried the goddess's small image, which signaled by its weight whether the flogging was hard enough. As was the case with the Artemis Taurpolos cult, the Spartan rite was understood to replace an original human sacrifice. It was famous throughout later antiquity and even attracted Roman tourists.

For girls and young women, Artemis guarded two passages, the entry into adolescence (becoming a *párthenos*) and the final passage to childbearing womanhood (becoming a *gunē*). At the age of about ten, girls retired for some time to a sanctuary outside the city where they danced or even performed athletic contests, as in the case of Brauron on the east coast of Attica where vase paintings show footraces of naked girls. When marrying, they dedicated the toys of their childhood, such as balls or dolls, in a shrine of Artemis. The goddess also helped with childbirth (often under the title of Lochia, "Lady of Birth"). A myth told how Artemis, born a day before her brother Apollo, helped her mother Leto give birth to him. Her shrine in Brauron received the garments of women who had died in childbirth; in other shrines, women dedicated garments to Artemis to thank her for safe delivery and in the hope of further births.

ANATOLIAN CULTS

A few Anatolian cults of Artemis are somewhat different from the above, most conspicuously the cult of Artemis in Ephesus. In the latter, Artemis combines aspects of the Anatolian Mountain Mother with her pan-Greek image. The famous many-breasted statue of Ephesian Artemis reproduces an archaic Near Eastern statue type. Already antiquity regarded her as many-breasted (*multimamma*);

modern scholars agree that they are not breasts, but disagree as to what they are.

ROMAN DIANA

Roman Diana shared mythology, iconography, and many cult details with Artemis, although Diana played no role as protector of young males, a role given mostly to Juno or Minerva. Diana's role as moon goddess, however, was more prominent in Rome and might be original. Like Artemis, Diana was regarded as protector of women and as protector of hunters whose dedications she received; animal heads could be suspended in her sanctuaries as a trophy, and a very important shrine was in a grove in the forests around Lake Nemi (Diana *Nemorensis,* "She of the Grove"). Unlike Artemis, however, she also played an important political role: Her sanctuary on the Aventine in Rome was the center of an age-old alliance of Latin cities under Rome's leadership. In Christian belief, she became the demon of witchcraft because she shared, as goddess of wilderness and transitions, traits with the goddess Hecate; as such, she is still worshipped among contemporary Wiccas and neopagans.

SEE ALSO *Anahita.*

BIBLIOGRAPHY

"Artemis" and "Diana." 1996. In *The Oxford Classical Dictionary,* ed. Simon Hornblower and Antony Spawforth. 3rd edition. Oxford: Oxford University Press.

Burkert, Walter. 1985. *Greek Religion: Archaic and Classical.* Oxford: Blackwell.

Ginzburg, Carlo. 1991. *Ecstasies: Deciphering the Witches' Sabbath,* trans. Raymond Rosenthal. New York: Pantheon Books.

Fritz Graf

ARTIFICIAL INSEMINATION

Artificial insemination refers to the techniques of fertilization employed for reproductive purposes by means other than sexual intercourse. Artificial insemination began in the 1700s and in most cases was used for livestock reproduction. The first attempt at human artificial insemination took place in 1780, when the Scottish surgeon John Hunter impregnated a woman by transferring semen from husband to wife with a syringe. Later attempts were relatively unsuccessful until the 1940s because little was known about the female reproductive cycle. Not until 1936 did the scientist C. G. Hartman determine that the menstrual cycle of a female is approximately twenty-eight days, with the most fertile period occurring eleven to fourteen days after the first day of the cycle. That knowledge greatly increased the odds of fertilization, and by 1955 approximately 55,000 women had become pregnant through artificial insemination despite the fact that the practice was condemned by religious institutions as unnatural and immoral.

THE FOUR TYPES OF ARTIFICIAL INSEMINATION

Artificial insemination (AI), or assisted reproductive technologies (ART), continues to become more sophisticated. By 2006 artificial insemination took the form of four medical procedures, with each progressing to a more invasive form: intravaginal (in the vagina), intracervical (in the cervical canal), intrauterine (in the uterine cavity), and intratubal (in the fallopian tubes).

Intravaginal insemination (IVI) is the least invasive artificial insemination technique although it is not often performed in fertility clinics due to the ease of performing the technique at home. Semen is placed directly into the vagina using a sterile syringe. There it enters the cervical opening, traveling through the cervix, uterine tract, and fallopian tubes to the egg waiting for fertilization, replicating to a certain degree the process that occurs during sexual intercourse. IVI is most often used in cases where women choose to become pregnant using donated sperm, or in cases where the male partner is not able to sexually perform.

Although not the least intrusive method, intrauterine insemination (IUI) usually is considered the most common method because of its success rate. This procedure bypasses the cervical opening by using a surgical catheter and places the sperm directly into the uterine tract to increase the chances that the sperm will reach the egg (ovum) and achieve fertilization. Six attempts may be required for fertilization to take place.

Intracervical insemination (ICI) is another common procedure for artificial insemination. Sperm is placed directly into the cervix to increase the chance that the sperm reaches the ovum. This technique is most successful when there is no underlying medical issue contributing to infertility in the woman. Those using sperm donors in the absence of or due to a fertitlity problem in the male partner often utilize ICI. This procedure is painless and non-invasive.

Intratubal insemination (ITI) places sperm directly into the fallopian tubes in order to increase the chance the sperm reaches the ovum. ITI is the least performed artificial insemination technique due to the level of invasiveness and expense. It is performed either through the insertion of a surgical catheter through the vagina, cervix, and uterine tract into the fallopian tubes, or through a laparoscopic procedure where an incision is made in the abdomen and guided by a surgical camera to allow the surgeon to insert the sperm directly into the fallopian tubes. This procedure is more painful than IUI or ICI and is most often recommended after IUI or ICI have failed.

IN VITRO FERTILIZATION (IVF)

If artificial insemination procedures are unsuccessful, in vitro fertilization (IVF) is usually the next step. In vitro means "in the lab," and babies conceived by this means have been commonly referred to as "test tube babies." IVF is most often used in conjunction with fertility drugs to produce multiple mature eggs during ovulation. These eggs are then surgically removed from the ovaries and fertilized with sperm from the male partner/donor in a petri dish. When embryos are produced, the embryos are surgically implanted into the uterus of the female in hopes that at least one of the embryos will remain viable and produce a child. Most often embryos are cultured three to five days before being implanted. While IVF is one of the most utilized of procedures, it is also the most controversial.

With each IVF procedure, multiple embryos are produced while only two to five embryos are implanted in the uterus. Often couples will preserve a few extra embryos in case they choose to expand their family at a later date. Additional embryos either become the property of the clinic where the IVF procedure was performed, are destroyed or donated to other infertile couples. Religious leaders, ethicists, and some science communities view the destruction of embryos as the destruction of a living human being, often equating the act as equivalent to abortion, or more extreme, as genocide. As property, embryos are often used for genetic and stem cell research, which brings up ethical issues around the preservation of human life as well as issues surrounding the selection of desired characteristics and the elimination of others through genetic modification methods currently being researched using these embryos. These issues also extend to the couples using IVF.

While the hope is that the couple undergoing IVF will have at least one embryo implant and develop into a full pregnancy, with better retrieval, culturing, and transfer techniques, many couples are confronted with multiple embryos implanting and developing. Couples are confronted with having to choose between having multiple births or selecting certain embryos/fetuses to abort and determining the criteria by which to eliminate. Many factors weigh in on these decisions including religious, political, economic, and social pressures.

ETHICAL ISSUES

When artificial insemination became a medical practice in the 1940s, controversy arose over the fact that the act of fertilization occurred outside the act of coitus. The use of donor semen (artificial insemination donor) was deemed a form of adultery and any offspring resulting from the procedure were considered illegitimate despite its use solely in cases of a husband's infertility, with written consent from both the husband and the wife. One way of bypassing this condemnation was by mixing the sperm of the husband with that of the donor in an artificial insemination center (AIC) so that the paternity of the offspring was uncertain.

State court cases began surfacing in 1964 when Georgia became the first state to declare a child legitimate if the husband gave written consent. In 1968 *People* v. *Sorensen* held that a man who had been convicted for not supporting a child conceived with his consent through donor insemination was legally obligated to support the child, relieving the donor of any financial responsibility. In 1973 the American Bar Association adopted the Uniform Parentage Act, which viewed the woman's husband as the natural father of a child conceived with donor insemination if the husband consented and if it was done under the supervision of a physician. The use of donor sperm in unmarried women did not occur until the 1970s.

The women's liberation movement of the 1970s ushered in a new wave of women's independence. As women started to question and challenge the roles and expectations of their sex, many women began to redefine what it means to be a woman. Unmarried women who desired children but not the marriage that traditionally preceded it, as well as lesbian couples, sometimes resorted to a home-based method of artificial insemination. Using a turkey baster or a syringe with a donor's semen, women would impregnate themselves. By the late 1970s sperm banks allowed unmarried women to receive sperm from an unknown donor.

LEGAL ISSUES

Although purchasing sperm remains a relatively easy task, finding a specialist to perform the insemination is more difficult. The decision whether to inseminate an unmarried woman, regardless of her sexual orientation, resides with the individual physician. Physicians in private practice have the right to refuse to serve any individual. The right to refuse under the Hyde-Weldon Amendment signed unto law under the 2005 Omnibus Appropriations Bill (HR 4818) extends the "conscience clause" to apply to any public health entity from health management organizations to individuals working for a public health service to refuse to perform services such as birth control, abortion, eugenics, and infertility services on the basis of religious or moral objections. The attention given to this clause has been focused mainly on birth control and abortion, but the clause also affects the ability of unmarried and nonheterosexual people to receive insemination services. These obstacles can be circumvented through home-based artificial insemination, but the complex legal issues that surface in cases of nontraditional insemination are becoming more politically charged.

Same-sex parenting and adoption, surrogate rights as well as the rights of a couple using a surrogate, legal protection of known donors, and the rights of offspring to receive donor identity are issues that have begun to surface in the courts and vary from state to state. For example, in a 2002 Pennsylvania case, *Ferguson* v. *McKiernan*, which was granted an appeal by the Pennsylvania Supreme Court in 2005, the lower court found McKiernan responsible for the support of two children he had fathered through donor insemination. The courts decided that the "rights" of an interested third party (the children) cannot be "bargained away" even if the third-party interests are not present at the time the contract is made. The ramifications of this ruling could extend to sperm bank donors as well as known donors and surrogates. A donor's right to anonymity also has been challenged; in 2006 only eight states recognized the parental rights of a nonbiological parent besides the stepparent in a heterosexual marriage, granting sole custodial rights to the biological parent or, in the case of the death or disability of that parent, to a family member of the biological parent rather than the same-sex partner even if the children were conceived as a couple. The relative ease of artificial insemination has created complex social issues that have begun to surface in public debate.

BIBLIOGRAPHY

Carbone, June. 2005. "The Legal Definition of Parenthood: Uncertainty at the Core of Family Identity." *Louisiana Law Review* 65: 1295–1334.

Fader, Sonia. 1993. *Sperm Banking: A Reproductive Resource.* Available from http://www.crybank.com.

Human Rights Campaign. "Donor Insemination Laws: State by State." Available from http://www.hrc.org.

Shapo, Helene S. 2006. "Assisted Reproduction and the Law: Disharmony on a Divisive Social Issue." *Northwestern University Law Review* 100(1): 465–497.

Regina M. Salmi

ARTISTS, WOMEN

There are far fewer well-known women artists than there are male artists throughout history. This is partly because women artists were often overlooked or their works were attributed to male teachers or relatives. It is also because, women have, for various reasons, been prevented from pursuing and developing the sustained careers by which artists gain reputation. Most women lacked the financial and social independence to develop artistic skills. They rarely had access to training either because training was considered to be inappropriate for females, or they had neither the money nor the freedom to take advantage of opportunities to work with and learn from established painters and sculptors. Marriage and childbearing often interrupted artistic careers, preventing women from spending time producing works of art. Women were also not educated in math and science, areas deemed necessary for successful careers in art.

Many women who did have careers as artists were often the relatives of male artists and thus could learn artistic skills in the household. When women did have the opportunity to produce art, their work was often fragile and portable—miniatures and manuscript illuminations—and did not survive or was not considered to be the substance of truly fine artistic expression. Because female artists could not paint from nude male models, the subject matter of women's paintings was often portraits and still lives instead of the more admired historical or religious painting by which fine art was defined. Even with great skill and mastery, women's art simply did not comply with what the art world deemed important. Only since the mid-1990s have women been popularly recognized for their work, a shift enabled by liberalized attitudes about women as well as changes in ideas about what art is.

RISE OF WOMEN ARTISTS: FROM THE RENAISSANCE TO THE NINETEENTH CENTURY

There have always been women artists, though few from ancient history are remembered. Women artists are described working in ancient Greece, and a few women are noted through the Middle Ages. The first women to emerge as artists with reputations and works that have survived came from renaissance Italy in the sixteenth century. The increased emphasis on the individual produced by renaissance ideas about art and education shifted the focus of painting from religious scenes to portraiture, where women excelled. Baldassare Castiglione's influential book, *The Courtier* (1528), which argued for the more complete education of upper-class women, made it socially acceptable, if not necessary, to train such women in drawing. Several female portraitists emerged from the Italian Renaissance, including Sofonisba Anguissola (c. 1532–1625), Lavinia Fontana (1552–1614), and Fede Galizia (c. 1578–1630). There was also a women sculptor, Properzia de' Rossi (c. 1490–1530). Fontana became an official painter in the papal court of Pope Clement VIII and was elected to the Roman Academy of Arts. Following the Italians, the northern center of the Renaissance, Holland, also yielded a few women painters, including Caterina van Hemessen (1528–c. 1587) and miniaturist Lavina Teerlinc (c. 1520–1576).

In the seventeenth and eighteenth centuries, women artists benefited from the increased interest in still life painting and portraits. Italy and Holland still dominated artistic production during the baroque era. In Italy painters Artemesia Gentileschi (1593–c. 1652), a follower of Michelangelo Merisi (known as Caravaggio), painted large-scale religious scenes, and Elisabetta Sirani (1638–1665) painted large portraits and historical scenes. Several women specialized in paintings of natural history, including the Italian painter Giovanna Garzoni (1600–1670) and Swiss watercolorist Sibylla Merian (1647–1717). In France Louise Moillon (1610–1696) was renowned for still lives of fruit; in the Netherlands Rachel Ruysch (1664–1750) and Maria van Oosterwyck (1630–1693) painted still lives of food and flowers and Judith Leyster (1609–1660) painted portraits. In the eighteenth century, the policies of art academies became more restrictive, limiting the number of female members. Nonetheless women artists persisted as renowned portraitists, including Italian Rosalba Carriera (1675–1757) and Angelica Kauffman (1741–1807) from Switzerland, and French artists Elisabeth Vigée-Lebrun (1755–1842), famous for her portraits of Marie Antoinette; Adélaïde Labille-Guiard (1749–1803); Françoise Duparc (1726–1778); and painter Jean-Honoré Fragonard's sister-in law, Marguerite Gérard (1761–1837).

THE IMPORTANCE OF WOMEN ARTISTS INTO THE TWENTIETH CENTURY

Women's increasing independence and education in the nineteenth and twentieth centuries allowed more women to pursue careers as artists, though the gender biases of European and North American culture still did not deem such art to be sophisticated or important. Although the genres of painting—the kinds of topics seen as acceptable subjects for painting—expanded, permitting more women to be taken seriously as artists, they still lacked access to studios and art education in general. Women were barred from membership in the British Academy of Arts. English and American art became more prominent in the nineteenth century and the advent of Impressionism in the 1870s spurred some women artists to experiment with new painting styles. However, as before, most women who pursued careers in art were the daughters of wealthy families who often had connections with male artists. The expansion of acceptable painting subjects facilitated recognition of such English painters as Sophie Anderson (1823–c. 1898) and Emily Marie Osborn (1834–c. 1893), as well as American painters Lilly Martin Spencer (1822–1902) and Margaretta Angelica Peale (1795–1882), and French painters Marie-Eléonore Godefroid (1778–1849) and Rosa Bonheur (1822-1899). There were more women sculptors in the nineteenth century as well, including Americans Anne Whitney (1821–1915), Harriet Hosmer (1830–1908), Edmonia Lewis (c. 1844–c. 1911), and Gertrude Vanderbilt Whitney (1875–1942); French sculptor Camille Claudel (1864–1943); and German sculptor Elisabet Ney (1833–1907).

Impressionism, a style of painting interested in conveying the impression of light and atmosphere, moved painting away from photographic realism to brighter, more dynamic scenes of figures and landscapes. French painter Berthe Morisot (1841–1895) and American Mary Cassatt (1844–1926) were both part of the core group of painters who formulated and developed Impressionism. Another French painter, Eva Gonzalez (1849–1883), a close friend of Edouard Manet, also participated in the move away from a more somber realistic style. Impressionism influenced other painters, especially American painters Lilla Cabot Perry (1848–1933), Helen Turner (1858–1958), and Cecilia Beaux (1855–1942).

In the early twentieth century rapid advances in science and technology permitted more women to travel, gain educations, and work in studio settings. As with Impressionism, the various avant-garde art movements of the twentieth century included women as members of their founding coterie. In the first part of the twentieth century, Paris was still the center of artistic activity, and women as well as men traveled to Paris to explore the most innovative ideas about art. Painting and sculpture had begun to move away from realistic representations to the more abstract styles of Fauvism (a short-lived painting movement whose adherents used bright, violent colors, simple direct lines, and dramatic energy) and Expressionism (the expression of emotions through the use of color and line). French painter Suzanne Valadon (1865–1938) was influenced by both Fauvism and Expressionism, using a wide and brilliant palette as well as more abstracted figures in her paintings. Sonia Terk Delaunay (1885–1979) developed her own form of abstract painting as did another Russian émigré, Natalya Goncharova (1881–1962). Swiss multimedia abstractionist Sophie Taeuber-Arp (1889–1943) was a member of the Dada movement (an anti-art art movement that ridiculed bourgeois art production); the Surrealists (artists who depicted dreamlike irrational, but often realistically painted, images) included American Kay Sage (1898–1963) and Spanish painter Remedios Varo (1913–1963). German painter and sculptor Käthe Kollwitz (1867–1945) produced sociopolitical commentaries on the human condition, while Vanessa Bell (1879–1961), English writer

Virginia Woolf's sister, and Romaine Brooks (1874–1970) painted portraits and scenes influenced by post-Impressionist simplicity.

In the United States Georgia O'Keeffe (1887–1986) set out to discern her own style of painting, producing stark, simple, yet striking minimalist or abstract images. Lois Mailou Jones (1905–1998) pursued an abstract painting style that included images familiar to African-American populations. Irene Rice Pereira (1907–1971) produced abstract paintings; Mexican painter Frida Kahlo (1907–1954) developed her own style of painting that reflected the colors and images of Mexico.

WOMEN ARTISTS INTO THE TWENTY-FIRST CENTURY

Since the middle of the twentieth century, women artists have become increasingly prominent, not only because the means of artistic production has become more universally available, but also because feminist movements encouraged women's art and provided a market for it. Abstract expressionism (painting as an assertion of the individual through abstract images) had several accomplished American female practitioners, including Helen Frankenthaler (b. 1928) and Lee Krasner (1908–1984). Other women artists sought to define their own styles. Portraitist Alice Neel (1900–1984) painted frank, unromanticized portraits; Elaine de Kooning (1918–1989) and Joan Mitchell (1926–1992) developed their own abstract styles. British painter Bridget Riley (b. 1931) developed a form of Op (or Optical) Art, and Judy Chicago (b. 1939) worked through paint, ceramics, and embroidery to create group projects on feminist themes.

Women sculptors also flourished in the twentieth century, adopting the abstract and simple forms of painting. Becoming as interested in pure form in sculpture as they were in abstract painting such sculptors as the Russian expatriate Louise Nevelson (1899–1988), British sculptor Barbara Hepworth (1903–1975), and French sculptor Louise Bourgeois (b. 1911) began the move toward less representational sculpture using a wide variety of materials. The evolution of sculpture continued with American Dorothy Dehner (1901–1994), the French Venezuelan Marisol (b. 1930), Chryssa (b. 1931), and the French Niki de Saint Phalle (1930–2002), whose work moved toward installation art, which became prominent in the 1970s.

In the early twenty-first century women are recognized as prominent installation artists as well as photographers and multimedia specialists. Much of this art involves social commentary and invites viewer involvement. Installation artists set up multimedia displays in a variety of spaces. Using photography, sculpture, painting, text, and everyday objects, these installations typically render wry commentary on commodities, gender roles, social class, commercialization, power and oppression, and art itself. Installation artists include Americans Eleanor Antin (b. 1935), Jenny Holzer (b. 1950), Barbara Kruger (b. 1945), French artist Annette Messager (b. 1943), the Germans Rebecca Horn (b. 1944) and Kiki Smith (b. 1954), Palestinian Mouna Hatoum (b. 1952), and Brazilian sculptor Jac Leirner (b. 1961). Performance art, related to installation art, includes live performance, sound effects, text, and other multimedia components. Prominent American performance artists are Laurie Anderson (b. 1947) and Kathy Rose (b. 1949).

Other women artists continue to work in more traditional media, including still life painters Americans Audrey Flack (b. 1931) and Janet Fish (b. 1938), and

"Crucifixion," Sculpture by Niki de Saint-Phalle, 1963. *Mixed media, woman, her upper torso made from faux flowers and discarded toys, wearing rollers in her hair, pink garter belt, yarn and dolls with out-reached arms, patchwork girdle, black chantilly lace stockings, black heels, merkin made from tangled yarn painted black.* MUSEE NATIONAL D'ART, GIRAUDON/ART RESOURCE, NY.

abstract painters Elizabeth Murray (b. 1940), Susan Rothenberg (b. 1945), and Mandy Martin (b. 1952). Catalan Sculptor Susana Solano (b. 1946) creates art out of everyday objects. American photographers Cindy Sherman (b. 1954) and Sandy Skogland (b. 1946) produce staged photographic portraits and events that comment both on the art of photography and the political and gendered slant of images. Other women artists, such as American Howardena Pindell (b. 1943), concentrate on collage.

Although women artists in the early twenty-first century are still not considered innovators by many in the hierarchy of art criticism, their work is gaining attention and critical acclaim. Observers recognize their work not only as expert and insightful, but as an entirely new expression of the human experience, important in its vision.

BIBLIOGRAPHY

Broude, Norma, and Mary Garrard, eds. 1994. *The Power of Feminist Art: The American Movement of the 1970s, History and Impact.* New York: H. N. Abrams.

Chadwick, Whitney. 2002. *Women, Art, and Society.* 3rd edition. New York: Thames and Hudson.

Grosenick, Uta. 2003. *Women Artists (Icons).* New York: Taschen.

Heller, Nancy G. 2003. *Women Artists: An Illustrated History.* 4th edition. New York: Abbeville Press.

Slatkin, Wendy. 2001. *Women Artists in History: From Antiquity to the Present.* 4th edition. New York: Prentice Hall.

Judith Roof

ASEXUALITY

The definition of the term *asexuality* depends on what one means by the term *sex*. One definition of sex is the physical differentiation between males and females. Therefore, to be biologically asexual an individual must lack either male or female reproductive organs and perhaps the corresponding secondary characteristics, such as breasts or facial hair. In this sense, *asexual* may be distinguished from *androgynous*, which can mean having neither set of sexual characteristics or having a mixture of both. However, asexual also has come to mean having a greatly diminished libido or even a lack of desire for sex. It is in this social rather than morphological sense that asexuality became a popular subject of discussion in the popular media in the first decade of the twenty-first century.

Asexuality is not synonymous with celibacy or chastity. Celibate people abstain from sexual activity for a variety of reasons, whereas chaste people refrain from religiously proscribed sexual activity (outside of marriage, for instance). In neither case is desire for sex in question. In fact, the celibate and the chaste are subjects of interest and reverence precisely because they are engaged, or are imagined to be engaged, in an internal battle with normal or even rampant sexual desire. For the asexual, the obverse is the case. Although asexuals may engage in sexual activity, perhaps including autoerotic stimulation, and may even have children, they do not desire sex with the intensity or frequency of sexual persons. That is, celibacy and chastity describe acts and choices, whereas asexuality describes desire or, rather, indifference. It is important to note that lack of interest in sex does not mean a lack of romantic involvement or amorous feelings, which may be directed toward members of the same sex, the opposite sex, or both. Thus one can speak of gay, straight, and bisexual asexuals.

Some research suggests that asexuality is rare, occurring in perhaps one percent of the adult population (Bogaert 2004). Until recently, social asexuality generally was seen as a disorder with either a psychological or a biochemical etiology: a past trauma such as abuse or a hormonal disorder, for instance. Medically, for asexuality to be seen as a disorder, either the asexual person or his or her partner must find the lack of desire a problem or must find that it marks a loss of normal desire. The logical consequence for these requirements, some people reason, is that if the persons in question do not see a problem and if there has been no loss of sexual desire, such asexuality is not a disorder but a sexual orientation like heterosexuality or homosexuality and should be respected as such. Far from being a programmatic rejection of human sexuality or a reaction to recent sexual revolutions, asexuality has simply become more visible in contemporary cultural and political environments.

SEE ALSO *Celibacy.*

BIBLIOGRAPHY

Asexuality Visibility and Education Network. Available from http://www.asexuality.org.

Bogaert, Anthony F. 2004. "Asexuality: Prevalence and Associated Factors in a National Probability Sample." *Journal of Sex Research* 41(3): 279–287.

Westphal, Sylvia Pagan. 2004. "Glad to be asexual." *New Scientist.* October 14. Available from http://www.newscientist.com.

Erick Kelemen

ASHERAH

SEE *Judaism.*

Athena on Amohora. *An amphora featuring the goddess Athena.* THE ART ARCHIVE/MUSEO NAZID TARANTO/DAGLI ORTI.

ATHENA

One of several virgin goddesses in ancient Greek religion, Athena was nonetheless most frequently associated with males. Already at her extraordinary birth from the head of her father Zeus (who swallowed his pregnant consort Metis, or wise counsel), she assumed a military aspect that would be her most identifiable iconographic feature. Although in physique and dress a female, her image bristles with masculine attributes: shield, spear, helmet, and the protective aegis given to her by Zeus, onto which she later attached the fearsome head of the gorgon Medusa. In literature as well as art she is often at the side of heroes (e.g., Odysseus, Hercules, Theseus, Jason) as an adviser and goddess of warfare. In Aeschylus's play *Eumenides*, she states: "There is no mother anywhere who gave me birth and, but for marriage, I am always for the male with all my heart, and strongly on my father's side." Athena made her first appearance in the Bronze Age as a goddess of the citadel, and she continued as the guardian of high places such as the Athenian Acropolis or the Capitoline in Rome (as Minerva). Later she is often depicted fighting alongside her father and the hero Hercules, fending off the mighty giants who threatened to take control from the Olympians. Because of her strong allegiance to males, namely her father and most mythological heroes, Athena was always a popular deity in the patriarchal, male-dominated world of ancient Greece.

Although her first loyalty was to men, Athena also had numerous female associations. Her reputation for technical skill (*sophia*) derived not only from warfare but also from handicrafts, as in her contest with the weaver Arachne. At the Panathenaia, her chief festival in Athens, her cult statue was presented with a new robe, or *peplos*, specially woven by select girls and women of the city. As tutelary goddess of the city she was associated with its small owls (one of her epithets is "owl-eyed") and the olive tree, her winning gift to the city in a contest with the sea god Poseidon. Although steadfastly a virgin, Athena served a maternal role in the rearing of the earth-born Athenian king Erichthonius, who was the result of her attempted rape by the smith god Hephaestus. In one temple in Athens, the Hephaesteum, they were jointly worshiped as patron deities of craftsmanship.

Not without Near Eastern and Indo-European parallels, Athena has affinities with the Egyptian goddess Neith and the Indian war goddess Durgā. After antiquity she has lived on in images of armed females such as the personifications of Roma and Britannia. In modern psychology as formulated by Sigmund Freud, the gorgon head on Athena's aegis was intended to make her unapproachable and to repel all sexual desires. Combining as she does the characteristics of the male world (rationality, wisdom) with those of the female realm (creativity, practicality), Athena is a goddess of polarities, a complex figure of female power and authority.

BIBLIOGRAPHY

Deacy, Susan, and Alexandra Villing, eds. 2001. *Athena in the Classical World.* Leiden, Netherlands: Brill.

Kerényi, Karl. 1978. *Athene: Virgin and Mother in Greek Religion*, trans. Murray Stein. Dallas: Spring Publications.

Neils, Jenifer, ed. 1996. *Worshipping Athena: Panathenaia and Parthenon.* Madison: University of Wisconsin Press.

Jenifer Neils

ATOSSA

SEE *Queens.*

AUTOMOBILES

The introduction of the gasoline-powered automobile at the end of the nineteenth century provided a mobile platform for sexual adventure and a focal point for the development of a new kind of sex culture. Although courtship already involved forms of transportation—romantic walks, buggy rides, bicycles built for two, and train trips—the automobile offered a new kind of mobility, separation, and privacy to couples who wanted to take romance beyond hand holding, dancing, and perhaps the chaste kiss that once constituted publicly acceptable courtship behaviors. In addition, automobiles are both sexy and symbols of sexuality in the increasingly technological culture of the last hundred years.

EARLY AUTOMOBILES

It took a few years for the automobile to evolve from a barely motorized buggy owned by a wealthy few to a widely affordable mode of transportation. Although versions of the automobile were introduced in Europe and the United States in the 1890s, it was only through Henry Ford's innovations in mass production that the automobile became widely available to working-class families. The first "surrey" cars in the 1890s lacked tops and had high benchlike seats that were hard and uncomfortable. By adding tops and then windows and heaters, car manufacturers moved toward a more comfortable and impervious interior space with bigger, longer, and more padded seats and upholstered doors. By the 1920s enclosed cars whose interiors could be used as mobile beds were being fitted with running boards and fenders that also served as sites for sexual encounters. Some cars came with matching tents or removable seats that made them ideal for camping, transport of goods and people, or sexual activity. By 1927 more than 15 million Model T Fords had been sold.

AUTOMOBILES AS SITES FOR SEXUAL ENCOUNTERS

As automobiles became more enclosed, blocking passengers from prying eyes and weather, they also become increasingly convenient sites for sexual behavior. As more people could afford to purchase automobiles, cars become increasingly available to younger people as vehicles for dating. Because most young people lived with their parents until marriage, romance was limited to what was publicly permissible. The mobility of the automobile, however, enabled new possibilities for sexual encounters, permitting couples to go where they wanted, providing a new site for sexual encounters away from public places such as the parks, church socials, porches, and living rooms that had previously given courting couples opportunities to get to know one another. Couples could move around together, going from social venues, such as a drive-in restaurant, where they could eat alone together with other automotive couples, to lovers' lanes and other parking spots, where the privacy of darkness and the solitude of the closed car permitted explorations away from the eyes of family members and neighbors.

During the first thirty years of the automobile, roadside culture also evolved to accommodate the automobile and its touring passengers. As automobiles became more numerous and reliable, more people began taking road trips and needed places to stay along the road because a tent was not everyone's idea of desirable accommodations. Roads, which had been poorly built, began to improve to accommodate automobile traffic. Food and lodging industries developed specifically for the needs of the automobile tourist, who often found it inconvenient to park in the environs of midcity hotels. Motor courts and motels emerged along popular automobiling routes and provided another trysting place designed specifically for vehicular access. Although most motor courts provided lodging for travelers, some quickly saw the benefits of hosting the sexually adventurous, renting rooms by the hour and asking few questions.

LEGAL REACTIONS

The increased opportunity for sexual behavior was not without detractors. Lawmakers began defining the kinds of activities permissible in automobiles. Although most lovers' lane activities were tolerated or, at worst, lovers were shooed away by the police, some municipalities passed laws against various degrees of sexual activity in cars, including kissing and masturbating while watching other people have sex in cars. In Clinton, Oklahoma, such self-servicing activities were banned in drive-in movie theaters. Chicago enacted a series of statutes, including one that made the car a "public place," which, taken together, essentially outlawed making love in cars. In Carlsbad, New Mexico, couples having sex in a parked vehicle during lunch hour had to have the curtains drawn. If couples having sex in parked cars in Liberty Corner, New Jersey, accidentally blew the horn, they could be put in jail. In Detroit car sex was banned unless the car was parked on the participants' own property. In Coeur d'Alene, Idaho, police officers who suspected that a car's occupants were engaged in sexual activity had to honk their horns three times and wait for two minutes before investigating. What the presence of such laws indicates is the pervasiveness of sex in cars. Those laws testify to the range of social situations sex in cars has produced.

OTHER ASSOCIATIONS WITH SEXUALITY

Automobiles and the culture of the road are associated with sexual behaviors in other ways as well. Prostitution has become associated with automobiles as one of the prime sites for business. Prospective clients cruise for prostitutes, and prostitutes use particular roads, intersections, truck stops, and rest areas as places to attract customers. As a strategy for curtailing prostitution, municipalities such as Los Angeles began seizing the automobiles of citizens suspected of soliciting prostitutes.

Hitchhiking also has become associated with sexuality as sexual appeal has become a pretext for hitching a ride—a tendency exploited in films such as *It Happened One Night* (1934)—and especially as it relates to the opportunity for and risk of potentially dangerous sexual encounters. The phrase "hitchhiking to heaven" refers to male masturbation.

Automobiles not only are sites for sexual activity; they also may produce sexual stimulation. In *Three Essays on Sexuality* (1905), written during the era of trains, the psychoanalyst Sigmund Freud noted the way "the shaking produced by driving in carriages and later by railway travel" results in a link "between railway travel and sexuality" produced by the "pleasurable character of the sensations of movement." The same sensation of movement has a sexual connection to the automobile, whose movement and shape, character, and symbolism bespeak sexuality, potency, and allure.

In western culture automobiles long have been thought of as sex symbols both as markers of masculinity and as a marketing strategy. Long, lean, powerful speedy machines became phallic symbols as well as indicators of wealth, style, and sexual prowess. Automobile enthusiasts annually list cars with the greatest sex appeal: Corvettes, Ferraris, Lamborginis, Mustangs, Porsches, and Mazda RX-8's, among others. These cars join more classic expressions of powerful sexiness that often are associated with specifically masculine characters in films, such as James Bond with his Aston Martin DB5 in *Goldfinger* (1964). Sports cars in particular, with their streamlined speed, have been associated with virility, as have jalopies, racing cars, and other custom vehicles whose power relates to the mechanical aptitude and bravado of their drivers. Films featuring drag races, such as *Rebel without a Cause* (1954), *Le Mans* (1971), and *Days of Thunder* (1990), show the ways in which cars, speed, and machismo have become linked in western culture.

In addition to the sexiness of automobile design, sex is used as a way to market automobiles. The association of sexy cars with sexually alluring women is presumed to attract male customers. Phallic automobiles are caressed by ultra sexy female car show models, and although they may have all but disappeared from television advertisements, women still figure prominently on automobile-theme calendars. Advertising tactics that emphasize sleek auto body lines, class status, power, and performance produce an association between the phallic, masculine characteristics of the automobile and its prospective owner, as does nomenclature such as the "muscle" car. Muscle cars such as Pontiac GTOs, Mustangs, and Camaros are automobiles that have been modified to gain maximum horsepower from the engine. They appear bulky and rumbling and outperform normal cars. The status of the car becomes that of the owner. Males are assumed to have driving skills that match the capabilities of their vehicles, and expert speedy driving is associated with masculinity.

At the same time, women are assumed to be poor drivers. Whereas in many advertisements the automobile is an outward sign of the owner's masculinity, few cars are marketed to women on the basis of intrinsic sex appeal. Instead, cars are advertised to women on the basis of practicality, ease of use, and safety.

Cars have also become symbols of courtship and romance, especially in popular culture. Car radios were invented in 1929 and were sold separately (the resulting combination of movement and sound produced the brand name Motorola). Even before the combination of the car and the radio, pop music about sex and romance was circulating, from early favorites such as Irving Berlin's "Keep Away from the Fellow Who Owns an

Automobile" to the Nylons' "Little Red Corvette" and Queen's "I'm in Love with my Car." Sex has been associated with automobiles in films that include *It Happened One Night*, the jalopy culture of *Rebel without a Cause* and *American Graffiti* (1973), and more recently *Crash* (2004).

BIBLIOGRAPHY

Flink, James J. 1988. *The Automobile Age*. Cambridge, MA.: MIT Press.

Freud, Sigmund. 1953–1974. "Three Essays on the Theory of Sexuality." In *The Standard Edition of the Complete Psychological Works*, ed. and trans. James Strachchey. London: Hogarth. (Orig. pub. 1905.)

Michael, Robert T.; John H. Gagnon; Edward O. Laumann; and Gina Kolata. 1994. *Sex in America: A Definitive Survey*. New York: Warner Books.

Wolf, Winifred. 1996. *Car Mania: A Critical History of Transport*. trans. Gus Fagan. London: Pluto Press.

Judith Roof

AVUNCULAR

Literally, avuncular means *like an uncle*. Its nominative form, avunculate, refers to the specific relationship between male children and their maternal uncle. The word avuncular has been redefined as a gender position by Eve Kosofsky Sedgwick. She conceives of the avuncular as a range of relatives, male and female, who are related to children but who are not their parents. In this way they have a relationship and a responsibility to these children, usually the offspring of cousins or siblings, but their relationship is by its very nature tangential, or nonnormative. For Sedgwick this places the avuncular in the realm of the *queer*, and establishes a normative link to the queer within the family unit. In *Tendencies* (1993), she writes, "Because aunts and uncles (in either narrow or extended meanings) are adults whose intimate access to children needn't depend on their own pairing or procreation, it's very common, of course, for some of them to have the office of representing noncomforming or nonreproductive sexualities to children" (p. 63). The male relative is part of a spectrum of older men who serve to offer "a degree of initiation into gay cultures and identities" (p. 59). This is not to suggest that there is necessarily a physical relationship between avuncular males and their young relatives, but that they serve as a kind of model for possible alternative sexualities. The female avuncular (often an aunt), serves as a kind of *camp* figure whose presence emphasizes the erotic nature of the male avuncular.

SEE ALSO *Family*.

BIBLIOGRAPHY

Levi-Strauss, Claude. 1963. *Structural Anthropology*, trans. Claire Jacobson and Brooke Grundfest Schoepf. New York: Basic Books.

Savoy, Eric. 1999. "Embarrassments: Figure in the Closet." *The Henry James Review* 20(3): 227–236.

Sedgwick, Eve Kosofsky. 1993. *Tendencies*. Durham, NC: Duke University Press.

Brian D. Holcomb

B

BACKROOM

Backroom refers to a type of illicit sexual practice that is defined by its location: the back room of a bar, club, or other establishment with an otherwise nonsexual function. This is a type of setting that allows for opportunistic sex: Contact is made in the front, or public part, of the bar or club, and then the back room is used for sexual activity. Back rooms are usually dark, and often mazelike. This configuration allows for a person to walk past a large number of other people to look for sex, or to *cruise*. The darkness also allows for a degree of anonymity. Group sexual activity is common in such locations.

Backroom sex is popular mostly with people who are excited by exhibitionism and voyeurism, or by those who are looking for casual anonymous sex. It is most common in bars and clubs with a primarily gay male clientele, although it takes place in heterosexual and lesbian establishments as well. Back rooms are most commonly associated with the leather and bondage and discipline, domination and submission, sadism and masochism (BDSM) communities, but are not confined to them. Because backroom activity is often spontaneous and anonymous, it is considered a risky sexual behavior. Much of the campaign against HIV/AIDS and other sexually transmitted diseases has focused on back rooms and other locations of casual sexual encounters.

Backrooms as sites for sexual encounters produce a complex legal situation because they are neither public nor private. Bathhouses and sex clubs are often private, and their primary function is sexual activity. Therefore, people who enter them are likely to be aware of their purpose and what kinds of activity they may encounter. Public restrooms (called *tearooms* when used for illicit sexual activity), parks, and other such locations are clearly public and have no intended sexual function. Sexual activity in these locations is illegal in almost all cases. Backrooms are usually in public facilities but are not part of the public space of those facilities. Sexual activity in backrooms is usually considered illegal, but is rarely prosecuted. When police raids of backrooms occur, it is usually in the name of public health enforcement, but is often considered a veiled form of homophobia.

BIBLIOGRAPHY

Colter, Ephen Glenn, ed. 1996. *Policing Public Sex: Queer Politics and the Future of AIDS Activism.* Boston: South End Press.

Leap, William L., ed. 1999. *Public Sex/Gay Space.* New York: Columbia University Press.

Scott, D. Travers, ed. 1999. *Strategic Sex: Why They Won't Keep It in the Bedroom.* New York: Harrington Park Press.

Brian D. Holcomb

BAHA'I FAITH

Baha'u'llah, the prophet-founder of the Baha'i faith, was born in Teheran, Iran, in 1817. The religion he founded grew out of nineteenth-century Shiite messianic expectations, much as Christianity grew out of similar expectations within Judaism. In claiming to be the latest messenger from God with new divinely revealed laws, Baha'u'llah irremediably separated the new religion from its Islamic background.

Among the principles promulgated in Baha'i writings was the equality of women and men. That equality does not refer solely to the spiritual plane, for Baha'i scriptures explicitly state that education for women and men should be identical and that women should be active in political affairs. The major exception to that principle is women's exclusion from service in the Universal House of Justice, the Baha'i community's supreme governing body. Nonetheless, representation of women in top Baha'i administrative positions is high. According to statistics cited at the Fourth World Women's Forum in Beijing in 1995, women constituted about 30 percent of the Baha'i leadership at the national level and about half of those serving in local Baha'i communities.

WOMEN IN BAHA'U'LLAH'S WRITINGS

The writings of Baha'u'llah unequivocally proclaim the equality of men and women, asserting that "in this Day the Hand of divine grace hath removed all distinction. The Servants of God and His handmaidens are regarded on the same plane." Elsewhere he suggests that differences between the sexes are the result of vain imaginings and idle fancies that have been destroyed with the new revelation. Baha'u'llah further insists on the education of girls, a requirement that Baha'u'llah's son, 'Abdu'l-Baha, took further by giving girls preference in cases in which not all children could be educated.

The *Kitab-i-Aqdas*, the book that contains Baha'i sacred law, was written in Arabic, a language that requires the use of the male gender for collective terms. For that reason most of its admonitions and laws appear to be addressed to men. Baha'is, however, generally have not understood the greater part of the *Aqdas* in this manner. 'Abdu'l Baha, for instance, insisted that although the *Aqdas* appears to allow bigamy, this is conditioned on equal treatment of both wives, an impossibility that made monogamy alone permissible. Shoghi Effendi, who led the Baha'i community between 1921 and 1957, stated that women have the same rights as men to sue for divorce and that in most cases the laws in the *Aqdas* apply to persons of both sexes except when the context makes this impossible. For instance, since the *Aqdas* allows but does not encourage a man to divorce his wife if she falsely represented herself as a virgin before marriage, a woman may divorce a man in the same circumstances.

When read within the context of nineteenth-century Iran, the *Kitab-i Aqdas* presents startling contrasts to the norms of male-female relations. Although the *Aqdas* makes it optional for women to perform the obligatory prayers or fast during their menses, within Islam they are not permitted to do so at all because they are regarded as ritually unclean at such times, a concept that is not found in Baha'i teachings. Perhaps more surprising is Baha'u'llah's treatment of sexual issues. The sexuality of women in both Judaism and Islam has been seen as a potentially dangerous force that threatens the honor of the family and indeed the entire social fabric. For this reason adultery historically carried very high penalties, usually death. In contrast, according to the *Aqdas*, adulterers are subject to a fine, not the death penalty. There are some minor disparities between men and women in matters of inheritance, with the presumption being that men will provide the major means of support for the family. However, the laws in the *Aqdas* apply only to cases in which the deceased did not leave a will as required by Baha'i law. This leaves Baha'is free to make adjustments in accordance with their individual situations.

As in Islam, women have independent property rights even when they are married. The dowry or bride-price is presented by the groom to the bride, but there are strict limits on the amount of the dowry, making it a largely symbolic payment. Couples are required to obtain parental permission before marriage but are expected to select their own partners. Monogamous marriage between members of the opposite sex is regarded as the only acceptable outlet for sexual relations; thus, both premarital sex and homosexual conduct are not allowed. Procreation is regarded as the primary purpose of sex. Baha'is place no value on celibacy for its own sake, and monasticism is forbidden. Baha'is are encouraged to marry and live productive lives.

It has been argued that the exclusive use of the male gender in referring to God leads to a perpetuation of male dominance. Although Baha'u'llah's Arabic writings necessitated the use of the male gender in reference to God, the Persian language has no gender. However, thus far references to God have been translated using the male gender regardless of the original language. Perhaps more interesting is Baha'u'llah's treatment of the symbol of the Heavenly Maiden, or *huri*. In the Qur'anic vision of paradise black-eyed damsels, or *huri*s, are thought to serve believers. Within the Baha'i context of fulfilled eschatology the *huri* comes to symbolize the holy spirit, the personification of Baha'u'llah's revelation and the vehicle through which he receives it.

WOMEN AND BAHA'I ADMINISTRATIVE INSTITUTIONS

Initially the prohibition against women serving in houses of justice was thought to apply to all administrative institutions, but in 1909 'Abdu'l-Baha stated that it applied only to the Universal House of Justice. In Iran their inclusion was implemented very gradually. Although women were allowed to vote in the Iranian Baha'i community, it was not until 1954 that they were permitted to serve in Baha'i institutions.

ABORTION AND DOMESTIC VIOLENCE

According to the Universal House of Justice, abortion "merely to prevent the birth of an unwanted child is strictly forbidden" (from a letter written on behalf of the Universal House of Justice to the National Spiritual Assembly of Ireland, March 16, 1983). However, abortion is permitted for medical reasons and in cases of rape. Domestic violence is condemned in the strongest terms.

BIBLIOGRAPHY

Baha'u'llah. 1992. *Kitab-I Aqdas*. Haifa, Israel: Baha'i World Centre.

Maneck, Susan. 1994. "Women in the Baha'i Faith." In *Religion and Women*, ed. Arvind Sharma. Albany: State University of New York Press.

Women. 1986. Compilation issued by the Universal House of Justice. Oakham.

Susan Stiles Maneck

BAKER, JOSÉPHINE
1906–1975

The concepts of gender and race are often perceived as discrete components of an individual's social identity. Yet the official discourse on "women of color," in a racialized and patriarchal order, only magnifies this order's implicit assumptions on women in general. Joséphine Baker's tumultuous life and career in twentieth century-Europe is a reflection of women's broader struggle for acceptance in modernity.

An icon of black female eroticism in interwar Europe, Baker simultaneously submitted to European colonial construction of the *abject* (in Bulgarian writer Julia Kristeva's terms) other, and subtly reframed her performances to fit into an African-American tradition of social commentary through parodic dancing, as exemplified most notably by the cakewalk. The tension between these two dimensions of Baker's persona is summed up in one of her frequently quoted sentences: "Since I personified the savage on the stage, I tried to be as civilized as possible in daily life."

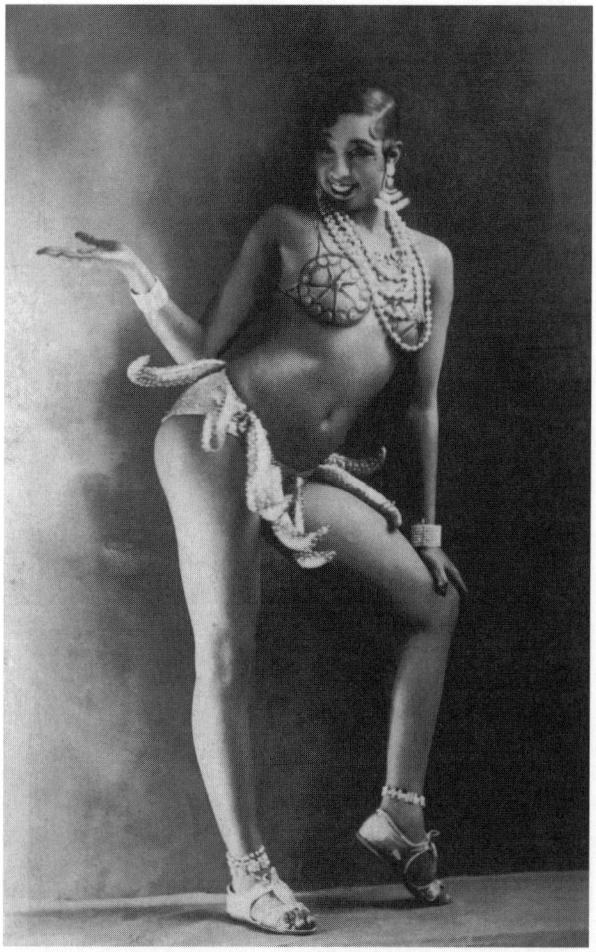

Joséphine Baker. *Joséphine Baker in her famous banana dance costume.* HULTON ARCHIVE/GETTY IMAGES.

FROM ST. LOUIS TO THE PARISIAN LIMELIGHT

Born Freda Joséphine McDonald on June 3 in Saint Louis, Missouri, to a bar singer, Baker grew up fatherless and in poverty. At eleven she witnessed the East Saint Louis race riots, an experience that may have prompted her to escape the segregated United States later in life. At thirteen she married for the first time. She also landed her first job as a dancer for Southern vaudeville troupes, the Jones Family Band and the Dixie Steppers (1919), and began touring the country. Baker divorced but was soon remarried to a Pullman porter named William Baker and was hired to perform in two Broadway musicals, *Shuffle Along* (1921) and *The Chocolate Dandies* (1924), distinguishing herself in the all-black casts by her constant buffoonery.

Selected for *la Revue Nègre*, a musical production that opened in Paris in 1925, Baker stole the show with her comic rendition of a new dance, the Charleston, and her passionate execution of the *Danse sauvage*, in front of crowds that included the most notable literati of the time. In line with primitivist shows performed in the trendy nightclubs of Harlem's "Jungle Alley," *la Revue Nègre* also exploited the European obsession with the alleged radical alterity of African people—former slaves and now colonial subjects. The craze over Sartjee Baartman, the "Hottentot Venus" of the 1810s, and

Baker, known as the Black Venus in the 1920s, suggests that women's bodies were thought to be the privileged locus of this alterity. Baker's nudity on stage, enhanced by exotic paraphernalia—feathers and jewelry, a banana belt, boa scarves and even a live jaguar—attracted scores of admirers to her shows, to the restaurant she owned in the Montmartre section of Paris, and to the movies she starred in. Worshiped by the primitivist modernists, she posed for Spanish painter Pablo Picasso and American artist Man Ray, and inspired French painter Paul Colin's lithographies. Writers Ernest Hemingway, F. Scott Fitzgerald, Erich Maria Remarque, and Paul Morand paid tribute to her talent.

But her seemingly compliant impersonation of the feminized subaltern earned her harsh criticism in a time of heightened pan-African consciousness. Indicted for being "an agent of minstrelsy," and "prostituting Negro talent" (Borshuk 2001, p. 42), Baker was also rebuked for sporting the dubious title of Queen of the 1931 Exposition Coloniale, while starring in a show at the Casino de Paris designed to celebrate the French Colonial Empire. Many criticized her Tragic Mulatto roles in French films, such as *Sirène des Tropiques* (1927), *Zouzou* (1934), and *Princesse Tam Tam* (1935).

A trend-setter, Baker left her mark on the French fashion of the Années Folles with her corset-free clothing, perfume, and short hairstyle. She even marketed a hair gel, the Bakerfix. As the embodiment of the emergent model of woman liberated from social norms popularized by Victor Margueritte in his novel *La Garconne* (1922), Baker sometimes performed in a deliberately androgynous way, and was rumored to be bisexual. Her alleged affair with Mexican painter Frida Kahlo is briefly mentioned in American director Julie Taymor's movie *Frida* (2002).

Having attained some autonomy as an artist by the mid-1930s, Baker began asserting her talent and philosophy in a more personal way. After a devastating visit to the United States in 1936, where she experienced racial discrimination anew, she married a sugar magnate, Jean Lion. Now a French citizen, she continued touring Europe in an often hostile prewar climate. Recruited as a spy at the onset of World War II, she participated in the Resistance movement both in France and North Africa with such distinction that she was made a lieutenant of the female division of the French Air Force and awarded the Légion d'honneur. Her health began to deteriorate after a hysterectomy in 1941.

LATER CAREER AND SOCIAL IMPACT

After the war Baker, again single, married her bandleader Jo Bouillon with whom she wanted to create a transracial model community in her manor in Dordogne, France. She adopted twelve children of various nationalities and religious backgrounds. But Baker managed her finances poorly, and became heavily indebted. Bouillon left her in 1957, and she was expelled from her manor in 1969, although her friend Princess Grace of Monaco helped her secure another home for her Rainbow Tribe.

During two trips to the United States, in 1951 and 1963, she used her fame to fight racial discrimination. She insisted on having an integrated audience at the Copa City in Miami, the first in the club's history; attacked the Stork Club in New York City for refusing her patronage; and participated in the March on Washington in 1963. She also gave benefit concerts in support of the civil rights movement.

Due to her financial difficulties, Baker could not leave the stage, but performed until the end of her life with great gusto and to much acclaim. She appeared at the Olympia Theater in Paris in 1959; in Monte-Carlo in 1969; at Carnegie Hall in New York in 1973; and at the Bobino Theater in Paris in 1975. The show at the Bobino Theater, a musical retrospective of her life and career, was cancelled when Baker died of a brain hemorrhage on April 12, four days after the opening. She was given a state funeral at the Eglise de la Madeleine in Paris and is buried in the Cimetiere de Monaco.

Baker's spectacular trajectory from the slums of St. Louis to the limelight of the European art scene has inspired several biographies, among which *Hungry Heart* (1993), written by her adoptive son Jean-Claude Baker, figures prominently. Jacques Abtey, Baker's partner in the Resistance described her underground activities in *La Guerre Secrète de Joséphine Baker* (1949). She personally authored a series of autobiographies that included various versions of her life story.

Baker's participation in her own objectification in the first phase of her career in France remains a troubling issue. Her expert self-promotion as the Vogue Nègre's ultimate object of both male and female desire points to her ability to mimic (and expand on) the conventional black female. As Michael Borshuk argues, in adapting an African-American tradition of parodic dancing to the context of European colonial triumphalism, Baker may have intended to subvert race and gender-based stereotypes. Or, as Samir Dayal contends, she may have been "a black subjectivity divided between conflicting self-representations" (Dayal 2004, p. 36). In any case Baker's own comments indicate that she was fully conscious of her contribution to the "blackening" of Europe. In 1927, she wrote: "Since *la Revue Nègre* has hit the Gay Paris, I would say that Paris is getting more and more black" (Colin 1927).

SEE ALSO *Dance.*

BIBLIOGRAPHY

Abtey, Jacques. 1949. *La Guerre secrète de Joséphine Baker, avec une lettre autographe du Général de Gaulle* [The secret war of Joséphine Baker, with a signed letter by General de Gaulle]. Paris: Siboney.

Baker, Jean Claude, and Chris Chase. 1993. *Josephine: The Hungry Heart.* New York: Random House.

Borshuk, Michael. 2001. "An Intelligence of the Body: Disruptive Parody though Dance in the Early Performances of Josephine Baker." In *EmBODYing Liberation: The Black Body in American Dance,* ed. Dorothea Fischer-Hornung and Alison D. Goeller. Hamburg, Germany: LIT Verlag.

Colin, Paul. 1927. *Tumulte Noir.* Paris: Art Succes.

Dayal, Samir. 2004. "Blackness as a Symptom: Joséphine Baker and European Identity." In *Blackening Europe: The African American Presence,* ed. Heike Raphael-Hernandez. New York: Routledge.

Kristeva, J. 1982. *Powers of Horror. An Essay on Abjection.* Columbia Univeristy Press.

Stovall, Tyler. 1996. *Paris Noir: African-Americans in the City of Light.* New York: Houghton Mifflin.

Sylvie Kandé

BALDWIN, JAMES
1924–1987

James Baldwin, novelist, essayist, and political and cultural activist, was one of the finest American intellectuals of the twentieth century. His works not only detail the particular struggles faced by intellectuals, bohemians, and racial and sexual minorities, but they also continually celebrate the fundamental truth of everyone's common humanity and the absolute necessity of the erotic in the maintenance and reproduction of the human community.

Born in Harlem on August 2, 1924, Baldwin passed through a difficult childhood as the eldest of nine children in a strict Pentecostal household. Becoming a preacher at age fourteen, Baldwin honed his gifts as a public speaker until he stepped down from the pulpit after three years, eventually leaving the church altogether. At this stage of his life, the young writer believed that he needed to distance himself from his parochial background in order to "preach the gospel" to a wider audience and he thought that he could most effectively reach that audience through his writing. Thus just out of his teens he began to write and publish in earnest, developing relationships with some of the most important literary journals in the United States. This continued until 1948, when with the support of the novelist Richard Wright, Baldwin received a Rosenwald Fellowship that allowed him to travel to Paris that same year.

In Paris Baldwin became part of the vibrant community of American expatriates who had made their way across the Atlantic in search of artistic opportunity as well as relief from the base insults meted out to racial and sexual minorities in the conservative, segregated, and intensely homophobic United States. He made good use of his Rosenwald Fellowship, publishing perhaps his most significant piece of literary criticism, "Everybody's Protest Novel," in his very first year as an expatriate. This work cast a highly critical eye upon the "protest tradition" that

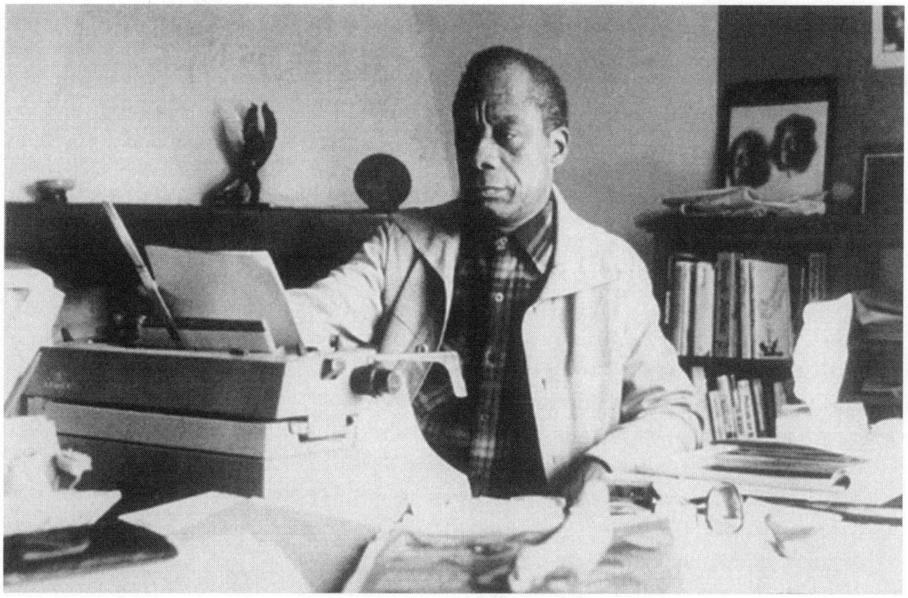

James Baldwin. *James Baldwin in his home office.* AP IMAGES.

Baldwin suggested began with Harriet Beecher Stowe's *Uncle Tom's Cabin* (1851–1852) and reached its zenith with Wright's *Native Son* (1940). Indeed the essay announced Baldwin as one of the most significant American cultural critics of his time. It also went a long way toward souring his relationship with Wright. There is, however, a sense among many scholars that part of what drove this disagreement between Wright and Baldwin was the way in which the two great American intellectuals seemed almost certain to clash because of their presumably incommensurate sexual "leanings." The younger, effeminate, homosexual, and northern Baldwin was always, one is led to believe, destined to confront the older, macho, heterosexual, and southern Wright. Indeed it seemed that Baldwin's confrontation with his erstwhile mentor had as much to do with a need to end certain silences about sexuality (particularly matters of homosexuality and interracialism) as with any personal antipathy for Wright.

This idea of confronting the silences enacted by one's elders is the theme of Baldwin's first novel, *Go Tell It on the Mountain* (1953), a largely autobiographical work, in which John Grimes, the stepson of a dictatorial Pentecostal preacher, reaches deep into black religious and cultural tradition to challenge his father's authority and create a more comfortable environment in which to explore his budding sexuality. It seems strange then that so many found the publication three years later of Baldwin's gay novel, *Giovanni's Room*, so unsettling. This text, a treatment of a tortured love triangle between the white American, David, his fiancée, Hella, and his Italian male lover, Giovanni, reiterates the theme of a necessary break with long-established tradition as Baldwin "abandons" the subject of race identity and oppression to create a work in which the pursuit of individual freedom and desire is all important.

The great paradox of Baldwin's life, however, was the fact that even though he made some of the finest calls ever heard for the necessity of personal freedom for the creative intellectual he nonetheless became known as a particularly effective *representative* spokesman for the black American community. After returning to the United States in 1957 at the height of the U.S. civil rights movement, Baldwin came to national prominence in 1963 with the publication of *The Fire Next Time*. Released one hundred years after the Emancipation Proclamation, this work is a breathtakingly rendered indictment of the racism that still eats away at the heart of the United States. The difficulty, though—a paradox that would plague Baldwin for the remainder of his career—was that Baldwin's fiery denouncements of racism and hypocrisy came to stand in for the whole of his corpus. After 1963 it became possible to ignore the fact that Baldwin had produced two novels that treated questions of individuality and desire with such care and precision. Instead an increasingly hungry and insistent American audience wanted nothing but fire and more fire from Baldwin as they stumbled through the worst days of the civil rights movement.

This helps one to understand better the famously homophobic critique of Baldwin by the Black Panther minister of information, Eldridge Cleaver. In his epoch-making work, *Soul on Ice* (1968), Cleaver takes Baldwin to task for the "queerness" on display in his wildly successful 1962 novel, *Another Country*. Indeed Cleaver suggests that throughout Baldwin's corpus he takes an unmanly and even sychophantic stance toward whites, while maintaining an awkward and even hostile pose toward blacks. Baldwin is indicted by Cleaver for not reproducing the image of an antisocial and presumably antiwhite black masculinity that he finds in both Norman Mailer's controversial essay, "The White Negro" (1957), as well as within *Soul on Ice* itself. Baldwin's insistent focus on love and reconciliation is read by Cleaver as a species of internalized racism that represented a particularly sad peculiarity of the black homosexual.

Fortunately such small-minded readings became less and less common in American culture as Baldwin, who died in Saint-Paul-de-Vence, France, on November 30, 1987, entered the last stage of his career. The efforts of gays, lesbians, and feminists helped not only to secure Baldwin's place as one of the most significant writers of his generation but also to allow him more leeway in his efforts to break away from suffocating notions of how black Americans should comport themselves as sexual actors. After *Another Country* Baldwin continued to write furiously, producing *Tell Me How Long the Train's Been Gone* in 1968, *If Beale Street Could Talk* in 1974, *Just Above My Head* in 1979, and *The Evidence of Things Not Seen* in 1985. All these works continued many of the themes of love, interracialism, and individual freedom that Baldwin began early in his career. Indeed Baldwin attempted throughout his life to wean the American public from its costly tendencies to overprivilege presumably natural distinctions between persons of differing sexualities and genders, while also championing the oppressed and celebrating the beauty of our shared humanity.

SEE ALSO *Homosexuality, Male, History of; Literature: IV. Gay, Creative.*

BIBLIOGRAPHY

Cleaver, Eldridge. 1968. *Soul on Ice*. New York: McGraw-Hill.

Leeming, David. 1994. *James Baldwin: A Biography*. New York: Knopf.

Mailer, Norman. 1957. *The White Negro*. San Francisco: City Lights Books.

McBride, Dwight A., ed. 1999. *James Baldwin Now*. New York: New York University Press.

Troupe, Quincy, ed. 1989. *James Baldwin: The Legacy*. New York: Simon and Schuster.

Robert F. Reid-Pharr

BARBIE

In 1959 the world of toys changed forever with the introduction of the Barbie (full name Barbara Millicent Roberts) doll at the American International Toy Fair in New York City. The doll proved to be popular with both children and adult collectors, and by 2000 annual sales of Barbie-related products reached $1.9 billion. In the same year Mattel was the fourth largest clothing manufacturer, and from 1959 to 1990 more than two thousand different styles and colors of shoes were available for Barbie. The average American girl owns ten Barbie dolls, and the dolls are sold worldwide. Every second two dolls are sold somewhere in the world (*I, Doll* 1996). In addition to sales of the dolls (Barbie, her friends, and her family members), a massive wardrobe, and various accessories, there have been Barbie television shows and films, games, video games, computer systems, and Web sites.

Adult collectors are numerous, buying and selling various generations of Barbie dolls, clothing, and accessories. For adults there are collectors' sites on the Internet, conventions, stores, and auctions.

The Barbie doll has maintained its popularity as a result of the regular updating of its hair, wardrobe, and accessories. For each generation since 1959 Barbie has served as a symbol of American popular culture. As both a doll and an icon Barbie is both loved and hated.

THE ORIGIN OF BARBIE

Created by Ruth Handler (1916–2002), the cofounder of the Mattel toy company, Barbie was the result of a convergence of two experiences. During a trip to Europe, Handler saw the Lili doll. A popular item in Germany among adult men, Lili was a young sexy single woman, often described as quasi-pornographic, who was sold dressed in lingerie or swimsuits. The Lili doll was an offshoot of a comic of the same name published in the newspaper *Die Bild-Zeitung*. Within a few years and with a few modifications, that doll intended for an adult male audience in Germany became one of the most popular toys for girls.

Handler's sighting of the Lili doll was fortuitous. She had wished her daughter could have a doll that was not an infant or a toddler but the type of young woman her daughter could become. Until that time the toy industry had offered dolls that encouraged girls to play "mother"; the dolls were babies or young children. Dolls representing adults were typically paper dolls. Handler wanted a three-dimensional doll with which her daughter could create a make-believe world of a teen or young adult woman, including the ability to dress the doll. Barbie was a doll that would allow young girls to utilize their imagination in regard to their future possibilities, to be more than mothers in playtime. Barbie was named for Handler's daughter, Barbara.

In addition to being the first mass-produced young-adult doll, Barbie represented a shift in the traditional marketing of toys. Rather than advertising to parents as the purchasers of their children's toys, Mattel focused its marketing effort on children and used television advertising to a great extent. As a result the company created a significant demand for its product.

THE EVOLUTION OF BARBIE

Barbie has evolved over time. A multitude of siblings and friends have been sold by Mattel, along with houses, cars, a recreational vehicle, and a wardrobe representing a plethora of careers. The basic body shape has not changed, however. If the doll were expanded to five feet ten inches in height, its measurements would be thirty-nine inches (bust), twenty-three inches (waist), and thirty-three inches (hips), and it would weigh 110 pounds.

Although Barbie had no eye color in 1959, within two years her eyes became and have remained blue. Although Barbie's eyes were set askance in the 1959 model, they focused farther forward and became wider over time. By the 1990s Barbie had become a doe-eyed innocent. The shape of Barbie's nose—small and upturned at the end—has not changed. She did not speak until 1967, the same year she was able to twist and turn (she was able to bend even more by the 1970s). Barbie smiled for the first time in 1971, the same year she first appeared with a tan. Although the hairstyle has changed to reflect the fashion of the day, she has remained a blonde since the 1960s.

Barbie's friends (by 1996 more than three dozen had been issued) reflect social change. Although her friends look a great deal like Barbie in body shape and general features, her friendship base became more diverse in 1967 with the introduction of the first African-American friend, "Colored Francie." That doll simply utilized the white features of the Francie doll with darker skin tones. In response to criticism, Mattel introduced Chrissy within a year. Chrissy's features more accurately represented her African heritage. Later additional African-American dolls were issued, as were Asian and Latina dolls (Miko in 1987, Teresa in 1988, and Nikki in 1989). In 1996 Mattel issued Becky, a paraplegic in a wheelchair. Unfortunately, Barbie's Dreamhouse remained inaccessible to Becky until the company redesigned the house in 2000.

BARBIE: FEMINIST IDEAL OR HARMFUL ROLE MODEL?

Some would argue that Barbie is and continues to be a positive toy for young girls. From this perspective Barbie represents a strong image of young womanhood. Each Barbie set revolves around an activity, a theme, or a

Barbie Dolls. *Two sisters playing with their Barbie dolls.* AP IMAGES.

career. Barbie has been an astronaut, a stewardess, and a ballerina. She also has been a veterinarian and in 1992 became a presidential candidate. Barbie has represented feminist aspirations for women as independent wage earners with positions equivalent to those of men. Girls who play with Barbie can imagine themselves as young adults pursuing those careers. Mirroring the increasing presence of women in the workforce, Barbie's career roles have evolved over time. Whereas she was outfitted as a nurse in 1961 (with Ken serving as the doctor), she was a physician in her own right by 1973.

Barbie represents more than career aspirations for young women. She is a single independent woman with many friends and a romantic interest (Ken, named for Handler's son, first appeared in 1961). Barbie has her own house and car, travels widely, and enjoys what appears to be a very busy social life. Her fashion tastes are impeccable, reflecting the latest styles from Hollywood and leading fashion designers.

Barbie also celebrates the athletic contribution of women, something that could encourage girls to see physical activity as normal for women. To this end Barbie has been a member of the World Cup women's soccer team and an Olympic champion swimmer. An advertising jingle from television commercials in the 1970s included the line "we girls can do anything" (*I, Doll* 1996).

Criticisms of Barbie focus on the body image the doll presents to girls. Because Barbie's proportions are replicated on the figures of her friends, for many feminists the dolls represent an impossible beauty standard. Because millions of girls play with the dolls as an example of young womanhood, they may believe that Barbie's good life (her friends, careers, and clothing) is connected with her appearance and size. Although Barbie is only one part of a young girl's exposure to the beauty ideal in popular culture, her ubiquitous image has a great impact on the development of body image ideas in young girls.

There is a general focus on appearance that detracts from the advances Barbie has made in her career path. Barbie's outfits, which correspond to her various careers, tend to focus on her physical appearance rather than her occupation. There are tight clothes, a short skirt on the business executive Barbie, and tight belts or sashes added to apparel (such as the sash added to the medical scrubs) that serve no practical purpose. Also, the focus on cosmetics and fashion downplays the significance of Barbie's career achievements.

In 1992 a Barbie doll line was equipped with a recorded voice. While Barbie extolled the typically female pursuit of consumerism ("Let's Go Shopping!"), she also exclaimed, "Math class is tough!" The American Association of University Women (AAUW) protested, fearing that this would enlarge the math and science gap experienced by girls in the American public school system. Taking the AAUW protest a step farther, a clandestine group known as the Barbie Liberation Organization (BLO) highlighted the gendered stereotypes reinforced by children's toys. The BLO purchased talking Barbie dolls, switched the voice track with that of G.I. Joe action figures, and returned the toys to the store. The toys were resold to consumers, who found their G.I. Joe dolls asking, "Will we ever have enough clothes?" and Barbie shouting, "Eat lead, Cobra!"

BIBLIOGRAPHY

Barbie Nation: An Unauthorized Tour. 2003. Directed by Susan Stern. San Francisco, CA: El Rio Productions.

I, Doll: The Unauthorized Biography of America's Sweetheart. 1996. Directed by Tula Asselanis. New York: Women Make Movies.

Lord, M. G. 1994. *Forever Barbie: The Unauthorized Biography of a Real Doll.* New York: Morrow and Co.

McDonough, Yona Zeldis, ed. 1999. *The Barbie Chronicles: A Living Doll Turns Forty.* New York: Simon & Schuster.

Julie L. Thomas

BATHS, PUBLIC

This entry contains the following:

I. GRECO-ROMAN
Lee Fontanella

II. MUSLIM MIDDLE EAST
Hamid Bahri

III. WEST, MIDDLE AGES–PRESENT
Jason Prior

I. GRECO-ROMAN

The Greek baths at Olympia date to the early fifth century BCE. The first baths were pools of unheated water, but baths grew more complex technically and later were heated by coal fires or hot rocks. The region of Laconica gave its name to *laconica*, or hot-air baths. Men and women bathed separately or at different hours of the day. As Greek baths grew in sophistication, specialty bathing developed, including individual tubs, footbaths, and even showers. Customarily, exercise, often in the nude, preceded ablutions, and some baths grew into centers of intellectual activity. Most notably the baths were communal, not totally private.

Those more cultivated aspects of Greek baths were retained by the Romans, who by the second century CE sometimes added libraries and elaborate artistic decorations to their baths. Roman males probably did not exercise in the nude, and it is not certain what they wore while bathing. Communal bathing (*thermae*) was the norm for free Romans, and *thermae* came to occupy huge tracts of urban land. A few people owned private baths (*balneae*) that could be used by others for an entry fee. As in Greece men and women had distinct bathing areas or bathed at different times of the day: women before the early afternoon and men in the late afternoon before dining.

Roman state-owned baths (the *thermae*) were a logical by-product of the construction of water-supply routes into the urban center. By 19 BCE Agrippa exerted sufficient control over the water supply to build an aqueduct and baths. Following the Greek style he combined pools for swimming with Turkish baths. Apart from Rome there is subterranean evidence of elaborate layouts for bathing at sites such as Bath Spa, Somerset, England, where architectural remnants point to the distinct stages of public bathing: perspiring heavily while exposed to steam, soaping and shampooing, and then massaging and cooling.

Nero (37–68 CE) ordered the building of the Thermae Neronianae, and emperor Titus (40–81 CE) built his baths on Nero's baths; later Trajan (52–117 CE) built the Thermae Suranae on the earlier baths. The later baths were enlarged under Vespasian, and all are said to have been highly elaborate in artistic decoration. In the second decade of the second century CE, Caracalla (188–217 CE) completed the baths that his father, Septimius Severus (146–211 CE), had begun: gigantic structures whose remains have been incorporated as a backdrop for performances of Verdi's *Aïda*. In 305 CE Diocletian (r. 284–305 CE) built baths even larger than those; his baths later were converted into the church Santa Maria degli Angeli.

Probably because the baths were so popular and so varied in terms of their social activities, they grew noisy, as the Roman philosopher and writer Seneca complained. Repasts were shared in some. They became locales plagued by petty thieves, and bathers' belongings had to be guarded by a servant in the changing rooms; some were said to become haunts for prostitutes.

Such elaborate processes of ablution, often in sumptuous surroundings, became the stuff of imaginative prose and the visual arts, especially in periods in which people indulged in prurience, possibly because outward social ethics and morality called for the opposite type of behavior. Most evidence suggests that in addition to the obvious hygienic benefits of the baths, their applications were highly varied, and they were used primarily for physical and intellectual cultural activities. In modern times the baths inspired writers and visual artists and were even used as movie sets, but in their time they were fundamentally practical, and their recreational aspects tended to be on a high level.

BIBLIOGRAPHY

Cary, M., and H. H. Scullard. 1975 [1935]. *A History of Rome Down to the Reign of Constantine.* London: Macmillan.

Lanciani, Rodolfo. 1979 [1897]. *The Ruins and Excavations of Ancient Rome.* New York: Bell.

Yegül, Fikret. 1992. *Baths and Bathing in Classical Antiquity.* Cambridge, MA: MIT Press.

Lee Fontanella

II. MUSLIM MIDDLE EAST

Public bathhouses, or *hammams*, are predominant in the Arab-Islamic world. A hammam is made up of mosaic floors and three tiled rooms, each offering a different level of heat and steam. They are called steam baths in Arabic, or Turkish baths in English.

Aakand (1978), Dow (1996), and Ecohard and Le Coeur (1942–1943) have noted that although hammams were modeled on Greco-Roman baths, it is with the advent of Islam that hammams gained prominence and acquired a new significance. It was after the Prophet Muhammad's recommendation that hammams multiplied and became second only to mosques. The prophet's "Hadith," which means "hygiene is part of faith," played a great role in inscribing the ritual of cleanliness where the faithful performed their prescribed ablutions before prayers; therefore, frequenting hammams became a prelude to entering the mosque.

Dow (1996), Al-Ghazali (1999), and Ecochard and Le Coeur (1942–1943) agree that the first and oldest Islamic hammams were in Syria, capital of the Umayyad Empire at the time, where a number of Syrian bathhouses have been preserved as historic monuments (Kayyal 1986). Ibn Khaldun mentions the existence of thousands of hammams during the reign of the Abbassid Caliph Al-Ma'mun (Ibn Khaldun n.d.) who chose Baghdad as his capital.

Hammams have seldom been seen as a source of profit. Their owners are often considered altruistic people since they allow people to purify their bodies and souls after sexual acts, "wash their bones" as the expression goes, and prepare to enter mosques (Ecochard and Le Coeur 1942–1943). There are several maintenance workers for each hammam. *Dallaak*, or *kassal*, is the masseuse who scrubs and washes bathers' bodies.

During the early days, there was much emphasis on covering one's private parts and not allowing any masseuse to clean them or touch them (Al-Ghazali 1999). The dark rooms and hot water served two functions; they cleanse the body and remind the bathers of hell's heat and thus make them closer to their God (Al-Ghazali 1999).

At the dawn of Islam, women were forbidden from entering hammams unless they were pregnant, ill, or done menstruating for the month (Munawi 1987). On Muhammad's recommendation, men were not to accompany their wives to the hammam (Al-Ghazali 1999) lest they engaged in depraved sexual acts (Munawi 1987). In the early twenty-first century, the bride and the groom have to go to the hammam before their wedding day. It is also customary for women to bathe forty days after giving birth.

Throughout the Arab world, each small neighborhood has at least one hammam. Whereas men's main forums are cafes, women's forums remain the hammams, which have evolved into beautification centers and social clubs where women bond with each other whether or not they have previously known each other. Hammams have become crucial to women particularly because many laws have been established to curtail their movement. Women bathers socialize with their friends during entire afternoons and exchange secrets far from men's gazes. They bring with them dried fruits and sweets that they share with the tenants and workers of the hammam (Ecochard and Le Coeur 1942–1943). The hammam is also the best social forum where mothers scrutinize unsuspecting potential brides for their sons. Kayyal (1986) and Aaland (1978) have noted that the mother would provide a thorough visual examination of the likely bride and memorize the minutest details about her breath, walk, and even the smoothness or roughness of her skin.

Entering the hammam is a defining moment in a man's childhood. When he reaches the age of seven, he is no longer allowed to accompany his mother or other women to the hammam. He is then entrusted to the company of his father, uncle, or a close adult male. Men rush to hammams on the eve of religious holidays and on Fridays at dawn before the prayers. Hammams have been known to be a sanctuary for the homeless and the poor and certain individuals stricken by illnesses (Ecochard and Le Coeur 1942–1943).

In the 1960s and 1970s, a hammam site was shared by men and women at different times of the day. Women could use hammams generally after midday prayers and afternoons (Ecochard and Le Coeur 1942–1943). In the early twenty-first century men and women have their own hammams where they could bathe day and night. Sometimes, affluent men or women rent an entire hammam and invite their close friends and families for a celebration.

In the Islamic tradition, using hammams has been associated with healing and curing a number of illnesses, such as indigestion, exhaustion, and diarrhea (Munawi 1987). One of the main drawbacks to going to hammams

Turkish Bath in Gaza City. *Two men relax in the Hamam Samra Turkish bath, in Gaza City.* © AHMED JADALLAH/REUTERS/CORBIS.

is loss of appetite. Arabic poetry is laden with chanting the rewards of going to the hammam where steaming naked bodies arouse pleasure seekers. Some equated a trip to the hammam to a long day of lasting desire. It is attributed to Abu Jaafar, a poet from Seville, courting a handsome young man in the hammam (Munawi 1987).

Though the hammam is entrenched in the Islamic tradition, baths in modern homes have lessened the number of hammams' clients, particularly among the wealthy.

BIBLIOGRAPHY

Aaland, Mikkel. 1978. *Sweat: The Illustrated History and Description of the Finnish Sauna, Russian Bania, Islamic Hammam, Japanese Mushi-buro, Mexican Temescal, and American Indian & Eskimo Sweatlodge*. Santa Barbara, CA: Capra Press.

Al-Ghazali, Abu Hamid. 1999. *Ihya' ulum al-Din* [The Revival of the Religious Sciences]. Beirut, Lebanon: Dar-al-Fikr.

Dow, Martin. 1996. *The Islamic Baths of Palestine*. Oxford, UK: Oxford University Press.

Ecochard, Michel, and Claude Le Coeur. 1942–1943. *Les bains de Damas; monographies architecturales*. Beyrouth, Lebanon: Institut français de Damas.

Ibn Khaldun, Abd-arahman. n.d. *Al-Muqaddimah* [An Introduction to History]. Beirut, Lebanon: Dar al-Fikr.

Kayyal, Munir. 1986. *Al-Hammamat al-Dimashqiyah* [Damascus Baths]. Damascus, Syria: Matba'at Ibn Khaldun.

Manderscheid, Hubertus. 2004. *Ancient Baths and Bathing: A Bibliography for the Years 1988-2001*. Portsmouth, RI: Journal of Roman Archeology.

Munawi, Abdalrauf ibn Tajal Arifin. 1987. *Nuzhah al-zahiya fi ahkam alhammam al-shari'yah wa-al-tibbiyah* [Promenade/ Excursion of the Vainglorious in the Rules of the Hammam'a Medical Jurisprudence], ed. and intro. Abdal-Hamid Salih Hamdan. Al-Qahirah, Egypt: al-Dar al-Misriyah al-Lubnaniyah.

Hamid Bahri

III. WEST, MIDDLE AGES—PRESENT

Public bathing was strongly discouraged in the early Middle Ages by such Christian moralists as Jerome. Nevertheless, it remained a common practice. Medieval illustrations of people in public baths are not infrequent and bathing seems to have been a social activity, involving both sexes, who, at times, banqueted and exchanged intimacies. Some baths allocated separate bathing days to men and women; however, such a

A Medieval Bathhouse. THE GRANGER COLLECTION, NEW YORK.

separation is not seen in all drawings. In the Middle Ages and the Renaissance, public baths were a common place for sexual encounters: men and women as well as men and men, women and women, and men and boys, although the last is rarely talked about in the early twenty-first century. Michael Rocke notes of fifteenth-century Florence: "Many men and boys consummated their sexual relationships ... in the several public baths spread across the city" (1996, p. 160) in a sexual culture in which roles were based on a hierarchical model of male sexual relations strictly defined by age, in which boys were passive and those older were active. While the sociability of the public baths was distinctly different from the sociability of the brothel, the baths were often used for prostitution. A blurring of lines may have been facilitated in the fourteenth century, when cities such as London tried to segregate prostitution by banishing it to areas outside the city where "stews" and bathhouses were found. From the fourteenth century, the term *stew*—another word for a bathhouse with hot baths—also became slang for brothel, as did *bagnios* (similar to modern Turkish baths) in the sixteenth century.

During the sixteenth and seventeenth centuries, public baths as places of pleasure and encounter fell out of fashion until the nineteenth century when bathhouse culture experienced a revitalization among Western cultures, particularly in Australia, New Zealand, and North America. Several factors contributed to this boom: the discovery of germ theory in the 1880s; the building of baths for the poor that were often heavily policed, segregated, time-limited and aimed at safeguarding their health and improving their moral character; and the development of curative and regenerative baths which sought to revive the sociability of such establishments as the Turkish baths—hammams.

Surveillance hampered, but did not prevent, opportunities for sexual encounters.

By the late nineteenth century, some bathhouses within such cities as New York and Sydney were known to tolerate sex between men. In the early twentieth century, when bathhouse patronage declined due to the emergence of private bathrooms, proprietors saw benefit in actively supporting the use of public baths as sites for furtive sexual encounters between men. These bathhouses were distinct from baths which just tolerated sex between men, in that their management excluded non-gay customers and safeguarded—rather than merely tolerated—homosexual activity.

In the later 1960s with the emergence of gay culture, a new generation of bathhouses became established as major gay institutions. In addition to standard cubicles and baths, other spaces such as theaters, restaurants, specialist rooms, mirrors, porn rooms, and mazes were introduced to foster sexual experimentation and exploration, as well as cultural and social activities. Such places as New York's Continental Baths and Sydney's Roman Baths were renowned for opulent interiors dripping with ferns—and men. Although designed for men, these baths would, on occasion, have women-only nights. In these new environments, Michel Foucault, among others, saw a potential starting point for the development of a culture that could invent new ways of relating, types of existence, types of values, types of exchanges between individuals that had been impossible within the world outside the baths at that time; a culture in which sexuality and pleasure were imbedded in sociability in a similar way to that which had existed in the Roman *thermes*.

The arrival of AIDS in the 1980s represented a possible crisis point in the acceptance of gay bathhouses, not only by authorities but by patrons themselves. Baths in the United States were closed in the belief that they spread contagion. Baths in other countries such as Australia and Belgium, however, continued to flourish and remained open on the basis that, if properly managed and designed, they could operate as venues for the practice of safe sex and dissemination of safe sex education. During the 1990s, this approach in Sydney, Australia, resulted in formal legal recognition of the importance of bathhouses to the city's sexual culture, and recognition of the distinct consensual environment they provided for male sexual encounters severing the blurring of lines between the sociability of the brothel and bathhouses that emerged in the Middle Ages.

BIBLIOGRAPHY

Bell, Arthur. 1978. "The Gay Bath Life Gets Respectability." In *Lavender Culture*, ed. Karla Jay and Allen Young, 77–84. New York: Jove Publications.

Berube, Allan. 1996. "The History of Gay Bathhouses." In *Policing Public Sex: Queer Politics and the Future of AIDS Activism*, ed. Ephen Glenn Colter, et al., 187–220. Boston: South End Press.

Bolton, Ralph; John Vincke; and Rudolf Mak. 1994. "Gay Baths Revisited: An Empirical Analysis." *GLQ: A Journal of Gay and Lesbian Studies* 1 (3): 255–273.

Chauncey, George. 1994. "The Social World of the Baths." In *Gay New York: Gender, Urban Culture, and the Making of the Gay Male World, 1890-1940*, 207–227. New York: Basic Books.

Gallagher, Bob; Alexander Wilson; and Michel Foucault. 1984. "An Interview: Sex, Power and the Politics of Identity." *The Advocate Los Angeles, California* 400 (August): 26–30, 58.

Halperin, David. 1995. *Saint Foucault. Towards a Gay Hagiography*. New York: Oxford University Press.

Karras, Ruth Mazo. 1996. *Common Women: Prostitution and Sexuality in Medieval England*. New York: Oxford University Press.

Karras, Ruth Mazo. 2005. *Sexuality in Medieval Europe: Doing unto Others*. New York: Routledge.

Prior, Jason. 2005. "Sydney Gay Saunas 1967–2000: Fights for Civic Acceptance and Experiences beyond the Threshold." Ph.D. dissertation, University of New South Wales.

Rocke, Michael. 1996. *Forbidden Friendships: Homosexuality and Male Culture in Renaissance Florence*. New York: Oxford University Press.

Rumaker, Michael. 1979. *A Day and Night at the Baths*. Bolinas, CA: Grey Fox Press.

Styles, Joseph. 1979. "Outsider/Insider: Researching Gay Baths." *Urban Life: A Journal of Ethnographic Research* 8 (2): 135–153.

Weinberg, Martin, and Colin Williams. 1975. "Gay Baths and the Social Organization of Impersonal Sex." *Social Problems: Official Journal of the Society for the Study of Social Problems* 23 (2): 124–136.

Jason Prior

BEARD

The beard occupies a significant symbolic terrain across time and cultures, and can be metonymical of the male person or of maleness, although this association is at times complicated by signs of cultural identity.

Thus, Hittite iconography, confirmed by Egyptian representations, indicates that while Hittite men, including warriors and priests, remain beardless with long hair (Haroutunian 2002, pp. 47–50), the mountain gods, weather gods, and vegetation gods represented at Yazilikaya rock sanctuary are bearded, signifying manliness, fertility, and power (Haroutunian 2002, p. 51).

The ancient cult of a bearded Ishtar may have combined the morning warrior star with the evening erotic star, but both the Cypriote Aphrodite (Krappe 1945) and the Venus Calva worshipped in Rome (Eitrem 1923) were coded as androgynous, with a beard and a comb. Both appear connected to marriage and fertility.

The beard could focalize anxious struggles between men over masculinity and virility, acting as an object of symbolic sexual transference. This is evident in the old Spanish *Poema de Mio Cid*, where the Cid grabs his beard and swears an oath by "this beard that no one has ever plucked" to avenge his daughter of the affront done to them (vss. 2829–2832, 3185–3186). Before appearing at court to confront the insulters, in a careful performance of power and manliness, he covers his hair with a coif so no one can pull it, and ties up his long beard with a cord, safeguarding it from attack, "to protect his entire person from direct personal physical insult"(vss. 3085–3100). He then insults an enemy by boasting of having pulled out his beard instead (vss. 3273–3290). This conflation of personal honor with manliness, virility, power, and the beard has been claimed in relation to other cultures throughout the Mediterranean basin and the Middle East, ranging from early modern Byzantium (Horowitz 1997) to modern Syria (McCartney 1938). Insistence on the beard as proof of virility and hostility towards beardless men are rife in the early medieval West. In the early twelfth century, shaving one's beard lumped a man with priests and women, and the new Christian militia, the Templars, was enthusiastically praised by Bernard of Clairvaux as a manly brotherhood, celibate and bearded, eschewing the effeminacy of worldly knights (McNamara 1994, pp. 9, 17). In the fabliau of the "Santier battu" (beaten path) a lady berates an unresponsive knight as beardless and effeminate: he bests her, claiming that she has no pubic hair "because grass does not grow on a beaten path" (Montaiglon 1973, R 3:247). Beyond insults, the text underscores that beard and hair are simulacra located in sex.

Yet, perhaps as a result of fashion, or because of ambiguity attached to facial hair, the Western European fifteenth century was largely beardless—a fact attested to in painting, as in the portrait of Pierre II, Duke of Bourbon by the Master of Moulins (Moulins cathedral) circa 1500, or of Etienne Chevalier by Jean Fouquet, circa 1450 (Berlin, Deutsches Museum)—apparently reflecting a conscious intent of setting oneself apart from those familiar "Others," Jews and Muslims, represented as very bearded. However, with the travels to the New World, and the encounter of Native American populations who seemed to carefully eschew any bodily hair, another European discourse of othering associated beardlessness, sodomitical tendencies, and an alleged inferiority that would justify enslavement and imprisonment of Native Americans. European men thus returned to wearing the beard in the sixteenth century (Horowitz 1997).

The beard marked enforceable gender-differentiation in the United States in the late nineteenth and early twentieth century. There was a post–Civil War campaign for male rights and the new masculinity, reflecting anxiety about the status of women. Thus, clergyman Horace Bushnell's 1869 tirade against women's suffrage extolled masculinity and the distinguishable emblems of a man's authority over women, specifically, "...the base in his voice and the shag on his face...." For him, women who sought the right to vote were such a "radical revolt against nature," that "the claim of a beard" could be no worse. Gender conservatives in the 1900s attacked pictorial portrayals of Jesus for showing him as too feminine, with "a womanly sweetness," as if the portrayal was that of "Christ with a woman's face, and an added beard," such a "scant beard" almost suggesting "a bearded lady" (Morgan 2005, pp. 213–215).

"Why do men have beards?" asked Arthur Schopenhauer (1788–1860). The answer, that a beard is a mask made necessary to combat the wiles of women, may reflect "... a worldwide mythology of great complexity" (Taussig 1995, p. 108). The rituals of secrecy enacted and enforced by men have created a "theater of men making men," and justify another "theater of concealment and revelation playing with ... the gender line fatefully implicating holiness and violence." This theater is real "as long as the men are looked at by women not as men acting but what it is they represent" (p. 113).

Thus, when women have beards, gender borders are dramatically raided, and the "natural" gender order is literally "defaced." The bearded androgyny of crucified female saints in the Middle Ages has been interpreted variously as linked to marriage rituals (Krappe 1945) or to fears of pollution and female danger (Sautman 1995, pp. 78–79). But late-nineteenth-century and early-twentieth-century Western sexology theorized transgendered women as deviant and abnormal, enshrining the natural order as stable and unidirectional. Their views were unshaken by the existence of actual bearded women, and the bearded woman was relegated to and contained by the status of freak and anomaly. Thus "bearded women" in carnival and circus midways were and are a rich and contentious site of visual culture and gender construction. The fascination exercised by the bearded woman, including her eroticization, is paralleled by attempts to recuperate and soften anomaly by feminizing it (Adams 2001, pp. 117, 222). However, the bearded woman has remained a resilient icon of denaturized sex and gender. In the late twentieth and in the twenty-first century, bearded women have exercised strong agency to revisit and correct their marginal and disavowed status, offering radical readings of gender, especially in modern U.S. lesbian communities. The performance work of Jennifer Miller, active in the Coney Island counterculture "freak shows," is a strong expression of this perspective (Adams 2001, pp. 135–136, 219–228).

SEE ALSO *Androgyny; Masculinity: I. Overview; Sex Roles.*

BIBLIOGRAPHY

Adams, Rachel. 2001. *Sideshow U.S.A. Freaks and the American Cultural Imagination.* Chicago: University of Chicago Press.

Eitrem, S. 1923. "Venus Calva and Venus Cloacina." *The Classical Review* 37(1/2): 14–16.

Haroutunian, Hripsime. 2002. "Bearded or Beardless? Some Speculations in the Function of the Beard among the Hittite." In *Recent Developments in Hittite Archaeology and History*, ed.

K. Ashlian Yener, Harry A. Hoffner, and Simrit Dhesi. Winona Lake, IN: Eisenbrauns.

Horowitz, Elliott. 1997. "The New World and the Changing Face of Europe." *Sixteenth-Century Journal* 28(4): 1181–1201.

Krappe, Alexander H. 1945. "The Bearded Venus." *Folklore* 56(4): 325–335.

McCartney, Eugene S. 1938. "On Grasping the Beard in Making Entreaties." *The Classical Journal* 33(4): 211–16.

McNamara, Jo Ann. 1994. "The Herrenfrage: The Restructuring of the Gender System, 1050–1150." In *Medieval Masculinities: Regarding Men in the Middle Ages*, ed. Clare A. Lees. Minneapolis: University of Minnesota Press.

Montaiglon, Anatole de, and Gaston Raynaud, eds. 1973. *Recueil général et complet des fabliaux des XIIIe et XIVe siècles*, 6 vols. Geneva: Slatkine Reprints. (Orig. pub. 1872–1890.)

Morgan, David. 2005. *The Sacred Gaze: Religious Visual Culture in Theory and Practice*. Berkeley: University of California Press.

Pidal, Ramon Menéndez, ed. 1975. *El Cid Campeador: Poem of the Cid*, trans. W. S. Merwin. New York: New American Library. (Orig. pub. 1959.)

Sautman, Francesca Canadé. 1995. *La Religion du quotidien. Rites et croyances populaires de la fin du Moyen Age*. Firenze: Olschki.

Taussig, Michael. 1995. "Schopenhauer's Beard." In *Constructing Masculinity*, ed. Maurice Berger, Brian Wallis, and Simon Watson. New York: Routledge.

The Poem of the Cid: A New Critical Edition of the Spanish Text. 1975. Intro. and notes Ian Michael, trans. Rita Hamilton and Janet Perry. Manchester, UK: Manchester University Press.

Francesca Canadé Sautman

BEATRICE
1265–1290

Beatrice Portinari is the central figure in Dante Alighieri's *Vita Nuova* (New life, c. 1294), in his *Divine Comedy* (1308–1321), in several other lyric poems outside of the *Vita Nuova,* and in Book III of the *Convivio* (The Banquet, 1308). The *Vita Nuova* was assembled after Beatrice's death as a book of memory with the author's love poems for her. Beatrice is historically identified by Giovanni Boccaccio (1313–1375) in his *Life of Dante* as the daughter of Folco Portinari, an eminent figure in the City of Florence, and as wife of Simone dei Bardi, a member of a rich Florentine banking family. Folco died in 1289 and his will records that monna Bice (lady Beatrice) born Florence, Italy, was one of his eleven children.

Within the *Vita Nuova*, a "libello" (little book) that is at once a psychological confession and work of self-examination as well as an experiment in the craft of poetry, there are sufficient biographical references to justify the historical existence of the lady Beatrice Portinari whom the poet idealized and sublimated as Beatrice. The author states that he first saw her when he was nine and at the beginning of her ninth year, and that she became: "the glorious lady of my mind, who was called Beatrice (she who brings bliss) even by those who did not know what her name was" (Musa 1973, p. 3). From this point to when she bids him adieu from the Celestial Rose of the Empyrean (*Paradiso* Canto XXXI: 58–93), Beatrice remained the narrator's inspiration to undertake his spiritual rebirth (new life) both as a man and as a poet.

Beatrice is the figuration of an earthly woman who, breaking all traditions, achieves the highest, most sublime symbolism of a divine being, a "figura Christi" and "typus Trinitatis" (a figure of Christ and a type of the Trinity). This process can be traced throughout the *New Life*: thus, Dante, quoting Homer, labels her "daughter not of a mortal, but of God"; when she denies him her greeting ("saluto"), for him the summation of all bliss (Dante plays with the words *saluto, salute, salutare,* both as greeting or salutation and spiritual health), he feels empty of any joy and beatitude (Musa 1973, p. 16). The elevation of Beatrice to divine-like status is at the core of the *Vita Nuova*, and intensifies in the canzone (song) "Donne ch'avete intelletto d'amore" (Ladies who have intelligence of love), in which the Blessed dare tell God that Heaven lacks perfection because of her absence (Ch. XIX). This both announces her death and the composition of the *Divine Comedy*. Further, in Chapter XXIV, the author proposes an analogy between Beatrice and Christ, as he sees Beatrice in a dream preceded by Giovanna Primavera (the lady of Guido Cavalcanti, Dante's oldest friend to whom the *Vita* is dedicated), as John the Baptist preceded Jesus: "since the name Joan (Giovanna) comes from the name John (Giovanni) who preceded the True Light" (Musa 1973, p. 52). This is followed with the most famous of Dante's sonnets, "Tanto gentile e tanto onesta pare" ("So winsome and so worthy seems to me"), Chapter XXVI, in which he writes: "... sweetly and mantled in humility,/ away she walks from all she's praised by,/ and truly seems a thing come from the sky/ to show on earth what miracles can be" (Alighieri 1992, p. 51). The symbolism of Beatrice as a type of the Trinity is reinforced upon her death (1290) when Dante speaks of her as number nine—that is, a miracle (Ch. 28, p. 62): "this lady was accompanied by the number nine so that it might be understood that she was a nine, or a miracle, whose root, namely that of the miracle, is the miraculous Trinity itself." In the last chapter of the *Vita Nuova*, Dante prepares the reader to the presence and role of Beatrice in the *Commedia*, stating that he hopes to say of her "that which has never been said of any woman."

This is the link to Beatrice's appearance in *Inferno* (2:52–108) within a type of Feminine Trinity who has descended unto Limbo, urging Virgil to come to the rescue of the pilgrim Dante lost in the dark wood, the *selva oscura*. Beatrice is moved by a love, "Amor mi mosse che mi fa parlare," which originated with Mary, "donna è gentil nel ciel" (there is a gentle lady in heaven), who asked a second woman, Lucia, "nemica di ciascun crudele" (enemy of any cruelty), to plead with a third one, Beatrice, sitting in heaven next to the ancient Rachel, and to rescue the one "who loved you so much" (II, 100–108). Dante the author thus builds a feminine Trinity and Godhead: Mary; Saint Lucy, patron saint of Syracuse and of eyesight; Beatrice. Thus begins the role of Beatrice as a divine guide and teacher for the pilgrim Dante, to take over from Virgil in the last three cantos of the *Purgatory* and in the *Paradiso*. She comes to embody not only the Divine Guide but also Theology, Divine Grace, Revelation, and the one who, transcending gender (as evidenced in the image of the Admiral in *Purgatory* 30:58) never loses her power as earthly woman (catalyst of courtly love at first) while being transformed into a divine one.

SEE ALSO *Allegory; Dante Alighieri.*

BIBLIOGRAPHY

Alighieri, Dante. 1992. *Dante's Lyric Poems*, trans. Joseph Tusiani, intro. and notes by Giuseppi C. Di Scipio. New York: Legas.

Barbi, Michele. 1954. *Life of Dante*, trans. and ed. Paul G. Ruggiers. Berkeley: University of California Press.

Ferrante, Joan. 2000. "Beatrice." In *Dante Encyclopedia*, ed. Teodolinda Barolini, et al. New York: Garland.

Musa, Mark. 1973.*Vita Nuova: A Translation and an Essay.* Bloomington: Indiana University Press.

Scott, John. 1972. "Dante's Admiral." *Italian Studies* 27: 28–40.

Singleton, Charles. 1949. *An Essay on the Vita Nuova.* Cambridge, MA: Harvard University Press for the Dante Society.

Singleton, Charles. 1958. *Journey to Beatrice.* Baltimore: John Hopkins University Press.

Giuseppe Di Scipio

BEATRICE OF THE KONGO
1686–1706

The relative paucity of clergy in African religions, imputable to their decentralized and non-proselytizing modes of worship, may have obscured women's leadership in the spiritual realm. When missionaries brought Christianity to Africa, women sometimes resolved to combine selected aspects of the imported religion with the previous system of beliefs—in which they occupied key positions as founding ancestors, oracles, mediums, rainmakers, healers, midwives, and initiation moderators—and emerged as larger-than-life prophets of a new syncretic faith propagated through an independent church.

Dona Beatriz Kimpa Vita was such a charismatic woman who, at the turn of the eighteenth century, spearheaded a messianic movement in the name of Saint Anthony and on behalf of Kongolese peasants of both sexes. She was born into aristocracy in 1686, two centuries after the conversion of the king of the Kongo, João I, to Catholicism under Portuguese influence (1491), and twenty years after the defeat of Mbwila (or Ambuila, 1665) in which King Antonio I was killed by the Portuguese army. Kongolese political factions soon began vying for succession in a series of civil wars that left the capital city, San Salvador, depopulated, and the region open to European slave traders. This religious and political context informed Beatrice's push for the restoration of a unified Kongo and for the Africanization of Christianity.

Beatrice began her religious career as a *nganga marinda,* a priestess specializing in the social dimension of illness. In 1704 Saint Anthony possessed her and revealed her new mission: He instructed her to save Kongo from its current chaos. Beatrice, who claimed direct communication with the divine, established her headquarters in San Salvador where she attracted flocks of followers with her sermons and miracles. Bernardo da Gallo, one of the two Italian Capuchins whose diaries record Beatrice's epic, thus acknowledged her popularity when he wrote: "… The false saint became the restorer, ruler and lord of the Congo, and was acclaimed, adored and esteemed as such by everyone" (Thornton 1983, p 109, note 60).

Much of her power resided in the hybrid nature of her teachings and mission. She proposed a rich vision of a new kingdom of Kongo where Christianity would be the instrument of liberation from foreign yoke and internecine strife. Her symbolic death, dream, and communication with a "lesser spirit" through possession were in line with African religious experiences. Her sense of entitlement in nominating the king among rival lineages similarly derived from a local notion of high priesthood. She also insisted on relocating the founding episodes and major actors of Christianity into sacred Kongolese sites: Jesus was born in San Salvador and Mary in Nsundi. Moreover, Beatrice readily reenacted specific moments of Christianity, such as Christ's death, the foundation of a church, the establishment of a dogma, and she dispatched emissaries, the "little Anthonies," to preach her Gospel throughout the land. Yet she rejected both the "fetishes," including the cross (that had indeed been appropriated by *ngangas* under the Kongoized name *kuluzu*) and the main Christian sacraments (namely baptism, confession, and even marriage), and often revised official prayers.

Beatrice's fate was sealed when she unsuccessfully approached King Pedro IV for national reconciliation and nominated to the throne Pedro Constantinho da Silva, who provided the ever-growing Antonine movement with an army. Concerned over the effect of Antonianism on Catholicism and the colonial project, Capuchin missionaries colluded with politicians to arrest Beatrice and her newborn child, whose existence challenged her claim to sainthood. While the infant was whisked away by the priests, the "false Saint Anthony" was burnt at the stake as a heretic and a witch on July 1, 1706, and her remains were reburnt the next day.

In spite of Pedro's two campaigns in 1709 and 1715, the Antonian movement survived probably until the 1720s in rural strongholds. Many of the prisoners taken during the Kongolese civil wars were deported as slaves to South Carolina and Saint-Domingue (later Haiti). Kongolese veterans, Catholic and Antonian alike, may then have contributed to the Stono rebellion (1739) and to the Haitian revolution (1791).

Beatrice's project of Africanizing Christianity is reminiscent of the Donatist movement in the third century in North Africa. It was also a blueprint for Kimbanguism in the 1920s Belgian Congo. Often compared to Joan of Arc, Beatrice of the Kongo is one of the many African women, such as Nehanda, Nongqause, Mai Chaza, and Alice Lenshina Mulenga, who best exemplify the spiritual dimension of anticolonial resistance.

SEE ALSO *Africa: I. History; Colonialism; Virginity.*

BIBLIOGRAPHY

Balandier, Georges. 1968. *Daily Life in the Kingdom of the Kongo from the Sixteenth to the Eighteenth Century*, trans. Helen Weaver. New York: Pantheon.

Coquery-Vidrovitch, Catherine. 1997. *African Women: A Modern History*, trans. Beth Gillian Raps. Boulder, CO: Westview Press.

Thornton, John K. 1983. *The Kingdom of Kongo: Civil War and Transition, 1641–1718.* Madison: University of Wisconsin Press.

Thornton, John K. 1998. *The Kongolese Saint Anthony: Dona Beatriz Kimpa Vita and the Antonian Movement, 1684–1706.* Cambridge, UK: Cambridge University Press.

Sylvie Kandé

BEAUTY PAGEANTS

Displaying young unmarried women in a ritual competition, beauty pageants crown one of the contestants as queen. She might be Miss America or Miss Ghana, Miss Gay IU (actually a male competition), Miss Rodeo Idaho, or even Miss Penitenciária. Although fictional, the title carries rewards ranging from large sums of cash, flashy cars, and scholarships to the symbolic power of representing one's community or nation and the pride inherent in being the one chosen above all the others. In all of its multiple variations, the beauty contest reflects the interests, purposes, values, and goals of the organizers and their perceived audiences. The majority of these values concern gender roles. In the social process of defining the ideal woman, queen contests often become the site of debates—particularly those concerning femininity and masculinity and the roles assigned to women and men. Consequently, the contests respond to pressures by incorporating changes. In some instances, however, differences may develop into major controversies and lead to unanticipated outcomes.

THE LOCAL AND THE GLOBAL

Classified as popular culture, beauty pageants are nevertheless viewed around the world as events that embody modernity and signify Western values. Consequently, every nation state that aspires to be modern holds a competition and forwards its winners to the annual television-mediated global competitions, Miss Universe and Miss World. Being represented on the global stage of national beauties and competing against world powers in a ritual performance of symbolic females creates the illusion of full participation in the global arena for those nation states that might otherwise be accorded second rank.

In addition to the national hierarchical stand-alone competitions culminating in the selection of the queen of the universe or the world, beauty contests are organized within events such as county or state fairs and rodeos, and by institutions, organizations, and industries. They also are produced as the expressions of identity for social groups and to recognize age groups, and to bring recognition and fundraising to churches and schools, businesses, and any socially organized unit that can be imagined. The power and money generated by these competitions accrues to the sponsors and participants as well as the winners; moreover, the event can be replicated with ease on a very small scale or a very grand one, and the subject (young women) is available as an infinite resource at no cost. This combination makes it possible for every variation of human organization to produce beauty contests and pageants.

GENDER ROLES AND THE INTRODUCTION OF CHANGE

The creation of gender roles is a dynamic process, negotiated among members of specific communities in response to historical and socioeconomic circumstances. Beauty contests bring this process into the public eye, revealing contradictions, conflicts, and changes as they are evolving. Tracking the modifications in the Miss America contest reveals a close parallel with changing gender issues in the larger culture. Major transformations have affected the pageant since it began in 1921 as the "Fall Frolic on the Boardwalk," an attempt by Atlantic City to continue to draw crowds after the summer season. The swimsuit competition has been the most controversial and debated issue over the years, confusing "wholesomeness with sex appeal, creating a paradox that still exists," as Angelina Saulino Osborne explains. As identified by Susan Powell, Miss America 1981, the platform concept forced a major change because the contestants then had to be willing to contribute time and energy to a worthwhile cause. An equally momentous change occurred with the introduction of scholarships (1945), supporting the contestants in the pursuit of higher education. The scholarships sent a different message and also attracted more serious contestants. Bess Myerson, a music major at Hunter College, entered because of the scholarship and became Miss America that year. She also was the first and only Jewish Miss America. It was not until 1983 that the first African-American Miss America, Vanessa Williams, was chosen. When Heather Whitestone won the contest and became Miss America in 1995, she represented a new recognition of people with disabilities as she is deaf. In 2006 a reality show component was announced in the hope of boosting waning ratings.

Change in any contest results from negotiation. Not acknowledged as such, however, this cultural process elicits the ideas, values, and opinions of those involved in the production, or it may engage opinions expressed through media, protests, organizations, money, and other modes. With regard to the Miss America Pageant, this latter process became transparent when the CEO of the organization was fired in 1999. The action occurred just after the CEO and the Pageant Board had revoked the ban on divorce and abortion for contestants in order to comply with state laws against discrimination. In response, state pageant directors, former winners, and other traditionalists vehemently opposed the change, and the CEO was removed. This controversy reflects similar ones throughout the country around the turn of the twenty-first century as debates over women's sexuality and reproductive rights, the female body, marriage, and the ideal woman have continued. In one instance, a crisis developed at a small midwestern university in 2000 when a queen was forced to give up her title because it was discovered that some years previously she had been raped, became pregnant, and then miscarried. Pageant rules in the United States generally stipulate an age group (late teens through early twenties), and a rule against marriage and pregnancy. (These rules were clarified for the Miss America Pageant in the early twenties after several married women with children entered.)

Perhaps no change has been as significant as the role of the sponsors, which expanded throughout the twentieth century. Sponsors are businesses and corporations that provide vast sums of money for the pageant and the queen, who then tours for and appears with the sponsors, adding her glamour to their products for the full year she wears the crown.

COMPETITION AND REPRESENTATION

Beauty contests motivate both contestants and audiences through competition and representation. Young women compete against each other in a ritualized competition. The competition creates a system of signification in which women are expected to embody values that symbolize the ideal female. The contests constitute a secular ritual due to the repetition of their form and purpose, the enactment of social/gender relationships, and the transformation that occurs: one of the contestants is judged to be more ideal than the others and she is crowned the queen, receiving recognition, rewards, and responsibilities. The other contestants are also affected by the ritual: they appear before an audience in a variety of attire, participate in the competition, and submit to being judged.

Ritual often develops as a response when transition, ambiguity, or conflict threatens the status quo, especially the structure of social relations such as that between male and female. Distinctions between adult and child and between female and male are fundamental to all societies, and are generally established through rituals of initiation. As the competitions to select a queen function to define and distinguish females who have reached maturity and present them to the public, they function like initiation rites in modern societies, defining femininity and the ideal woman.

In beauty contests ritual links the individual to society through the process of sponsorship by a business or political unit such as a town, state, nation, or organization. The contestant then represents that entity and learns her role as the symbol of something other than herself. Obfuscated by the glitz and glamour of bodies, lights, and music, the flow of money through sponsorship links the ideal unmarried woman to the social relations of capitalism. In the beauty pageant economy funds are exchanged through: entry fees for the contestants; wardrobe, accoutrements, and travel; tickets for the public; and prizes awarded the winners. The selection process determines that a contestant must obtain the support of a sponsor (a business, a community, or another public

Miss Universe 2006 and Miss Indonesia 2005. *Miss Universe 2006 Zuleyka Rivera Mendoza (R) of Puerto Rico and Miss Indonesia 2005 Nadine Chandrawinata pose for photographers.* © MAST IRHAM/EPA/CORBIS.

entity). The sponsor then provides the entry fee and other expenses if the contest is a large one, and the name of the sponsor is indicated on the ribbon the contestant wears across her body.

One privately organized pageant in 1998 in a small but economically upscale town offered a contest with three segments: a swimsuit preliminary, an evening gown preliminary, and a final contest. Tickets were $20 for each event or $50 for all three, and the entry fee for contestants was $795.00. The contestants sought sponsors at the national and the local level. At a state level contest or a very large event, thousands of dollars will be necessary to support a queen candidate. Sixteen businesses were required to support the campaign of Miss Rodeo North Dakota in 2004, and many more sponsors were required to send her to the national competition.

INNOVATION AND VARIATION

As twentieth-century immigrant groups have settled into the United States and become citizens, they have introduced innovation into the beauty contest paradigm. These groups have now established contests with the titles Miss Vietnam USA, Miss Ethiopia North America, Miss India USA, Miss Liberia USA, Miss Asian America, Miss Latina U.S., and Miss Haiti USA. These are not the first contests to recognize cultural identities, however. Native American groups have long produced a variation of the beauty contest. In a pan-Indian event considered to be the largest in the United States, the annual Gathering of Nations Pow Wow in Albuquerque, New Mexico, native women from all over the United States, Canada, Mexico, and Central America compete in a contest titled "Miss Indian World Pageant." With a female mistress of ceremonies directing the pageant, the contestants compete on stage by performing traditional skills, dressed in native costumes. Young Native American women can also compete for the title of Miss National Congress of American Indians in a contest in which individual tribes send their representative princesses to perform both a traditional and a modern skill.

The queen contests that involve the majority of young women in the United States and other countries as well are those localized contests attached to the annual festival celebrated in almost every small town and suburb.

Closely linked to the town and the festival, these queens have specialized names and are known to their audiences. At the Rattlesnake Roundup in Sweetwater, Texas, the winner of the beauty contest receives the title "Miss Snake Charmer," and is rewarded with the opportunity to handle a rattlesnake. In contrast to the annual events, some contests may be held in conjunction with a one-time special event. This was the case in Ghana, where organizers of the celebration to mark the forty-year anniversary of the creation of the Brong Ahafo region featured a beauty contest in 1999. The Anniversary Beauty Queen was awarded a trip to London, cash, and a television.

Yet another variation of the beauty contest, with quite a different focus on the body, are the bodybuilders' contests. In a turn-of-the-twenty-first-century phenomenon, both females and males engaged in building muscular bodies compete in contests that display them for the public. However, females in these contests develop massive physiques that are not consistent with the viewing public's concept of femininity, confusing it with masculinity. Consequently, bodybuilding shows added two other sporting events in the mid-nineties: Ms. Fitness (showcasing athletic women softer than their bodybuilding counterparts who perform routines in stiletto heels) and Ms. Figure (in which contestants are not bodybuilders but have good muscle tone and also wear stiletto heels).

Whatever purpose they claim to serve, beauty contests address the question of gender with seriousness. For gay men, who do not conform to the heterosexual model of female and male, the beauty contest provides an excellent opportunity to challenge assumptions about sexuality and satirize sanctioned gender roles. Defining themselves as women and producing the event, the participants in a gay beauty contest perform lip synch to recordings of female singers, give themselves female names, and include an evening gown competition, modeled on the mainstream contests. Paralleling the Miss America contest, gay men produce the Miss'd America Pageant, held in Atlantic City, on the night following the original pageant. While the performance is a satire, it takes its fundraising seriously and raises thousands of dollars annually for AIDS programs. Also familiar is the annual New York City contest featured in the award-winning documentary *Paris is Burning* (1990), in which the costumes reflect the dreams and hopes of the participants. University campuses and gay bars are also sites of gay male contests. At Indiana University in Bloomington, the contest is titled Miss Gay IU and attracts straight as well as gay audience members, female as well as male. Like similar events, in 2006 this one emphasized awareness of AIDS and donated the considerable contribution from the audience to YouthAIDS, an organization dedicated to educating youth about AIDS. In the Southern Philippines a very different system of signification applies, given that transvestite men have traditionally played a role of ritual specialist and performer. There, gay men combine the cultural concept of *bantut* (referring to a long established tradition of performers in the Muslim Tausug and Sama communities in the Philippines who are designated with the term *bantut* who are considered to be men who act like women) with the contemporary concept *gay*, and perform in "international" contests in which they dress in the costume of nations and ethnicities. In the Philippines as elsewhere, transvestite performances challenge hetereosexual concepts of gender, both masculine and feminine, reversing and rearranging them on stage.

DEBATE AND CONTROVERSY

Debate and controversy have followed beauty contests since P.T. Barnum proposed them in the nineteenth century. Depending on the site of the contest, the scale, and the system of signification in place, debate may be expressed on the local level. But in instances where the event is large scale, as it was in India when the Miss World pageant was held there in 1996, the controversy was nationwide and became international news. Protests were staged by conservative religious groups, political parties, feminist activists, student groups, and secular intellectuals, but the global contest went forward in the city of Bangalore and state of Karnataka. In São Paulo, Brazil, where 603 female inmates from ten prisons competed in the Miss Penitenciária pageant in 2005, some individuals felt the prisoners were being glorified instead of punished (Prada 2005). In Nigeria, the Miss World global contest set off political and religious debates in 2002 when it was scheduled during the Muslim holy month of Ramadan. Riots were triggered when a newspaper article claimed that the Prophet would have chosen some of the beauties for wives. Coinciding with the contest was the sentencing of a young mother to death by stoning for adultery by an extremely conservative Islamic court. Though ultimately she was not killed, others died during the ensuing riots. Even in war zones beauty contests are adapted to local circumstances. The first contest to select the Beauty of Chechnya in 2006 was held amidst controversy after Muslim clerics gave their approval, and the swimsuit competition was ruled out.

Riddled with contradictions and a subject of considerable controversy, the first recorded children's contest was a P.T. Barnum baby show in 1855, attended by 61,000 patrons. Children's beauty contests are common in small towns and suburbs and often take place in shopping malls in the midst of an ordinary weekend. Some locations include all ages, beginning with a division for babies that will include boy babies as well as girls. The next two divisions only have females (six to nine years, and ten to thirteen years). In small towns parents may organize these events, but entrepreneurs have also developed them as profit-making ventures, capitalizing on young parents' eagerness to gain recognition for their small children, as well as the photographs that are often associated with the process. In either case, very young children are often made up with lipstick and mascara, in an attempt to give the appearance of mature young women as they stroll down the runway, eliciting praise from some parents and adjectives like "disturbing" from others. Children's and girls' pageants differ in this regard from the first half of the twentieth century when contests were often held, but no attempt was made to portray children as adults.

The most significant debates in Europe and North America center around issues raised by the feminist movement, religious groups, and others, who have objected to the display of the female body, often comparing it to a cattle auction. These criticisms forced changes in the Miss America pageant, shifting the focus from the measurements of a woman's body to the contestants' abilities to think and to speak, and the swimsuit competition was removed for several years, though it has since been reincorporated. In 1997 the Miss America Organization issued a list of word substitutions in an attempt to improve the image of the event, which was losing popularity, proposing "scholarship program" in place of "beauty contest." Again in 2001 it attempted a major overhaul, labeling the swimsuit competition as the "Lifestyle and Fitness" event. These changes have succeeded in attracting serious young women as contestants, many of whom have become doctors or media stars or performers. In the 2007 talent contest, even opera was to be featured (the winner of Miss Indiana 2006 was a music student). Not the first talent competition to feature classical music, Bess Myerson, also a music major, performed Gershwin and Grieg in 1945 when she won the crown and the first scholarship ($5,000).

In spite of these language changes and success in attracting serious and talented young women, the focus remains on the body, indicated by the fact that some contestants have undergone cosmetic surgery, although this is not openly debated. Once again, the contest reflects a practice from the larger society.

Because cultures differ in their definitions of gender and how values are assigned, and the same culture can change these values and definitions, a beauty pageant must be considered in view of the social and historical context in which it occurs. The meaning it is assigned, the debates it generates, and the outcomes it produces will be determined by the hierarchy of values in place in the culture. Thus the meaning of a beauty pageant can only be understood within the system of signification in the culture where it has been produced. In the United States in the early twenty-first century, opposing views on femininity and the role of women are struggling to establish dominance, and these are debated in and through beauty pageants.

SEE ALSO *Physical Culture.*

BIBLIOGRAPHY

Banet-Weiser, Sarah. 1999. *The Most Beautiful Girl in the World: Beauty Pageants and National Identity.* Berkeley: University of California Press.

Borland, Katherine. 1996. "The India Bonita of Monimbo: The Politics of Ethnic Identity in the New Nicaragua." In *Beauty Queens on the Global Stage,* ed. Colleen Ballerino Cohen, Richard Wilk, and Beverly Stoeltje. New York: Routledge.

Burbick, Joan. 2002. *Rodeo Queens and the American Dream.* New York: Perseus Books Group.

Cohen, Colleen Ballerino; Richard Wilk; and Beverly Stoeltje, eds. 1996. *Beauty Queens on the Global Stage: Gender, Contests, and Power.* New York: Routledge.

Craig, Maxine Leeds. 2002. *Ain't I a Beauty Queen? Black Women, Beauty, and the Politics of Race.* Oxford, UK: Oxford University Press.

Johnson, Mark. 1997. *Beauty and Power: Transgendering and Cultural Transformation in the Southern Philippines.* New York: Berg.

Orejuela, Fernando. 2004. "The Latino Body and Sports." In *The Encyclopedia of Latino Popular Culture,* ed. Cordelia Chávez Candelaria. Westport, CT: Greenwood.

Orejuela, Fernando. 2005. "The Body as Cultural Artifact: Performing the Body in Bodybuilding Culture." Ph.D. diss., Indiana University.

Osborne, Angela Saulino. 1995. *Miss America: The Dream Lives On.* Dallas: Taylor Publishing.

Parameswaran, Radhika. 2001. "Global Media Event in India: Contests Over Beauty, Gender, and Nation." *Journalism Communication Monographs* 3(2): 53–105.

Phelan, Peggy. 1993. *Unmarked: The Politics of Performance.* London: Routledge.

Prada, Paulo. 2005. "Felons All, but Free to Try Being Beauty Queen for a Day." *The São Paulo Journal* (Dec. 1). Available from http://www.nytimes.com.

Savage, Candace. 1998. *Beauty Queens: A Playful History.* New York: Abbeville Press.

Stack, Carol B. 1990. "Different Voices, Different Visions: Gender, Culture, and Moral Reasoning." In *Uncertain Terms: Negotiating Gender in American Culture,* ed. Faye Ginsburg and Anna Lowenhaupt Tsing. Boston: Beacon Press.

Stoeltje, Beverly. 1996. "The Snake Charmer Queen: Ritual, Competition, and Signification in American Festival." In *Beauty Queens on the Global Stage,* ed. Colleen Ballerino Cohen, Richard Wilk, and Beverly Stoeltje. New York: Routledge.

Stoeltje, Beverly. 1998. "Gender Representations in Performance: The Cowgirl and the Hostess." *Journal of Folklore Research* 25(3): 219–241.

Watson, Elwood, and Darcy Martin, eds. 2004. *There She Is, Miss America: The Politics of Sex, Beauty, and Race in America's Most Famous Pageant.* New York: Palgrave Macmillan.

Wilk, Richard. 1996. "Connections and Contradictions: From the Crooked Tree Cashew Queen to Miss World Belize." In *Beauty Queens on the Global Stage*, ed. Colleen Ballerino Cohen, Richard Wilk, and Beverly Stoeltje. New York: Routledge.

Beverly J. Stoeltje

BEAUVOIR, SIMONE DE
1908–1986

French philosopher and author, Simone de Beauvoir is most famous for her analysis of gender oppression in her 1949 study, *The Second Sex.* Friend and partner of the existentialist philosopher Jean-Paul Sartre, Beauvoir was a prolific writer and astute commentator on politics, existential philosophy, and society. She brought issues of sex and gender into intellectual consideration. In addition she wrote novels, biographies, and several volumes of memoirs. She is one of the most famous philosophers of the twentieth century, a major intellectual force in the emergence of the Women's movement in the 1960s and 1970s, and an example of her own arguments that women are as capable and valuable as men.

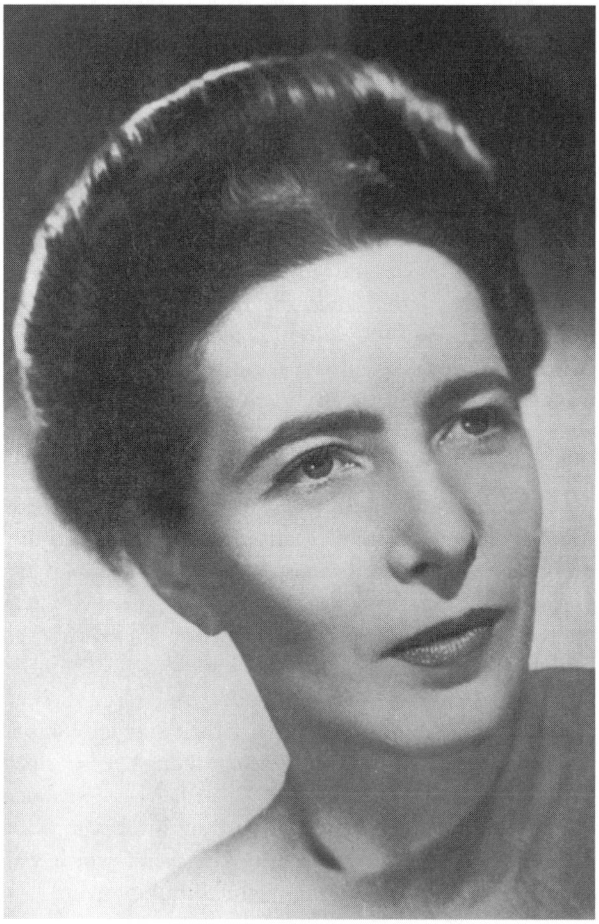

Simone de Beauvoir. EVENING STANDARD/GETTY IMAGES.

FORMATIVE YEARS

Born in Paris on January 9, 1908, Beauvoir was the elder daughter of a bourgeois Parisian family. In her childhood she was an enthusiastic devotee of all things normatively bourgeois: family, patriotism, religion. She loved teaching her younger sister, which she credited with developing her later pleasures in pedagogy and writing. Beauvoir was a superior student, passing baccalaureate exams in both mathematics and philosophy. She pursued the study of mathematics as well as language and literature, but philosophy was her main interest. She enrolled at the Sorbonne in 1926 to study philosophy and there met Sartre, who was taking classes at the Sorbonne while enrolled at the École normale supérieure. Beauvoir earned certificates in seven areas, including general philosophy, ethics, sociology, and psychology. She wrote a thesis on the German philosopher Gottfried Wilhelm Leibnitz and did her practice teaching with classmates Claude Lévi-Strauss and Maurice Merleau-Ponty. When she was twenty-one, though not enrolled at the École normale, she took second place in the philosophy exam, the youngest person ever to do so. First place went to Sartre.

Because of her success on the exam, Sartre asked to meet her, and Beauvoir became a part of Sartre's somewhat elitist group of intellectuals. Attracted to Sartre's intellect, which she felt was equal to her own, Beauvoir became Sartre's lifelong "essential" lover. Although they never lived together or had children, they remained partners until Sartre's death in 1980. They each had other "contingent" romantic relationships in addition, Beauvoir with both women and men, including the American novelist Nelson Algren and the French filmmaker Claude Lanzmann.

Beauvoir began teaching literature and philosophy in Marseilles, then moved to Rouen. She often discussed politics with the students, especially issues concerning the disparate treatment of women. She was reprimanded for her classroom critiques of patriarchy, was fired when the Nazis took over in 1940, and, returning one last time to teaching, was finally dismissed for a liaison with a female student.

WRITING CAREER

She turned to writing, which had always been her ambition. She began with a collection of short stories about women, *When Things of the Spirit Come First*, which was not published until she had become a more accomplished author. But she succeeded in publishing a novel about a triangular love relationship between a man and two women, *She Came to Stay* (1954). During the German occupation of France, she began writing fiction with a moral flavor, and with Sartre, Merleau-Ponty, and others founded a leftist political journal, *Les temps modernes* (Modern times). Although influenced by Karl Marx, Beauvoir did not have an unbothered relation to communism. She worried about the relation between politics and ethics, especially about what responsibility individuals had to themselves and to oppressed groups. Her writing consisted primarily of trying to work out an existentialist ethics in *The Ethics of Ambiguity* (1948) and "Must We Burn Sade?" (1955).

Beauvoir is best known for her landmark two-volume treatise on the oppression of women, *The Second Sex.* The book examines the assumptions of every relevant discipline and mode of social thought from science and biology to sociology, psychoanalysis, literature, and history. In the first volume, she traces what biologists, psychoanalysts, and Marxists have thought of women and how they have situated women within their own sets of assumptions. She also traces the history of how women have been treated in different kinds of cultures from the nomads to modern times. The first volume ends with an analysis of the myths surrounding women through history, in literature, and in everyday life. She points out whose interests are served by myths of women as emotional, illogical, and weak, and how those myths work as a system that elevates the male at the expense of and in relation to the female. In this way Beauvoir also works out the ways that cultural systems define and use the figure of the "Other" as a means of self-definition and promotion.

The second volume analyzes the reality of women's lives in the twentieth century, tracing the various roles and possibilities available to women through their lives from childhood, puberty, marriage, maternity, and old age to alternative roles such as prostitute and lesbian. Beauvoir examines various other positions available to women including being mystics, narcissists (i.e., being that which people like to look at), and lovers. She ends the book by considering the various possibilities for female independence.

Publishing *The Second Sex* established Beauvoir as a central feminist voice. The book itself was controversial, praised and criticized by both men and women. Beauvoir began working with feminist movements, helping to start the women's liberation movement in France, and writing and speaking about women. She also continued to write both fiction and philosophy. From the time *The Second Sex* was published to her death, she wrote an additional thirteen books, including her four-volume autobiography, which begins with her childhood in *Memoirs of a Dutiful Daughter* (1958). She also wrote a compelling description of Sartre's decline and death in *Adieux: A Farewell to Sartre* (1981). Unlike most philosophers, Beauvoir had become a visible public figure with the notoriety and attention expended on the famous. Disliking so much limelight, both Beauvoir and Sartre limited their associations to the close friends they had had since university. Beauvoir traveled, however, touring the United States and China. She also continued to think and write about oppressed groups, including the aged. In *The Coming of Age* (1970), which takes an approach similar to that of *The Second Sex,* Beauvoir traces the ways older people have been treated as less capable others.

After Sartre's death, Beauvoir continued to write. She also adopted the female companion who lived with her. Beauvoir died in Paris of a pulmonary edema on April 14, 1986.

BIBLIOGRAPHY

WORKS BY

Beauvoir, Simone de. 1953. *The Second Sex,* trans. and ed. H. M. Parshley. New York: Knopf.

Beauvoir, Simone de. 1984. *Adieux: A Farewell to Sartre,* trans. Patrick O'Brian. New York: Pantheon.

Beauvoir, Simone de. 1990. *She Came to Stay.* New York: Norton. (Orig. pub. 1954.)

Beauvoir, Simone de. 2000. *The Ethics of Ambiguity,* trans. Bernard Frechtman. New York: Citadel Press. (Orig. pub. 1949.)

Beauvoir, Simone de. 2005. *Memoirs of a Dutiful Daughter,* trans. James Kirkup. Repr., New York: Harper. (Orig. pub. 1974.)

WORKS ABOUT

Bair, Deirdre. 1990. *Simone de Beauvoir: A Biography.* New York: Summit Books.

Rowley, Hazel. 2005. *Tête-à-tête: Simone de Beauvoir and Jean-Paul Sartre.* New York: HarperCollins.

Judith Roof

BEGUINES

Beguine (Latin: *beguina*) was the name given in medieval Europe to a woman who led a religious life without taking solemn or perpetual vows. Although the Beguine lifestyle initially drew strong criticism and some Beguines were persecuted as heretics, they gained a certain respectability in parts of northwestern Europe, where the single-sex communities formed by such women (known as Beguinages) survived until the late twentieth century.

The earliest evidence of Beguine life can be found around 1200 in the region of what is now Belgium, where in various places lay women started to devote themselves to asceticism, charity, and prayer while living alone or with their families. By the 1230s, their numbers in cities like Liège, Leuven, Ghent, and Bruges had grown significantly, enabling them to pool their resources, buy property for communal residence, and create organizations for mutual support. While some Beguines continued to live as solitaries, most of them lived together in small Beguine convents or in larger Beguine courts (enclosed neighborhoods arranged around a church, a hospital, and other service buildings), which in many cities of the Low Countries and the adjacent Rhineland could house several hundreds to one thousand or more women. The Beguine movement spread before 1300 to the rest of Germany, Switzerland, and northern France, with extensions into southern France and central Europe.

The status of such women was controversial from the very beginning. Despite their evident religious interests, Beguines never formed a recognized religious order, and significant differences existed between the various communities, which drew up internal regulations and elected their own superiors independently from each other. Women who joined a Beguinage promised to obey such internal rules, to observe a simple lifestyle, and to refrain from sex, but they did not give up property, nor did they assume a lifelong obligation. The arrangement thus allowed single women to exercise a profession in the urban economy as laborers, nurses, or teachers, while participating in an informal religious life that was not only more flexible than traditional monasticism but also provided these women with greater opportunities to carve out their own spiritual itinerary, with the assistance of male clerics.

In a society deeply suspicious of female sexuality, adult women who were neither under the control of their husbands nor bound by perpetual monastic vows easily aroused skepticism and distrust, as the name *Beguina* (from the Indo-European root *begg-* signifying "to mumble," hence "to simulate") indicates. While certain clerics praised individual Beguines and even wrote hagiographical texts to support the movement (Jacques de Vitry's *Life of Mary of Oignies*, written in 1215, became the most popular of such vitae), the more conservative figures of the Catholic Church disapproved of their intellectual activities, in particular their teachings on mysticism, for which Beguine writers such as Hadewijch of Brabant and Mechtild of Magdeburg became well known in the thirteenth century. When in 1310 the French Beguine Marguerite Porète was condemned as a heretic for alleged antinomianism in her treatise *The Mirror of Simple Souls*, the movement as a whole became the target of large-scale investigations and sporadic persecution by Church authorities, resulting in the suppression of many Beguine communities. Beguines of northern France and the Rhineland were forced to adopt a recognized religious rule (usually the Third Rule of St. Francis) or to give up their lifestyle. The large court Beguinages of the Low Countries, financially more secure and often protected by influential members of the ruling classes, remained largely unscathed but gradually adopted stricter rules of discipline and submitted to greater outside control, especially under the influence of the Modern Devotion movement of the late fourteenth and fifteenth centuries.

The Reformation of the sixteenth century closed down the last Beguine houses in Germany and in most of the Netherlands. In Belgium and in the predominantly Catholic parts of the Netherlands, however, the Beguine courts were revived and even flourished again during the seventeenth-century Counterreformation, now with full support of the Catholic Church. In the late twentieth century, dwindling fervor for the religious life among Catholics finally put an end to Beguine traditions in Belgium and the Netherlands; a few small communities of women invoking the Beguine example were newly created in Germany, Switzerland, and the United States.

SEE ALSO *Monasticism.*

BIBLIOGRAPHY

Lerner, Robert E. 1972. *The Heresy of the Free Spirit in the Later Middle Ages.* Berkeley: University of California Press.

McDonnell, Ernest W. 1954. *The Beguines and Beghards in Medieval Culture, with Special Emphasis on the Belgian Scene.* New Brunswick, NJ: Rutgers University Press.

Simons, Walter. 2001. *Cities of Ladies: Beguine Communities in the Medieval Low Countries, 1200–1565.* Philadelphia: University of Pennsylvania Press.

Walter Simons

BEHN, APHRA
1640–1689

Aphra Behn is one of the more controversial and fascinating women writers of the English Renaissance. Virginia Woolf (1929) acknowledged Behn's contribution to the world of women's letters by suggesting "all women together ought to should let flowers fall upon [her] tomb ... for it was she who earned them the right to speak their minds" (1977, p. 63). Catherine Gallagher (1993), however, is less certain. She argues that Behn "did not take up the pen with fear and trembling, deeply impressed by its undoubted resemblance to a penis ... Nor do her writings reveal a hidden female culture or firm bonds of solidarity between women." Janet Todd's biography confirms that Behn "is not so much a woman to be unmasked as an unending combination of masks"

Aphra Behn. COURTESY OF THE LIBRARY OF CONGRESS.

(2000, p. 1). Her date and place of birth is uncertain, although it is thought she was born in Harbledon, on December 14, 1640. It is probable she grew up in Kent in the period of the Civil War and Commonwealth and was a royalist sympathizer. During her lifetime she was known as Aphra or Ann. But Astrea, the goddess of justice, was the name she adopted for herself as both spy and author.

To assist her family after the death of her father en route to a top administrative position in Surinam, the young Aphra Johnson married a German merchant, Mr. Behn (c. 1664). Little is known of Behn or the marriage, but by 1666 Aphra was an impoverished widow, a status that usefully enabled her to travel to Antwerp as a spy to gather information on Dutch activities in the West Indies for Charles II. Behn was poorly paid if at all, and she returned to England in 1667 penniless and confined in debtor's prison where she was forced to write to support herself. Her lack of visible means of support led many to conclude that she was a kept woman or prostitute, but there is no evidence for such a claim. Her "Memoirs" state that after Antwerp, her life was entirely dedicated to pleasure and poetry, writing, she said "for bread, fame and my cause." She is widely accredited with being the first English professional woman writer.

Behn supported herself mostly by writing for the theater. Nineteen plays were performed in her lifetime. The first was the witty *The Forc'd Marriage* (1670); the best known, *The Rover* (1677, 1681 parts 1 & 2), is still performed in the early twenty-first century. The theater, however, was never a secure living and Behn frequently endured financial crises. During her lifetime, her reputation was controversial but her talent never in doubt, winning her strong supporters like the Earl of Rochester, as well as powerful detractors. Later critics found her difficult to place. Algernon Charles Swinburne admired her as a "sweet songstress"; Julia Kavanagh argued that her plays were "so coarse as to offend even a coarse age." Behn's way of life as well as the topics she chose for her verse have often been criticized for their lack of propriety.

Behn is a writer of remarkable range. Her contemporary reputation was highest for her plays and prose writing; the latter has recently been acknowledged as contributing to eighteenth century developments in prose fiction. Her imperialist romance novella set in Surinam, *Oroonoko,* is notable; despite the Eurocentric beauty of its black slave hero, the piece lent its voice to the anti-imperial and anti-slavery movement of its time. Behn's provocative verse remains as problematic as it was in the seventeenth century, for different reasons. While she describes the circuit of female desire, she does not directly promote a female cause. In *The Norton Anthology of Literature by Women* (1988), Sandra Gilbert and Susan Gubar include only five of her poems, all featuring a distinctly female voice or ungendered speakers. Janet Todd's more recent edition of the complete poems suggests, however, that it is hard to detect a consistent poetic persona or sustained voice, in part because many of the poems are loosely adapted from French originals often employing the male voice. Even her original pieces are frequently occasional, written as poetic exchanges among friends or in praise of another writer's work. A favorite poetic form is the pastoral, but, against the idealizing bent of the mode, Behn frequently depicts relationships that degenerate into something closer to the comic, as in *The Disappointment.*

Despite the controversial nature of her writing, Behn's professional reputation was such that she was asked to write a poem commemorating the ascension of William III to the British throne; she stood by her principles, however, as a partisan of the Stuart cause rather than the House of Orange, and refused. She died on April 16, 1689, shortly after William's coronation, and was buried in Westminister Abbey—an odd triumph! The inscription on her tomb is fitting: "Here lies a Proof that Wit can never be/ Defence enough against Mortality."

BIBLIOGRAPHY

Gallagher, Catherine. 1993. "The Networking Muse: Aphra Behn as Heroine of Frankness and Self-Discovery." *Times Literary Supplement.*

Hobby, Elaine. 1988. *Virtue of Necessity: English Women's Writing 1649–1688.* London: Virago Press.

Spencer, Jane. 1986. *The Rise of the Woman Novelist: From Aphra Behn to Jane Austen.* Oxford, UK: Blackwell.

Todd, Janet. 1996. *The Secret Life of Aphra Behn.* Cambridge, UK: Cambridge University Press.

Todd, Janet, ed. 1992–1996. *The Works of Aphra Behn.* 7 vols. Columbus: Ohio State University Press.

Todd, Janet. 1998. *The Critical Fortunes of Aphra Behn.* Columbia, SC: Camden House.

Woolf, Virginia. 1977. *A Room of One's Own.* London: Granada Publishing Limited. (Orig. pub. 1929.)

Claudia Marquis

BESTIALITY

SEE *Sexual Practices.*

BETA MALE

SEE *Male.*

BETTY BOOP

If Mickey Mouse is the world's most recognizable male animated character, Betty Boop must be his female equivalent. Though Betty Boop films were in production for fewer than nine years in the 1930s, the character gained a following that has extended into the twenty-first century.

Betty Boop was created in 1930 to play opposite a lecherous, piano-playing dog character, Bimbo, in the Fleischer Brothers' "Talkartoons" series. In her first appearance in an episode called "Dizzy Dishes," she was an ugly half-dog, half-human creature. By the ninth episode in the series, "Minding the Baby," she had metamorphosed into the completely human, Jazz Age sexpot, the role for which she became famous, and she was given her name. Henceforth, the cartoons were renamed the "Betty Boop" series.

Rather quickly, Betty Boop became a significant popular culture figure, attracting "appearances" by jazz musicians such as Cab Calloway and Louis Armstrong, spinning off into daily and Sunday comic strips and a national radio show, *Betty Boop Fables,* and supporting a line of merchandise that included dolls, clothes, and dishes. Some American women adopted her famous hairdo, and people everywhere echoed her famous "Boop-oop-a-doop" line.

Known for their humor, sexual innuendoes, jazz-oriented scores, and the squeaky voice of Mae Questel, some Betty Boop cartoons are now cult classics, particularly "Minnie the Moocher" (1932), "Snow White" (1933), "The Old Man of the Mountain" (1933), and "Poor Cinderella" (1934). These and other cartoons between 1932 and 1934 featured Betty Boop at the peak of her popularity, when she was a fun-loving, not to-be-taken seriously female, who, at the same time, exhibited some of the early stages of liberation her gender was experiencing.

Before the Motion Picture Production Code took effect in 1934, Betty Boop cartoons were outrageous—extremely funny and sometimes racy, incorporating Cab Calloway soundtracks with references to drugs, alcohol, and sex and featuring lascivious male characters who ogled Betty Boop, threatened to take her boop-oop-a-doop away, and even touched her forbidden parts. Betty's attire was often provocative. In "Bamboo Isle" (1932), she appeared topless; in "Mysterious Mose" (1930), she revealed more than usual cleavage, and in all of the cartoons, her legs and trademark garter were exposed.

Betty Boop lost her appeal after the 1934 code lowered her hemline, removed the garter, raised her neckline, and generally took the fun out of the character. The cartoons thenceforth highlighted a demure woman in a long dress, and the stories revolved around less interesting characters such as a dog or Grampy or Fearless Fred. In 1939, with interest in the series waning, Max Fleischer retired his famous character.

Even without new cartoons produced, Betty Boop has stayed popular, her cartoons showing up on television in the 1950s and after, and her merchandise appealing to fans into the twenty-first century. In 1988 she appeared in the successful *Who Framed Roger Rabbit,* and anytime animation masterpieces are discussed, her name is evoked.

BIBLIOGRAPHY

Beck, Jerry, ed. 1994. *The 50 Greatest Cartoons: As Selected by 1,000 Animation Professionals.* Atlanta: Turner Publishing.

Cohen, Karl F. 1997. *Forbidden Animation: Censored Cartoons and Blacklisted Animators in America.* Jefferson, NC: McFarland.

Fleischer, Richard. 2005. *Out of the Inkwell: Max Fleischer and the Animation Revolution.* Lexington: University Press of Kentucky.

John A. Lent

BHAKTI

SEE *Hinduism.*

BIBLE, NEW TESTAMENT

Sex in the ancient world may be regarded as a biological identity. Gender is a "social construct" indicating the ways in which men and women are taught values and behaviors appropriate to gender roles and social expectations. Practicing *sophrosune,* for example, is self-control for men but discretion and even silence for women. The gender ideology of the public and the private implies leadership roles in the public sphere for men, while women's domain is the household. However, this differentiation cannot be taken too far because the ancient household was also a public space regardless of its size or economy.

IDEOLOGY AND INTERPRETATION

"Let a woman learn in silence with all submission," writes the author of I Timothy 2:12, imitating Paul. "I permit no woman to teach or to have authority over a man; she is to keep silent. For Adam was formed first, then Eve." However, the injunction reveals more about the writer than about the social position of women in early Christian movements. The focus in the text is on the problem of "women," and by means of such texts one can see the ideological uses of interpretation to authorize and sustain certain relationships of domination.

The ideal of restricted women's behavior in the public space is relevant to understanding the contradiction in Paul's first letter to Corinth on the proper role of women in worship and the harshness of the prohibition on women teachers (1 Timothy 2:11–12). Although Paul expected women to take an active role in worship in terms of prophetic speech (1 Corinthians 11:5), he also demanded women's silence in the assembly (1 Corinthians 14:34–35): "The women should keep silence in the churches. For they are not permitted to speak, but should be subordinate, as the law says. If there is anything they desire to know, let them ask their husbands at home. For it is shameful for a woman to speak in church."

In this context Paul can be seen as an orator adopting a role as head of household to preserve order in the Christian community through personal authority. This is best seen in the fiat in 1 Corinthians 11:16: "If any man will not be ruled in this question, this is not our way of doing things, and it is not done in the churches of God." Through the ordering and gendering of the household Paul exercised control over the community, placing special emphasis on particular hairstyles and veiling practices. This is also part of Paul's promotion of an ordered, moderate, upright community that reflected the "glory" of both Paul and God.

Thus, female conduct at Corinth or anywhere else was incidental to the main argument establishing Paul's domination and power over those constructed as being in need of control. Of course, the ecclesial body benefits from stability. However, the predominant cultural value system in which Paul was operating and that he inscribed on the Corinthian body and sought to promote as the basis for his own identity for the audience has to be seen from a Greco-Roman male perspective. Paul was trying to control women who prophesied. In the ancient world prophesying was anarchic and not gender-specific. Paul intended to counter what the early Church Fathers and he regarded as chaos with an ordered and structured Christian community in which women "know their place."

CONTROL OF BODIES AND HOUSEHOLDS

The argument begins with control of his own body (1 Corinthians 7), which is the starting point for domination of others (1 Corinthians 11). The female body in turn becomes the cultural and rhetorical battleground for the maintenance of custom in Paul. In so ordering the Corinthian "household" Paul realizes the stability of an ordered empire. Seen in this light, early Christian witnesses such as 1 Corinthians 11:2–16 become a powerful statement about Paul's status as head of household and maintainer of Corinthian order.

The household is the projection of Paul's ability to control, order, and dominate, and it becomes the model for the author of I Timothy.

Some scholars have proposed that the injunction of I Timothy is an interpolation on the basis of concerns about female modesty in the public space. I Timothy 3:5 describes an overseer (bishop) as the husband of one wife and the manager of the household, arguing: "For if a man has not the art of ruling his house, how will he take care of the church of God?" It can be suggested that the text serves as a witness to a reading of Paul's exclusion of women from the emerging leadership role of monarchical bishop and the use of a rhetoric of shame to ensure women's silence in public arenas.

Such understandings of Paul's letters to the Corinthians echo in analyses of his letter to the Romans and its condemnation of sexual relations between men and men and women and women. Bernadette Brooten concentrates on same-sex relations between women in the ancient world and shows that "throughout Western history we find the male creators of culture and of ideology wavering between assuming that sexual relations between women do not exist at all—indeed cannot exist—and imagining that if they do, then the women must be capable of penetration" (Brooten 1996, p. 190). In regard to that notion, "this focus on penetration as the principal sexual image led to a simplistic view of female erotic behavior and a complex view of the erotic choices of free men" (Brooten 1996, p. 49). In the Roman imperial era the phenomenon of female same-sex love received increased attention and then broad societal recognition. However, it is important to examine the source of that hostility.

In ancient Mediterranean concepts of sexuality "active and passive define what it means to be masculine/feminine" (Brooten 1996, p. 125; cf. p. 157, n. 43). If a female played the penetrating (i.e., active) role, she transgressed those fundamental categories, acting "contrary to nature." However, this was also the case if a woman allowed herself to be penetrated by another woman. The logic is skewed, but Brooten shows that "female homoeroticism did not fit neatly into ancient understandings of sexual relationships as essentially asymmetrical" (Brooten 1996, p. 76). Only Christians wanted homoerotic women to die and burn in hell. "Paul condemned sexual relations between women as 'unnatural' because he shared the widely held cultural view that women are passive by nature and therefore should remain passive in sexual relations" (Brooten 1996, p. 216).

It is important to realize that before the author of I Timothy wrote, women such as Phoebe were patrons in a community of Roman believers (Romans 16:1–2) and that there were female apostles before Paul, such as Junia (Romans 16:7). Lydia was a God fearer and wealthy householder who was baptized by Paul with her whole household. She was a patron to the house church and a traveling apostle (Acts 16:11–15).

Washing the feet of Jesus. *Mary Magdalene washes feet of Jesus Christ in this detail from the Meal at the house of Simon, c. 1560.* THE ART ARCHIVE/GALLERIA SABAUDA TURIN/DAGLI ORTI.

REPRODUCTION AND THE COMMUNITY OF GOD

Recent study of John's gospel demonstrates how the author sought to eradicate sex by envisaging the generation of new members of the Johannine community from not of God without conception and birth (John 1:12–13). In Chapter 1 Jesus exists as God's word. In Chapter 3 Nicodemus explores what being born anew (or from above) means. To be born from above or born anew does not mean entering the mother's womb a second time (John 3:4). As Jesus explains to a mystified Nicodemus, it means being born of water and the spirit.

If John's gospel describes human generation in a nonbiological way, one can see why Jesus' parents and family of origin are absent from the gospel. Jesus has a mother, but he never addresses her as such. Except at Cana neither of them makes claims on the other as family members in a way that those in the same household might be expected to, and even at Cana the claim is not framed in terms of family obligation. Jesus' words in John 2:4, "Woman, what have I to do with you?" distance him from his earthly mother and cause more distress to interpreters than to his mother. Moreover, Jesus distances women from men: To the Samaritan woman he says, "You are right in saying, 'I have no husband,' for you have had five husbands, and the one you have now is not your husband. What you have said is true" (John 4:17–18); to the woman taken in adultery he says, "No one has condemned you, neither do I," although the law condemns both the man and the woman (Leviticus 20:10; Deuteronomy 22:22). Similarly, in John's gospel parents separate or differentiate themselves from their children: The parents of the man born blind say, "Ask him, he is of age" (John 9:23).

At the crucifixion scene Jesus consigned the Beloved Disciple to replace him as son to his mother (John 19:25–26). Affiliation was not through birth; Jesus' mother is now mother or guardian to the prototypical disciple in whatever community exists after Jesus' death. From the cross, in a last will and testament, Jesus affiliated a new son to his mother. He created a mother-son bond through his last words. The new son takes his new mother into his realm (or house) and in so doing sustains the bond. Jesus creates through words a new family of his disciples: brothers, sisters, and friends he loves, the most prominent of whom becomes son to his mother. The

Beloved Disciple is thus a (re)born child of God not by desire, by man, or by the will of the flesh.

SEE ALSO *Bible, Old Testament or Tanakh; Christianity, Early and Medieval; Christianity, Reformation to Modern.*

BIBLIOGRAPHY

Brooten, Bernadette J. 1996. *Love between Women: Early Christian Responses to Female Homoeroticism*. Chicago: University of Chicago Press.

Good, Deirdre. 2006. *Jesus' Family Values*. New York: Seabury.

Jasper, Alison E. 1998. *The Shining Garment of the Text: Gendered Readings of John's Prologue*. Sheffield, UK: Sheffield Academic Press.

Penner, Todd, and Caroline Vander Stichele. 2004. "Unveiling Paul: Gendering Ethos in 1 Corinthians 11:2–16." *Lectio Difficilor* 12(2): 2–16.

Seim, Turid Karlsen. 2005. "Descent and Divine Paternity in the Gospel of John: Does the Mother Matter?" *New Testament Studies* 51(3): 361–375.

Skinner, Marilyn B. 2005. *Sexuality in Greek and Roman Culture*. Malden, MA: Blackwell.

Deirdre Good

BIBLE, OLD TESTAMENT OR TANAKH

The Hebrew Bible (known to Christians as the Old Testament and to Jews by the acronym *Tanakh*) is an anthology of religious literature of different genres written in various settings of Israelite society over a period of approximately one thousand years. This diverse collection of sacred books, which reached its final form in the first century CE, played a central role in the development of the post-biblical religious traditions of Judaism and in shaping attitudes about sex and gender in Western society.

The diversity of the Hebrew Bible on the topic of gender and human sexuality is evident in the two biblical creation stories at the beginning of Genesis. Genesis 1:1–2:3 recounts that both males and females (unspecified in number) were created simultaneously in the divine image and equally charged to multiply and to assume stewardship over the earth and their fellow creatures. Genesis 2:4–3:24 preserves a tradition of male priority, where woman is a subsequent and secondary creation, formed from the body of the uniquely created man to fulfill male needs for companionship and progeny (Gen. 2:24). Despite the pains of childbirth, a woman desires her husband sexually and he rules over her (Gen. 3:16). Until very recent times, this image of differentiated and unequal gender roles was far more influential in the post-biblical development of Judaism than the first, egalitarian vision.

Biblical narratives offer vivid portraits of fascinating and complex women who determined the national destiny (Sarah, Rebecca, Rachel, Miriam, Deborah, Yael, Hannah, Abigail, Bathsheba, and Huldah, among many others). However, biblical legislation assumed a woman was subordinate to the dominant male in her life, whether father or husband. This man controlled a woman's sexuality, including the right to challenge both her virginity and her marital faithfulness (Deut. 22:13–22; Num. 5:11–31). Legal concerns in the Hebrew Bible about women's sexual activity really have to do with relations between men. A man could be executed for having intercourse with another's wife (Lev. 20:10) because he had committed a crime of theft against a man; similarly, a man who seduced or raped a virgin had to pay a bride-price to her father and marry her (Deut. 22:28). Israelite society was polygynous, although biblical narratives display ambivalence about this practice in their frequent depictions of hostilities between co-wives and half-siblings.

In the patriarchal culture of ancient Israel, where women were essentially the daughters, wives, and mothers of particular men, women had virtually no property rights. Unmarried women inherited from their fathers only if they had no brothers; in such cases, women had to marry within their father's clan to prevent the dispersal of tribal property among outsiders (Num. 36:2–12). Widows did not inherit from their husbands but were dependent on their sons or the generosity of other heirs. According to the biblical practice of levirate marriage, childless widows were the legal responsibility of their husband's oldest brother (Deut. 25:5–10) or in some cases, his nearest male relative (Ruth 4:1–11). Some women were prostitutes, an occupation condemned in priestly texts but presented as part of the larger Israelite landscape in narratives about Rahab (Joshua 2, 5) and Tamar (Gen. 38), and the two women who brought their dispute to Solomon (1 Kings 3:16–28).

In the ritual regulations of Leviticus, menstruating and postpartum women were considered ritually impure and sexually unavailable to their husbands for prescribed periods of time (Lev. 12, 15), during which they could also render people and objects they touched ritually impure. A woman was ritually impure for a period of seven days after giving birth to a male child, and fourteen after a girl. For thirty-three additional days after a boy and sixty-six after a girl, she was forbidden to enter the Temple or to touch hallowed things (Lev. 12:1–8). Although such ordinances were part of a priestly system in which other genital discharges, male and female, could cause ritual impurity, they applied particularly to women, due to the biological consequences of fertility, pregnancy, and childbirth. After the destruction of the Second Temple in 70 CE, when most other forms of ritual impurity lapsed, the practice of separating menstruating and postpartum women from conjugal contact and communal religious life until their cleansing in a ritual bath continued in rabbinic Judaism.

Scholars suggest that so long as Israelite society was mainly agricultural, social and religious gender roles were relatively egalitarian. With the emergence of a monarchy, political state, and the institutionalization of religious life in the Temple cult and priestly bureaucracy (beginning in the tenth century BCE), women were increasingly excluded from the public arena and lost access to communal authority, a social approach maintained in the rabbinic Judaism of the post-biblical era.

Public religious rituals in ancient Israel were mainly male. The priesthood was a hereditary position, limited to men of the tribe of Levi. According to Leviticus 21:14, the high priest may not marry a widow, a divorcée, or a harlot, but only a virgin. Other priests may marry a widow. Women participated in communal festivals, brought sacrifices, and sang and danced at festivals and as part of victory celebrations (Exod. 15; Judg. 5:1–31; Judg. 21:19–23; I Sam. 18:6–7). Hannah, the mother of Samuel, Israel's last judge, is depicted as praying alone at the Tabernacle at Shiloh (I Sam. 1:19). Her prayer (I Sam 2:1–10) became the model for supplicatory prayer in rabbinic Judaism (*Babylonian Talmud: Berakhot* 31a). Women had no publicly recognized religious leadership roles in ancient Israel, although there are references to "wise women" (2 Sam. 12:1-6; 2 Sam. 14:1-20; 2 Sam. 20:16-22) who were consulted in times of crisis. A few women, including Miriam (Exod. 15:20), Deborah (Judg. 4:4), and Huldah (2 Kings 22:14–16), are designated as prophets.

Sexuality is affirmed in the Hebrew Bible as a powerful human force with both positive and negative potentialities. Channeled within marriage, heterosexual intimacy leads to both pleasure and progeny. The Song of Songs preserves an idyllic vision of human sexuality and an established vocabulary of female-male erotic love. However, from the early post-biblical period on, this book was read as an allegory of the divine-human relationship. Heterosexual love and potential betrayal also underlie the powerful biblical metaphor of God and Israel as husband and wife (e.g., Hosea). Conversely, Proverbs warns young men to shun the snares of enticing and seductive women (Prov. 5 and 7, 31:2–3), and post-biblical Jewish writings frequently represent women as temptresses and sexually unreliable. Male homosexual relations are forbidden in Leviticus 18:22 and 20:13 and this prohibition continued in rabbinic Judaism. There are no allusions to lesbian sexual activity in biblical legislative or narrative texts.

Contemporary Judaism exists in diverse movements; in recent years, Reform, Reconstructionist, and Conservative Judaisms have affirmed the equal status of women and men in all aspects of Jewish life, leadership, and ritual practice. Reform and Reconstructionist Judaisms also endorse the full participation of gay and lesbian Jews in every area of Jewish life. In the first decade of the twenty-first century, conservative Judaism continued to struggle with this issue. Orthodox Judaism, which also exists in many forms, professes separate (generally lesser) social, communal, and ritual roles for women and maintains traditional negative attitudes towards homosexuality.

SEE ALSO *Esther; Judaism.*

BIBLIOGRAPHY

Ackerman, Susan. 2005. *When Heroes Love: The Ambiguity of Eros in the Stories of David and Gilgamesh.* New York: Columbia University Press.

Baskin, Judith R. 2002. *Midrashic Women: Formations of the Feminine in Rabbinic Literature.* Hanover, NH: University Press of New England for Brandeis University.

Boyarin, Daniel. 1997. *Unheroic Conduct: The Rise of Heterosexuality and the Invention of the Jewish Man.* Berkeley: University of California Press.

Frymer-Kensky, Tikva Simone. 1992. *In the Wake of the Goddesses: Women, Culture, and the Biblical Transformation of Pagan Myth.* New York: Free Press.

Meyers, Carol L. 1988. *Discovering Eve: Ancient Israelite Women in Context.* New York: Oxford University Press.

Meyers, Carol L. 2005. *Households and Holiness: The Religious Culture of Israelite Women.* Minneapolis, MN: Augsburg Fortress Publishers.

Niditch, Susan. 1998. "Portrayals of Women in the Hebrew Bible." In *Jewish Women in Historical Perspective.* 2nd edition, ed. Judith R. Baskin. Detroit, MI: Wayne State University Press.

Trible, Phyllis. 1978. *God and the Rhetoric of Sexuality.* Philadelphia, PA: Fortress Press.

Judith R. Baskin

BIG BAD WOLF

Wolves get bad press, much worse than they deserve. Consider their much-vaunted fierceness: that of the big bad wolf that ate the first two little pigs; the dangers of a wolf in sheep's clothing; the foolishness of the boy who cried wolf; the need to keep the wolves at bay. In early versions of "The Three Little Pigs" (the first written edition of which appears in the late eighteenth century), the wolf devours the first two pigs, who built houses of straw and sticks, enabling the wolf to huff and puff and

An illustration from "Little Red Riding Hood." © CORBIS.

blow their houses in; the clever third pig, who built his house of bricks, outsmarts and eats the wolf. Walt Disney's little pigs might be foolish to sing "Who's Afraid of the Big Bad Wolf" in the immensely popular *Three Little Pigs* cartoon short (1933) and its sequels, yet Depression Era viewers adopted the song as their anthem, hoping to keep the wolf from the door. Despite attributions of dangerous ferocity, however, in North America at least, there have been few cases of healthy wild wolves attacking humans. (Europe and Asia are another matter, though attacks recorded there may have been by rabid or hybrid wolves.)

Then there's the wolf as sexual creature, especially as a sexual predator. Yet wolves do not in fact howl wolf whistles. Nor are they particularly rapacious: they pair off in long-term bonds and form cooperative packs that share in the care of the young. "Little Red Riding Hood," of course, promotes a rather different wolf. In different tellings, Red is simply eaten, as in Charles Perrault's cautionary version (1697); is released by a hunter from the wolf's belly, as the Grimm brothers would have it (1812); escapes her predicament through her own wits, as in the early oral versions of the story cited by Jack Zipes; or, as in Angela Carter's retelling in "The Company of Wolves" (1979), is dangerously yet deliciously complicit with the wolf, embracing sexuality. The sexual wolf—almost always male, almost always heterosexual—has been featured by artists too, from Gustave Doré to Sarah Moon.

For humans, in short, the wolf has represented embodiment, sexual and otherwise. It seemed the most humanlike of the animals with whom Europeans and North Americans came into contact, a convenient figure onto which to project needs and desires. It especially came to represent the physical body of humans, for good or ill. It could suckle Romulus and Remus and hence nurture Roman civilization. It could also represent the threats to civilization—not least as the sometimes-wolf, sometimes-human werewolf (perhaps most memorably embodied, during the twentieth century, by Lon Chaney Jr., in *The Wolf Man* [1941] and its sequels). More recently the wolf could represent an escape from the hyper-civilized, the freedom of running or dancing with wolves. The wolf is the physical human, whether we menace others, make love, or wolf down food: its representation raises questions about what it means to be human.

SEE ALSO *Fairy Tales; Little Red Riding Hood.*

BIBLIOGRAPHY

Mech, L. David, and Luigi Boitani, eds. 2003. *Wolves: Behavior, Ecology, and Conservation.* Chicago: University of Chicago Press.

Otten, Charlotte F., ed. 1986. *A Lycanthropy Reader: Werewolves in Western Culture.* Syracuse, NY: Syracuse University Press.

Smoodin, Eric. 1993. *Animating Culture: Hollywood Cartoons from the Sound Era.* New Brunswick, NJ: Rutgers University Press.

Zipes, Jack. 1993. *The Trials and Tribulations of Little Red Riding Hood.* 2nd edition. New York: Routledge.

Julia Biery
Beverly Lyon Clark

LES BIJOUX INDISCRETS

Denis Diderot (1713–1784), a towering philosopher of the French Enlightenment, published an early novel titled *Les Bijoux Indiscrets* ([Indiscrete jewels], translated as *The Indiscreet Toys* in an English edition of 1749) in January 1748 without an author or a publisher name. It recounts the lengthy divertissement of a bored sultan in an Orientalized Congo who is curious about the faithfulness of women, especially the favorite of his harem. He turns a magical ring on all the women of the realm, enjoying its ability to force the "jewel" hidden in their bodies—their sex—to speak frankly and unreservedly about its owner's exploits. This allows the sultan to observe the sexual profligacy of any and all of his subjects and the corruption, venality, hypocrisy, and mendacity of the entire culture: Women sell themselves to cover gambling debts, priests are the first to profit from promiscuity, and husbands seek advancement through their wives' lovers.

SOURCES

Bijoux belongs to the eighteenth-century genre of Orientalist fiction and generally is considered to be an imitation of *Le sopha-conte moral* (1740) by the fashionable Crébillon Fils (Claude Prosper Jolyot de Crébillon, 1707–1777) and perhaps of *Nocrion, conte allobroge* (1747), which has been attributed to Caylus (Anne Claude Philippe, Comte de Caylus, 1692–1765). However, *Bijoux* is also a direct heir to a medieval tradition and has been associated with a fabliau in which a knight makes women's sexual body parts speak, and Diderot might also have been influenced by Renaissance texts called *Blasons* in which a particular part of a woman's body is extolled and described in detail, sometimes as the result of an exploration by an outside force, which could be the eye, the hand, or even an emboldened insect.

LEGAL RECEPTION

Although the book was an immediate commercial success, Diderot was denounced to the chief of police on February 14, 1748. His bad reputation in matters of religion and morality had intensified before and after this publication. In 1746 he had completed the *Pensées philosophiques*, which marked his conversion to deism; that work was condemned roundly by the French parliament on July 7 of that year. On June 20, 1747, he was denounced to the police for irreligiousness for writing *De la suffisance de la religion naturelle* (published only in 1770) and the *Skeptic's Promenade* (published as late as 1830). On June 3, 1749, his *Lettre sur les aveugles, à l'usage de ceux qui voient* ([Letter on blindness, for the use of those who have their sight], which was translated in 1770) immediately garnered him the dangerous label of an atheist. This time the police searched his home, and he was arrested and jailed at Vincennes.

Subjected to an interrogatory, Diderot first denied any wrongdoing and then, on August 11, 1750, broke down and confessed his role, betraying his mistress, Madame de Puisieux (Madeleine d'Arsant de Puisieux, 1720–1798), as the responsible party. Somehow he got out of jail, probably through the distributors of the *Encyclopédie*, a massive project that Diderot and his friend d'Alembert (1717–1783) officially undertook in 1747 and whose first volume appeared in 1751.

While in Vincennes, Diderot began to blame *Bijoux* for his troubles. With time he increasingly disowned the work and publicly professed to have committed an embarrassing youthful error and to regret it as a respectable writer, moralist, philosopher, and art critic. His publisher, Naigeon, claimed that he lamented the work's existence every day of his life. However, that contrition might have been theatrical in that Diderot added material to the text well after 1750, including three chapters that went into the 1798 edition on his explicit instructions. In 1761 he still was apologizing for the work, calling it abominable and still blaming his mistress. He circulated an ugly story that she asked him for fifty louis that he did not have and that in despair he wrote the novel in a hurry and according to popular taste to earn that sum.

This was a murky episode in Diderot's relationship to Madeleine de Puisieux, a respectable author who wrote on pedagogy and manners and translated a work on the equality of women and men. Diderot fed the misogynist stereotypes of his time, casting Madeleine de Puisieux as the instigator and a prurient female lover of salacious literature, the force behind the indecent parts, whereas philosophical thinking remained the province of Diderot, the male, much as was the case with the characters in *Bijoux* (Rustin 1979).

CRITICAL RECEPTION

The work elicited massive invective in the early nineteenth century, followed by decades of silence and obscurity in the early twentieth century and then a more accepting attitude after the 1960s. However, the work still was treated with some discomfort by modern editors. Scholars in the late twentieth century recognized its importance and commented on it extensively, although they may focus less on the blatant sexual aspects of the work in relation to its other dimensions.

Already incontrovertibly linked to the history of erotic literature (Rustin 1979), *Bijoux* completely breached the bastions of propriety with a section that is one of the earliest European works of identifiable verbal pornography, in which a "traveling jewel" recounts its adventures in what seems to be the most explicit detail. But is it so explicit? Those pages are written in languages other than French: English, Latin, Italian, and Spanish. This creates a screen or the semblance of a screen for Diderot's educated contemporaries between the ribald and the literally obscene. Further, the degree of crude graphic rendition of sex acts varies considerably from text to text. The English version, for instance, is filled with the strings of sexual metaphors (both explicit and concealing) characteristic of erotic French literature since the late Middle Ages and certainly since the Renaissance. Diderot thus created at once a linguistic tour de force, a rhetorical experiment in verbalizing the obscene, and a representational puzzle, signaled by that deliberate act of veiling and unveiling.

All these aspects of the work have intrigued interpreters of Diderot's oeuvre, eliciting scholarly reflections on the interface of sexuality and textuality and on the scripting of desire in text (Creech 1979; Wall 1994). Michel Foucault used *Bijoux* to illustrate his thesis of the constant sex talk of modern Western European culture: "We willingly imagine ourselves under a 'victorian' regime," he wrote in a brief essay. "It seems to me instead that our kingdom is the one imagined by Diderot in *Les bijoux indiscrets*; a certain, nearly invisible mechanism makes sex speak in a virtually inexhaustible chatter. We are in a society of speaking sex" (Foucault 1978, p. 6). Foucault deemed the text extremely important for the history of sexuality and its discourses, for part four of the first volume of his *History of Sexuality* begins with the statement: "The aim of this series of studies? To transcribe into history the fable of *Les bijoux indiscrets*" (Foucault 1990, p. 77). Foucault saw the fable, and the device of the ring, as allegorical of the Western will to know about sex and make others speak about it, to understand "what is it that we demand of sex, beyond its possible pleasures, that makes us so persistent?" (p. 79).

Scholars have thus responded to Foucault's reading of *Bijoux*, making the sultan into a form of critic who adumbrates the will to see and know contained in the *Encyclopédie* (Creech 1986). Some have attempted to move beyond the ribaldry of the text or correct its apparent misogyny (Meeker 2003), stressing that in the end the virtue of women is upheld (Humphries 1989, Fowler 1997), or that, in fact, it is not about the sexuality of women at all, but about male desire (Fowler 2000). Others, on the contrary, have read it as an historical contribution to building the misogynistic view of woman as disease, specifically linked to the theme of smallpox (Goldberg 1984). Others have underscored its carnivalesque and operatic quality (Didier 1984), or showed its intrinsic connection to the wider philosophical problems addressed by Diderot elsewhere, in particular its relationship to libertine philosophy (Richard 1998, Meeker 2003) and to the critique of metaphysics (Deneys-Tunney 1999).

SEE ALSO *Pornography.*

BIBLIOGRAPHY

Beeharry-Paray, Geeta. 2000. "*Les Bijoux indiscrets* de Diderot: Pastiche, forgerie ou charge du conte crébillonien?" *Diderot Studies* 28: 21–38.

Creech, James. 1979. "Language and Desire in *Les Bijoux indiscrets*." *Eighteenth Century: Theory and Interpretation* 20: 182–198.

Creech, James. 1986. *Diderot: Thresholds of Representation.* Columbus: Ohio State University Press.

Deneys-Tunney, Anne. 1999. "La Critique de la métaphysique dans *les Bijoux indiscrets* et *Jacques le Fataliste* de Diderot." *Recherches sur Diderot et sur l'Encyclopédie* 26: 141–151.

Diderot, Denis. 1981. *Les Bijoux Indiscrets*, ed. Jacques Rustin. Paris: Gallimard Folio.

Didier, Béatrice. 1984. "L'Opéra fou des *Bijoux*." *Europe: Revue Litteraire Mensuelle* 661: 142–150.

Foucault, Michel. [1978] 1990. *The History of Sexuality*. Vol. 1, *An Introduction*. New York: Random House.

Foucault, Michel. 1978. "The West and the Substance of Sex," trans. Laurence E. Winters. *SubStance, Focus on the Margins* 6 (20): 6–8.

Fowler, J. E. 1997. "Diderot's Family Romance: Les Bijoux indiscrets Reappraised." *Romantic Review* 88(1): 89–102.

Fowler, J. E. 2000. *Voicing Desire: Family and Sexuality in Diderot's Narrative*. Oxford, UK: Voltaire Foundation.

Goldberg, Rita. 1984. *Sex and Enlightenment: Women in Richardson and Diderot*. New York: Cambridge University Press.

Humphries, Jefferson. 1989. "The Eighteenth Century Reinvents Virtue: A Reading of Diderot's *Bijoux indiscrets*." *French Forum* 14(1): 31–42.

Laborde, Alice M. 1984a. *Diderot et Madame de Puisieux*. Stanford French and Italian Studies, no. 36. Saratoga, CA: Anma Libri.

Laborde, Alice M. 1984b. "Madeleine de Puisieux et Diderot: De l'égalité entre les sexes." In *L'Egalité. Travaux du Centre de Philosophie du Droit de l'Université Libre de Bruxelles*. ed. Léon Ingber. Brussels: Bruylant.

Meeker, Natania. 2003. "'All Times Are Present to Her': Femininity, Temporality, and Libertinage in Diderot's 'Sur les femmes.'" *Journal for Early Modern Cultural Studies* 3(2): 68–100.

Mylne, Vivienne, and Janet Osborne. 1971. "Diderot's Early Fiction: *Les Bijoux Indiscrets* and *l'Oiseau blanc*." *Diderot Studies* 14: 143–166.

Richard, Odile. 1998. "*Les Bijoux indiscrets*: Variation secrète sur un thème libertin." *Recherches sur Diderot et sur l'Encyclopédie* 24: 27–37.

Rustin, Jacques. 1979. *Le Vice à la mode: Étude sur le roman français du XVIIIe siècle: De Manon Lescaut à l'apparition de La Nouvelle Héloïse: 1731–1761*. Paris: Ophrys.

Wall, Anthony. 1994. "Le Bavardage du corps ou *Les Bijoux indiscrets* de Denis Diderot." *Neophilologus* 78:3: 351–359.

Francesca Canadé Sautman

BINGEN, HILDEGARD OF
1098–1179

Born in 1098, the tenth child of Hildebert and Mechtild von Bermersheim, Hildegard of Bingen was a product of the German nobility. Hildegard is remembered as a mystic, a scholar, a playwright, a poet, and a musician. The earliest manuscript of her great visionary work, *Scito vias Domini*, better known to modern readers as *Scivias*, was illuminated with sensitive and creative images of her visions made in the scriptorium at Rupertsberg in 1165. Medieval evidence suggests that the illuminations were painted by a "gifted Rupertsberg nun, or perhaps a monk from St. Disibod" (Hart and Bishop 1990, p. 26). The illuminated *Scivias*, perhaps the best known of Hildegard's works, embodies in its unique artistic and theological approach the creativity, originality, and spirituality of Hildegard's life and work.

Hildegard began her spiritual life with Jutta von Spanheim, who lived as an anchoress at the Benedictine monastery in Disibodenberg. Although she is most famous for the visions that occurred "in the forty-third year of [her] earthly course," Hildegard confessed later in life that she had experienced visions beginning in early childhood. Sickly as a young child, she had much time for introspection and thought, and although she would not write about them until much later in life, her visionary experiences seem always to have been a part of how she approached God and her world. In 1106 Hildegard went to live with Jutta, and stayed with her for thirty years. She followed Jutta's example and served as abbess of Disibodenberg starting in 1136, and she founded two additional convents, at Rupertsberg near Bingen and at Eibingen.

Hildegard traveled throughout Germany and the Low Countries, and she was a prolific writer of letters. These letters—written to the leaders of her time, such as Eleanor of Aquitaine (1122–1204), Henry II of England (r. 1154–1189), Abbot Suger (1081–1151), and Frederick I, Holy Roman Emperor (r. 1152–1190); to friends, leaders, and to lay supporters and advocates—represent an excellent cross-section of twelfth-century society and culture, both within and beyond the circle of Church authority, and demonstrate Hildegard's contemporary reputation for wisdom and theological knowledge. Among her more well-known correspondents is the Benedictine nun, mystic, and author Elizabeth of Schönau (1129–1165). Hildegard's mystical authority was actually sanctioned by a pope, based on an investigation requested by Bernard of Clairvaux (1090–1153), who brought her work to the attention of Pope Eugenius III (r. 1145–1153).

In the early twenty-first century, Hildegard can be seen as participating in a literary tradition through such female authors and mystics as the ninth-century Carolingian writer Dhouda, the tenth-century playwright Hrotsvitha of Gandersheim, and the visions of the early Christian martyr Saint Perpetua (d. 203). However, these women were unknown to her (Hart and Bishop 1990, p. 9), so her independence and both her theological and literary authority have seemed, traditionally, to be anomalous for a woman of her time. Hildegard was also fairly well educated for a twelfth-century woman, although her Latin was imperfect and she questioned her own literary abilities. Thus, she dictated her works to several scribes, among whom the best known was Volmar; he transcribed her works until his death in 1151. Her final scribe, Guibert of Gembloux, was one of her most vocal admirers, including in his transcriptions some of his own opinions about Hildegard, such as comparing her to the Virgin Mary in her influence and sanctity.

During the time in which Hildegard flourished, female mysticism, as it has often been termed, was a new concept: much of what would later be attributed to this genre has its origin, to some extent, in the works of Hildegard. Two major influences on these works—the biblical Song of Songs and Bernard of Clairvaux's sermons on this text—seem to have influenced all devotional writers of the twelfth century but particularly the women who experienced mystical encounters and those who recorded those encounters. It is clear that Bernard's sermons reached Hildegard, who frequently uses the language of bridal mysticism in her works, particularly in *Scivias* and *Symphonia armonie celestium revelationum* (a separate publication that compiles the musical compositions found in part III of *Scivias*). Hildegard and Bernard probably never met, but Hildegard uses Bernard's own language from the sermons on the Song of Songs when she writes to him in 1147: "And so I beseech your aid, through the serenity of the Father and through His wondrous Word and through the sweet moisture of compunction ... and through the sublimity

Hildegard of Bingen. HULTON ARCHIVE/GETTY IMAGES.

of the Father, who sent the Word with sweet fruitfulness into the womb of the Virgin, from which He soaked up flesh, just as honey is surrounded by the honeycomb" (Baird and Ehrman 1994–2004, pp. 27–28). This is a clear echo of the Song of Songs: "Thy lips, my spouse, are as a dropping honeycomb, milk and honey are under thy tongue" (Canticles 4:11). Thus, although Bernard makes every effort to avoid sexualizing the relationship between the soul and Christ in his own works, he may have unwillingly influenced Hildegard's erotic imagery and, through her, the erotic language and sensual imagery of medieval mystical writers after the twelfth century, such as the authors of *Ancrene Wisse*, *Hali Meiðhad*, and the Wooing Group in England, as well as the works of Elizabeth of Schönau and Mechthild of Magdeburg, who allude directly to Hildegard in their own mystical writings.

The nature and impact of Hildegard's relationships with other women is still being investigated by scholars, some of whom interpret her affection and intimacy for her female companions as "queer," or at least as being edged with erotic desire. The most obvious case for this argument is her relationship with Richardis von Stade, a nun with whom she lived for several years, first in Disibodenberg and then in Rupertsberg when Hildegard became abbess. Richardis may have served as Hildegard's scribe for a time, and she is pictured with Hildegard (and her scribe Volmar) in a well-known miniature from the thirteenth century. Richardis had been a long-time companion and friend to Hildegard, nursing her through bouts of migraines and illness, and encouraging her writings. When, in 1151, Richardis was elected abbess of the neighboring convent of Bassum, Hildegard protested strongly to Richardis's family and to church authorities, including the pope, who deferred to Heinrich, Archbishop of Mainz (who had already clearly indicated his approval of Richardis's move to Bassum). In letters she wrote to Richardis, Hildegard seems to reveal her love for her, although the nature of that love is unclear. Some see their relationship as that of a mother and her prodigal daughter; some see it clearly as an articulation of lesbian desire between the two women. Susan Schibanoff, for example, has argued that Hildegard experienced a "homoerotic attachment" to Richardis (2001, p. 69). Citing Thomas Stehling, whose work includes a study of medieval "lesbian love letters," she argues that Hildegard's echo of Lamentations in her letters to Richardis ("let all who have sorrow like my sorrow mourn with me" [Baird and Ehrman, 1994–2004, p. 144]) follows the pattern of other homoerotic letters by medieval women that derive from Song of Songs, a source well known and frequently used by Hildegard.

Although it is not possible to fully understand Hildegard's relationship with Richardis, it is clear that the younger nun's absence generated for her, in Schibanoff's words, "a desperate and physical loneliness" (p. 54). In her work *Ordo virtutem*, composed about the time that Richardis was sent to Bassum, Hildegard seems to struggle with the power of the flesh and a desire to enjoy the pleasures of the world. This allegorical text tells the story of a virtuous soul who is tempted by the Devil and must be brought back to God through the virtues (such as chastity, humility, and patience). When the soul asks for salvation, she thus describes her sinfulness: "a scorching sweetness devoured me in my sins" (Zaerr translation 2005), indicating Hildegard's own knowledge of the seductiveness of sin and transgression. Homoerotic desire may also be present in Hildegard's *Symphonia* when she describes the beauty of the Virgin Mary using the language of erotic desire (she writes, for example, "the sweetness of all delights / is forever in you" in *O clarissima Mater*) (Gentile translation 2006). However, other scholars have countered that very often when desire, even erotic desire, was expressed for the Virgin Mary, it was not understood as erotic in the same way that such desire is understood or expressed for modern audiences—indeed, it has been viewed as not queer but "aheterosexual" (Holsinger 1993, p. 119)—and thus, although compelling, the homoerotic voice of Hildegard is difficult to ascertain in her works without extensive modern interpretation.

The impact of Hildegard's life and writings cannot be underplayed. As Barbara Newman noted, "if Hildegard had been a male theologian, her *Scivias* would undoubtedly have been considered one of the most important early medieval summas" (quoted in Hart and Bishop 1990, p. 23). Hildegard influenced Elizabeth of Schönau and Mechthild of Magdeburg directly, as well as any number of other authors, male and female, mystic and traditional, who have made use of her imagery, language, and theological insight for more than eight centuries. She is an important participant in the history and development of female experience, spirituality, and authorship, but her place in history is beyond the influence of gender and places her as a leading voice in the tradition of medieval spirituality and thought.

BIBLIOGRAPHY

Baird, Joseph L., and Radd K. Ehrman, trans. and eds. 1994–2004. *The Letters of Hildegard of Bingen*. 3 vols. New York: Oxford University Press.

Burnett, Charles, and Peter Dronke, eds. 1998. *Hildegard of Bingen: The Context of Her Thought and Art*. London: Warburg Institute, School of Advanced Study, University of London.

Cadden, Joan. 1984. "It Takes All Kinds: Sexuality and Gender Differences in Hildegard of Bingen's 'Book of Compound Medicine.'" *Traditio* 40: 149–174.

Dreyer, Elizabeth A. 2005. *Passionate Spirituality: Hildegard of Bingen and Hadewijch of Brabant*. Mahwah, NJ: Paulist Press.

Dronke, Peter. 1984. "*Vita* of Hildegard of Bingen." In *Women Writers of the Middle Ages*, ed. Peter Dronke. Cambridge, UK: Cambridge University Press.

Flanagan, Sabina. 1998. *Hildegard of Bingen, 1098–1179: A Visionary Life*. 2nd edition. London: Routledge.

Fox, Matthew. 1985. *The Illuminations of Hildegard of Bingen*. Santa Fe, NM: Bear & Co.

Godefridus. 1995. *Vita sanctae Hildegardis auctoribus Godefrido et Theodorico monachis*, trans. Adelgundis Führkötter and James McGrath, ed. Mary Palmquist and John Kulas. Collegeville, MN: Liturgical Press.

Hart, Columba, and Jane Bishop, trans. 1990. *Scivias*. Mahwah, NJ: Paulist Press.

Hildegard of Bingen. 2005. *Ordo virtutum*, trans. Linda Marie Zaerr. Boise State University. Available from http://english.boisestate.edu/lzaerr/Ordo%20Virtutum.pdf.

Hildegard of Bingen. 2006. "O clarissima Mater," trans. Norma Gentile. Healing Chants. Available from http://www.healingchants.com/hct.oclarissimamater.html.

Holsinger, Bruce Wood. 1993. "The Flesh of the Voice: Embodiment and the Homoerotics of Devotion in the Music of Hildegard of Bingen." *Signs* 19(1): 92–125.

Iversen, Gunilla. 1997. "'O Virginitas, in regali thalamo stas': New Light on the 'Ordo Virtutum': Hildegard, Richardis, and the Order of the Virtues." *Early Drama, Art, and Music Review* 20(1): 1–16.

Migne, J. P., ed. 1855. "Sanctae Hildegardis abbatissae Opera omnia." In *Patrologiae cursus completus*. Paris: Series Latina 197.

Newman, Barbara. 1987. *Sister of Wisdom: St. Hildegard's Theology of the Feminine*. Berkeley: University of California Press.

Newman, Barbara, trans. and ed. 1988. *Symphonia*. 2nd edition. Ithaca, NY: Cornell University Press.

Newman, Barbara, ed. 1998. *Voice of the Living Light: Hildegard of Bingen and Her World*. Berkeley: University of California Press.

Newman, Barbara. 1999. "Reviewed: Baird, Joseph, and Radd Ehrman. *The Letters of Hildegard of Bingen*, Vol. II: *Medieval Review*." Available from http://name.umdl.umich.edu/baj9928.9904.015.

Schibanoff, Susan. 2001. "Hildegard of Bingen and Richardis of Stade: The Discourse of Desire." In *Same Sex Love and Desire Among Women in the Middle Ages*, ed. Francesca Canadé Sautman and Pamela Sheingorn. New York: Palgrave.

Stehling, Thomas, trans. 1984. *Medieval Latin Poems of Male Love and Friendship*. New York: Garland.

Van Engen, John. 2000. "Letters and the Public Persona of Hildegard." In *Hildegard von Bingen in ihrem historischen Umfeld*, ed. Alfred Haverkamp. Mainz: Verlag Phillip Von Zabem.

Wiethaus, Ulrike. 1993. "In Search of Medieval Women's Friendships: Hildegard of Bingen's Letters to her Female Contemporaries." In *Maps of Flesh and Light: The Religious Experience of Medieval Women Mystics*, ed. Ulrike Wiethaus. Syracuse, NY: Syracuse University Press.

Susannah Mary Chewning

BIOLOGY

Biology is the scientific study of the processes of life. Biology gradually came into existence as a coherent field of study in the nineteenth century. It combined into a single field what had previously been called natural history and natural philosophy as well as elements of medicine, zoology, physiology, botany, chemistry, and pharmacology. Biology is an empirical, experimental science, which means that hypotheses made about the character and functioning of life processes are proven through repeatable experiment. Because biology is the science of life processes and reproduction is considered one of the key processes that defines life itself, biology has always been bound up with issues of sex and reproduction. Although biology is an empirical science, it has also long reflected cultural attitudes about sex and gender, both as foundational concepts for theories of life and as categories to be questioned and investigated. In its development of new theories about reproduction, physiology, behavior, and heredity, biology continues to grapple with understandings of sex and gender as well as the ways biological science has produced itself around and through gender and sexual difference.

The term *biology* combines the Greek root *bios*, or *life*, with the Greek *ology*, or *study of*, and was introduced in Germany in 1800 by German physiologist Karl Friedrich Burdach (1776–1847). The idea of combining botany and zoology was soon taken up simultaneously by both German naturalist Gottfried Reinhold Treviranus (1776–1837) in his 1802 book *Biology or Philosophy of Living Nature* and influential French botanist and early theorist of evolution Jean-Baptiste Lamarck (1744–1829), the major proponent of Lamarckism, or the idea that parents could pass on acquired traits. The concept of a science of life gained support throughout the nineteenth century, catalyzed through the discoveries of German botanist Matthias Schleiden (1804–1881) and German biologist Theodor Schwann (1810–1882) in 1838 that plants and animals were composed of cells. The idea of a single field of life studies was also advanced in 1858 by English naturalists Charles Darwin (1809–1882) and Alfred Wallace (1823–1913) whose development of a theory of evolution disagreed with Lamarck's idea that acquired traits could be passed from generation to generation. In the latter half of the nineteenth century, French biologist Louis Pasteur (1822–1895) developed the field of microbiology, demonstrating the connections between microorganisms and disease. Austrian Botanist Gregor Mendel (1822–1884) published his findings on patterns of heredity in 1866. Although his ideas were ignored until they were rediscovered in 1900, they formed the basis for the modern study of genetics.

Perceiving the continuities among what had been diverse fields of study enabled the development of more comprehensive theories of life, including Darwin's theory of evolution, but also including the germ theory of disease advocated by Pasteur, and the discovery of viruses in 1898. In the early twentieth-century American biologist Walter S. Sutton (1877–1916) and German Theodor Boveri (1862–1915) independently discovered that human chromosomes are paired and are the agents of heredity. In 1905 American researchers Edmund B. Wilson (1856–1939) and Nettie Stevens (1861–1912) independently discovered the chromosomes that determine the sex of humans. Working with fruit flies, American zoologist Thomas Hunt Morgan (1866–1945) linked heredity to evolution and developed ways to map genes on chromosomes and link specific genes to traits. With the invention of technology such as the X-ray in 1895 and the electron microscope in the 1930s, as well as advances in the fields of biochemistry, genetics, physiology, microbiology, and medicine, biologists were able to investigate phenomena happening on the smallest scale. With the development of sophisticated statistical methods, a better understanding of the geological history of the earth, and better modes of gathering data, scientists made advances in studies of paleontology, population genetics, ecology, and evolutionary biology.

The discipline of biology in the early twenty-first century examines molecular and cellular phenomena and issues involving whole organisms as well as their environments and interrelation with other organisms. Molecular biology studies life processes as matters of molecular chemistry and includes studies in biochemistry, biophysics, genetics, and cell biology. Studies involving whole organisms focus on the relations among organisms or between organisms and their environments—ecology, ethology—or on the evolution or development of organisms—evolutionary biology, paleontology, developmental biology, and population studies.

HISTORY OF CONCEPTS ABOUT LIFE, SEX, AND REPRODUCTION

From the time of the Greeks, natural philosophers, such as Aristotle (384–322 BCE), were interested in the nature of reproductive processes. They and those who followed devised a series of theories for how humans and other organisms reproduced, almost all of which assumed the superiority of the male contribution. As with other sciences, biology was influenced by cultural ideas about sex and gender, which it reflected in its assumptions, hypotheses, and theories. Until the mid 1950s most biologists assumed that the male of the species was the more developed and superior entity, and used the male as a model for most interrogations of life processes. They perceived the male as the source of form and intelligence and the female as the source of matter, ideas that indeed go back to ancient times. Assumptions about the character of genders across species have affected most aspects of zoological and biological inquiry from its study of cell processes to reproduction and even to its conceptions of DNA.

Ancient Greek philosophers such as Hippocrates (c. 460–c. 377 BCE), Plato (428–c. 347 BCE), and Aristotle considered the qualities and causes of life and offered various approaches to understanding the nature of existence. Hippocrates, who worked as philosopher and clinical physician, believed that nature could be explained through reason rather than through recourse to supernatural devices, and his approach to medicine involved observation and experience over theorizing. Hippocrates's theory of health was that healthy life required a balance and disease was evidence of an imbalance. Hippocrates believed that the body was governed by the actions of four fluids, or *humours*: black bile, yellow bile, phlegm, and blood. When these humours got out of proper balance and one or another dominated, illness ensued. Hippocrates's notion of the four humours persisted until the Enlightenment.

Plato thought that human life was split among spirit, reason, and appetites, each located in a specific organ: spirit in the heart, reason in the brain, and the appetites in the liver. Advocating measure in all things, Plato was far more a philosopher than an observer; the importance of observation was advocated by his pupil Aristotle. Aristotle believed in the reasoned and careful observation of all kinds of natural phenomena, from the weather to animals to plants. He believed that in nature everything had a function, and he sought to find both what caused phenomena and what those phenomena themselves caused. Aristotle dissected animals and discerned that the heart and blood seemed to be the first causes of life in living organisms.

Aristotle's empirical approach to nature enabled him to provide his own account of the agents of reproduction, which disagreed with the account formulated earlier by Hippocrates. Hippocrates had formulated the theory of pangenesis to account for how parental traits were passed on to offspring. He believed that sperm concentrated elements from all of the organs of the body as well as physical changes and traits that an individual acquired over a lifetime. Sperm then carried all of this forward in creating offspring. The female might also contribute her *seed*, though that contribution was also imagined to be like semen, because the female was understood to be a lesser-developed version of the male.

Aristotle introduced a different concept of how semen worked. He believed that semen had a *vital heat* that molded new individuals by its heating action on menstrual blood. He also believed that the parts of individuals developed gradually from this original heating action. Aristotle disagreed with Hippocrates's idea that acquired traits could be passed on, showing that individuals who lost limbs did not father limbless children. He, too, included the female as a part of the reproductive process, but as the contributor of brute matter upon which the shaping action of semen worked. The idea that semen was the primary determinant of the characteristics of a new generation persisted until the eighteenth century.

Galen (129–c. 199) was a Greek doctor who practiced and theorized about medical care during the Roman Empire. An enthusiastic anatomist, he identified the functions of many of the organs. In contrast to the Aristotelean model in which sexual difference was a matter of degree rather than kind, Galen envisioned two sexes whose genital parts were different but which were rearrangements of one another; the uterus, for example, was the counterpart of the scrotum. As with Hippocrates, Galen believed that reproduction was the result of the contribution of two seeds, both of which were versions of semen. During the Middle Ages, Islamic philosopher Avicenna (980–1037) picked up Aristotle's ideas about sexual difference, as well as the idea that sperm was like the agent that clots milk and female sperm like the milk itself.

During the Renaissance, which witnessed the revival of Aristotelean ideas in Europe, British physician William Harvey (1578–1657) introduced a refinement of Aristotle's theory about the mechanism of human reproduction: epigenesis. Epigenesis adopted Aristotle's idea that organs were not all present from the beginning, but developed gradually as the fetus developed. This was in contradistinction to another widely held theory about reproduction, preformationism, which held that each sperm contained a minute, fully formed individual, called a homunculus. The ideas of preformationists came from what early microscopists thought they saw when they looked at magnified sperm. Still there was no real role for the female in these theories. Partly this was because of cultural preconceptions about the superiority of the male. It was also partly because human eggs were not available to be observed through the microscope.

When scientists did look at eggs, as Aristotle had and as German anatomist Caspar F. Wolff (1734–1794) did in the late eighteenth century, they noticed that more seemed to occur in the egg than could be accounted for by a preformed, sperm-conveyed individual. By studying chicken eggs, Wolff reaffirmed Harvey's notion that individuals developed gradually. Mathematician and natural philosopher Pierre de Maupertuis (1698–1759) revived Hippocrates's notion of pangenesis, at least in so far as he believed that sperm carried particles from every organ. Maupertuis also assigned a role to the egg, although he believed that the qualities carried by the sperm were dominant.

Darwin also ascribed to a theory of pangenesis, believing that sperm carried gemmules from around the father's body that were passed on to offspring. Lamarck also believed in a theory of pangenesis. Only in 1863 did German biologist August Weismann (1834–1914) disprove the idea that parents passed on acquired characteristics.

The paternal bias of all of these theories of reproduction accompanied, paradoxically, the fact that without circumstantial corroboration, one could never be absolutely certain of who was a child's father. The role of the mother, so obvious in pregnancy and gestation of the fetus, was ignored or denied in the matter of passing on traits. The idea that maleness was the source of reason and form and that the female supplied only matter was so pervasive and unquestioned that only the invention of microscopy, the discovery of human chromosomes, the development of genetic studies, and diligent and unbiased observation finally showed that parents each contributed one-half of the genetic material for each child.

With the advent of sophisticated understandings of genetics as well as advanced concepts of physiology and development, the role of the female has become in many ways more central and important in human reproduction than the role of the male. Modes of artificial insemination and in vitro fertilization have made the contribution of genetic material less a challenge than the gestation of a child. The interaction of genetic contributions from each parent has become a matter of hypothesis and study, especially as the x chromosome, contributed by the female, carries many traits that are only expressed by male children.

SEXUAL DIFFERENCE AND PHYSIOLOGY

Theories about human reproduction depended upon and reflected ideas about the differences between the sexes. Understandings of reproduction as the action of formative semen upon the more material female required an understanding of the sexes as being the same, different only in degree of development. From the time of the ancient Greeks until the eighteenth century, male and female anatomies were seen as counterparts of one another that differed only in their relative arrangement and size. Male reproductive parts had equivalents among female reproductive parts. Both males and females contributed semen; both had testes. Male testes, however, were large; female testes were small. According to Galen, the penis and vagina were homologous, and the female's exterior genitalia (labia, clitoris, vulva) were analogous to the head of the penis at the end of a vagina shaft.

The one organ that was considered to be specifically female was the uterus (despite Galen's attempts to compare it to the scrotum). The uterus was believed to generate a host of ills and female diseases, as it was also believed to be the repository of poisons that caused female diseases. Even through the nineteenth century, many believed that the uterus could get loose and wander around the body, causing a number of symptoms—a condition referred to as *hysteria* from the Greek word for womb. Speculation about the nature and functioning of the uterus produced a number of theories—from the idea that the character of the uterus determined the sex and quantity of offspring, to the notion that it had a chamber for every day of the week, to the theory that it was divided into male-producing and female-producing sides (and sometimes with a center section that produced hermaphrodites), to the hypothesis that women had two uteruses that matched the number of breasts, to the belief that the uterus had horns—all gleaned from analogies to mammalian physiology. Anxieties about female difference were displaced on to the uterus as the locus of difference. At the same time, quandaries about the origins of sexual difference and disease were resolved by recourse to the mysterious qualities of the uterus.

The male reproductive system did not receive the same kind of fascinated attention, partly because the organs were visible and partly because they served as the norm against which the female differed. Because both males and females were believed to have semen, much more attention was devoted to trying to discern its origin. Where did semen originate: In the brain? From blood? The persistent notion of male and female commonality also supported the belief that if males lost portions of their reproductive anatomy, they would become like females. Venetian surgeon Alessandro Benedetti (c. 1450–1512) noted that when males lost their testicles, they became more like women, an opinion seconded a few centuries later by Harvey. Until the Renaissance many anatomists also believed that females could turn into males at puberty, having their interior organs drop out.

Only in the sixteenth century did scientists discover more details about the female anatomy, which made it much more difficult to support the idea that men and women were two versions of the same sex. In 1559 anatomist Realdo Colombo (1515–1559) identified the clitoris, which undid the neat symmetry that Galen had contrived. Anatomist Gabriele Falloppio (1523–1563) described the fallopian tubes, though their function was a mystery. By the latter half of the seventeenth century, Dutch anatomist Reinier de Graaf (1641–1673) found what he thought were the eggs of the human female (but which were in fact the ovarian follicles). De Graaf's discovery of the follicles and naming of the ovaries, however, supplied a new source for the possible location of a preformed homunculus in the egg and challenged the notion that females contributed little other than matter to the reproductive project.

SEXUAL DIFFERENCE, HORMONES, AND BEHAVIOR

In most patriarchal cultures, sexual difference has been interpreted as a difference in the intrinsic qualities and capabilities of individuals. Male and female have been regarded as oppositions and as complementary to one another. Males have been perceived as strong, wise, reasonable, intelligent, governing, aggressive, and generally more developed than females, who have been considered correspondingly weak, less wise, less intelligent, followers, of a passive disposition, and generally less developed than males. Males were form; females were matter. The biological basis for these differences was for centuries thought to be a difference in development instead of anatomy. But from the Renaissance, with its burgeoning studies of human anatomy, internal differences between males and females, such as the uterus, offered other bases for understanding sexual difference.

In the late nineteenth century and the twentieth century, the discovery of hormones and their regulatory roles provided another way to understand the differences between the sexes based on the effects of hormones that derived from the reproductive organs. In 1849 German physiologist Arnold Berthold (1803–1861) demonstrated that testes secreted a substance into the bloodstream. Other glands and their role in the body became a topic of interest, particularly the thyroid gland, which was affected by goiters, but also the adrenal gland and adrenaline, which was the first hormone to be synthesized outside of the body. The term *hormone* was introduced in 1905, and research continued into the role of the pituitary gland (linked to growth), the hypothalamus (linked to regulation of the pituitary), and the pancreas and its production of insulin.

Sex hormones were also a subject of interest. The part played by the testes had been suspected for a long time, because Renaissance anatomists noticed the effects the loss of testicles had. Because the testes were visible and their effects known, male sex hormones such as androsterone and testosterone received initial attention. Testosterone was isolated and synthesized in the 1930s by scientists who ground up animal testicles. Female sex hormones were more difficult to isolate, partly because they came from more than one source in the body—the ovaries, the follicles—and menstrual cycles and pregnancies involved a more complex interplay of several hormones—progesterone, progesterol, estrogen, estriol, and estradiol. Discovering and understanding the role of hormones in body development and regulation enabled the development of pregnancy tests and the birth control pill.

In the early twenty-first century scientists attributed many gender characteristics to the actions of hormones, although these attributions still reflect old ideas about the inferiority of women. Testosterone endows strength, whereas estrogen causes irrational emotion, unreliability, and moodiness. These ideas come from the differences sex hormones produce in their actions on the body. Androgens, estrogens, and progestins, which both males and females have in differing amounts, spur sexual development in the womb and at puberty, regulate sex drive, and control reproduction. Androgens such as testosterone, produced by the testes but also by the adrenal gland, influence the apparent sex of a fetus. Androgens present in the womb stimulate the development of male genitalia, which even occurs in female embryos if too much testosterone is present. Male fetuses that develop in the womb without sufficient androgens will not develop normal male genitals.

At puberty high concentrations of sex hormones (testosterone for males, estrogen for females) spurs the development of secondary sex characteristics, such as facial and body hair and vocal chord and genital growth in males, and the development of body hair, growth of breasts, and the onset of menstruation in females. Sexually mature males have a constant supply of testosterone, whereas mature females experience menstrual cycles governed by the complex interplay of estrogen and progestin that govern uterine lining, the release of eggs, and the shedding of the uterine lining. Pregnancy is also governed by sex hormones: When the ovaries reduce their production of estrogen, female humans enter into menopause, which is when menstrual periods cease.

SEXUAL DIFFERENCE AND GENETICS

Even the production of sex hormones is itself an effect of the actions of genes, whose discovery and function have been the object of much research since the twentieth century. Sexual difference plays through genetics in two main ways. First, the sex of individuals is determined by the kinds of chromosomes they receive from their parents. One set of the twenty-three pairs of human chromosomes is called the sex chromosomes, and this pair consists of two different kinds of chromosome—an X chromosome and a Y chromosome. Females have two X chromosomes and males have one X chromosome and one Y chromosome. Gametes (eggs and sperm) each carry one-half of a set of chromosomes. Female parents contribute gametes with X chromosomes only. Sperm can carry either an X or a Y chromosome. X chromosomes are longer than Y chromosomes and contain more genes. In the other pairs of chromosomes, the genes from each of the pair are matched, which means that dominant and recessive forms of a gene often temper one another. Recessive genes for various diseases may not be fully expressed when the other gene of the pair is a normal variant.

In the pairing of X and Y chromosomes, however, the recessive traits for such problems as colorblindness and hemophilia have no corresponding gene on the Y chromosome, and so they express themselves in male children. These traits are called sex-linked traits and involve primarily males. Occasionally gametes may carry more than one sex chromosome as the result of a mistake. Children born with three or more sex chromosomes express different varieties of sex/gender traits. Some individuals are born with genes for both male and female sex organs; these individuals are called hermaphrodites.

A growing belief in the genetic basis for behaviors also offers a way to understand the differences between genders. Genders—feminine and masculine—represent one way cultures and individuals have interpreted the qualities of sexual difference—a difference in reproductive gonads and roles. Femininity and masculinity have been considered effects of nurture and culture instead of nature since the work of Austrian Austrian psychoanalyst Sigmund Freud (1856–1939) and other psychologists and sexologists at the turn of the twentieth century. Discovering that the behaviors of fruit flies were partly determined by genes, genetic researchers turned to human behavior, looking for genes that account for aggressiveness, antisocial behavior, nurturing, and homosexuality. Because human behaviors are far more complex than the behaviors of fruit flies, and because behavior is also culturally taught and reinforced, genes can likely only partly explain gender behavior.

The second way sexual difference plays through the genes is in the ways genes from each parent govern different developmental or life processes, with genes from the father, for example, governing the development of the placenta or social skills and genes from the mother dominating matters of brain function. Research continues into how genes affect one another, how they influence sex and gender expression and behaviors, and the vast variation there is in the possible combinations of sex and gender in human beings.

BIOLOGY AND GENDER

As with all sciences, biology is affected by cultural ideas and preconceptions. For example, the kinds of phenomena scientists choose to examine are sometimes defined by their ideas of what phenomena are important, which is in turn influenced by assumptions about the relative centrality of males and females. Twentieth-century investigations of heart disease, for example, focused on males, not only because males were believed to be more afflicted by heart disease, but also because females were still assumed to be lesser versions of males. Studies of reproduction in females lagged behind understandings of male contributions. Only by the late twentieth century did scientists begin to undertake more systematic studies of major diseases specifically in women, acknowledging the differences between female and male biology and physiology. The understanding that some processes and diseases are specific to females or males has also enabled a wider recognition of male-specific disorders, such as prostate problems.

Feminist scholars such as Evelyn Fox Keller, Anne Fausto-Sterling, and Sandra Harding have examined the ways scientists, including biologists and geneticists, incorporate presumptions about sexual difference into the ways they define issues to examine and hypotheses to offer, how they decide to test these hypotheses, and the relative importance of various issues. The argument that female reproductive mechanisms are more monstrous and less influential than male contributions delayed research into female anatomy as well as specifically female diseases such as ovarian cancer. The assumption that all mammals pattern their behaviors on human sexual difference skewed the ways zoologists understood the complexities of animal social organizations, such as packs. Assuming the empirical truth of a cultural phenomenon such as gender (instead of sexual difference) turns objective empiricism into a protocol marred by biases. Assuming that there are only two sexes produces the conclusion, for example, that hermaphroditic or intersex children must be made to conform with cultural gender norms, a conclusion that then supports invasive surgeries and other types of coercion aimed toward making the children comply with a rigid type. Assuming that culturally defined genders and sexualities are natural spurs some scientists into looking for genes that produce such behaviors.

Perhaps the greatest problem of all is the way females have long been understood as irrational and emotional and thus not good scientists. The bias of the sciences toward a rational, empirical norm that barely veils the masculinist assumption has made it difficult for female scientists to contribute to scientific research. The result is a dearth of important female scientists and the consequent marginalization of influential biologists, such as Barbara McClintock (1902–1992), in the scientific community.

BIBLIOGRAPHY

Fausto-Sterling, Anne. 1992. *Myths of Gender: Biological Theories about Women and Men.* New York: Basic Books.

Harding, Sandra. 1986. *The Science Question in Feminism.* Ithaca, NY: Cornell University Press.

Keller, Evelyn Fox. 1985. *Reflections on Gender and Science.* New Haven, CT: Yale University Press.

Laqueur, Thomas. 1992. *Making Sex: Body and Gender from the Greeks to Freud.* Cambridge, MA: Harvard University Press.

Porter, Roy. 1998. *The Greatest Benefit to Mankind: A Medical History of Humanity.* New York: Norton.

Ridley: Matt. 2003. *The Red Queen: Sex and the Evolution of Human Nature.* New York: Perennial.

Rodgers, Joann. 2003. *Sex: A Natural History.* New York: Owl Books.

Judith Roof

BIRTH

For most of human history, birth was exclusively the work of women who labored to push their babies from the private inner world of their wombs into the larger world of society and culture. Yet in the early twenty-first century, increasing numbers of babies are pulled from the vaginal canal with forceps or vacuum extractors, or are cut from their mothers' wombs via cesarean section. The medical definition of birth is the emergence of a baby from a womb—a definition that ignores women's involvement and agency.

BIRTH AND HUMAN EVOLUTION

Higher primates walk on all fours and have pelvises wide enough to allow the direct descent of the fetal head, making for easy labors and uncomplicated births. When humans began to walk upright, the pelvis narrowed, so that the human baby has to rotate as it descends through the birth canal. Non-human primate babies can climb onto their mothers' backs and cling immediately after birth. But the larger brains of human infants make it necessary for them to be born earlier in the developmental cycle, ensuring that human babies are relatively helpless at birth and require immediate nurturing. These factors encouraged the evolution of birth as a highly social process; women give birth alone and unaided in very few societies.

Evolutionary scientists postulate that midwifery evolved along with human birth. The presence of other women at a birth would have enhanced the success of the birth process, as these women acquired skills such as turning the baby in utero to ensure the optimal position for birth, assisting rotation of the head and shoulders at birth, massaging the mother's uterus and administering herbs to stop postpartum bleeding, and facilitating breastfeeding. For these reasons, more mothers and babies survived in societies that developed midwifery traditions early on, giving them a distinct evolutionary advantage.

BIRTH, CULTURE, AND WOMEN'S STATUS

Although childbirth is a universal fact of human physiology, the social nature of birth and its importance for survival ensure that this biological and intensely personal process carries heavy cultural overlay, resulting in wide variation in childbirth practices: Where, how, with whom, and even when a woman gives birth are increasingly culturally determined. In 1908 French ethnographer Arnold van Gennep (1873–1957) noted that cultures ritualize important life transitions—of which birth is a prime example. Birth practices reflect and reveal the core values and beliefs of the culture, telling the observer a great deal about the way that culture views the world and the place of women in it. Many religions, including Judiaism and Zoroastrianism, regard birth as polluting and require ablution and isolation for purification afterward.

Where women's status is high, a rich set of nurturant traditions tends to develop around birth; where it is low, the opposite may occur. For example, in the highly patriarchal Islamic society of Bangladesh in which the status of women is low, childbirth (like menstruation) has traditionally been regarded as highly polluting. Before modernization, women gave birth on dirty linens, attended only by female relatives or traditional midwives who were themselves regarded as polluting. In contrast, in the matrilineal societies of Polynesia where the status of women is high, pregnant women are pampered and nurtured. Skilled midwives administer frequent full-body massages during pregnancy and have a rich repertoire of techniques for assisting women during labor and birth.

THE EFFECTS OF PLACE OF BIRTH

Anthropologist Brigitte Jordan's comparative study of birthing systems in the Netherlands, Sweden, the

United States, and Mexico's Yucatan, originally published in 1978, was the first to comprehensively document the wide cultural variations in birth. Her biocultural approach utilized the definition of birth, the place of birth, birth attendants, artifacts utilized to facilitate or control birth, and differences in knowledge systems about birth as foci for cross-cultural comparison.

Among these factors, place of birth has emerged as most salient for how birth happens. In home settings across cultures, from huts to houses, childbirth occurs according to the natural rhythms of labor and women's social routines. In early labor, women move about at will, stopping their activities during the 45 seconds or so per contraction, and then continuing their activities (which may include doing chores, chatting, walking, eating, singing, and dancing). Such activities subside as the women begin to concentrate more on the work of birthing, often aided in this labor by massage and emotional support from their labor companions, who are usually midwives. Many cultures have set patterns about who should be present at the birth (sometimes the father, sometimes only women, sometimes the whole family and/or friends), how labor support should be provided, what rituals should be performed to invoke the help of ancestors or spirits, and what herbs and hand maneuvers may be helpful to assist a birth or stop a postpartum hemorrhage. When birth is imminent, women at home usually take upright positions, squatting, sitting, standing, or balancing on hands and knees, often pulling on a rope or pole or on the necks or arms of their companions, and work hard to give birth. Postpartum practices vary widely: Some cultures encourage early breastfeeding, some define colustrum as harmful and feed the baby other fluids until breastmilk comes in (a practice now known to be medically dangerous—many babies die from imbibing contaminated water). Steam and herbal baths and periods of postpartum confinement are often culturally prescribed, varying in length from a few to forty days.

Where freestanding birth centers exist staffed by professional midwives, the experience of birth is resonant with the experience of birthing at home—a free flow. There are no absolute rules for how long birth should take. As long as the mother's vital signs are good and the baby's heartbeat is relatively stable, trained attendants allow the birth process to proceed at its own pace, keeping their focus on the needs of the mother, encouraging her to eat and drink at will, and to move about freely, adopting positions of her choice.

Birth in the hospital is an entirely different experience. The biomedical model dominant in hospitals demands that birth follow a certain pattern, including cervical dilation of 1 centimeter per hour—an arbitrary rule unsupported by science but consistent with industrial patterns of production. Ensuring the mechanical consistency of labor requires frequent manual checking of cervical dilation, which, if determined to be proceeding too slowly, will be augmented by breaking the amniotic sac and intravenous administration of the synthetic hormone pitocin (syntocinon) to speed labor. Women are often not allowed to eat or drink, and thus are routinely hydrated through intravenous lines, which also facilitate the administration of pitocin and other drugs. Electronic fetal monitoring to record the strength of the mother's contractions and the baby's heartbeat is pervasive in hospitals in developed countries, in spite of the fact that its routine use does not improve birth outcomes but does significantly raise cesarean rates because hospital personnel often misinterpret the monitor tracings, seeing an impending crisis where there is none. (Intermittent auscultation by a nurse, doctor, or midwife has been proven to be far more effective in identifying emerging problems.) Episiotomies to widen the vaginal outlet at the moment of birth are also common, although scientifically demonstrated to be unnecessary in 90 percent of births. Such routine obstetric procedures have been interpreted by cultural anthropologist Robbie Davis-Floyd as rituals that symbolically enact and display the core values of the technocracy, which supervalues progress through the development and application of increasingly advanced technologies to every aspect of human life, including reproduction.

IMPACT OF THE BIOMEDICAL MODEL ON BIRTH IN DEVELOPING COUNTRIES

The growing worldwide supervaluation of high technologies has induced many developing countries to suppress viable indigenous birthing systems and import the biomedical model from developed nations even when it is ill suited to the local situation. Hospitals built in the Third World may lack basic supplies such as bandages, clean sheets, and fresh needles yet be stocked with high-tech equipment. Hospital staff often has little understanding of or respect for local birth traditions and values, with the result that local women often avoid such hospitals. From northern India to Papua New Guinea to Mexico, indigenous women voice concerns about biomedical hospitals and clinics in both rural and urban areas: "They expose you;" "they shave you;" "they cut you;" "they leave you alone and ignore you, but won't let your family come in;" "they give you nothing to eat or drink;" and "they yell at you and sometimes slap you if you do not do what they say." Ironically none of the rules and procedures

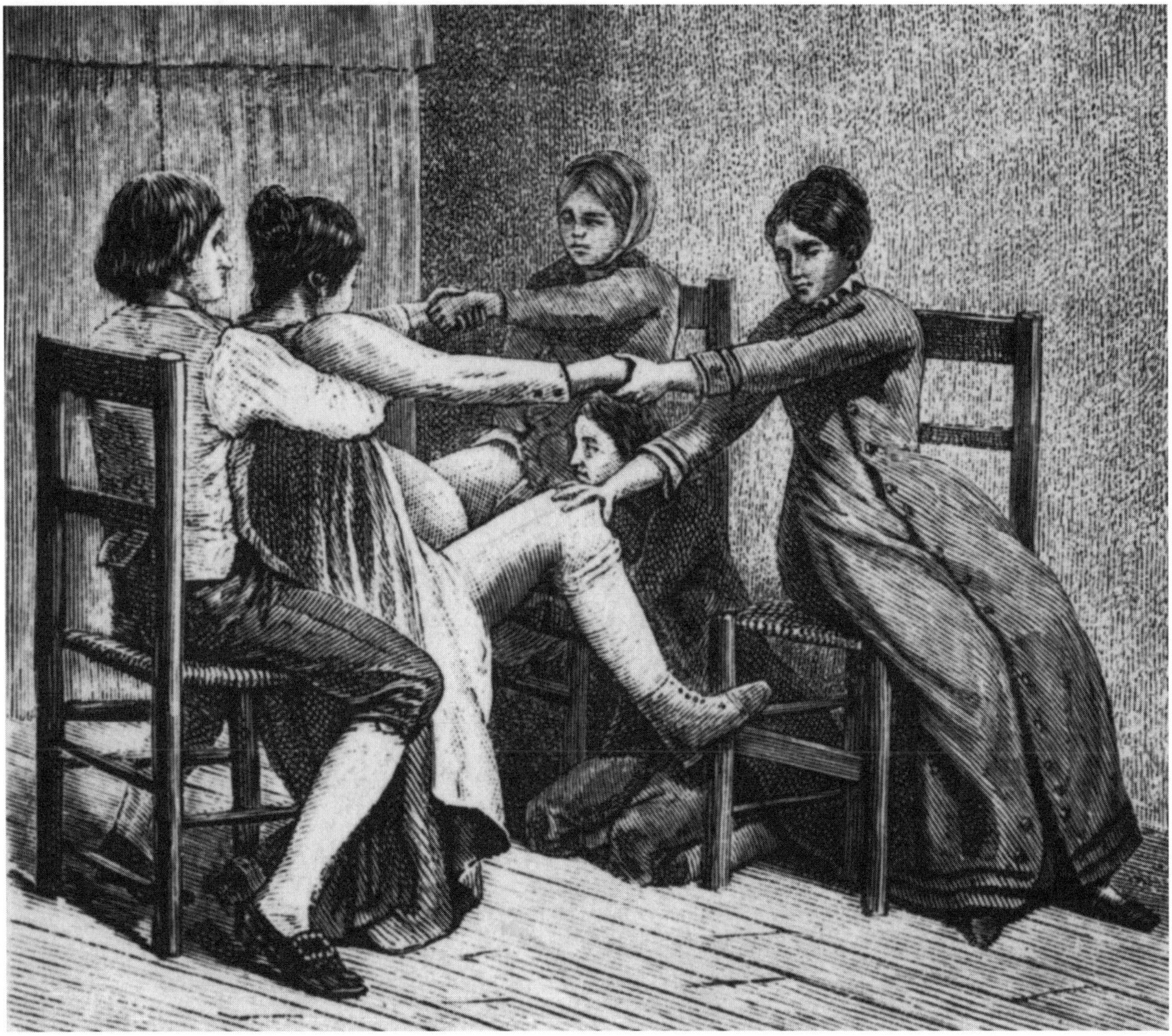

Colonial Childbirth. *Illustration of a colonial woman in childbirth.* © BETTMANN/CORBIS.

these women find so alarming are essential to good obstetric care; rather they reflect the importation of the culturally insensitive technocratic approach.

The transglobal imposition of this model on childbirth, sold to goverments as *modern health care* and to women as *managing risk* and *increasing safety in birth*, has resulted in an explosion of technological interventions in birth unprecedented in human history, including numbers of cesarean sections. Despite the World Health Organization's (WHO) demonstration that cesarean rates should never be above 15 percent, cesarean rates for Taiwan, China, and Puerto Rico are well above 40 percent; for Mexico, Chile, and Brazil are at around 40 percent; for the United States are 30.2 percent, and for Canada and the United Kingdom are 22 percent. Physician convenience and economic gain, combined with deeply ingrained medical beliefs that birth is a pathological process that works best when technologically controlled, are other factors in the recent rise in the number of cesareans performed. The WHO standard is met in the Netherlands, with a cesarean rate of 12 percent, and is reinforced by the excellence of birth outcomes in that country. This success is entirely cultural: The definition of birth as a normal physiological process in the Netherlands, in combination with Dutch cultural values on family, midwifery care, and careful attention to scientific evidence, have led to minimal interventions in hospital birth and the high home birth rate (30%) in that country. In contrast, in most of the developed world, home birth rates hover around 1 percent, despite the demonstrated efficacy and safety of a planned, midwife-attended home birth.

CONTESTING BIOMEDICAL HEGEMONY

The massive disparity between the scientific evidence in favor of less intervention in birth and the increasing interventions in actual practice reflect widespread acceptance of the technocratic model of medicine—a model developed by white male physicians—as *the* model on which to base developing health care systems. The hegemony of this approach is ensured by the political and economic benefits to physicians and technocrats from the imposition of the model, the forces of globalization and their concurrent trends toward increasing technologization, and women's concomitant faith in the model as the safest practice.

Nevertheless this hegemony is heavily contested. In addition to the thousands of local birthing systems, two other paradigms for contemporary childbirth exist throughout the world: The humanistic and holistic models. The highly patriarchal technocratic model of biomedicine metaphorizes women's birthing bodies as dysfunctional machines and encourages aggressive intervention in the mechanistic process of birth. The reform effort located in the humanistic model stresses that the birthing body is an organism influenced by stress and emotion and calls for relationship-centered care; respect for women's needs and desires; and a physiological, evidence-based approach to birth. The more radical holistic model defines the body as an energy system, stresses spiritual and intuitive approaches to birth, and places high value on the feminine. In dozens of countries, humanistic and holistic practitioners and consumer members of growing birth activist movements are utilizing scientific evidence and anthropological research to challenge the technocratic model of birth. They seek to combine the best of indigenous and professional knowledge systems to create healthier, safer, and more cost-effective systems of birth care.

Yet, from a crosscultural point of view, the focus on care of the individual limits all three paradigms. For example mortality resulting from birth is widely recognized as a massive global problem; more than 529,000 women die annually from complications of pregnancy and birth (including unsafe abortion). Biomedicine identifies conditions such as hemorrhage and toxemia as major causes of maternal death, and advises investment in doctors, hospitals, and rural clinics to provide prenatal care to prevent toxemia, and active intervention immediately after birth (i.e., administration of pitocin, cord traction for rapid removal of the placenta) to prevent hemorrhage. This biomedical approach makes it appear that problems inhere in individuals and should be treated on an individual basis, patient by patient, hospital by hospital. In contrast social science research in countries with the highest maternal mortality rates highlights the general poor health of women, who in many patriarchal societies suffer from overwork, exhaustion, anemia, malnutrition, and a variety of diseases resulting from polluted water, showing that the most important interventions required for improving women's health and for increasing safety in birth are clean water, adequate nutrition, and improved educational and economic opportunities for women.

BACK TO THE FUTURE: SCIENCE AND MIDWIFERY CARE

In the United States, obstetricians solidified their control over birth during the first half of the twentieth century and nearly eliminated midwifery by the 1950s. Since then the demands of many women for natural childbirth, coupled with scientific research into the dangers of interventionist hospital birth and the benefits of planned, midwife-attended births at home or in freestanding birth centers have generated a midwifery renaissance. Indeed in the four countries in which infant perinatal mortality statistics are the lowest in the world—Japan, the Netherlands, Sweden, and Denmark—more than 70 percent of births are attended by midwives who serve as the woman's primary caregiver throughout pregnancy, birth, and the postpartum period.

SEE ALSO *Anthropology; Fatherhood; Motherhood.*

BIBLIOGRAPHY

Davis-Floyd, Robbie E. 1992. *Birth as an American Rite of Passage*. Berkeley: University of California Press.

Davis-Floyd, Robbie E., and Carolyn Sargent, eds. 1997. *Childbirth and Authoritative Knowledge: Cross-Cultural Perspectives*. Berkeley: University of California Press.

DeVries, Raymond; Edwin van Teijlingen; Sirpa Wrede; and Cecilia Benoit, eds. 2001. *Birth by Design: Pregnancy, Maternity Care and Midwifery in North America and Europe*. New York: Routledge.

Jordan, Brigitte (1993). *Birth in Four Cultures: A Cross-Cultural Investigation of Childbirth in Yucatan, Holland, Sweden and the United States*. 4th edition. Prospect Heights, IL: Waveland Press.

Kalpana, Ram, and Margaret Jolly, eds. 1998. *Maternities and Modernities: Colonial and Post-Colonial Experiences in Asia and the Pacific*. Cambridge, UK: Cambridge University Press.

Lukere, Vicki, and Margaret Jolly, eds. 2002. *Birthing in the Pacific: Beyond Tradition and Modernity*? Honolulu: University of Hawaii Press.

Murphy-Lawless, Jo. 1998. *Reading Birth and Death: A History of Obstetric Thinking*. Bloomington: Indiana University Press.

Van Hollen, Cecilia. 2003. *Birth on the Threshold: Childbirth and Modernity in South India*. Berkeley: University of California Press.

Robbie Davis-Floyd

BIRTH CONTROL

SEE *Contraception: III. Methods.*

BISEXUALITY

The concept of bisexuality is notoriously unstable. Historically, the term has signified a wide range of often-contradictory definitions, many of which have shifted in line with transformations of Western paradigms of sexuality. There are at least five meanings of the term:

1. A synonym for biological hermaphroditism;
2. A form of psychological androgyny;
3. A psychological capacity of individuals to sexually desire both men and women;
4. A sociological adjective describing sexual behaviors or practices;
5. A collective and political identity category.

Although these five meanings of bisexuality might at first glance seem somewhat disparate, contingent, and unrelated, there is a series of important historical and epistemological relationships and continuities among them (Angelides 2001).

A SYNONYM FOR BIOLOGICAL HERMAPHRODITISM

Bisexuality appears to have been first used as a biological concept. In nineteenth century evolutionary and embryological theories it was widely used to refer to the state of human primordial hermaphroditism. Evolutionists such as Charles Darwin and his contemporaries assumed bisexuality was the missing link in the descent of humans from invertebrate organisms. Some "remote progenitor of the whole vertebrate kingdom," declared Darwin, "appears to have been hermaphrodite or androgynous" (Darwin 1901, p. 249). Within this paradigm, human development was thought to pass through various stages beginning with a state of originary bisexuality (or biological hermaphroditism), wherein the embryo displayed both sets of sexual organs before the atrophy of one of them after the third month of development (Darwin 1901). It was believed that the more advanced a racial group, class, or civilization, the more they had progressed beyond this phase of primordial hermaphroditism. In other words, the so-called "higher" races, classes, and cultures were seen to exhibit greater degrees of sexual differentiation. There was, of course, also a gender difference in this model, and men were deemed more advanced than women by virtue of having developed further beyond biological bisexuality. Existing racist and sexist social hierarchies were legitimated with this evolutionary paradigm, revealing the ways in which both "nonwhites" were sexualized and Western notions of sexuality racialized.

With the advent of sexology in the latter part of the nineteenth century, men of science such as Richard von Krafft-Ebing (1840–1902), Havelock Ellis (1859–1939), and their contemporaries appropriated the theory of bisexual evolution in order to explain deviations of the "sex instinct." Individuals exhibiting homosexual desire were believed to have either regressed to, or be developmentally arrested at, this ancestral bisexuality. It was partly on the basis of this concept of embryological bisexuality that the nineteenth century classification of individuals into two opposing types, the homosexual and the heterosexual, hinged. As Ellis, the venerated sexologist, noted around the turn of the nineteenth century, "Embryologists, physiologists of sex and biologists generally, not only accept the idea of bisexuality, but admit that it probably helps to account for homosexuality" (Ellis 1928, p. 314). Bisexuality was not itself considered a separate ontological typology or identity category but was rather that out of which either homosexuality or heterosexuality developed.

A FORM OF PSYCHOLOGICAL ANDROGYNY

Sigmund Freud (1856–1939), the founding father of psychoanalysis, inherited the theory of primordial bisexuality and made it the bedrock of his psychoanalytic framework. Aiming to erect a psychological theory of gender and sexuality that would complement the biological foundations of psychoanalysis, he posited a kind of psychological bisexuality as an analogue to evolutionary notions of embryological bisexuality. Borrowing the idea from his friend Wilhelm Fliess (1858–1928), Freud argued that just as primordial bisexuality manifests physically in every individual by "leaving behind only a few traces of the sex that has become atrophied" (Freud 1905, p. 141), so too does it manifest mentally such that each individual is "made up of masculine and feminine traits" and desires (Freud 1925, p. 255). For Freud bisexuality also played a pivotal role in the theory of the Oedipus complex. "It would appear ... that in both sexes the relative strength of the masculine and feminine dispositions is what determines whether the outcome ... shall be an identification with the father or with the mother. This is one of the ways in which bisexuality takes a hand in the subsequent vicissitudes of the Oedipus complex" (Freud 1923, p. 33).

Freud also referred to the third meaning of bisexuality—what is often referred to as a bisexual orientation—that is, the psychological capacity of individuals to sexually desire both men and women. However, like the sexologists, he also to a large extent foreclosed the possibility of a bisexual orientation or identity, in spite of his theory of psychological bisexuality (masculinity and femininity). This was because it was difficult to reconcile, on the one hand, bisexuality as both cause (biological) and effect (psychological), and on the other, an individual being capable of simultaneously desiring and identifying with the same gender. That is, in the Freudian schema an individual could only sexually desire the opposite of his or her gender identity. In order to be bisexual in the third meaning of the term, therefore, an individual had to have a shifting gender identity.

In the three decades following Freud's death the concept of biological bisexuality (and its role in psychological androgyny and bisexual desire) was largely repudiated within the disciplines of psychoanalysis and psychiatry (for example, Rado 1940; Bergler 1962; Bieber 1962). This coincided with a shift toward environmental or adaptational approaches to the study of sexuality. Rather than view an undeveloped embryonic structure as bisexuality, Sandor Rado (1900–1980) argued that it ought instead to be viewed as possessing "bipotentiality of differentiation." "Under normal developmental conditions, as differentiation proceeds and one type of reproductive action system grows to completion, the original bipotentiality ceases to have any real significance" (Rado 1940, pp. 143–144). The notion of a capacity to be sexually attracted to both sexes was also largely denied by psychologists and psychiatrists at this time. Psychoanalyst Edmund Bergler described it as "a state that has no existence beyond the word itself" (Bergler 1962, p. 80). People were assumed to be at core heterosexual, resorting only to homosexual sex as a result of neurosis, stress, or in instances when the opposite sex was not available. As psychoanalyst Irving Bieber, a widely touted expert in the 1960s, put it, "We assume that heterosexuality is the *biologic* norm and that unless interfered with all individuals are heterosexual. Homosexuals do not bypass heterosexual developmental phases and all remain potentially heterosexual" (Bieber 1962, p. 319).

Despite its apparent irrelevance to dominant twentieth century psychological theories of sexuality, bisexuality has been shown to be instrumental in propping up a binary model of sexuality by virtue of its erasure as an authentic sexual identity (Angelides 2001).

A SOCIOLOGICAL ADJECTIVE DESCRIBING SEXUAL BEHAVIORS OR PRACTICES

Although hegemonic psychiatric and psychoanalytic discourses rejected bisexuality, the concept played an important role in describing individual biographies of sexual practice with both men and women. Within the discipline of sociology, several important studies demonstrated the prevalence of bisexual practices and the need for more expansive terminology for describing the variability of human sexuality than that provided by the rigid and exclusive binary of hetero/homosexuality.

The groundbreaking studies of Alfred Kinsey (1894–1956) and his associates in the late 1940s and 1950s spearheaded an implicit challenge to what he perceived as the normative and homogeneous psychomedical categories of hetero- and homosexuality. Bisexuality was recast in the sense of the third meaning noted above, as "the capacity of an individual to respond erotically to any sort of stimulus, whether it is provided by another person of the same or of the opposite sex." This, it was argued, "is basic to the species" (Kinsey 1948, p. 660). Kinsey backed up this claim with data that revealed around 46 percent of men and up to 14 percent of women had engaged in both heterosexual and homosexual activities in the course of their adult lives. Eschewing psychomedical concepts of "normal," "abnormal," "homosexual," and "heterosexual," Kinsey instead referred to sexualities as mere "statistical variations of behavioral frequencies on a continuous curve" (1948, p. 203). The Kinsey seven-point scale was created to describe more accurately this statistical variation. The aim was "to develop some sort of classification which could be based on the relative amounts of heterosexual and homosexual experience or response in each [person's] history" (1948, p. 639). Notwithstanding the broad-ranging critiques made of Kinsey's methodology, his data revealed for the first time the reality of widespread bisexual behaviors in American society.

Other researchers have attempted to refine Kinsey's scale and further his efforts to provide an alternative to the binary model of sexuality that might incorporate a more accurate concept of bisexuality. The most notable of these is Klein's Sexual Orientation Grid (Klein 1978). The shift away from viewing sexualities as reflective of ontological typologies and toward viewing them as reflective of behavioral variations was also bolstered by cross-cultural and cross-species research, which similarly revealed that bisexual variability was the norm and not the exception (Ford and Beach 1951). More recently, burgeoning global HIV/AIDS research has reinforced the need for thinking about bisexuality as an important sociological category for describing (usually) men who have sex with men but who do not identify themselves as homosexual (Aggleton 1996).

A COLLECTIVE AND POLITICAL IDENTITY CATEGORY

The emergence of a collective and political identity category of bisexuality has certainly been constrained, if not often foreclosed, by the history of bisexual erasure within Western binary models of sexuality. Until at least the 1970s (if not beyond) a prevailing psychomedical view was that bisexuality did not constitute a sexual identity or "orientation." Instead it was routinely envisioned as a form of immaturity, a state of confusion, or a transitional state on the way to either hetero- or homosexuality. This is in stark contrast to homosexuality, which has formed the basis of collective self-identification at least since the late nineteenth century. However, it was not until the 1970s and 1980s that bisexuality constituted a palpable collective and political identity category in many Western societies. In addition to a perceived absence in the historical and cultural record, self-identified bisexuals were animated to assert a political identity due to the experience of marginalization within gay liberation and lesbian feminist movements in the 1970s and 1980s (Rust 1995).

With steadily expanding bisexual activism, identities, organizations, and publications, activists and theorists of bisexuality have issued wide-ranging critiques of binary models of sexuality. They have attempted to expose how the historical neglect or cultural trivialization of bisexuality has been fuelled not by scientific "fact" but by misleading historical, cultural, and political assumptions. Terms such as "biphobia" and "monosexism" have been coined as a way of highlighting the cultural, political, and theoretical bias against people who sexually desire (or who have sexually desired) more than one gender in the course of their lives (Ochs 1996). Activists and theorists of bisexuality have also attempted to interrogate the political, theoretical, and cultural interconnections between feminism and bisexuality (Weise 1992), and between bisexuality and gay, lesbian, and queer cultures and theories. (Hall and Pramaggiore 1996; Angelides 2001).

Existing research has demonstrated that, far from being marginal to broader representations and practices of sexuality, bisexuality is in fact centrally implicated in the Anglophone epistemology of sexuality and the global production of sexual desires, behaviors, and identities.

SEE ALSO *Sexuality.*

BIBLIOGRAPHY

Aggleton, Peter, ed. 1996. *Bisexualities and AIDS: International Perspectives*. Bristol: Taylor & Francis.

Angelides, Steven. 2001. *A History of Bisexuality*. Chicago: University of Chicago Press.

Bergler, Edmund. 1962. *Homosexuality: Disease or Way of Life?* New York: Collier Books.

Bieber, Irving, et al. 1962. *Homosexuality: A Psychoanalytic Study*. New York: Basic Books.

Darwin, Charles. 1901. *The Descent of Man and Selection in Relation to Sex*. London: John Murray.

Ellis, Havelock. 1928. "Studies in the Psychology of Sex" In Vol. 2, *Sexual Inversion*. 3rd rev. and enlarged. Philadelphia: F.A. Davis.

Ford, Clellan S., and Frank A. Beach. 1951. *Patterns of Sexual Behavior*. New York; Harper & Row.

Freud, Sigmund. 1905. *Three Essays on the Theory of Sexuality*. In *The Standard Edition of the Complete Psychological Works of Sigmund Freud*, 24 volumes, ed. and trans. James Strachey. London: Hogarth Press, 1953–1974.

Freud, Sigmund. 1923. *The Ego and the Id*. In *The Standard Edition of the Complete Psychological Works of Sigmund Freud*, Vol. 19, ed. and trans. James Strachey. London: Hogarth Press, 1953–1974.

Freud, Sigmund. 1925. "Some Psychical Consequences of the Anatomical Distinction Between the Sexes." In *The Standard Edition of the Complete Psychological Works of Sigmund Freud*, Vol. 19, ed. and trans. James Strachey. London: Hogarth Press, 1953–1974.

Hall, Donald, and Maria Pramaggiore, eds. 1996. *Representing Bisexualities: Subjects and Cultures of Fluid Desire*. New York: New York University Press.

Kinsey, Alfred C.; Wardell B. Pomeroy; and Clyde E. Martin. 1948. *Sexual Behavior in the Human Male*. Philadelphia: Saunders.

Kinsey, Alfred C., et al. 1953. *Sexual Behavior in the Human Female*. Philadelphia: Saunders.

Klein, Fritz. 1978. "*The Bisexual Option: A Concept of One Hundred Percent Intimacy*. New York: Arbor House.

Krafft-Ebing, Richard von. 1965. *Psychopathia Sexualis: A Medico Forensic Study*, trans. Harry E. Wedeck. New York: Putnam.

Ochs, Robyn. 1996. "Biphobia; It Goes More Than Two Ways." In *Bisexuality: The Psychology and Politics of an Invisible Minority*, ed. Beth A. Firestein. Thousand Oaks, CA: Sage, 217–239.

Rado, Sandor. 1940. "A Critical Examination of the Concept of Bisexuality." *Psychosomatic Medicine* 2: 459–467.

Rust, Paula C. 1995. *Bisexuality and the Challenge to Lesbian Politics: Sex, Loyalty, and Revolution*. New York: New York University Press.

Weise, Elizabeth Reba. 1992. *Closer to Home: Bisexuality & Feminism*. Seattle, WA: Seal Press.

Steven Angelides

BLACK ARTS MOVEMENT

Hailed by its practitioners, pundits, and critics as the cultural "aesthetic and spiritual sister of the Black Power concept" (Neal 1989, p. 62), the Black Arts Movement marked black Americans' turn away from a white, Western paradigm to embrace their own "Black Aesthetic" during the tumultuous era of the 1960s. Perhaps the Black Arts Movement, like its political double, is rooted in U.S. blacks' collective exasperation with the perceived inadequacy of nonviolence as a response to the vicious persistence of violent racism in the "dominant American culture" (Heacock 1995, p. 34). Amiri Baraka says that the 1964 Broadway play *Blues for Mr. Charlie* by James Baldwin (1924–1987) "announced the Black Arts Movement" (1996, p. 96). Critic Houston Baker Jr. (1994) cites Baraka himself as its progenitor, stemming from Baraka's unsparing and scathing critique of the *middle-classness* of "Negro literature" in his 1962 article,

"The Myth of a Negro Literature." Early on, when he was still LeRoi Jones, Baraka had termed the West "a grey, hideous space" (Jones 1964, p. 62), and thus a bankrupt model to which black writers should owe no allegiance. Henry Louis Gates Jr., no lover of Baraka, says it is Baraka's founding of the Black Arts Repertory Theatre/School in Harlem in 1965 that ignites this movement for a Black Aesthetic (1987, p. xxvii). This period, both for the Black Arts and Black Power movements, is as crucial to the politics of U.S. black culture as the modernist Harlem Renaissance, because of its rate of cultural production and because of its role in transforming the consciousness of a whole generation of post–World War II African-American women and men.

Poetry was the cultural engine of change for the Black Arts and Black Power movements. Dudley Randall (1914–2000), who was dubbed the "father of black poetry" by *Black Enterprise Magazine* in 1978, established Broadside Press in 1965 in Detroit. Between 1965 and 1984, Broadside Press published the poetry of more than two hundred black poets in broadsides, individual collections, anthologies, records, and tapes, including Sonia Sanchez, Nikki Giovanni, Gwendolyn Brooks, Margaret Danner, Haki R. Madhubuti, Etheridge Knight, Carolyn Marie Rodgers, Everett Hoagland, Stephany, Melvin W. Dixon, as well as Baraka, and many other less well-known writers during the period. "Broadside Press [was] a cultural marker of an epic generation" (Clarke 2005, p. 172), and it cornered the market on the publication of Black Arts Movement poetry.

The Black Arts Movement is also marked by critical innovations in jazz, notably in the music of Sun Ra (1914–1993), John Coltrane (1926–1967), and Pharoah Sanders (b. 1940), among many others. During the late sixties, poet Jayne Cortez (b. 1936) also became well known for combining her lyric verse and jazz music in explosive critique and exhortation of the black world, as did the immortal Last Poets collective; both are progenitors of the spoken word genre (Nielsen 1997, p. 221).

Even though the first books of Nikki Giovanni (*Black Feeling, Black Talk*, 1968), Audre Lorde (*The First Cities*, 1968), Carolyn M. Rodgers (*Paper Soul*, 1968), and Sonia Sanchez (*Homecoming*, 1969) are each synonymous with Black Arts aestheticizing, the Black Arts Movement was still a story of black heterosexual manhood's coming of age, with black womanhood standing at the edges of the birthing stool, greeting the entry of the angry infant, hollering down the birth canal of the new blackness. Yet each of the afore-named books attests to black women's vibrant militant literacy. Giovanni's critique of the "nigger" in black people and Sanchez's cautionary censure of the West and its cultural inventions were as strong and strident as the work of any black male poet of the time.

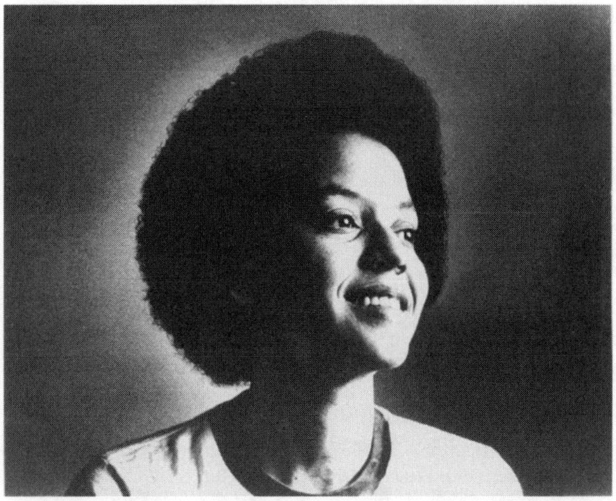

Nikki Giovanni. *Author of Black Feeling, Black Talk.* AP/WIDE WORLD PHOTOS.

Gwendolyn Brooks, upon witnessing students' adulatory responses to the poetry of Baraka at a black writers' conference at Fisk University in 1967, decided that she must stand in blackness with her poetry. Her 1968 book *In the Mecca* marked her final publication with Harper's, her press for twenty-five years. This collection was also Brooks' swan song to the lyric (i.e., the sonnet). Her subsequent collections were published by Broadside Press and then, after 1985, Haki Madhubuti's Third World Press.

Cortez's first book of poems, *Pissstained Stairs and the Monkey Man's Wares*, was self-published in 1969, and uttered profane critiques of racism and colonialism with vatic intensity.

With the publication of *The Black Woman, An Anthology*, Toni Cade Bambara's 1970 anthology of writings by black women, readers began to notice black women's contributions as writers, revolutionists, and theorists of this militant turn of cultural events in the black American world. Emergent black feminism influenced the understanding of black women's role in leading and endorsing this hallmark period of black American creativity.

Lesbian feminist poet Audre Lorde's third book, *From a Land Where Other People Live* (1973), was published by Broadside and nominated for a 1974 National Book Award along with those of two other feminist poets, Adrienne Rich's *Diving into the Wreck* and Alice Walker's *Revolutionary Petunias*. Rich's book won, but she demanded that Lorde and Walker share the award. Alexis Deveaux, in *Warrior Poet*, her biography of Lorde, reveals that Randall requested that Lorde omit "Love Poem" from this collection, because of its explicit reference to sex between women. Lorde acquiesced, feeling betrayed by her desire for the "prospect of another published book" and "her own need for the black community's embrace" (p. 131). This is an indication of how proscribed were gender and sexuality within the Black Arts Movement. Yet the sharp angle of the period's critique of the racism and colonialism of the West still continues to influence black cultural production.

BIBLIOGRAPHY

Baker, Houston A., Jr. 1994. "Generational Shifts and the Recent Criticism of Afro-American Literature." In *Within the Circle*, ed. Angelyn Mitchell. Durham, NC: Duke University Press. (Orig. pub. 1981.)

Baraka, Amiri. 1996. *Eulogies*. New York: Marsilio.

Clarke, Cheryl. 2005. *"After Mecca": Women Poets and the Black Arts Movement*. New Brunswick, NJ: Rutgers University Press.

Deveaux, Alexis. 2004. *Warrior Poet: A Biography of Audre Lorde*. New York: W. W. Norton.

Gates, Henry Louis, Jr. 1987. *Figures in Black: Words, Signs, and the "Racial" Self.* New York: Oxford University Press.

Heacock, Maureen Catherine. 1995. "Sounding a Challenge: African American Women's Poetry and the Black Arts Movement." Ph.D. diss., Minneapolis: University of Minnesota.

Jones, LeRoi. 1964. "Black Dada Nihilismus." In *The Dead Lecturer*. New York: Grove Press.

Jones, LeRoi. 1966. "The Myth of a Negro Literature." In *Home: Social Essays*. New York: William Morrow.

Neal, Larry. 1989. "The Black Arts Movement." In *Visions of a Liberated Future: Black Arts Movement Writings*. New York: Thunder's Mouth Press.

Nielsen, Aldon Lynn. 1997. *Black Chant: Languages of African-American Postmodernism*. Cambridge, UK: Cambridge University Press.

Cheryl Clarke

BLADDER INFECTIONS

SEE *Sexually Transmitted Diseases.*

BLAXPLOITATION FILMS

Blaxploitation films—action films with black subject matter made in the 1970s—have powerfully shaped the vocabulary of images of black masculinity and femininity in American culture. Blaxploitation's roots might be found in the growing political consciousness of the civil rights movement. In contrast to past successful black film figures of respectability, such as Sidney Poitier or Diahann Carroll, the heroes and heroines of blaxploitation privileged the style, language, music, and social landscape of everyday black America, eschewing assimilation into the white world.

Melvin Van Peebles's *Sweet Sweetback's Baad Asssss Song* (1971), produced through Van Peebles's guerilla tactics of borrowed equipment, actors, and time, sparked the genre. *Sweetback*'s odyssey is a defense of black masculinity by any means necessary: the murder of white cops, subterfuge, revenge, hand-to-hand combat, rape, and consensual sex with white women and with black women. Whether police, pimp, or pusher, the blaxploitation heroes that followed were similarly tactical and spectacular in their performance of masculinity, from *Shaft*'s suave John Shaft to *Superfly*'s mack-daddy Priest to the ghetto gangster title character in *Black Caesar*. According to the cultural historian Stephane Dunn, these films' defense of black manhood reflects contemporary nationalist discourse that called for the restoration of the black man's place on top in the black family and community. For Van Peebles and fans such as Huey Newton, films such as *Sweetback* were revolutionary. Yet many saw this construction of the sexualized and often violent black hero as a none-too-revolutionary revision of the black buck stereotype, the "Superspade," in Thomas Cripps's terms (1978). In 1972 the Congress of Racial Equality (CORE) and the National Association for the Advancement of Colored People (NAACP) led boycotts protesting blaxploitation films' use of sexualized violence and their limited range of black heroes (Guererro 1993).

While women's bodies were a key selling point in posters and other advertisements, in many blaxploitation films women waited in the background as "local color"—flat stereotypes of bitches, mammies, and whores. But a few standout performances remain. In *Cleopatra Jones* (1973) and its sequels, for example, Cleopatra is a crime-fighting, butt-kicking superheroine, the central figure of justice and revenge. Many of Pam Grier's films, including *Coffy* (1973), *Foxy Brown* (1974), and *Friday Foster* (1975), reverse the hierarchy of heroism in sometimes radical ways. Like Van Peebles's Sweetback, Grier's Coffy uses her body as a means of power. Within the same scene Coffy's body might be depicted bared and vulnerable to the eyes of the viewer and then used to avenge an act of sexual violence. Grier herself attributes the films' success as part of a larger zeitgeist: "All across the country, a lot of women were Foxy Brown and Coffy. They were independent, fighting to save their families, not accepting rape or being victimized" (Martinez 1998, p.53). Blaxploitation heroines have been a significant site of spectatorship for many black women. The continued cult status of Coffy, Foxy, and Cleopatra is evident in the work of many black artists and thinkers, from the rappers Lil' Kim and Foxy Brown to feminist critics such as bell hooks and Jennifer Brody, to the filmmaker Cheryl Dunye.

Cleopatra Jones. *Tamara Dobson, seen here in 1973, played Cleopatra Jones in two blaxploitation films.* AP IMAGES.

BIBLIOGRAPHY

Baad Asssss Cinema: A Bold Look at 70's Blaxploitation Films. 2002. Directed by Isaac Julien. Independent Film Channel.

Berry, S. Torriano, and Venise T. Berry. 2001. *The 50 Most Influential Black Films.* New York: Citadel Press.

Brody, Jennifer DeVere. 1999. "The Returns of Cleopatra Jones." *Signs* 25(1): 91–121.

Cripps, Thomas. 1978. *Black Film as Genre.* Bloomington: Indiana University Press.

Dunn, Stephane. Forthcoming. "Baad 'Bitches' and Sassy Supermamas: Race, Gender, and Sexuality in Black Power Action Fantasies." Urbana: University of Illinois Press.

Grant, William R., IV. 2004. *Post-Soul Black Cinema: Discontinuities, Innovations, and Breakpoints, 1970–1995.* New York: Routledge.

Guerrero, Ed. 1993. *Framing Blackness: The African American Image in Film.* Philadelphia: Temple University Press.

Martinez, Gerald; Diana Martinez; and Andres Chavez. 1998. *What It Is . . . What It Was! The Black Film Explosion of the '70s in Words and Pictures.* New York: Hyperion.

Royster, Francesca T. 2003. *Becoming Cleopatra: The Shifting Image of an Icon.* New York: Palgrave Macmillan.

Francesca T. Royster

BLOOD

As the fluid of life, blood has abundant literal and metaphorical meanings that vary across cultures and genders. Women's blood and men's blood differ in both composition and cultural associations, and this distinction is most often linked to women's menstruation. In sexual practice, blood can be an erotic fluid comparable to other bodily fluids. Blood also designates family relations and racial distinctions, both based on genetic material in blood.

PHYSIOLOGY

The heart pumps blood throughout the body, where the blood delivers nutrients and oxygen to organs and tissues and removes waste products such as carbon dioxide and lactic acid. Physiologically, the blood of men and women differs in the amount of hemoglobin, which carries iron and oxygen to the body's cells. This difference is due largely to women's loss of blood through menstruation and to men's greater muscle mass. It also means that women are more likely to become anemic, and this illness is a particular danger to pregnant women. Babies born to anemic mothers are at high risk of being developmentally retarded. Leonard Shlain (2003) argues that women's need for iron, most readily available in red meat, encouraged the development of hunting in pre-modern society.

FEMININE AND MASCULINE BLEEDING

Cultural connotations of blood reveal its relation to gender stereotypes, so that women's blood is feminine and weak, whereas men's blood is masculine and virile. Women's blood is most often associated with their reproductive ability and is thus linked to menstruation, the loss of virginity, childbirth, and menopause.

Menstruation has disparate meanings in different cultures. It is considered variously as a simple act of elimination, a positive experience linked to fertility of women and of the earth, and an unclean process that is regulated by taboos. One euphemism used in the United States and elsewhere, "the curse of Eve," reflects sentiments that menstruation is an unwelcome experience for women and an uncomfortable topic of discussion for men. A symbol of the arrival of puberty, a woman's first menstruation is called the *menarche.* As a rite of initiation, some cultures celebrate this flowing of blood; in many Western cultures, this event goes largely unacknowledged. In tribal cultures such as the Loango of East Africa, menstruating women are isolated from the rest of the community in menstruation huts. The Bible, in Leviticus, warns against associating with or having sex with menstruating women for fear of contamination with the unclean fluid. Some feminist critics argue that the taboos on and fear of menstruation are a suppressive reaction to the implicit procreative power to which menstruation attests.

Many women bleed when they lose their virginity, since sexual intercourse can break the hymen, a membrane covering the vaginal opening. However, other activities, including the use of tampons and involvement in sports, may stretch or break the hymen before initial intercourse. Despite knowledge that the existence of the hymen is not an infallible indicator of virginity, many Mediterranean, African, and Islamic cultures require proof that a woman is a virgin on her wedding night, asking for evidence of the broken hymen by such means as a bloody sheet displayed to wedding guests. Other feminine bleeding occurs during and after childbirth due to straining and tearing of the genital area and the uterus. Women thus bleed both at regular intervals—through menstruation—and at significant moments in their reproductive lives. At menopause, with the cessation of menstruation, women's sexually associated bleeding ceases.

Men's blood is generally associated with wounds resulting from physical conflicts and war, and thus is a symbol of heightened masculinity, virility, or dominance. Representations of violence normally include blood, and film and television may be censored for extreme violence as demonstrated by excessive amounts of blood. Barbara Ehrenreich (1997) argues that the link between violence, blood, and masculinity, supported by the prevalence of phallic weapons, may have replaced previous mythical representations of vaginas as both bleeding wounds and predatory, bloody mouths.

Some tribal cultures have rituals for men that parallel menstruation, in which men make a small incision on their penises and allow a certain amount of blood to flow out before bandaging the wound. In Judaism, as Lawrence A. Hoffman (1996) points out, the circumcision of infants is a similar male initiation rite that involves the symbolic loss of blood from the genitals. Ehrenreich (1997, p. 106–107) lists many other cultural practices that compare women's vaginal bleeding with ritual acts of bloodletting for men:

> In Papua New Guinea, the self-induced ritual nosebleeds are seen as parallel to menstruation; the Australian Aborigines who subincise their penises reopen the wounds regularly in order, they say, to simulate menstruation. In ancient Hawaii blood sacrifice was understood to be a "man's childbearing," just as childbearing was a "woman's sacrifice," and the Aztecs similarly equated men's death in war to women's death in childbirth. War as a kind of ritual bloodletting is linked to menstruation in the myths of the Ndembu people of Africa, and the Plains Indian mythology studied by Claude Lévi-Strauss.

SEXUAL PRACTICES AND BLOOD

Sexual fetishes involving blood are termed *blood play* or *blood sports*; these involve individuals licking or drinking the blood of their sexual partners after cutting or otherwise wounding them. This practice is related to bloodletting, vampirism, and self-mutilation. Such practices are grouped with other sexual activities based on sadomasochist tendencies or sexual dominance and submissiveness.

Vampires, mythic figures who drink the blood of the living to maintain their own lives after death, are highly sexualized in cultural representations. The act of drinking another person's blood involves seduction to attain physical proximity and a life-threatening "kiss" that transfers bodily fluid. While representations of female vampires exist, most are men, a stereotype that relies on the connection between violence, sexual aggression, and masculinity.

In Japanese anime and manga, male characters who are sexually aroused are shown to have nosebleeds. The exact reason for this connection is unclear, but one theory is that the rush of blood to the genitals is so intense that it floods the whole body and spills out through the nose. The depiction of blood and sex is common in Japanese culture, which is notable for its eroticization of violence, usually against women.

BLOOD-BORNE SEXUALLY TRANSMITTED DISEASE

Many sexually transmitted diseases, such as herpes and AIDS, are carried in the blood as well as in other bodily fluids like semen. Beginning in the late twentieth century, AIDS became a major concern for citizens of all countries. Originally considered a gay male disease, due to its initial prevalence among gay men and the ease with which gay sex transmits the virus, AIDS was rarely spoken of nor were treatments readily available. After discovering this disease can be transmitted through heterosexual encounters and blood transfusions, the United States took a more active role in educating the public about the virus, including advocating safe sex with condoms. In Africa, AIDS is an epidemic due to a lack of knowledge about virus transmission and ineffective folk remedies. One such remedy, the belief that an infected man may cure himself by having sex with a virgin female, has led to the mass rape and infection of young women.

BLOOD RELATIONS: KINSHIP AND BLOODLINES

As the carrier of genetic material, blood is linked to family or clan identity and racial groups. Thus, kinship is often referred to as bloodlines, distinguishing bonds of blood relationship from friendship or marriage. People who are not related by blood but who want to symbolize their strong connection with each other may become *blood brothers* or *blood sisters* by partaking in various rituals that may involve sharing or commingling their blood.

Bloodlines establish taboos on marrying or having sex within one's immediate family, a practice known as incest, or within larger groups or relations such as clans, also defined as endogamy. Such taboos are practical for cultural and health reasons. Culturally, the ban on endogamous relations helps create connections among multiple clans or families, which can increase wealth or form protective alliances. In addition, bans on incest maintain harmony within smaller family units by both discouraging any natural sexual attraction to one's immediate relatives, such as the Oedipal desire of a son for his mother, or the Electra complex (in which a daughter is sexually attracted to her father), and reinforcing natural aversions to such sexuality. Physiologically, continued incestuous relations lead to problems such as a diminished gene pool and increased susceptibility to disease. One such disease is hemophilia, or the inability for blood to clot properly, which notoriously affected members of the royal families of Europe beginning with Queen Victoria of England (r. 1837–1901). It can also be traced back to the Talmud and other Jewish religious texts, dating from the second to fifth centuries CE, that regulate circumcision based on previous family members who bled to death following the act. Hemophilia is most often manifested in men, while women are almost always only carriers.

In Western society, bloodlines and kinship are marked by patrilineal naming, so that fathers pass their surnames on to their children and thus show the continuation of their bloodlines. Several anthropologists argue that patriliny has not always been the standard mode of determining kinship. In 1861, J. J. Bachofen published *Das Mutterrecht* (Mother right), in which he argued that matriliny, which figures the mother-child relation as the basic social unit, preceded patriarchy and patriliny. Patriliny and patriarchy followed to demonstrate and secure the father's role in reproduction, family, and society.

In the United States, the historical preoccupation with racial difference, particularly the distinction between white and black Americans, resulted in the "one drop of blood" rule, which holds that a single drop of blood from a non-white ancestor results in a non-white person. During slavery, this rule kept many mixed-race individuals in bondage, and often the white male slave owners had sex with or raped their female slaves to increase their property and wealth. Following slavery, racial discrimination continued to categorize mixed-race individuals as black and relegate them to an inferior social status. Due to increased mixed-race births, such emphasis on racial groups as categories of identity has waned. To account for this demographic and social change, the 2000 U.S. census was the first census to offer respondents the opportunity to classify themselves as belonging to more than one racial group.

SEE ALSO *Female Genital Mutilation; Incest; Menstruation; Miscegenation; Vagina; Vampirism.*

BIBLIOGRAPHY

Bradburne, James M., ed. 2001. *Blood: Art, Power, Politics and Pathology.* New York: Prestel.

Buckley, Thomas, and Alma Gottlieb, eds. 1988. *Blood Magic: The Anthropology of Menstruation.* Berkeley: University of California Press.

Ehrenreich, Barbara. 1997. *Blood Rites: Origins and History of the Passions of War.* New York: Metropolitan Books.

Hoffman, Lawrence A. 1996. *Covenant of Blood: Circumcision and Gender in Rabbinic Judaism.* Chicago: University of Chicago Press.

Pasternak, Burton; Carol R. Ember; and Melvin Ember. 1997. *Sex, Gender, and Kinship: A Cross-Cultural Perspective.* Upper Saddle River, NJ: Prentice Hall.

Shlain, Leonard. 2003. *Sex, Time, and Power: How Women's Sexuality Shaped Human Evolution.* New York: Viking.

Wolf, Arthur P., and William H. Durham, eds. 2004. *Inbreeding, Incest, and the Incest Taboo: The State of Knowledge at the Turn of the Century.* Stanford, CA: Stanford University Press.

Michelle Veenstra

BLOW JOB

SEE *Oral Sex; Sexual Practices.*

BLOW-UP DOLL

SEE *Sex Aids.*

BLUES

Blues is a genre of American popular music that attained national prominence in the 1910s and 1920s. Coinciding with the advent of the recording industry, blues helped foster a distinct cultural sphere in the mass media for African Americans. Often mistakenly interpreted as an unmediated expression of individual sorrow, blues is a highly stylized and constantly evolving art form that affirms the lives and communal values of its audiences. Although it commonly is perceived as "folk" music, in its first few decades blues was synonymous with a variety of types of black popular music and thus cannot be characterized by style alone.

ORIGINS AND INCEPTION

The blues is an African-American invention that was a reworking of European-derived conceptions of song form, melody, harmony, and meter along African cultural lines. Musical techniques born of that negotiation include bent or "blue" notes, syncopation, and the twelve-bar blues form. As a commercial genre, blues emerged in the 1900s from ragtime. Songwriters who were looking for the next big craze began to combine the vernacular music of African Americans with Tin Pan Alley song forms. Foremost among those musical entrepreneurs was W. C. Handy, the self-proclaimed "Father of the Blues," who set off a publishing explosion in 1912 with "Memphis Blues."

Black vaudeville theaters and the traveling tent shows that visited remote areas of the South were the main institutions that supported early blues. As blues gained notice through sheet music sales, popular singers, both black and white, fashioned themselves as purveyors of authentic "Negro" blues. Popular dance bands in northern cities such as James Reese Europe's New York–based orchestra began arranging blues numbers for a mainly white middle-class audience.

RACE RECORDS AND BLUES QUEENS

In 1920 the success of Mamie Smith's "Crazy Blues" proved the existence of an African-American audience for recorded blues, and record companies rushed to develop "race record" catalogues, targeting the musical preferences of the black working class. The biggest stars of that period were women, the majority of whom had honed their talent on tent show and black vaudeville stages, environments that demanded they cultivate powerful voices and commanding stage presences. Backed by the most sophisticated jazz bands of the day, singers such as Gertrude "Ma" Rainey, Bessie Smith, and Ida Cox used their recordings to create larger-than-life personae, singing as women who were glamorous, sexually independent, and often rowdy. Their bravado was full of entertaining off-color humor, yet the music also provided a way for its predominantly African-American female audience to confront issues of gender and sexuality: Ma Rainey's sarcastic "Prove It on Me Blues" (1928) laid claim to a lesbian identity, and Bessie Smith's "Hard Time Blues" (1926) asserted independence from a no-good man.

BLUES AS A MALE-DOMINATED GENRE

For African-American women after the blues queens greater fame and fortune could be found in more mainstream jazz and pop genres. Singers from Billie Holliday to Dinah Washington sang blues numbers throughout their careers but were not associated exclusively with blues. Thus, blues became largely male-dominated, a genre in which competing versions of masculinity vied for popularity. From 1926 until his untimely death in 1929 the best-selling blues artist was the Texas-born guitarist and singer Blind Lemon Jefferson, whose "down home" guitar style and moaning vocals began a boom in recordings by country blues artists. Songs such as "Black Snake Moan" (1927) used thinly veiled metaphors to express sexual yearning ("some pretty mama better come and get this black snake soon"). Not all sexual content in country blues, however, was heterosexual. Although not big hits, recordings such as Charlie Jordan's "Keep It Clean" (1930) and Kokomo Arnold's "Sissy Man Blues" (1934) celebrated homosexual desire.

As African Americans continued to migrate north, blues took on an increasingly urban character. The piano-playing crooner Leroy Carr exploited the potential of microphone recording, crafting smooth, seductive blues that earned him legions of female admirers and dozens of male imitators. In contrast, virtuosic boogie-woogie pianists such as Pine Top Smith were mainstays at late-night Chicago parties, using a steady bouncing beat to encourage women to "shake that thing" on the dance floor. Fusing the rhythmic drive of boogie-woogie with humorous double entendre, as in the song "Let Me Play with Your Poodle" (1942), the guitarist-singer Tampa Red created a smart-talking version of blues known as hokum. A notable exception to the overwhelming male bias was Memphis Minnie, whose guitar technique and strong singing voice earned the respect of her male peers.

BLUES AS THE DEVIL'S MUSIC

Blues musicians rejected the puritanical attitude toward matters of sexuality and bodily pleasure that marked early American culture. Whether one hears the ubiquity of sexual topics in blues as the legacy of an African worldview or understands it as a matter of class and race (working-class blacks were not expected to adhere to normative moral standards and were thus "freer" to refer to sexuality in music), blues made many people uncomfortable enough to charge that it was Devil's music.

Certainly some of those charges were the result of well-meaning guardians warning young girls (or boys) to stay away from the sexually charged atmosphere of blues clubs. Some scholars argue, however, that direct references to the Devil in blues demonstrate the survival of African and circum-Caribbean religious beliefs. They

John Lee Hooker. *John Lee Hooker on stage playing a B. B. King "Lucille" brand guitar.* JACK VARTOOGIAN.

maintain that blues betray a familiarity with African-American "cult religions" such as hoodoo in which African deities such as Eshu-Elegbara were reinterpreted as the Devil. Other scholars disagree, charging that white fans, eager to hear blues as "dangerous" and "primitive," blew the Devil myth out of proportion. According to this camp, most references to the Devil were meant as humorous gestures, not serious religious incantations.

PRESENCE IN AFRICAN-AMERICAN LITERATURE

Some of the artists and intellectuals of the Harlem Renaissance (c. 1920–1930) took an interest in blues. For example, the poet Langston Hughes and the writer Zora Neale Hurston considered blues an authentic expression of "Negro" subjectivity. They defended the music against middle-class highbrow critics in the hope that they and other black artists would be able to use blues as a foundation for their own works. Blues also have figured prominently in the work of more recent African-American writers and critics. Alice Walker's award-winning novel *The Color Purple* (1982) contains a character modeled on an early blues queen, and the scholar Houston A. Baker, Jr., has made blues a focal point for creating an African-American school of literary criticism.

IMPACT AND LEGACY

Since the 1960s white enthusiasts largely have shaped the history of the blues. Their preference for Mississippi-style country blues performers such as Robert Johnson and for electrified Chicago-based musicians such as Muddy Waters resulted in a skewed historiography that gave short shrift to significant and commercially successful figures such as the blues queens and Leroy Carr. At the same time blues has been displaced by newer genres of popular music. However, despite their greater appeal to younger generations, genres such as rock 'n' roll and soul drew heavily on blues. Rock 'N' Roll pioneers such as Chuck Berry, Jerry Lee Lewis, and Elvis Presley all used blues forms. "The Godfather of Soul," James Brown, who always maintained that he hated blues, based hits such as "Papa's Got a Brand New Bag" (1965) on twelve-bar blues patterns. More recently hip-hop artists have modeled a style of ostentatious display, braggadocio, and irreverence that harks back to the days of the blues queens. The impact of blues on American popular music has been far-reaching and undeniable.

BIBLIOGRAPHY

Abbott, Lynn, and Doug Seroff. 1996. "'They Cert'ly Sound Good to Me': Sheet Music, Southern Vaudeville, and the Commercial Ascendancy of the Blues." *American Music* 14(4): 402–454.

Baker, Houston A., Jr. 1984. *Blues, Ideology, and Afro-American Literature: A Vernacular Theory.* Chicago: University of Chicago Press.

Baraka, Imamu Amiri. 1963. *Blues People: Negro Music in White America.* New York: W. Morrow,.

Carby, Hazel V. 1999. "'It Jus' Be's Dat Way Sometime': The Sexual Politics of Women's Blues." In *Keeping Time: Readings in Jazz History,* ed. Robert Walser. New York: Oxford University Press.

Murray, Albert. 1976. *Stomping the Blues.* New York: McGraw-Hill.

Palmer, Robert. 1981. *Deep Blues.* New York: Viking Press.

Wald, Elijah. 2004. *Escaping the Delta: Robert Johnson and the Invention of the Blues.* New York: Amistad.

Robert Walser
Loren Kajikawa

BOBBITT CASE

SEE *Castration.*

BOCCACCIO, GIOVANNI
1313–1375

Giovanni Boccaccio. COURTESY OF THE LIRBARY OF CONGRESS.

Born in Paris, according to legend, but most likely in Florence in 1313, the son of Boccaccio di Chellino, an agent of the Bardi bank, Giovanni Boccaccio was brought up in Certaldo, near Florence where he died on December 21, 1375 in Certaldo. His stepmother, Margherita dei Mardoli, was related to Beatrice Portinari's family. Early on Boccaccio developed a fondness for literary studies; he also studied banking in the Bardi establishment in Naples from 1325 to 1330. The time he spent at the Anjou court greatly influenced his life as a man and as a writer. There Boccaccio met and fell in love with the woman he called Fiammetta, who became his muse. His love lyrics, or *Rime,* which were influenced by the style of Dante Alighieri and Petrarch, are mostly dedicated to Fiammetta. *La caccia di Diana* (c. 1334; Diana's hunt), to be read by women, is a long poem in a mythological frame contrasting Venus and Diana, love and chastity, and presenting Neapolitan maidens in a hunt. It may very well contain the *senhal* (an allusive pseudonym) of Fiammetta that appear in his subsequent works. *Il filostrato* (1335), a poem in octaves, is the story of the tragic love of Troilus and Cressida derived from Benoît de Sainte-Maure (fl. twelfth century) and his *Roman de Troie. Il filocolo* (c. 1338), a prose romance in five books, written at the behest of Fiammetta, recounts the story of the pagan Florio and his Christian love Biancofiore. *Teseida* (c. 1340–1341), the first epic poem in the Italian vernacular, in twelve cantos, retells the love of Arcita and Palemone for Emilia, the Amazon princess. Next came the *Commedia delle ninfe,* or *Il ninfale d'Ameto* (1341–1342; Ameto's story of the nymphs), an allegorical work with a number of amorous confessions, and the *L'amorosa visione* (1342–1343; The amorous vision), prose verse in Dantean terza rima celebrating the triumphs of fame, wealth, and love. The *Elegia di Madonna Fiammetta* (1343–1344) is considered the first Italian psychological realistic novel dealing with the torments of a woman jilted by her lover, and is dedicated to ladies in love. His two works in the vernacular are the *Decameron* (1349–1353) and *Il Corbaccio* (1353-1355). The latter is a novella containing a bitter invective against women, a seed of which can be found in the *Decameron,* day VIII, story 7, the tale of a misogynistic scholar who takes his revenge on the woman who scorned him.

Boccaccio's close relationship with Petrarch and his devotion to classical studies led him to write several treatises in Latin, among them the *De genealogia deorum gentilium* (1350–1375; On the genealogy of the gods of the gentiles), which affirms his aesthetic doctrine as well as his notion of poetry as a sacred science and as theology. The mythological content of the work fosters the inclusion of a number of women. Boccaccio's views of women are represented cogently and exemplified in his masterpiece, the *Decameron*, a collection of 100 tales dedicated to women, for their entertainment and relief. The cornice, or author's foreword, places the narrative during the plague of 1348, when seven young Florentine maidens and three young men repair to a villa outside Florence (Fiesole) to escape the ravages of the pestilence, symbol of death and decrepitude, and to opt for life and joy by telling tales for ten days, each day with a different theme. He also titles his work "The Book of Prince Galahad," alluding to Guinevere and Lancelot's go-between, as an analogy with his role as writer/intermediary with his female audience.

Boccaccio's fascination with women is unique among the authors of the Middle Ages, but his views are also ambiguous and perhaps influenced by his religious fears and prejudices. This ambiguity is noticeable from the *Decameron* to the Latin compendia, specifically *De claris mulieribus* (c. 1360–1374), his treatise on famous women. In the preface to the latter work, Boccaccio states that "women are endowed by nature with soft, frail bodies and sluggish minds," and thus one cannot fail to admire them when they have acquired "a manly spirit and if with keen intelligence [they] have dared undertake and have accomplished even the most difficult deeds." Indeed, the *Decameron* reflects these deeds and exalts women, for the power of love and nature cannot be hindered by any force or law. A bevy of women embody a new conception of womanhood and the loftiest form of femininity, including the Marchioness of Monferrato who reproaches the king of France (day I, story 5), the lady of Gascogne who ennobles the king of Cyprus (I, 9), Madam Beritola (II, 6), Alatiel (II, 7), the wife of Bernabò (II, 9), Ghismonda (IV, 1), Elisabetta of Messina (IV, 5), and Ginevra (X, 10). Yet they remain subjected, reverent, and obedient to men, as stated by Elissa in the introduction and again by Emilia (IX, 9).

Boccaccio's *Decameron* provides a complete picture of society in a mercantile and bourgeois world. The author reveals the eroticism present in every level of human society, including religious people. He also alludes to incest in the tales of Titus and Gisippus (X, 8) and that of Ghismonda and her father Tancredi (IV, 1), and to homosexual practices (V, 10), all as part of a natural process. Boccaccio remains constant in his strong belief that intelligence, reason, wit and the power of love and nature are found in everyone (IV, 7). Thus Madam Philippa (VI, 7), who is about to be burnt at the stake for adultery, convinces the judges that the laws are wrong and that they should spare her because she never refused her sexual services to her husband, and what then should she have done with what was left? Another commanding figure is Alatiel, the sultan's daughter, who manages to survive and find a happy ending after so many misadventures and unwanted lovers (II, 7). The entire seventh day is a triumph of women and their ingenuity, tact, and intelligence in pursuit of the sexual pleasures to which they are entitled. The typology of Boccaccio's tales may not be novel, but his approach to and characterization of women certainly are. Nevertheless, Boccaccio returns to the misogynistic conception of women in *Il Corbaccio*, already present in the tale of the scholar (VIII, 7) or in the stupidity of Calandrino who regularly beats and abuses his wife (VIII, 3). In *De claris mulieribus*, his portrayal of women is more synthetic and critical, and in *De genealogia deorum gentilium*, more faithful to sources. In the former, for example, Dido is portrayed different from that of the Virgilian tradition—she is courageous, decisive, and coherent—and the author seizes the opportunity to moralize on the virtue of widowhood.

Overall, Boccaccio offers a mixed picture of traditional misogyny and some fresh views. Most importantly, he opens a door to a more complex characterization of women, and at the very least initiates an enduring debate with readers on the question of women.

BIBLIOGRAPHY

Barolini, Teodolinda. 1983. "Giovanni Boccaccio." In *European Writers: The Middle Ages and the Renaissance*, ed. William T. H. Jackson. New York: Scribners.

Bergin, Thomas G. 1981. *Boccaccio*. New York: Viking Press.

Branca, Vittore. 1976. *Boccaccio: The Man and His Works*, trans. Richard Monges and Dennis J. McAuliffe. New York: New York University Press.

Di Scipio, Giuseppe. 2000. "Decameron" and "Novella." In *Medieval Folklore: An Encyclopedia of Myths, Legends, Tales, Beliefs, and Customs*, ed. Carl Lindahl, John McNamara, and John Lindow. Santa Barbara, CA: ABC-CLIO.

Forni, Pier Massimo. 1996. *Adventures in Speech: Rhetoric and Narration in Boccaccio's "Decameron."* Philadelphia: University of Pennsylvania Press.

Hollander, Robert. 1977. *Boccaccio's Two Venuses*. New York: Columbia University Press.

Kirkham, Victoria. 1993. *The Sign of Reason in Boccaccio's Fiction*. Florence: Olschki.

Smarr, Janet Levarie. 1986. *Boccaccio and Fiammetta: The Narrator as Lover*. Urbana: University of Illinois Press.

Giuseppe Di Scipio

BODHISATTVAS

SEE *Buddhism.*

BODY, DEPICTIONS AND METAPHORS

Frequently asked questions and issues concerning the social, cultural, and physical aspects of the human body and its metaphorical projections include the following: What is a human body? Historically, what have been the most prominent representations of the body? What are the predominant body metaphors (basic images and schemata of the body)?

Throughout history the human body has been a source of inspiration for artists and scholars in different disciplines. It has received considerable attention in fields such as anthropology, feminist theory, history, law, philosophy, and sociology, among others. Since the mid-1980s there has been an intensified interest in notions of embodiment; that interest has coincided with enormous changes in modern society.

WHAT IS A HUMAN BODY?

It is difficult to define the human body and the ways in which people conceptualize it because that definition constantly is modified and reconstructed. From Egyptian and Sumerian depictions of the ideal human form, through the Greek and Roman idea of the balanced and symmetrical human body, to the medieval image of the body functioning to confine the soul, the body has been a primary source of information about society and culture.

In premodern societies the body, both male and female, was an important site on which cultural and social values were inscribed through painting, scarification, piercing, and tattooing. Those bodily markings carried a wide range of different meanings referring to social status, gender, and identity.

As soon as people are born, they are designated as male or female. This dualism has been reflected in differences in the treatment of men and women, cultural practices, and metaphorical projections. Women's identity traditionally was associated with the sinful, mortal, irrational body, and men's identity with mind, immortality, and reason. Many images of the female body were influenced by religious beliefs.

REPRESENTATIONS OF THE HUMAN BODY

The human body is perceived universally as a composite of the physical body and the mind and/or soul. Since the ancient Greek philosophers Western tradition has supported the view that the mind and the body are opposites (mind-body dualism). The body was conceived as a "prison of the soul" and mind. This concept can be traced back to Plato, Aristotle, and the Christian tradition, all of which supported a mind-body dualism in which the soul was associated with immortality and the body and/or flesh was associated with sinfulness and mortality. Shakespeare and many other authors held similar views.

The consequences of this negative perception of the physical body are far-reaching and often are expressed in social, cultural, and linguistic practices. In contrast, the Eastern perception of the body as it is expressed in Taoism and Zen Buddhism advocates the nondualistic nature of the human body. This concept sees the human being as a union of body and mind working together.

By the late fifteenth and early sixteenth centuries more naturalistic images of the body resulted from growing interest in the human form, especially among artists such as Leonardo da Vinci and Michelangelo. Vitruvian man is a symbol of the ideal and symmetrical human body, demonstrating perfection through harmonious proportion.

Until the end of the eighteenth century the human body was perceived mainly as an ungendered, universal, and generic body. The male body and/or man was considered the norm, and female characteristics were conceptualized on the basis of masculine parameters. The residues of that conceptualization are still visible in modern language, for example, "All men are equal in the eyes of law" and the "evolution of man." In these metaphors *man* refers to all people, male and female.

In the nineteenth and twentieth centuries a revolutionary reconceptualization of sexual difference emerged. The discourse on the body shifted from man-made language to neutral naming. In that period the linguistic landscape of the female body changed; for example, in referring to a woman, *postal worker* became *post officer* and then *postwoman*. An emerging vocabulary has been used to signify new identities: *gay, lesbian, bisexual, heterosexual,* and so forth.

In modern society the form of the human body has changed through practices such as bodybuilding, cross-dressing, and cosmetic surgery. Virtual reality and its vocabulary disseminate the image of a new body in terms such as *robots, android, cyborgs, cyberterrorists,* and *computer nerds.* Donna Haraway (1991) claims that the cyborg functions as a metaphorical projection of the disintegration of traditional boundaries.

BODY METAPHORS

There is a growing body of evidence that conceptual metaphor is a pervasive imaginative structure in human understanding of the world (Lakoff and Johnson 1980). Metaphors are used particularly frequently when new experiences are introduced. They allow the unfamiliar (technical terms) to be grasped in terms of the familiar (body terms). Examples of these terms include *grabber hand*, *palmtop*, and *nipple*. Body metaphors reveal that apart from male-female differences, all human beings have a common set of concepts based on their common body structure and sensual experiences.

Symmetry and Balance The human body is symmetrical and balanced. It can be folded over in the middle into left and right halves (vertical axis). The experience of balanced posture gives rise to metaphors such as *balanced personalities*, *balanced views*, *the balance of power*, *justice*, and *inner balance*.

Interior-Exterior The view of the body as a physical object presupposes its three-dimensional form in space and time. In the majority of metaphorical projections the body functions as a container. It consists of many entities: mind, soul, words, emotions, thoughts, and so forth. In proverbial and figurative speech people reach their inner part through their eyes: "Eyes are the window of the soul."

Up-Down The posture that is regarded as typical of the human body is upright. This concept is universally accepted. Accordingly, activities that are viewed positively are expressed as up (a higher value, an improvement). Metaphorically, if someone is down, that person is in a weak, desperate position: "Tim has been feeling down."

Front-Back The posture of the human body is such that the senses are directed predominantly forward (the eyes, nose, and mouth). This experience generates the view that the front part is equivalent to progress, dignity, and knowledge: "Seeing is believing."

These embodied linguistic patterns do not remain the private property of the person who experiences them. They become shared cultural and linguistic models of experience.

When the body is mentioned in literature, philosophy, and similar disciplines, it often is conceptualized as a *plant*, an *animal*, a *cage* or *confinement of the soul*, a *machine*, a *container of emotions*, a *computer*, a *communication network*, and so on. Some metaphorical projections of the human body are widely used. For example, Plato describes humankind as a "heavenly plant," and women often are perceived as fragile flowers or small animals. The human body often is used as a metaphor for society (the head of the state, the face of the law, etc.). The explosion of human-machine images in science fiction has changed human thought and perception.

Besides the concept of the body functioning as an integrated system of experiences, the body parts have individual functions. They can become symbolic models of stable meanings in different parts of a person's experience. For example, the head is thought of as the seat of the intellect: a director, a leader, and a container of thoughts, ideas, and memories. The heart is considered the seat of emotion (sadness, fear, and love) and the center of bravery. The hand is thought of as an agent of power and control as in the expression "to have someone in one's hands."

Linguistic and visual categorization of the body reveals that all human beings have a common set of conceptual metaphors that are based on their common body structure and sensual experiences. At the same time the body and its individual parts are used in metaphorical projections as symbols of specific cultural and social values.

People unconsciously project their own bodies into the external world, describing it in terms of their own measures: the *leg of a table*, the *arm of a chair*, the *foot of the mountain*, and so on.

The ideology of gender studies has been constantly focused on efforts to understand and study bodies and body dichotomies: male-female, mind-soul. This division between male and female will inevitably be based on cultural and social explanations. Concepts that were considered masculine—such as light, straight, good, reason, mind, spirit, power, and the public sphere—are opposed to concepts associated with femininity: darkness, left, bad, irrationality, body, emotion, passivity, inferiority, and the private sphere. These associations have been perpetuated within Western languages and cultures. A reconception of sexual difference is visible with changes in society, and sexual awareness.

SEE ALSO *Body Modifications*.

BIBLIOGRAPHY

Harraway, Donna Jeanne. 1991. "A Cyborg Manifesto: Science, Technology, and Socialist-Feminism in the Late Twentieth Century." In *Simians, Cyborgs, and Women: The Reinvention of Nature*. New York: Routledge.

Johnson, Mark. 1987. *The Body in the Mind: The Bodily Basis of Meaning, Imagination, and Reason*. Chicago: University of Chicago Press.

Kövecses, Zoltán. 2005. *Metaphor in Culture: Universality and Variation*. Cambridge, UK, and New York: Cambridge University Press.

Lakoff, George. 1987. *Women, Fire, and Dangerous Things*. Chicago: University of Chicago Press.

Lakoff, George, and Mark Johnson. 1980. *Metaphors We Live By*. Chicago: University of Chicago Press.

Lakoff, George, and Mark Johnson. 1999. *Philosophy in the Flesh: The Embodied Mind and Its Challenge to Western Thought*. New York: Basic Books.

O'Neill, John. 1985. *Five Bodies: The Human Shape of Modern Society*. Ithaca, NY: Cornell University Press.

Spender, Dale. 1998. *Man Made Language*. London and New York: Pandora.

Danica Skara

BODY IMAGE

The expanding body of work available on the connection between body image, sexuality, and gender is a direct result of the progress made by the feminist movement and gender studies in twentieth-century European and North American culture. When people discuss sexuality and gender, it is very likely that the dialog will turn to the subject of body image. The links between body image and sexual practice, performance, and preference have increased during the twentieth century, largely due to the widespread consumption and availability of media images. These links can be identified in a body-building culture, or the *hard body* aesthetic, in the increased visibility of eating disorders such as anorexia nervosa, bulimia, and overeating, and in the rise of subcultural groups that directly relate their sexual practices to body image. These subcultures include the feeder/feedee culture, sadomasochistic or dominant/submissive culture, and transsexual and transgender cultures. In the late twentieth and early twenty-first centuries, reality television programs made the effects of *extreme* self-improvement more accessible and visible. Viewers witness the physical transformations of *regular* people (as opposed to celebrities), whether these people have lost several pounds or have undergone plastic surgery in order to drastically alter their appearances.

Although how one develops a body image is debatable, there is no doubt that the individual experience of body image is directly related to the subjective interpretation of other bodies. Body image affects sexual practices, drives, and performance, and there is a relation between body image and sexual preference.

LINKS BETWEEN BODY IMAGE AND SEXUAL PRACTICES

The increasing visibility of different representations of bodies both complicates the process of and opens up greater possibilities for exploring sexual practices. Indeed such visibility is essential in describing any sociocultural link to body image. In addition a greater number of sexual subcultures is evolving, largely due to the increased availability of media images (i.e., the Internet) and the mainstreaming of pornography. Further the visibility of *extreme* bodies, whether excessively thin or excessively obese, continues to grow. As subcultures evolve and overlap, the topic of body image and its links to sexual practices continues to evolve.

Whereas body image evokes the interface between the inner and outer representation of any gender, it is also potentially connected to an individual's notion of identity. For example an anorectic individual does not usually say, "I feel fat," but rather, "I am fat." An anorectic person sees a fat body in the mirror, whereas to other people, that same body appears to be skeletal. A characteristic of the eating disorder anorexia nervosa is that the inner image depends on the outer reflection in the mirror as well as how the individual is seen by others. The anorectic's perspective is affected by a collection of images, or bodily ideals, that are dictated by the dominant media: film, television, and advertisements in magazines. In addition widespread research shows that young women in European and North American cultures are particularly influenced by these images because they have been exposed from childhood to the popular notion that the thin female body is a signifier of desire. According to Leslie Heywood, anorexia, "mental or physical, is central to the self-definition of most women, particularly educated women attempting to gain access to the *white male power* that requires them to cancel out their bodies" (Heywood 1996, p. 33). The goal of the anorectic adolescent girl (usually white) is, arguably, to be a woman who is not yet a woman, which suggests sexual timidity or fear. At the very least confusion is often experienced by one whom has an eating disorder because the degree to which one is desired seems to directly correspond to the degree to which one has conformed to the contemporary bodily ideal. Childhood sexual abuse may also account for many cases of eating disorders in women (and increasingly in men).

Body Image and Sexual Practice If anorexia nervosa is a means by which people attempt to deny desire, both for others and as directed toward themselves, then feeder/feedee culture, which is the exact opposite of anorexia nervosa, is concerned with concrete connections between food and eroticism. In the context of *fat fetishism*, the feedee is the submissive counterpart to the feeder. As part of the relationship, the feedee is fed, either for the purpose of gaining weight, or for the sheer pleasure of the act. According to Octavio Paz, "[t]he erotic industry is the younger sister of the food industry. Private business expropriates utopia. During its ascendancy capitalism exploited the body; now it has turned it into an object of advertising. We have gone from prohibition to humiliation" (Paz 1972, p. 81).

As the numbers of obese people increases in the early twenty-first century, especially in North America, the emergence of a *fat acceptance*, or *fat admiration* culture has become more visible. The feeding subculture is often denounced by the mainstream fat acceptance community as misogynistic, because the submissive partners are almost exclusively women. The fat acceptance community also sometimes regards feeder relationships as pathological.

The growth of feederism paralleled the development of feeder pornography, with the increase of Internet websites not unlike those devoted to the celebration of the skeletal beauty of anorexic bodies. On these focused websites, the fed or starved chart their *progress*, whether losing or gaining weight, and have admirers that contact them. The dominant/submissive relationship lies at the heart of feeder/feedee culture, whereas the sadist and the masochist both reside in the anorectic's sense of body image. While the anorectic may deny food as a metaphor for denying sex, or the desire for sex, the feeder/feedee relationship to food functions as a metaphor for the unchecked immersion into unbridled desire.

FORCE FEEDING

Force feeding has had frightening connotations for women throughout history, particularly during the suffrage movement in the United States during the early twentieth century. In the Victorian era, such extreme outward displays, especially by women, of bodily expression such as that which occurred during the suffragettes' public protests, were subdued by police, who arrested the women, and doctors, who force fed them. Many women engaged in hunger strikes because it was the most powerfully visible way to attract attention to the immediacy of the suffrage movement. According to Barbara Green, "no image has been more provocative than the image of the forcibly fed woman.... The gesture of making public the private experience of the female body, exposing its secrets, describing its invasion, takes place in the realm of the spectacular, produces a speaking subject who is embodied, and who speaks from the female body in pain" (Green 1993, p. 71–72). This condition is at the heart of the dominant/submissive tension, where it involves body image and sexual practice. The act of bringing to the outside what has formerly been inside evokes fear, wonder, fascination, horror, and desire. The depiction of a hunger striker forcibly fed—that is, choking, spitting, and vomiting as food is forced down her throat—creates a body image that, due to its spectacular availability, can be considered pornographic.

LINKS BETWEEN BODY IMAGE, SEXUAL PERFORMANCE, AND PREFERENCE

The widespread availability of pornography, or its mainstreaming, has reinforced a hard body aesthetic in terms of body image. Since the late twentieth century, the increased use of plastic surgery, as well as demand for enhancements, such as anal bleaching, which were previously unheard of outside the pornographic film industry, have demonstrated society's growing interest in *perfect* bodily symmetry. Obviously, the term *perfect* is problematic due to its subjective and illusory meaning, but it is the term people of every gender often use to describe the kind of bodies they desire and/or want to attain.

According to Tom Venuto, a body builder, body symmetry "refers to the qualities of balance, proportion, shape and classical aesthetics. It was first described by the Greek philosopher Pythagoras, who explained it in terms of mathematical relationships" (Venuto 2004, p. 1). Venuto lists several male body builders who have historically fit this shape. The key physical qualities include low body fat; a tiny waist; broad shoulders; a wide, tapering back; slab-like pectoral muscles, developed top to bottom with a sharply defined, lower pectoral line; small hips and glutes; and the appearance of long legs. Some theorize that the quality of symmetry is what makes an individual sexually desirable, regardless of gender or sexual preference. Further a healthy, toned, clean body is often considered a signifier of virility and strength.

Whether addressing sexual drive, performance, or practice, and regardless of sexual orientation and gender, the discussion of body image will eventually turn to the issue of visibility and invisibility. Body image is based on a visual representation (inner and/or outer) of an individual. Philosopher Michel Foucault described the body as constantly "in the grip" of cultural practices (Foucault 1988, p. 55). Bodies, no less than anything else human, are influences by culture.

Stereotyping about sexual preference, performance, and gender is especially influenced by the practices of the dominant culture. However, the subject of sexual orientation, performance, and body image is complicated by culturally coded stereotypes that exist beyond the *normal* pressures imposed by the dominant culture on ideal body types.

SEE ALSO *Eating Disorders.*

BIBLIOGRAPHY

Bordo, Susan. 1988. "Anorexia Nervosa: Psychopathology as the Crystallization of Culture." In *Feminism and Foucault: Reflections on Resistance*, eds. Irene Diamond and Lee Quimby. Boston: Northeastern University Press.

Bordo, Susan. 1993. *Unbearable Weight*. Berkeley: University of California Press.

Green, Barbara. 1993. "Spectacular Confessions: 'How It Feels to Be Forcibly Fed.'" *Review of Contemporary Fiction* 13: 3.

Foucault, Michel. 1988. *An Introduction.* Vol 1 of *Histoire de la sexualité* [History of sexuality], trans. Robert Hurley. New York: Vintage Books.
Heywood, Leslie. 1996. *Dedication to Hunger.* Berkeley: University of California Press.
Jeffords, Susan. 1994. *Hard Bodies.* New Brunswick: Rutgers University Press.
Orbach, Susie. 1986. *Hunger Strike.* New York: Norton.
Paz, Octavio. 1972. "Eroticism and Gastrosophy." *Daedalus* 101(4): 81.
Venuto, Tom. "How to Develop a Classical Body Shape." Bodybuilding and Fitness Portal. Available from http://www.bodybuilding-fitness.net.

Amy Nolan

BODY MODIFICATIONS

Uniting both the physical and the symbolic, the natural and the cultural, the human body is an important medium through which social mores, ideals, and values are expressed. Deliberate modifications to the physical form of the human body serve to communicate a wide variety of information about an individual's gender, age, status, rank, group affiliation, occupation, position in the life cycle, acceptance or rejection of social norms, and so forth. Body modifications thus serve primarily symbolic purposes, although some may be undertaken for therapeutic or ritual reasons in which the final result is less important than the experience itself. Every human society has practiced some form of body modification, from Polynesian tattooing to Chinese foot binding to breast implants, and other contemporary cosmetic surgeries. Such modifications exhibit varying degrees of permanence, severity, and visibility and are undertaken for various reasons. They may be chosen by an individual or compelled by the force of law, tradition, religion, sanction, convention, or social pressure.

Broadly one may divide body modifications into those processes that modify the body's contours or form, and those that mark the body's surface. Procedures that alter the body's form include the following:

- Metabolic manipulation through weight-lifting, exercise, dieting, and use of drugs or hormones
- Cosmetic surgery (liposuction, face-lifts, rhinoplasty) and other chemical processes to firm or plump skin (botox)
- Genital surgery (male and female circumcision) and sex reassignment surgery
- Restriction or compression (corsets, belts, foot binding)
- Abrasion (filing of teeth, scourging, flagellation)
- Elongation (neck, lips, earlobes, penis, testes, labia)
- Partial or full removal of body parts (digits, breasts, testes, penis, clitoris, lips, ears, nose, organs, ribs)
- Implantation of foreign objects (silicone implants, decorative items under the skin)
- Prosthetics (false limbs, fingernails, pacemakers, valves, lenses)

Processes that alter, inscribe or adorn the body's surface include the following:

- Tattooing
- Piercing or perforation and the use of earrings, nose-rings, lip plugs, and other adornments
- Painting, staining, bleaching, tanning
- Scarification and cicatrization (the production of raised scars or keloids)
- Branding or cautery
- Hair removal or addition

The symbolic function of most body modifications means that the social and historical context is fundamental to determining the meaning of a particular practice. For example the ancient Greeks, Romans, Iranians, and Celts employed tattooing for punitive purposes and to indicate ownership: identifying criminals, military conscripts, prisoners of war, and slaves. By contrast early Christians throughout the eastern Mediterranean acquired tattoos voluntarily as a sign of their devotion to Christ or after completing a pilgrimage. Among various indigenous groups in Africa, Asia, India, North America, and the South Pacific, tattooing was performed in the context of rites of passage; to indicate status, tribal, or caste affiliation; or in the course of healing and mourning rituals. Thus the practice of tattooing holds a plurality of meanings, and has been employed to communicate a wide range of socially salient information by different groups at different points in time.

While body modifications may be performed for various purposes—punitive, commemorative, aesthetic, therapeutic—nearly all express socially and historically specific understandings of identity. Because gender may be understood as a socially-determined identity putatively linked to an individual's biological sex, body modifications constitute an important means through which gender differences are constructed and communicated. Physical alterations make a society's gender norms evident in the very material flesh of the body: in its contours (muscular or rounded, lean or curvy), textures (absence or presence of hair, roughness or softness of skin), size (large or small, robust or delicate), and surface (tattoos, scarifications). For example Victorian notions of femininity were exemplified in the tiny waist, exaggerated bosom, and delicate constitution achieved through the use of a tightly laced corset. Similarly contemporary models in the United States of masculinity emphasize a powerful physique attained through long hours of weight training and the use of dietary supplements.

One of the clearest examples of body modification as a process of engendering is female circumcision (also called female genital mutilation). In the early twenty-first century the practice is found primarily in Africa and areas of the Middle East, as well as among immigrant communities from these regions in Europe and North America. Among groups that practice female circumcision, male circumcision is also performed, for the operation is seen as necessary to produce socially acceptable women and men. Circumcision typically occurs at puberty or immediately prior to marriage, although in some cases it may be performed on infants or small children. In most cases a woman cannot marry until she has been circumcised, and often the practice is said to be necessary for reproduction, or to ensure female purity and fidelity by reducing sexual pleasure.

Among the Mende of Sierra Leone, circumcision is performed on girls and boys in the context of traditional puberty rites. The practice is understood to rid the female body of the male element, located in the clitoris, and the male body of the female element, located in the foreskin. The result is a woman and a man who can then unite in marriage for the purposes of reproduction. It is thus the practice of circumcision itself that fully genders the body, and those who have not undergone the operation are unable to participate in the adult world of marriage and family life.

Like circumcision body modifications in traditionally-oriented societies tend to be obligatory, collective, and performed in the context of life-cycle transitions or other transformations in an individual's status. By contrast in Europe and North America tattooing and other body modifications are often undertaken by individuals to indicate their membership in a stigmatized subculture (sailors, the working class, criminals, punk rockers), to express their rejection of the dominant cultural norms of the body, or to affirm an alternative identity or sensibility. Contemporary practitioners describe their modifications as a way of taking control of their body and redefining it to accord with their own sense of self. The notion that the body is an object for endless transformation and a vehicle for individual expression is closely linked to a market-driven consumer culture, which has resulted in the increased popularity of piercing and tattooing in Europe and North America. Whether freely chosen or compelled by social pressure, physical modifications to the human body communicate salient aspects of an individual's identity. The diversity of practices and purposes associated with these modifications suggests that the human body cannot be understood apart from the particular social and historical contexts that give it meaning.

SEE ALSO *Body Image.*

BIBLIOGRAPHY

Caplan, Jane, ed. 2000. *Written on the Body: The Tattoo in European and American History.* Princeton, NJ: Princeton University Press.

Featherstone, Mike, ed. 2000. *Body Modification.* London: SAGE.

Pitts, Victoria. 2003. *In the Flesh: The Cultural Politics of Body Modification.* New York: Macmillan.

Rahman, Anika, and Nahid Toubia, eds. 2000. *Female Genital Mutilation: A Guide to Laws and Policies Worldwide.* New York: Zed Books.

Kelly E. Hayes

BODY, THEORIES OF

The phrase *theories of the body* refers to philosophical and medical-scientific discourses as well as politically informed cultural critiques such as feminist and queer studies. In all these cases the body emerges as a concept marked by internal division in terms of sex and gender, age, size, and color as well as a word that signals its difference from its implied opposite: mind, spirit, psyche, soul, or any other term used to describe personhood outside its material manifestations.

BODIES AS ORGANISMS AND BODIES AS SOCIAL PHENOMENA

The internal differentiation of the body has been the starting point for most current theorizations of the body in critical cultural studies. The division between the body and its external material context, along with its difference from the immaterial mind, soul, or spirit, has been the subject of philosophical and religious speculation since the beginnings of Western history. The emergence of modern scientific thought in the seventeenth century heralded a new form of interest in the body as organism and as social phenomenon.

The distinct perspectives on the body occasionally become so entwined that they become indistinguishable. However, the different interests these discourses bring to their object of speculation inevitably lead to equally divergent theoretical constructions of the elusive phenomenon at the focus of their attention: the human body. Because no theory of the body is disinterested, contemporary theories of the body should be assessed against the conceptual entanglement of bodies as organisms and bodies as social phenomena.

THE MIND-BODY DISTINCTION

Current critical analyses of the body usually take the eighteenth-century medicalization of the body or the seventeenth-century philosophical preoccupation with the mind-body distinction as their point of departure to call into question what has been characterized as the inalienable dualist nature of Western thought. There are problems with both approaches. Although it may be claimed that from the ancient Greek philosopher Plato (427–347 BCE) to the French philosopher, mathematician, and scientist René Descartes (1596–1650) prevailing Western notions of the body have evolved largely from a split between mind and body, spirit and flesh, psyche and soma, there has been an alternative line of analysis in which the immaterial aspects of human being have been conceptualized as having an intrinsic interrelation with the matter of bodies, inseparable from the flesh.

As early as 360 BCE the Greek philosopher Aristotle (384–322 BCE), investigating the soul and its properties in *De Anima*, claimed that the soul is a "first actuality of a natural organic body" (Aristotle 1987, p. 60), thus introducing a notion of nondualist embodied being that was taken up and elaborated on by a series of later philosophers, including Baruch Spinoza (1632–1677), Friedrich Nietzsche (1884–1900), and Giambattista Vico (1668–1744).

Even in Plato the dualist mind-body distinction is complicated by that philosopher's additional supposition of the soul as the directing force of the body (Plato 2005). Plato believed that the body and the mind exist separately and often stand in opposition to each other in that the interests of the body are mere physical needs and sensual pleasures whereas the mind has the ability and will to gain real knowledge of ideal forms. However, it is the soul that tries to bind mind to body, attempting to make them run together rather than allowing them to be pulled in contradictory and opposite directions. Although its undeniably dualist character came to prevail in most modern theories of the body, the complications of Plato's tripartite model reemerge in theological and religiously inspired theories of the body in the period immediately preceding the rise of modern philosophy, that is, in the middle ages and the early Renaissance.

THE MIDDLE AGES AND THE RENAISSANCE

Late mediaeval theologians such as Thomas Aquinas (1225–1274) used the Aristotelian concept of the soul as life principle, locating knowing, feeling, and experiencing in the body and thus categorizing human beings in accordance with a threefold principle in which the differences between the levels of spirit and soul often were seen as more important than those between soul and body. The pervasive influence of Christian doctrine in that period may have reinforced a Platonic devaluation of the (sinful) flesh in favor of the higher faculties of the soul or spirit; the medieval fascination with the flesh did not imply a simple rejection of the body to celebrate the soul as a separate entity. That would have been a conceptual and a doctrinal impossibility in the context of a religion that revolved around the divine offering redemption by becoming flesh (Bynum 1995).

Whereas early fourteenth-century theologians tended to follow Aquinas in positing the soul as that which carries the structure of a person if the body is absent, in the normal or desired situation personhood was thought to be determined equally by body and soul. Rather than an unambiguously dualist line running uninterruptedly through theories of the body from Plato to Descartes, it is more accurate to suggest that the newly emerging mathematical and natural sciences spurred seventeenth- century philosophers to develop a rigorous theory of personhood that would install the split between mind and body and continue to predominate in debates for the next three hundred years.

In an attempt to break free from the speculative neo-Aristotelian notions of the person that had triumphed within the Catholic Church and the theological circles of his day, Descartes introduced a reduction of truth to that which can be apprehended by the mind exclusively operating with its own resources (Descartes 1984). Truth thus becomes the product of a self-referential system of cognition that is dependent on nothing but itself: thinking. The elevation of mind over body that follows from this premise institutes the dualist framework in which mind and body are conceived of as separate, self-contained spheres, incompatible and mutually exclusive substances. The Cartesian mind is set up as the essence of the person, existing entirely independently of the body.

The mathematical security Descartes gained from the absolute separation of mind and matter came at the cost of several forms of ontological reduction that it has taken centuries of philosophizing to reconcile. The positing of consciousness—Descartes's term for the earlier notion of soul—as an entity in and of itself that is amenable only to first-person knowledge made it unfeasible to think through any form of interaction between consciousness and body as manifested in movement, for instance, or in the body's response to conceptual demands or requirements. Also, the presumed self-referential nature and radical independence of consciousness renders it autotelic, i.e., having itself as its sole purpose, to the extent that any knowledge or awareness of other people's minds or even of other persons is in effect a logical impossibility. After Descartes the human body has tended to be explained entirely in mechanical terms without any reference to life forces.

The power of the Cartesian heritage can be seen in the fact that until fairly recently the body as matter, as a self-moving automaton, has been marginalized in the history of modern Western philosophy, which has been preoccupied with theories of mind. The fact that certain conceptions of mind may be used to explain the body does not detract from the reductionism of this concept, for whether the mind is reduced to the body or the body is reduced to the mind, either strategy serves to bridge the irreducible gap or explain away the impossibility of explicating their interaction within a rationalist framework. The influence of Descartes is palpable in the fact that since the onset of modernity the body as organism has been regarded primarily as an object of investigation for the life sciences, biology, and medicine (Grosz 1994).

When the body has been studied outside the natural sciences, it often has been treated as a mere extension or map of the human faculties or behaviors that are amenable to the human sciences, for instance, as a cartographic resource for symptoms in psychology, a variably meaningful entity in anthropology, and a transformational force in sociology. In political-philosophical discourses the Cartesian tradition is sustained by the focus on the body as an instrument or tool at the disposal of consciousness or, alternatively, as the possession or property of an autonomous subject. The fact that several of Descartes's fundamental assumptions have continued to prevail through the history of (post)modernity, however, does not mean that there have not been alternative voices that have attempted to overcome the limitations of rationalist reductionism.

ATTACKS ON CARTESIAN DUALISM

The first serious attempts to subvert Cartesian dualism occurred in the nineteenth century among thinkers such as Georg Friedrich Wilhelm Hegel (1770–1831), Karl Marx (1818–1883), Nietzsche, and Søren Kierkegaard (1813–1855). Each of these thinkers tried to overcome the mind-body distinction that still dominates approaches to embodied personhood in much of analytic philosophy of mind, cognitive psychology, and artificial intelligence programs. It was not until the rise of phenomenology in the twentieth century, with representatives such as Edmund Husserl (1859–1938) (Husserl 1967), Martin Heidegger (1889–1976) (Heidegger 1962), Jean-Paul Sartre (1905–1980) (Sartre 1956), and Maurice Merleau-Ponty (1908–1961) (Merleau-Ponty 1962, 1964), however, that an effective counterdiscourse developed that could be reworked and extended by post-structuralist and feminist thinkers such as Jacques Lacan (1901–1981), Michel Foucault (1926–1984), Julia Kristeva (b. 1941), and Luce Irigaray (b. 1930), among others.

Phenomenology Phenomenologists reject the (post) Cartesian biological-mechanistic approach to the body as physical object (*Körper*), instead focusing on the lived body (*Leib*) as it functions in the world: With phenomenology the question of the body shifts to the question of embodiment. By investigating and illuminating the interrelation between the body, actions, and perceptions, phenomenology overcomes the reductionism of Cartesian dualism and lays the foundations for theories of the body that supplement philosophical thought with insights from psychoanalysis, social history, literary theory, and gender and sexuality studies.

Freud and Lacan Although his work on soma and psyche was steeped in contemporary medical-scientific frameworks, Sigmund Freud (1856–1939), the founder of psychoanalysis, complicated prevailing notions of the body by stipulating the difference between the body as organism and the human subject as a psychosomatic being (Freud 1995). The human organism, Freud maintains, knows only needs that must be fulfilled to safeguard its survival. The human subject of desire, in contrast, comes to know itself both in its embodiedness and in its relations to other bodies and other objects under the aspect of the psyche. The human ego derives its primary experience of itself through its corporeal interactions with the outside world, mainly through sense perception. To perceive of the body as mere outside or shell of an independent interiority thus fails to do justice to the irreducible complexity of psychosomatic being. The fact that in his clinical practice Freud came to regard the body as a map from which symptoms of the subject's interior could be gleaned does not detract from the importance of his earlier insight into the irreducibility of the person to soma or psyche.

When Jacques Lacan analyzed Freud's theories in the 1940s, one of his major aims was to integrate a psychoanalytic account of the ego with an account of the body. For Lacan the human infant is nothing more than a "body in bits and pieces" (Lacan 1953, p. 13) until the moment between ages six and eighteen months when the infant becomes capable of recognizing the image of his or her self in the mirror, having its first anticipation of itself as a unified and separate individual (Lacan 1977a). Imaginary from the start and fundamentally dependent on the perception and experience of that which is other—both other human beings and the scene of otherness in which the mirror recognition occurs—the subject's sense of embodiment is marked by alienation and is of a profoundly transitive nature. A further form of alienation takes place when the child enters the realm of language, the symbolic order, in which she or he is assigned her or his predetermined role on either side of the sexual divide. While Lacan's theorization of the human ego, which is "structured like a language" (p. 20) appears to depart even further from the body as matter or flesh than Freud's distinction between the body as organism and the embodied ego, it is the importance of the mirror stage in the Lacanian ego's development that points to the critical role of the body as matter in its imaging of itself as well as the internal connection of the ego to other bodies (Lacan 1977b).

Foucault One of the most influential theorists of the body in the late twentieth century was the social historian and philosopher Michel Foucault. Harking back to phenomenological insights into the intertwining operations of structures and forces to produce the reality and experience of the lived body in the world without a controlling center, Foucault situates the body as a production caught in a network of power relations, each in its own way shaping and disciplining its materiality in accordance with historically shifting standards of normalization and intelligibility (Foucault 1970, 1972). Because the power relations at the focus of his analysis are not the large-scale structures of the economy and the state but the micro-level power relations represented by, for instance, hospitals, schools, and prisons, Foucault identifies the body as the principal target of modern power, that is, power operating in a capillary fashion throughout the social body; this can best be grasped in its concrete and local effects on the human body and in the everyday practices by which established power relations generally are reproduced and sustained (Foucault 1990).

Queer Theory Taking their lead from Foucault (1995), most contemporary queer theorists aim their critiques at the disciplinary and constraining medical and juridical discourses that at the end of the nineteenth century produced the pathologically sexed, perverse, or homosexual body (Ellis 1897, Krafft-Ebing 1939). Aiming at denaturalizing the notion of a biologically sexed and/or sexualized body, such critiques have shown that rather than being biologically given or emerging in nature, differentiated forms of embodiment, whether in terms of gender, sexuality, ethnicity, race, and/or class, are generated by the socially and discursively constructed frameworks of interpretation or grids of intelligibility that establish and maintain dominant power relations and inscribe strict boundaries between normal and abnormal, healthy and pathological, conceptually and socially viable and nonviable (Laqueur 1990, Davidson 1992).

Although such queer critiques have helped liberate the pathologized homosexual body from the naturalizing disciplinary practices of medicine and the law, they also have demonstrated that discursive practices are productive rather than merely prohibitive, enabling certain categories of being to come into their own rather than repressing or regulating them. However, in their effort to locate the emergence of the category of the sexualized body historically, those theories tend to presume a kind of stability or even a singular quality in such (abnormal) sexualities as sexualities. This not only threatens to result in the kind of essentialization of deviant bodies that these critiques set out to dismantle, it also fails to do justice to the complex interrelations between medical and juridical discourses on sexuality and the equally significant, often contradictory discourses on race, gender, primitivism, and degeneration that undergird early modern biological discourses (Nordau 1990). In other words, the exclusive focus on the medical construction of a deviant sexual body threatens to obscure the operations of the multiple and shifting sociopolitically interested frameworks in which these scientific discourses function and develop (Terry 1995, Somerville 1994, Seitler 2004).

Feminism The problems posed by most mainstream (male-authored) theories of the body for feminist theorists, including contemporary critics, derive partly from the general neglect of the specificity of female bodies and the traditional reduction of women to their bodies as distinct from and secondary to the primary (male) powers of the mind. Female sexuality and women's reproductive capacities traditionally formed the parameters of misogynist definitions of femininity. This explains why the first generation of second-wave feminist theorists resisted reexaminations of (theories of) the body and instead tried to achieve equality on intellectual or conceptual grounds (de Beauvoir 1993, Firestone 1970).

With the gradual establishment of poststructuralist theory and the introduction of so-called French feminist thought (Kristeva 1980, 1986; Irigaray 1977), however, a generation of feminist theorists emerged with a much more positive attitude toward the body, seeing it not as a biological obstacle but as an object of representation and signification in which the markings of masculinity and femininity both find expression and function in the practices of everyday life, although in radically different and unequal ways. Some poststructuralist feminists maintain a relatively strict split between mind and body by recasting dualism as the sex-gender distinction in which the sexed body is seen as the biological base from which the cultural meanings of gender derive and on which they are inscribed (Gallop 1988, Spivak 1988). Others reject the distinction between biological sex and cultural gender and see the gendered body not as passive matter but as a lived phenomenon thoroughly entwined with constitutive systems of signification and representation (Butler 1990, 1993; Grosz 1994).

Although the need to escape from biological determinism initially led to a relative downplaying of the body in the development of feminist theory, an increasing awareness of the body as a site of contestation in a range of economic, political, sexual, and philosophical struggles has resulted in a number of feminist theorists directing their attention to the body from a wide range of disciplinary perspectives. Reacting against a history in which the body has been devalued because of its primary association with femininity, as distinct from the more valuable masculine mind, the more philosophical and theoretical branch of 1990s corporeal feminism posits the body as a primary site of gender constitution whose negation has produced a seemingly immutable sexual difference (Gatens 1996, Grosz 1994). Particularly influential has been notion of the body as a performative act, that is, the idea that gendered bodies are a material production, the result of the repetition and reiteration of preexisting rules and regulations that render certain forms of embodiment culturally intelligible and socially viable while excluding and devaluing alternative forms of corporeality (Butler 1990, 1993). Such excluded bodies, for instance, those marked as lesbian, come to function as that which is abjected from dominant culture. In both of these views the female body is seen as something that must be retrieved from a repressive and negating masculinist metaphysics that situates the female body as a kind of limit point outside representation.

Countering the inherent negativity of corporeal feminist critiques, a more positive approach to the body is offered by contemporary feminist theorists who take their cue from the French philosophers Gilles Deleuze (1925–1995) and Félix Guattari (1930–1992). Warning against the risk of essentializing the female body as a metaphysical limit case and thus precluding an examination of the specific historical regimes that regulate bodies, these theorists offer a positive feminist ethics in which thought, reason, and discourse are seen as bodily events and in which the body figures as the event of expression (Bray and Colebrook 1998, Buchanan and Colebrook 2000). Rejecting the idea that corporeality, materiality, and sexual difference are anterior to thought or are negated by representational regimes, these theorists claim that both bodies and representations are aspects of an ongoing process of negotiation and reconfiguration in which no single event fully determines the meaning or materiality of any body and in which practices of signification function in a positive, enabling manner as much as they may limit or constrain the event of corporeal becoming. The extent to which this positive ethics will help bring about change in oppressive bodily practices in different sociocultural domains remains to be seen. What it does offer is a theory of (female) embodiment that leaves room for both corporeal agency and creative practices of (im)material becoming.

BIBLIOGRAPHY

Aristotle. 1987. *De Anima*, trans. H. Lawson-Tancred. Harmondsworth, UK: Penguin.

Beauvoir, Simone de. 1993. *The Second Sex*, trans. H.M. Parshley. New York: Knopf.

Bray, Abigail, and Claire Colebrook. 1998. "The Haunted Flesh: Corporeal Feminism and the Politics of (Dis)Embodiment." *Signs: Journal of Women in Culture and Society* 24(1): 35–67.

Buchanan, Ian, and Claire Colebrook, eds. 2000. *Deleuze and Feminist Theory*. Edinburgh, Scotland: Edinburgh University Press.

Butler, Judith. 1990. *Gender Trouble: Feminism and the Subversion of Identity*. New York: Routledge.

Butler, Judith. 1993. *Bodies That Matter: On the Discursive Limits of "Sex."* New York: Routledge.

Bynum, Caroline. 1995. "Why All the Fuss about the Body: A Medievalist's Perspective." *Critical Inquiry* 22 (Autumn) 1–33.

Davidson, Arnold. 1992. "Sex and the Emergence of Sexuality." In *Forms of Desire: Sexual Orientation and the Social Constructionist Controversy*, ed. Edward Stein. New York: Routledge.

Deleuze, Gilles, and Félix Guattari. 1983. *Anti-Oedipus: Capitalism and Schizophrenia*, trans. Robert Hurley, Mark Seem, and Helen R. Lane. Minneapolis: University of Minnesota Press.

Deleuze, Gilles, and Félix Guattari. 1987. *A Thousand Plateaus: Capitalism and Schizophrenia*, trans. Brian Massumi. Minneapolis: University of Minnesota Press.

Descartes, René. 1984. *The Philosophical Writings of Descartes*, trans. John Cottingham, Robert Stootfhoff, and Dugald Murdoch. Cambridge and New York: Cambridge University Press.

Ellis, Havelock. 1975. *Sexual Inversion*, ed. John Addington Symonds. New York: Arno Press.

Firestone, Shulamith. 1970. *The Dialectic of Sex: The Case for Feminist Revolution*. New York: Morrow.

Foucault, Michel. 1970. *The Order of Things: An Archaeology of the Human Sciences*. New London: Tavistock.

Foucault, Michel. 1972. *The Archeology of Knowledge and the Discourse on Language*, trans. A. M. S. Smith. New York: Pantheon.

Foucault, Michel. 1990. *The History of Sexuality*. Vol. 1: *An Introduction*, trans. Robert Hurley. New York: Vintage.

Foucault, Michel. 1995. *Discipline and Punish: The Birth of the Prison*, trans. Alan Sheridan. New York: Vintage.

Freud, Sigmund. 1995. *The Basic Writings of Sigmund Freud*, ed. and trans. A. A. Brill. New York: Modern Library.

Gallop, Jane. 1988. *Thinking through the Body*. New York: Columbia University Press.

Gatens, Moira. 1996. *Imaginary Bodies: Ethics, Power, and Corporeality*. London and New York: Routledge.

Grosz, E. A. 1994. *Volatile Bodies: Toward a Corporeal Feminism*. Bloomington: Indiana University Press.

Heidegger, Martin. 1962. *Being and Time*, trans. John Macquarrie and Edward Robinson. New York: Harper & Row.

Husserl, Edmund. 1967. *Cartesian Meditations: An Introduction to Phenomenology*, trans. D. Cairns. The Hague, Netherlands: Martinus Nijhoff.

Irigaray, Luce. 1977. "Women's Exile." *Ideology and Consciousness* 1: 61–76.

Irigaray, Luce. 1985. *This Sex Which Is Not One*, trans. Catherine Porter. Ithaca, NY: Cornell University Press.

Krafft-Ebing, Richard von. 1939. *Psychopathia Sexualis: A Medico-Forensic Study*. New York: Physicians and Surgeons.

Kristeva, Julia. 1980. *Desire in Language: A Semiotic Approach to Literature and Art*, trans. Leon Roudiez. New York: Columbia University Press.

Kristeva, Julia. 1986. "Women's Time." In *The Kristeva Reader*, ed. Toril Moi. New York: Columbia University Press.

Lacan, Jacques. 1953. "Some Reflections on the Ego." International Journal of Psychoanalysis 34: 11–17.

Lacan, Jacques. 1977a. *The Four Fundamental Concepts of Psycho-Analysis*, ed. Jacques-Alain Miller. London: Hogarth Press.

Lacan, Jacques. 1977b. *Écrits: A Selection*, trans. Alan Sheridan. New York: Norton.

Laqueur, Thomas. 1990. *Making Sex: Body and Gender from the Greeks to Freud*. Cambridge, MA: Harvard University Press.

Merleau-Ponty, Maurice. 1962. *Phenomenology of Perception*, trans. Colin Smith. London and New York: Routledge & Keegan Paul.

Merleau-Ponty, Maurice. 1964. *The Visible and the Invisible*, trans. Alphonso Lingis. Evanston, IL.: Northwestern University Press.

Nordau, Max. 1993. *Degeneration*. Lincoln: University of Nebraska Press.

Plato. 2005. *The Symposium*. Harmondsworth, UK: Penguin Books.

Sartre, Jean-Paul. 1956. *Being and Nothingness: An Essay on Phenomenological Ontology*, trans. and intro. Hazel E. Barnes. New York: Philosophical Library.

Seitler, Dana. 2004. "Queer Physiognomies; Or, How Many Ways Can We Do the History of Sexuality." *Criticism* 46(1): 71–102.

Somerville, Siobhan. 1994. "Scientific Racism and the Invention of the Homosexual Body." *Journal of the History of Sexuality* 5(2): 243–267.

Spivak, Gayatri Chakravorty. 1988. *In Other Worlds: Essays in Cultural Politics*. New York: Routledge.

Terry, Jennifer. 1995. "Anxious Slippages between 'Us' and 'Them': A Brief History of the Scientific Search for Homosexual Bodies." In *Deviant Bodies: Critical Perspectives in Science and Popular Culture*, ed. Jennifer Terry and Jacqueline Urla. Bloomington: Indiana University Press.

renée c. hoogland

BOGOMILS AND CATHARS

The Bogomils and Cathars were radical dualistic Christian sects that differed from mainstream Christianity on a number of important doctrinal issues. The Bogomils and Cathars challenged traditional medieval Christian views about marriage, sex, and the religious authority of women. Although both groups ultimately were dismissed as heretical, the alternative notions of sex and gender they purposed had an impact on the development of Christianity.

ORIGINS

The Bogomils emerged in the late tenth century when a Bulgarian priest who took the name *Bogomil*, meaning "worthy of the pity of God," broke with mainstream Roman Catholicism and professed a belief in a dualistic form of Christianity. He preached about a world starkly divided between the forces of good (God) and those of evil (Satan). That interpretation of Christianity quickly spread throughout medieval Europe. In Languedoc in southern France dualistic Christians eventually adopted the name *Cathari*, "the Pure Ones," or Cathars (also known as Albigensians for the town of Albi, which had a high concentration of Cathars). The rest of this entry will employ the designation *Cathar*. By the twelfth century CE the Cathars were the most popular sect in the Christian world and were persecuted vigorously as heretics by the Roman Catholic authorities.

THEOLOGY

The Bogomils and Cathars were Christians who believed in the salvific power of Jesus Christ but differed from mainstream Christianity in their emphasis on a radically dualistic worldview. At the center of Bogomil and Cathar doctrine was the belief that existence is predicated on a battle between good and evil.

That dualism took two forms. The first was a mitigated dualism in which God (the force of good) is the ultimate authority and Satan (the force of evil) is God's subordinate. The other form was an absolute dualism that maintained that good and evil have always coexisted. In both systems the Cathars believed that God is the creator of the spiritual realm but Satan is responsible for material creation, including the earth and bodily existence. The soul technically belongs to the spiritual realm, but it fell and was imprisoned by Satan in the human body. According to Catharism, Adam and Eve were the first captured souls. Cathar myth describes Adam and Eve succumbing to Satan through sexual seduction. Cathar belief also held that the fall of spiritual souls is strongly linked to the expression of sexuality and that imprisonment in the body is punishment for the overt sexuality of the fallen soul. The goal of Cathar religious practice was for the soul to do penance for its sexual transgression so that it could be freed from its bodily prison and return to the spiritual realm.

The Cathar understanding of creation and the plight of humanity shares significant details with Gnostic and particularly Manichaean mythology and its aversion to sex and sexuality. This has led a number of scholars to speculate that Cathar doctrine was influenced by remnants of underground Gnostic communities that migrated to Turkey and central Eurasia after their eradication by the Roman Empire. Others have argued that dualism was an inherent aspect of central European culture and that Catharism was a product of indigenous beliefs.

Because the Cathars regarded the material world as the evil creation of Satan and believed that sexuality plays a significant role in separating the soul from its true nature, Cathar practice focused on antimaterialist asceticism. The Cathars rejected anything related to sex or materialism. Their refusal to marry was meant as a repudiation of sexual intercourse. They also refused to consume foods that they regarded as products of sexual generation. This included eggs, meats (as the product of sex), and most dairy products (owing to their connection to reproductive milk). The Cathars also disengaged themselves from worldly matters such as war, politics, and the swearing of oaths.

The rigorous asceticism of Cathar belief proved impractical for all but a few members of the Cathar community. The few Cathars who actually followed the prohibitions on sex, food, and worldly involvement formed an elite group known as the Perfecti, "the Perfect Ones." The majority of Cathars lived lives similar to those of mainstream Christians, accruing spiritual benefits from their contact with and support of the Perfecti.

THE ROLE OF WOMEN

Unlike the Roman Catholic priesthood, both men and women could become Perfecti. The ritual of initiation known as *Consolamentum*, or spiritual baptism, was open to both men and women and could be administered by both. Cathar women also were allowed to perform priestly duties such as hearing confession, absolving people of their sins, and leading communal prayers. The highly visible role of women in Cathar ritual has caused scholars to speculate that women made up a large proportion of the Cathar community and that women may have provided support to Catharism. The equality with which women participated in Cathar ritual as well as the repudiation of marriage and sex also may indicate that Catharism did not subscribe to traditional notions of gender. It is possible that because the Cathars saw gender distinctions as a by-product of the unfortunate material embodiment of the soul, such distinctions do not reflect the true nature of the soul and therefore categories of male and female and the rules and restrictions associated with gender were of no consequence to the Cathars. This is only speculation: It is impossible to know with certainty how the Cathars viewed gender, but their inclusion of women in rituals definitely deviates from the position of contemporaneous mainstream Christianity on appropriate gender roles.

PERSECUTION

The departure of Catharism from normative Roman Catholic beliefs and practices caused the Cathars to be branded as heretics. In 1208 the Roman Catholic pope instigated a crusade against the Cathars. Known as the Albigensian Crusade, it lasted twenty years and decimated the Cathar community. The few Cathar men and women who survived the crusade were subjected to the Inquisition. By the middle of the fourteenth century Catharism essentially had disappeared, leaving only traces of its thoughts and practices to continue to be debated and disavowed within the mainstream Christian community.

SEE ALSO *Christianity, Early and Medieval.*

BIBLIOGRAPHY

Hollister, C. Warren. 1994. *Medieval Europe: A Short History*. 7th edition. New York: McGraw-Hill.

Peters, Edward. 1980. *Heresy and Authority in Medieval Europe*. Philadelphia: University of Pennsylvania Press.

Jennifer Hart

BONAPARTE, MARIE
1882–1962

Great-grandniece of Napoleon Bonaparte, Princess Marie Bonaparte was a writer, psychoanalyst, and devotee of Sigmund Freud. Not a medical doctor, Bonaparte worked in France to help establish groups, including the Société Psychoanalytique de Paris (SPP), for nonmedical psychotherapies. Interested in issues of sexuality, lay analysis (the practice of psychoanalysis by analysts without medical degrees), and frigidity, as well as a translator of essays and Freud's correspondence with Dr. Wilhelm Fliess, Bonaparte used her influence to help Freud escape from the Nazis in 1938. She also maneuvered to get Freud the Nobel Prize, but did not succeed.

The wealthy daughter of Prince Roland Bonaparte and Marie-Félix Blanc, daughter of Monte Carlo real estate developer François Blanc, Marie Bonaparte married Prince George of Greece in 1907 and had two children. Concerned about her own sexual frigidity, Marie consulted Freud, and then trained to become an analyst. She had affairs with Rudolf Lowenstein, who later served as psychoanalyst Jacques Lacan's analyst, with whom she cofounded the SPP; as well as with leading French politician Aristide Briand. Bonaparte used her wealth and social position as a platform from which she could study psychoanalysis and anthropology, and approach sexual issues unapologetically. Endowed by Freud with a confidence typically enjoyed in this era only by men, Bonaparte became the most prominent woman psychoanalytic authority in France. Throughout her career, she would battle to empower forms of lay psychotherapy while at the same time advocate to ground psychoanalysis in biology and encourage psychoanalysis to adopt the ethics of medicine.

Lay analysis was an issue particularly bound up with the ability of women to practice as psychotherapists. Most women did not have access to a medical education during the first part of the twentieth century, thus their ability to work as psychoanalysts was hampered if a medical degree was required. Psychoanalysis, itself a young practice, sought simultaneously to secure the professional rigor of the medical community. Part of the importance of the SPP was that it provided some support to practicing lay analysts, such as Bonaparte. In 1934 Bonaparte financed an Institute for the Instruction of Analysts, and she served for many years as both officer and honorary president of the SPP.

Bonaparte is perhaps best known as a friend and sponsor of Freud and as an author and translator. She wrote a psychoanalytic study of the life and works of Edgar Allan Poe, a treatise on female sexuality, a commentary on child psychology, and a book on war and those lost in war. She was interested in the relation between psychoanalysis and folklore as well as in the organic bases for psychical phenomena.

In *The Life and Works of Edgar Allan Poe: A Psychoanalytic Interpretation* (1933), Bonaparte began with Freud's idea that dreams and creative writing derive from the same unconscious sources. She analyzed Poe's creative work in the same way that Freud analyzed dreams. Freud theorized that dreams were wish fulfillments often made up of memories and problems suffered by individuals as infants. Much of that infantile material, according to Freud, was sexual. By finding sets of recurrent patterns and preoccupations, an analyst might begin to hypothesize about the character of an individual's infantile material and unconscious memories. In analyzing Poe's writing in relation to his life, Bonaparte tried both to develop a significant practice of psychoanalysis based on an individual's literary production and an understanding of Poe himself as an author whose works reflect Oedipal conflicts and the repeated satisfaction of thwarted childhood sexual curiosity, as evidenced in the clever deductions of Poe's fictional detective, Auguste Dupin.

In *Female Sexuality* (1951), Bonaparte takes up the question of female sexuality that baffled Freud throughout his career. Like Freud, Bonaparte believed individuals begin with bisexual potential, but that females can follow one of two paths to sexual development. Depending on the innate sensitivity of the clitoral and vaginal zones, girl children may either experience excitement and orgasm through the seductions of cleansing and fondling or through masturbation. The method and zone of early excitement establishes itself as a primary sexual pathway for the female who then seeks to repeat the satisfying experience in later sexual encounters. Bonaparte believed that infantile experience marks individuals for life.

Not many psychoanalytic practitioners took up Bonaparte's theories about female sexuality, but her work on Poe did influence the ways some critics analyze literary works as keys to the author's preoccupations.

SEE ALSO *Freud, Sigmund.*

BIBLIOGRAPHY

WORKS BY

Bonaparte, Marie. 1949. *The Life and Works of Edgar Allan Poe: A Psycho-analytic Interpretation,* trans. John Rodker. New York: Humanities Press.

Bonaparte, Marie. 1951. *Female Sexuality*, trans. John Rodker. New York: Grove Press.

WORKS ABOUT

Roudinesco, Elisabeth. 1990. *Jacques Lacan & Co.: A History of Psychoanalysis in France, 1925–1985*, trans. Jeffrey Mehlman. Chicago: University of Chicago Press.

Judith Roof

BONDAGE AND DISCIPLINE

Bondage and discipline refers to the consensual physical restraint of a sexual partner for the purpose of inflicting pain, punishment, or humiliation. Bondage and discipline is part of Bondage and Discipline, Domination and Submission, Sadomasochism (BDSM), a larger category of sexual activities based in erotic power exchange. Bondage is a common fantasy for both men and women, and it appears that many couples have at one time or another experimented with bondage. Bondage and discipline, however, is practiced by a much narrower portion of the general population and is commonly engaged in by men and women participating in sadomasochism and domination and submission activities.

For the person being bound (generally referred to as the submissive or *bottom*) bondage can generate sexual excitement from the vulnerability associated with being subject to the will of another and from the mental freedom of having given up control of the situation. Some people enjoy the sensation of struggling against bonds; others may enjoy and derive sexual pleasure from the pain and humiliation inflicted by their partner. Bondage may also incorporate an element of torturous sexual teasing that many find stimulating.

For the partner doing the binding (usually called the dominant or *top*), the sight of a bound nude or seminude body may be particularly stimulating, as is the excitement of having a person sexually available and at one's mercy. The power exchange involved in having a submissive capitulate to the will of the dominant and in having the dominant take responsibility for the safety and pleasure of the submissive can be highly exciting to both parties, even when sexual intercourse or genital stimulation does not form part of the bondage and discipline play.

TYPES OF BONDAGE

Bondage may pull parts of the body together (as in the binding of wrists and ankles or some breast and genital binding); separate body parts (as with use of a spreader bar to keep the legs apart); bind a person to an object; suspend a person in midair; restrict movement; or completely wrap (or mummify) the body.

Bondage materials range from the commonly available to the homemade to the professionally manufactured and sold. The most basic bondage item is rope, which is both pliable and adjustable enough to perform a variety of functions. Leather cuffs, handcuffs, and chains are also often used to bind the extremities together or to a stationary object, to tie a submissive in a spread-eagle position, or to hogtie a person with the ankles and wrists both bound behind the back. Gags, blindfolds, ear plugs, and hoods may be used to enhance a sense of isolation, confinement, vulnerability, and helplessness in the victim, as well as to induce a certain amount of sensory deprivation. Eyebolts are often mounted both on furniture and on walls or ceilings to aid in tying down or suspending a submissive. Mummification, or the wrapping of the body in such materials as bandages, plastic wrap, or cloth, completely immobilizes the body and allows the dominant the option of leaving the submissive in a state of sensory deprivation or of stimulating him or her while immobilized. The binding of genitals or breasts is also common and may or may not be done in conjunction with other forms of bondage. Both genital and breast binding (in men and women) may be done so as to prevent or to facilitate access to the body part in question.

TYPES OF DISCIPLINE

The term discipline is often used to refer any kind of sadistic or dominant activity performed in a BDSM context. Such discipline might be as simple as the infliction of pain on the bound submissive. Alternatively activities that both parties consider pleasurable (such as oral sex) might be cast by the dominant as something the submissive must perform or undergo as punishment for some misbehavior. Discipline might also take the form of role-playing in which the dominant takes on authoritarian role (parent, teacher, police officer) and punishes the submissive for some infraction. Such forms of discipline act more as sexual titillation than as punishment per se.

More specifically, however, discipline refers to the training or punishment of a submissive by a dominant. Because the role of the submissive is to please the dominant (whether as a part of master/slave lifestyle or as part of a specific scenario two people are enacting), it is generally accepted that the submissive will require a certain amount of training and discipline in order to best serve the dominant. This discipline might take the form of withholding of a reward, such as orgasm; demanding that the submissive perform a service or degrading act for the dominant; or inflicting physical pain, such as whipping, spanking, or beating. Bondage itself can also be a form of discipline, if administered as a punishment.

SOCIAL CONTEXTS

In the United States bondage seems first to have emerged publicly through gay leathermen, who imitated post-World War II biker culture. In the 1960s bondage began to move into heterosexual culture, where the forerunners of current-day BDSM clubs developed as a means of exploring bondage and the BDSM lifestyle. Western bondage has been influenced by *shibari*, a Japanese style of bondage that originated as a mechanism of restraining and torturing prisoners. *Shibari* techniques emphasize the aesthetics of the bondage and utilize binding that, rather than simply immobilizing the submissive, stimulates him or her sexually by applying pressure to the breasts or genitals.

Though scientific and sociological studies of bondage and discipline are scattered, evidence suggests that many mainstream couples take part in bondage. The fascination that bondage holds for the general population is demonstrated by its prominence in mainstream erotica and pornography and by its frequent mention in mainstream popular culture.

Bondage and discipline in the strictest sense, however, is much more likely to be limited to the BDSM community, a loose conglomeration of individuals and institutions that self-identify as participating in sadomasochistic sexual play. Within this community, bondage and discipline often forms part of a core of common BDSM sexual activity and tends to not be particularly distinguished from other types of domination and submission behaviors; some individuals, however, more specifically fetishize bondage and its accoutrements.

BIBLIOGRAPHY

Bean, Joseph. 1994. *Leathersex: A Guide for the Curious Outsider and the Serious Player.* San Francisco: Daedalus.

Brame, William; Gloria Brame; and Jon Jacobs. 1996. *Different Loving: An Exploration of the World of Sexual Dominance and Submission.* New York: Villard.

Midori. 2001. *The Seductive Art of Japanese Bondage.* San Francisco: Greenery Press.

Miller, Philip, and Molly Devon. 1995. *Screw the Roses, Send Me the Thorns: The Romance and Sexual Sorcery of Sadomasochism.* Fairfield, CT: Mystic Rose Books.

Wiseman, Jay. 2000. *Jay Wiseman's Erotic Bondage Handbook.* San Francisco: Greenery Press.

Maureen Lauder

BORAN

SEE *Queens.*

BOSCH, HIERONYMUS
1453–1516

Jheronymus [Hieronymus] van Aken was born in Dutch Brabant in the small town of Hertogenbosch, whose name he adopted, becoming known as Bosch. From an artists' family, he was familiar with the workshop mode of painting, and some of his works were completed in a workshop environment. His comparatively small oeuvre was enormous in its impact on immediate contemporaries and followers for more than a century, creating a "Bosch style" exemplified by numerous imitators (Koldeweij, Vandenbroek, and Vermet, 2001, pp. 11–28). Many of his sources and models were identified in the 1930s by Charles de Tolnay (1937).

The themes in Bosch's work are mostly religious: *Temptation of Saint Anthony, The Adoration of the Magi, The Last Judgment, Saint Jerome at Prayer, Saint John at Patmos, The Seven Deadly Sins, The Garden of [Earthly] Delights*, and works such as the allegorical *Haywain.* He favored the triptych as a medium providing the structural support for complex compositions that organized time and space in a symbolic and relational diachrony.

THEMES AND INTERPRETATIONS

In Bosch's depictions of hell and demonic assemblies hybrid creatures that combine human or animal features with objects or reassembled body parts engage in a pandemonium of taunting, violence, torture, and sexual assaults on apparently helpless, and usually naked, human bodies. The intense visionary quality of his work, and the often disturbing brutality of these scenes, the symbolic surcharge of allegorical figurations, elicited more commentary than for other early modern artists, as art historians have sought the interpretation that would finally shed light on the hidden meaning of this oeuvre.

Bosch has been claimed as an anti-orthodox opponent of Church doctrine, and ascribed connections to heretical sects such as the Brothers of the Common Life and the Brothers of the Free Spirit (Fraenger 1952). He has also been read as expressing the orthodox, perhaps mystical, religious piety of an outraged observer of sin (Gombrich 1967). He has been interpreted according to the symbols of alchemy—one of the more convincingly documented readings (Dixon 1981)—and according to alchemical/Gnostic readings (Mettra 1977). It also has been claimed that he merely transmitted the fantastic art of the "grylls" of antiquity and revisited classical models, especially through glyptic art (Baltrusaitis 1981). In spite of the many approaches and the wealth of erudition displayed, the case has not been closed, and no single one is so compelling as to effectively silence the others.

Bosch's vision is rife with intriguing representations of women and gender: In *The Haywain* armed female figures appear to be as violent as the men. In scenes with sinners there is a current of sexual (in)difference in the way some of the naked bodies are represented as markedly androgynous. The mermaids in armor and closed helmets floating on the pools of the Garden of Delights also code androgyny.

THE GARDEN OF DELIGHTS

The Garden of Delights stands out in his oeuvre, a consummate achievement both as a work of art and as an enigmatic composition with multiple elements of sexual and religious symbolism.

The *Garden* was not apparently meant for display in a religious building; as art historians are confident that it was the painting displayed a year after the artist's death in the palace of Henry III of Nassau. It was described by an Italian visitor, Antonio de Beatis, and this contemporary view assigned no particular meaning to the work, taking note of the mixed landscapes of land and sea, the black and white men and women, "*de diversi acti e modi*" (in diverse actions and guises, or comportments; *diversi* also can mean "strange"), birds and animals depicted with great realism ("*naturalitá*"), a work both "*piacevole*" and "*fantastiche*" (Gombrich 1967, pp. 403–404). An often-quoted commentary on Bosch's whole oeuvre close to his time is that of Siguenza in 1605, who also saw nothing untoward or heretical in his work. Trying to

The Garden of Earthly Delights by Bosch. *Detail from the central panel of* The Garden of Earthly Delights *by Hieronymus Bosch.* © FRANCIS G. MAYER/CORBIS.

decipher a hidden and overarching meaning in it has been a conceit of the twentieth century.

The outside panels of the *Garden* triptych show a transparent ball of glass or a bubble encasing the world, an apparently peaceful landscape surrounded by waters and dominated high up by a minute figure of God the creator done in grisaille. It illustrates the verse of the psalm "*Sicut in utrem aquas maris*" (God gathered the waters of the seas in a flask) (Dempsey 2004). The left panel depicts Paradise, in which Christ shows a newly formed Eve to a seated Adam, who stares fixedly at her; the Fall is implied with details of violence in the animal realm: Peace among them is fissured, as the cat walks off with a mouse in its mouth.

On the right panel, there is a vision of hell, filled with the familiar violent, hybrid figures. However, this section focuses on the discordant noise of the place, and it is the human sense of hearing that is assaulted. It shows the mutilation and martyrdom of ears, bodies strung across giant musical instruments as in a crucifixion, and naked sinners singing in a chorus with a monstrous kapellmeister, reading music from the posterior of a human figure. Merely identifying the panel as "Hell" does not do justice to its symbolic complexity.

The central panel is a vividly erotic but coded rendition of the Garden. However, this garden is not the "*hortus conclusus*," or "closed-off garden," which in medieval symbolism often was an iconographical attribute of the Virgin Mary, whose untouched womb, without breach or rupture, was likened to it. Instead, it contains many enclosures. Its space is defined by concentric pools of water. In the farthest region of the canvas a small pool contains black and white female figures bathing together. Around the largest pool a cavalcade of naked men and women gallop astride giant animals, including camels, stags, boars, cats, and birds. On the pools float various ephemeral conveyances containing amorous couples, including a black man with a pale white woman, and other couples swim together or peer out of nooks and crannies of fruit. Behind it loom the ambiguous horned structures found in much of Bosch's oeuvre, built of spikes and protuberances, architectural marvels made of matter that appears vegetal or carnal—because of its pink hue—rather than made of stone: Some embracing couples are walking toward them. Fruit is of paramount importance, mostly in the form of the gigantic strawberry or split pomegranate: Figures hold them or embrace them or hide in them; one holds the fruit between outstretched legs. In the busy forefront another well-known sexual symbol of that time is the mussel, here containing a couple with intertwined legs. In the far right corner a group of naked figures, one black, stands and watches. Prominent among them is a wild woman, hands on hips, in the observer position.

The overwhelming proliferation of images and the strong sexual content of the work have been noted by critics, often with distaste for unnamed practices—probably a reaction to the few instances of sodomitical representations: a male figure extracting roses from the anus of a leaning and sexually undefined figure and a bird's beak at work on the anus of one of the riders, an image familiar in Medieval manuscript marginalia. The easiest way to interpret the conundrum presented by the *Garden* has been to see it sequentially: From the left, with the ominous presence of Eve, the eye moves to acts not condoned by religion or law and then, to the right, to punishment. Thus, the central panel can be seen as a florid description of the temptations of sin. The nakedness of the figures has been adduced as proof of that interpretation (Glum 1976), yet Laurinda Dixon has countered that the structure of the triptych is identical to "the basic alchemical allegory" (Dixon 1981, p. 99).

One cannot indeed overlook that male and female figures are depicted in the Garden with sustained attention to the beauty of the body and the harmony of its proportions. While the stain of luxury and wantonness may be present, the expression of soft physical beauty underscored by the predominance of curves (bodies, pools of water, bubbles, fruit) exudes an exuberant expression of the erotic that may transcend sin, or at the very least, sequentially add to and expand on it. Indeed, in Bosch's work, demons are hybrid forms, as in the models identified by Baltrusaitis (1981), mostly grotesque, sporting slimy scales and the tails of rodents—symbols of evil (Glum 1976)—and engaged in terrifying acts. There is no such suggestion in the central panel of *The Garden of Delights*, and it seems that the search for interpretative clues must continue. Particularly suggestive are readings that take into account Bosch's multiple layerings between the religious and the profane (Kessler 1997), perhaps a reflection of his painting technique, which used transparent layers of color, visible groundsel, and visible drawing lines to create a sort of palimpsest in his work (Koldeweij, Vandenbroek, and Vermet, 2001, pp. 11–13).

SEE ALSO *Erotic Art.*

BIBLIOGRAPHY

Baltrusaitis, Jurgis.1981. *Le Moyen Age fantastique: Antiquités et exotismes dans l'art gothique* [The fantastic in the Middle Ages: Antiquities and exoticism in Gothic art]. Paris: Flammarion.

Dempsey, Charles. 2004. "*Sicut in utrem aquas maris:* Jerome Bosch's Prolegomenon to the Garden of Earthly Delights." *MLN* 119(1): S247–S270.

Dixon, Laurinda S. 1981. "Bosch's Garden of Delights: Remnants of a 'Fossil' Science." *Art Bulletin* 63(1): 96–113.

Fraenger, Wilhem. 1952. *The Millenium of Hieronymus Bosch: Outlines of a New Interpretation*, trans. Eithne Wilkins and Ernst Kaiser. London: Faber and Faber.

Glum, Peter. 1976. "Divine Judgment in Bosch's Garden of Earthly Delights." *Art Bulletin.* 58(1): 45–54.

Gombrich, E. H. 1967. "The Earliest Description of Bosch's Garden of Delight." *Journal of the Warburg and Courtauld Institutes* 30: 403–406.

Kessler, Erwin. 1997. "Le Jardin des Délices et les fruits du mal" [The Garden of Earthly Delights and the fruits of evil]. In *Flore et jardins: Usages, savoirs et représentations du monde végétal au Moyen Age: Etudes reuniés et publiées par Pierre-Gilles Girault* [Flora and gardens: Uses, knowledge and representations of the vegetal world in the Middle Ages], ed. Pierre-Gilles Girault. Paris: Leopard d'Or.

Koldeweij, Jos, Paul Vandenbroek, and Bernard Vermet, eds. 2001. *Hieronymus Bosch: The Complete Paintings and Drawings*. Amsterdam: Ludion Ghent; Rotterdam: NAi; New York: Harry N. Abrams.

Mettra, Claude. 1977. *Jérôme Bosch*. Paris: Henri Screpel.

Tolnay, Charles de. 1937. *Hieronymus Bosch*. Basel and Leipzig: Editions Holbein.

Francesca Canadé Sautman

BOSWELL, JOHN
1947–1994

John Boswell was perhaps one of the most controversial and influential figures in the fields of the history of sexuality, religious studies, and medieval history in the late twentieth century. Born in 1947 in Boston, he attended the College of William and Mary, and after earning his Ph.D. from Harvard in 1975, he joined the Yale history department as an assistant professor. He became full professor in 1982 and was named the A. Whitney Griswold Professor of History in 1990. A popular teacher and lecturer, Boswell frequently spoke on issues concerning gay rights. In 1987 he was instrumental in creating the Lesbian and Gay Studies Center at Yale. He died of an AIDS-related illness in 1994.

His groundbreaking work *Christianity, Social Tolerance, and Homosexuality: Gay People in Western Europe from the Beginning of the Christian Era to the Fourteenth Century* (1980) won the National Book Award for History in 1981. In it Boswell challenges an idea that had become a commonplace: that Christianity had always considered homosexual acts morally wrong and that it had a longstanding tradition of homophobic practices. He stresses that there had been tolerance for homosexual acts in Greek, Roman, Hebrew, and early Christian societies. He further maintains that neither scripture nor early Christian society demanded a negative response to same-sex relations. He posits that "gay subcultures" existed in both ancient and medieval times, and explores the twelfth century as a period when homoerotic relationships flourished, even among members of the clergy. He positions the rise of homophobia in the late twelfth and thirteenth centuries, when Christian writers read their attitudes back into earlier texts. By applying the term *gay* to the past, Boswell suggested a transhistorical identity.

Boswell's research, critical perspective, and conclusions sparked a variety of responses—not all positive. Boswell, himself a converted Catholic, was criticized for advocacy scholarship. He was labeled an apologist for Christianity, attempting to read homophobia out of Christianity. At the opposite end of the spectrum, Catholic and conservative Christian readers attacked his work as a distortion of fundamental Christian principles. His study heightened the essentialist–social constructionist debate over the understanding of same-sex relationships in the past. Boswell stressed that his use of *gay* was not anachronistic; rather he selected the term to indicate individuals who chose same-sex relations. Scholars who disputed this usage advocated the Foucauldian notion that the concept of sexual identity did not become a functional category until the nineteenth century. Criticism also came from feminist scholars, who noted the absence of a serious discussion of women in his study, and viewed it as reinscribing the marginality of lesbian experience and confirming the medieval misogynistic viewpoint.

In his later work, *Same Sex Unions in Pre-Modern Europe* (1994), Boswell contends that the Christian Church had sanctioned same-sex unions and had complex rituals for these unions, thus offering an historical precedent for same-sex marriage. Basing his analysis on a wide range of manuscripts reflecting practices in the Mediterranean, Boswell draws a parallel between heterosexual marriage and voluntary same-sex unions between males. What remains unclear in these couples is whether their bond was only emotional, not physical. Although none of the evidence that Boswell uncovered in the manuscripts ever indicated an erotic relationship, one may have existed. Some critics maintain that the *adelphopoiesis* (brother-making) rituals were ceremonies pledging loyalty and brotherhood between men.

The controversy that Boswell's studies elicited raises the issue of how we interpret medieval responses to same-sex relationships. Whether one rejects or supports his conclusions, Boswell's work reopens the debate of understanding medieval sexuality.

SEE ALSO *Gay; Homosexuality, Male, History of.*

BIBLIOGRAPHY

Boswell, John. 1980. *Christianity, Social Tolerance, and Homosexuality: Gay People in Western Europe from the Beginning of the Christian Era to the Fourteenth Century.* Chicago: University of Chicago Press.

Boswell, John. 1982–1983. "Revolutions, Universals, and Sexual Categories." *Salmagundi* 58: 89–113.

Boswell, John. 1994. *Same-Sex Unions in Premodern Europe.* New York: Villard.

Johansson, Warren; Wayne R. Dynes; and John Lauritsen. 2003. *Homosexuality, Intolerance, and Christianity: A Critical Examination of John Boswell's Work.* Pink Triangle Trust Library. Available from http://bibpurl.oclc.org/web/7484.

Kuefler, Mathew, ed. 2006. *The Boswell Thesis: Essays on Christianity, Social Tolerance, and Homosexuality.* Chicago: University of Chicago Press.

Edith Joyce Benkov

BOYS, CONSTRUCTION OF

Boy is a gender assigned to most male children at or before birth. As early as two years old, boys have a sense of themselves as boys and have begun understanding other people in terms of sexual difference. By early adolescence, boys have often begun to emulate the masculine behavior of older boys and to identify themselves more as "guys" or, in the United Kingdom, "lads." Though the term *boys* is sometimes used to refer to teenagers and adult men, it is usually associated with physical and mental immaturity and thus, in reference to adults, is used either ironically or disdainfully.

In the first half of the twentieth century, the term boys was often used to evoke a group of men linked by a certain male camaraderie, as in "one of the boys," "boys will be boys," or the use of boys to refer to the armed forces. This usage has largely been replaced by the use of *guys* in the United States and *lads* in the United Kingdom, terms that encompass a wide age range and can connote participation in a male-oriented, masculine culture.

The common association between immaturity and boys sets up a power dynamic in which boys are subordinated to adult men. This power imbalance is implicit in the nineteenth-century American usage by whites of the term boy to refer to adult male slaves and by its British usage until the mid-twentieth century to refer to native men from the colonies.

Because this power dynamic places the gender boy opposite adult masculinity, boys occupy a somewhat feminized position, and much of young boys' gender negotiations in school revolve around establishing their difference from girls. These gender negotiations begin as early as preschool, by which time young children have already internalized a gender identity and have begun categorizing others as boy or girl. Boys often reject games and activities they associate with girl behaviors, and they very quickly form a community based on the exclusion of girls. They will similarly often refuse to allow girls to participate in games, such as soccer or baseball, that they consider to be the province of boys.

BOYS' ASSERTION OF POWER AND MASCULINE PRIVILEGE

Many researchers have remarked on the degree to which the way boys construct and regulate their gender identities in school depends upon the assertion of power and masculine privilege, which has been noted as early as kindergarten and is directed both at other students and at teachers. Among themselves, boys tend to engage in a great deal of physical violence, usually couched as play fighting, including poking, slapping, hitting, and wrestling. Even routine physical contact, by the fifth grade, has shifted from touching and hugging to hand slapping, shoving, and poking. Though boys are less likely to physically fight girls, there is a well-documented pattern of sexual aggression, both verbal and physical, directed at girls. Girls, it appears, also learn early not to complain too loudly about such aggression. Though girls sometimes strike back at boys or band together to drive them from a common area, they only infrequently report the behavior to authority figures. The behavior is often chalked up to boyish antics (by both girls and adults), but girls in many cases have also learned that telling tales will earn no redress. Female teachers also receive sexually or physically aggressive comments, even from very young boys, which they often choose to ignore rather than engage. Though this phenomenon is fairly common, Barrie Thorne (1993) and others also caution against overgeneralizations about the level and type of boys' aggression. The most assertive and aggressive boys are also the ones who call the most attention to themselves as objects of study, and researchers who have focused on less visible students have found that boys negotiate and assert their masculinity and gender identities in a multiplicity of ways.

GROUPING BEHAVIOR

Although boys commonly interact with girls outside of school, girls and boys are inclined, when possible, to self-segregate in school. On playgrounds, boys tend to coalesce in larger, more visible groups. They generally control some 90 percent of the playground area and concentrate in outlying areas, such as sports fields, rather than areas close to the school building. They are usually more physically aggressive than girls, apparently more competitive, hierarchically organized, and often gravitate toward team sports during playtime. As Thorne comments, however, there is great variability in these patterns. Whereas the most popular and most visible boys tend to be sports-oriented and competitive, more marginal boys may form smaller friendship groups and participate in different playground activities; girls, moreover, may not be less competitive or hierarchical than boys, but rather express these things in terms (such as being nice) that appear more cooperative. Despite this variability in the mechanisms by which boys establish their gender identities, too much deviation from established norms is consistently policed: Boys who spend too much time with girls or who play girls' games are subject to accusations of effeminacy or homosexuality (wimps, sissies, queers, or fags).

Compared to girls, boys tend to interact very differently with authority. Rule transgression and the use of forbidden language is an important part of boys' play activities. Regulations are often flouted in more or less plain view of authority figures. Researchers have noted that boys tend to organize in quite large groups, rather than pairs or triplets, and that much of the thrill of rule breaking seems to stem from doing it in front of witnesses. These groups provide a level of anonymity that often enables individual boys to escape punishment for violating rules. Boys similarly experiment with sex and sexuality in such groups where the excitement of viewing illicit pornography or telling a dirty joke is enhanced by the presence and encouragement of witnesses.

FORMATION OF GENDER IDENTITY

As is the case with girls, researchers have found that the formation of gender identity in boys is as much a project in establishing heterosexuality as it is establishing gender. Whereas girls constitute their identities as heterosexual with consistent reference to what boys will find desirable, boys are more inclined to construct their genders in terms of homophobia and avoidance of the homosexual. Thus, improperly masculine behaviors are often deterred by charges of homosexuality, even when the accusers do not understand the sexual implications of epithets such as "queer" or "fag." As with girls, much of boys' gender construction is concerned with negotiating or maintaining the boundaries between boys and girls. These boundaries are often tested and reinscribed by coed games such as catch and kiss, cooties, and invasions of the girls' side of the playground. Interaction with girls is thus constructed as exciting, but also dangerous and possibly polluting (cooties, for example, usually originate with girls). The culture of boyfriends and girlfriends, which starts as early as kindergarten, is thus somewhat problematic for boys: Romantic contact and success with girls can be one method by which a boy asserts his masculinity, but it also bears the danger of contamination by femininity and possible teasing or ostracization by other boys.

Girls are sexualized early in childhood and tend to construct their genders and identities explicitly in relation to male desire. They initially understand heterosexual pairings in terms of romance, and they actively engage in pairing themselves and classmates in nominally boyfriend/girlfriend relationships. In contrast, boys usually first conceive of heterosexual pairings in terms of sexual bodies and activities, which conception is later modified to include romance and intimacy. (It is noteworthy, however, that for both girls and boys this initial contact with male–female relationships occurs in groups of the same sex, with heterosexual interest and desire being performed for a homosocial audience.) Unlike girls, however, boys largely negotiate gender identities as a homosocial group. For girls, male desire is a crucial aspect of the construction of gender identity, whereas boys establish masculinity and power primarily in relation to other boys. Girls are used as a controlling mechanism in this construction, but the gender identity of boys is created and performed first for other boys. Romantic relationships with girls are thus one option for establishing a heterosexual, masculine gender identity before a boy's peers, but it is not the only one.

SEE ALSO *Butch/Femme; Girls, Construction of.*

BIBLIOGRAPHY

Blaise, Mindy. 2005. *Playing It Straight: Uncovering Gender Discourses in the Early Childhood Classroom.* New York: Routledge.

Kimmel, Michael S., and Rebecca F. Plante, eds. 2004. *Sexualities: Identities, Behaviors, and Society.* New York: Oxford University Press.

Lehr, Susan, ed. 2001. *Beauty, Brains, and Brawn: The Construction of Gender in Children's Literature.* Portsmouth, NH: Heinemann.

Renold, Emma. 2005. *Girls, Boys, and Junior Sexualities: Exploring Children's Gender and Sexual Relations in the Primary School.* London: RoutledgeFalmer.

Thorne, Barrie. 1993. *Gender Play: Girls and Boys in School.* New Brunswick, NJ: Rutgers University Press.

Maureen Lauder

BRAIN

The literature on brain, gender, and sexuality is subject to an array of interpretations. For example, it is known that individuals can be born with the "external parts" of one sex despite the fact that their cells contain the chromosomal pattern of the other sex or that those "external parts" can present ambiguously at birth as a result of genetic disorders, hormonal aberrations, or trauma, creating a condition called *intersexual.* However, even though technology continues to provide information with increasing degrees of precision, these matters often are confused because of the common misuse of the terms *sex* and *gender* as synonyms. David Haig chronicled this confusion in the academic literature and concluded that the increased use of the term *gender* "appears to be the result of well-meaning attempts to signal sympathy with the ideas and goals of feminism. This has had the paradoxical outcome of undercutting and blurring the distinction which feminists sought to emphasize by distinguishing sex from gender" (Haig 2000, p. 373).

SEX AND GENDER

Although gender controversies probably are as old as the human species, they were not labeled as such until John Money's 1955 adoption of the word *gender* from linguistics and grammar, where it was used to classify nouns. Money's graduate work was with intersexuals, or hermaphrodites as they were referred to at that time. Before he changed the lexicon, the only word or concept available was sex, and that created a dilemma in dealing with intersexuals. An example of that difficulty would be provided by a phenotypic male with the outward appearance of a male, including many male secondary sexual characteristics, and the genotype of a female, with ambiguous genitalia and therefore with no functioning male sex organ. Such an individual would not have a male sexual role in the sense of completing the act of penetration (Money used a new term for that role: *sexuoerotic*). However, that person would be able to present in public performing a male sexual (sociosexual) role consisting of masculine or manly attitudes, behaviors, interests, and actions.

Sex thus is the more restrictive term, tied to biology, and represents one's identification as a male, female, or intersexual on the basis of one's external genitalia. Gender is one's identification as male/man/masculine or female/woman/feminine on the basis of somatic and behavioral criteria. Gender thus is the more inclusive term and can be used to address genital sex, erotic sex, chromosomal sex, and gonadal sex and the expression of those factors as they are presented to society.

THE NUMBER OF SEXES

Anne Fausto-Sterling (2000) proposed, partly to be provocative, the concept of five sexes. Although the concept has caught on more than the terminology has, that terminology can be helpful in understanding the group—intersexuals themselves—that appears to be promoting the term intersexual. The five sexes are male and female, with the addition of herms, formerly called true hermaphrodites, who are born with both a testis and an ovary; merms, formerly called male pseudohermaphrodites, who are born with testes and some form of female genitalia; and ferms, formerly called female pseudohermaphrodites, who are born with ovaries combined with some form of male genitalia. Fausto-Sterling revised her earlier estimation of the prevalence of intersexuality down from 4 percent to 1.7 percent, or seventeen in every 1,000 live births. She agrees with Suzanne J. Kessler (1998) that her paradigm of five sexes still gives primacy to genitalia when in fact gender is attributed to individuals in their everyday lives without knowledge of what is underneath their clothing and is performed by those individuals regardless of the idiosyncratic configuration of their genitalia.

SCIENTIFIC STUDIES

The attempt to understand brain, gender, and sexuality has resulted in an enormous literature primarily involved in studying the differences between male and female biology and behavior. In the search for anatomical differences, gross and microscopic anatomical postmortem studies have given way to computerized axial tomography (CAT), positron emission tomography (PET), and magnetic resonance imaging (MRI), including functional MRI (fMRI), which allows increased spatial and temporal resolution.

In adults the male brain weighs 11 to 12 percent more than the female brain, and the male head is about 2 percent bigger than the female head. However, MRI demonstrates that in the frontal and parietal lobes the female brain has more folds; it is more convoluted and thus has a larger surface area. Neural and synaptic density is a function of surface area, not volume, and so the female brain has greater cortical complexity.

No area of the male brain is more complex than the female brain. MRI studies of adolescent brains have shown different sizes and maturation rates, with larger volumes found in the male cerebellum, putamen, and globus pallidus and a larger caudate nucleus found in the female. The corpus callosum in very early studies was said to have a greater surface area in the male brain; however, a 1982 study reported thicker fibers in the corpus callosum in female brains. MRI studies have found no differences in this structure in male and female brains. In the hypothalamus the preoptic area (POA), which is known to be involved in mating behavior in animals, is twice the size in the male and has twice as many cells. Functional imaging has demonstrated some different patterns of use of the parts of the brain.

Some research in brain and nervous-system function has involved the structures involved with sexual reproduction. The technical term for the differences between the two genders in the service of sexual reproduction is *sexual dimorphism.* Sexually dimorphic structures have been found in all parts of the neuraxis. Two that have been studied extensively are the sexually dimorphic nucleus, the spinal nucleus of the bulbocavernosus muscle (SNB), and the sexually dimorphic nucleus of the preoptic area (SDN-POA). The peripheral SNB clearly influences sexual behavior. The SDN-POA has confused investigators because although the destruction of the entire POA impairs reproductive behavior, little effect results from selectively lesioning its SDN.

BEHAVIORAL AND COGNITIVE STUDIES

Studies in sex differences in human behavior have focused on social behaviors in children, especially play behavior; social behavior in adults, especially aggression and child rearing; cognitive abilities; and sexual behavior. The studies most pertinent to gender issues and the brain are those of juvenile play behavior, cognitive function, and sexual behavior.

Studies of juvenile play behavior in nonhuman animals show that sex differences can be modified by alterations in prenatal hormones. *Rough-and-tumble* play in males has been linked to prenatal or perinatal testosterone. The administration of androgens in female species such as the rat prenatally and/or postnatally results in more play fighting in juveniles. Early castration in the first week of life *feminizes* this behavior in male rats; later castration does not. In the brain the amygdala has been associated with this sexually differentiated play behavior. In primates only manipulations in the prenatal period can *masculinize* play behavior. In humans studies have reported boys displaying a higher level of play activity with more rough-and-tumble, as well as a preference for male playmates and transportation and construction toys versus dolls, kitchen supplies, and crayons. Such findings appear in many cultures. An *experiment of nature* involving females born with congenital adrenal hyperplasia has revealed similar changes, which often are referred to as *tomboyism.* In both animal experiments and human observations, psychosocial variables that include but are not limited to maternal care, expectations, and general environmental variables are acknowledged as influencing all the sex differences that have been reported.

In terms of cognitive function, although claims have been made in both directions, the question of which sex is more intelligent appears to have been declared a draw. There are, however, particular areas of cognition, thinking, and problem solving that garner much attention. Women most often are reported to perform better in tests of verbal abilities, especially verbal fluency, speech production, language decoding, and spelling; perceptual speed and accuracy; and fine-motor skills. Men do better on tests of spatial abilities, quantitative abilities, and motor strength. Virtually every study, regardless of its bias, includes some form of the same disclaimer, which is stated and then ignored: (1) the range of differences within each sex was usually larger than the average difference between the sexes; (2) sex differences are most marked at the extreme end of the range of ability, such as the most skilled; (3) differences often are found only at specific ages; and (4) the results may be affected by the measurement technique, such as multiple-choice questions, fill-in-the-blank prompts, or essay responses. Studies using meta-analysis have led many researchers to conclude that there are no significant differences between men and women in cognition; others report confirmation of some of the classically reported trends.

SEXUAL BEHAVIOR

Sexual behavior is one area where concrete findings would be expected and have been reported consistently. Although the fact is often forgotten, sex is not about reproduction but is the process by which DNA from two different members of the same species is exchanged and/or combined for purposes of repair and/or to achieve genetic variation. Sexual recombination of DNA involves differentiation into two genders: male and female. In fusion sex (as opposed to conjunction sex), in which two gametes fuse (as in humans), the female brings to the union nuclear DNA and cytoplasmic organelles such as mitochondria that contain DNA, and the male delivers only nuclear DNA.

All living things have sex, from viruses to multicellular eukaryotes, including humans. In humans but not in all species, sex and reproduction are obligatorily linked. Although the behavior necessary for procreation often is called *having sex*, technically, only the gametes have sex. Fusion takes place after the gametes have been released and the two bodies that produced them have separated. The body serves at the pleasure of the gametes, which are directed by genes. The genes live on, and the body dies. However, it is the body, directed by the brain, that performs the behaviors that allow sex to occur. Those behaviors are modified in each body (partner, gender) so that the bodies can find each other, join, release their gametes, and separate.

PET scans in human males and females have shed light on female orgasm. There is no convincing evidence of an evolutionary purpose for female orgasm. Evidence that shows the difficulty women have in achieving orgasm, especially during intercourse, has been replicated sufficiently to have strong credibility. The role of the clitoris, the homologue of the penis, became muddled by fruitless debates about the supremacy of vaginal versus clitoral orgasm dating back to Viennese psychiatrist Sigmund Freud (1856–1939); this line of argument continued long after data on vaginal insensitivity made it moot. Personal reporting and indirect psychophysiological recording have had to suffice as evidence of the occurrence of orgasm in human females.

However, G. Holstege et al. were successful in performing PET scans in both men and women during orgasm. It has been known for some time that orgasm is closely associated with a series of perineal-pelvic contractions. Holstege reported, "These results demonstrate that, similar to ejaculation and orgasm in men, during female orgasm activation occurs primarily in subcortical parts of the brain. The meso-diencephalic junction comprises the reward-related ventral tegmental area, which might produce the pleasure aspect of orgasm. The finding of involvement of the PAG [periaqueductal gray matter] is interesting, because this area has been shown to play a role in female cat, rat, and hamster sexual behavior. Faking an orgasm only activated parts of the voluntary motor system" (Holstege 2003).

Typical of media fascination with sex differences, this historical identification of a central marker localizing "orgasm in the lower brain stem" was ignored, and attention was concentrated on less dramatic, subtle cortical events as it was announced that women fall into a *trance* during orgasm.

REDUCTIONISM AND APPROPRIATENESS

Studies have demonstrated that differences in learning, cognition, and success in school can be influenced by simple things. For example, it has been shown that there are innate differences in the ways girls and boys see and hear. In his article titled "Six Degrees of Separation: What Teachers Need to Know about the Emerging Science of Sex Differences" (2006) Leonard Sax maintained that *six degrees of separation* between the sexes in ambient temperature produces dramatic effects, leading him to suggest more attention to same-sex schooling.

In regard to understanding gender and its multivariate influences, Money's work let the genie out of the bottle. Haig stated, "Although Money explicitly adopted an interactionist position ... his work was implicitly read as lying at the nurture-end of the spectrum" (Haig 2004, p. 93). Although biologists, psychologists, and social scientists all *know* that the formation and expression of gender point toward the inadequacy of the term *multivariate*, they often yield to the temptation to bolster their viewpoint, discipline, or prejudice by blurring the boundaries of nature and nuture.

Societies have been rigid in their maintenance of *appropriateness* in regard to issues of sex and gender. For some—the transgendered/transsexuals—this has produced a conundrum that can be resolved only by what many consider mutilating solutions. Others—intersexuals—often have had to have Solomon-like decisions made for them concerning what has been felt to be corrective surgery. Others, whose sexual preferences come into conflict with an unaccepting world, seek legal solutions to establish their rights. At times the battle seems endless between visions that coalesce into opposing factions: the tyranny of the dichotomous versus the anarchy of the androgynous.

BIBLIOGRAPHY

Bleie, Tone. 2003. "Evolution, Brains and the Predicament of Sex in Human Cognition." *Sexualities, Evolution and Gender* 5(3): 149–189.

Fausto-Sterling, Anne. 2000. "The Five Sexes, Revisited." *Sciences* 40(4): 18.

Haig, David. 2000. "Of Sex and Gender." *Nature Genetics* 25: 373. Available from http://www.nature.com/.

Haig, D. 2004. "The Inexorable Rise of Gender and the Decline of Sex: Social Change in Academic Titles, 1945–2001." *Archives of Sexual Behavior* 33: 87–96.

Halpern, D. F. 2004. "A Cognitive-Process Taxonomy for Sex Differences in Cognitive Abilities." *Current Directions in Psychological Science* 13(4): 135–139.

Holstege, Gert; A. A. T. Reinders; A. M. J. Paans; L. C. Meiners; J. Pruim; and J.R. Georgiadis. 2003. "Brain Activation during Female Sexual Orgasm." Program No. 727.7. Abstract Viewer/Itinerary Planner. Washington, DC: Society for Neuroscience. Available from http://sfn.scholarone.com.

Hyde, Janet Shibley. 2005. "The Gender Similarities Hypothesis." *American Psychologist* 60(6): 581–592.

Kessler, Suzanne J. 1998. *Lessons from the Intersexed.* New Brunswick, NJ: Rutgers University Press.

Money, John. 1955. "Hermaphroditism, Gender and Precocity in Hyperadrenocorticism: Psychologic Findings." *Bulletin of the Johns Hopkins Hospital* 96: 253–264.

Sax, Leonard. 2006. "Six Degrees of Separation: What Teachers Need to Know about the Emerging Science of Sex Differences." *Educational Horizons* 84: 190–220.

Schuiling, G. A. 2002. "Sex, Gender and Reproduction." *Journal of Psychosomatic Obstetrics and Gynecology* 23: 83–88.

Benjamin Graber

BRANTÔME
1540–1614

The son of a nobleman from Perigord, Brantôme spent his youth at the royal court. Educated first at the College of France in Paris and later at the University of Poitiers, he resumed life at the court sometime around 1556. The next year he was granted the Abbey of Brantôme and assumed the title of abbot despite his interest in pursuing a military career. A riding accident in 1584, coupled with a break with Henry III in 1582, isolated him from the court but left him the time to begin writing his memoirs of the Valois kings.

Brantôme's reputation as a memoirist rests primarily on three works: the *Vies des grands capitaines* [Lives of great captains] and two volumes treating women, *Les dames illustres* [Lives of illustrious ladies] and *Les dames galantes* [Lives of gallant ladies]. The *Grands capitaines* focus primarily on an idealized version of the courts of Francis I and Henry II, and the *Dames illustres* paints a similar portrait of the women at those courts. The *Dames galantes,* a blend of gossip, rumors, and well-known stories, depicts an erotic counterpoint of the court, often reporting on the same figures. The manuscript versions left by Brantôme were published posthumously in 1665–1666.

Brantôme's *Dames galantes* can be viewed as an encyclopedia of scandal. The focus of the text is *galanterie,* the amorous and sexual adventures of the members of the French court. In essence Brantôme equates sex and court life. Although it is clear that the veracity of much of his account cannot be verified, he raises questions about and offers models for gender relations and sexuality in mid-sixteenth-century France.

Divided into "discourses," each with multiple anecdotes, the *Dames galantes* treats a wide range of themes. The first discourse, titled "On Women Who Make Love and Cuckold Their Husbands," examines extramarital relations. The discussion includes a lengthy subsection on female homoerotic relations. Brantôme combines references to classical antiquity, such as Martial and Lucian, with gossip about women at the French and other courts as well as examples from exotic countries such as Turkey.

Brantôme specifically refers to Sappho, and in that section the first concrete use of the term *lesbian* to designate women who engage in same-sex relations appears. There is a notable tension in Brantôme's attitudes toward those "lesbians." On the one hand the significance of such relationships is downplayed somewhat; indeed, Brantôme emphasizes their utility as preludes to heterosexual sexual relationships while maintaining a woman's chastity. On the other hand he mentions some women who maintain long-term relationships. The sexual ambiguity of such women proves more troubling. A marked anxiety in his discussion of women who use prosthetic devices in sex acts is played out in his cautions about the risk of debilitating illness or even death for those women. Nonetheless, Brantôme concludes that erotic relations between women do not constitute cuckoldry, reinforcing a gender system aligned with biological sex. The only true sexual relations are heterosexual ones.

The discourses range from topics such as "On Married Women, Widows and Girls, as to Which Are Warmer in Love Than the Others" to "On One Must Never Speak Ill of Woman and the Consequences of So-Doing." Despite Brantôme's apparent affection for women and the request "Ladies ... excuse me if I have offended you," his overarching position in the *Dames galantes* reinforces gender stereotypes.

BIBLIOGRAPHY

Brantôme. 1933. *Lives of Fair & Gallant Ladies*. New York: Liveright.

Brantôme. 1955. *Les dames galantes*, intro. Maurice Rat. Paris: Editions Garnier Freres.

Brantôme. 1991. *Recueil des dames, poésies et tombeaux*, ed. Etienne Vaucheret. Paris: Gallimard.

Coats, Catharine Randall. 1993. "Drink Deep from the Text: Wooing and Warning the Reader in Brantome's 'Dames galantes' and 'Dames illustres.'" *Modern Language Studies* 23(2): 84–91.

Cottrell, Robert D. 1970. *Brantôme: The Writer as Portraitist of His Age*. Geneva: Librairie Droz.

Daumas, Maurice.1998. *Le système amoureux de Brantôme*. Paris: L'Harmattan.

Lazard, Madeleine. 1995. *Pierre de Bourdeille, seigneur de Brantôme*. Paris: Fayard.

Holly E. Ransom

BUDDHISM

Buddhism began in what is now northern India with the life of its founder, Siddhārtha Gautama of the Śākya tribe (c. 563–483 BCE), simply referred to as the Buddha (a title meaning "the enlightened one"). Traditional accounts say he was born the son of a king. At the time of his birth a holy man predicted that he would either rule the world or renounce it. In order to ensure his glorious future as a great king, the Buddha's father brought him up in luxury and prevented him from seeing anything unpleasant. When he was about twenty-nine years old, however, the Buddha traveled outside the palace grounds and was radically changed by four visions created by the gods: He saw a sick man, an old man, a dead man, and a wandering male ascetic, four aspects of human experience that his father had prevented him from seeing. The ascetic represented the solution of the existential problem of suffering posed by the first three visions. He would become an ascetic and seek a way to liberate himself from the repetitive cycle of birth, death, and rebirth that is inevitably attended by sickness and aging. He abandoned worldly life and sought enlightenment, a profound shift of consciousness that frees one from the worldly desires that lead to continual reincarnations. This story is told in all the major biographies of the Buddha along with the other main events of his life: his miraculous conception and birth, life in his father's palace, his years of ascetic practices, and, after great effort, his enlightenment. A pivotal event is the Buddha's departure from home, when he abandons not only his wife but also the many women of his harem. This is a popular textual and iconographic scene that represents women both as sexual temptresses and as physically disgusting when the Buddha sees them asleep, lying in awkward positions, drooling and snoring.

For six years after leaving home the Buddha practiced such severe forms of asceticism that he was near death. His dead mother, Queen Māyā, descended from heaven to remind him of his spiritual destiny, and at her prompting the Buddha decided on a more moderate path, the "middle path," between the severe asceticism he had been practicing and the worldly life of pleasure he had led as a prince. To this end, he accepted the food offered to him by a young village woman named Sujātā. His five male followers, who later became the first monks, doubted that he would now achieve enlightenment, and abandoned him to food and females. Left alone, the Buddha continued his process of reconciliation with females from all realms of existence—human (living and dead), divine, and animal; not only was he refreshed and strengthened by this process, he also reintegrated positive experiences of women and female forces and reversed his earlier rejection of them. Then, and only then, was he ready to move toward the Bodhi tree under which he battled the demon Māra, a battle that turned in his favor only when he met Māra's challenge to find a witness for his merit by calling on the Earth herself, which he did by extending his right hand downward. Iconographically this is one of the most popular Buddha images, called the *bhūmisparśa*, the earth-touching pose. This is the main icon of the Buddha's supreme achievement, enlightenment, and by the gesture of his right hand it signals the necessary female component of that achievement. Historically, however, the Buddhist community has only intermittently lived up to the equalitarian possibilities of this vision.

EARLY BUDDHISM

Most information about the early Buddhist community comes from canonical sources, for instance, the Pali Canon, a multivolume collection of sermons, rules, folklore, philosophical discourses, and poems. The Pali Canon was compiled and edited by Theravāda monks in Sri Lanka (formerly Ceylon) beginning around the first century BCE from much earlier oral sources, although additional material continued to be added until at least the fifth century CE. A significant part of this literature is the shared canon of all Buddhists, although compilers of the Mahāyāna and Tantric canons made additions. In general, at least two basic points need to be made about this literature. First, comparisons of the same events described in different canons show gendered disjunctions that are suggestive of conflicting views about women. For example, in the Pali canon women are absent from the Buddha's funeral, whereas in the *Mūlasarvāstivādin Vinaya* (completed about the third century CE) women held the processional canopy over the Buddha's bier, which was carried by the men. Second, as with most of the world's religious texts, the Buddhist canons have been compiled and written by men and have a misogynist edge. Thus, the existence of any information at all on early Buddhist women is strong evidence for the persistence of a powerful female presence and suggests that much more material has been lost. In spite of the foregoing, the canons reveal what Buddhists have believed about women for centuries and provide authority both for women seeking to reform sexist tendencies in Buddhism and those who oppose such reforms. The information provided by these texts gets slippery, however, as they move with an easy fluidity between myth and real life, blurring any distinction between the two, and therefore they must be grounded in the archaeological, epigraphic, and iconographic evidence that documents women's participation, especially as donors (Findly 2003, Schopen 1997).

After his enlightenment the Buddha established a religious community that practiced his ideas, and he continued to preach and shape this community until his death at age eighty, forty-five years later. Its center was composed of the nuns and monks who renounced worldly life. hey were celibate, ate only one meal per day, begged for their food from the laity, and spent most of the year wandering from place to place in order not to become attached to one spot. This path is a model for a moderate life that emphasizes meditation as a way to change one's conscious perception of the world in order to reach enlightenment in this life. Included in this community were the lay supporters who gained merit by giving to the monastics, which helped the former to be reborn in a position deemed more favorable to spiritual progress. The lay supporters adopted five precepts: no taking of any life (animal or human), no stealing, no illicit sex, no lying, and no intoxicating substances. In the early twenty-first century, the Buddhist community retains this general outline with the exception that monasteries were later established as permanent communities and the goal of enlightenment was eventually seen as less attainable in one lifetime. Of interest with regard to stationary versus wandering nuns and monks is a third group, solitary forest-dwellers. Among Buddhists there was and remains an enduring conflict between the ideal of the solitary forest monastic, who may attract a few disciples, and that of monastics settled in monasteries in or near towns who offer time-consuming services to the laity such as being educators and performing rituals. It is widely believed that certain charismatic forest-dwellers achieve greater states of wisdom and power than their city-dwelling brethren. Traditionally, the forest has been a place of greater religious freedom, whereas large monasteries tend to routinize practice and absorb the energies of its members in the numerous activities involved in running a large institution. Significantly, the spiritual abilities of women were more accepted among forest-dwelling renunciants than among those settled in monasteries (Ray 1994).

The Buddha's first female disciple was his stepmother and aunt (his mother's sister), Mahāprajāpatī. She is an important figure in early Buddhism because she became the first Buddhist nun and maintained a lifelong relationship with the Buddha. Although the textual record of her ordination is highly problematic, many scholars accept as historical fact the story that the Buddha was initially reluctant to ordain her and that he created eight additional rules for nuns. Actually this story is quite possibly a later interpolation and/or just a dramatic device (Sponberg 1992, Walters 1994, Young 1994). It is descriptive of existing conditions, the subordination of the nuns to the monks, rather than a prescription by the Buddha that this is the way it should be. Of note, however, is the propagation of this story as fact throughout the Buddhist world and the eventual decline of the nuns' ordination lineage. This whole scenario is perhaps best viewed in light of the routinization of charisma whereby followers eventually retract the innovations of charismatic leaders—in the case of the Buddha, the prominent role of women. Additionally, the legend of the first ordination of women needs to be understood within the context of contemporaneous activities of other ascetic women, such as the Jain order of nuns and their rather different history (Young 2004). Significantly, through this first ordination the Buddha affirmed women's ability to achieve enlightenment, and Mahāprajāpatī's own biography is a testament to that ability (Walters 1994) as are the nuns' poems in the *Therīgāthā*. The main goal is enlightenment, and here women are equal to men, though this was and remains a highly contested issue (Young 2004).

The Buddha's wife, or wives (depending on the tradition), also deserves careful attention, not necessarily for what may have been her actual relationship to the Buddha, but for what various traditions have done with her as a symbol of womanhood (Shaw 1994, Strong 1997, Young 2004, Zelliot 1992). She is also a particularly intriguing figure in the *jātakas*, the past life stories of the Buddha, most of which he shared with her.

Buddhist Monks. *A group of young Buddhist monks standing in line after a flower offering.* AP IMAGES.

In early Buddhism the maleness of the Buddha took on an exaggerated importance that culminated in enduring debates as to whether women are capable of achieving enlightenment or if they must first reincarnate as men. Such a view is not limited to Buddhists; it was part of a pan-Indian view in which male superiority most often looked to female inferiority for validation. In fact, it is all too familiar in the religions of the world as well as in other cultural constructs. Buddha's maleness, which belonged to his historical identity, was misinterpreted as essential to his salvational role. Thus, existing male social privileges were confirmed, in part because male privileges went beyond what was socially permissible for women, and in part because the greater physical accuracy of men's resemblance to the Buddha led to an identification with the Buddha that was physically impossible for women.

Yet the Buddha's life is a redefinition of masculinity, one that introduces new masculine values and reinterprets some old ones, such as the heroic masculine ideals of his early life that were based on his royal status. He chose instead to build on the Indian ideal of the virile ascetic whose sexual abstinence is the source of his power. Indian stories abound with examples of ascetics who by withholding their semen gained tremendous power and even threatened the gods. Though there were stories about female ascetics, and even though many of the early Buddhist nuns are said to have achieved enlightenment, the belief arose that men alone are capable of fully representing and/or achieving what the Buddha did. The power to expound and enact this ideology resided within a male, monastic hierarchy that questioned women's access to ordination, gave official voice and visibility primarily to men, controlled the texts of the tradition, and finally, so completely marginalized women's monastic participation that the ordination of nuns completely ceased throughout South and Southeast Asia.

In early-twenty-first-century Sri Lanka and Southeast Asia there are communities of Buddhist women referred to as eight- or ten-precept nuns. These are women who take the precepts of an ordained monk without an ordination ceremony. They dress all in white, as opposed to the yellow/orange robes of the monks, and most often act as servants to the monks, though some choose to live independently and pursue good works and meditation (Bartholomeusz 1994). The ordination ceremony for nuns did survive in East Asia, where there are flourishing communities of fully ordained nuns.

TYPES OF BUDDHISM

Innovations in doctrine occurred slowly over the centuries, with various schools distinguishing themselves, most of which eventually disappeared. This early period of Buddhism is best described as Nikāya or Sectarian Buddhism. By around the first century BCE two distinct schools of Buddhism had been established. The first is Theravāda, the only surviving school of the early period, which spread south from northern India into Sri Lanka and eventually east to Burma, Thailand, Cambodia, and Laos. Its ideal type is the arhat, a nun or monk who has achieved enlightenment. The other school is Mahāyāna, which grew out of various sectarian groups, taking shape as a separate school of Buddhism in northern India around the first century BCE; it is the form of Buddhism that spread north to Tibet and east to China, Korea, and Japan. This school understands itself to contain the esoteric doctrine of the Buddha—his nonpublic teachings—and its religious ideal is the bodhisattva, an enlightened being of infinite compassion who postpones final personal enlightenment in order to continue to reincarnate and help all other beings to achieve enlightenment. Bodhisattvas can be human or divine, female or male, thus leaving the path of spiritual accomplishment open to women, though they often met with the usual difficulties of sexist societies and religious hierarchies.

Human bodhisattvas strive to perfect themselves through giving, developing patience, making an effort in whatever they do, practicing meditation, and developing their wisdom. Celestial bodhisattvas are divine beings who can be supplicated by human beings. One of the best known and most complex is Avalokiteśvara, the great protector from all manner of physical danger. In the process of *his* dissemination throughout Asia he was transformed into a female deity known as Kuan Yin in China and Kannon in Japan, and was referred to as the Goddess of Mercy. In Tibet he remained male but is associated with Tārā, a female celestial bodhisattava well known for her compassion and her ability to protect those who appeal to her.

Mahāyāna emphasizes contemplation, visualization, and, most importantly, recitations of the name of particular *male* celestial buddhas such as Amitābha. This had great appeal to a laity who, for various reasons, could not or would not become monks or nuns. Celestial buddhas are believed to have achieved enlightenment many eons ago, long before the time of Gautama Buddha. They, too, were originally human bodhisattvas who, when they made their vow to become a buddha, described the Pure Land they would create. A Pure Land is a celestial realm that has been purified by the presence and teachings of a buddha, in contrast to impure lands that lack a buddha and his teachings.

The Pure Land of Amitābha Buddha, called Sukhāvatī, is the Pure Land encountered most often in literature and art. It is depicted as a sweet-smelling and beautiful garden with lotus ponds and trees made of precious jewels, where all the needs of its inhabitants are satisfied. Rebirth here can be achieved by a combination of good deeds and repeating, in some cases just hearing, the name of Amitābha Buddha. Rebirth in this paradise is one's final incarnation, as it is inevitable that buddhahood will be achieved here, but only males are born in Sukhāvatī. Reincarnating beings gestate and are born from lotuses, thereby circumventing the need for wombs. Pure Land Buddhism became an extremely popular and widespread form of worship throughout Asia.

VAJRAYĀNA BUDDHISM

A third school of Buddhism, variously called Esoteric Buddhism, Vajrayāna, and/or Tantra began sometime around the fourth century CE. This movement had its roots in the popular religions of northern India that contained many magical and shamanistic features as well as in the worship of goddesses such as Tārā and Vajrayoginī and spread throughout the Buddhist world. It stresses enlightenment in one lifetime in contradistinction to the idea of gradual enlightenment over several lifetimes, which had developed in some sects of Mahāyāna and Theravāda, and it emphasizes individual visionary experiences. Its ideal type is the *siddha*, who could be women or men, but most often the tradition is described from the male point of view.

Eventually, Tantra was institutionalized into mainstream Buddhist practice, though the more unruly *siddha* tradition continued to flourish among individual wandering yogis. Tantric practices involve ritually ingesting forbidden substances, such as wine and meat, and engaging in sexual intercourse. Generally, Tantric monks maintained their vows of celibacy by resorting to visualization in Tantric rituals, although many famous, nonmonastic Buddhist saints did the actual practice.

Tantra spread throughout South, Southeast, Central, and East Asia and survives in the early twenty-first century among Buddhists in the Himalayan countries of Tibet, Nepal, and Bhutan; in Japan in the Shingon and Tendai schools of Buddhism; and among exiled Tibetans everywhere. Not all Vajrayāna Buddhists participate in its esoteric rituals. Laypeople and many monks and nuns are content with less complicated practices such as circumambulating sacred structures, going on pilgrimage, chanting, and performing meritorious acts.

Women, both lay and monastic, were instrumental in spreading all three schools of Buddhism as missionaries (Bode 1893, Findly 2003), teachers, practitioners, and donors. Because of the historical importance of royal support in the spread and maintenance of Buddhism, the contributions of royal women were tremendously important. Most of this support, however, was directed toward monks, not nuns. This hinges on the concept of merit (Skt.: *puṇya;* Pali: *panna*), the idea that donations whether monetary or through actions and prayers create merit that will lead to better future lives in Buddhist heavens or other circumstances that will be conducive to achieving enlightenment. In practice merit is usually dedicated to the good of all sentient beings or to the donor's parents, but the donor also receives spiritual benefits. At issue is the belief that monks make a better, more productive, field of merit than nuns, from which inevitably followed, and continues to follow, the wealth of male establishments and the poverty of nuns. Despite such views about the qualities of actual women, important Buddhist values were often conceived in feminine terms such as compassion (*karuṇā*) and wisdom (*prajñā*).

MODERN BUDDHISM IN ASIA

Buddhism was very successful in adapting itself to many diverse cultures, in part because rather than opposing indigenous religious practices, it incorporated them. Modern Buddhism in Asia begins around the sixteenth century with the shock of European colonialism and the consequent rise of nationalism. In Cambodia and Laos the Communist takeovers of the governments were disastrous for Buddhism, especially in Cambodia where tens of thousands of monks were executed and innumerable monasteries destroyed. In the early twenty-first century, Buddhism is slowly recovering in these countries.

In China the rise of the Communist regime in 1949 led to the confiscation of Buddhist properties and forced many nuns and monks to return to lay life. When, in 1950, the Chinese took over Tibet, monks and nuns were imprisoned, tortured, and humiliated for years. In early-twenty-first-century Tibet many of the monasteries have been rebuilt, though some are more like tourist shops than monasteries. The Chinese authorities carefully monitor the monasteries and nunneries, which they continue to view with suspicion because nuns and monks are still active in seeking Tibetan independence. In India there are approximately 100,000 Tibetan refugees, who have rebuilt their monastic institutions there and have established a government-in-exile under the Dalai Lama.

In 1868 the Japanese emperor was restored to power, and this government was initially quite hostile to Buddhism. It took over a great deal of Buddhist property and changed the face of Japanese Buddhism in two important ways. First, it issued a decree that all Buddhist monks should be allowed to marry, with the end result that there are few celibate monks, although nuns have maintained their vows of celibacy. The second change developed in relation to the government's expansionistic and militaristic policy. A new generation of Buddhist scholars redefined Buddhism in relation to Japanese nationalism and Western rationalism and science.

When Japan annexed Korea in 1910 as part of its program of military expansion it changed Korean Buddhism in order to have Japanese Zen be dominant. They also wanted Buddhist monks to renounce their vows of celibacy and to marry. This led some Korean monks to oppose the Japanese, but many did get married. The legacy of this is a divided Buddhist monastic community. After the Japanese left in 1945 those monks who remained celibate demanded that the monks who had married be thrown out of their monasteries and out of the order. Subsequently, the married priests formed their own order.

In the early twenty-first century, Asian Buddhists are deeply involved with social and political issues along with meditation practices and the search for enlightenment. Monks and nuns were involved in opposing the Vietnam War, and in Thailand, Myanmar, Sri Lanka, and Vietnam they are actively participating in social welfare and education programs. Additionally, throughout South and Southeast Asia nuns are striving to raise their status as monastics.

Throughout Asia there is a remarkable acceptance of Western converts, who are welcomed at pilgrimage sites and accepted as disciples. For approximately 2,500 years Buddhism has been a religion that seeks converts of any race or faith. Its enduring success can be seen in the West today, where Buddhist centers have been established by Asian immigrants and by Western converts. Gender can be a hot topic among Western converts who are not comfortable with traditional Asian views of women's place, though some female converts feel feminism conflicts with their spiritual goals (Klein 1995). Other Westerners have embraced what is termed Engaged Buddhism—active involvement with the political and social needs of the larger community such as advocating for world peace and assisting the disadvantaged. Buddhism in the West is a complex of 2,500 years of practices and beliefs as preserved and modified by many different Asian cultures.

BIBLIOGRAPHY

Bartholomeusz, Tessa J. 1994. *Women under the Bō Tree: Buddhist Nuns in Sri Lanka*. Cambridge, UK: Cambridge University Press.

Bode, Mabel. 1893. "Women Leaders of the Buddhist Reformation." *Journal of the Royal Asiatic Society*: 517–566, 763–798.

Cole, Alan. 1998. *Mothers and Sons in Chinese Buddhism*. Stanford, CA: Stanford University Press.

Davidson, Ronald M. 2002. *Indian Esoteric Buddhism: A Social History of the Tantric Movement.* New York: Columbia University Press.

Falk, Nancy Auer. 1980. "The Case of the Vanishing Nuns: The Fruits of Ambivalence in Ancient Indian Buddhism." In *Unspoken Worlds: Women's Religious Lives in Non-Western Cultures*, ed. Nancy Auer Falk and Rita M. Gross. San Francisco: Harper and Row.

Faure, Bernard. 1998. *The Red Thread: Buddhist Approaches to Sexuality.* Princeton, NJ: Princeton University Press.

Findly, Ellison Banks. 2003. *Dana: Giving and Getting in Pali Buddhism.* Delhi: Motilal Banarsidass.

Gutschow, Kim. 2004. *Being a Buddhist Nun: The Struggle for Enlightenment in the Himalayas.* Cambridge, MA: Harvard University Press.

Horner, I. B., trans. 1938–1966. *The Book of the Discipline.* 6 vols. London: Oxford University Press.

Klein, Anne Carolyn. 1995. *Meeting the Great Bliss Queen: Buddhists, Feminists, and the Art of the Self.* Boston: Beacon Press.

Norman, A. K., trans. 1971. *The Elders' Verses.* 2 vols. London: published for the Pali Text Society by Luzac & Co.

Pao-Chang, Shih, comp. 1994. *Lives of the Nuns: Biographies of Chinese Buddhist Nuns from the Fourth to Sixth Centuries*, trans. Katherine Ann Tsai. Honolulu: University of Hawaii Press.

Paul, Diana Y. 1985. *Women in Buddhism: Images of the Feminine in the Mahāyāna Tradition.* 2nd edition. Berkeley: University of California Press.

Ray, Reginald A. 1994. *Buddhist Saints in India: A Study in Buddhist Values and Orientations.* New York: Oxford University Press.

Schopen, Gregory. 1997. *Bones, Stones, and Buddhist Monks: Collected papers on the Archaeology, Epigraphy, and Texts of Monastic Buddhism in India.* Honolulu: University of Hawai'i Press.

Shaw, Miranda. 1994. *Passionate Enlightenment: Women in Tantric Buddhism.* Princeton, NJ: Princeton University Press.

Sponberg, Alan. 1992. "Attitudes toward Women and the Feminine in Early Buddhism." In *Buddhism, Sexuality, and Gender*, ed. José Ignacio Cabezón. Albany: State University of New York Press.

Strong, John S. 1997. "A Family Quest: The Buddha, Yaśodharā, and Rāhula in the *Mòlasarāstivāda Vinaya.*" In *Sacred Biography in the Buddhist Traditions of South and Southeast Asia*, ed. Juliane Schober. Honolulu: University of Hawai'i Press.

Tsomo, Karma Lekshe, ed. 1988. *Sakyadhītā: Daughters of the Buddha.* Ithaca, NY: Snow Lion Publications.

Walters, Jonathan S. 1994. "A Voice from the Silence: The Buddha's Mother's Story." *History of Religions* 33(4): 358–379.

Young, Serinity. 1994. "Gendered Politics in Ancient Indian Asceticism." *Union Seminary Quarterly Review* 48(3–4): 73–92.

Young, Serinity. 2004. *Courtesans and Tantric Consorts: Sexualities in Buddhist Narrative, Iconography, and Ritual.* New York: Routledge.

Zelliot, Eleanor. 1992. "Buddhist Women of the Contemporary Maharashtrian Conversion Movement." In *Buddhism, Sexuality, and Gender*, ed. José Ignacio Cabezón. Albany: State University of New York Press.

Serinity Young

BUGGER, BUGGERY

For centuries the colloquial terms *bugger* and *buggery* have referred to homosexuals and homosexual activity, particularly anal intercourse. The term appears to have entered Western European usage in the twelfth and thirteenth centuries, in connection with various dualist heresies that had started in Bulgaria. Thus bugger, or the Old French *bougre*, may have evolved from Bulgar or, alternatively, from Bogomil, a heresy that developed in Bulgaria in the early tenth century. The Bogomils were dualists who believed that God had two offspring: Satan and Christ. Their beliefs can be linked back to the Manichean sects of late antiquity. By the mid-twelfth century, there were multiple heretical sects, similar to the dualist Bogomils, in Latin Europe, including the Albigensians and the Cathars. Christians, especially the leaders of the Roman Catholic Church, related these heresies to sexual improprieties, especially sodomy. As early as the mid-eleventh century, in the *Liber Gomorrhianus* (*Book of Gomorrah*), Peter Damian had linked homosexual acts with heresy and the work of the devil. This conjunction ultimately extended to witchcraft and became increasingly prevalent throughout the Middle Ages and into the sixteenth and seventeenth centuries.

The connection between heresy and sex resulted in homosexual acts, especially anal penetration, being characterized as buggery. Church leaders, in particular, tried to slander the ascetic practices of heretical leaders. The Cathar *perfecti*, who were reputed to abstain from meat and marriage, were accused of practicing sodomy within their group, even though they abstained from sex with women. Thus the heretics, the *bougres*, were also sodomites. Variations of the words buggery and bugger, indicating anal intercourse and those who practice it, occur in romance languages, for example, *buggerone* in Italian and *bugarón* in Spanish. The Germanic languages contain the same conceptual relationships, for example, the German term for heretic, *Ketzer*, can also refer to sodomites.

Much of the rhetoric that linked heresy and sodomy was formal and formulaic. There is very little evidence to support the conclusion that heretics practiced sodomy or that men prosecuted for sodomy also held heretical beliefs. One example, however, is found in the inquisitorial registers of Bishop Jacques Fournier. In the 1320s, Fournier investigated the survival of Catharism in the area around Montaillou in southern France. One of the accused, Arnold of Verniolle, revealed that he had engaged in multiple sexual relationships with young men and boys. Arnold, however, carefully described acts of interfemoral rubbing and masturbation as opposed to anal penetration. Perhaps this explains why he was sentenced to life in prison rather than executed.

SEE ALSO *Homosexuality, Defined.*

BIBLIOGRAPHY

Boswell, John. 1980. *Christianity, Social Tolerance, and Homosexuality: Gay People in Western Europe from the Beginning of the Christian Era to the Fourteenth Century.* Chicago: University of Chicago Press.

Goodich, Michael. 1979. *The Unmentionable Vice: Homosexuality in the Later Medieval Period.* Santa Barbara, CA: ABC-Clio.

Puff, Helmut. 2003. *Sodomy in Reformation Germany and Switzerland 1400–1600.* Chicago: University of Chicago Press.

Rocke, Michael. 1996. *Forbidden Friendships. Homosexuality and Male Culture in Renaissance Florence.* New York: Oxford University Press.

Jacqueline Murray

BULIMIA

SEE *Eating Disorders.*

BULLDAGGER

Bulldagger is pejorative slang for a very masculine lesbian, which often carries a more racialized meaning than its synonyms *bulldyke*, *bulldiker*, and *diesel dyke*. Bulldaggers are associated with physical strength, sexual prowess, emotional reserve, and butch chivalry. The term has roots in African-American communities of the early twentieth century, especially with 1920s Harlem where sexual and gender mores were more flexible. As a queer butch gender, bulldagger is distinguished from lesbian androgyny or femme and, in lesbian-feminist reclamation of the term, helps to enrich what has been a white-washed lesbian history beginning with the figure of Sappho (c. 625–570 BCE) (Bogus 1994).

As Eric Garber argues in "A Spectacle in Color: The Lesbian and Gay Subculture of Jazz Age Harlem," American 1920s blues culture "accepted sexuality, including homosexual behavior and identities, as a natural part of life"(1989, p. 320). Songs such as "Sissy Man Blues" and "B.D. [bulldike or bulldagger] Women Blues" dealt explicitly with the gender-bending types who populated this world. Harlem's most famous bulldagger, openly gay jazz singer Gladys Bentley, performed in tuxedos, dated glamorous women, and infused jazz standards with her own lesbian sizzle.

Despite tolerant recognition in 1920s Harlem, bulldagger became an increasingly homophobic and racist expression used to disparage empowered, butch, or openly lesbian African-American women. Thus, the bulldagger exists as a symbol of strength and ridicule in the black lesbian tradition. Scholar, poet, and essayist SDiane A. Bogus explains, "The Black Bulldagger is a link to our ancient and recent Black woman-loving past, and the predecessor of today's Black lesbian. She is a character, an idea, a woman who loved women but was heavily male-identified more often than not. She was the unattractive girl, the tomboyish teen, the independent woman, or any Black sister who repulsed the advances of men" (1994, pp. 30–32). In this sense, the bulldagger of the African-American cultural imagination exposes the intersectionality (the overlap of race, class, sexuality, and gender) inherent in the category of lesbian and offers a past and precedent for lesbians of color. Chicana cultural theorist Gloria Anzaldúa's mythic "La historia de una marimacha" (1993), which was translated into English as "A Bulldagger's Tale," attests to a comparable overlap of racialized butchness and lesbianism in a Latina context.

The linguistic origins of bulldagger, as with the lesbian monikers dyke and the earlier bulldike, are uncertain. Linguist Susan A. Krantz (1995) has theorized that bulldike (with dike a variant of dick, and 1920s American slang bull for *untruthful talk*) could be equated with *false penis*, a meaning that extends to bulldagger, given the dagger's analogous relation to the male sexual organ. From a more lesbian–feminist perspective, writer and poet Judy Grahn (1984) connects the words bulldike and bulldagger with Queen Boadicea (later, Grahn claims, pronounced "Boo-uh-dike-ay"), who led a successful Celtic uprising against Roman colonizers in 61 CE and was a priestess associated with bull sacrifices.

Audre Lorde's *Zami, A New Spelling of My Name* (1982) and Leslie Feinberg's *Stone Butch Blues* (1993) are autobiographies that grapple with the term bulldagger in race- and class-conscious historical contexts.

SEE ALSO *Butch/Femme; Dyke; Lesbian, Contemporary: I. Overview.*

BIBLIOGRAPHY

Anzaldúa, Gloria. 1993. "La historia de una marimacha" [A bulldagger's tale]. In *The Sexuality of Latinas*, ed. Norma Alarcón, Ana Castillo, and Cherríe Moraga. Berkeley, CA: Third Woman Press.

Bogus, SDiane A. 1994. "The Myth and Tradition of the Black Bulldagger." In *Dagger: On Butch Women*, eds. Lily Burana, Roxxie, and Linnea Due. Pittsburgh, PA: Cleis Press.

Garber, Eric. 1989. "A Spectacle in Color: The Lesbian and Gay Subculture of Jazz Age Harlem." In *Hidden from History: Reclaiming the Gay and Lesbian Past*, ed. Martin Bauml Duberman, Martha Vicinus, and George Chauncey Jr. New York: New American Library.

Grahn, Judy. 1984. "Butches, Bulldags, and the Queen of Bulldikery." In *Another Mother Tongue: Gay Words, Gay Worlds*. Boston: Beacon Press.

Krantz, Susan E. 1995. "Reconsidering the Etymology of Bulldike." *American Speech* 70(2): 217–221.

Omosupe, Ekua. 1991. "Black/Lesbian/Bulldagger." *Differences: A Journal of Feminist Cultural Studies* 3(2): 101–111.

Emma Crandall

BUNDLING

Bundling (or "tarrying") comprises a number of socially condoned courtship practices primarily documented among northern and northeastern European Christian communities as well as among homogeneous, non-urban Christian communities in the United States. The practice is documentable from the late Middle Ages until its dwindling in the nineteenth century, with some anecdotal evidence of its continued existence into the early twentieth century. The practices of bundling revolve around a young, unmarried man sleeping, fully clothed, in the same bed as a young, unmarried woman. These non-urban communities are usually small in scale and primarily practice agriculture. Communities practicing bundling were close-knit, in that the young men and woman knew each other, as did their respective families.

Details of this practice vary from whether the woman wore clothes or a night dress, was sewn into a sack (bundling sack), lay under the covers and the male above the covers, both lay under the covers or both were on top, whether there was a board placed between them (bundling board), whether the couple was sleeping in the same room or same building as the guardians or in a separate building, whether there was a candle in a particular window, and whether the door or the window must be rapped upon in a particular way. The young man and woman were not normally joined by other young men and women. This practice contrasts with the practice of inviting all the young people of the community to a festival which included sleeping in the same barn or outbuilding.

Bundling was performed with the full knowledge and assent of families and the community. Many reasons are given for this practice: finding compatible marriage partners, permitting courtship while not wasting firewood and candles, and communal recognition of sex without penetration among the young in courting. Another reason given in the United States is that distances between homesteads on the frontier required a young man to spend the night when courting a woman.

BIBLIOGRAPHY

Aurand, A. Monroe, Jr. 1941. *Little Known Facts about Bundling in the New World*. Harrisburg, PA: Author.

Fischer-Yinon, Yochi. 2002. "The Original Bundlers: Boaz and Ruth, and Seventeenth-Century English Courtship Practices." *Journal of Social History* 35 (3): 683–705.

Hoffman, W. J. 1888. "Folk-Lore of the Pennsylvania Germans, Part I." *The Journal of American Folklore* 1(2): 125–135.

Gjerde, Jon. 1985. *From Peasants to Farmers: The Migration from Balestrand, Norway, to the Upper Middle West*. Cambridge: Cambridge University Press.

Leeuwen, Marco H.D. van. 2002. "Partner Choice and Homogamy in the Nineteenth Century: Was There a Sexual Revolution in Europe?" *Journal of Social History* 36 (1): 101–123.

Carol E.B. Choksy

BURCHARD OF WORMS

965–1025

Burchard of Worms, born to a wealthy Hessian family, was bishop of the diocese of Worms (south of Frankfurt) from 1000 until his death. He is mainly remembered for his *Decretum*, an encyclopedic collection of Church canons or regulations, which he and his assistants completed by 1023.

For most of the Middle Ages the regulation of marriage and all other forms of sexual behavior fell predominantly to the Church. As the most comprehensive and systematic compilation of Church canons up to that time, Burchard's *Decretum* constitutes a valuable, authoritative resource for attitudes toward sexuality in the early Middle Ages (that is, the period from the sixth century to the eleventh). Textual evidence suggests that Burchard's work continued to be consulted until the end of the Middle Ages. Two sixteenth-century print versions remain extant, and Book 19, a self-contained penitential manual known as the *Corrector*, served as a source for the *Milan Penitential*, compiled after the Council of Trent (1545–1563) by one of the leading architects of the Counter-Reformation, Cardinal Saint Charles Borromeo (1538–1584). Thus Burchard's *Decretum* also provides important evidence for continuities between early-medieval sexual beliefs and those that existed from the later Middle Ages into early modernity.

THE *DECRETUM*: CONTENT AND INFLUENCE ON CANONICAL LAW

Modern scholars have generally viewed Burchard's *Decretum* as part of the prehistory of the discipline of canon law, which begins with the appearance of canon lawyer Gratian's *Decretum* in 1140. However, the work itself explicitly orients itself toward penance. In his preface Burchard explains that he has compiled the work to aid priests in their administration of penance, and penitential concerns are as prominent throughout the work as juridical or ecclesiological issues. Indeed, even at its most juridical, canon law typically retains some penitential cast, and as canon law grew more systematic in the later Middle Ages, and ecclesiological courts grew more purely juridical in outlook and procedure, precepts that had begun as penitential doctrine became regularized and routinized. Burchard's *Decretum* consists of twenty books. Nine concern Church orders, the nature and sources of Church authority, Last Things (death, judgment, heaven, and hell) and the sacraments of Baptism, the Eucharist, and the Anointing of the Sick. One book deals with magic. Burchard returns to this topic later, and, concentrating on female magic, is concerned both with proscribing a variety of folk rituals associated with women and denying their efficacy. Four books deal with criminal offenses and legal procedures and punishments, in particular excommunication. The remaining six books are all entirely penitential and most of them concern sexual behavior, marriage, and marital status. Book VII adumbrates the basic framework of the extensive incest prohibitions advocated by the early medieval Church—intermarriage forbidden up to the seventh degree of relatedness. Books VIII and IX discuss forms of celibacy, those in clerical orders and for virgins and widows; Book XVII deals with all forms of fornication.

Book XIX, or the *Corrector*, covers some of the same ground as the earlier books, though it does so in the form of interrogatories, or lists of questions confessors should ask penitents. Consistent with penitential doctrine on sexuality, the only form of sexual activity that the *Corrector* does not view as sinful is that which takes place within marriage for the sole purpose of reproduction. Nonreproductive sexual acts, such as oral sex, are sinful even between married partners. The same is true of sex when a wife is menstruating or pregnant. Though intercourse from the rear "in the manner of a dog" (*canino more*) is reproductive, it too is sinful, perhaps because of its visual analogy with nonreproductive anal intercourse. Christianity had established the teleology of reproduction in marriage as the sole justification for sex in the Pauline letters, that is, in the earliest texts in the New Testament. The penitential writings of the early Middle Ages distinguish themselves from what came before, and most of what came afterward, mainly in the anatomical specificity and detail with which they apply this teleological, reproductive rationale. In his aspiration to provide an authoritative statement of the entire tradition, Burchard is, if anything, even more explicit than his predecessors.

Burchard's treatment of homosexuality offers perhaps the most striking instance of this tendency. Homosexuality has traditionally been known as the love that dare not speak its name; in more properly Christian terms, as an unspeakable sin. Since the late twentieth century, following French philosopher Michel Foucault (1926–1984), many scholars have viewed sodomy as "an utterly confused category." Nevertheless, the penitential tradition of the early Middle Ages provides a counterexample of some considerable duration, when the category was neither confused nor unspeakable. The *Synod of the Grove of Victory*, written by penitentials in Wales in the mid-sixth century, defines sodomitic fornication as comprising four distinct sexual acts: anal intercourse, interfemoral intercourse, mutual masturbation, and masturbation. This definition remained stable for the next five centuries.

Burchard's discussion in Book XX may well be the most explicit in the entire tradition. His confessor is to ask penitents, "Have you committed fornication as the Sodomites committed it, have you thus inserted your rod (*virgam*) in male backsides and posteriors, and have you thus coupled with them in the Sodomitical custom?" And then, with equal specificity, "Have you committed fornication with yourself, as some do, such that you take your male member in your hand, drawing away your foreskin and rubbing so that through this pleasure semen rushes out of you?" Some thirty years later, a more subdued version of this four-fold definition began Peter Damian's *Book of Gomorrah* (1049), arguably the most important treatment of homosexuality in the entire medieval period, and the text which may have coined the actual term *sodomy* (*sodomia*). Nevertheless, the influence of this definition waned, especially in the period after the Fourth Lateran Council (1215), as subsequent penitential tradition sought to limit discussion of the topic and offered more abstract definitions.

SEE ALSO *Homosexuality in the Christian Church; Homosexuality, Contemporary: II. History; Sodomy.*

BIBLIOGRAPHY

Austin, Greta. 2004. "Jurisprudence in the Service of Pastoral Care: The *Decretum* of Burchard of Worms." *Speculum* 79: 929–959.

Burchard of Worms. 1990. "Selections from the *Corrector and Physician*." In *Medieval Handbooks of Penance: A Translation of the Principal "Libri Poenitentiales" and Selections from Related Documents*, ed. and trans. John T. McNeill and Helena M. Gamer. New York: Columbia University Press. (Orig. pub. 1938.)

Burchard of Worms. 1997. "Corrector" In *Medieval Popular Religion 1000–1500: A Reader*, ed. and trans. John Shinners. Peterborough, Ontario: Broadview Press.

Burchard of Worms. 1998. "Preface to the *Decretum*." In *Prefaces to Canon Law Books in Latin Christianity: Selected Translations, 500–1245*, trans. Robert Somerville and Bruce C. Brasington. New Haven, CT: Yale University Press.

Hamilton, Sarah. 2001. *The Practice of Penance, 900–1050*. Rochester, NY: Royal Historical Society, Boydell Press.

Rampton, Martha. 2002. "Burchard of Worms and Female Magical Ritual." In *Medieval and Early Modern Ritual: Formalized Behavior in Europe, China and Japan*, ed. Joëlle Rollo-Koster. Boston: Brill.

Larry Scanlon

BURLESQUE

Burlesque, like nearly all of American popular culture, began in the hurly-burly of the Victorian age. Industrialization, the creation of a large working class in opposition to a newly powerful middle class, a new mass culture of consumption, and a system of racial and national hierarchies within an empire created the perfect climate for burlesque, a working-class entertainment in which all rules could be broken for comic effect and profit. Indeed, it was exactly this "slap in the face" aspect of burlesque that made it such an important part of the growing entertainment industry. Burlesque routines rewrote so-called higher art forms, such as opera, as comedy and farce. For instance, one of the most popular burlesque acts in America was Lydia Thomson and the British Blondes, whose 1868 production of the Greek myth Ixion attracted large crowds not because of its classical cachet, but because all the women in the show wore body-revealing costumes.

Thumbing their noses at the pretentiousness of bourgeois culture was surely part of burlesque's appeal, but its real naughtiness, and therefore its real attraction, was how it laughed at the Victorian myth of the ideal woman. The ideal woman was emotional (not rational), engaged in the domestic sphere (not the market), innocent of sexual desires, and lily white. (Women of color were not part of this idealized version of femininity because part of the cultural work of the ideal woman was to show that whites were superior.) Burlesque slapped the ideal woman in the face by allowing white women to strut their desires and their bodies across stages all over North America and Europe. Not only were the actresses scantily clad, but they were also aware of their sexual power in ways that made critics rage and audiences blush. In Victorian America, these vamping women in flesh colored tights could shock and thereby attract huge crowds.

As the Victorian age dissolved into the twentieth century, however, competition from other forms of entertainment, including a burgeoning movie industry, pushed burlesque from a primarily satirical art form to a primarily erotic one. The evolution eventually resulted in what has become known as the striptease. Although no one knows exactly when or how the striptease developed, by the late 1890s, burlesque performers were regularly disrobing on stage. Perhaps stripping began accidentally, when a performer's strap broke, as many sources would have it, or perhaps it began at Chicago's Columbian Exhibition in 1893 when a Syrian belly dancer, Fahreda Mahzar (1849–1902), billed as *Little Egypt*, set off a national craze of *hootchy-kootchy* dancers.

Regardless of how the striptease began, the incorporation of scantily clad women into popular culture owed much to the carnival midway, dime museums, and other displays of curiosities. One of the first such erotic acts was brought to the American public by none other than P. T. Barnum (1810–1891). As early as 1864, Barnum was looking for a woman from the Caucasus to display in his American Museum. Playing on Victorian notions of racial types and purity, Barnum sought the whitest of white women, thought to be from Circassia in the Caucasus (thus the term Caucasian). Because the Caucasus were imagined as the center of white racial purity and were simultaneously next to the Ottoman Empire, Barnum concocted a story of a girl nearly sold into sexual slavery to a Turk, but rescued by white men and brought to New York for his audience's viewing pleasure. As Linda Frost notes, "The unsullied purity of the Circassian Beauty therefore seems in part to represent a Northern anxiety about racial mixing, particularly in regard to the anticipated effects of emancipation" (Frost 2005). The quote might help explain why the hundreds of Circassian beauties who popped up around the country were, in fact, not clearly white given that they always had large, bushy hair; nor were they clearly pure, given that Circassian beauties were also displayed in their undergarments.

The craze for Circassian beauties in the 1860s set the tone for consuming white women as sexual objects while simultaneously reinscribing them as racially and sexually pure. (The beauty had been saved from the beastliness of the Turks who would have sexually enslaved her.) The fact that the Circassian beauties were also clearly gaffs, that is, fakes, who spoke English, but had mysteriously forgotten their native tongue, was part of Barnum's general mode of display. In Barnum's freak shows, it was all completely true unless it was not, and then it was a good joke. This Barnumesque wink and nod was so thoroughly familiar to a Victorian audience, that the humor of burlesque was derived directly from Barnum and the American tradition of displaying bodies for fun and profit.

Thus as the striptease developed into the central component of burlesque, it was always mixed with the comedic, "just in good fun" character of earlier modes of display. By the 1920s and 1930s, burlesque was enjoying its golden age, with comedic starts such as Jackie Gleason (1916–1987), Red Skelton (1913–1997), and (Bud) Abbott (1897–1974) and (Lou) Costello (1906–1959) in addition to striptease legends such as fan dancer Sally Rand (1904–1979) or Gypsy Rose Lee (1914–1970), who paired stripping with highbrow recitation, making it both funny and sexy. However, as with many working-class pleasures, a moral panic developed among middle-class reformers about the supposed dangers of burlesque. In New York City, the center of burlesque, Mayor Fiorello LaGuardia (1882–1947) managed to shut down the last of the remaining burlesque theaters by 1937. By then, many performers had moved from burlesque and vaudeville into the film industry. Those who did not make it in Hollywood moved from the theaters of burlesque to the backrooms of strip joints and into the two-dimensional spaces of illicit photograph and film.

Although in the 1970s there were still approximately 7,000 women working as stripteasers, the occupation was considered to be *dirty* and *immoral*, even by the performers themselves. Burlesque as a grand theatrical expression of working-class mockery of bourgeoisie prudishness was dead. As a ghost of its former self, stripping survived at the edges of so-called respectability, refusing to disappear. Yet, stripping could not be incorporated into popular culture the way other pieces of burlesque had been. Then, in the 1990s, just when cable television and satellite dishes made stripping and pornography as everyday as sitcoms, burlesque was reborn. The New Burlesque came out naughtier, more clearly critical of the ruling elites, and funny enough to make nearly everyone laugh. At the same time burlesque was being reborn, so were many of the other earlier forms of mass culture, such as freak shows and circuses. In part, people interested in live theater were interested in saving these dying art forms. In part, a post-feminist, post-politically correct, and highly ironic sensibility allowed people to both perform as freaks and hootchy-kootchy girls and simultaneously make fun of the racism and sexism that created these performances in the first place.

One of the best examples of this New Burlesque and its illegitimate marriage to the New Circus is the Bindlestiff Family Cirkus, a New York City troupe started in 1995 as a hybrid of vaudeville, circus, burlesque, and sideshow. Early Bindlestiff performances included classic burlesque routines, such as plate spinning, but the plates were spun not with fingers, but by attaching the pole to a dildo, inserting the dildo into the vagina of Ring Mistress Philomena (Stephanie Murano), and by the contraction of Philomena's kegel muscles. Other New Burlesque performers started showing up for regular Friday night performances at the Coney Island Sideshow, a traditional ten-in-one freak show started in 1983. Coney Island Friday night burlesque also included old burlesque routines, such as Dirty (Linda) Martini's fan dance, and bathing the dancers in red wine at the end and serving it to the audience after their bodies had been washed in it, a homage to an early twentieth-century Coney Island performer named Tirza.

These acts were not necessarily for the audience's unadulterated pleasure. Often New Burlesque was just as interested in invoking disgust as it was desire. For instance, Bambi, the Corn Star, would come out dressed like a chicken (itself a homage to Tod Browning's [1880–1962] classic 1932 horror film *Freaks*), squat, lay a hard-boiled egg out of her vagina, peel it, and force-feed it to an audience member. Across the country, in Los Angeles, Michelle Juliette Carr, creator of the Velvet Hammer Burlesque, was putting on shows with post-punk and postmodern performers of all shapes and sizes debating feminism and swilling champagne in G-strings and pasties. All this edgy performance occurred alongside a general critique of the government, capitalism, and greed as well as a variety of novelty acts from sword swallowing to playing music on tampon applicators.

Unlike the shocking burlesque of the Victorian era, or the sleazy burlesque of the early twentieth century, the New Burlesque has attracted a variety of middle-class fans, from artists, photographers, and performers, to academics and activists. It is both straight (the majority of acts are still performed by genetic females) and queer (the production of straight femininity is poked fun at, for instance, by female to female impersonator BOB). The audiences are mixed women and men, straight and queer. The New Burlesque is generally controlled by the women on stage (i.e., not necessarily exploitative) and it is not necessarily for profit (i.e., none of the performers are getting rich on burlesque).

If burlesque has come back to reintroduce the promise and pleasure of the striptease, it has also come back to reinvent that striptease as a way out of the messiness that seemingly comes along with flesh and desire. In a culture where there is an increasing demand that all bodies look the same and all female bodies be constantly on display, the New Burlesque puts women of all shapes, sizes, and bodily configurations on stage who can hootchy-kootchy even while they make fun of themselves and their audience for wanting them to perform. These are women able to laugh at femininity and the heterosexual imagination even while they celebrate it. Most importantly of all, it shows women who cannot liberate themselves from the chains of sexism and racism, but who can, nevertheless, twist and turn and even jump rope with those chains, all the while tying their audience into knots of painful laughter.

SEE ALSO *Clothing; Hierarchy.*

BIBLIOGRAPHY

Allen, Robert C. 1991. *Horrible Prettiness: Burlesque and American Culture.* Chapel Hill: University of North Carolina Press.

Buszek, Maria-Elen. 1999. "Representing 'Awarishness': Burlesque, Feminist Transgression, and the Nineteenth-Century Pinup." *TDR: The Drama Review* 43(4): 164.

Essig, Laurie. 2005. "The Pleasure of Freaks." *Proteus* 22(2): 19–24.

Frost, Linda. 2005. *Never One Nation: Freaks, Savages, and Whiteness in American Popular Culture, 1850–1877.* Minneapolis: University of Minnesota Press.

Kasson, John F. 1978. *Amusing the Million: Coney Island at the Turn of the Century.* New York: Hill and Wang.

Latham, Angela J. 1997. "The Right to Bare: Containing and Encoding American Women in Popular Entertainments of the 1920s." *Theatre Journal* 49(4).

Skipper, James K., and Charles H. McCaghy. 1970. "Stripteasers: The Anatomy and Career Contingencies of a Deviant Occupation." *Social Problems* 17(3): 391–405.

"The Golden Days of Burlesque Historical Society." Available from http://www.burlesquehistory.com

Laurie Essig

BUTCH/FEMME

Butch/femme (sometimes called butch/fem) is a form of sexual and gender practice primarily associated with United States and British working-class lesbian communities in the middle of the twentieth century. The term describes an erotic and affective dynamic between women who adopt either a primarily masculine (or butch) gender style or a primarily feminine (or femme) style. Although the relationship between butch/femme and heterosexual (male/female) relations has been a matter of contention, it is important to understand butch/femme as a lesbian cultural form with its own history and specific forms of practice.

ROOTS OF THE BUTCH/FEMME CULTURE

It is difficult to say where butch/femme culture came from. While it is possible to trace similar behaviors and identifications in different cultures and in various historical moments, the importance of gender cross-identification in understanding same-sex relations spiked in Germany, England, and the United States at the end of the nineteenth century with the rise of sexology, a pseudo-scientific study of sex and gender. The writings of important sexologists such as Richard von Krafft-Ebing, Karl Heinrich Ulrichs, and Havelock Ellis focused on the figure of the sexual invert: the woman who was *actually* a man, and the man who was *actually* a woman. In these writings, the female invert emerges as the iconic figure of female same-sex desire. With her active sexual desires and masculine gender style, she longs for a feminine partner with whom she can complete herself as a man. What is much harder to explain within the sexological framework is the desire of a feminine woman for a masculine woman (or female invert).

Sexology does not, however, provide an adequate explanation for the rise of butch/femme in the twentieth century. As several historians have shown, this practice became dominant in communities that had no exposure to medical accounts of inversion where butch/femme developed as a popular form of identity. In their important history of the lesbian community in Buffalo, New York in the 1940s and 1950s, social anthropologist Elizabeth Lapovsky Kennedy and activist and historian Madeline D. Davis suggest that butch/femme is a survival strategy within a violently homophobic (as well as classist and racist) culture. They argue that butch/femme roles are "the only vital alternative for working-class lesbians" and that they were "the key structure for organizing against heterosexual dominance" (Kennedy and Davis 1994, p. 395). While other (gender-normative) options were available to more privileged women, working-class lesbians in the twentieth century largely embraced the gender-dichotomous roles of butch/femme in order to announce their difference from the heterosexual norm and to claim public space.

Another important account of the emergence of butch/femme can be found in American writer Esther Newton's 1984 article, "The Mythic Mannish Lesbian" in which she describes the importance of masculine identification in the forming of a modern public lesbian identity. Because, as Newton points out, women in the nineteenth century were not associated with sexuality or desire (but rather with its absence), looking like a man was one clear strategy for twentieth-century lesbians to signal their desire for other women. Newton considers the importance of masculinity in a novel that has served as a touchstone for modern lesbianism and for butch/femme, Radclyffe Hall's *The Well of Loneliness* (1928). This novel features an introductory note from the Ellis attesting that it is a realistic account of the life of a female invert. It traces the fortunes of Stephen Gordon, a masculine woman who longs to live her life as an English gentleman, but who is instead cast out as a gender and sexual misfit. Exiled from her ancestral home, Stephen can neither fight in World War I nor marry the woman she loves. *The Well of Loneliness* was banned in a public obscenity trial in London the year it was released, but underground copies of the novel circulated in lesbian circles until the ban was lifted in the 1960s. Despite the novel's dark portrait of Stephen's tragic fate, it remains the most widely read lesbian novel of all time.

Butch/Femme Couple. *A lesbian couple preparing to go to a gay youth prom.* © MARK PETERSON/CORBIS.

FEMINIST RESPONSE

Butch/femme *roles* (as they were called) came under attack during the height of the women's liberation and gay liberation movements. Many feminists and lesbian-feminists objected to butch/femme culture, arguing that it imported the worst of heterosexuality and patriarchy into lesbian relationships. In women's groups in the 1970s, many butches and femmes were encouraged to adopt a more normative feminine or gender-neutral style. For butches this meant departing from an image of working-class masculine style; for femmes it meant toning down a hyper-feminine style and asserting themselves as empowered women. Women were also encouraged to promote equality and sameness within their relationships. For many such arguments were based on a dubious logic of *false consciousness* and *internalized oppression*, or the idea that women who adopted such roles must not know what their true desires were. Lesbian feminists were imposing a specific form of white middle-class sexuality and gender presentation as a universal standard, particularly for working-class women and women of color.

While butch/femme (along with pornography and sadomasochism) came under attack during the 1970s and the sex wars of the 1980s, the practice regained visibility in the 1990s. Perhaps the key text in renewing attention to butch/femme in the period was Leslie Feinberg's popular autobiographical novel, *Stone Butch Blues*. The novel traces the difficulties of a Jewish working-class butch named Jess Goldberg growing up in the bars, streets, and factories of Buffalo, New York in the years leading up to Stonewall, the riot that sparked gay liberation. Feinberg recounts the terrible violence, harassment, and stigmatization that Jess is exposed to on a daily basis as a masculine woman. In response to such experiences, Jess becomes more and more *stone*, a word that refers both to a sexual practice (a refusal of sexual vulnerability or nakedness in bed) and to an emotional state, a hardness that is a form of self-protection.

EFFECT ON AND IMPORTANCE IN QUEER STUDIES

Butch/femme has also played a significant role in the turn to queer studies in the academy. During the sex wars, a range of pro-sex feminists and lesbians made arguments about the inevitability of power in sexual relationships; early work in queer studies emphasized the impossibility of escaping from social power in any arena of social or intimate life. Philosopher Michel Foucault's account of the imbrication of power, knowledge, and sexuality in the first volume of *The History of Sexuality* (1976) profoundly influenced queer studies, and led to interest in topics like butch/femme, camp, drag, public sex, and gay shame. These stigma-inflected aspects of queer life were understood not as utopian escapes from homophobia and patriarchy, but rather as deeply ambivalent sites of resistance.

Writer Judith Butler made both butch/femme and drag central in one of the founding work of queer studies, *Gender Trouble* (1990). At stake in Butler's attention to butch/femme was a familiar charge that butch/femme was an imitation of heterosexuality. Drawing on her own personal experience, Butler wrote in "Imitation and Gender Insubordination," "I suffered for a long time from being told that what I *am* is a copy, an imitation, a derivative example, a shadow of the real" (Butler 1991, p. 20). Rather than argue that butch/femme gender was original, Butler used it to argue that all gender is derivative. Drag and butch/femme were for her sites of gender disruption that make visible how all gender is performative, a copy without an original.

In *Female Masculinity* (1998), gender theorist Judith Halberstam is primarily interested in the way that masculine gender style signifies on a biologically female body. She takes a long historical perspective, considering figures from the eighteenth-century tribade to the contemporary drag king scene. Unlike people such as Newton who provide a historical and cultural frame for the emergence of the butch at the beginning of the twentieth century, Halberstam argues for the durability of this form of gendered embodiment over time. If in the 1990s the figure of the butch came into her own, discussions of femme identity lag somewhat behind. Representing the specific experiences of femmes has proved difficult over the course of the twentieth century. With their inherently heterosexual understanding of desire, the sexologists failed to account for the desire of the feminine woman attracted to other woman: she remains a cipher in their accounts. In many twentieth-century fictional accounts of butch/femme desire, the emphasis often falls on the butch as desiring and suffering hero. The writings of Joan Nestle (*A Restricted Country* [1987]) and Amber Hollibaugh (*My Dangerous Desires: A Queer Girl Dreaming Her Way Home* [2003]) and the 1999 film *But I'm a Cheerleader* stand as notable exceptions to this rule; there have also been a couple of significant collections on femme experience. However the problem of femme invisibility continues to plague both fictional and theoretical accounts of butch/femme experience.

One of the most persistent tropes of butch/femme representation is the sanctuary that an erotic and intimate relation offers from a hostile world. In a dialogue framed as a response to the denigration of butch/femme by lesbian-feminists, "What We're Rollin Around in Bed With" (1983), Amber Hollibaugh and Cherríe Moraga discuss their personal experiences as working-class women both inside and outside the feminist movement. In speaking to Moraga (who identifies as butch), femme-identified Hollibaugh stresses the importance of butch/femme erotic practice as a response to a hostile world: "You see, I want you as a woman, not as a man; but I want you in the way you need to be, which may not be traditionally female, but which is the area that you express as butch. Here is where in the other world you have suffered the most damage. Part of the reason I love to be with butches is because I feel I repair that damage" (Hollibaugh and Moraga 1983, p. 401). While some women have written about the limits of butch/femme as a response to violence and inequality, this persistent notion of *repairing the damage* has marked it as a practice characterized by both extraordinary difficulties and extraordinary intimacy.

GLOBAL PERSPECTIVES IN THE TWENTY-FIRST CENTURY

The significance of butch/femme was transformed by several developments in queer culture in the twentieth-century. A shift in perspective in queer studies from a primarily American focus to a more global focus calls for a rethinking of the meanings of butch/femme in a range of national and transnational contexts. While critics and historians have written about the importance of some gender-transitive practices across the globe (*travesti* in Brazil; *berdache* in Native American cultures), early-twenty-first century work has attempted to think through the meeting of contemporary American queer culture and specific gender and sexual formations around the globe.

The meaning of butch/femme has also been transformed by the visible emergence of a transsexual and transgender politics and community since the 1990s. As more women decide to transition and live as men, the limits of butch identity as well as the stability of the butch/femme identity come into question. The mainstreaming of gay and lesbian identity in the late 1990s and early part of the twenty-first century also raises important questions about the relationship between butch/femme culture and social stigma. Understanding butch/femme primarily as evolving in a social context that is intensely threatening and in which it is difficult to signal active desire through a feminine style, one might be tempted to conclude that butch/femme will wither away as a practice as feminism and gay and lesbian activism transform the public sphere. In a 1998 collection on butch/femme, lesbian critic Sally Munt questions the transformation of butch/femme from a way of life to a lifestyle, as she asks "why a primarily working-class identification has become colonized as middle-class, white, and chic" (Munt 1998, p. 4).

The testimonies of several young black and Asian working class women interviewed in the documentary film *The Aggressives* (2005) make it clear that butch/femme is not a style that came and went in the middle of the twentieth century. The women interviewed testify to a deeply-felt masculine identification. At the same time, their stories of hostility and rejection on the street, by their families, and in the workplace, as well as their creative responses to such difficulties testify to the ongoing role that butch/femme practices play as a strategy of survival and visibility.

SEE ALSO *Lesbian, Contemporary: I. Overview.*

BIBLIOGRAPHY

Bannon, Ann. 1962. *Beebo Brinker*. Repr., San Francisco: Cleis Press, 2003.

Bannon, Ann. 1975. *I Am a Woman*. New York: Arno Press.

Burana, Lily Roxxie, and Linea Due, eds. 1994. *Dagger: On Butch Women*. San Francisco: Cleis Press.

Butler, Judith. 1991. "Imitation and Gender Insubordination." In *Inside/Out: Lesbian Theories, Gay Theories*, ed. Diana Fuss. New York: Routledge.

Butler, Judith. 2000. *Gender Trouble: Feminism and the Subversion of Identity*. New York: Routledge.

Case, Sue-Ellen. 1993. "Toward a Butch-Femme Aesthetic." In *The Lesbian and Gay Studies Reader*, eds. Henry Abelove, Michele Aina Barale, and David Halperin. New York: Routledge.

Cvetkovich, Ann. 2003. *An Archive of Feelings: Trauma and Lesbian Public Cultures*. Durham, NC: Duke University Press.

De Lauretis, Teresa. 1994. "The Lure of the Mannish Lesbian." In *The Practice of Love: Lesbian Sexuality and Perverse Desire*. Bloomington: Indiana University Press.

Doan, Laura. 2001. *Fashioning Sapphism: On the Making of an English Subculture*. New York: Columbia University Press.

Duggan, Lisa, and Kathleen McHugh. 1996. "A Fem(me)inist Manifesto." *Women and Performance* 8:2, no. 16: 150–60. Special issue "Queer Acts," eds. José Esteban Muñoz and Amanda Barrett.

Duggan, Lisa, and Nan Hunter. 1995. *Sex Wars: Sexual Dissent and Political Culture*. New York: Routledge.

Feinberg, Leslie. 1993. *Stone Butch Blues: A Novel*. Los Angeles: Alyson Books.

Foucault, Michel. 1990. The History of Sexuality. Vol. I: *The Will to Knowledge*, trans. Robert Hurley. New York: Vintage. (Orig. pub. 1976.)

Gopinath, Gayatri. 2005. *Impossible Desires*. Durham, NC: Duke University Press.

Halberstam, Judith. 1998. *Female Masculinity*. Durham, NC: Duke University Press.

Halberstam, Judith, and C. Jacob Hale. 1998. "Butch/FTM Border Wars: A Note on Collaboration." *Gay Lesbian Quarterly* 42.

Hall, Radclyffe. 1990. *The Well of Loneliness*. Repr., New York, Anchor Books, 1928.

Hollibaugh, Amber. 2000. *A Queer Girl Dreaming Her Way Home*. Durham, NC: Duke University Press.

Hollibaugh, Amber, and Cherríe Moraga. 1983. "What We're Rollin Around in Bed With: Sexual Silences in Feminism." In *Powers of Desire: The Politics of Sexuality*, ed. Ann Snitow, Christine Stansell, and Sharon Thompson.

Jeffreys, Sheila. 1989. "Butch and Femme, Now and Then." In *Not a Passing Phase: Reclaiming Lesbians in History 1840–1985*, ed. Lesbian History Group. London: The Women's Press.

Kennedy, Elizabeth Lapovsky, and Madeline D. Davis. 1994. *Boots of Leather, Slippers of Gold: The History of a Lesbian Community*. London: Penguin Books.

Lorde, Audre. 1982. *Zami: A New Spelling of My Name*. Watertown, MA: Persephone Press.

Munt, Sally, ed. 1998. *butch/femme: Inside Lesbian Gender*. London: Cassell.

Nestle, Joan. 1987. *A Restricted Country*. Ithaca, NY: Firebrand Books.

Nestle, Joan, ed. 1992. *A Persistent Desire: The Femme-Butch Reader*. Boston: Alyson Publications.

Newton, Esther. 1984. "The Mythic Mannish Lesbian: Radclyffe Hall and the New Woman." *Signs* 9(4): 557–575.

Newton, Esther. 2000. *Margaret Mead Made Me Gay: Personal Essays, Public Ideas*. Durham, NC: Duke University Press.

Prosser, Jay. 1998. *Second Skins: The Body Narratives of Transsexuality*. New York: Columbia University Press.

Rich, Adrienne. 1980. "Compulsory Heterosexuality and Lesbian Existence." *Signs* 5(4): 631–660.

Rubin, Gayle. 1984. "Thinking Sex: Notes for a Radical Theory of the Politics of Sexuality." In *Pleasure and Danger: Exploring Female Sexuality*, ed. Carole S. Vance. New York: Routledge.

Snitow, Ann; Christine Stansell; and Sharon Thompson, eds. 1983. *Powers of Desire: The Politics of Sexuality*. New York: Monthly Review Press.

Heather Love

BUTTOCKS

Buttocks are fleshy protuberances at the rear of the pelvis. They occur in many quadruped species, but are common to primates. The human buttocks are composed of the three gluteal muscles (commonly referred to as the *glutes*), the gluteus maximus, gluteus minimus, and gluteus medius, as well as the fatty tissue that covers them. They are among the strongest muscle groups in the human body, comparable in strength to the thigh muscles. Their general function is to connect the leg muscles to the trunk of the body. In doing so, they provide stability to the core muscles of the trunk, as well as allow for flexibility of the hip muscles and articulated movement of the legs. This muscle group is significant partly because it is separated into two parts by the gluteal crease (the double hemispheres of the buttocks). Thus, this group can work together or allow independent movement of the legs. The gluteal crease is also the location of the anus, which is both the site of excretion of solid waste matter from the body and an erogenous zone. The anus, sphincter, and rectum contain numerous nerve endings, making them sites of potential pleasure and pain. Anal sex, which often involves the insertion of the penis, finger, or an object into the anus, is a common practice, although it is often considered taboo. The rectum shares a muscular wall with the vagina in females and with the prostate gland in males—both sensitive areas that are particularly stimulated by anal intercourse or stimulation.

EVOLUTION AND FUNCTION OF BUTTOCKS

The human buttocks are distinctive among all species in that they are continuously present. The erect stature of humans causes the pelvis to project to the rear of the spinal column, which forces the muscles and fatty tissue of the buttocks into their common configuration. Other species that alternate between an erect stance and walking on all fours have visible buttocks only when their posture allows. Some anthropologists have gone so far as to suggest that the buttocks are responsible for the development of the human brain. The buttocks allow for the upright, two-legged stance distinctive to humans. This stance in turn accommodates two important developments, the freedom of the forearms (previously used for walking on all fours) and the alignment of the spinal column. The use of the arms and hands for tasks other than balance encouraged the development of a complex brain capable of problem solving. Simultaneously the erect stature of humans caused the brain to rest atop the spinal column instead of in front of it, making the frame able to support a larger brain, which in turn was capable of higher-order functions and cognition. There is considerable disagreement about the role the development of buttocks played in initiating the development of the human brain, but it is generally agreed that the unique development of human buttocks was necessary to allow their brain development.

In most primate species, the female buttocks are linked with reproduction. Females signal their readiness to mate by displaying their buttocks, which have become enlarged and swollen. As their menstruation cycle progresses, the swelling becomes more pronounced and, in some species, the color of the buttocks changes to a deep red or purple. After the fertile period of the cycle, the buttocks lose their vivid coloration, and the swelling disappears. The buttocks return to their usual state of being flat and unremarkable. The buttocks of the human female do not change noticeably with the menstrual cycle and have no particular function in the reproductive process. Unlike other primates, the human female is also capable of having intercourse at any time, not just during her menstrual cycle. The configuration of the buttocks and the pelvis orients the human genitalia more to the front of the body than is true in other primates, making face-to-face intercourse possible.

The buttocks contain large amounts of fatty tissue, which gives them their distinct rounded shape. This fatty layer is generally greater in females than in males, which gives the human sexes similar, yet distinct, buttocks and also contributes to the typically wider female hips. This difference in fatty tissue is also apparent in human breasts, which in males are typically lean and flat whereas in women they are fuller and rounder. Anthropologists such as Desmond Morris have linked the development of the human female breasts to the loss of the sexual function of the buttocks. In other mammals, the female breasts are typically flat except when pregnant or nursing. In humans, the female breasts are continuously present, like the buttocks, although they may increase in size during menstruation, pregnancy, or nursing. Morris claims that "the female breasts evolved, quite simply, as buttock mimics" (Morris 1994, p. 122).

The human buttocks became unnecessary for sexual function but remained a site of sexual interest to potential mates. The forward-facing genitalia, however, made the buttocks less apparent, and the breasts developed to resemble the shape of the buttocks and take their place as a visible sexual signal. This is reinforced by the general lack of function of the bulk of human breast tissue. The female breasts are primarily rounded globes of fatty tissue, like the buttocks, and serve little purpose in the manufacture of milk or in aiding breast feeding. Morris further claims that other structures, such as the typically smooth, rounded, facial cheeks typical of female humans similarly mimic the buttocks and are also located in a more prominent, front-facing position.

BUTTOCKS AS AN EROGENOUS ZONE AND IN SEXUAL ACTIVITY

The buttocks have long been an erogenous zone and a source of sexual pleasure and fascination. The shape of the buttocks is pleasing to many and is an often-rendered physical feature in painting and sculpture. As a physical feature common to both men and women, buttocks do not carry the same type of gender-specific taboos typical of the genitals or the female breasts. Because of the excretory function of the anus, however, there is a taboo based in abjection associated with the area. Many people distinguish between the buttocks and the anus, finding one appealing and the other not. Others are stimulated by the taboo associated with the anus as much as by the shape of the buttocks themselves, and take pleasure in both. The popularity of the buttocks as a site of attraction is evident in the proliferation of nicknames for them, including butt, booty, backside, bum, buns, ass, and arse. Fanny is also a nickname for buttocks in American English, but in British English, it is vulgar slang for the female genitals.

In homosexual males, the anus serves as an orifice for intercourse, which makes the buttocks and anus a primary site of sexual activity. Gay men are often divided into groups based upon their preference in anal sexual practice: The receptive partner is called a *bottom*, while the insertive partner is called a *top*. Those who enjoy both positions are called *switch* or *versatile*. Lesbian anal intercourse is also common, and is usually practiced with a hand-held sex toy (often a dildo) or with the use of a strap-on prosthesis. Because the anus has no natural lubrication, anal intercourse always carries greater potential for tissue rupture than does vaginal intercourse or other sexual activities. It is thus considered a high-risk activity for the transmission of disease, and protection (usually in the form of a condom covering the penis or prosthesis) is usually advised. In cultures where women's virginity is valued highly, (heterosexual) anal intercourse has often substituted for vaginal intercourse as a means of being sexually active while remaining technically virginal. This difference, of course, depends wholly upon the way that virginity is defined. Heterosexual anal intercourse, however, is not strictly a substitute for vaginal intercourse. It is also practiced as a primary form of sexual activity among some couples and as an alternate or occasional activity among others. There are few reliable studies on anal intercourse among heterosexuals, but anecdotal references indicate that it is somewhat common.

The buttocks also figure in sexual practices other than intercourse. Anilingus (also known as *rimming*) involves one partner licking the anus of the other with their tongue. Massage of the buttocks is common and often a form of foreplay. The buttocks also are involved in a number of fetishistic practices. Clothing designed to reveal, conceal, or accentuate the buttocks is a feature of some fetish activities. Underwear that has been worn and retains the smell of the body parts it covers (including the buttocks) is a primary form of clothing fetishism. This differs from tactile fetishes, which are more concerned with the feel of the clothing item. According to Valerie Steele, "Smelly fetishes may indicate an obsession with bathroom functions, which would seem to imply an 'infantile' perspective on sexuality" (1996, p. 124). Spanking, or striking the buttocks with the hand or an implement of some sort (often a paddle, strap, or whip), is often cited as a common sexual fantasy, although little data exists to demonstrate the degree to which it is actually practiced. *Fisting* involves the insertion of the entire hand into the anus. It is practiced among heterosexuals, lesbians, and homosexual males, although it is most common to homosexual males. Because the diameter of the human hand and arm (fisting often involves insertion of the arm up to the elbow) is far greater than that of the average human penis or any common sexual prostheses, it involves significant stretching of the sphincter and can be quite painful. It is sometimes incorporated into bondage and discipline/sadomasochism (BDSM) activities or other sexual practices in which inflicting pain or demonstrating dominance over another is desirable.

BUTTOCKS IN HISTORY

The buttocks, particularly of the female, have been the subject of much discussion, fascination, and artistic representation. Some of the earliest examples of human art include carvings of fertility goddesses with extremely ample breasts and buttocks. The most famous example is the Venus of Willendorf, a Paleolithic statuette discovered in Austria in 1908 believed to date back to 24,000–22,000 BCE. Buttocks have also famously been depicted in such varying works of art as Donatello's sculpture *David* (1425–1430) and Paul Cezanne's *Large Bathers* (1899–1906). Fashion over time has alternately hidden and emphasized the buttocks. The most notable example of the buttocks in fashion is the bustle, popular primarily from 1882 to 1888 in Europe and the United States. This structure (made of fabric but often internally supported by a metal frame) was worn behind the waist, giving its wearer a highly exaggerated silhouette. The effect was meant to be evocative rather than to echo an actual human shape, and while short-lived, it is one of the most recognizable fashion trends in history. Anticipating the bustle was the brief celebrity of Saartjie Baartman, a Khoikhoi woman from South Africa who was brought to Europe and exhibited under the name *Hottentot Venus* from 1810 to 1815. She was famous primarily for her buttocks, which were enormous by European standards but thought to be typical of her native people. They projected from her pelvis at an angle almost perpendicular to her back and were several times larger than the average buttocks of European women. She was valued both as an oddity and as a representation of ideal female fertility.

BIBLIOGRAPHY

Hennig, Jen-Luc. 1995. *The Rear View: A Brief and Elegant History of Bottoms through the Ages*, trans. Margaret Crosland and Elfreda Powell. New York: Crown Publishers.

Holden, Angus. 1935. *Elegant Modes in the Nineteenth Century: From High Waist to Bustle*. London: George Allen & Unwin.

Morris, Desmond. 1994. *The Human Animal: A Personal View of the Human Species*. New York: Crown Publishers.

Russell, Pamela. 1998. "The Palaeolithic Mother-Goddess: Fact or Fiction?" In *Reader in Gender Archaeology*, eds. Kelley Hays-Gilpin and David S. Whitley. London: Routledge.

Standring, Susan, ed. 2004. *Gray's Anatomy: The Anatomical Basis of Clinical Practice*. 39th edition. New York: Churchill Livingstone.

Steele, Valerie. 1996. *Fetish: Fashion, Sex and Power*. New York: Oxford University Press.

Vlasopolos, Anca. 2000. "Venus Live! Sarah Bartmann, the Hottentot Venus, Re-Membered." *Mosaic: A Journal for the Interdisciplinary Study of Literature* 33(4): 129–143.

Brian D. Holcomb

BUTT PLUG

SEE *Sex Aids.*

BYZANTIUM

The civilization of Byzantium, centered on Constantinople (modern Istanbul), was unquestionably patriarchal throughout its long history (330–1453), and Byzantium's self-appointed role as the preserver of Christian Orthodoxy led to a focus on virginity, celibacy, and asceticism as the highest social ideals.

CELIBACY AND ASCETICISM

Total sexual abstinence was always considered the highest state. The early church maintained an order of virgins as a class, and female ascetics would generally take a vow of perpetual virginity. The same standard of virginity existed for holy men, though self-castration for the purposes of moral purity was considered a sin. Monks and nuns, of course, did not marry, though it was not uncommon for men and women to marry young and then separate to different monastic institutions after their children had grown up. Priests and deacons were allowed to have wives, provided that they married prior to taking orders; bishops had to separate from their wives before their appointment, and their wives had to retire to a monastery. A priest was not allowed to remarry after his wife's death. Double monasteries, separate communities of men and women within the same institution, initially common, were finally prohibited in the eighth century because of the dangers caused by the proximity of monks and nuns.

Although all monastics were expected to follow an ascetic regime, it could be taken to extremes by hermits and stylites (*pillar dwellers*), who were committed not only to celibacy and fasting but to mortifying their flesh with hairshirts and chains, self-flagellation, sleeping on the floor or in caves, and continual prayer in pursuit of attaining apatheia (or *freedom from emotion*). Such ascetics (women in early Byzantium as well as men) frequently became saints and are shown as totally immune to sexual temptation. The true holy man is thus capable of indifference even to female nudity, and in hagiography, women often make sexual advances to the holy man, in real life or in dreams, to corrupt him by their devilish wiles. The naked body is seldom depicted in art, and Byzantine costume was careful to conceal what lay beneath.

MARRIAGE, DIVORCE, AND ADULTERY

Some of the more fundamentalist Christian sects, such as the Marcionites and Gnostics, considered marriage contrary to the message of the Gospels and as the work of the devil. Mainstream Orthodoxy, however, worked out a compromise between the total rejection of marriage and the type of free marriage normal in the late Roman Empire. The church fathers decreed that marriage was a divine institution (though inferior to celibacy) instituted for the procreation of children and the prevention of fornication. Girls could marry at the age of twelve (though this was not the norm) and boys from fourteen; parental consent was essential. Women (and ideally men) were expected to preserve physical virginity until their wedding night; when possible, to avoid seduction, daughters were kept segregated and chaperoned, meeting only the men of their own family.

Second marriages were permitted a decent interval after the death of a spouse, but a third was generally considered undesirable (St. Basil the Great [c. 329–379] termed a third marriage as prostitution) and was only permissible under certain circumstances (such as childlessness). Third marriages were legislated against by certain emperors, such as Leo VI (r. 886–912)—who, in order to have a legitimate heir, was later in the embarrassing position of himself taking a fourth wife in the teeth of monastic opposition. Divorce was increasingly restricted throughout the empire, and from the eighth century was only permissible on the grounds of a wife's adultery, attempted poisoning, or the lengthy impotence of the husband. The late Roman practice of concubinage was considered as quasi-prostitution and was abolished by Leo VI, though in practice it still continued in some areas. Punishments for adultery could vary, but the eighth- century law code, the Ekloga, specified that the adulterous couple should have their noses cut off, and the woman could be confined in a monastery.

Despite this moral code, immorality and mistresses were often rife at the imperial court and were little frowned on by the church as long as they did not threaten the sacred institution of marriage. The Moechian (*adulterous*) controversy sparked when Constantine VI (r. 780–797) divorced Maria Amnia and married his mistress, Theodote; the situation was unusual in that it provoked extreme monastic opposition, and many churchmen considered the remarriage uncanonical. Constantine's mother, Irene, later used his unpopularity over this as a factor in deposing and blinding him and ruling on her own account (797–802). But emperors, married or unmarried, often publicly kept mistresses. Leo VI married two of his mistresses after the death of his first and third wives, and Constantine IX Monomachos (r. 1042–1055) was nearly lynched in 1044 because the people thought he intended to divorce or exile his elderly wife, Zoe, in favor of his mistress, Maria Skleraina. Illegitimate children could also be recognized at court. Manuel I Komnenos (r. 1143–1180), whose mistress (and niece), Theodora, had a retinue greater than that of the empress, gave his illegitimate son by her high rank at court in default of a legitimate heir. This was not an unknown practice and, under the Palaiologue dynasty (1259–1453), illegitimate daughters were frequently married to Asian rulers, such as Turks and Mongols, as dynastic pawns.

PROSTITUTION

On the streets of the capital itself, prostitution remained a stable feature of Byzantine society, and prostitutes could be found both in organized brothels and in the inns, baths, theaters, and hippodrome (actresses and other female entertainers being considered prostitutes by definition). The church regularly outlawed prostitution, and emperors attempted to provide protection and escape, such as *houses of repentance*, for those girls forced into it, but it was never eradicated. The empress Theodora (wife of Justinian, 508–548), herself an ex-hippodrome performer, founded the Monastery of Repentance for such unfortunates in the sixth century, and saints' lives told of repentant prostitutes attaining sanctity, such as Pelagia the Harlot and Mary of Egypt, following the exemplum of Mary Magdalene.

THE BYZANTINE FAMILY

The family was the fundamental unit of Byzantine society, and though—because of the idealization of celibacy, attitudes toward women were ambivalent—wives and mothers were increasingly seen as playing a decisive role within the household. Unless women went into monastic life, their major preoccupations were expected to be marriage and children. Women in theory were a marginalized group not to be seen or heard in public, and segregation of the sexes was the ideal, but this seldom took place in practice. The women's quarters in the palace and noble homes were not areas to which women were confined but where they could enjoy some privacy and engage in female occupations such as spinning and weaving. While these areas were generally staffed with eunuchs, males were not excluded, but those from outside the immediate family would not enter without invitation. The majority of the female population was often out in public and mingling on the streets as part of their daily routine, and women were deeply involved in retail trade. Aristocratic women could be shop owners or supervise a workshop in their home, and they were expected to take an active role in the maintenance of their household and supervision of family, servants, and property. Byzantine women also had very important rights: A woman possessed her dowry and daughters could inherit equally with their brothers in cases of intestate succession.

Whatever their social status, within the church women were prohibited from giving instruction or from holding any priestly functions. However, the church acknowledged that women were spiritually equal to men, and the Theotokos (Mary, *the God-bearer*) was always a central figure in the devotion of both men and women. Women, moreover, could play an important role as abbesses, and noble ladies frequently founded monasteries to which they could retire upon widowhood.

EUNUCHS: BYZANTIUM'S THIRD GENDER

Byzantium also possessed a third gender: that of eunuchs, a class inherited from the late Roman Empire and from the civilizations of Asia. They could play an important part at court and in the church (and even in the army). Certain high positions within the palace hierarchy, such as that of the Grand Chamberlain, were reserved for eunuchs, who could also be found working in aristocratic families. Considered trustworthy because they were unable to take the throne and distinguished by their marked physical characteristics, they maintained a high profile in the palace, including the women's quarters, and generally acted as the officials of ruling and regent empresses as well as for most emperors prior to the late eleventh century. Although legislation banned castration, the operation was often performed on children and adults—in the case of children, sometimes by their own families to ensure them a glittering future at court. Illegitimate children within the royal family—such as Basil the Nothos (*Illegitimate*), son of Romanos I (r. 920–944)—could be castrated and promoted through the bureaucracy to work alongside the future emperor, their legitimate half brother. Other eunuchs were imported from the Caucasus and the Slav and Arab worlds. Eunuchs were in charge of the imperial bureaucracy until the late eleventh century.

Eunuchs are often linked to the practice of homosexuality and, in sharp contrast to the generally *laissez faire* attitude toward extramarital relationships, church fathers denounced this as the *sin of sodomy*. It could be punishable by death according to criminal law. Homosexual practices are documented in both male and female monasteries, and

Theodora and Her Court. *This mid-sixth century mosiac depicts Byzantine empress Theodora and her court.* THE GRANGER COLLECTION, NEW YORK.

several monastic institutions refused access to beardless youths or eunuchs to avoid temptation for the monks, and they also tried to limit physical contact between members of the monastic community. However, there were monasteries especially for eunuchs: the monastery of St. Lazaros in Constantinople was restricted to eunuchs by Leo VI when emperor, and there were other communities of eunuch monks at various periods. Eunuchs were prominent as bishops, abbots, and patriarchs, the last being Eustratios Garidas (r. 1081–1084).

SEXUALITY AND ROMANCE

In general, erotic or romantic love between the sexes was viewed with suspicion. Indeed, sexuality and carnal love were seen in Byzantium as inspired by the devil and as tending to lead to fornication, and worse yet, adultery. But conjugal love was praised, though the church fathers, often recommended limitations on conjugal sex. The Byzantines knew of erotic literary genres. The ancient romances continued to be read in Byzantium, though episodes of extramarital sex within them are severely criticized, and Byzantine readers seemed to have interpreted these works as metaphorical descriptions of the soul's struggle for salvation. Similarly, the terminology of erotic love is often transferred to the relationship between God and man. The romance as a literary genre, however, reappears in the twelfth century, perhaps influenced by contacts with European literature during the crusades, whereas more popular, orally transmitted works from the fourteenth century adapt European plots and love themes into a Byzantine setting. It can therefore be assumed that the later Byzantine public, literate or illiterate, had a taste for love stories and fictional romances despite the negative attitude toward sexuality that prevailed in Byzantium.

BIBLIOGRAPHY

Evans, J. A. S. 2002. *Empress Theodora, Partner of Justinian.* Austin: University of Texas Press.

Garland, Lynda. 1988. "The Life and Ideology of Byzantine Women: A Further Note on Conventions of Behaviour and Social Reality as Reflected in Eleventh and Twelfth Century Historical Sources." *Byzantion* 58: 361–393.

Garland, Lynda. 1999. *Byzantine Empresses: Women and Power in Byzantium AD 527–1204.* London: Routledge.

Garland, Lynda, ed. 2007. *Byzantine Women: Varieties of Experience 800–1200*. Aldershot, UK: Ashgate.

Herrin, Judith. 1983. "In Search of Byzantine Women: Three Avenues of Approach." In *Images of Women in Antiquity*, ed. Averil Cameron and Amelie Kuhrt. Detroit, MI: Wayne State University Press.

Herrin, Judith. 2001. *Women in Purple: Rulers of Medieval Byzantium*. Princeton, NJ: Princeton University Press.

Holum, Kenneth G. 1982. *Theodosian Empresses: Women and Imperial Dominion in Late Antiquity*. Berkeley: University of California Press.

Kalavrezou, Ioli, ed. 2003. *Byzantine Women and Their World*. New Haven, CT: Yale University Press.

Laiou, Angeliki E. 1985. "Observations on the Life and Ideology of Byzantine Women." *Byzantinische Forschungen* 9: 59–102.

Laiou, Angeliki E. 1992. *Gender, Society and Economic Life in Byzantium*. Aldershot, UK: Variorum.

Nicol, Donald M. 1994. *The Byzantine Lady: Ten Portraits 1250–1500*. Cambridge, UK: Cambridge University Press.

Ringrose, Kathryn M. 1994. "Living in the Shadows: Eunuchs and Gender in Byzantium." In *Third Sex, Third Gender: Beyond Sexual Dimorphism in Culture and History*, ed. Gilbert Herdt. New York: Zone Books.

Ringrose, Kathryn M. 2003. *The Perfect Servant: Eunuchs and the Social Construction of Gender in Byzantium*. Chicago: University of Chicago Press.

Talbot, Alice-Mary. 1996. *Holy Women of Byzantium: Ten Saints' Lives in English Translation*. Washington DC: Dumbarton Oaks.

Talbot, Alice-Mary, et al., eds. 2004. "Bibliography on Women in Byzantium." Dumbarton Oaks. Available from http://www.doaks.org/WomeninByzantium.html.

Lynda Garland

C

CALL GIRL

A call girl is a female prostitute whose clients contact her by telephone to arrange meetings. Call girls typically charge higher prices than street prostitutes and exercise a great deal of discretion over which clients they accept. A call girl will generally meet with a client in her own home, in his home, or in a hotel room; meetings are arranged in advance, usually by telephone—hence the term *call* girl. Depending on the wishes and needs of the client, sessions may be brief, with the sole purpose of bringing the client to orgasm, or much more protracted, involving conversation, cuddling, leisurely lovemaking, extended role-playing scenes, or even a traditional dinner date.

Though the term *call girl* is often used interchangeably with *escort,* there are significant differences between the two. Clients make contact with escorts through publicly available means: They may arrange for a meeting through an escort service, or they may find escorts advertised in magazines and newspapers. Call girls generally accept clients by referral only; clients may be referred by a madam (a woman who manages a house of prostitution), by other call girls, or by other clients. This referral system helps protect call girls from the danger of soliciting an undercover police officer and helps ensure discreet clients, thus allowing them to remain more or less invisible to the public. As such, call girls, of all illegal prostitutes, run the least risk of arrest and prosecution.

THE BUSINESS

Call girls are generally considered to be a higher class of prostitute than streetwalkers, escorts, and brothel workers. The most successful call girls are often well educated, intelligent, stylish, sophisticated, and—above all—discreet. Though comprehensive demographic data is largely lacking, existing studies and anecdotal evidence suggest that call girls are overwhelmingly white and that their clientele tends to be middle or upper class. The profession is lucrative, and call girls generally dress and live well. Much of the allure of the call girl stems from her conventional outer appearance, and most call girls, therefore, look very much like the kind of smart, successful woman that the general populace cannot imagine being a prostitute.

As with many sex workers, call girls consider themselves first and foremost to be professionals. In order to best serve their customers and to encourage repeat business, call girls pay close attention to their clients' desires—both expressed and unvoiced. More so than with street prostitutes, whose circumstances often dictate a hurried sexual encounter, call girls are selling a fantasy. Successful call girls are cognizant not only of what sexual activities their clients desire but also of what kind of persona he will find most attractive and exciting in a lover. A call girl might play the role of a first-time call girl, an experienced dominatrix, a raunchy schoolgirl, or a comforting caregiver. She might be passive or demanding, pliant or controlling, depending on the wishes and moods of her client. Often it is left to the call girl to discern which response is most appropriate. As such, call girls are often accomplished at reading and responding to their clients' hidden desires at a moment's notice.

Call girls acquire clients almost exclusively by referral, thus necessitating a close connection to other women in the profession. Many call girls begin by working for a madam, who provides contacts with screened clients—and sometimes a location for the meeting—in exchange for a substantial cut (usually 40 to 50 percent) of the call girl's earnings. Women employed by a madam will often try to develop their own client lists; such women might try to circumvent the madam's participation in the transaction by providing the client with their direct contact information—a practice understandably discouraged by madams—or they might purchase a "book," or client list, from a call girl who is leaving the profession. Self-employed call girls expand their client bases by exchanging referrals. A call girl who is unable to meet with a client might send him to another girl, or she might send a client to another girl in exchange for that girl's previous participation in a threesome or in a role-playing or fantasy scenario.

CALL GIRLS VERSUS STREET PROSTITUTES

Although both call girls and street prostitutes may see the same clients for years, call girls tend to spend more time per session with their clients; this may be because sessions are almost always conducted in a safe and secure location, often a private home. Additionally, call girls are much more likely to engage in conversation and other nonsexual activity with their clients. Whereas street prostitution often aims to bring the client to climax as quickly as possible, call girls and their clients are much more likely to engage in extended foreplay, as well as activities, such as oral and vaginal stimulation, that are aimed ostensibly at female as well as male pleasure.

THE CLIENTS

Studies of call girls and their clients are necessarily somewhat difficult to come by, as call girls' business and safety depend on their own discretion, as well as that of coworkers and clients. Available studies suggest, however, that men may visit call girls for somewhat different reasons than they visit street prostitutes. Though sexual activity is almost always a component of a visit to a call girl, conversation is often also a significant aspect of the session. Call girls frequently report discussing their clients' business and personal lives and often provide support and commiseration after a bad day. Reasons for visiting a call girl vary widely, but for a significant percentage of men this kind of emotional interaction is crucial. Married men may report being able to converse with a call girl about topics they will not discuss with their wives, while single men sometimes indicate that a call girl is an easy alternative to a girlfriend, citing readily available sex and intimacy without the time commitment of a romantic relationship. As Janet Lever and Deanne Dolnick (2000) have suggested, men's visits to call girls are often as much about intimacy and connection as they are about sex.

BIBLIOGRAPHY

Buchwald, Laura. 2001. "A Conversation with Tracy Quan." *Bold Type* 5.4 (September). Available from http://www.randomhouse.com/boldtype/0901/quan.

Bullough, Vern, and Bonnie Bullough. 1987. *Women and Prostitution: A Social History*. Buffalo, NY: Prometheus Books.

Lever, Janet, and Deanne Dolnick. 2000. "Clients and Call Girls: Seeking Sex and Intimacy." In *Sex for Sale: Prostitution, Pornography, and the Sex Industry*, ed. Ronald Weitzer. New York: Routledge.

Ringdal, Johan Nils. 2004. *Love for Sale: A World History of Prostitution*, trans. Richard Daly. New York: Grove Press.

Stein, Martha L. 1974. *Lovers, Friends, Slaves . . .: The Nine Male Sexual Types, Their Psycho-sexual Transactions with Call Girls*. New York: Berkley Publishing.

Maureen Lauder

CAMILLE, MICHAEL
1958–2002

Born in Yorkshire into a working-class family, Michael Camille earned a first-class B.A. (1980), an M.A. (1982), and a Ph.D. (1985) at Cambridge University. He then moved to the University of Chicago, where he taught medieval art history until his death of a brain tumor.

From the start, Camille's work took up questions of marginality, shifting attention from "official" culture and the great monuments of the past to images and objects that had previously been ignored by mainstream art history. In doing so, Camille was concerned to analyze representations—especially "monstrous" representations connected to marginalized, "othered" sexualities and religious groups—that exceeded and resisted, but also potentially bolstered, dominant cultural constructions. Camille's first book, *The Gothic Idol: Ideology and Image-Making in Medieval Art* (1989), considered depictions of idols and idolatry that showed Christianity grappling with, and in many ways demonizing, its religious and sexual others—homosexuals or sodomites, pagans and heretics, Muslims and Jews. Here, he emphasized how closely related to each other were medieval sexual and religious otherness. Camille's next book, *Image on the Edge: The Margins of Medieval Art* (1992), moved even more fully to examine scandalous, scatological, and sexual images in the margins of architecture and manuscript illustration. Camille developed a complex argument that shares much with queer theory about how the center or dominant depends for its very existence upon the abjected and disavowed material pushed to the margins. *Master of Death: The Lifeless Art of Pierre Remiet, Illuminator* (1996), while it shifted its attention away from sexuality, continued to think about how the

Middle Ages represented bodies—here, bodies subjected, often grotesquely, to old age, death, and decay. Considering the time of the Black Death, the book might also be read as reflecting Camille's experience as a gay man living during the AIDS crisis. In addition, Camille coedited, with Adrian Rifkin, *Other Objects of Desire: Collectors and Collecting Queerly* (2001), a volume on the collecting of art as a queer practice.

Late in his life, Camille was engaged intensively in thinking about disallowed medieval sexualities, working on an unfinished book entitled *Stones of Sodom*, which was to trace medieval representations of sodomy. Glimpses of what this project might have looked like are available in some of Camille's later published work. Thus, in "The Pose of the Queer: Dante's Gaze, Brunetto Latini's Body" (2001), Camille closely examines one manuscript illumination of the circle of the sodomites in Dante's *Inferno*, analyzing the physical pose given there to Dante's former teacher Brunetto Latini as Dante the pilgrim gazes down at Brunetto's body. Comparing Brunetto's pose, one arm akimbo, to twentieth-century visual stereotypes of gay men, Camille's essay reflects on the resonances and differences between the medieval moment, with its understanding of sodomy, and the modern moment of gay identity, concluding that "I would rather call Brunetto a queer or a queen than a homosexual (or a heterosexual), precisely because these terms do not so much define modern rigid stereotypes as open up possibilities" (p. 79).

SEE ALSO *Gay.*

BIBLIOGRAPHY

Boeye, Kerry. 2002. "A Bibliography of the Writings of Michael Camille." *Gesta* 41(1): 141–144.

Camille, Michael. 1989. *The Gothic Idol: Ideology and Image-Making in Medieval Art.* Cambridge, UK: Cambridge University Press.

Camille, Michael. 1992. *Image on the Edge: The Margins of Medieval Art.* Cambridge, MA: Harvard University Press.

Camille, Michael. 2001. "The Pose of the Queer: Dante's Gaze, Brunetto Latini's Body." In *Queering the Middle Ages*, edited by Glenn Burger and Steven F. Kruger. Minneapolis: University of Minnesota Press.

Steven F. Kruger

CAMP

Camp celebrates the stylistic and emotional excesses of mainstream popular culture as they are interpreted and redefined by homosexual subcultures. Camp emphasizes that all comportment is artifice; to camp it up is both to behave artificially and to celebrate and call attention to artificiality in everyday life. The word *camp* is associated with excessive displays of gesture and emotion; it was used in J. Redding Ware's 1909 *Passing English of the Victorian Era*, a dictionary of Victorian slang, to describe the showy, theatrical behaviors, affectations, and gestures associated with persons of so-called low character. This exaggerated comportment, or campiness, in which theatricality calls attention to the artificiality of all behavioral conventions, constituted a specifically homosexual set of codes, styles, and gestures in the early and middle twentieth century.

Those codes have been used by gay subcultures since that time to accentuate the distance that exists for queer people between what most people insist are natural behaviors and what gay men and lesbians traditionally have seen as little more than cultural norms. Aspects of camp that play up effeminacy and drag in particular are thought to have been favored by homosexual subcultures because their emphasis on role playing resonated with those for whom acting heterosexual meant playing a role.

THE INFLUENCE OF OSCAR WILDE

Oscar Wilde is considered one of the modern fathers of camp sensibility; his effete comportment and witticisms helped revive the cult of the dandy in the late nineteenth century. His 1890 novel *The Picture of Dorian Gray*, a bible of aestheticism, constantly undercuts the moral tale of a superficial sociopath with passages celebrating the protagonist's devotion to surface beauty and individual style. His stage comedies, especially the 1895 *The Importance of Being Earnest*, are rife with campy epigrams and double entendres.

Wilde's epigrams, in which conventional sentiments are read backward, adapted, or tweaked slightly so that they are both familiar and strange, are examples of a camp take on mainstream culture in which audiences are forced to reread normative practices through the eyes of a skeptical, if affectionate, outsider. The aphorisms "Divorces are made in heaven" and "In marriage, three is company, two is none," from *The Importance of Being Earnest*, make fun of the sanctity of marriage. The first alters the conventional description of the ideal heterosexual union as "a match made in heaven," and the second alters the cliché that celebrates the couple form as preferable to any other social arrangement: "Two's company; three's a crowd." By flipping these sayings over to suggest that the opposite is true, that divorce is far more heavenly than marriage and that any company at all is a welcome relief from the everyday tedium of married life, Wilde declares that contrary to Victorian popular sentiment, traditional marriage is both hellish and boring. The fact that Victorian audiences found those observations hilarious when they were made in Wilde's plays signifies that they not only appreciated Wilde's wit but relished his send-up of institutionalized heterosexuality.

LATER CAMP

Later examples of camp favored excess as an expressive mode, whether it was the maniacal choreography and extraordinary overhead camera shots signifying a point of view that no audience of a supposed stage musical would ever have of a Busby Berkeley musical, the lurid color palette and tragic melodrama of a Douglas Sirk tearjerker, or the menacing, bitchy femininity of Joan Crawford or Bette Davis. Divas who cultivated a monumental stage presence, such as Maria Callas and Diana Ross, or a histrionic theatricality, such as Bette Midler and Liza Minelli, are camp figures, as are feminine personalities whose extreme artificiality shows that they are aping versions of themselves, such as Marilyn Monroe, Paul Lynde, and Barbra Streisand. The diva's camp artificiality can encompass physical excessiveness as well; Dolly Parton's and Jane Russell's breasts are camp, as is Phyllis Diller's or Michael Jackson's face and the porn star Ron Jeremy's comically hairy and chubby physique.

SONTAG'S ANALYSIS OF CAMP

Although camp remained a homosexual subcultural language and style for decades, it achieved mainstream recognition as a theory of culture, or interpretive lens, with the publication of Susan Sontag's 1964 essay "Notes on 'Camp,'" which remains the best-known essay on the subject. Sontag (1983) argues that camp is a mode of aestheticism, a sensibility and a badge of identity, and a way of seeing that emphasizes texture, decorative surface, style, and frivolity. Among the objects she lists as camp, ostensibly because their design and execution epitomize an over-the-top excessiveness, are Tiffany lamps, Bellini operas, flapper costumes of the 1920s, Flash Gordon comics, the movie *King Kong,* and all things art nouveau. She differentiates naïve camp from intentional camp, insisting that only naïve camp—camp that is trying to be serious and meaningful but fails—can be considered real or pure camp. She discusses the camp sensibility that recognizes objects of value gleaming among the detritus of popular culture, stating that in its appropriation of the low, vulgar, tasteless, and extravagantly tacky as beautiful, camp challenges the hegemony of high culture, setting itself up as a more urban, sophisticated, and generous sensibility.

It generally is acknowledged that Sontag appropriated camp from homosexual subcultures in the essay only to dismiss those subcultures, though that gesture itself is part of the cultural and historical closeting of homosexuality among the 1960s avant-garde. Much of Sontag's essay rests on the work of homosexual and lesbian writers, artists, filmmakers, and actors. She sets herself the task of expanding what she terms a "lazy" definition published ten years earlier in Christopher Isherwood's *The World in the Evening*, she dedicates the essay to Oscar Wilde, and her examples of camp include Noel Coward plays, Aubrey Beardsley drawings, Jean Cocteau films, Oscar Wilde epigrams, Greta Garbo's beauty and lack of dramatic depth, Barbara Stanwyk's and Tallulah Bankhead's mannish acting style, Caravaggio's paintings, Genet's ideas, and the dandyism of Wilde and the aesthetes, to which she dedicates four of her fifty-eight "notes." Though all these figures are gay or lesbian, she never infers, except in her insistence on the camp sensibility of those artists, that their sexual identities place them within the homosexual vanguard.

Sontag was not open about her lesbianism, and this helps explain some of the distance from and ambivalence toward homosexuality the essay expresses as well as its substitution of a Jewish interpretive standpoint for a homosexual one. She does not mention homosexuals or homosexuality until note fifty; in note fifty-one she concedes that homosexuals are in the "vanguard" of camp sensibility; in note fifty-two she equates that sensibility with the Jewish moral sensibility; and by note fifty-three the parallel to a more moral Jewish sensibility allows her to declare camp an oppositional "solvent of morality" (Sontag 1983, p. 118) in which style always trumps content and politics.

OTHER CRITICAL ANALYSES

Sontag's interest in the "mere" surface politics of camp has been contested by cultural critics. Many gay critics have accused her of appropriating a queer style of resistance and neutralizing its politics through her definition of camp as an aesthetic sensibility and moral solvent. Andrew Ross (1989), for example, has countered that camp is political in a Marxist sense in that it registers historical shifts in modes of production. He defines camp as an "effect" created when outmoded products recirculate in contemporary culture and become available for new value and new meaning. Thus, mid-twentieth-century films such as *Sunset Boulevard* are campy because they use aging film stars from the silent era to create melodramatic metanarratives about aging film stars from the silent era. *What Ever Happened to Baby Jane?* is similarly campy in its use of the over-the-hill leading ladies, rivals, and icons of the big studio era Bette Davis and Joan Crawford, pitted against each other in a gothic scenario shaped by sibling rivalry. Moe Meyer (1994) is even more literal than Ross about the politics of camp, defining it as "queer parody," arguing that it played a crucial role in the theatrics of gay activist groups such as ACT-UP and Queer Nation, and insisting that any attempts to define camp as

"Hairspray" Opens on Broadway. *Harvey Fierstein, Marissa Jaret Winokur, and the cast of the musical "Hairspray" on stage for curtain call after the opening night performance at the Neil Simon Theater in New York.* © GREGORY PACE/CORBIS.

merely aesthetic undermine its political force as a strategy of queer resistance to normative models of identity, respectability, gender, sexuality, and class.

Noting that most of the leading lights in the pantheon of camp figures are women, recent feminist critics such as Pamela Robertson (1996) have questioned the notion of a one-way exchange in camp in which gay men supposedly appropriate female stars and female styles but women do not appropriate a gay male aesthetic. To see exchanges between women and gay men is to imagine, Robertson argues, that feminism can have a similar critical distance from and opposition to mainstream popular cultural forms. Thus, Mae West's camping could parody 1890s traditions of burlesque and female impersonation to contest contemporary female stereotypes in the 1930s.

DRAG QUEENS AND KITSCH

One of the most recognizable forms of camp has long been the female impersonator, or drag queen. The drag queen performs a reading of culture by invoking the femininity of certain film stars and famous singers and performers past and present and parodying those traits by exaggerating them. Thus, Judy Garland's overly painted face might be parodied to the point of clownishness by huge red lips and gigantic false eyelashes, her need to be loved by her audience reduced to a grotesque and sexualized begging by the drag performer down on his knees in front of the audience, and her signature vibrato amplified to the point of quavery croaking, all of it suggesting both the hardness and the pathos of an over-the-hill performer unwilling to relinquish the limelight. Although such impersonation was read in the past as making fun of women, it is possible to interpret the masquerade of femininity as the butt of the impersonator's joke; indeed, one of the things camp drag emphasizes is the enormous effort it takes to be a woman and a performer. Female drag impersonators are usually effeminate gay men whose femininity has served as a source of both oppression and pride for them, and their camp take on the dignity and burden of femininity is often profoundly sympathetic and identificatory as well as parodic.

That type of drag was even more political and oppositional in the days when it was illegal to dress in the clothes of the opposite sex. In the era when police could arrest men or women who did not have on at least three items of gender-appropriate clothing, the theatricality of drag protected gay female impersonators from the violence meted out to effeminate men who were not in costume and makeup. Other forms of camp, such as the arch enthusiasm for kitschy, sentimental items such as Hummel statues, velvet paintings, onion-head children with huge eyes, and baby animal figurines, signify other kinds of opposition, the cultivation of an aesthetic that rejects the institutionalization of "high" art and instead celebrates the lowbrow, the ugly, and the general trashiness of mass-manufactured collectibles. This type of camp is political insofar as it rejects the self-improving class politics of bourgeois aesthetics. At the same time it takes a certain level of sophistication to appreciate the lowbrow as lowbrow; thus, the camp appreciation for kitsch risks accusations of condescension in its appropriation of lowbrow sentimentality as something that is interesting mostly because it is bizarre.

Whether camp remains a specifically gay aesthetic is debatable only because camp has permeated mainstream culture to such a profound degree since Sontag's essay. Camp has transformed itself dramatically from the camp of an earlier era. The secret language of camp melodrama and emotional excess, in which a group of homosexual insiders and their friends once read Mae West's suggestiveness as nelly effeminacy, Joan Crawford's hard femininity as drag queen hauteur, or Judy Garland's brave vulnerability as the broken-hearted optimism of the gay romantic heart, has become ubiquitous in popular culture. The distinction between naïve and intentional camp Sontag insisted on has disappeared as mainstream audiences have grown more sophisticated.

The best examples of camp from the latter decades of the twentieth century were usually intentional products rather than naïve accidents, whether the invitation to subcultural revelry of *The Rocky Horror Picture Show,* which makes fun of the straightest characters and rewards the naughty ones; the B-movie vulgarity of *Showgirls*, with its cheesy dialogue and over-the-top bad acting; the sissy boys and drag queens playing heterosexual men and women in a John Waters film; or the tongue-in-cheek retro style of *But I'm a Cheerleader*, much of it taken from Waters, in which heterosexual normativity is portrayed as cultish and bizarre. Television series such as the night-time soap opera *Desperate Housewives* deliberately cultivated a camp critical distance between viewers and the characters, encouraging audiences to judge the everyday pursuits of suburban families as bizarre, excessive, and highly entertaining. Reality television became adept at exploiting the camp effect of contestants frantically trying to become famous, its judges acting as critics who ridiculed talentless people who were willing to do anything for money and attention. By recognizing and creating a market of viewers who would tune in week after week to watch people embarrass themselves, reality television read the excessive desire for fame on the part of everyday people as ubiquitous, excessive, outrageous, queer, kitschy, ridiculous, and touching, creating a new take on an old culture of spectacular display in which everyone and anyone, regardless of identity, can imitate the performing style of his or her favorite star and be queen for a day. If camp has become the hip sensibility of contemporary popular culture, it remains to be seen whether the camp gesture or way of reading culture can continue to operate as oppositional or subversive. It is uncertain whether camp has been assimilated to the degree that if everything is camp, nothing is, or whether, instead, if everything is camp, everything is.

SEE ALSO *Dandyism; Drag Kings; Drag Queens; Garland, Judy; Wilde, Oscar.*

BIBLIOGRAPHY

Meyer, Moe. 1994. "Introduction" and "Under the Sign of Wilde: An Archaeology of Posing." In *The Politics and Poetics of Camp,* ed. Moe Meyer New York and London: Routledge.

Robertson, Pamela. 1996. *Guilty Pleasures: Feminist Camp from Mae West to Madonna.* Durham, NC: Duke University Press.

Ross, Andrew, 1989. "The Uses of Camp." In *No Respect: Intellectuals & Popular Culture.* New York: Routledge.

Sontag, Susan. 1983. "Notes on 'Camp.'" In *A Susan Sontag Reader.* New York: Vintage.

Jaime Hovey

CANCER, BREAST

In 1971 U.S. President Richard M. Nixon declared a war on cancer and poured more than $100 million into cancer research due to public outcry against the disease. Cancer kills more than half a million Americans each year (American Cancer Society [ACS] 2006, p. 4). One of the most common types of the disease was also one of the first identified in humans, breast cancer. Physicians have recognized it for thousands of years. However years of research and hundreds of millions of dollars have not resulted in an exact cause or cure. Breast cancer is still a major health problem in the early-twenty-first century and one out of eight American women was diagnosed with the disease in 2005 (ACS 2006, p. 14; Olson 2002; Surveillance, Epidemiology, and End Results Program [SEER] 2002, p. 1). The history of breast cancer is filled with controversy because of the highly gendered nature of the disease and the status of the female breast as a cultural symbol of sexuality.

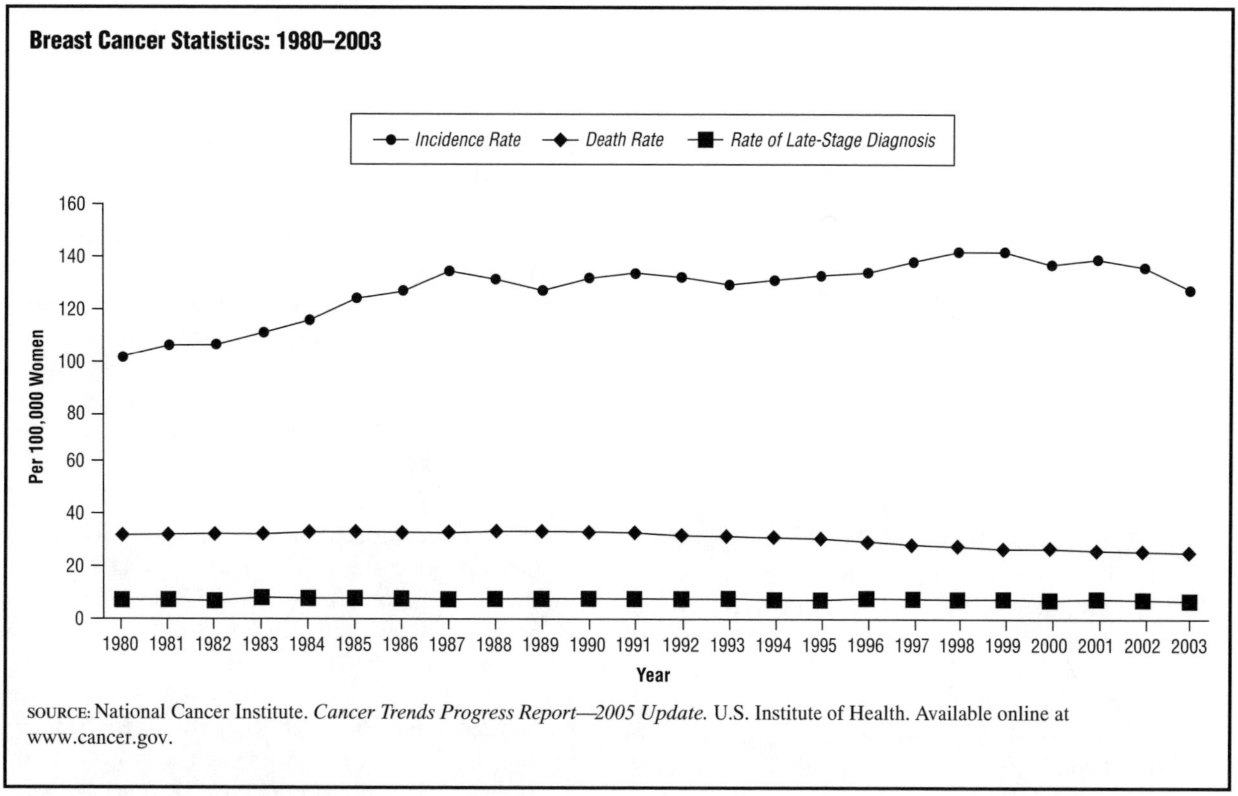

Breast Cancer Statistics, 1980-2003. THOMSON GALE.

INCIDENCE RATE, MORTALITY RATE, AND TREATMENT OPTIONS

Breast cancer is the leading cancer diagnosis among American women, accounting for nearly one in three cancers in that group (ACS 2006, p. 1). Figure 1 depicts incidence of and death rates from female breast cancer and rates of late-stage breast cancer diagnosis in the United States from 1997 to 2002. Cancer incidence is measured as the number of new cases each year for every 100,000 women while the death rate is measured as the number of deaths each year for every 100,000 women. Overall these figures seem promising; the declining fatalities and increasing five-year survival rates indicate that larger numbers of women survive a cancer diagnosis. However the incidence of female breast cancer has steadily increased since 1980. The increase is largely attributed to more mammography screenings in women ages forty and over. For example, 29 percent of women in the forty and over group were tested in 1987 as compared to 70 percent in 2000. Although the mortality rate declined during the 1990s, rates of late-stage (metastases) breast cancer diagnosis have remained stable since 1980 and hover around 7 per 100,000 women (National Cancer Institute [NCI] 2005a, p.1). Patients diagnosed in later stages are less likely to benefit from treatments or recover as easily as those whose diseases were discovered at earlier stages.

Cancer-related health disparities remain among population subgroups in the United States. Both incidence and death rates generally increase with age—more that 95 percent of new cases occurred in women forty and older. The average age at diagnosis is sixty-one. Caucasian women have the highest incidence of breast cancer (141.1 per 100,000, 1998–2002) but black women have the highest rate of breast cancer death (34.7 per 100,000). Hispanics, Asians, and women of other minority groups have lower incidence of and death from breast cancer (ACS 2006, p. 2). A recent study also confirmed treatment disparities between Caucasian and minority women; minority women with early-stage breast cancer received fewer cycles of cheomotherapy than Caucasian women (Bickell, Wang, Oluwole, et al. 2006).

Early remedies for the cancer were surgical or conservative. Doctors preferred conservative treatment, which included purging, specific diets, bloodletting, and medicines. In the nineteenth century, Viennese surgeon Theodor Billroth confirmed that breast cancer traveled to regional lymph nodes before spreading to other parts of the body. As a result radical mastectomy, also known as Halsted mastectomy, was the major treatment for breast cancer until 1979. The radical mastectomy removes the breast and the underlying muscle in the chest wall or pectoral muscle. In the 1980s modified radical mastectomy became standard, while breast conservation therapy (BCT) was the preferred treatment in the 1990s (Altman 1996, Olson 2002). BCT combines a lumpectomy with radiation therapy. A modified radical mastectomy removes the whole breast, some axillary lymph nodes, and possibly part of chest wall muscle. A lumpectomy removes only the tumor and a rim of normal surrounding breast tissue (NCCN 2005).

Therapies in the early twenty-first century are based on a number of factors, including age, onset of menopause, severity, histologic and nuclear grade of the primary tumor, estrogen-receptor (ER) and progesterone-receptor (PR) status, measures of proliferative capacity, and HER2/neu gene amplification. Patients can choose between standard treatments and clinical trials. Standard treatments include surgery, radiation therapy, chemotherapy, and hormone therapy. Typical surgeries include lumpectomy, partial mastectomy, total mastectomy, modified radical mastectomy, and radical mastectomy. In 1990 the National Institutes of Health (NIH) Consensus Development Panel concluded that BCT provided the same survival rates as women who chose total mastectomy and axillary dissection. Accordingly the NIH recommends BCT for women with early-stage breast cancer (stages I and II). Despite the NIH recommendation, the modified radical mastectomy remains the most common surgical procedure for women diagnosed with early-stage breast cancer (Altman 1996, NCI 2005b). A recent study concluded that more patient involvement in treatment decision making was associated with greater use of mastectomy (Katz, Lantz, Jamz, et al 2005). Concern about disease recurrence was cited as the most influential factor when women chose mastectomies over BCT.

Radiation therapy uses high-energy x-rays or other forms of radiation to destroy cancer cells in the breast, chest wall, or lymph nodes. It is generally used after surgery, especially as part of BCT. The treatment commonly follows a mastectomy in cases with either of the following conditions, a tumor larger than five centimeters in size or positive lymph nodes. There are two different types of radiation therapy: external beam and internal. External beam therapy, which is most common, uses an external machine to deliver the radiation, while a radioactive substance (usually sealed in needles, seeds, wires or catheters) is inserted into the body in or near the tumor in the internal method (NCCN 2005, NCI 2005b).

Chemotherapy and hormone therapy are systemic treatments, meaning they both use drugs to stop the growth of cancer cells. Chemotherapy can be used before surgery (neoadjuvant treatment) and after surgery (adjuvant therapy). The goal for neoadjuvant treatment is to shrink the tumor enough to make surgical removable possible, especially for women who have a large tumor and prefer to undergo BCT. Adjuvant therapy kills cancer cells that break away from the primary tumor and spread through the bloodstream, and do not show up on diagnostic tests such as an X-ray and CT scan or can not be felt during the physical examinations by physicians (NCCN 2005, NCI 2005b). Systemic treatment can be given intravenously or orally and is more effective when combinations of more than one drug are used together. Chemotherapy has been recommended for women with positive lymph nodes since 1985, but younger women are more likely to receive chemotherapy than older women. For example, in 2000, 86 percent of women ages twenty to sixty-four with node-positive breast cancer received chemotherapy as compared to 45 percent of women sixty-five and up with similar conditions. For women whose breast cancers have spread to other organs in the body (metastases, stage IV), systemic treatment is the main treatment.

For women with estrogen- and progesterone-receptor positive tumors, hormone drugs are given after standard treatment to prevent recurrence. There are two types of hormone drugs, anti-estrogen drugs and aromatase inhibitors. Tamoxifen is the most commonly used of the anti-estrogen drugs, which act to block estrogen after it is produced. It is often prescribed for five years. Aromatase inhibitors, which interfere with the production of estrogen, have the same or better effects, but fewer side effects compared with tamoxifen. Accordingly they are the preferred adjuvant hormone therapy for postmenopausal women (NCCN 2005).

In addition to standard treatments, patients can also participate in clinical trials testing promising treatments. A new treatment is normally studied in three phrases of clinical trials before it is eligible for approval by the Food and Drug Administration (FDA). The last phase involves enrolling thousands of patients with one group receiving the standard treatment and the other group receiving the new treatment. Between 2000 and 2005, a clinical trial tested the effectiveness of trastuzumab (also called Herceptin) on women who have tested positive for the HER2/neu receptor. The study enrolled more than 3,300 patients with early-stage breast cancers and positive axillary lymph nodes and concluded that patients who received trastuzumab combined with standard chemotherapy had a 52 percent decrease in disease recurrence compared to patients treated with standard chemotherapy alone. Because of this finding, trastuzumab has become part of standard chemotherapy treatment for about 20 to 25 percent of breast cancer women whose tumors are HER2/neu receptor positive (NCI 2005c).

SOCIAL CONSTRUCTION OF BREAST CANCER

Gender-roles in a patriarchal society are established with man in mind and female sexuality is constructed to complement male sexuality. Thus a woman's breast performs both reproductive and sexual functions; a nutrition source for infants also serves as erotic draw for men. Women's subordinate position also manifests itself in breast cancer treatment, where patients tend to be female and physicians male. In the disease's early history, women often delayed seeking medical treatment because of shame and stigma. After diagnosis women usually left the treatment decision entirely in the hands of their male physicians. This paternalistic relationship between breast cancer patient and physician persisted until major social changes transformed medical practice in the 1960s and 1970s (Casamayou 2001, Olson 2002, Young 1998).

At the macro level, post-World War II economic affluence led to significant cultural and structural changes in the United States. As suggested by political scientist Ronald Inglehart, people became more sensitive to quality of life issues such as social justice, equity, and citizen participation in the public decision-making process. Economic affluence also created more than 72 million baby boomers during the period from 1946 to 1964. Social movements in the 1960s such as civil rights, environmental, and feminist movements as well as the anti-Vietnam War movement, were products of these cultural and social changes. These macro-level changes set a new stage for patient advocates to challenge the medical establishment and demand the federal government reexamine issues related to women's health and patient's rights.

At the micro level, the federal government did not have a formal policy about cancer until public concern about the disease replaced fear of infectious diseases in the 1930s. As a result of the new public interest, the NCI was established in 1937. Funding for biomedical research emerged as the heart of federal health policy after the World War II—a triple alliance among congressional representatives, executive agency personnel, and lobbyists was formed to secure funding. Key congressional supporters included John Fogarty, chair of the Labor-Health, Education, and Welfare subcommittees of the appropriations committees of the House and Senate, and Lister Hill. Outside the government, health activist Mary Lasker formed the first lobbyist group for cancer research with her own wealth after her husband died of cancer. Backed by the triple alliance, the medical establishment basked in an unprecedented position of prestige and power over patients.

However other social forces emerged during the 1970s that changed paternalistic relationships between patients and physicians. First media coverage of prominent women's diagnoses and cancer treatments led to a societal openness toward the disease. These women included actress and diplomat Shirley Temple Black; Betty Ford, wife of President Gerald Ford; Happy Rockefeller, wife of politician Nelson Rockefeller; and writer Betty Rollin. Second the 1960s feminist movement created a new generation of educated women with professional and organizational skills. One of them was Rose Kushner whose breast cancer experience led her to become the first patient consumer advocate. She campaigned to change the one-step (biopsy and mastectomy) process to a two-step process of breast cancer diagnosis and surgery, and promoted the patients' rights to shop for the surgeon after diagnosis. Other survivors and advocates shared similar views and believed that more funding was needed to further lower breast cancer deaths and that patients should have greater involvement in treatment decision making. Many were also disturbed by the 1977 FDA policy that banned fertile women from toxicity studies and from initial safety and efficacy studies. Under the guise of *protecting the fetus*, this policy resulted in excluding many women from accessing major clinical trials. Angered and frustrated with unfair medical practices, breast cancer survivors formed grassroots patient advocacy organizations; eventually national breast cancer advocacy groups like the National Alliance for Breast Cancer Organizations (NABCO) in 1986, Y-ME in 1978, Susan B. Komen in 1982, National Breast Cancer Coalition in 1991, and Living Beyond Breast Cancer in 1991 were established. The grassroots breast cancer movement led to the biggest increase in federal funding for breast cancer research. For example, in 2005, the NCI alone invested $570 million in breast cancer research, while the entire public funding for breast cancer research was about $600 million in 1993 (Casamayou 2001, NCI 2006, Oberman 1994).

BREAST CANCER AND THE IMAGE OF WOMEN'S BODY

Breast cancer diagnosis and its related treatment inflict physical as well as psychosocial discomfort on patients. Some discomforts such as fatigue and hair loss are transitory, but others such as weight gain, premature menopause, and the loss of a breast linger on. Research focuses most of its attention on the effect of breast surgery on women's sexuality and body image. The mystique of a woman's breast in popular culture has deeply affected how women and men view themselves and their partners. Popular media reinforces these images by linking a woman's beauty to a slim, fit body with large breasts (Altman 1996, Dinnerstein and Weitz 1998, Olson 2002). Even the ACS held breast cancer survivors to these standards of beauty. During the 1980s, Darlene Betteley, a volunteer for the Reach to Recovery Program, was required to wear a prosthesis for hospital visits because the ACS did not want women who just had a mastectomy to be reminded of how the surgery changed a woman's exterior. According to the ACS, a woman without a breast is not a *normal* woman and volunteers were expected to look normal during hospital visits (Batt 1998).

Contrary to popular belief, a majority of women who had mastectomies did not undergo breast reconstruction,

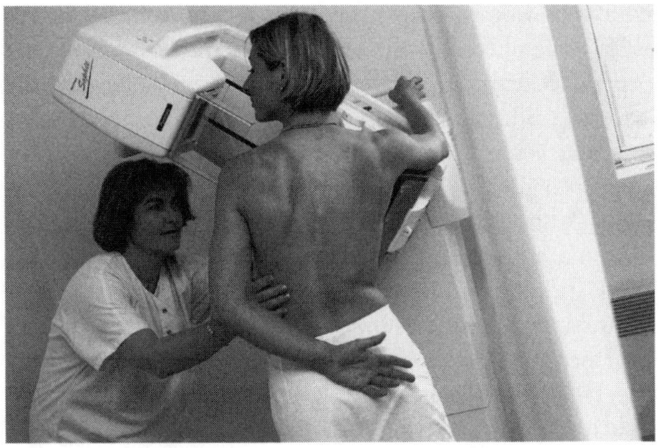

Mammography. *A woman undergoes a mammography, a test that screens for breast cancer.* PHANIE/PHOTO RESEARCHERS, INC.

even when the procedure would be covered by medical insurance. Empirical studies on the impact of breast surgery on the quality of life among survivors revealed mixed findings. Some reported that women who had lumpectomies were more satisfied with their body image and marital relationships than women who had mastectomies, but others reported no significant differences between the two groups in terms of psychological well-being and marital relationships (Altman 1996; Fung, Lau, Fielding, Or, and Yip 2000; Lichtman, Taylor, and Wood 1988). Another effect of breast cancer treatment on a woman's body is weight gain. Studies confirmed that weight gain and obesity are common in women diagnosed with breast cancer. Weigh gain was also related to higher rates of breast cancer recurrence and mortality, in particular in women who had never smoked (Irwin, McTiernan, Baumgartner, et al 2006; Kroenke, Chen, Rosner, Holmes 2005).

The post-World War II generation of women transformed societal reactions toward breast cancer because of their own breast cancer experiences. These courageous women challenged cultural norms about women's breasts and empowered patients' rights in breast cancer treatment. Today breast cancer research and survivors receive unprecedented support from governments and communities. Early-twenty-first-century studies also confirmed that the quality of post-treatment life was better for women who were actively involved in the treatment planning (Hack, Degner, Watson, and Sinha 2006). New patient advocacy organizations targeting specific groups such as Sisters Network Inc and Young Survival coalition were established in the late-1990s. Despite this progress, the incidence of breast cancer remains higher than it was in the mid-1970s and cancer-related disparities remain among population subgroups. Future study should focus on how certain cultural practices or beliefs affect breast cancer diagnosis and treatment decisions. Finally women who are uninsured or underinsured are less likely to receive the same quality of treatment as their peers, which may contribute to these disparities.

BIBLIOGRAPHY

Altman, Roberta. 1996. *Waking Up, Fighting Back: The Politics of Breast Cancer.* Boston: Little, Brown.

American Cancer Society. 2006. *Breast Cancer Facts and Figures 2006.* Atlanta: American Cancer Society, Inc.

Batt, Sharon. 1998. "'Perfect People': Cancer Charities." In *The Politics of Women's Bodies,* ed. Rose Weitz. New York: Oxford University Press.

Bickell, Nina A.; Jason J. Wang; Soji Oluwole; et al. 2006. "Missed Opportunities: Racial Disparities in Adjuvant Breast Cancer Treatment." *Journal of Clinical Oncology* 24(9): 1357–1362.

Casamayou, Maureen Hogan. 2001. *The Politics of Breast Cancer.* Washington, DC: Georgetown University Press.

Dinnerstein, Myra, and Rose Weitz. 1998. "Jane Fonda, Barbara Bush, and Other Aging Bodies: Femininity and the Limits of Resistance." In *the Politics of Women's Bodies,* ed. Rose Weitz. New York: Oxford University Press.

Fung, Kin Wah; Yvonne Lau; Richard Fielding; et al. 2000. "The Impact of Mastectomy, Breast-Conserving Treatment and Immediate Breast Reconstruction on the Quality of Life of Chinese Women." *ANZ Journal of Surgery* 71(4): 202–206.

Hack, Thomas F.; Lesley F. Degner; Peter Watson; and Luella Sinha. 2006. "Do Patients Benefit from Participating in Medical Decision Making? Longitudinal Follow-Up of Women with Breast Cancer." *Psycho-Oncology* 15(1): 9–19.

Inglehart, Ronald. 1990. *Culture Shift in Advanced Industrial Society.* Princeton, NJ: Princeton University Press.

Irwin, Melinda L.; Anne McTiernan; Richard N. Baumgartner; et al. 2006. "Changes in Body Fat and Weight after a Breast Cancer Diagnosis: Influence of Demographic, Prognostic, and Lifestyle Factors." *Journal of Clinical Oncology* 23(4): 774–782.

Katz, Steven J.; Paula M. Lantz; Nancy K. Jamz; et al. 2005. "Patient Involvement in Surgery Treatment Decisions for Breast Cancer." *Journal of Clinical Oncology* 23(24): 5526–5533.

Kroenke, Candyce H; Wendy Y. Chen; Bernard Rosner; and Michelle D. Holmes. 2005. "Weight, Weight Gain, and Survival After Breast Cancer Diagnosis." *Journal of Clinical Oncology* 23(7): 1370–1378.

Lichtman, Rosemary R.; Shelley E. Taylor; and Joanne V. Wood. 1988. "Social Support and Marital Adjustment after Breast Cancer." *Journal of Psychological Oncology* 5(3):47–74.

Light, Paul C. 1988. *Baby Boomers.* New York: W. W. Norton & Company.

National Comprehensive Cancer Network. "Breast Cancer Treatment." 2005. Available from http://www.nccn.org/patients/patient_gls/_english/_breast/5_treatment.asp.

National Cancer Institute, NIH, DHHS. 2005a. "Cancer Trends Progress Report: 2005 Update." Available from http://progressreport.cancer.gov.

National Cancer Institute, NIH, DHHS. 2005b. "Breast Cancer (PDQ®): Treatment. Health Professional Version." Available from http://progressreport.cancer.gov.

National Cancer Institute, NIH, DHHS. 2005c. "Herceptin® Combined with Chemotherapy Improves Disease-Free Survival for Patients with Early-Stage Breast Cancer." Available from http://www.cancer.gov/newscenter/pressreleases/HerceptinCombination2005.

National Cancer Institute, NIH, DHHS. 2006. "A Snapshot of Breast Cancer." Available from http://planning.cancer.gov/disease/Breast-Snapshot.pdf.

Oberman, Michelle. 1994. "Real and Perceived Legal Barriers to the Inclusion of Women in Clinical Trials." In *Reframing Women's Health*, ed. Alice J. Dan. Thousand Oaks, CA: Sage Publications.

Olson, James S. 2002. *Bathsheba's Breast: Women, Cancer & History*. Baltimore, MD: The Johns Hopkins University Press.

Surveillance, Epidemiology, and End Results Program. 2002. "Cancer Facts & the War on Cancer." Available from http://training.seer.cancer.gov/module_cancer_disease/unit5_war_on_cancer.html.

Young, Iris Marion. 1998. "Breasted Experience: The Look and the Feeling." In *The Politics of Women's Bodies*, ed. Rose Weitz. New York: Oxford University Press.

Furjen Deng

CANCER, PROSTATE

Prostate cancer is the growth of malignant cells in the prostate gland, one of the male sex glands. The prostate, which produces a fluid that becomes semen, is walnut-sized, lies below the bladder, and surrounds the urethra. Prostate cancer is the most common cancer found in men and usually occurs after age fifty, with the vast majority of cases diagnosed after age sixty-five. This cancer is usually slow growing; however, it can be aggressive, especially in younger men.

Although the cause of prostate cancer is unknown, several risk factors are associated with the disease: age; African-American heritage; family history (especially a brother or father diagnosed and especially if the cancer occurred at an early age); high fat diet; and frequent exposure to rubber or cadmium. In addition, high plasma testosterone levels may be associated with increased risk.

Although prostate cancer may present no symptoms and may be found in routine physical exams, common symptoms include: problems with urination (e.g., frequent, difficult, or painful); difficulties with erection or ejaculation; blood in semen or urine; and stiffness or pain in thighs, hips, or back. However, these symptoms are associated with other noncancerous conditions as well.

Prostate cancer is curable if detected early, but a lack of symptoms can lead to later detection. The two most common screening methods are digital rectal exams (physician inserts finger in rectum) and blood tests (checking prostate-specific antigen or prostatic acid phosphatase). Other testing methods include urine tests (checking for blood or infection), transrectal ultrasonography (using rectal probe producing sound waves to try to locate tumors), intravenous pyelogram (X-rays of urinary tract), cystoscopy

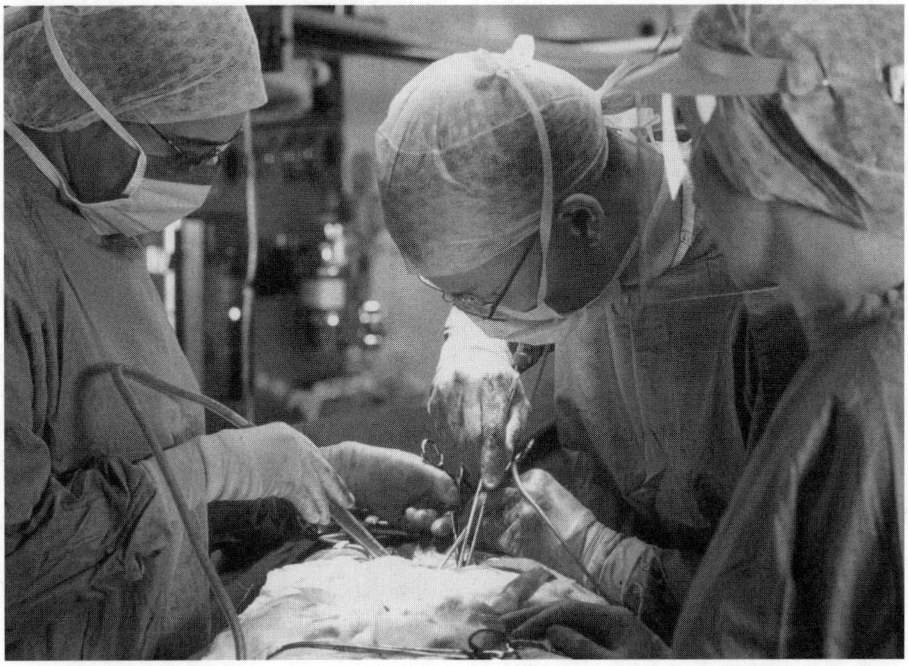

Prostate Cancer Surgery. *Doctors perform surgery to remove a cancerous prostate gland.*
COLIN CUTHBERT/PHOTO RESEARCHERS, INC.

(examining the urethra and bladder with a lighted tube), and biopsy (removing and examining prostate tissue sample). A biopsy is the most definitive test.

Treatment recommendations vary based on the extent of the cancer, a person's age and health, and the amount of risk involved in the procedure. For cancer that is detected early and growing slowly, watchful waiting (periodic assessment of the cancer growth without actively treating it) may be the best approach—particularly for older patients and those with other medical problems. Removing the cancer, adjacent tissue, and possibly close lymph nodes through surgery is another option. This treatment is usually reserved for those under seventy and in good health. Risks involved in surgery include impotence and compromised stool and urine control.

Radiation, which targets malignant cells and shrinks tumors, is another common combatant to prostate cancer. It can be external (targeted from outside of the body) or internal (implanted into the prostate) and may also result in impotence and problems with urination. Hormone therapy is a fourth option that lowers male hormone levels, which can slow cancerous growth and shrink tumors. It can involve surgery (the removal of one or both testicles), taking drugs to help lower or prevent male hormone production, or both. Side effects for this type of procedure include hot flashes, bone weakening, impaired sexual function, heart attacks, and strokes. Among the other options to choose from are chemotherapy, cryosurgery, focused ultrasound, experimental radiation therapies, herbal treatment, and biological therapy.

Generally, agencies recommend that men have yearly digital rectal exams and blood tests after the age of fifty. Men with greater risk factors should begin screening earlier.

BIBLIOGRAPHY

American Cancer Society. Available from http://www.cancer.org.

National Cancer Institute. "Prostate Cancer." Available from http://www.cancer.gov/cancertopics/types/prostate.

Prostate Cancer Foundation. Available from http://www.prostatecancerfoundation.org.

Joy L. Hart

CANNIBALISM

Cannibalism, which is practiced by humans and other animals, is the act or practice of consuming any part of the body of a member of one's own species. In some cultures the practice is sacrosanct; in others, including the majority of those in the West, it is taboo. Although the origins of cannibalism are unclear, "archeological evidence suggests that cannibalism was practiced as far back as the Neolithic Period and Bronze Age in what is now Europe and the Americas" (Bell 2006, p. 2). According to William Arens's *The Man-Eating Myth: Anthropology and Anthropophagy* (1980), the word stems from an expedition to the West Indies led by Christopher Columbus during which he and his crew purportedly learned of the ritualistic consumption of human flesh among members of the Carib tribe. "The explorers mispronounced the name of the tribe and referred to them as 'Canibs,' which was over time changed to 'canibales,' meaning thirsty and cruel in Spanish. The English translation of the Spanish word became cannibalism," whereas "the Latin form of the word cannibalism is anthropophagy and is a term used mostly in anthropology and archeology" (Bell 2006).

TYPES OF CANNIBALISM

Survival cannibalism (the consumption of flesh to survive a desperate situation) is exemplified by the 1846 Donner Party expedition through the Sierra Nevada Mountains and the 1972 crash in the Andes of the airplane carrying the Uruguayan rugby team, the story of which was told in the 1993 film *Alive*. The most prominent forms of ritualistic cannibalism are epicurean and/or nutritional (practiced for the taste or nutritional value of the consumed flesh), exocannibalism (cannibalizing members outside one's social group), and endocannibalism (cannibalizing members within one's social group).

Exocannibalism usually is associated with violence and the belief that consuming the flesh of an enemy endows a cannibal with the spirit and/or abilities of the deceased. Commonly based on the same belief, endocannibalism most frequently is practiced in the form of mortuary cannibalism (consumption of the already deceased) and may be referred to as compassionate cannibalism. Prominent historical examples include the ancient Aztecs of Mexico, who employed all these forms in their cannibalization of several thousand individuals per year, and the Iroquoian North American Indian tribe, which is thought to have engaged in exocannibalism as recently as 1838. Certain tribes in Papua New Guinea practiced all three types of ritualistic cannibalism until the 1950s and 1960s. Such practices were accompanied by the spread of kuru, a deadly and highly infectious illness similar to mad cow disease. Large-scale ritualistic cannibalism was curtailed by the early 1900s, largely as a result of the activities of Christian missionaries.

Sexual cannibalism (sexualized consumption of one's own species), although widely considered a psychosexual disorder, is not listed in the *Diagnostic and Statistical Manual of Mental Disorders*. *Vorephilia* (sexual interest in things eating other things) may involve sexual cannibalism, although it typically does not (Adams 2004). In 2002 the psychologist Steven Scher of Eastern Illinois University conducted an atypical research study regarding cannibalism

Jeffrey Dahmer. *Serial killer Jeffrey Dahmer may be classified as a sexual cannibal.* AP IMAGES.

and sexual interests in which he and his team "found that people were more likely to eat someone that they were sexually attracted to" (Bell 2006, p. 5). Modern serial killers who may be placed under the heading of sexual cannibalism include Andrei Chikatilo, Jeffrey Dahmer, Albert Fish, Robin Gecht and the Chicago Rippers, Ed Gein, Georg Grossman, Fritz Haarmann, Edmund Kemper, Armand Meiwes, Issei Sagawa, and Sascha Spesiwtsew.

MODERN CANNIBALS

The Russian Andrei Romanovitch Chikatilo (1936–1994), known as the Rostov Ripper, was convicted of and executed for the murders of fifty-two women and children. After his first killing in 1978 Chikatilo was unable to achieve sexual arousal separate from violence, and he was known to mutilate and consume parts of his victims, including their breasts and sexual organs. Furthermore, "Chikatilo claimed that he was disgusted by the 'loose morals' of many of his victims, who served as painful reminders of his own sexual incompetence" (Bell 2006, p. 5).

The American Albert Fish (1870–1936), known as the Moon Maniac, the Gray Man, and the Brooklyn Vampire, was a self-mutilating sadomasochist who enjoyed driving sharp objects deep into his genital region. Although Fish apparently never harmed his six children, whom he raised largely by himself, he tortured and/or killed numerous other children, whose flesh, urine, blood, and excrement he admitted to consuming for sexual pleasure. Fish referred to his implements of torture as "instruments of hell" and used a belt studded with nails to tenderize the flesh of his victims before cooking and consuming them. Fish pleaded insanity in 1935 but was found sane and guilty and electrocuted in Sing Sing Prison in 1936, an experience he predicted would be the "supreme thrill." Fish's final words apparently were "I don't know why I'm here."

The advent of the Internet brought the worldwide subculture of cannibalism fetishism to the surface through a myriad of websites and bulletin boards where individuals can post classified advertisements. The advertisers have been mostly homosexual males seeking men or heterosexual men seeking women. In 2001 such postings translated into actual cannibalistic activities when the forty-one-year-old homosexual computer administrator Armin Meiwes of Rotenburg, Germany, placed an advertisement on the Internet searching for "young, well-built men aged 18 to 30 to slaughter" and received a promising reply (one of approximately two hundred) from the forty-three-year-old Bernd-Jurgen Brandes (BBC: "German Cannibal" 2003). The ensuing activities, which were videotaped by Meiwes, began with the two attempting to flambé, then fry, and then consume Brandes's penis at Brandes's request and ended with Meiwes slowly killing, dissecting, and partially consuming Brandes as well as storing parts of the deceased in his freezer. Meiwes was caught after he again advertised on the Internet ten months later. As in most industrialized nations there are no laws directly governing cannibalism in Germany. Meiwes was charged with murder for "sexual satisfaction," convicted of manslaughter in January 2004, and sentenced to jail for eight and a half years. In 2005 the gay filmmaker Rosa von Praunheim turned Miewes's case into a feature entitled *Your Heart in My Brain.*

BIBLIOGRAPHY

Adams, Cecil. 2004. "Eat or Be Eaten: Is Cannibalism a Pathology as Listed in the DSM-IV?" Chicago Reader. Available from http://www.straightdope.com/columns/040702.html.

Arens, William. 1980. *The Man-Eating Myth: Anthropology and Anthropophagy.* New York: Oxford University Press.

BBC News. 2003. "German Cannibal Tells of Fantasy." Available from http://www.news.bbc.co.uk/2/hi/europe/3286721.stm.

BBC News. "German 'Cannibal' Tells of Regret." Available from http://www.news.bbc.co.uk/2/hi/europe/3230774.stm.

Bell, Rachel. 2006. "Cannibalism: The Ancient Taboo in Modern Times." Court TV Crime Library. Available from http://www.crimelibrary.com/criminal_mind/psychology/cannibalism/index.html.

"Rosas Biografie." 2006. Available from http://www.rosavonpraunheim.de/bio/bio_engl.html.

Sanday, Peggy Reeves. 1986. *Divine Hunger: Cannibalism as a Cultural System*. Cambridge, UK: Cambridge University Press.

Whitney Jones Olson

CANON LAW

Canon law is the law of the church. Prior to the Reformation in the sixteenth century, canon law was used across Christendom. Beginning as early as the second century CE, the church developed legal norms that it attempted to enforce on the faithful. During the Middle Ages (between approximately 500 and 1400), canon law pertained to virtually every aspect of human activity, although, after the Reformation, with the development of the modern nation-state, the purview of canon law constricted as secular law courts became dominant. Canon law continues to govern many aspects of the life of members of the Catholic, Lutheran, Orthodox, and Anglican churches, primarily in areas influenced by religious belief and morality, especially areas of human sexual activity.

James A. Brundage, the foremost historian of medieval canon law governing sex and sexuality, identified three patterns used to categorize and evaluate sex. The first was according to the reproductive function of sex, which formed the basis for evaluating various sexual activities as natural or unnatural. Second, sex was perceived as a source of impurity, leading to feelings of shame by the participants, or a perception that those who engaged in sex were defiled and required ritual cleansing. Finally, sex was viewed as a source of intimacy and a means of expressing and enhancing love within a married couple. These perspectives influenced various aspects of the moral code governing sex and sexuality as it was enshrined in canon law.

HISTORICAL DEVELOPMENT

Canon law developed out of a wide array of sources over the course of many centuries. In the early Christian church, councils were convened to settle doctrinal controversies, and their pronouncement or decision was termed a canon. Gradually, multiple councils issued canons clarifying a wide variety of questions, some quite broad with others directed to specific difficult cases. Another means to clarify doctrine or resolve disputes was through ecclesiastical legislation implemented by a bishop. The letters and decisions of the pope, called decretals, carried particular weight. The writings of church fathers, those early theologians who expounded upon the implications and application of religion in daily life, were another source for law. Finally, a body of literature known as penitentials began to appear in western European Christendom between the sixth and tenth centuries. Penitentials were lists of sins, that is, transgressions against the Christian moral code, accompanied by the appropriate penance. All these sources circulated throughout the early Middle Ages and carried varying degrees of authority. That the various sources frequently contradicted each other added to this proliferation and confusion. Thus, early canon law was a complex of disparate documentation that did not provide a consistent interpretation of doctrine or penalties for transgression.

By the eleventh century there were attempts to collect the various canons and pieces of legislation. Two of the earliest attempts, which influenced the subsequent development of canon law, were the *Decretum* of Burchard of Worms (c. 950–1025), which drew significantly on the penitentials, and the *Decretum* of Ivo of Chartres (c. 1040–c. 1116), which drew together numerous patristic texts. It was not until the mid-twelfth century, however, that canon law was collected and systemized. Around the year 1140, the canon lawyer Gratian (d. before 1159) laid the foundations of a systematic approach to canon law with the publication of his *Concordia discordantium canonum* (Concordance of disconcordant canons). This work, popularly known as the *Decretum*, included patristic authorities, early church council decrees, and papal decisions, organized according to topic or theme. Gratian organized these varied and contradictory sources and subjected them to logical analysis, reconciling their discrepancies in his own commentary. Through the juxtaposition of various views and assisted by his own critical analysis, Gratian produced a synthetic and systematic summary of church law.

Whereas the *Decretum* formed the foundation of canon law, pronouncements by church councils and bishops and decretals by the popes continued to be issued. As a result canon law continued to grow, and the *Decretum* soon needed updating. In 1234 a new collection of canon law appeared based on new legislation and the thousands of decretals that had been issued after Gratian finished his compilation. Raymond of Peñafort (c. 1185–1275), a famous canon lawyer, was appointed by Pope Gregory IX to compile this new collection, known as the *Decretales Gregorii* or the *Liber extra*. Subsequently, at intervals, similar collections were published to cope with ensuing legislation. The last of these appeared in 1500. Shortly afterward the collections were bundled together and, along with Gratian's *Decretum*, formed the complete collection of canon law, the *Corpus juris canonici* (Body of canon law), which endured from the later Middle Ages until it was revised in 1917. The code of canon law was again revised in 1983. Medieval canon law, then, had currency well into the modern world, formed the basis of western European and North American morality and

A Manucript Page from Gratian's Decretum. **© COURTESY OF THE MUSEUM OF BIBLIOTECA CAPITUAL TORTOSA; RAMON MANENT/CORBIS.**

informed the values of secular law codes across those societies into the twenty-first century.

ENFORCEMENT

From the initial appearance of organized Christian communities, church leaders attempted to impose rules to govern the sexual behavior of the faithful. In his letters, written in the mid-first century, the apostle Paul certainly admonished Christians to embrace chastity and avoid the libidinous excesses that characterized Roman society. As a marginal group Christian communities had only informal, internal mechanisms to control the behavior of their members. When Christianity was recognized as the official religion of the Roman Empire in the fourth century, however, church leaders began to hold councils and issue canons, and they developed effective mechanisms of enforcement that were more effective.

Christian sexual morality was built upon the fundamental tenet that legitimate sexual activity could occur only within marriage and for the purpose of procreation. Although some argued that a married couple could seek an outlet for sexual desire with their spouse or engage in sexual activity as a means of developing intimacy and reinforcing marital love, such acts were considered to be somewhat sinful, albeit permissible. Thus, not every sex act that was sinful was necessarily illegal. The distinction, however, between sexual sin and sexual crime was clarified, and some sexual irregularities were relegated to the internal forum of confession and penance. So, for example, canon law did not comment on the phenomenon of men's nocturnal emissions, although this was considered to be a matter of considerable moral concern. Similarly, although masturbation was a prohibited sex act, it was considered to be relatively minor and private, and better left to the confessional. These examples illustrate how the theological and canonical approaches to sexuality were closely linked and mutually influenced each other.

The ecclesiastical courts, charged with enforcing canon law, concerned themselves with more egregious breaches of the moral code, especially those infractions that were public. For example, adultery was a serious crime, not only because it breached the sexual fidelity that was central to marriage, but also because it could result in the birth of illegitimate children who could challenge the laws of inheritance and defraud legitimate children. Canon law considered adultery as if it were a crime pertaining primarily to women. Men were rarely punished for adultery, although they might be required to perform penance for their sin. A woman convicted of adultery, however, suffered disgrace, and could be relegated to a convent, thrown out of her home, deprived of her children and dowry, and reduced to penury.

Frequently, the only economic recourse for an adulterous wife, as for other impoverished women, was prostitution. Although prostitution was also considered a crime under canon law, for both the prostitute and the client, the medieval church tended to treat it relatively leniently. For example, although a prostitute both sinned and committed a crime, she was also a worker and as such was owed her wages. A client who tried to avoid paying her was guilty of theft. The church tended to tolerate prostitution because it was considered a lesser evil. Without prostitutes men's unbridled lust would have no outlet, and honorable matrons and respectable virgin daughters would be subject to harassment on the streets or even to abduction and rape. This indicates some of the compromises that canon law made to accommodate the realities of daily life. Whereas a man who consorted with a prostitute committed the sexual crime of fornication, or adultery if either were married, this act was preferable to the alternative.

If sexual crimes were public and notorious rather than private and secret, the church needed a means to prosecute the wrongdoers. As a result ecclesiastical courts appeared in the early thirteenth century designed, among other things, to regulate and control the sexual behavior of the laity. The attempt to regulate sexual activity was particularly directed at the unmarried, those men and women who committed fornication. Whereas fornication was considered one of the least serious of the sexual transgressions, it was also believed to be the most widespread. The church developed a system of regulation that permitted court officials to summon people to account for their behavior on the basis of rumor or general suspicion. For convicted couples the punishments were relatively minor and could range from paying a small fine to being whipped three times around the church or local marketplace. The church courts could also require a couple who engaged in habitual fornication to marry, assuming there were no impediments to prevent legal marriage.

LAWS: MARITAL SEX

Although many of the provisions of canon law were concerned with constraining sexual activity outside of marriage, others governed sexual relations between married people. One of the requirements for a legal marriage was the ability of each partner to engage in sexual relations. Although, according to various decretals issued by Pope Alexander III (r. 1159–1181), a couple did not need to consummate a marriage for it to be considered legitimate and indissoluble, sexual relations had to be possible. Hence, an impotent man or a woman with malformed genitals that prevented intercourse was prohibited from marrying. This requirement underscored the importance of procreation as the appropriate goal of marriage and sexual intercourse.

The church revealed its ambivalent attitude toward sex in numerous regulations that prohibited sexual relations, even within marriage. Most of these were related to the notion that sex caused impurity and pollution. This accounts for the imposition of clerical celibacy in the eleventh century. Reformers feared that a married priest would perform the sacraments while still polluted by sexual relations with his wife. Even the married laity faced strict limits on when and where they could engage in sex. Based on blood taboos and ideas about ritual purity inherited from Judaism, sex was forbidden when a woman was menstruating, lactating, or pregnant and after giving birth before she had been ritually cleansed by churching. Concerns about how to exclude polluted people from the sacraments and sacred spaces led to prohibitions on intercourse on Saturdays, Sundays, Wednesdays, Fridays, and feast or fast days, and during holy seasons such as Lent or Advent. All of these prohibitions left on average about twenty-two days per year for legitimate marital intercourse. A couple was also forbidden to have sex in a church or cemetery, which would be polluted by the emission of semen. All these prohibitions, however, could be overridden by the doctrine of the conjugal debt.

The conjugal debt recognized that marriage provided the only legitimate outlet for sexual desire. Either spouse was required to grant the other sexual intercourse whenever and wherever it was demanded. This requirement was more important than the prohibitions of time or place or the woman's physical condition. The rationale was similar to the toleration of prostitution: If a spouse did not have a legitimate sexual outlet when needed, he or she might be tempted to engage in adultery. Although the conjugal debt was reciprocal in theory, the real concern was to channel men's lust and protect them from committing more serious sexual crimes such as rape, homosexuality, or bestiality. In practice it relegated wives to being perpetually available for sex, regardless of their personal wishes.

LAWS: EXTRAMARITAL SEX

Canonists were in general agreement that there was a hierarchy of sexual crimes, although they differed on the relative seriousness of different acts. In general fornication was considered the least serious offense because it did not breach the vows of marriage or chastity. Moreover, there was always the possibility that the man and woman would marry in the future. Adultery was more serious because it ruptured the sacramental bonds of marriage. Fornication and adultery, while illegal, were nevertheless considered to be natural. Far more serious were so-called unnatural sex acts that overthrew the natural order. These imperiled the souls of the individuals and destabilized the social order. There were four categories of unnatural acts: masturbation, bestiality, sex between a man and a woman in an unconventional manner, and sodomy. Masturbation, as a solitary and private act, was considered to be the least serious and was not prosecuted by the ecclesiastical courts. Bestiality, sex acts involving animals, had been considered a relatively minor crime in the rural society of the early Middle Ages. By the twelfth century, however, bestiality was the most serious of unnatural acts because it blurred the distinction between human and animal. Although bestiality carried severe penalties, including killing the animal and lifelong penance for the human actor, it rarely appears in the court records.

Adopting variant sexual positions during sexual intercourse was considered a serious offense, although this issue may have figured more prominently in the confessional than in court. The general suspicion regarding the virtually unavoidable pleasure that resulted from intercourse meant that canonists strove to regulate sex positions that might enhance pleasure and exacerbate the sinfulness of the sex act. The only licit position for intercourse was the so-called missionary position: vaginal intercourse, with the woman lying supine and the man prone on top of her. Any other positions were prohibited, although occasionally a writer might concede some variation, such as sitting or standing, if it would increase the probability of conception or if a disability prevented normal intercourse. Standards of morality dictated that a husband should not see his wife naked or engage in foreplay. Fellatio, cunnilingus, and anal intercourse were utterly forbidden because they were judged to be both contraceptive and unnatural.

Sodomy was an ill-defined category of sexual transgression. For most of the Middle Ages and into the early modern and modern periods, the term referred to sexual acts between two men, particularly anal intercourse. Sometimes the term denoted a wide array of *unnatural acts*, including mutual masturbation, interfemoral rubbing, fellatio, and cunnilingus. Sodomy sometimes included sex between women, but because such activity did not involve vaginal penetration and the emission of semen, it was not considered as serious a sexual crime as sex between men. Sex between women was more serious if one of the participants cross-dressed or used a dildo to imitate the male role. After the mid-thirteenth century sex between women was considered generally equivalent to that between men.

Although as early as the eleventh century homosexuality had been denounced by reformers such as Pier Damiani (Peter Damian) seeking to impose clerical celibacy, it was not until the thirteenth century that fear of homosexuality led to widespread prosecutions. Sex between men came under increasing scrutiny, and the pace of accusations and prosecutions increased. Sodomy was considered a capital offense by the secular legal system. Some of the men convicted of sodomy by the religious courts were turned over to secular authorities for execution because capital punishment was forbidden under canon law. The persecution of homosexuals that increased during the early modern and modern periods grew out of cooperation between church and state to enforce the Christian moral code.

FROM THE MIDDLE AGES TO THE MODERN WORLD

The canon laws governing sex and sexuality developed over the course of a thousand years were systematized and codified in the twelfth and thirteenth centuries and were enforced across western Europe by ecclesiastical courts. Although in the sixteenth century the Protestant Reformation ruptured the seamless system of canon law and ecclesiastical courts, there was remarkably little change to the laws governing sexual activity. Throughout the sixteenth and seventeenth centuries, the older regulations governing sexual activities endured, with perhaps only an increase in the prosecution of both male and female same-sex activities. In continental Europe the regulation of sex gradually moved from religious to secular jurisdiction. In England ecclesiastical courts endured through the breach with Rome, and church courts continued to enforce canon law with remarkably little deviation from their Catholic roots. In Roman Catholic areas, the ecclesiastical courts were more centralized in the wake of the Council of Trent (1545–1563), although the canon laws regarding sex were maintained. It was not until the eighteenth century that church courts ceased to be the main mechanism for the enforcement of sexual norms, even as canon law continued to enunciate those norms.

The principle features of medieval canon law were carried into the modern world and into the secular court systems of modern states. The vestiges of medieval canon law endured in European and North American values and legal systems into the twentieth and twenty-first centuries. Many jurisdictions in the United States retain sodomy laws that prevent sexual activity between men; some prohibit anal sex within marriage or between any consenting adults. Only in the 1980s and 1990s was the concept of spousal rape recognized. Prior to that the doctrine of the conjugal debt continued to influence society's understanding that a husband had an absolute right to sexual relations with his wife. In some places adultery and fornication remained illegal until the 1960s. Even in the early twenty-first century, the argument endures that the primary goal of marriage is procreation, and consequently, a married man and woman should receive special recognition, status, and privileges from the state. The procreative aspect of marriage is used as a rationale to prohibit same-sex unions. This view can be traced back to the fourth century, when the church argued that the primary role of marriage and sexual intercourse was to produce children. Vestiges of medieval values are found throughout European and North American societies and in those societies that have been influenced by European and North American law and Christianity. Only in the late twentieth century were many of the medieval perspectives on sex and sexuality challenged. Even so, some, such as the prohibition against bestiality, remain deeply embedded in North American and European society's understanding of sexual morality.

BIBLIOGRAPHY

Brundage, James A. 1987. *Law, Sex, and Christian Society in Medieval Europe*. Chicago: University of Chicago Press.

Brundage, James A. 1993. *Sex, Law, and Marriage in the Middle Ages*. Aldershot, UK: Variorum.

Brundage, James A. 1996. "Sex and Canon Law." In *Handbook of Medieval Sexuality*, ed. Vern L. Bullough and James A. Brundage. New York: Garland.

Flandrin, Jean-Louis. 1979. *Families in Former Times: Kinship, Household, and Sexuality*, trans. Richard Southern. Cambridge, UK: Cambridge University Press.

Friedberg, Emil, ed. 1955 *Corpus iuris canonici.* 2 vols. Graz, Austria: Akademische Druck- und Verlagsanstalt. [Orig. pub. 1879–1881.]

Noonan, John T., Jr. 1986. *Contraception: A History of Its Treatment by the Catholic Theologians and Canonists.* Rev. edition. Cambridge, MA: Harvard University Press.

Payer, Pierre J. 1984. *Sex and the Penitentials: The Development of a Sexual Code, 550–1150.* Toronto: University of Toronto Press.

Reid, Charles J., Jr. 2004. *Power Over the Body, Equality in the Family: Rights and Domestic Relations in Medieval Canon Law.* Grand Rapids, MI: Eerdmans.

Sheehan, Michael M. 1996. *Marriage, Family, and Law in Medieval Europe: Collected Studies,* ed. James K. Farge. Toronto: University of Toronto Press.

Jacqueline Murray

CANON, REVISING THE

One might best define canon formation as the process by which works of literature come to be considered *classics*. Although the value of particular authors or works has always been debated, it was not until the emergence of feminism and the social movements for racial justice of the 1960s and 1970s, and the academic disciplines they have spawned (women's studies, black and ethnic studies, multicultural studies), that the process of canon formation itself has been questioned. Until then, the canon remained a firmly entrenched exclusionary category whose very raison d'être was to seem unmovable. The higher education curriculum, in particular through such courses as "great books," or rhetorical categories such as "masterpieces," maintained a vision of cultural heritage that was overwhelmingly male, white, and European-derived, and in which the political and aesthetic effects of sexual orientation were carefully concealed. The canon thus enshrined "great men" and projected an ideological message of "greatness" inseparable from normative views about sex and gender and, in literary themes, of a safe handling of women as the objects of writing.

This questioning and the debates it has given rise to form one of the most important critical controversies of late-twentieth-century literary scholarship. In fact, challenging and changing the canon remains one of the principal issues for some literary scholars, whereas staunchly defending it is the objective of others. Charles Altieri, for example, sees the canon as both curatorial and normative, preserving a varied and rich cultural heritage, providing what he calls a "cultural grammar for interpreting experience" (Altieri 1983, p. 47). However, one can also argue that exclusion from the curriculum of works reflecting their gender or ethnic identities makes students feel disenfranchised, or irrelevant, an important aspect of the struggle to open the canon. In the traditional canon, far from finding a "shared heritage," many students—and instructors—do not hear voices that reflect experiences closer to theirs.

WHAT IS THE CANON?

Canon formation has to do with how practices of reading and writing are organized by society, and academic institutions provide the primary contexts within which the canon is formed and revised. The reproduction and legitimating of texts, the regulation of what and how one reads is, to a large degree, determined by the academy, and also by the media and publishing industry. It is through the syllabus and curriculum that works are granted their status as *great* works. Canonical works appear more frequently in anthologies and on class syllabi. They are, typically, studied more often than other works in articles, books, and dissertations. They are more readily accessible in editions and translations, which, in turn, make them more accessible to future generations of students and scholars. They are, then, more present in the collective awareness. "They are culturally important because they have been culturally important" (Scholes [paraphrasing Smith] 1992, p. 148). There is thus a circular, self-perpetuating aspect to canon formation that accounts, in part, for the enormous influence of the canon and for the difficulties involved in reshaping it.

The etymology of the term *canon* provides some useful insight into both its function and its power. The ancient Greek *kanon,* meaning straight rod, bar, ruler, standard, or instrument of measure, eventually acquired a secondary sense of law or rule. Moreover, rich resonances can also be found in the word's relationship to the ancient Greek *kanna* (reed), and its descendant *cane,* which suggest the idea of severity or imposition of power as in "to cane" or beat with a stick (Scholes 1992, p. 139). In Alexandrian times, *kanon* referred to a body of superior texts, models of style and composition (Scholes 1992, p. 140). In the fourth century CE the canon came to signify, in particular, the accepted Christian sacred writings (as opposed to the apocrypha). In a similar vein, individuals seen to have lived exemplary lives were and are *canonized.* Thus, the notions of power, exemplarity, orthodoxy, and of a body of received, institutionally fixed texts are implicit in our current usage of *canon.*

Homogeneity is central to any categorization, including canon-formation. Canonical works are precisely that because they are perceived to share certain timeless qualities. Thus some critics suggest that the alternative to homogenizing works in this static manner involves historicizing them, and the process by which they were canonized in the first place (Guillory 1990). Rather than as repositories of truth and beauty, canonical texts can be seen as the embodiment of certain historically grounded critical practices that privilege one type of reading, and therefore one type of text, over another. For example, New Criticism's valuing of certain types of poetic discourse over others can be seen as promoting the work of the critic. That is to say, complex texts fraught with ambiguity, tension, and irony require the interpretation of the literary scholar as they are not readily accessible to the masses. In addition, the emphasis placed by the New Critics on masterpieces—individual works of art—rather than tendencies, led to disinterest in the social and cultural context in which all works are created. Thus a canon was formed which at once served the interests of the critic and dehistoricized the works of which it was comprised (Lauter 1991).

Texts can be made canonical against an author's full range of beliefs, and certain works can be carefully excluded, in fact, obliterated, from the canon. A case in point is provided by the posthumous fate of the French symbolist poet Paul Verlaine (1844–1896). Primarily seen as producing a dreamy, evanescent, melancholic evocation in rhythmic verse of loss and the passage of time, Verlaine also authored fierce, vengeful, political poetry denouncing the massacres of the 1832 and 1834 insurrections, and the repression of the Paris Commune (in which he participated), praising the insurrectional leader Louise Michel (1830–1905) (Choury 1970). He also penned sexually aggressive and explicit erotic poetry such as *Les Amies* (1867), where he depicts lesbianism (Milech 1994), and *Hombres* (1891), in which he perhaps coded his homosexual orientation (Minahen 1997). All these works are excluded from the "canonization" of this author in school manuals and even university curricula, and rarely, if ever, written about.

Further, a study published in 1998 suggests that graduate reading lists are more idiosyncratic than one would think. Of a survey of fifty-six Spanish graduate course reading lists, only *Lazarillo de Tormes* (1554) and *Don Quixote de la Mancha* (1605) appeared on all lists. Among the authors' conclusions are that a substantial canon does not exist within Hispanism, and that canon formation "appears to take place only in microcosm; the canon for each institution evidently is shaped independently at the departmental level. The large numbers of authors and works that appear once only among fifty-six reading lists indicate that in many cases, individual convictions about the canon are just that—the opinion of one language faculty or perhaps even one specialist at a single university" (Brown and Johnson 1998, p. 6). This data suggests, then, that to some degree canons are shaped by the individual ideological and critical preferences of the members of the profession, who then implicitly reinforce and perpetuate the selection through course curriculum, exam questions, dissertation topics, and so on.

CHANGING THE CANON

In the 1980s and early 1990s, the canon was energetically challenged in higher education across North America. With respect to sex and gender, battle lines were drawn over the greater inclusion of women in this institutionalized selection. Another issue was the inclusion, not merely of lesbian and gay figures per se (writers such as Walt Whitman [1819–1892], Emily Dickinson [1830–1896], or Colette [1873–1954] were already part of the canon), but, rather, of sexual orientation and queer sensibilities as crucial to artistic and intellectual production. Important female literary figures that had been heretofore neglected became, themselves, canonic. Examples of canon reformation are found throughout the various languages and literatures. In American literature, for instance, poets like Audre Lorde (1934–1992), named State Poet of New York from 1991 to 1992, Adrienne Rich (b. 1929), and Muriel Rukeyser (1913–1980) enjoyed recognition beyond belonging to a feminist/lesbian canon. French medieval author Christine de Pizan (1364–1430) went from being a mere sideline in the medieval canon to becoming a foundational and authoritative figure (Quilligan 1991) of medieval and early French letters, whose work gives rise to many reinterpretations (Richards et al 1992, Desmond 1998, Brownlee 2005) and to substantial international conferences (Hick et al 2000). In Spanish literature, María de Zayas (1590–c. 1661) is an excellent case in point. Although she was a bestseller in seventeenth-century Spain, she was all but unknown until the 1970s and the veritable explosion of Zayas criticism that followed in the 1980s and 1990s. Because of critical attention paid to her, mostly by female scholars, she has become recognized as an important foundational figure in Spanish women's writing (a status previously enjoyed by only St. Teresa of Avila [1515–1582] and Sor Juana Inés de la Cruz [1648–1695]—and not always, at that) and is routinely included in graduate reading lists as well as undergraduate and graduate curricula. In the Luso-Brazilian field, Clarice Lispector (1920–1977) had long been the sole woman writing in Portuguese to be represented in anthologies and reading lists (indeed, she remained the sole Lusophone author included in the 2003 *Norton Anthology of World Literature*), but by the turn of the twenty-first century graduate courses and reading lists were making room for other Brazilian authors such as Nélida Piñon (b. 1937) and Lídia Jorge (b. 1946). Yet the Argentinian poet Alfonsina Storni (1892–1938) is the only twentieth-century female author writing in Spanish included in the 2003 edition of the *Norton Anthology of World Literature.*

However, even with more inclusive bodies of texts, the critical tendency to make normative claims while silencing differences among texts remains prevalent. The Latin American canon has expanded in various ways to include earlier authors like Teresa de la Parra (1889–1936), virtually unknown until rescued by critics, and the many women writing since the 1980s, contributors to the so-called "*boom femenino.*" Yet this growing body of work by Latin American women has prompted critical and theoretical generalizations that tend to homogenize texts in their attempts to define and categorize them (Shaw 1997). Deborah Shaw argues, "Notions of multiplicity, diversity, and *mestizaje* are crucial if we are to avoid the overgeneralized pronouncements on the literary production of the mythical Latin American woman" (p. 170).

The far-reaching modifications of the canon as a result of these debates and interventions vary immensely, as some cultural attitudes are tougher to break than others. There is indeed a big difference between simply adding women to lists of authors or artists and actually destabilizing the gender order, or debunking assumptions about sex and sexual orientation. Homophobia in the classroom itself continues to severely affect the ability of instructors to present new texts, particularly those that address homosexuality and AIDS. There are also regional, local, and educational tier (community college versus university) differences that continue to shape the canon in terms of what is taught regarding sex and gender in relation to local politics and the degree of conservative political control over the curriculum (Eisner 1999).

In terms of general curricular reformation, colleges and universities throughout the United States are transforming their course of study as it is generally recognized that knowledge about diversity both at home and internationally is crucial to students' intellectual formation. In addition, students in U.S. universities themselves constitute a larger and more diverse group than ever before. Data gathered by the American Association of Colleges and Universities suggests that a majority of institutions of higher education either already have in place or are in the process of instituting some type of diversity requirement. At some colleges, women's and gender studies courses comprise one element of a multifaceted diversity requirement. At other institutions, students are required to take one or a number of courses addressing diversity in its various aspects (ethnic studies, multicultural studies, women's and gender studies). Research suggests that diversifying the undergraduate curriculum has had positive effects and that, contrary to the claims of some critics, is resulting in a more rigorous program of study for students (Humphreys 1998).

ART AND THE CANON

Similarly, the place of women artists in movements, schools, and moments, albeit contested, is secure enough to prevent their total exclusion, even if the criteria for defining "great" or "leading" artists remained similar to those of literature. The importance of women like expressionists Käthe Kollwitz (1867–1945) and Paula Modersohn-Becker (1876–1907), the lesbian-identified surrealist Claude Cahun (Lucy Schwob, 1894–1954), abstract expressionist sculptor Louise Berliawsky Nevelson (1899–1988), French-American sculptor Louise Bourgeois (b. 1911), painters Georgia O'Keeffe (1887–1986) and Judy Chicago (b. 1939), is evident in special museums, museum collections, retrospectives, and art histories. Mexican artist Frida Kahlo (1907–1954) was not only rediscovered by feminist art and cultural critics, but her work has been vastly popularized. A Web site dedicated to her ("Frida Kahlo and Contemporary Thoughts" by Daniela Falini) includes a "cult" button in its menu, and countless plays, musical and dance performances, art exhibits, films, and installations celebrate or echo her life and work.

Yet it was as late as the 1970s that women artists openly challenged their exclusion from the art pantheon (Broude and Garrard 1994). In 1971 Judy Chicago and Miriam Shapiro (b. 1923) founded the CalArts Feminist Art Program and one of the first feminist art shows, Womanhouse (30 January–28 February 1972). The first women's gallery, A.I.R., was founded at that time. Feminist scholars such as Mary Ann Caws, Linda Nochlin, Mary Garrard, and numerous others rewrote the history of art itself. Women artists of all stripes were being regularly rediscovered and reinterpreted, for instance in the Los Angeles County Museum of Art retrospective of 1976. Women artists, revalued through careful attention to their associations and learning environments (Weisberg and Becker 1999), are no longer viewed as muses, models, and understudies for men, but as actual producers of art (Caws 2000, on Dora Maar; Bal 2005, on Artemisia Gentileschi).

From the "eccentrics" of modernism (Caws 2006) to contemporary artists, in the face of a male canon that excluded them, independent, original, groundbreaking women have inspired an influential counter-canon of their own, sustained by international recognition. These might include multimedia artist, sculptor, painter, and philosopher Adrian Piper (b. 1948), conceptual artist Barbara Kruger (b. 1945), or installation artist Jenny Holzer (b. 1950), who takes art into the public sphere through LCD displays such as in New York City's Times Square or stickers with texts on parking meters and telephone booths. Her interactive web installation "Please Change Beliefs," which invites viewers to click on a constant string of textual material that challenge truisms, illustrates the often rebellious character of women's art. Yet, while the canon of art has thus changed, the representation and status of women artists remains on an average still below that of men, and is contested by cultural agitprop groups like the Guerrilla Girls, with highly visible public actions such as their intervention at the 2005 Venice Biennale, cartoon-style books that lambaste the male stranglehold on art and the place of women in major art museums, for instance through posters asking such questions as "Do women have to be naked to get into the Met. Museum?" (http://www.guerrillagirls.com).

ONGOING ISSUES

In effect, while the cultural revolutions of the last few decades have greatly modified the literary canon, the canon is not about to disappear. It is in of itself an insidious notion that is difficult to shed: it creates an intellectual safety net of comfort, convenience, protection that "great works" are permanent, familiar, and easily accessible, as well as imparting to a large readership the notion of a shared culture.

Attention to gender, women's, and ethnic studies has also brought to light that there is not one single unified, but several, canons. Some of these can have a venerable history of their own, in turn affected by ongoing debates on gender and sexuality. If there is an African American "canon," it has included women all along (Foster 1997). African American literature indeed counts women such as Phillis Wheatley (1753–1784), Harriet Ann Jacobs (1813–1897), and Frances Ellen Watkins Harper (1825–1911) among its founding figures, and gay men such as James Baldwin (1924–1987), or internationally acclaimed women authors such as Toni Morrison (b. 1931) among its defining authors. It has a different relationship to establishing the contours of a community of readers and a collection of "great works" than the dominant white male canon. As a literature priding itself in a resistant role to racial and social injustice, it has been very often willing to embrace the exposure of the relation between structures of power and sex and gender, between racism and patriarchy, and forms of exclusion based on gender and sexuality, even in its "canonic" works.

Even though the canon of the past appears to have been seriously damaged and impaired, tensions remain between change and backlash initiatives. It remains to be seen whether twenty-first-century government attempts (the Spellings Commission Report of 2006, for example) to regulate colleges and universities in the name of greater accountability and higher standards will have the effect of reinstituting a more restrictive canon, or perhaps undoing some of the gains made since the 1980s by groups underrepresented in the traditional canon. The proposed standardized testing for the goal of outcomes assessment aims to address, among other things, what some see as the cultural illiteracy of early twenty-first-century college students. Critics fear that the establishment and application of single sets of criteria to all colleges and universities will discourage not only institutional diversity, but curricular diversity as well.

BIBLIOGRAPHY

Altieri, Charles. 1983. "An Idea and Ideal of a Literary Canon." *Critical Inquiry* 10(1): 37–60.

Bal, Mieke, ed. 2005. *The Artemisia Files: Artemisia Gentileschi for Feminists and Other Thinking People*. Chicago: University of Chicago Press.

Broude, Norma, and Mary D. Garrard, eds. 1994. *The Power of Feminist Art: The American Movement of the 1970s, History and Impact*. New York: Abrams.

Brown, Joan L., and Crista Johnson. 1998. "Required Reading: The Canon in Spanish and Spanish American Literature." *Hispania* 81(1): 1–19.

Brownlee, Kevin. 2005. "Christine de Pizan: Gender and the New Vernacular Canon." In *Strong Voices, Weak History: Early Women Writers and Composers in England, France, and Italy*, ed. Pamela Joseph Benson and Victoria Kinkham. Ann Arbor: University of Michigan Press.

Caws, Mary Ann. 2000. *Dora Maar: With and Without Picasso: A Biography*. London: Thames and Hudson.

Caws, Mary Ann. 2006. *Glorious Eccentrics: Modernist Women Painting and Writing*. New York: Palgrave Macmillan.

Choury, Maurice, ed. 1970. *Les Poètes de la Commune*. Paris: Seghers.

Desmond, Marilynn, ed. 1998. *Christine de Pizan and the Categories of Difference*. Minneapolis: University of Minnesota Press.

Eisner, Douglas. 1999. "Homophobia and the Demise of Multicultural Community: Strategies for Change in the Community College." *ADFL Bulletin* 31(1): 54–59.

Falini, Daniela. "Frida Kahlo and Contemporary Thoughts." Available from http://www.fridakahlo.it.

Foster, Frances Smith. 1997. "Canonization." *In The Oxford Companion to African American Literature*, ed. William L. Andrews, Frances Smith Foster, and Trudier Harris. New York: Oxford University Press.

Guerrilla Girls, Inc. Available from http://www.guerrillagirls.com.

Guerrilla Girls. 2004. *The Guerrilla Girls' Art Museum Activity Book*. New York: Printed Matter.

Guillory, John. 1990. "Canon." In *Critical Terms for Literary Study*, ed. Frank Lentricchia and Thomas McLaughlin. Chicago: University of Chicago Press.

Harris, Ann Sutherland, and Linda Nochlin. 1976. *Women Artists, 1550–1950*. Los Angeles: Los Angeles County Museum of Art.

Hicks, Eric; Diego Gonzalez; and Philippe Simon, eds. 2000. *Au Champ des Escriptures: Actes du IIIe Colloque International sur Christine de Pizan*. Paris: Honoré Champion.

Holzer, Jenny. "Please Change Beliefs." Available from http://www.adaweb.com/project/holzer/cgi/pcb.cgi.

Humphreys, Debra. 1998. "Diversity and the College Curriculum: How Colleges and Universities Are Preparing Students for a Changing World." Available from http://www.diversityweb.org/diversity_innovations/curriculum_change/principles_and_practices/curriculum_briefing.cfm.

Lauter, Paul. 1991. *Canons and Contexts*. New York: Oxford University Press.

Lawall, Sarah, ed. 2003. *The Norton Anthology of World Literature*, Vol. F: *The Twentieth Century*. New York: Norton.

Milech, Barbara. 1994. "'This Kind': Pornographic Discourses, Lesbian Bodies, and Paul Verlaine's *Les Amies*." *Men Writing the Feminine: Literature, Theory and the Question of Genders*, ed. Thaïs Morgan. Albany: State University of New York Press.

Minahen, Charles D. 1997. "Homosexual Erotic Scripting in Verlaine's *Hombres.*" *Articulations of Difference: Gender Studies and Writing in French*, ed. Dominique D. Fisher and Lawrence R. Schehr. Stanford, CA: Stanford University Press.

Nochlin, Linda. 1988. *Women, Art, and Power: and Other Essays.* New York: Harper and Row.

Quilligan, Maureen. 1991 *The Allegory of Female Authority: Christine de Pizan's Cité des dames.* Ithaca, NY: Cornell University Press.

Richards, Earl Jeffrey, with Joan Williamson, Nadia Margolis, and Christine Reno, eds. 1992. *Reinterpreting Christine de Pizan.* Athens: University of Georgia Press.

Scholes, Robert. 1992. "Canonicity and Textuality." In *Introduction to Scholarship in Modern Languages and Literatures*, ed. Joseph Gibaldi. 2nd edition. New York: Modern Language Association of America.

Shaw, Deborah. 1997. "Problems of Definition in the Theorizing of Latin American Women's Writing." In *Gender Politics in Latin America: Debates in Theory and Practice*, ed. Elizabeth Dore. New York: Monthly Review Press.

Smith, Barbara Herrnstein. 1988. *Contingencies of Value: Alternative Perspectives for Critical Theory.* Cambridge, MA: Harvard University Press.

Von Hallberg, Robert, ed. 1984. *Canons.* Chicago: University of Chicago Press.

Weisberg, Gabriel P., and Jane R. Becker, eds. 1999. *Overcoming All Obstacles: The Women of the Académie Julian.* New Brunswick, NJ: Rutgers University Press.

Diana Conchado
Francesca Canadé Sautman

CAPELLANUS, ANDREAS

SEE *Courtly Love, Western.*

CARAVAGGIO, MICHELANGELO MERISI DA
1571–1610

The Italian painter Michelangelo Merisi was born in or near Milan in late 1571, and died at age thirty-eight in Port'Ercole on July 18, 1610. During his brief but nonconformist life, Caravaggio, who laid the foundations of the baroque style, earned notoriety as much for his hot-tempered violence and bisexuality as for his painting, which was both popular and controversial. Critics were quick to connect his life of brawling, murder, and illicit sex with his art: It was rumored that he used a prostitute or mistress as a model for the Virgin Mary, and rival Giovanni Baglione accused him in court of keeping a young male model as lover. Caravaggio represents a landmark in the history of sexual expression both for his innovative subject matter and for his biography, one of the first that enables correlation of a body of homoerotic images with both individual personality and social milieu.

Michelangelo Merisi da Caravaggio. MANSELL/TIME LIFE PICTURES/GETTY IMAGES.

After absorbing the north Italian tradition of detailed, unvarnished realism, Caravaggio made his reputation in Rome among a circle of patrons with bisexual tastes, principally Cardinal Francesco del Monte. These men commissioned subjects from mythology (Bacchus, Cupid) that offered pretexts for beautiful, partially nude males. The models for their androgynous fantasies were often the same working-class adolescents who entertained at the aristocrats' gatherings; Caravaggio also recorded these youths more objectively in genre scenes, as musicians and, implicitly, bedmates. His pictures preserve the self-image of an embryonic homosexual subculture, an urban network of patrons, artists, and models of the type increasingly visible in the following century. Even with classical justification, such images were potentially subversive, as the nobleman Vincenzo Giustiniani evidently knew. He commissioned *Amor Victorious* (c. 1602)—an allegory of the power of eros in which nude Cupid, an unidealized urchin, grins lasciviously while fondling a phallic arrow and trampling symbols of men's serious pursuits—but hung it with a curtain that could be discreetly drawn when official visitors required greater decorum.

Similar sensibilities animated the artist's religious works, which spotlighted undraped angels and young saints in the warm light and dramatic shadows labeled "caravaggesque." This style aimed to fulfill Counter-Reformation demands for emotional images with a sensuous appeal to broad audiences; in Caravaggio's hands, however, that very intensity blurred the boundaries separating spiritual from physical ecstasy. Commissioned to depict Matthew inspired by an angel, he imagined another androgynous winged boy intimately entwined with the saint's limbs; the client rejected the picture and demanded a less suggestive replacement.

Despite lingering claims that meager documentation makes his legend unverifiable, the artist's fame as unapologetic bisexual and celebrator of male beauty has made him a cultural icon to post-Stonewall gays, celebrated in the poetry of Thom Gunn (1929–2004) and Derek Jarman's film *Caravaggio* (1986). The centrality of forbidden sexuality and gender ambiguity in his art provides a lens to examine the links and tensions between earthly and heavenly rapture. Through it one can glimpse, philosophically, an early moment when divine love could be manifested in homoerotic form; psychologically, an artist who openly represented his homosexual desire, including revealing self-portraits; and culturally, an audience whose patronage and reception of his work are identifiable.

SEE ALSO *Art.*

BIBLIOGRAPHY

Hibbard, Howard. 1983. *Caravaggio*. New York: Harper and Row.

Varriano, John. 2006. *Caravaggio: The Art of Realism*. University Park: Pennsylvania State University Press.

Wittkower, Rudolph. 1999. *Art and Architecture in Italy 1600-1750, Vol. 1. Early Baroque*, rev. J. Connors and J. Montagu. New Haven, CT: Yale University Press.

James M. Saslow

CARLINI, BENEDETTA
1590–1661

Abbess of the Theatine convent Holy Mary of Pescia Italy, Benedetta Carlini was born January 20th in Vellano and figures in the *Miscellanea Medicea*, a file containing short transcripts, letters and summaries of documents no longer extant (Brown 1986). Carlini appears in the file as a result of clerical inquiries (*processi*) concerning her claims of mystical visions and miracles. Beginning in 1619 and continuing through 1623, these inquiries focused on whether Carlini might be a saint and the investigators tried to determine the validity of her spiritual experiences, which included receiving the stigmata (the marks associated with the wounds inflicted on Christ at his crucifixion), exchanging hearts with Christ, and becoming Christ's bride in a public ceremony in which Christ praised her through her own mouth. The testimony of several nuns later established that Carlini had not only faked her stigmata and flirted with a priest, but engaged in a same-sex relationship with Bartolomea Crivelli, another nun.

First written about in Judith Brown's *Immodest Acts: The Life of a Lesbian Nun in Renaissance Italy* (1986), Carlini's case is intriguing and has sparked much debate. Lesbian historian Lillian Faderman faults Brown's work for the "calculated sensationalism of its name" (Faderman 1987, p. 576). Brown explains her use of "lesbian sexuality" and "lesbian nun" for "reasons of convenience to describe acts and persons called 'lesbian' in our own time" (Brown 1986, p. 171). That language, however, contextualizes Carlini only in modern terms of sexual identity, not in seventeenth-century Italian categories. Since the investigation considered sodomy, the clerics themselves might have categorized Carlini as a tribade.

After reexamination of the archival documents, historian Rudolph Bell launched a spirited exchange with Brown concerning her manuscript readings. He disagrees that the crossed out passages and unsteady handwriting associated with descriptions of the sexual acts reveal the male investigator's anxiety and interprets them as evidence of the erratic narrative of Crivelli. Further whereas Brown contends that the investigations were reopened in 1622, resulting in the collection of damaging evidence, Bell sees the entire period from 1619 to 1623 as one process that initially sought to confirm Carlini's status as a holy woman, but evolved into a political stratagem to eliminate a problematic abbess. Bell cites evidence that Carlini had long had problems establishing her authority and had called upon the Medici family for support. Moreover the 1622 and 1623 interviews document the dissatisfaction of the abbey's nuns who, according to Bell, wished to unseat Carlini.

During those interviews Crivelli, who had earlier corroborated the Carlini's visions, confessed that the two had engaged "in the most immodest acts" for more than two years, several times per week (Brown 1986, p. 117). Their sexual practices included kissing and genital rubbing but involved no instruments. Crivelli's version claimed Carlini took the persona of a male angel, Splenditello, when she "sinned with her by force" (Brown 1986, p.122). As Splenditello, the abbess allegedly told her companion their acts were not sin, since "it was the Angel Splentidello and not she that did these things" (Brown 1986, p. 119).

The entire account relies on Crivelli's testimony since Carlini never admitted she had engaged in sexual acts. Instead of eliciting accusations of sodomy, the affair was quietly resolved: Carlini, agreeing to charges of possession, was removed as abbess. Though the presumed diabolical origin of her sexual activities was paramount, Carlini's outing as a lesbian contributed to her removal, and for the following thirty-five years until her death on August 7, 1661, she lived in solitary confinement.

SEE ALSO *Monasticism.*

BIBLIOGRAPHY

Bell, Rudolph M. 1987. "Renaissance Sexuality and the Florentine Archives: An Exchange." *Renaissance Quarterly* 40(3): 485–511.

Brown, Judith. 1986. *Immodest Acts: The Life of a Lesbian Nun in Renaissance Italy.* New York: Oxford University Press.

Faderman, Lilian. 1987. "Review of *Immodest Acts: the Life of a Lesbian Nun in Renaissance Italy* and *Lesbian Nuns: Breaking Silence.*" *Signs* 12(3): 576–579.

Karras, Ruth Mazo. "Review of *Immodest Acts: the Life of a Lesbian Nun in Renaissance Italy* and *Holy Anorexia.*" *American Journal of Sociology,* 93(1): 234–236.

Holly Ransom

CASANOVA, GIACOMO
1725–1798

It is hard to distinguish between the writer Giacomo Casanova, born in Venice in 1725, and the protagonist of his monumental *Story of My Life* ("neither the story of a famous man nor a novel"), the multi-volume source of his fame as a symbol of unabashed, libertine sexuality; and it is harder still to neglect the countless other books and films that have contributed to fashioning his sexual persona, a carnival mask that has taken on a life of its own.

Ever since the *Histoire* (written from 1785 until his death in Bohemia, where he worked as the Count of Waldstein's librarian) was acquired by the publisher Brockhaus of Leipzig in 1821, another history has unfolded, that of its publication in various editions and languages: Only from 1960 to 1962 was the original French text released in its entirety (Casanova 1960–1962). Marie Françoise Luna has provided the best reconstruction to date of Casanova's "autobiographical project": not simply the confessions of a libertine and free thinker, but the self-portrait of a writer mining his own memory. The result is an original Franco-Italian mixture of styles and genres: epic and erotic, picaresque and sentimental, in a literary tradition stretching back to Boccaccio, Ariosto and Aretino.

Casanova was allegedly the illegitimate son of Michiel Grimani, the aristocratic owner of the theater where his parents, both actors, worked. Entrusted by his absentee mother at age eight to his grandmother after the death of his actor father, he had a memorable encounter with magic: a "witch" in Murano "cured" him of a chronic bleeding nose. François Roustang links Casanova's earliest childhood recollections to a precocious identification with archetypical women—the witch and the bedeviled madwoman, the latter Casanova's first seducer, Bettina (he was twelve and she seventeen). Prone to "hysterical fits," Bettina was repeatedly exorcised and diagnosed with a uterine ailment. Yet, she was neither crazy nor possessed, Casanova writes. This formative episode remained with him: In 1772, in a dispute with two professors at the Medical School of Bologna, he came to the ironic defense of the so-called "thinking uterus": he wrote, "Woman has a uterus and man has sperm, that's all the difference ... why incriminate the uterus and not the sperm? ... The education and the condition of the woman are the two causes that make her different ..." (*Lana Caprina*). As Marta Cavazza (2003) has written: "Casanova's playful and impertinent little book is one of the first to pose indirectly, though clearly, the distinction between sex and gender" (p. 256). From women, Casanova learns "how superior the eloquence of nature is to that of the philosophical mind" (Casanova 2000, p. 81).

His formative years were spent mainly in Italy, between Venice and Padua, with intervals in Corfù and Constantinople. As the protégée of several substitute father figures, he studied literature, violin and the law, between sexual escapades and short-lived stints in the clergy and the army. With his first trip to Paris in 1750, Casanova's horizons dramatically widened. He became (and remained for much of his life) a nomad, a strolling player of Eros in the cosmopolitan Europe of his times, joining the Freemasons, trying his hand at diplomacy (as an envoy of the King of France), entrepreneurship (managing a lottery), scholarship (writing historical works), all while pursuing numerous sexual adventures with women of all social stations (the written catalogue stops at one hundred and twenty-two). Finally, in 1774 (the year his memoirs end) he made his way back to a diminished Venice, only to be forced to flee once more, this time for good, after a dispute over a debt with his bastard half-brother, Giovan Carlo Grimani. He spent his final years in exile in Bohemia, writing obsessively, publishing a novel (the *Icosameron,* a sort of utopian fantasy) and leaving behind, in addition to the *Histoire,* a trove of unpublished manuscripts.

Philosopher or charlatan, magician or trickster, confidant or spy, seducer or seduced, Casanova's life contains multitudes. He crossed paths with legendary figures on both sides of the Enlightenment: Voltaire, Cagliostro, and Saint Germain. His fame as a cabalist gained him the patronage of powerful Venetians and, later in Paris, of old Madame d'Urfé, who wanted him to impregnate her with her own masculine reincarnation. These practices landed him in the *Piombi* (Leads), the infamous jail under the roof of the Doge's palace (1755). The story of his escape (like that of a duel he fought in Poland) became legendary throughout Europe: He wrote his own account of both episodes to set the facts straight (or fuel his legend). Yet, his free-thinking attitude toward superstition was ambivalent: The pleasure he took in duping fools, husbands, and lovers (deception that cut both ways: "... when love has a hand in things, each party usually dupes the other," he writes, adding "I continued to be the dupe of women until I reached the age of sixty"), may well hide a deeper level of repressed belief and sexual anxiety (Casanova 2000, pp. 3, 42). This ambivalence provides the ground for Casanova's flexible (and modern) philosophy: "To be a chameleon, a Proteus, a Tartuffe, an impenetrable comedian, to behave lowly, feign everything, appear cool ..." (Mangini, p. 155; Casanova 1966–1971, vol. 1, pp. 257–258).

As a sex symbol, the comparison with Don Juan is unavoidable—and overplayed. Both are old-fashioned serial lovers, *ancien régime*. Yet, classical Spain and romantic Venice are distant worlds: For Don Juan, a rich aristocrat, "sex is an anarchic power that challenges order in all forms: social, moral, and especially religious" (Tournier 1998, p. 9); for Casanova, a poor commoner who can rely only on his personal charm, sex is a passport that opens many doors. Indeed, Casanova (a friend of Mozart's librettist Da Ponte) likely provided the inspiration for that "aura of joy" that pervades Mozart's *dramma giocoso*: "The famous *odor di femmina* (scent of a woman) was his creation" (Tournier 1998, p. 9). Casanova claimed that four-fifths of his pleasure lay in making women happy, even though at least one affair ended so unhappily as to drive him close to suicide.

Casanova's name, unlike those of Sade or Sacher Masoch, does not designate a "perversion," but a sort of old-fashioned, exuberant sexual "normalcy," or "depravity" (Thomas 1985, p. 75). "Happy are those who can achieve pleasure without harm to anyone," he writes. When "he encounters a tender, erotic bond between two women," he accepts his role as "alternately a complicit instigator, a voyeur, and an ambiguous victim" (Thomas 1998, p. 179). This picture is somewhat complicated by recent findings about homosexual encounters (self)-censored from the memoirs. Revealingly, in one episode of the memoirs he is madly inflamed by the ambiguity of a woman disguised as a *castrato* (a castrated male singer).

Giovanni Casanova. **KEYSTONE/GETTY IMAGES.**

Master and slave of dissipation (Abirached 1961) or disguise (Roustang 1988), soulless sexual athlete (Fellini 1976) or reincarnation of the "pagan cheerfulness of love" (Zweig 1998, p. 100), as a modern heroic-comic symbol of masculinity, Casanova is inseparable from his melancholy double: a priapic, carnivalesque ghost who lived a life on the run, a consummate conjurer in the profane cabbala of sex.

BIBLIOGRAPHY

WORKS BY

Casanova, Giacomo. 1960–1962. *Histoire de ma vie*, ed. Angelika Hübscher. Wiesbaden-Paris: Brockhaus-Plon.

Casanova, Giacomo. 1966–1971. *History of My Life*, ed. and trans. Willard R.Trask. New York: Harcourt, Brace & World

Casanova, Giacomo. 1986. *"Icosameron," or, The Story of Edward and Elizabeth: Who Spent Eighty-OneYears in the Land of the Megamicres, Original Inhabitants of Protocosmos in the Interior of Our Globe*, ed. and trans. Rachel Zurer. New York: Jenna Press.

Casanova, Giacomo. 1993. *Histoire de ma vie*, ed. François Lacassin. Paris: Laffont.

Casanova, Giacomo. 1999. *Lana Caprina. Une controverse médicale sur l'Utérus pensant à l'Université de Bologne en 1771-1772*, ed Paul Mengal. Paris: Champion.

Casanova, Giacomo. 2000. *Story of My Life*, ed. Gilberto Pizzamiglio, trans. Stephen Sartarelli and Sophie Hawkes. New York: Marsilio.

Casanova, Giacomo. 2003. *The Duel*, trans. J. G. Nichols. London: Hesperus.

WORKS ABOUT

Abirached, Robert. 1961. *Casanova; ou, la dissipation*. Paris: Grasset.

Cavazza, Marta. 2003. "Women's Dialectics, or the Thinking Uterus: An Eighteen-Century Controversy on Gender and Education." In *The Faces of Nature in Enlightenment Europe*, ed. Lorraine Daston and Gianna Pomata, 237–257. Berlin: BWV.

Childs, Rives J. 1961. *Casanova: A Biography Based on New Documents*. London: Allen and Unwin.

Childs, Rives J. 1988. *Casanova, a New Perspective*. New York: Paragon House Publishers.

Ellis, Havelock. 1898. *Affirmations*. London: Walter Scott.

Fellini, Federico. 1976. *Casanova*. Motion Picture.

Luna, Marie-Françoise. 1998. *Casanova memorialiste*. Paris: Champion.

Macchia, Giovanni. 1989. "Casanova e il *Don Giovanni* di Mozart." *Tra Don Giovanni e Don Rodrigo*, 147–163. Milan: Adelphi.

Mangini, Nicola. 1960. "Giacomo Casanova." *Dizionario biografico degli italiani*. Roma: Istituto della Enciclopedia italiana.

Pizzamiglio, Gilberto, ed. 2001. *Giacomo Casanova tra Venezia e l'Europa*. Firenze-Venezia: Olschki.

Roustang, François. 1988. *The Quadrille of Gender. Casanova's Memoirs*. Stanford, CA: Stanford University Press.

Thomas, Chantal. 1985. *Casanova. Un voyage libertin*. Paris: Dénoel.

Thomas, Chantal. 1998. "The Role of Female Homosexuality in Casanova's *Mémoirs*." *In Libertinage and Modernity. Yale French Studies*, ed. Catherine, Cusset (94) 179–183.

Tournier, Michel. 1998. "Don Juan and Casanova." In *The Mirror of Ideas*, trans. Jonathan F. Krell, 8–9.

Zweig, Stefan. 1998. *Casanova. A Study in Self-Portraiture*. London: Pushkin Press. (Orig. pub. 1928.)

Massimo Riva

Farinelli *Farinelli, one of the most famous castrati.* © ARCHIVO ICONOGRAFICO, S.A./CORBIS.

CASTRATI

Castrati are male singers, castrated before puberty in order to preserve a strong soprano singing voice. In the seventeenth and eighteenth centuries, castrati were used extensively in Italian church choirs and were famous throughout Europe as stars of the Italian opera.

Castrati were generally castrated between the ages of eight and ten, or before their voices broke, by removal of the testicles. As a castrato's larynx doesn't descend at puberty and his Adam's apple doesn't develop, the vocal chords remain closer to the cavities of resonance, creating a clearer sound and a higher-pitched vocal timbre. Castrati voices were distinctive: Neither female nor childish, clear, strong, high-pitched, flexible, and powerful, they were often likened to the imaginary voices of angels.

The use of castrati in religious ceremonies dates to at least the third or fourth century. Castrati were used frequently in Byzantine church music, and this practice spread into the West, particularly southern Italy and Sicily. By the sixteenth century, the Roman Catholic Church had long condemned the practice of castration and thus employed children and falsettos for soprano parts in its choirs (women being prohibited from performing on stage). Castrati were commonly used in church choirs in Spain, however, and by 1599, the Vatican had begun to allow castrati in the Papal choir. By 1625, the pope had replaced all the Papal Choir's falsettos with castrati, who were now lauded as "natural" sopranos.

Castrati were generally Italian, from lower-class families, and were usually trained in Italian conservatories. Though castration by no means ensured a high-quality voice or a successful singing career, many families deemed the risk of an unsuccessful operation worth the benefits that might accrue to a castrato. Successful castrati were well compensated, received expensive gifts from rulers and nobles, mingled freely with the upper classes, and might become famous throughout Italy and Europe. In the seventeenth century, choirs and conservatories spread throughout Italy, and there was great competition to attract and retain castrati. The birth of opera in the same period provided an additional source of competition for musical talent. As the fame of Italian opera grew in Europe during the seventeenth and eighteenth centuries, so too did the fame and wealth of the castrati, who were feted by the nobility and became known for their romantic escapades with noble women.

By the turn of the nineteenth century, however, society's attitude toward the castrati had begun to change. Enlightenment thinkers—particularly among the French, who had long considered the castrati an abomination—criticized the practice of castration for its barbarism, deeming it an insupportable infringement of the rights of man in a modern, enlightened civilization. In 1798, Pope Pius VI (r. 1775–1799) revoked the ban of women on the stage, reducing the need for castrati, and in the early nineteenth century Napoleon I (1769–1821) began working to end the practice of castration in Europe. Although papal choirs continued to use castrati throughout the nineteenth century, the baroque operas of the castrati were now out of favor. In 1902, Pope Leo XIII (r. 1878–1903) banned the use of castrati in Church music. In the years following the papal ban, the last seven castrati left the Sistine Chapel choir. Alessandro Moreschi (1858–1922), the last castrato, left the choir in 1913, leaving behind the only existing recordings of a castrato's voice.

SEE ALSO *Castration; Eunuchs.*

BIBLIOGRAPHY

Barbier, Patrick. 1996. *The World of the Castrati: The History of an Extraordinary Operatic Phenomenon*, trans. Margaret Crosland. London: Souvenir Press.

Scholz, Piotr O. 2001. *Eunuchs and Castrati: A Cultural History*, trans. John A. Broadwin and Shelley L. Frisch. Princeton, NJ: Markus Wiener.

Maureen Lauder

CASTRATION

Castration refers to the removal of the testicles of a human or animal so as to render him infertile. Although castration technically refers to only removal of the testicles, the term is sometimes used to refer to the removal of the penis. In many cultures castration of humans is used as a punishment for crimes, while some religious sects have practiced castration as a means of dedicating the body to a god. In Asia and the Middle East, castrated men, known as eunuchs, were charged with protecting the harems of wealthy or powerful men from incursions by other men. As such eunuchs had a unique proximity to centers of power and often wielded enormous influence in their societies. In seventeenth and eighteenth-century Europe, gifted male singers, known as castrati, were castrated before puberty to prevent their voices from deepening and changing registers. In spite of the elevated social status of eunuchs and castrati in earlier times, however, castration more recently tends to be utilized primarily as punishment for or prevention of sexual offenses.

PHYSIOLOGY

Generally speaking castration refers to any method whereby a male loses the use of his testes. Historically the most common means of castration involved the removal of the testicles from the body. The most important effect of castration is sterility. In the prepubescent, castration generally results in a less muscular frame, lack of sex drive, an undeveloped prominentia laryngea (Adam's apple), and a high-pitched voice. Men who undergo castration after puberty normally experience a reduced sex drive, but such men can sometimes maintain an erection.

HISTORY

Human castration seems to have originated during the Stone Age, and archaeological evidence of eunuchs appears to follow the same distribution and chronology as animal domestication and human conquest. Thus as stable civilizations and communities spread from the Middle East outward to China and India, so too did eunuchs begin to appear in areas where humans settled. The first humans to be castrated were most likely prisoners of war who were enslaved rather than killed after capture.

It appears that the earliest institutional use of castration may have been the consecration of castrated slaves to Inanna, the Sumerian goddess of war. The followers of the goddess Cybele, a religious cult that dates from around 750 BCE and persisted into the early Christian era, voluntarily castrated themselves as a means of dedicating themselves to their goddess; evidence of the castration practice appears as early as 415 BCE.

Early Christians also occasionally saw castration as a means to spiritual salvation. The most famous of these, Origen, castrated himself circa 209 in an effort to follow the New Testament scripture Matthew 19:12, which refers to eunuchs "who have made themselves eunuchs for the kingdom of heaven's sake." Argument over the interpretation of this biblical passage raged among Christians for hundreds of years. At least one Christian sect required compulsory castration, but in 325 the Council of Nicaea condemned self-castration. In the fifth century, Saint Augustine pushed for an interpretation of Matthew's text that read castration as an allegory for celibacy, a position that the Church espoused informally for several centuries before codifying it in 1139 with the outlaw of clerical marriage. In spite of the church's attempt to read castration as mere celibacy, however, Pierre Abelard, a twelfth-century philosopher who was castrated by the outraged relations of his young lover, Heloise, firmly believed that his castration was divinely ordained and had brought him closer to God.

Although the Church had long since outlawed self-castration and though eunuchs were not a common feature of Western European medieval life, church choirs—which prohibited singing by women—utilized castrati. In this the Roman Catholic Church mimicked the Byzantine Church, in which eunuch choirs were traditional for hundreds of years. As noted castration prevented a boy's voice from changing and deepening; in addition as he developed, the size and power of the castrato's ribcage and lungs, combined with an unusually high vocal range, created a highly prized, unique singing voice. The castrati were regular features of church choirs by the sixteenth century and were common until the end of the nineteenth century. In the seventeenth and eighteenth centuries, many castrati moved out of church choirs and into Italian opera houses, where their singing became a well-known, popular entertainment.

In contrast to the limited positions available to European eunuchs, castrated men in Asian, African, and Middle Eastern societies often wielded considerable social and political power. Eunuchs were often employed as household servants, entrusted with the personal care of the ruler. Expanding on the practices of their Roman, Byzantine, and Persian predecessors, medieval Muslim rulers used eunuchs not only to control their concubines and legitimate wives, but also in a variety of other domestic and ceremonial functions. Eunuchs were considered to be more loyal to their masters than intact men and, indeed, often were, as their positions close to society's rich and powerful accorded them a certain level of prestige and influence. In many eastern cultures, including the Byzantine Empire, China, and Assyria, some of the most renowned commanders of armies and navies were eunuchs. In Greece, Persia, Rome, and China, household servants and palace guards were often eunuchs, sometimes organized into elaborate hierarchies. In one African state, eunuchs administered justice in the king's name and controlled the line of succession. In both China and Vietnam, rulers trusted only eunuchs to fill the highest ranks of civil servants, believing that because they couldn't reproduce, eunuchs would be less likely to try and establish their own dynasties. Nonetheless, it appears that Chinese eunuchs at times wielded considerable political power, and in seventeenth century Persia, palace eunuchs gained such effective control that for a number of years they ruled the country under a series of figureheads. In many cultures, most notably the Ottoman Empire, eunuchs were employed to guard the harems of the richest and most powerful men, thereby acquiring for themselves a social status and access to power that placed them close to the upper tiers of society.

By the nineteenth and twentieth centuries, in contrast to the powerful positions occupied by many eunuchs throughout history, societies in Europe and North America viewed castrated men primarily as weak, effeminate non-men. Even as early as Augustine's fifth-century commentaries on eunuchs, the Christian European world had begun to regard the castrated man as something profoundly unnatural.

In 1908 psychoanalyst Sigmund Freud developed his theory of castration anxiety, which hypothesizes that a normal part of male childhood development includes the belief that girls have no penis because they have been castrated, thereby instituting a lifelong, subconscious anxiety on the part of the male that he too will lose his penis. While Freud's theory has been largely discredited, it is noteworthy insofar as it signals a shift in thinking about castration. Until the twentieth century, castration referred almost exclusively to the removal of the testicles; Freud's theory equates castration with the loss of the penis and, coupled with the theory's female corollary, penis envy, situates the penis at the crux of masculine privilege and power. This understanding of the centrality of the penis can be seen at work in popular uses of the term castration, including as a metaphorical reference to a real or perceived lack of power on the part of male and to the emasculating effect of a powerful woman on a man.

CASTRATION AS PUNISHMENT AND TREATMENT

Castration has long been used as a method of punishment for criminal acts in many societies. It was frequently used in the waging of war, as a means of punishing, controlling, or subjugating a fallen enemy. In the United States, in the decades following the Civil War, castration often accompanied the lynching of black men in the South as a simultaneous punishment for and warning against miscegenation, whether real or imagined. Castration was also used as a criminal sentence in many societies. In some cases, only the testicles were removed; in others all the genitalia were excised, often condemning the victim to a painful death. Prior to the eighteenth century, castration was often written into the law as punishment for certain crimes or specifically designated as the sentence for a particular crime. In Europe during the Middle Ages and Renaissance, criminals were sometimes sentenced to death followed by dismemberment and castration.

In the nineteenth and twentieth centuries, sterilization was often used to control criminal populations and to punish or treat sex offenders. The development of vasectomy techniques (which sterilize by blocking the connection between the testicles and prostrate rather than by removing the testicles) in the nineteenth century meant that castration as such was no longer employed for treatment or punishment of criminals; the scientific nature of the new procedure appears to have made sterilization generally more palatable. In the early-twentieth century, the United States experimented with a number of procedures—often performed without the knowledge or consent of the victims—and sterilization laws designed to reduce the criminality of the general population and help maintain the purity of bloodlines in the face of high United States immigration rates. The discovery after World War II that Nazi doctors had experimented with similar sterilization techniques and policies dampened popular enthusiasm for the project. More recently chemical castration, which temporarily reduces testosterone production, has been attempted on a number of sex offenders, and, in the early-twenty-first century, the possibility and ethicality of legislating such treatment is under debate.

SEE ALSO *Castrati; Eunuchs; Hijrās; Penis.*

BIBLIOGRAPHY

"Image Archive on the American Eugenics Movement." Eugenics Archive. Available from http://www.eugenicsarchive.org/eugenics.

Kuefler, Mathew. 2001. *The Manly Eunuch: Masculinity, Gender Ambiguity, and Christian Ideology in Late Antiquity.* Chicago: University of Chicago Press.

Monick, Eugene. 1991. *Castration and Male Rage: The Phallic Wound.* Toronto: Inner City Books.

Ringrose, Katherine M. 2003. *The Perfect Servant: Eunuchs and the Social Construction of Gender.* Chicago: University of Chicago Press.

Scholz, Piotr O. 1999. *Eunuchs and Castrati: A Cultural History,* trans. John A. Broadman and Shelley L. Repr., Frisch. Princeton, NJ: Markus Wiener, 2001.

Taylor, Gary. 2000. *Castration: An Abbreviated History of Western Manhood.* New York and London: Routledge.

Maureen Lauder

CATALINA DE ERAUSO
c. 1592–1650

Catalina de Erauso was a Basque noblewoman who, just before taking final vows to become a nun at age fifteen, escaped from the convent in San Sebastián where she had lived since the age of four. Using the name Francisco de Loyola, Erauso lived successfully as a man for almost twenty years, for a brief period in Spain and later in the New World using the name Alonso Díaz Ramírez de Guzmán. Although she was distinguished for her fearless deeds as a soldier fighting for the Spanish empire in Peru and Chile, Erauso's memoirs showcase her propensity for

Catalina de Erauso HULTON ARCHIVE/GETTY IMAGES.

violence, gambling, and womanizing. However rebellious Erauso may seem, once she confessed her previous identity as Catalina, she quickly became the celebrity known as the "Lieutenant Nun" and was rewarded for her gender transgression in 1626 with a soldier's pension from the Spanish monarch Philip IV and dispensation from Pope Urban VIII to continue dressing in men's clothing. In 1630 she returned to the New World and spent the last twenty years of her life in Mexico working as a muleteer, using the name Antonio de Erauso, until her death in 1650.

There is no evidence from seventeenth-century documents that she was believed to possess any irregularities in primary sexual characteristics. After her shocking revelation, the matrons who examined her body for confirmation of her female anatomy declared her to be an "intact virgin" (Erauso 1996, p. 66). Other witnesses, nonetheless, described certain secondary sexual traits in terms of maleness. Erauso admitted, for example, to having used a poultice or plaster mixture spread on a cloth to flatten her chest. This invasive technique testifies to her intention to live permanently as a man, unlike the temporary cross-dresser who sooner or later returns to female garb.

By the end of the twentieth century, scholarship on Erauso began to show an increasing awareness of the identity politics implicit in narrating the lives of individuals who transgress traditional prescriptions for gender roles and sex assignment. Early modern historian Mary Elizabeth Perry, for example, alternates gender pronouns when writing about Erauso: "It seems neither fair nor accurate, however, to use exclusively feminine pronouns to refer to the Nun-Lieutenant, who worked so diligently to make herself into a man... it could be argued that Catalina de Erauso should be identified as a male who did not allow his family's mistaken identity of him nor his lack of some of the physiological characteristics of males to undercut his own understanding of himself" (Perry 1999, p. 395). Michele Stepto, on the other hand, reminds researchers of the colonialist, manipulative, and bigoted nature of Erauso's profile (Erauso 1996).

Given the contradictions inherent in Erauso's life (as a transgendered individual associated with colonial exploitation, violent crimes, same-sex desire, and so forth), it is not surprising that the Lieutenant Nun can be upheld as hero or enemy by competing ideological and identitarian positions, whether Catholic, transgender, lesbian, hetero-biased, feminist, misogynist, colonial, racist, classist, and nationalist (Spanish, Basque, or Latin American) ideologies. In this way, Erauso remains an ambivalent icon: a rebel and conformist, a hero and an outlaw, able to represent either side of many controversies.

BIBLIOGRAPHY

Erauso, Catalina de. 1996. *Lieutenant Nun: Memoir of a Basque Transvestite in the New World*, trans. Michele Stepto and Gabriel Stepto. Boston: Beacon Press.

Perry, Mary Elizabeth. 1999. "From Convent to Battlefield: Cross-Dressing and Gendering the Self in the New World of Imperial Spain." In *Queer Iberia: Sexualities, Cultures, and Crossings from the Middle Ages to the Renaissance*, ed. Josiah Blackmore and Gregory S. Hutcheson. Durham: Duke University Press.

Vallbona, Rima de, ed. 1992. *Vida I sucesos de la Monja Alférez: Autobiografía atribuida a Doña Catalina de Erauso*. Tempe: Arizona State University.

Velasco, Sherry. 2000. *The Lieutenant Nun: Transgenderism, Lesbian Desire & Catalina de Erauso*. Austin: University of Texas Press.

Sherry Velasco

CATHERINE THE GREAT
1729–1796

Sophie Friederike Auguste of Anhalt-Zerbst, later Empress Catherine II of Russia and called Catherine the Great, was born in Stettin, Prussia (now Szczecin, Poland), on May 2 (April 21, old style), 1729, and died in Tsarskoye Selo, near St. Petersburg, on November 17 (November 6, O.S.), 1796. Young Sophie was betrothed to Grand Duke Peter, heir to the throne of Russia, on July 10 (June 29, O.S.), 1744 as a result of a political scheme organized by King Frederick II of Prussia and accepted by Empress Elizabeth (r. 1741–1762; Peter's childless aunt) in order to strengthen the relationship between the Franco-Prussian axis and Russia, at the expense of Austria and other European powers. Sophie converted to the Russian Orthodox faith, and engaged in a strenuous study of Russian language, culture, and mores. This "Russification" would appear even more remarkable in contrast to the Germanophile attitudes and Protestant faith of Grand Duke Peter. Upon her conversion, she changed her name to Yekaterina Alexeyevna, in honor of Empress Elizabeth's mother.

Catherine the Great. AP IMAGES.

The marriage (celebrated on September 1 [August 21, O.S.], 1745) never developed into a romantic or intimate relationship, and Peter, weakened and disfigured by smallpox and other diseases (including a birth impairment that probably made him sterile), kept a semiofficial mistress (Elizabeth Vorontsova), while Catherine conceived her son Paul (later Tsar Paul I; 1754–1801; r. 1796–1801) with Sergei Saltykov, one of her lovers. Upon Elizabeth's death, on January 5, 1762 (December 25, 1761, O.S.), Peter ascended to the throne. Through a coup d'état masterminded with the help of Grigory Orlov (her then lover) and his brothers, Catherine had her husband overthrown and was proclaimed empress on July 9 (June 28, O.S.),

1762. Peter's death in prison (officially of a sudden sickness, in fact murdered by some of the conspirators who had deposed him) on July 17 (July 6, O.S.), cast a long-lasting shadow on Catherine's reputation, as did the demise of former (deposed) Tsar Ivan VI in 1764. It seems, however, that Catherine was not directly involved in either assassination.

Catherine's reign was marked, in addition to the relentless pursuit of territorial expansion, by a constant oscillation between impulse for reform and rational codification of laws, and the conservation of autocratic, traditionally Russian attitudes toward power and government. Her *Great Instruction* (1767), the major theoretical output of what she defined her "Legislomania," was inspired by a peculiarly antiliberal and absolutistic interpretation of the works of such philosophers as the Baron de Montesquieu and Cesare Beccaria, while her literary and practical concerns on the education of children of both sexes (which also resulted in the creation of foundling homes, hospitals, and educational institutions) drew on the ideas of John Locke and Jean-Jacques Rousseau. Catherine entertained a frequent epistolary relationship with both Voltaire (whose library she purchased at his death in 1778) and Denis Diderot. The latter paid her a long visit in 1773. For more than twenty years, she corresponded with Friedrich Melchior Grimm (1723–1807), an important figure in European literary circles, and her most dedicated confidant. This frequentation of Enlightenment figures (together with the legacy of her Lutheran upbringing), probably accounted for her aversion to traditional Russian superstitions. In 1768 she had herself inoculated against smallpox, a gesture that was immediately used and amplified for image-bolstering and political propaganda across Europe.

Catherine worked relentlessly on the construction of her public persona, often playing with gender-related attributes both in normative/traditional and in unconventional ways. On one hand, she was customarily referred to as "Little Mother" and tried to cast herself in the tradition of the four other female rulers who had preceded her. On the other, she cultivated and exhibited masculine attitudes—from riding horses astride and not sidesaddle, to her frequent use of male attire (a penchant she shared with her predecessor, Elizabeth). Even more complex are the issues related to her relationship with a long list of male "favorites," some of whom acquired significant positions in government and military leadership (from Stanisław Poniatowski, later installed as king of Poland, to Grigory Potemkin and Peter Zavadovsky, to name a few), while others, especially toward the end of her life, seemed to have possessed lesser intellectual and political skills.

Catherine seems to have established a system of "favoritism" that went beyond the promiscuity and multiple affairs of Elizabeth and other female rulers. It was a system that developed into a sort of career pattern in which her lovers would eventually be rewarded with substantial severance pay and pensions.

This comportment became an attribute popularly attached to Catherine's persona, together with other perceivably excessive and obsessive attitudes of hers ("legislomania," in her own definition, and "graphomania"). The reaction to the "reversal of traditional sex roles" (Alexander 1989, p. 211) inherent in her favoritism generated (especially in foreign countries) innumerable pamphlets, satires, or blatantly slanderous books that transformed Catherine's perceived sexual voracity into sinister or pornographic legends (with allegations ranging from uxoricide to bestiality), drawing on consolidated historiographical paradigms of character construction (the ones anciently applied to such figures as Sammuramat, Cleopatra, and Messalina, or, in later times, to María Luisa of Parma). From the literary point of view, besides government-related works and some occasional narrative and theatrical works, her most remarkable achievements are considered her epistolary and her French *Mémoires*.

BIBLIOGRAPHY

Alexander, John T. 1989. *Catherine the Great: Life and Legend.* New York: Oxford University Press.

Catherine the Great. 2005. *The Memoirs of Catherine the Great,* trans. Mark Cruse and Hilde Hoogenboom. New York: Modern Library.

De Madariaga, Isabel. 2002. *Catherine the Great: A Short History.* 2nd edition. New Haven, CT: Yale University Press.

Troyat, Henri. 1980. *Catherine the Great,* trans. Joan Pinkham. New York: Dutton.

Paolo Fasoli

CATHOLICISM

The term *Catholic*, which etymologically means universal, is used within Christianity to differentiate it from other Christian communions such as the Protestant or Russian and Greek Orthodox Churches. The Catholic Church maintains that it is One, Holy, Catholic and Apostolic, as the Nicene Creed states, and that the Bishop of Rome, the Pope, is the head of Christianity, the Supreme Pontiff of the Church of Christ. Consequently, it is common, not only for Catholics but for others, to refer to the Catholic Church as "the Church." Besides the Latin rite which has several subdivisions such as the Ambrosian (Milan, Italy), the Mozarabic (Toledo, Spain), the Lyonnais, the Braga and the Monastic rite, the Catholic Church includes Eastern rites such as the Byzantine, Alexandrian, Armenian, Chaldeian, and Antiochene.

The term Catholic was first employed by Saint Ignatius Martyr (d. 107 CE) in an epistle to the Church of Smyrna, when he said: "Ubi Christus, ibi catholica Ecclesia"("There where Christ is, is the Catholic church"). Christianity began in Palestine, stemming from the words and deeds of Jesus of Nazareth, son of Mary and Joseph the carpenter, who was baptized by John the Baptist in the river Jordan around the year 28 CE (Matthew 3:1-17). This is the very Jesus who declared himself the Messiah, the Christ, at the beginning of his public life. In Nazareth, attending Sabbath service at the synagogue, he attributed to himself the words of the Scriptures: "The spirit of the Lord is upon me / because he has anointed me; / he has sent me to announce/ good news to the poor..."(Luke 4:16-20). Jesus was crucified in April of the year 30 CE by command of the Roman Procurator Pontius Pilate, and after his resurrection his disciples undertook the evangelization of the world, following their teacher's command as stated in the Gospel of Matthew: "Full authority in heaven and on earth has been committed to me. Go forth therefore and make all nations my disciple; baptize all in the name of the Father, the Son and the Holy Spirit, and teach them to observe all that I have commanded you. And be assured, I am with you always, to the end of time" (Matthew 28: 16-20).

The Apostle who did the most to spread the word of this new religion among the Gentiles was Paul of Tarsus, born Saul. A rabbinical student of the Jewish Diaspora and a Roman citizen, he died martyred with the Apostle Peter in Rome under the rule of the Emperor Nero, circa 67 CE. Paul had evangelized part of Asia Minor, Palestine, and Syria, and his disciples brought the word to Greece, Macedonia, Egypt, and Northern Africa. Wherever there were Jews living in the Diaspora, there was a fertile ground for converts to Christianity. Slowly, evangelization reached very large numbers of people, including the Roman Imperial family. Since Rome was the capital of the Roman Empire, it was chosen as the center of Christianity and this became a well entrenched ideology (Kantorowicz 1981).

Up to the fourth century, however, the Eastern Churches of Ephesus, Antioch, Alexandria Caesarea, and Carthage retained great importance. Early Church Fathers such as Iraeneus (b. c.190–195), Tertullian (b. c. 160 in Carthage), and Origen (185–254 CE) lent their prestige to Rome by asserting the supremacy of the Universal Church. At the time of Origen, the Roman Empire was in total political chaos and decadence; thus, one could conceive of Christianity as an alternative that could rescue the positive values of the Empire. The Emperor Constantine's 313 Edict of Milan ended the persecution of Christians, and the conversion of the Emperor himself completed the victorious journey of the new religion. Rome, now the center of Christianity and Catholicism, with the establishment of the papacy and the Holy See, saw its central role reaffirmed with the crowning of Charlemagne aHoly Roman Emperor in the year 800. The Bishop of Rome therefore claims his authority as conferred to Peter by Christ: "You are Peter and on this rock I will build my Church" (Matthew 15:18).

The Oriental Churches, such as the Greek and Russian Orthodox, had also been growing and had become centers of Christianity in their own right for political and religious reasons. Divisions within Christianity were further accentuated with the Protestant Reformation (1517) led by Martin Luther (1483–1586) who, in protest against the practice of indulgences, posted his 95 theses on the door of the Palast Church in Wittemberg, Germany, and later by John Calvin, who began the Reformation (1532) in France. The Church of England broke away from the Catholic Church under the reign of Henry VIII, after his divorce from Catherine of Aragon to marry Anne Boleyn (1533), and his excommunication by Pope Clement VII, bringing about the final rift between Rome and England. Like Protestantism, the Anglican Communion has maintained the necessity for the faithful to pray in the vernacular; thus Thomas Cramer (1552) produced its *Book of Common Prayer*. The Church, in response to several heretical currents throughout its history—for example the Cathar heresy resulting in the Albigensian Crusade in Southern France (1209–1229)—also established the Inquisition in 1233 CE and the Pope entrusted its powers to the Dominican order. A conviction of heresy could result in capital punishment and burning at the stake.

These rifts between Christian denominations are reflected in major differences regarding issues of vital religious, theological and social importance. The rift with the Reformation centered on clerical celibacy, the primacy of the Roman Pontiff, the practice of simony, the abuse of indulgences and the seven sacraments themselves, as well as the Eucharist. It was followed by a Catholic Reformation with the Council of Trent (1545–1564) which provided a reform of the clergy (establishment of seminaries for the preparation and instruction of priests), of evangelization, missionary work, and Catholicism itself. Sacerdotal celibacy and the exclusion of women in the priesthood were reaffirmed. The *Index of Prohibited Books* (*Index librorum prohibitorum*) was issued with papal approval along with the *Professio Fidei* (Profession of Faith) for all Catholics to follow.

The Second Vatican Council (1962–1965) was convened by Pope John XXIII in order to prepare the Church for the modern world. It dealt with issues such as the mission of laity, the nature of religious freedom, ecumenism, and liturgical reform such as the usage of the vernacular in liturgy. While the First Vatican Council

(1869–1870) reaffirmed the doctrine of Papal infallibility, based on the creed of the Pope as direct heir to St. Peter who received the office directly from Jesus, the Second Council was more inclusive, attempting to reach out ecumenically to all the Churches and even other religions. However, with the encyclical *Lumen gentium* (*The Light of the Peoples*) the Church claimed to be "the one Church of Christ which in the Creed is professed one, holy, catholic and apostolic ... which is governed by the successor of Peter and by the bishops in community with him"(Pope Paul VI, November 1964). Regarding salvation, the Council held to the notion that Christians and non-Christians might be saved by accepting and responding to the grace of God and in its revelation through the mercy of Christ, the "baptism of desire," a tenet that many Christian theologians and intellectuals had advocated. For instance, in his *Divine Comedy*, Dante exposed his conception of Limbo, and allowed the salvation of Cato, Rhipheus the Trojan, and the Emperor Trajan.

THE VIRGIN MARY

The Church has maintained that the Virgin Mary, as the human mother of Jesus, is the mother of all humanity, and that Catholics and others may intercede with her and the other saints in heaven through prayer: "The Blessed Virgin Mary can best be set forth as a most exalted Co-operatrix with Christ. Such a chapter would greatly enhance the glory of the Mother of God" (*The Sixteenth Documents*, p. 666). In Catholic tradition, the Virgin Mary became the figural fulfillment of Eve who has been blamed—by theologians from Saint Augustine to Jerome, to Aquinas and even Luther and up to the present—for the original sin, which has become primarily a sexual issue and foundational to misogyny in Christian cultures. Since the time of Augustine, the sexual urge has been proclaimed a sin and chastity is traditionally upheld. The Biblical Eve has become, in art and literature, the image of the *femme fatale*, while Mary has taken her place as mother of humanity and the symbol of life rather than death, as a means of salvation and the fruit of Redemption. In Catholic exegesis, Mary is a symbol and type of the Church (*typus Ecclesiae*) as are all the female figures of the Old Testament such as Rachel, Sarah, Rebecca, Ruth, Judith, and others (Di Scipio 1983, Pelikan 1996).

DISSENT

The Church, born under persecution during the Roman Empire, has always maintained pacifism in social teaching. In the modern era, however, some Catholics maintain that there may be a "just war," such as World War II against the evil of Nazism, but even such wars are meant to prevent or limit wars, not justify them. Pope John XXIII pointed the way with his encyclical *Pacem in Terris* (1963). Pope John Paul II adamantly opposed the Iraq War (begun 2003) and made a cornerstone of his pontificate a reconciliation with Jews, Muslims, and non-Christians, even apologizing to some for past errors committed by the Church of Rome. At the same time John Paul reaffirmed Church teaching against capital punishment in all instances as immoral.

The Catholic Church thus has a lively tradition of dissent on social issues such as pacifism and sexuality, as demonstrated by figures such as the Jesuit priest Robert Drinan (d. 2007) who served as a Representative to the U.S. from Massachusetts for five terms and hotly opposed the Vietnam War in the 1960s, and ignored the Church doctrine by supporting federal financing of birth control and abortion. Similarly, Auxiliary Bishop Thomas J. Gumbleton, who served as pastor in an inner city Detroit parish, co-founder of the peace ministry Pax Christi, broke ranks because of his teaching in favor of gay men and lesbians and the ordination of women, as well as his open lobbying in favor of victims of sexual abuses, and was forced to resign in an apparent act of retaliation by the Church (*New York Times*, January 26, 2007). Another controversial priest was the French-born Abbé Pierre (d. 2007), founder of the organization Emmaus International to help the homeless and the indigents. He served in World War II as a chaplain for the French Navy and also in the French Resistance, he helped Jews and others escape from the Nazis, was elected to the National Assembly, and received the French Legion of Honor which he gave back as a gesture to dramatize the issue of the homeless. The French President Chirac gave him another. He enraged the Catholic hierarchy by supporting gay marriage and revealing that as a young priest he had sex with a woman.

THE PRIESTHOOD, CELIBACY, AND WOMEN IN THE PRIESTHOOD

The Catholic Church follows the precept that everyone is equal in the eyes of God and restated this principle in Vatican Council II on the authority of Paul in Galatians 3:28 and Colossians 3:11: "There is, therefore in Christ and in the Church no inequality on the basis of race or nationality, social condition or sex because, 'there is neither Jew nor Greek: there is neither bond nor free: there is neither male or female. For you are all "one" in Christ Jesus'" (*The Sixteen Documents*, p. 143). But on the question of ordination, the Catholic Church upholds the *magisterium*, the position that priestly ordination can be conferred only on men. This was reaffirmed in Pope John Paul II's Apostolic Letter, *Ordinatio Sacerdotalis* (Sacerdotal Ordination, 1994) which states: "the Church has no authority whatsoever to confer priestly ordination on women and definitely held by all Church faithful." The Church saw it as necessary to restate this position in a subtle manner because of the challenge being posed in the late twentieth and early twentieth-first centuries by many women's groups who claim that Jesus had several women apostles, particularly Mary Magdalene, whom feminist scholars consider one of the first apostles as confirmed by the Gnostic Gospels, and of whom Augustine himself said that the Holy Spirit made the Apostle of the Apostles. The present Pope, Benedict XVI, as Cardinal Joseph Raztinger, head of the Office of Congregation of Faith, stated several times that the Church is God's Church, and that theologians cannot change this. Nevertheless, in the 1970s, Ludmila Javorova and other Czech women were ordained to serve the needs of women imprisoned by Communists.

Another important issue is priestly celibacy. Celibacy is a longstanding tradition in the Church from its origins with the example of Jesus himself and Paul. The Church has had to intervene repeatedly on this issue. Pope Leo the Great (440–461) decreed celibacy in the fifth century, as this rule was not being followed and many clergy kept concubines at home. It was reaffirmed in the eleventh century at the Synod of Poiters in 1074, when Pope Gregory VII excommunicated married priests. Celibacy was upheld again in the First Lateran Council (1124), and after the Protestant Reformation at the Council of Trent (1545–1563) which affirmed that celibacy and virginity are superior to marriage. It was restated at the Vatican Council II in 1965, and in the Encyclical Sacerdotalis Caelibatus of 1967 issued by Paul Pope VI, who also issued celibacy dispensations (frozen by Pope John Paul II in 1978), and in the Code of Canon Law of 1983.

Since Vatican Council II, the Catholic Church admits to the deaconate married men of mature age, but it does not permit ordained priests to contract marriage. It does allow men who have been married to enter the priesthood, provided they refrain from sexual intercourse, but it excommunicates those priests who have contracted marriage. This is constantly being challenged, as in the case of Archbishop Emmanuel Milingo from Zambia (b. Lusaka 1930) who married and, excommunicated, still ordained other married priests and founded an organization of former priests defrocked for having contracted marriage, such as Married Priests Now and the Association of Married Priests, founded by theologian Giuseppe Serrone. However, the Eastern Rites do ordain married men and the Vatican has admitted married clergy from the Anglican faith who have converted to Catholicism.

The Church faces great difficulties because of the decline in priestly ordination and the exclusion of women. Throughout the world, married priests are performing religious rites, such as the Easter service, as a response to this shortage and in rebellion against Rome. The Vatican has, through the eminent theologian Cardinal Martini, affirmed, on December 5, 2006, that nowhere in the New Testament is it stated that married men cannot be ordained, but the Church upholds the tradition that celibacy is the better choice, as stated by the Apostle Paul (I Corinthians: 7). Interestingly enough, during the period 2001 to 2006 many more young women have been entering convents, according to an article in *Time Magazine* (November 20, 2006, pp. 53–56), although since 1965, Catholics nuns have decreased in number from 179,954 to 67,773. The Church maintains, notwithstanding the sexual scandals that have affected it in the United States, that celibacy is not the cause for the decrease of priesthood. Yet sexual scandals have already caused entire dioceses to go bankrupt because of legal expenses for settlements of sexual abuses by clergy, one case being that of the Diocese of San Diego, which would be the fifth (*New York Times*, February 20, 2007, p. A14).

It must be noted that sexual abuse by the clergy is the domain of the Congregation of the Doctrine of Faith in Rome, not of local bishops. This is in accordance with the Apostolic Letter of John Paul II, *Scramentum sanctitatis tutela*, and the 1983 Code of Canon Law punishes sexual abuse of a minor with laicization and dismissal from the ministry. The Anglican communion (77 million members) faces similar debates regarding homosexuality, same-sex marriage and the ordination of women, as it discussed the actions of the Episcopal Church of the United States (its American branch is made up of 2.3 million members), which has ordained lesbian female bishops. Conservative bishops have refused to celebrate the Eucharist with Bishop Katherine Jefferts Schori, maintaining that this violates Scriptural teaching: "Facing a possible church-wide schism, the Anglican communion yesterday gave its Episcopal branch in the United States less than eight months to ban blessings of same sex unions or risk a reduced role in the world's largest Christian denomination" (*New York Times*, February 20, 2007, p. A1). The Catholic Church has vehemently opposed legislation favoring recognition of same-sex unions in the United States and other countries, and is in open conflict with the government, the Parliament and the Italian Constitution (*La Repubblica*, February 13, 2007, pp. 10–11). Pope Benedict XVI, in speaking to the faithful, has affirmed that "No human law can subvert the law of the Creator" (*La Repubblica*, February 12, 2007).

HUMAN LIFE, SEXUALITY, AND EUTHANASIA

The Church holds that human life is holy and that each individual, male and female, is equal and created in the image of God. It opposes abortion (Portugal is the latest Catholic country to allow abortion, beginning 2007), euthanasia, homosexuality, artificial birth control, artificial insemination, and same-sex marriage. The Church tells the faithful that sex is not sinful if contained within marriage and for reasons of procreation, but is a capital sin if practiced outside of marriage. Pope John Paul II, in his Theology of the Body (October 29, 1980), states that physical love allows one to understand "the meaning of the whole existence, the meaning of life." In essence this is a restatement of the Aristotelian and Thomistic principles of the perfection achieved in the unity of the body and soul, something that Dante Alighieri, for example, championed in his *Divine Comedy.* Since the Church considers Manicheism a heresy (the doctrine that the Spirit is good and the Flesh evil), the human body and sex are good within limitations. Yet it prohibits and considers sinful sexual relationship between men, between women, same-sex marriage, and the remarriage of divorced people.

Consequently the Church faces strong criticism and challenges on issues such as artificial contraception, artificial insemination, abortion (which may carry the penalty of excommunication), and sexuality in general, in particular for its ban on the use of condoms in the prevention of AIDS and teenage pregnancy. The Church maintains that abstinence is the only way to prevent unwanted pregnancies or the spread of AIDS. Studies indicate that most Catholics ignore the Church on these points, and that they generally make use of artificial contraception. Abortion is very high among Catholics in Latin American countries—with the highest number of Catholics in any continent—and condom distribution is widely practiced in Africa and other continents for AIDS prevention, even by Catholic missionaries. Cardinal Alfonso Lopez Trujillo, President for the Pontifical Council for the Family has restated that the Church has not changed its views on the use of condoms (Catholic News Agency, May 4, 2006). The Church is aware that most Catholics do not follow these precepts, but it remains consistent in its traditional teaching.

The Catholic Church also condemns euthanasia, which is allowed in the Netherlands and some other countries. In 2007, the Church was involved in a very serious controversy with the case of Welby, an Italian man suffering with Parkinson's Disease, who had requested to die, and was allowed to, when a Dr. Riccio from Cremona disconnected a respirator. Mr. Welby intentionally wanted to provoke a dialogue on this issue. The Church Vicariate in Rome then refused Mr. Welby a Christian burial (January 2007), and this caused a huge uproar; many Catholics were appalled and accused the Church of hypocrisy, for it permits religious services for notorious criminals and political figures, such as General Pinochet of Chile, while denying the same for a suffering person of the same faith. Cardinal Martini of Milan intervened and pointed out the difficulty of such a case and urged the government to pass a law similar to the one in France which prohibits, in such cases, the use of medical treatment with obdurate and unreasonable obstinacy (*Sole 24 Ore,* January 21, 2007). Yet statistics clearly indicate that most Catholics in Italy (68%) favor "a good death," that is, allowing one to die without prolonged suffering and unnecessary treatment.

In February 2007, Pope Benedict XVI reaffirmed the traditional Church policy on same-sex marriage, euthanasia, and abortion in his Sunday Sermon (Angelus) and to the Conference of Italian Bishops (CEI) on February 4, which was celebrating the Sacredness of Life Day. He also upheld the precept of the traditional family union through matrimony in response to an ongoing debate among the faithful on all these issues, claiming that his position is "based on the real needs of the couple"(*La Repubblica,* February 5, 2007, p. 13, U.S. edition). And he attacked once again all legislation favoring genetic manipulations, abortion, euthanasia, eugenics and selective diagnosis before birth (*La Repubblica,* February 24, 2005, p, 15). At the same time, in a Catholic country like Italy, the number of unmarried couples living together has risen from 192,00 in 1983 to 555,000 in 2005. Similar statistics hold for other countries, and the Church thus faces some very strong challenges—yet throughout the centuries, it has found ways to survive and adapt itself to its times.

SEE ALSO *Alan of Lille; Aquinas, Thomas; Christ; Damian, Peter; Marbod of Rennes; Marriage, Spiritual; Mary Magdalene; Monasticism.*

BIBLIOGRAPHY

Abbot, Elizabeth. 2000. *A History of Celibacy.* New York: Scribner.

Allen, John. 2005. *The Rise of Benedict XVI.* New York, Doubleday.

Cross, F. L., and Livingston, E. A., eds. 1997. *The Oxford History of the Christian Church.* New York: Oxford University Press.

Deedy, John. 1987. *The Catholic Fact Book.* Chicago: The Thomas Moore Press.

Di Scipio, Giuseppe C. 1983. "The Hebrew Women in Dante's Symbolic Rose." *Dante Studies* CI:. 111–121.

Greer, Rowan A., trans. 1979. *Origen.* 1979. New York: Ramsey; Toronto: Paulist Press.

Hefling Charles, and Cynthia Shattuck, eds. 2007. *The Oxford Guide of the Book of Common Prayer.* Oxford, UK and New York: Oxford University Press.

Kantorowicz, E. H. 1981. *The King's Two Bodies.* Princeton, NJ: Princeton University Press. (Orig. pub. 1957.)

Pelikan, Iaroslav. 1996. *Mary through the Centuries.* New Haven, CT, and London: Yale University Press.

Poodles, Leon, J. 2002. "Catholic Scandals: A Crisis for Celibacy?" *Touchstone,* April 2.

The Sixteen Documents of Vatican Council II and the Instruction on Liturgy with Commentaries by the Council Fathers, compiled by Rev. J. L. Gonzalez and the Daughters of St. Paul. 1965. Index by Charles Dollen. Boston: Magister Books: St. Paul Editions.

Giuseppe Di Scipio

CELESTINA

Celestina is the name of an old procuress in Fernando de Rojas's *Tragicomedia de Calisto y Melibea* (1499). Often referred to as *La Celestina*, the play concerns the lovesickness of a young man, Calisto, for Melibea, who appears to have no interest in him. At the encouragement of his valet, Calisto solicits the help of the old procuress Celestina as a skilled go-between. With much effort, Celestina secures Melibea's consent using a masterful rhetorical strategy that blends scientific argument with folkloric wisdom and acute insights into a young woman's sexual awakening. She also resorts to magic, though textual evidence that her success relies on the occult is scant. Melibea and Calisto consummate their passion thanks to Celestina's expert mediation. The play ends violently as Calisto falls to his accidental death, Melibea commits suicide, and Calisto's valets murder Celestina over an argument regarding payment, and are hanged for the crime.

The play is an exploration of sexual desire and the ways in which this is manifested in a young man and a young woman, aided by the verbal manipulation of a crafty procuress who makes a living facilitating illicit sexual encounters. Desire is portrayed as a primal drive, inevitable and necessary, able to inspire lofty courtly words as well as lewd and graphic remarks. It is shown at work among the higher and lower classes as one of the main forces that promotes interaction between people. Of particular importance to the issue of sexuality and gender is the play's representation of the seductive power of words, and the importance of a go-between for communication between men and women.

Celestina herself is drawn with such complexity and nuance that she occupies a special place in Spanish literature as a type: Able to speak eloquently on medicine, desire, magic, and sex, she occupies as much the role of teacher as that of go-between. But because she lives in constant fear of punishment (for her semi-illicit dealings) and poverty, she also represents the anxiety of early modern Spanish society. Rojas wrote *La Celestina* at a time when religious minorities felt increasingly pressured by the establishment, and previous models of coexistence between religions were fast being erased. Thus, while on one level the play is about sexuality and desire, on another it addresses the difficulties of living on the margins of an increasingly dogmatic society.

La Celestina inspired a number of continuations by other authors. It has also been translated frequently into many languages, and been represented in music and on stage as well as the visual arts. Mentions of Celestina and Celestina-like behavior are not uncommon in Spanish letters even in the early twenty-first century, and showcase the enormous attraction of art toward the figure of an old woman with an uncanny understanding of the workings of desire.

SEE ALSO *Homoeroticism, Female/Male, Concept; Lesbianism; Magic.*

BIBLIOGRAPHY

Corfis, Ivy A., and Joseph T. Snow, eds. 1993. *Fernando de Rojas and Celestina: Approaching the Fifth Centenary; Proceedings of an International Conference in Commemoration of the 450th Anniversary of the Death of Fernando de Rojas, Purdue University, West Lafayette, Indiana, 21–24 November 1991.* Madison, WI: Hispanic Seminary of Medieval Studies.

Gilman, Stephen. 1956. *The Art of "La Celestina."* Repr., Westport, CT: Greenwood Press, 1976.

Rouhi, Leyla. 1999. *Mediation and Love: A Study of the Medieval Go-Between in Key Romance and Near Eastern Texts.* Leiden, Netherlands: Brill.

Severin, Dorothy Sherman. 1989. *Tragicomedy and Novelistic Discourse in "Celestina."* Cambridge, UK: Cambridge University Press.

Leyla Rouhi

CELIBACY

Celibacy is the voluntary renunciation of sexual activity either for a specific period or for the remainder of one's life. It differs from virginity, the biological state of never having had sexual intercourse, because one can voluntarily commit to celibacy before or after having been sexually active. Celibacy also differs from chastity, which refers to refraining from inappropriate sexual activity. For example, a married person is chaste if she or he is monogamous and modest in social relationships. Thus, one can be chaste while not being celibate, and one can be celibate while not being a virgin.

Throughout history, from ancient times to the present, men and women in both the East and the West have opted to practice celibacy for a variety of reasons including the philosophical, religious, and practical. Some cultures believed that celibacy was the only way to rid oneself of the impurities of the body and its passions in order to attain holiness and ritual purity, an ideal still held by some in the twenty-first century. In former times, particularly in the Middle Ages, celibacy was also a means for women to escape the domination of a husband in a traditional marriage. In the mid- to late-twentieth century, however, celibacy became one way for many to assert their autonomy, redirect energy, and avoid disease.

NEGATIVE ATTITUDES TOWARD THE BODY, ITS PASSIONS, AND WOMEN

When celibacy is thought about in the twenty-first century, it is usually associated with negative attitudes towards the body, sex, and reproduction. In fact, such negativity was a factor in the origins of celibacy as an institution in both the Western and Eastern worlds.

In the West One of the major reasons for celibacy in the Western world is the belief that the body and its senses are obstacles to a moral life. The popularity of this line of thought can be attributed mainly to the Greek philosopher Plato who wrote in the fourth century BCE. His philosophy, known as dualism, holds that humans consist of two elements, a body and a soul. The soul is the seat of rational thought, while the body is the source of appetites and emotions, which hinder the rationality of the soul. Morality, for Plato, means being able to know the good through reason, but to do this one has to first control the sensual appetites of the body.

This philosophical dualism is also the basis of Greek mystery religions, whose adherents believed that the immortal soul is capable of knowing divine truths. Through observing secret rites and practicing asceticism—that is, the denial of sensual pleasures—one's soul could be released from its bodily prison and attain communion with the gods. This belief was adopted by the Essenes, a Jewish community that separated itself from the corrupt world to live a rigorously disciplined life at the beginning of the Common Era. Many members practiced celibacy to avoid being contaminated by sexual intercourse and to free their immortal souls from the bonds of the flesh. While some Essenes did marry, it was only to produce offspring; therefore, fertility was the chief requirement of a prospective wife. Most members, however, rejected marriage because they believed women to be disruptive and to create disharmony because of their sensuality. Woman's association with the body made her more emotional than men and hence an obstacle to his spiritual life. Celibacy was a means to avoid such negative influence.

That sexual activity distracts and prohibits one from having a spiritual life was a part of Christianity from its early years. The idea appears as early as Paul's first letter to the Corinthians written in the middle of the first century CE, in which he suggests that married people abstain from sex to leave themselves free for prayer (1 Cor. 7:5). An even better way, says Paul, is to be like him, that is, to remain celibate (1 Cor. 7:7), because an unmarried man can devote himself to the Lord's affairs (1 Cor. 7:32). While Christians were free to choose marriage, particularly if they were weak and liable to be tempted, Paul saw celibacy as the way of perfection. He also thought women capable of celibacy and included widows in his directive (1 Cor. 7:8). It is at this time that the first women celibates held special positions in the community, often as collaborators with the clergy.

In the fourth century, when persecution of Christians ceased and the ascetic life became institutionalized, monks and nuns committed themselves totally to God by fleeing to the desert and renouncing all earthly pleasures including sexual activity. Thus celibacy became an intricate part of monasticism. It was against this backdrop and with the knowledge of Plato's philosophy that the most influential Christian theologian, St. Augustine (354–430), lived and wrote. In his *City of God* (14:17–18) Augustine claims that the sexual impulse is a result of original sin and is, itself, a source of sin and shame. He reduced the role of sexuality to that of procreation and viewed any pleasure derived from the act as interfering with one's spiritual life. Celibacy, where the passions are always in control, is the ideal state by which to achieve union with God.

Both Plato and Augustine hold to the Greek view of the divided self, the higher part being the rational soul that governs the lower irrational part, the appetites, and passions. In the context of their writings, men have been associated with rationality and women with the passions and sexuality. Like the Essenes of ancient Judaism, these major thinkers believed that women's sole purpose was to bear and nurture children, and this purely physical function rendered it much more difficult for women to achieve holiness. They were also the source of sexual passion and, therefore, had to be controlled by men.

The Christian Church in the West continued to be influenced by these philosophies, and in the sixth century Pope Gregory the Great (r. 590–604), a former monk, strongly advocated celibacy among the clergy. It was not until 1074, however, that another former monk, Pope Gregory VII (r. 1073–1085), made it compulsory in the hopes of reforming the hedonistic Christian world with monastic asceticism (Abbott 2000). In the early twenty-first century, only the priests of the Roman Catholic Church are required to be celibate. There is little mention in the documents of the Second Vatican Council (1962–1965) about the sinfulness of the body, but negative attitudes are still present when the priest is told that, in order to serve the church well, he must mortify the deeds of the flesh in himself, that is, be celibate (Paul VI 1965).

Closely linked to the belief that sexual activity is sinful is the concept of ritual purity. In order for religious leaders to perform sacred ceremonies, they must be pure—in other words, have abstained from sexual activity. As far back as the seventh century BCE, there were vestal virgins serving Vesta, the goddess of the hearth, by tending Rome's sacred fire, a symbol of Rome itself. This task was of utmost importance because, were this fire to be extinguished, battles would be lost and Rome would be destroyed. This and other important duties had to be entrusted to one who was pure and incorruptible, and only the vestal virgin's celibacy could ensure such purity. Young girls were chosen from wealthy families at the age of ten and were committed to thirty years of celibacy after which they were free to marry,

St. Augustine. *St. Augustine believed that celibacy was the ideal state for Christian men and women.* HULTON ARCHIVE/GETTY IMAGES.

but, in fact, few chose to do so after having lived most of their life in a privileged celibate state (Abbott 2000). Ritual purity was also required in ancient Greece, where priests and priestesses were to remain celibate before performing sacred rites.

In Christianity, the celebration of the Eucharist was so sacred that, by the fourth century, it was believed that sexual intercourse would make the priest unworthy to perform the rite. Married priests would have to abstain from sex the night before Mass, and, eventually, when daily Mass became a common practice, would have to not marry at all, hence, the support for mandatory celibacy. Ritual purity remains a reason for celibacy in the Catholic Church as indicated in the Vatican II document *Decree on the Ministry and Life of Priests*, which states, "inasmuch as they celebrate the mystery of the Lord's death they should keep their bodies free of wantonness and lusts."

In the East While the cultures in India, China, and Japan value marriage and family, there are traces of negative attitudes toward the body and sexuality in the traditions of Hinduism, Buddhism, and Jainism. These religions believe that the body is a temporary home for the inner soul or, in the case of Buddhism, for the no-self, and is an impediment to ultimate liberation or enlightenment. In order to achieve these goals, therefore, one must renounce worldly attachments and bodily pleasures, including sexuality.

While there are many different strands of Hinduism, they are united by the common idea that one must be born again and again to ultimately reach final liberation, or *moksha.* One's soul, or atman, is ultimately united with divine reality, or Brahman, the source of all things, when it is freed from the body, which can be achieved in various ways. One common idea is that men of the upper castes follow four stages of life, two of which require celibacy. The first is the student life, *brahmacharya*, in which the student's discipline includes control over sexual passions in order to become mentally strong. In the second stage of householder, *grihastha*, one marries, has children, and participates in social and political life. The third stage is retirement, *vanaprastha*, when most financial responsibilities are over and it is time to slow down and practice meditation. The fourth and final stage, *sanyasa*, is the preparation for salvation when one severs all relationships and attachments and frees the mind of desires (Prinja 2002). Clearly, according to this schema, the Hindu believes that, because sexual activity distracts from both learning and attaining salvation, celibacy must be practiced both in the first and last stages of life.

Celibacy is also practiced by other renouncers in Hinduism such as *sādhus.* These are ascetics who leave a conventional lifestyle and undertake austerities in order to purify the mind and body. They are able to achieve liberation, or *moksha*, by dedicating themselves solely to meditation and contemplation of God. Some are wandering mendicants (beggars), some live alone in caves, forests, and temples, while still others join orders and live in communities, or *ashramas. Sādhus* are supported mostly by people who believe that their donations can rid them of bad karma and bring them closer to *moksha.* While the majority of *sādhus* are men, late-twentieth-century government census data indicate there are some concentrated populations of female renunciants called *sādhvīs* in parts of India (Clark 2005). According to Hindu philosophy, *sādhus, sādhvīs*, and others wanting to have a spiritual life must receive training from a guru, or mentor, who, in order to provide this training, must be pure and sinless, which, in Hinduism, requires celibacy (Prinja 2002).

There is another more philosophical strand of Hinduism called Vedanta, meaning after the Vedas, whose followers lead a celibate monastic life. This philosophy holds that the ultimate unchanging reality, or Brahman, dwells within people as the divine self, or atman, and one's goal in life is to realize this divinity within. One of the largest orders of Vedanta monks and nuns is that founded by Ramakrishna (1836–1886) in the nineteenth century and in the early twenty-first century has headquarters throughout the world. Ramakrishna required his followers to practice celibacy for two reasons: to conserve energy and redirect it to self-realization and to avoid distractions of the body so that one can unite one's spirit with God or Brahman.

Buddhism was an outgrowth of Hinduism in that the historical Buddha, Siddhārtha Gautama (c. 563–c. 483 BCE), finding that the ascetic practices of Hinduism did not answer his questions about the meaning of life, meditated under the bodhi tree until he found the answers. This moment of realization gave him the title *Buddha*, meaning "the enlightened one." As a result of this meditation he discovered and taught the four noble truths: (1) all life is suffering; (2) suffering is caused by desires; (3) to eliminate suffering one needs to eliminate desires; and (4) one eliminate desires by following the eightfold path, which consists of right view, right intention, right speech, right action, right livelihood, right effort, right mindfulness, and right concentration. These eight injunctions can be summarized in the basic moral principle of compassion through self-discipline. Buddhism is not dualistic like the philosophy of Plato but rather monistic, that is, there are not two ultimate realities of body and spirit but only one, nirvana, or the state of liberation from the cycle of death and rebirth. Nevertheless, Buddhism does say that the body and its cravings are "empty," that is, are not substantial or enduring and therefore must be transcended to achieve this liberation. Further, the idea of women being temptresses because of their uncontrollable sexuality and emotions exists throughout early Buddhist literature. For this reason the Buddha was reluctant to admit women to the monastic community, the *sangha*, and did so only if they submitted to the authority of the male monks (Paul 1985).

In Theravāda Buddhism practiced in Sri Lanka, Myanmar, Cambodia, Laos, and Thailand, the celibate male monk who has renounced the world and its desires is the one who is closest to liberation. Mahāyāna Buddhism, on the other hand, which exists in Tibet, China, Korea, and Japan, teaches that laypeople as well as monks can be enlightened and, therefore, places less importance on the necessity of celibacy. However, in approximately 100 BCE, when this type of Buddhism was in its early stages, women were so identified with bodily passions that they would have to be reborn as a man in order to attain liberation (Willis 1999).

A third religion growing from Hinduism is Jainism. Its founder, Mahāvīra (c. 599–527 BCE), established a community based on severe asceticism. The main tenet is non-violence, or ahimsa, which is accompanied by other disciplines, including non-attachment, or *aparigraha*, and celibacy, or *brahmacharya.* Like Buddhism, Jainism believes that passions, particularly sexual ones, are the root cause of unhappiness, and if indulged, they will lead to higher levels of dissatisfaction. Jainism, however, accepted women as nuns from the beginning and appeared to be much more egalitarian in its treatment of them, giving them access to education and the reading of sacred texts. But in spite of these divergences from tradition, this community still reflects the negative attitudes toward the body and its passions, and still requires nuns to be subordinate to monks regardless of their age (Balbir 1999).

CELIBACY AS A MEANS OF SOCIAL FREEDOM

Negative attitudes toward the body and sexuality were not the only motivations for celibacy throughout history. An understanding of past societies and their narrow definitions of gender roles provides a context within which to view celibacy as a means of freeing one from social constraints.

In the West Celibacy has also been embraced for positive reasons throughout history, especially by women. In cultures that limited their roles to wife and mother, celibacy freed women to devote themselves to lives of service and study. In the early Christian Church, some women committed themselves to the celibate life not only for spiritual reasons but also for freedom to serve the community. Widows, being allowed to keep their husband's inheritance, pulled together and formed an independent group who had considerable influence in the early communities (Ruether 1998).

Beginning in the fourth century, there were many female ascetics who left noble families and rejected marriage in order to form new communities for themselves and other women. Unlike their contemporaries, these religious females were educated in languages, the arts, and theology and were able to write prose and poetry and circulate them to other communities (Ruether 1998). Hence, posterity is now able to read and be inspired by the writings of Hildegard of Bingen (1098–1179), Mechthild of Magdeburg (1210–c. 1283), and Julian of Norwich (1342–after 1416).

With the advent of the women's movement in the mid-twentieth century, the idea of a committed celibate life no longer holds the same promise of freedom it once did. The modern woman has many opportunities for education, a profession, and, if she wishes, a life of service without necessarily embracing celibacy. As a result, the convents of nuns have far fewer applicants, and other celibate groups often have members who commit to them only for a limited period rather than for life.

In the East In India, women are expected to marry, often to someone chosen by their parents. However, there are stories of women throughout history who have deliberately rejected the role of wife and mother to be free to live a life of devotion. For example, Lalleshvari, who lived in the fourteenth century, sought freedom from an abusive marriage by seeking a guru to mentor her in the ascetic life (Johnsen 1994). Another woman, Mīrā Bāī (c. 1450–c. 1547), considered herself the bride of the god Krishna from a very early age. She wrote and sang songs as she wandered throughout India followed by many of her devotees. Legend has it that those who wanted her to marry a prince threatened her with death, but her resolve never wavered and she has become a model for early-twenty-first-century women who choose to reject marriage and live a celibate life.

In the early twenty-first century, there are many women saints of all ages in Hinduism, both in India and throughout the world, who are considered to be incarnations of the goddess Devi and are leading lives of celibacy and teaching and mentoring others on the spiritual path. Because widows are considered inauspicious in India, women who have lost their husbands often seek freedom from the oppression of society by becoming *sādhvīs* and embracing an ascetic lifestyle, which includes permanent celibacy (Clark 2005).

The traditions of Jainism and Buddhism developed as heretical sects that allowed women to join monastic communities and lead ascetic lives. The overwhelming number of women who followed the strict asceticism of Jainism (one source gives 36,000 female ascetics to 14,000 males under its founder Mahāvīra in the sixth century BCE) suggests that women followed a spiritual yearning that freed them from traditional societal demands (Murcott 1991). Around the same time, during the early years of Buddhism, women who joined Buddhist *sanghas* were also going against prevailing social norms. According to historians, these Buddhist nuns, or *bhikṣuṇīs*, freely left a family life to obtain spiritual realization unavailable to the woman who was a traditional wife and mother. Even as Buddhism spread to China and Tibet, cultures where most women were illiterate, women realized that going to a monastery afforded them freedom from unwanted marriages and provided security and educational opportunities. Buddhist nuns historically were scholars, a vocation that no woman of ancient times could hold in the outside world (Abbott 2000). While in the twentieth and early twenty-first centuries not all Buddhist nuns have been celibate for life, their value of asceticism allows freedom from the pull of modern materialistic societies driven by passions and possessions. Hence, in the early twenty-first century, monasteries are not located only in Asia: They are growing in first-world Europe and the United States at a rapid rate.

CELIBACY FOR INDEPENDENCE, ENERGY, AND HEALTH

Since the sexual revolution of the 1960s, society has become more and more sexually oriented. Teenagers are having sex at a younger age, and teen pregnancies have risen. The television, movie, and music industries, knowing that sex sells, are pushing the sexual content of their products to new limits. Cosmetics and clothes are all geared to keeping men and women looking, smelling, and feeling sexy, and the pharmaceutical industry is dedicated to producing products that enhance sexual activity. This sex-focused culture, however, is also giving rise to a record number of sexually transmitted diseases, including the pandemic of AIDS. Against this backdrop, celibacy has acquired new meaning. While it is apparently counter to all that is socially acceptable, it is being embraced by many for just that reason. Since the mid-1980s there have been a growing number of people, especially women, who view sexual liberation as no liberation at all. Rather than freeing them to make choices, it requires them to make one choice, to have sex and to maintain their sexual attractiveness.

In her 1993 study of celibacy among women, Sally Cline reveals that many women believe that celibacy offers them strength, a sense of personal identity and independence, and creative time and energy for growth and work, which conventional sexual activity has not allowed them. Men also recognize that casual relationships, promoted by the image of the male stud, are no longer satisfying and that hormonal energy can be channeled into higher experiences. Celibacy can also be, for men and women alike, the ultimate expression of individuality and independence (Poulter 2006). With the advent of the Internet, these ideas are appearing more and more frequently on web pages, in chat rooms, and in online articles. The fear of sexually transmitted diseases, while always a motivator for abstaining from sexual activity, has become only one of many reasons to embrace celibacy, if not for a lifetime, at least for a period of time in which one has a chance to discover one's self, be free from conventional pressures, and experience autonomy in a new way.

It seems as though history is repeating itself. Gender roles, once so rigid in the Middle Ages, seem just as rigid in the early twenty-first century except in opposite ways. Forced marriages and confinement to family life for both men and women have given way to forced sexual activity, extramarital sex, and the pressure of sexual performance. In both these situations, celibacy has been a way to move out of social expectations and into a more meaningful sense of self. It appears that, far from being outdated, celibacy is a state that will always have its advocates and practitioners.

BIBLIOGRAPHY

Abbott, Elizabeth. 2000. *A History of Celibacy*. New York: Scribner.

Balbir, Nalini. 1999. "Jainism." In *Encyclopedia of Women and World Religion*, ed. Serinity Young. New York: Macmillan Reference USA.

Clark, Matthew. 2005. "Sadhus and Sadhvis." In *Encyclopedia of Religion*, ed. Lindsay Jones. 2nd edition. Detroit: Macmillan Reference USA.

Cline, Sally. 1993. *Women, Passion, and Celibacy*. New York: Carol Southern Books.

Johnsen, Linda. 1994. *Daughters of the Goddess: The Women Saints of India*. St. Paul, MN: Yes International Publishers.

Murcott, Susan. 1991. *The First Buddhist Women: Translations and Commentary on the Therigatha*. Berkeley, CA: Parallax Press.

Paul, Diana Y. 1985. *Women in Buddhism*. 2nd edition. Berkeley: University of California Press.

Paul VI. 1965. *Decree on the Ministry and Life of Priests*. December 7. Vatican City: Vatican. Available from http://www.vatican.va.

Poulter, Martin. 2006. "The Celibate FAQ." *Celibate Webring*. Available from http://www.glandscape.com/celibate.html.

Prinja, Nawal K., ed. 2002. *Explaining Hindu Dharma: A Guide for Teachers*. 2nd edition. Surrey, UK: Vishwa Hindu Parishad.

Ruether, Rosemary Radford. 1998. *Women and Redemption: A Theological History*. Minneapolis, MN: Fortress Press.

Willis, Janice D. 1999. "Buddhas, Bodhisattvas, and Arhats." In *Encyclopedia of Women and World Religion*, ed. Serinity Young. New York: Macmillan Reference USA.

Maura O'Neill

CELLINI, BENVENUTO
1500–1571

Benvenuto Cellini, who was born in Florence on November 1, 1500, and was one of the most renowned sculptor-goldsmiths of the Renaissance, crafted numerous works celebrating the nude body, male and female, with mannerist elegance and erotic undertones. He is equally renowned in the early twenty-first century for his swashbuckling bisexual life and his socially revealing, if exaggerated and self-justifying, autobiography and other writings. The memoir, which he began to dictate while he was sentenced to house arrest for sodomy from 1557 to 1561, selectively details his eventful career in Florence, Rome, and France. Although Cellini boasts about his often casual or exploitative female affairs, when he gossips about the libertine sodomy among clergy, aristocrats, and artists and their youthful assistants, he omits or denies his own relations with young men, documented in court archives (he was convicted twice, first in 1523).

After 1545, as the Counter-Reformation tightened sexual and artistic mores, the lighthearted hedonism of Cellini's youth met increasing hostility. Commissioned that year by Cosimo I de' Medici, the duke of Florence, to complete a classical fragment of a nude youth, Cellini suggested adding symbols to identify the marble boy as Ganymede, the mythical prince loved by Jupiter, who had been the premier symbolic justification of pederasty since antiquity. The sculptor Baccio Bandinelli, exploiting his rival's well-known weakness, blurted out, "Shut up, you filthy sodomite!" Cellini's witty retort both denied the specific charge and dignified the general custom:

Benvenuto Cellini. COURTESY OF THE LIBRARY OF CONGRESS.

"I wish to God I did know how to indulge in such a noble practice; after all, we read that Jove enjoyed it with Ganymede in paradise, and here on earth it is the practice of the greatest emperors and ... kings" (Cellini 1956). Evidently few believed him; a sonnet, written a decade later while in jail for assault, acknowledged persistent rumors: "Some say I'm here on Ganymede's account" (Saslow 1986).

Although Cellini's masterpiece, a bronze Perseus brandishing the head of Medusa (1545–1554), exposed a colossal male nude in Florence's central piazza, it was officially a political allegory of Duke Cosimo. In contrast, his marbles from the same years frankly appeal to the homoerotic gaze. Besides Ganymede, two other nude statues represent myths of male love: a seductive Narcissus and an Apollo ruffling the hair of his beloved Hyacinthus. Neither was commissioned, and he kept them in his studio all his life, indicating strong personal investment in their theme; another sonnet compared Apollo's female beloved Daphne unfavorably to Hyacinthus, who was more willing to accept "the incurable wound" of love.

Late in life, Cellini converted to the newly prevailing orthodox piety, marrying his mistress and shifting to more acceptable religious subjects, but his emphasis on the male body still unsettled traditional decorum. His marble crucifix (1556–1562) atypically depicted Jesus totally nude; when puritanical Philip II of Spain received it as a gift, he hastily covered its genitals with his handkerchief.

Cellini died in Florence on February 13, 1571. His writings, among the first detailed autobiographical evidence from an artist, offer important evidence of sexual practices and attitudes, and show the evolution of his art and emotional life as the High Renaissance tolerance for classically inspired pederasty gave way to renewed moral conservatism.

SEE ALSO *Art; Homoeroticism, Female/Male, Concept; Homosexuality, Male, History of.*

BIBLIOGRAPHY

Cellini, Benvenuto. 1956. *Vita, Book 2.* Chapters 70-71, trans. George Bull. Harmondsworth, UK: Penguin.

Gallucci, Margaret A. 2003. *Benvenuto Cellini: Sexuality, Masculinity, and Artistic Identity in Renaissance Italy.* New York: Palgrave Macmillan.

Saslow, James M. 1986. *Ganymede in the Renaissance: Homosexuality in Art and Society.* New Haven, CT: Yale University Press.

James M. Saslow

CENSORSHIP

This entry, concentrating on censorship of sexual content in the United States, initially defines censorship. It then explores different rationales for censorship and the various means and modes that it can take. In addition to addressing the censorship of pornography and obscene speech, it examines censorship of broadcast indecency in the United States by the Federal Communications Commission (FCC) and other common censorship battles, including those involving self-censorship by private entities and businesses.

DEFINING CENSORSHIP: GOVERNMENT CENSORSHIP AND PRIVATE CENSORSHIP

Censorship is the prohibition, suppression, and restriction of speech, be it the printed word or other forms of expression such as images, broadcasts, and Internet postings. It generally is found in two distinct modes in the United States—government censorship and private censorship. The former typically occurs when a government official or government entity either creates a law or seeks a court order, such as an injunction, that prohibits and bans the utterance and/or dissemination of speech on a particular topic, subject, or idea. Likely targets of censorship in the early twenty-first century are content such as military or security secrets, obscenity, broadcast indecency, and true threats of violence. The government, in brief, is the agent of the censorship—it plays the role of censor—and thus this form of censorship can also be called official censorship. People who violate censorship laws—laws that forbid the communication of certain messages and topics, such as federal statutes in the United States prohibiting the creation and dissemination of images of child pornography—and court orders face criminal penalties including fines, incarceration, and contempt.

Conversely, in private censorship—what might be called unofficial censorship—the censorship agent is not a government actor or government entity but is, instead, a private individual, a private business, or a corporation. For instance, private censorship takes place when a corporation or business acts as censor and decides not to sell or to rent a speech product such as a sexually explicit adult magazine such as *Hustler*, a violent video game such as *Grand Theft Auto*, or a profanity-laced rap CD by Eminem because the corporation or business objects to the content, subject matter, or message in the speech product. The individuals running a corporation or business that engages in such censorship may personally object to the messages in question or, from an economic and business standpoint, they may fear boycotts by consumers and religious groups if they sell the censored products. This may be thought of as a particular variety of private censorship called corporate censorship. Corporate censorship also occurs when a corporate-owned radio station refuses to play the songs of a certain musical group because the radio station's owners object to the group's political viewpoint or find the group's lyrics offensive. For instance, in 2003 many radio stations in the United States refused to play songs by the Dixie Chicks, a pop-country musical trio, after lead singer Natalie Maines made comments critical of President George W. Bush during a concert in England. In addition to corporate censorship, private censorship transpires when an individual who desires to speak nonetheless refrains from doing so voluntarily because of fear that his or her speech could lead to some form of punishment, retaliation, or retribution at the hands of others, including but not limited to the government. This is known as self-censorship; rather than risk possible reprisals for expressing a viewpoint or message, people play it safe, forgo speaking, and censor themselves. It thus is often said that a "chilling effect" on speech occurs when fear leads to self-censorship.

What unite both government censorship and private censorship are the notions of control over communication and the silencing of speech. In the case of government censorship, the control may come in the form of a prior restraint on speech—an order stopping speech before it can be released or sold to the public at large or to a specific segment of the public such as children. A court order restraining speech before it can be heard is a form of a judicial decree known as an injunction. In the United States, the First Amendment to the U.S. Constitution stands as a bulwark against most forms of government censorship. It provides in relevant part that "Congress shall make no law ... abridging the freedom of speech, or of the press." The U.S. Supreme Court has interpreted the word *Congress* to mean not simply the U.S. Congress, but any federal, state, or local government entity or official. The First Amendment thus creates an ethos and spirit of free expression that is dramatically and diametrically opposed to government censorship. Indeed, prior restraints on speech are presumptively unconstitutional and the government faces a heavy burden when attempting to justify them (*New York Times Co. v. United States*, 1971). Private censorship, however, is immune from the First Amendment guarantees of free speech and press. Thus there is no constitutional protection against private censorship, and private businesses and corporations are free not to sell or rent those speech products to which they object.

Even the First Amendment does not completely prohibit government censorship. The U.S. Supreme Court, the ultimate arbiter of the meaning of the First Amendment, has long held that some forms of speech—obscenity, child pornography involving real children, fighting words, true threats of violence, and incitements to violence—fall outside the scope of First Amendment protection and thus can be suppressed and censored. In addition and as described later, the FCC engages in censorship of certain sexually explicit content on broadcast television that it deems to be indecent.

Therefore, despite the presence of the First Amendment protection of free speech and press, both government censorship and private censorship occur in the United States. The constitutional law scholar and professor Rodney A. Smolla (1992) calls censorship "a social instinct," observing that "governments in all places at all times have succumbed to the impulse to exert control over speech" (p. 4). Other scholars agree that "throughout history governments have sought to, and succeeded, in banning material that they consider injurious" (Green 1990, p. vii) and "studies in communications, anthropology, sociology, and economics support the claim that censorship is an enduring feature of human communities" (Jansen 1991, p. 181). It thus should come as no shock that "censorship has been a constantly recurring social phenomenon" (Garry 1993, p. xv) in the United States. In fact, only seven years after the First Amendment took effect in 1791 with its protection of freedom of speech, "the federalist party under President John Adams obtained passage of the Alien and Sedition Acts of 1798, which attempted to silence any criticism levied against

Anthony Comstock. *Anthony Comstock was made a special agent of the U.S. Post Office charged with enforcing the Comstock Act, an anti-indecency law named for him.* COURTESY OF THE LIBRARY OF CONGRESS.

it by Thomas Jefferson's emerging Republican-Democratic party" (Garry 1993, p. 19).

Given such historical tendencies and social instincts toward censorship, it is not surprising that there is a long history of censorship of sexual content in the United States. In 1821 Massachusetts successfully prosecuted Peter Holmes, publisher of a version of an erotic novel by the English novelist John Cleland called *Fanny Hill; or, Memoirs of a Woman of Pleasure* (1748–1749), because government authorities found it to be "lewd, wicked, scandalous, infamous, and obscene" (Heins 2001, p. 25). The book, describing "a young woman's successful rise from destitution to a middle-class life through a career in prostitution" (Lane 2000, p. 11), was censored because it would allegedly put lustful desires in the minds of both minors and adults. In 1842 Congress enacted the first federal statute that allowed the censorship of obscene material. Congress in 1865 passed another law prohibiting the use of the mail to convey obscene pictures and books because it was "concerned about the consumption of pornography in the [military] ranks during the Civil War" (Lane 2000, p. 15).

The first dramatic move toward the large-scale censorship of sexual content in the United States, however, came in 1873 with the passage of the so-called Comstock Law, named for Anthony Comstock, a crusader in New York State against indecent material. This act "made it a crime knowingly to send information and advertisements about obscene publications, contraception, or abortion through the mails" (de Grazia 1992, p. 4), and Comstock was made a special agent of the U.S. Post Office charged with enforcing it—something he did quite vigorously. Forty years after the act's passage, Comstock claimed to have "destroyed more than 160 tons of obscene literature and had convicted enough individuals to fill nearly 61 passenger cars with 60 seats each" (Lane 2000, p. 15). Comstock had great power, in part, because the act did not define terms such as *obscene*, *lewd*, and *indecent*, thus giving him wide latitude to subjectively enforce the obscenity censorship law as he saw fit. The postal service remains one the primary enforcers of obscenity laws in the early-twenty-first-century United States, with postal inspectors monitoring mails for obscene content under federal law (18 *U.S. Code* § 1461).

Censorship of sexual content continued in the twentieth century, and it was not until 1966 that the U.S. Supreme Court finally held that the book *Fanny Hill* was not obscene and thus could be legally distributed (*A Book Named "John Cleland's Memoirs of a Woman of Pleasure" v. Massachusetts*). A major victory against censorship occurred in 1933 when a federal judge held that James Joyce's book *Ulysses* was not obscene (*United States v. One Book Called "Ulysses"*). But that decision did not stop efforts to censor speech that government authorities considered to be obscene. Between 1957 and 1977, the nation's high court heard arguments in nearly ninety different obscenity prosecutions. During the administration of President Bill Clinton, however, there were no federal obscenity prosecutions, as the Justice Department under Clinton focused instead on the proliferation of child pornography on the World Wide Web and congressional efforts turned to censoring nonobscene yet explicit sexual content on the web. The administration of President George W. Bush began a new federal crackdown on obscenity, launching two major prosecutions, one in 2003 and the other in 2006.

RATIONALES FOR CENSORSHIP: FEAR AND POWER

Rationales for censorship of expression often are based upon fears—realistic or imaginary—about the supposedly dangerous and deleterious effects that particular messages might have on the audience that receives them. For instance, those in power in government may want to censor messages of opposing political parties because they fear the opposition's messages will undermine their authority and control. Likewise, the government may want to censor messages with sexually explicit content because it fears that young children would be harmed or corrupted by viewing the content. For instance, a public high school—a government entity—may ban books with sexual content from its shelves or remove selected pages from them, clear acts of government censorship.

Private censorship also may be based on a fear rationale. For instance, a company may decide not to sell a particular rap CD because it fears consumer backlash in the form of boycotts and protests were it to carry the CD. Alternatively, the rationale for private censorship may not be based on fear but simply on the premise that the individual engaged in the censorship truly objects, based on personally held beliefs, to the content in question and thus decides not to sell or rent it.

Ultimately, censorship is about power and control of information. By preventing people from receiving certain information and knowledge, individuals and government entities acting as censors exert control over the information-deprived individuals. The maxim that "knowledge is power" goes double with censorship, as censorship is the suppression of knowledge with this suppression entrenching the power of those who control the flow of information. Government censorship of sexual content in books, magazines, and videos therefore is a means of power and control over sexual practices and sexual mores of the population, as censorship of this material both reduces what people know about sexual conduct and makes clear to them that some sexual practices are forbidden, scandalous, or taboo.

MODERN RATIONALES FOR CENSORSHIP OF SEXUAL CONTENT

In the early-twenty-first-century United States, there are two primary and distinct rationales for censoring sexual content and, in particular, for censoring sexual content that is commonly thought of as pornography, such as that found in such magazines as *Hustler*, *Taboo*, and *Barely Legal.*

First, antipornography feminist legal scholars such as Catharine A. MacKinnon (1993) believe that such sexual content represents "the power of men over women, expressed through unequal sex, sanctioned both through and prior to state power" (p. 40). Under this view, the sexual content found in adult magazines, videos, and DVDs should be censored because it objectifies and exploits women and, in turn, conveys an ideology that sustains male power. In addition, this strand of antipornography feminism contends that censorship is necessary not only because pornography subordinates women to men but also because it changes how women feel about themselves. As the late feminist scholar Andrea Dworkin (2004) wrote, "the pornography industry has managed to legitimize pornographized sexuality and to make it the duty of every woman to perform sexually as a prostitute. Partly, the voyeurism of the pornography industry changes the way in which women are seen. This includes how we see ourselves" (p. 141). It is worth noting that not all feminists are in favor of censorship of sexually explicit pornography; in fact, there is a group in the United States called Feminists for Free Expression (FFE) that is decidedly anticensorship and believes that "while messages reflecting sexism pervade our culture in many forms, sexual and nonsexual, suppression of such material will neither reduce harm to women nor further women's goals" ("FFE Mission").

The second primary rationale for censoring sexual content is that the content undermines moral and religious values, while concomitantly corrupting children and harming social institutions such as the family and marriage between a man and a woman. This view is commonly associated with the conservative and religious right movement in the United States. Groups such as Citizens for Decent Literature, founded in the 1950s by Charles Keating, and the American Family Association, founded in 1977 and headed in the early twenty-first century by the Reverend Donald Wildmon, are examples of censorship advocates subscribing to this rationale.

Beyond these two primary rationales for censorship of sexually explicit content are arguments that pornography: (1) exploits the women who are used in making it; (2) is addictive and ruins the lives of those who consume it, along with the lives of their family members; and (3) desensitizes users and negatively changes their beliefs and behaviors about healthy sexual relationships. Both antiporn feminists and antiporn conservatives may embrace these arguments, depending on the particular individual.

Very different rationales for censorship of sexual content are found when the individuals featured in the content are children. In particular, child pornography is censored in the United States—it is not protected by the First Amendment, and it is a violation of both federal and state laws to distribute it and to possess it—because the minors used in child pornography: (1) do not have the mental capacity to understand the ramifications of their participation in it and thus are not capable of giving informed consent to making it; (2) are both physically and emotionally harmed by participating in it; and (3) could be haunted later in their adult lives by the permanent record of their participation in child pornography if someone years or decades later discovers the magazine, video, or DVD in which they appeared. In addition, another rationale for censorship of child pornography is that its use by pedophiles whets their appetite to sexually molest and abuse children.

Finally, another rationale for censoring sexual content is political expediency. In particular, politicians may call for censorship of sexual content not because they really fear that it causes any harm to those who would view it or read it, but because such a pro-censorship stance against sexual content may win them support from voters and public interest groups such as Focus on the Family. Viewed in this light, support of censorship can be seen as little more than a cynical form of political pandering to the electorate.

TYPES OF CENSORED SEXUAL CONTENT: OBSCENITY, CHILD PORNOGRAPHY, INDECENCY

The First Amendment does not protect obscene speech, and thus it may be censored by the federal government in the United States. The U.S. Supreme Court created a three-part test in 1973 for determining when material is obscene (*Miller v. California*). That test, known as the *Miller* test after the name of the legal case in which it was created, asks the jury in an obscenity prosecution to determine whether the material in question: (1) appeals to a prurient interest in sex, when taken as a whole and as judged by contemporary community standards from the perspective of the average person; (2) is patently offensive, as defined by state law, in its display of sexual conduct; and (3) lacks serious literary, artistic, political, or scientific value. Only if a jury finds that each of these three components is satisfied by the sexual content in question will it be deemed to be obscene. Once deemed obscene, the censorship and suppression of further distribution of the material is permissible. The rationale for censorship of obscenity, as reflected in the *Miller* test's use of terms such as *prurient interest* (defined by the U.S. Supreme Court as a morbid or shameful interest in sex) and *patently offensive*, is premised on the conservative argument described above that it harms morals and values.

Child pornography involving real minors—not computer-generated ones—also is not protected by the First Amendment, and thus it too may be censored by the government. Significantly, however, there is not a uniform or standard definition of child pornography, in contrast with the *Miller* test for obscenity. What courts have made clear is that the sexual content need not rise to the level of obscenity under *Miller* or be as graphic or explicit if children are depicted in it. For instance, an image depicting the lascivious exhibition of the genitals or pubic area of a minor constitutes child pornography under federal statutory law embodied in the *United States Code* even if the minor is not engaged in a sex act (18 *U.S. Code* § 2256).

A third category of sexual content that may be censored by the government in the United States is broadcast indecency. In particular, the U.S. Supreme Court ruled in 1978 that the FCC could censor the over-the-air broadcast, on both radio and television during certain periods of day, of sexual content that it deemed to be "indecent" even though the content does not rise to the level of obscene speech under *Miller* (*Federal Communications Commission v. Pacifica Foundation*). In 2006 the FCC defined *broadcast indecency* as speech that, in context, depicts or describes sexual or excretory activities or organs in terms patently offensive as measured by contemporary community standards for the broadcast medium. This is a two-part test that first requires a determination of whether the speech in question depicts or describes sexual or excretory activities or organs. If it does include such content, then it must be determined whether the depiction or description is patently offensive. In deciding if material is patently offensive, the FCC generally weighs three factors: (1) whether the description or depiction is explicit or graphic; (2) whether the material dwells on or repeats at length descriptions or depictions of sexual or excretory organs; and (3) whether the material appears to pander or is used to titillate or shock. No single factor controls the analysis; each is weighed in context in a totality-of-the-circumstances approach.

In 2006 the FCC raised by ten times the amount that it could monetarily fine a broadcaster for a single instance of an indecency violation, from $32,500 to $325,000. Broadcasters do not face such liability, however, if they air indecent content between 10:00 P.M. and 6:00 A.M. This eight-hour window when indecent content is permitted on the broadcast airwaves is known as the safe-harbor period; it gives adults a chance to receive such indecent content during a period when the FCC believes that fewer children are in the audience and thus are less likely to be exposed to it. In essence, this safe-harbor period is designed to strike a balance between the First Amendment interest of adults to receive indecent speech, on the one hand, and the government interest in helping parents shield their children from indecent content, on the other.

In 2004 the FCC vigorously applied its indecency standard when it issued an aggregate $550,000 fine against various CBS television stations for airing that same year the Super Bowl XXXVIII halftime show. It was, at the time, the largest indecency fine ever levied. The FCC focused its inquiry on Janet Jackson and Justin Timberlake's performance of the song "Rock Your Body." The duet concluded with Timberlake's removal of a portion of Jackson's leather bustier, briefly exposing her breast to the camera, at the precise moment when Timberlake finished the song's last lyric, "gonna have you naked by the end of this song." In reaching its decision that the broadcast was indecent, the FCC initially found that the halftime broadcast culminated in on-camera partial nudity with Jackson's exposed breast, thus constituting a depiction of a sexual organ under its definition of indecency. It then concluded that this depiction was patently offensive because, although it lasted less than one full second on the air, it was designed to shock and titillate and it was graphic and explicit. In 2006 the FCC upheld this order after CBS appealed it (FCC 2006b).

In 2006 the FCC issued a new record-setting aggregate fine of more than $3.6 million against CBS affiliates for airing an episode of the show *Without a Trace* that, in the FCC's determination, was indecent because it graphically depicted teenage boys and girls participating in a sexual orgy. The episode had aired at 9:00 P.M. in the central and mountain time zones, thus placing it outside the safe-harbor period. Although no nudity was shown and the sex was merely simulated, the FCC nonetheless found that it was indecent, reasoning that the episode "contains numerous depictions of sexual conduct among teenagers that are portrayed in such a manner that a child watching the program could easily discern that the teenagers shown in the scene were engaging in sexual activities, including apparent intercourse. The background sounds, which include moaning, add to the graphic and explicit sexual nature of the depictions" (FCC 2006a). The FCC does not monitor the airwaves looking and listening for indecent content that it would like to censor. Rather, it considers and evaluates whether a broadcast is indecent only after receiving a formal complaint from a listener or viewer. By 2006, organizations such as the Parents Television Council actively monitored the airwaves, and its members had filed thousands of complaints for alleged indecency violations with the FCC.

To escape the FCC's censorship of indecent sexual content in the early twenty-first century, some radio show hosts such as Howard Stern abandoned over-the-air radio and moved to subscription-based satellite radio where the FCC does not censor indecent content. This demonstrates that the effect of censorship of sexual content may not be to eradicate it but simply to shift it to another venue or mode of communication.

This section has so far described the U.S. government's censorship powers over three distinct types of sexual content: obscenity, child pornography, and broadcast indecency. One might wonder what its censorship powers are over adult pornography. The problem here is that there is not a precise legal definition of pornography in the United States; rather, it is a catchall term that means many different things to many different people. *Hustler* magazine may be considered pornographic by many people because of its sexual content, but that is not a legal determination. Obscenity and pornography thus are not the same thing; the former is a legal term, the latter is not. Something may be pornographic in the eyes of many yet not be obscene under the *Miller* test in a court of law.

WARDING OFF GOVERNMENT CENSORSHIP WITH SELF-REGULATION AND SELF-CENSORSHIP

In order to ward off government censorship of sexual and violent content in their media products, many entertainment-based industries have adopted and employed voluntary ratings systems that provide consumers and viewers with package-affixed labels and warnings about the content in a particular product. While such voluntary ratings systems do not constitute private censorship to the extent that the content of the product itself is not altered by the imposition of a rating or warning label, they do amount to good-faith and self-regulatory efforts to monitor content to fend off censorship. For instance, the Motion Picture Association of America (MPAA)—a nongovernmental organization—has a voluntary rating system, first adopted in 1968, that rates movies, taking into account factors such as theme, language, violence, nudity, and sex. Although no film company is forced to submit a film for rating to the MPAA, the vast majority opt to do so. The video game industry also has a voluntary rating system run by the Entertainment Software Rating Board. For instance, a video game rated AO (Adults Only) means that the content may include prolonged scenes of intense violence and/or graphic sexual content and nudity. In the music industry as well, the Recording Industry Association of America (RIAA) places voluntary warning labels on CDs. In each case, the hope of these industries is that enforcement of their own voluntary rating system will be sufficient to prevent and stave off official government censorship of their content.

Such voluntary rating systems, however, can actually lead to private self-censorship. For instance, most movie producers do not want an NC-17 (No One 17 and Under Admitted) rating on a movie because most large theater chains will not show such movies on their screens, thus reducing the amount of potential box-office revenue to the take from only a tiny number of theaters nationwide and effectively spelling the kiss of death for the movie. Thus a producer of a film that initially receives an NC-17 rating might choose to go back and re-edit the movie, voluntarily eliminating certain graphic sexual scenes in order to obtain a less severe R (Restricted: Under 17 Requires Accompanying Parent or Adult Guardian) or the even more lucrative and family-friendly PG-13 rating (Parents Strongly Cautioned: Some Material May Be Inappropriate for Children Under 13) which is "by far the most profitable rating that a movie can receive" (Mundy 2003, p. W12). Even advertisements for movies may be subject to self-censorship as a result of a voluntary rating system. For instance, in 2006 the MPAA, which approves advertising for the films it rates, called for the producers of a documentary titled *The Road to Guantánamo* to change a movie poster that showed "a man hanging by his handcuffed wrists, with a burlap sack over his head and a blindfold tied around the hood" (Kennicott 2006, p. C1). Although not government censorship, this is a clear case of self-censorship by the movie industry.

The voluntary ratings also can lead to corporate censorship. This occurs when large retailers and distributors use the ratings as the criteria for refusing to sell products with a specific warning label or rating. The Harvard University law professor Paul C. Weiler (2006) writes that Wal-Mart, the largest seller of record albums, not only will "not stock any NC-17 or X-Rated videos, but it will not sell any record albums that carry an RIAA 'parental advisory' rating. Needless to say, one cannot buy albums by gangsta rap artists like Snoop Doggy Dogg or Tupac Shakur at a Wal-Mart outlet" (p. 128). In some cases, religious organizations and advocacy groups such as the National Institute on Media and the Family put pressure on corporations to engage in such censorship. For instance, in 2005 retailer Best Buy, acting "under pressure from religious groups, unveiled one of the toughest policies yet to keep violent and sexually explicit video games out of the hands of children" (Serres 2005, p. 2D). Specifically, Best Buy implemented a program that secretly monitors its employees and then fires the ones who sell video games rated M (Mature) to minors. Other retailers refuse to even stock M-rated games under such pressure from some religious and pro-family advocacy groups.

Even when a product is not rated, some corporations simply refuse to sell it. For instance, "many groups have warred against *Playboy*, successfully getting it pulled from magazine stands in places including Wal-Mart and some 7-Eleven stores. The religious right has rallied against the magazine from the pulpit and in books" (Guerrero 2003, p. 12).

SHIFTS IN COMMUNITY VALUES AND EFFECTS OF CENSORSHIP ON SEXUAL MORES

By 2005 the *Adult Video News*, an adult trade industry publication, estimated that adult entertainment was a $12.6 billion industry in the United States. Adult sexual content was clearly popular among many people—in addition to such massive revenue figures were indicators such as the appearance in 2004 on the *New York Times* Best Sellers list of the porn star Jenna Jameson's memoir, *How to Make Love Like a Porn Star*, and the proliferation across the country of clean, well-lighted adult content stores called Hustler Hollywood. Nevertheless, censorship efforts continued. The administration of President George W. Bush launched two high-profile federal obscenity prosecutions targeting the companies Extreme Associates, Inc., and JM Productions.

Community standards about sexual practices are critical in such obscenity prosecutions, as the *Miller* test for obscenity asks jurors to consider whether material is obscene in light of contemporary community standards. Importantly, the term *contemporary* means that what might have once been obscene may not be in the early twenty-first century; likewise, the term *community* means that what may be obscene in one state (and thus subject to censorship there) may not be obscene in another state. Indeed, the *Miller* test does not use a nationwide community standard but leaves it up to juries in the states to determine what their contemporary standards are and what can and cannot be censored. Some members of the adult entertainment industry in the early twenty-first century are thus cautious about shipping content into conservative states such as Utah and Georgia. Such a decision by companies to not to mail content to certain states is an example of self-censorship. It also means that picking the right venue—a more sexually conservative one—by the government in a federal obscenity prosecution can result in a censorship-friendly verdict and conviction. As time goes on, it remains to be seen how shifting values and mores about sexual practices in the United States will affect the government's censorship efforts. If citizens become more tolerant of different sexual practices that once were considered taboo and become more comfortable in viewing images of sexual conduct, then it will, in turn, become increasingly difficult for the government to win obscenity convictions and censor sexual content.

BIBLIOGRAPHY

A Book Named "John Cleland's Memoirs of a Woman of Pleasure" v. Massachusetts, 383 U.S. 413 (1966).

Coetzee, J. M. 1996. *Giving Offense: Essays on Censorship.* Chicago: University of Chicago Press.

de Grazia, Edward. 1992. *Girls Lean Back Everywhere: The Law of Obscenity and the Assault on Genius.* New York: Random House.

Dworkin, Andrea. 2004. "Pornography, Prostitution, and a Beautiful and Tragic Recent History." In *Not for Sale: Feminists Resisting Prostitution and Pornography*, ed. Rebecca Whisnant and Christine Stark. North Melbourne, Australia: Spinifex Press.

Federal Communications Commission v. Pacifica Foundation, 438 U.S. 726 (1978).

Feminists for Free Expression (FFE). "FFE Mission." Available from http://www.ffeusa.org/html/mission/index.html.

Garry, Patrick. 1993. *An American Paradox: Censorship in a Nation of Free Speech.* Westport, CT: Praeger.

Green, Jonathon. 1990. *The Encyclopedia of Censorship.* New York: Facts On File.

Guerrero, Lucio. 2003. "50 Years Later, Playboy Still Swinging." *Chicago Sun-Times*, November 28, p. 12.

Heins, Marjorie. 2001. *Not in Front of the Children: "Indecency," Censorship, and the Innocence of Youth.* New York: Hill and Wang.

Jansen, Sue Curry. 1991. *Censorship: The Knot that Binds Power and Knowledge.* New York: Oxford University Press.

Kennicott, Philip. 2006. "MPAA Rates Poster an F." *Washington Post*, May 17, C1.

Lane, Frederick S., III. 2000. *Obscene Profits: The Entrepreneurs of Pornography in the Cyber Age*. New York: Routledge.

MacKinnon, Catharine A. 1993. *Only Words*. Cambridge, MA: Harvard University Press.

Miller v. California, 413 U.S. 15 (1973).

Mundy, Liza. 2003. "Do You Know Where Your Children Are?" *Washington Post*, November 16, W12.

New York Times Co. v. United States, 403 U.S. 713 (1971).

Post, Robert C., ed. 1998. *Censorship and Silencing: Practices of Cultural Regulation*. Los Angeles: Getty Research Institute for the History of Art and the Humanities.

Serres, Chris. 2005. "Best Buy Toughens Its Policy on Sale of Violent Video Games." *Minneapolis Star Tribune*, May 20, 2D.

Smolla, Rodney A. 1992. *Free Speech in an Open Society*. New York: Knopf.

Soley, Lawrence. 2002. *Censorship, Inc.: The Corporate Threat to Free Speech in the United States*. New York: Monthly Review Press.

U.S. Federal Communications Commission (FCC). 2006a. *Complaints against Various Television Licensees Concerning Their December 31, 2004 Broadcast of the Program "Without a Trace."* FCC 06-18, File No. EB-05-IH-0035 (March 15, 2006).

U.S. Federal Communications Commission (FCC). 2006b. *Complaints against Various Television Licensees Concerning Their February 1, 2004 Broadcast of the Super Bowl XXXVIII Halftime Show*. FCC 06-19, File No. EB-04-IH-0011 (March 15, 2006).

United States v. One Book Called "Ulysses," 5 F.Supp. 182 (S.D. N.Y. 1933), *aff'd* 72 F.2d 705 (2d Cir. 1934).

Weiler, Paul C. 2006. *Entertainment, Media, and the Law*. 3rd edition. St. Paul, MN: Thomson/West.

Clay Calvert

CHANCRE

SEE *Sexually Transmitted Diseases.*

CHASTITY

Chastity is a concept found in the three Abrahamic religions—Judaism, Christianity, and Islam. It refers to purity of one's thoughts and deeds, particularly as they apply to sexual relations. To be chaste means that one is a virgin until marriage and engages in sex only with one's lawful spouse. For Catholic priests and nuns, chastity includes, but is not limited to, sexual abstinence; the goal of chastity is to eliminate all carnal desires so that one can fully concentrate one's mind and body on serving God.

Some Christians argue that married couples should also remain chaste, that is, abstain from sex, except for the purpose of reproduction. However, this was not its original meaning. The confusion over whether chastity refers to complete abstinence or only abstinence outside of marriage stems from the religious emphasis placed on chastity as a moral state of mind. The chaste person is first and foremost modest, simple in expression, and acts in accordance to religious moral precepts. Restraint in sexual behavior is a consequence of, rather than a synonym of, chastity.

In Islam the concept of chastity refers only to sexual abstinence among unmarried men and women. There is no order of religious priests in Islam and all religious leaders are permitted to marry. In Judaism, rabbis are permitted to marry and the injunction on sexual abstinence is limited to unmarried Jews. In Buddhism, Hinduism, and Jainism, monks and nuns take a vow of chastity (*brahmacharya*) for life. In these three Eastern religions the goal of chastity is to eliminate all attachments to other humans and to all bodily desires so that the person liberate themselves from earthly pleasures, focus on religious service, and eventually attain nirvana or *moksha*. Nirvana and mochas refer to finally getting off of the wheel of death and rebirth (*samsara*) and reuniting with the universal godhead. In Zoroastrianism, chastity is expected only until marriage after which married couples—including priests, who are permitted to marry—are expected to have children to continue the faith. So, for all religions, chastity refers to sexual abstinence out of wedlock and purity of mind.

THE MEDIEVAL IDEAL OF CHASTITY

The modern Western idea of chastity is rooted in the ideal of courtly love that originated in southern France in the eleventh century. At that time, most marriages among the nobility were arranged and lacked intimacy. Courtly love served as a way for women to be sexually faithful to their contracted husbands, while at the same time having a chaste romantic relationship with a suitor. The suitor, usually of a lower class than the woman, was motivated not only by love but also by prestige and economic gain. Courtly love relationships were romantic and could even be expressed in public without shame and with the consent of the husband. However, such relations always had to be chaste, thus explicitly separating love from sex. When courtly love ceased to be chaste it caused both social and personal disruption, even destruction. The prototypical story of courtly love and chastity is that of Sir Lancelot and his love for King Arthur's wife, Guinevere. Their love was expressed publicly with the approval of King Arthur; it was when their love ceased to be chaste that it led to the dissolution of King Arthur's court. The two ideas of courtly love—that romantic love is pure when it is independent of sexual desire and that the conjunction of the two is frequently socially and psychologically dangerous—survive in the early twenty-first century.

PRESENT-DAY FORMS OF CHASTITY

There are three different forms of chastity that are popular: the first, and by far the most organized and largest of these, is rooted in various religiously based movements that encourage teenagers and singles to remain chaste until marriage; the second, which is not organized but which is also popular especially among youths, is the idea that youths should channel their sexual energy to noble nonreligious causes, such as poverty, the environment, self-actualization, and so on; the third movement is, in many ways, the perverse inverse of the religious ideal of chastity, and extols chastity as a means to heighten sexual pleasure. What these three different cultural versions of chastity have in common is the belief that chastity purifies the mind and allows one to focus on good deeds. Each of these three different modern-day cultural versions of chastity is discussed below.

RELIGION AND CHASTITY

The chastity movement in modern-day America began in 1940 when fifty Jesuit priests convened to write a booklet aimed at college-bound youths. The key theme of this booklet was that chastity is the queen of Christian virtues. Young adults were enjoined to resist sexual temptation by reminding themselves that the body is the temple of the Holy Spirit and therefore a shrine to God. Sex out of wedlock is the same as desecrating the house of God. Chastity does not mean celibacy for married couples but it does imply that sex should not be done to satisfy lust and that wife and husband should remember that the body belongs to Christ and not to one's spouse. After a couple has borne children they are encouraged to practice perfect or absolute chastity so that each can be closer to God.

In the 1980s and 1990s the Jesuit view of chastity was popularized by national chastity movements, the largest of these is called True Love Waits (TLW). TLW was founded as part of a Christian sex education campaign in 1987 by Jimmy Hester who was joined in 1992 by Richard Ross, a Baptist pastor. The success of TLW hinges on a four-pronged strategy: first are frequent meetings by peers; second are personal testimonials; third are symbols of commitment to chastity; and fourth is peer and parental pressure to encourage young adults to make a commitment to chastity. Members of the TLW movement are encouraged to meet regularly and recruit friends into the movement. Unlike the Jesuit booklet, TLW counselors and speakers directly address such intimate issues as whether or not looking at a swimsuit magazine, kissing, oral sex, or homosexuality are permitted.

The chastity movements in the United States are generically Christian rather than Catholic and are frequently associated with right-to-life and anti-abortion campaigns. Akin to medieval courtly love, the contemporary chastity movement separates romantic love from sex, emphasizing not only that sex can destroy romantic love, but that romantic love is purer when the couple is chaste.

CHASTITY AND NOBLE CAUSES

In a study of New England college students who chose to be chaste, Victor de Munck (2001) discovered that as many as 50 percent of them chose to do so because of their commitment to a noble cause. These students were so devoted or committed to their particular cause(s) that they simply had neither time nor immediate desire to enter into a committed relationship. Their attitude was identical to that of a Catholic monk who chooses to be celibate in order to serve God, except that they chose to serve a secular ideological calling. Unlike the college students who chose chastity for religious reasons, these students did not consider virginity a moral requirement or virtue but chose it for pragmatic reasons—it took time and was potentially troublesome.

CHASTITY AS SEXUAL PRACTICE

Although chastity belts are commonly associated with the medieval era, they were first made in the 1600s. Chastity belts were sometimes worn by females (usually from the upper class) either to keep them virgins or ensure fidelity whenever their husbands went away for an extended period of time. As Western medical practices had long considered masturbation deleterious to a man's health, chastity belts were also made for young men.

In recent years chastity belts have made a comeback as part of an alternative sexual lifestyle involving bondage, dominance, sadism, and masochism (BDSM). Chastity belts are usually made of plastic, stainless steel and leather, with a key lock in the center. There are a number of specialty shops that make custom-made chastity belts. Among practitioners of BDSM, chastity belts are used to prevent penetrative-receptive sex or masturbation in order to heighten sexual desire and ultimately sexual pleasure. Periods of sexual denial may be short or long-term. In either case the goals are to gain control over one's own or one's partner's sexual desire, and to frustrate that desire in order to achieve a stronger orgasm.

Chastity belts for men or women are bought or, more typically, ordered online from adult stores or specialty shops, the latter making customized belts. They are usually consensually used by a monogamous couple. There is a division of labor: one partner wears the belt and the other possesses the key to the belt. The person with the key usually plays the dominant role (called *dom*), whereas the person wearing the chastity belt plays the submissive role (called *sub*).

In order to have the chastity belt removed, the person wearing it must obey the commands of the keyholder.

Contemporary culture is more complex and varied than it was during the 1950s. The concept of chastity has been interpreted in surprising ways depending on the interests and personal dispositions of the individual. Regardless of the differences in the adoption of the concept of chastity, all three groups described above define chastity as a state of mind that is intended to discipline the body in order to bring the person into a closer relationship with the object of his or her love.

SEE ALSO *Abstinence; Virginity.*

BIBLIOGRAPHY

De Munck, Victor C. 2001. "Cultural Schemas of Celibacy." In *Celibacy, Culture, and Society: the Anthropology of Sexual Abstinence*, ed. S. Bell and E. J. Sobo. Madison: University of Wisconsin Press.

Kelly, Gerald. 2002. *Chastity: A Guide for Teens and Young Adults.* Harrison, NY: Roman Catholic Books.

"Lifeway Student Ministry (True Love Waits)." Available from http://www.lifeway.com/tlw/.

Victor de Munck

CHASTITY BELT

One common and popular assumption about chastity belts is that they were a medieval device, designed by men and worn by women, to ensure that wives would remain faithful while their husbands went into battle and were away from home for long periods of time. Whether or not the medieval ironclad, lock-and-key chastity belts ever existed remains unknown (there is no concrete evidence that they did exist), but the mythology of the chastity belt survives into the twenty-first century.

In Renaissance poetry, largely written by men for women, chastity belts surfaced as symbols or pledges of fidelity. In William Collins's "Ode on the Poetical Character" (1747), the poet describes a "zone" or girdle that functions as a stand-in for virtue and moral purity:

> "That girdle gaue the virtue of chast loue,
> And wiuehood true, to all that did it beare;
> But whosoeuer contrarie doth proue,
> Might not the same about her middle weare,
> But it would loose, or else a sunder teare."
>
> *(Jung 2006, p. 17)*

Sandro Jung's study of William Collins's "girdle poems" reveals the chastity belt to be a "magical" device

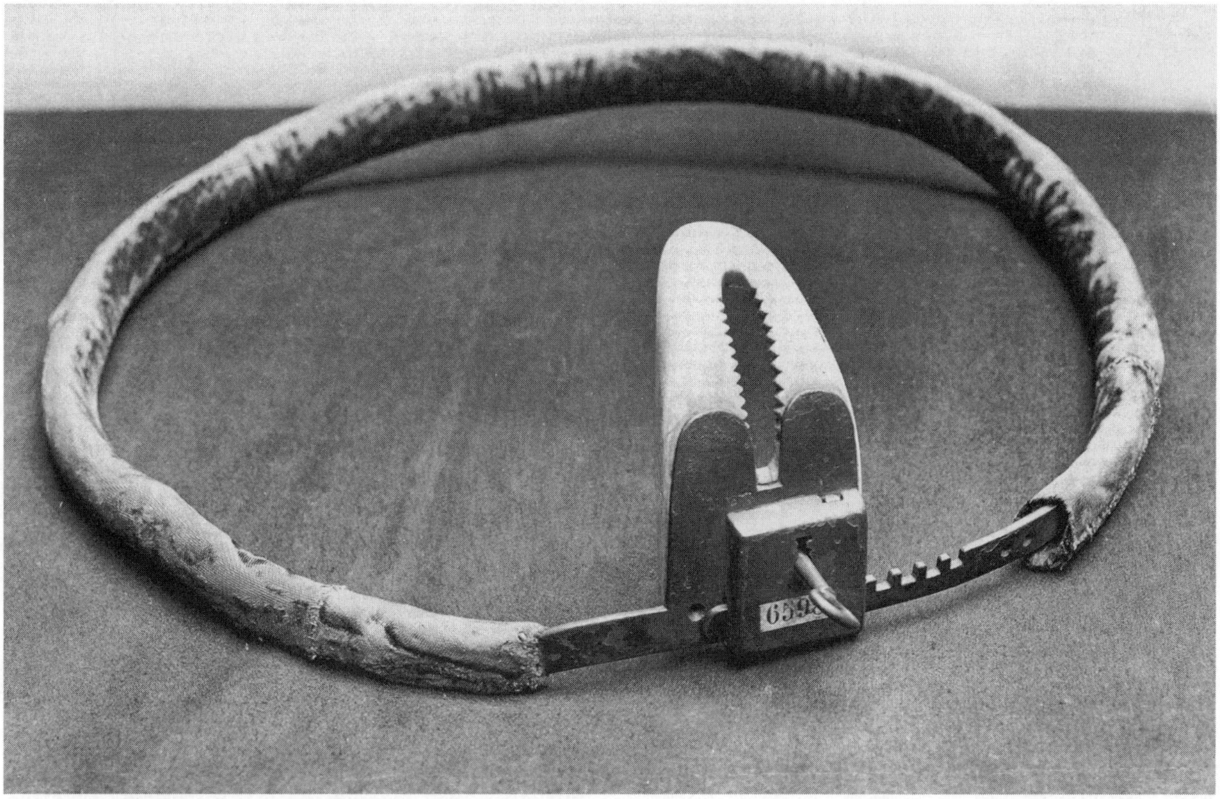

A Medieval Chasity Belt. ND/ROGER VIOLLET/GETTY IMAGES.

that represents purity and a "constancy of love" that reinforces the elevation of romantic love as existing above all other forms (2006, pp. 17–18).

The voluntary and "pleasurable" bondage of romantic love that the girdle represents in the Renaissance is literalized in the Victorian era, when actual belts were created in order to ensure that people would not venture too far from virginity. The very word *chastity* was often used in Victorian poetry to refer to a woman's sexual discretion, and ability to be faithful to her husband.

During the Victorian era, cloth and leather chastity belts were sometimes prescribed to prevent both male and female youth from masturbating, which at the time was thought to be physically and morally harmful. In addition, women of this era sometimes wore cloth chastity belts in order to avoid the consequences of sexual harassment in the workplace. In two hundred years' time, the idea, as well as the form, of the chastity belt had transformed from being a symbolic emblem of romantic love to a literal and repressive medical device to be used to distance people from their bodies.

The Roman Catholic Church had condemned masturbation before the Victorian era, but during the late nineteenth and early twentieth centuries, according to Planned Parenthood, "physicians involved in the social hygiene movement ... continued to diagnose and treat conditions thought to be sequelae of masturbation [especially female masturbation]" (2003, p. 3). Among these treatments was the use of chastity belts, "or toothed urethral rings that would prick the penis if it became erect, metal strap-on-and-lock sheaths to cover the penis or vulva, or electric alarms that promised to put an end to wet dreams" (Planned Parenthood 2003, p. 3). During the mid-twentieth century, however, thanks to Freudian theory and Alfred Kinsey's published results on human sexuality, the medical community acknowledged the beneficial effects of masturbation.

In the late twentieth and early twenty-first centuries, the chastity belt returned in the form of "Forget Me Not Panties." Actually a hoax and never truly for sale, these were a line of women's underwear which "was advertised by its creators as a way to keep track of girlfriends, wives, or daughters. It was an instant hit" (Deziel 2006, p. 41). The creator of the "Forget Me Not Panties," Leba Haber Rubinoff, intended to create a "humorous way to get people talking about gender" (Deziel 2006, p. 41). This satirical version of the chastity belt indicates a shift toward playing with, and thus questioning, traditional and widely accepted notions of sex and gender roles.

SEE ALSO *Chastity; Masturbation; Virginity.*

BIBLIOGRAPHY

Denziel, Shanda. 2006. "The Smartypants Scam." *Macleans* 119(2): 41.

Dingwall, Eric John. 1931. *The Girdle of Chastity: A Medico-Historical Study.* London: Routledge.

Jung, Sandro. 2006. "William Collins and the 'Zone.'" *ANQ* 19(2): 17–22.

Kinsey, Alfred; Wardell B. Pomeroy; Clyde E. Martin; et al. 1948. *Sexual Behavior in the Human Male.* Philadelphia: W.B. Saunders.

Kinsey, Alfred, et al. 1953. *Sexual Behavior in the Human Female.* Philadelphia: W.B. Saunders.

Planned Parenthood Federation of America. 2003. "Masturbation: From Myth of Sexual 'Health.'" *Contemporary Sexuality* 37(3): 1–7.

Stengers, Jean, and Anne Van Neck. 2001. *Masturbation: The History of a Great Terror,* trans. Kathryn A. Hoffmann. New York: Palgrave.

Amy Nolan

CHAT ROOM

Chat rooms provide a form of online communication where people interact on a one-to-one or many-to-many basis in real time (synchronously). Chat rooms have been a popular form of online communication since the early days of the Internet. Individuals can chat using special programs (e.g., Internet Relay Chat) or servers may offer chat rooms (e.g., America Online [AOL]). However Web-based chat rooms are also increasingly available, so that users do not need a special program to enter them. Some chat rooms require registration, others are open. There are chat rooms to cover practically any topic, from gardening to politics, as well as for particular demographics, such as children or teens. People may start chatting in a general chat room and after introduction and flirtation split off to a private room in which the participants are limited. A significant number of chat rooms cater to people who specifically want sexual encounters.

According to Aaron Ben-Ze'ev, who does interdisciplinary work on emotion, people coming to chat rooms for sex are looking for the following: to experiment with online sex within an existing relationship; to develop an online relationship that could transfer into an offline relationship at some point; or to have short online affairs. Sex online is known as cybersex or *cybering*. During cybersex, two or sometimes more people exchange messages describing sexual acts and their own feelings, which are aimed at evoking both self-arousal and that of other parties. Often partners masturbate while exchanging text messages. Advances in technology are making voice and video chat increasingly available and affordable. This development may replace text chat, and chat rooms may become areas in which participants watch something captured on a single webcam, or where two people in a private chat watch each other via webcam. However in his essay "Text Talk" (1997), John Suler, a clinical psychologist of cyberspace, makes the case that text chat has some characteristics that will ensure its ongoing popularity, such as its anonymity and minimalism, which allow for creative solutions like emoticons and for a communication that feels like it connects speakers very directly.

One of the positive characteristics of cybersex in chat rooms is that a number of the offline obstacles that restrain people from engaging in sexual relations do not exist. Text chat does not communicate physical appearance or disability (or a person's age or gender). Ben-Ze'ev comments: "If, in the good old days, an ideal desired person was tall and beautiful, in cybersex the ideal is a smart person who can type fast with one hand" (Ben-Ze'ev 2004, p. 11). Thus all one needs to be attractive in a chat room is a way with words and good typing skills. Sociologist Mary Chayko and Ben-Ze'ev also cite the anonymity of chat rooms as a benefit. People who otherwise might feel inhibited often feel sexually liberated in chat rooms because no one knows who they are offline. Another advantage of sex in chat rooms is that, while cybering allows for many casual encounters, becoming pregnant and acquiring sexually transmitted infections are not possible.

The anonymity and casual nature of contacts in chat rooms also form their greatest disadvantage or danger. While the sex online is virtual, real emotions are involved. Ben-Ze'ev gives numerous examples of heartache caused when individuals involved in romantic relationships developed in chat rooms were suddenly abandoned by their online partners. The anonymity of the chat room allows participants to keep other online or offline relationships secret, so deception is not uncommon. Anonymity also allows people to lie about their gender, and permits sexual predators to lure vulnerable parties, especially children, into dangerous offline situations.

BIBLIOGRAPHY

Ben-Ze'ev, Aaron. 2004. *Love Online: Emotions on the Internet.* New York: Cambridge University Press.

Chayko, Mary. 2002. *Connecting: How We Form Social Bonds and Communities in the Internet Age.* Albany: State University of New York Press.

Suler, John. 1997. Text Talk: Psychological Dynamics of Online Synchronous Conversations in Text-Driven Chat Environments. Available from http://www.rider.edu/suler/psycyber/texttalk.html.

Barbara Postema

CHAUCER, GEOFFREY
c. 1340–1400

Widely considered the first great poet in the English tradition, Geoffrey Chaucer was the son of a wine merchant. He was attached in his youth to aristocratic and

Geoffrey Chaucer. PUBLIC DOMAIN.

royal households, later holding several important public positions—controller of customs, justice of the peace, member of Parliament, clerk of the King's works—and traveled to France, Italy, and Spain, probably on official business (the Italian trips also contributed to his poetic development, introducing him to the work of Dante, Petrarch, and Giovanni Boccaccio). Chaucer received regular annuities and grants from the royal family; these recognized his political service but also perhaps his poetry. About Chaucer's private life, we know less: he was married to Philippa Roet, also in service to the royal family, and he had several children. Chaucer jokes in his poetry about his ineptitude as a lover, his portly physique, and the trials of marriage, but one should not read these as reliably autobiographical.

Chaucer's major works include dream visions—the *Book of the Duchess* (c. 1369), the *House of Fame* (c. 1379–1380), the *Parliament of Fowls* (c. 1380–1382); a long courtly romance, adapted from Boccaccio, *Troilus and Criseyde* (ca. 1385); a collection of mostly classical stories about "good" women and unfaithful men, *The Legend of Good Women* (the Prologue of which is a fourth Chaucerian dream vision, c. 1386); and a more various collection of stories, framed within the account of a pilgrimage from London to Canterbury, *The Canterbury Tales* (1388–1400).

Most of Chaucer's poetry touches on questions about sex, gender, and sexuality. The dream visions all interrogate romantic love, though sometimes obliquely. Susan Schibanoff argues in *Chaucer's Queer Poetics* (2006) that the dream poems provide a site for the development of a queer Chaucerian aesthetics. *Troilus and Criseyde* traces the process by which its title characters fall in love and ultimately lose each other; the poem's center includes an elaborate bedroom scene in which they consummate their love, helped by Troilus's friend (and Criseyde's uncle) Pandarus, who serves as the go-between in their affair. As Tison Pugh (in *Queering Medieval Genres* [2004]) and Richard Zeikowitz (2003) have emphasized, the poem explores not only courtly love but also male-male homosocial/affective bonds. *The Canterbury Tales* depicts men and women from various social positions thrown together on a pilgrimage during which they tell stories. Several female characters—the Wife of Bath, the Prioress, the Second Nun—narrate tales. And almost all the tales focus their attention on male-female relationships and on marriage. Those few that don't—the *Friar's*, *Pardoner's*, and *Canon's Yeoman's Tales*—instead thematize male-male bonds. George Lyman Kittredge, in *Chaucer and His Poetry* (1915), proposed that one sequence of tales—*The Wife of Bath's*, *Clerk's*, *Merchant's*, and *Franklin's*—constitutes a "Marriage Group"; this has provided an important framework for reading the *Canterbury Tales.*

The explicit concerns of Chaucer's poetry have thus made it impossible for criticism to ignore questions about sex, gender, and sexuality. But it was not until the rise of feminist theory in the 1970s and 1980s that critics began to look more fully at the ways in which gender shapes Chaucer's work; and it was not until the 1990s and the elaboration of queer theory that the same became true for sexuality. In both feminist and queer criticism of Chaucer, many readings have focused on individual characters whose representation seems to raise especially poignant questions about gender and sexuality. The Wife of Bath, married five times and outspoken in her comments about male-female relations, has been of particular interest to feminist readers. Similarly, the Pardoner, compared to both "a geldyng" (castrated horse) and "a mare," has been at the center of much queer inquiry. As early as 1980, Monica McAlpine proposed that the Pardoner be read as akin to a modern homosexual ("The Pardoner's Homosexuality and How It Matters," *PMLA* 95 [1980]: 8–22); this was followed by a series of denials and then by analyses influenced by queer theory, beginning with Glenn Burger's "Kissing the Pardoner" (*PMLA* 107 [1992]: 1142–56).

The most thought-provoking feminist and queer Chaucerian work has recognized that it is not only in the depiction of particular characters but also in the deeper concerns of Chaucer's poetry that gender and sexuality matter. Carolyn Dinshaw's groundbreaking *Chaucer's Sexual Poetics* (1989) argues that Chaucer inherited, interrogated, and reshaped a longstanding hermeneutical tradition in which the literary text was figured as a female body under male control. Elaine Tuttle Hansen's *Chaucer and the Fictions of Gender* (1992) argues that Chaucer represented female characters like the Wife of Bath not out of some protofeminist impulse but instead to resolidify masculine authority. Queer-inflected Chaucerian work often takes off from such feminist criticism, but it emphasizes—instead of gender—the complex ways in which Chaucer engages with sexualities (not the modern categories of homo/heterosexuality, but instead medieval ones such as sodomy, celibacy, courtly love, and conjugality).

In *Getting Medieval* (1999), Dinshaw considers how non-normative, dissonant sexualities are represented in the Middle Ages by authors like Chaucer, how the "touch of the queer" disturbs medieval hegemonies, and how medieval queernesses resonate with the postmodern world. Karma Lochrie, in *Covert Operations: The Medieval Uses of Secrecy* (1999) and *Heterosyncrasies* (2005), emphasizes female sexuality, arguing that the category of sodomy was applied to women as well as men; she also critiques work that unreflectively brings modern categories of analysis (even commonsensical ones like "normality" and "normativity") to bear on the premodern. The fullest queer analysis of Chaucer is Glenn Burger's *Chaucer's Queer Nation* (2003). Burger examines explicitly sexualized moments in the *Canterbury Tales* (the conclusion of the bawdy *Miller's Tale*; the Pardoner's queer performance), but he also reads queerly what might seem the more "normal" (and "heterosexual") relations of conjugality in the tales of the Marriage Group, the Wife of Bath's "female masculinity," and the religious/eschatological conclusion of Chaucer's Canterbury pilgrimage.

Other important work on gender and sexuality in Chaucer includes that of Alcuin Blamires, Catherine S. Cox, Susan Crane, Sheila Delany, Aranye Fradenburg, Allen J. Frantzen, Steven Kruger, Anne Laskaya, Jill Mann, and Robert S. Sturges.

BIBLIOGRAPHY

Burger, Glenn. 1992. "Kissing the Pardoner." *PMLA* 107: 1142–56.

Burger, Glenn. 2003. *Chaucer's Queer Nation.* Minneapolis: University of Minnesota Press.

Crane, Susan. 1994. *Gender and Romance in Chaucer's Canterbury Tales.* Princeton, NJ: Princeton University Press.

Dinshaw, Carolyn. 1989. *Chaucer's Sexual Poetics.* Madison: University of Wisconsin Press.

Dinshaw, Carolyn. 1999. *Getting Medieval: Sexualities and Communities, Pre- and Postmodern.* Durham: Duke University Press.

Hansen, Elaine Tuttle. 1992. *Chaucer and the Fictions of Gender.* Berkeley: University of California Press.

Lochrie, Karma. 2005. *Heterosyncrasies: Female Sexuality When Normal Wasn't.* Minneapolis: University of Minnesota Press.

McAlpine, Monica. 1980. "The Pardoner's Homosexuality and How It Matters." *PMLA* 95: 8-22.

Schibanoff, Susan. 2006. *Chaucer's Queer Poetics: Rereading the Dream Trio*. Toronto: University of Toronto Press.

Zeikowitz, Richard. 2003. *Homoeroticism and Chivalry: Discourses of Male Same-Sex Desire in the Fourteenth Century*. New York: Palgrave Macmillan.

Steven F. Kruger

CHICANA MOVEMENT

A Chicana movement began as a series of actions through which women organized collectively in the late 1960s and 1970s to challenge unequal treatment within the Chicano civil rights and power movements of that era. In the mid-1960s Mexican Americans in the United States experienced an awakening of consciousness, identity, and ethnic pride in a broad-based "Chicano movement" that encompassed several efforts toward social change, including farm workers', land grant, urban, youth, and student movements.

Those efforts raised awareness of the conditions facing Chicano communities as a result of long-standing racism and discrimination, including unequal access to education, discrimination in housing, underemployment, police brutality, and a lack of political power. The term *Chicano* referred to a collective identity based on militant cultural and political consciousness of a history of racialization of Chicanos as Mexicans in the United States.

Early in the development of the Chicano movement at the First Annual Denver Youth Conference, March 27–31, 1969, Chicana student activists called for a thoughtful consideration of their roles in the movement. After hearing the declaration "The Chicana woman does not want to be liberated," many women activists began to question the limitations inherent in that statement, pointing out the significant involvement and contributions of women to the Chicano movement in actions such as the 1968 high school walkouts in East Los Angeles and the formation of student organizations on college campuses.

Subsequently, the ideology of cultural nationalism emphasized the maintenance of culture as a form of resistance to pressure from the dominant society to assimilate by promoting an image of the traditional family as an ideal to be upheld by movement participants. In that traditional family, men were the breadwinners and women were helpmates whose role was to raise the children and maintain the home. Chicanas adopted a variety of strategies for reconfiguring the symbolics of male-centered and male-dominant cultural nationalism, including the recovery and reinterpretation of key figures in Mexican history such as the *solda-deras* and *soldadas*—women who participated in the Mexican Revolution of 1910—and *Malintzin Tenepal*, or *la Malinche*—the indigenous woman translator for the Spanish conquerer Hernán Cortés.

As Chicana students and community activists observed patterns of inequality in the treatment and inclusion of women in organizations such as *Movimiento Estudiantil Chicano de Aztlan*, *La Raza Unida Party*, and the Brown Berets, they began to develop their own spaces to challenge gender inequality and sexism. For example, in Texas women in *La Raza Unida Party* organized as *Mujeres por la Raza Unida* and sponsored women candidates for political office. In California Chicana students at California State University at Long Beach founded *Hijas de Cuahtemoc*, an autonomous women's organization. Also in California, *Comision Femenil Mexicana* was founded to advocate for women's advancement in the community and the workplace. *Comision Femenil Mexicana* also sponsored the Chicana Service Action Center, a resource for employment opportunities as well as services for survivors of domestic violence. A Chicana rights project gathered information about the economic, educational, and employment status of Chicanas and litigated cases for women.

Many women activists wrote poetry or essays expressing their critique of unequal treatment by men in the movement, racism in U.S. society, and racism in the mainstream women's movement of that era. Among the prominent activist women who raised their voices and pens from the late 1960s to mid-1970s were Francisca Flores, founder of *Comision Femenil Mexicana*; Ana Nieto-Gómez, a student at Long Beach and an educator in southern California; Marta Cotera, the Texas-based author of *Diosa y Hembra* and a participant in *Mujeres por la Raza Unida*; and Enriqueta Vasquez, a writer for *El Grito del Norte*, a newspaper in New Mexico. Although there were differences among women in the movement, a broad-based Chicana movement advocated for women's perspectives on a variety of issues, including child care, reproductive rights, welfare rights, educational justice, employment opportunities, and an end to the war in Vietnam.

The main period of organizing as a broad-based movement tapered off in the middle to late 1980s, but a Chicana movement continued to evolve in the late 1980s and early 1990s through the higher education organization *Mujeres Activas en Letras y Cambio Social* [Women Active in Letters and Social Change] and the literary emergence of writers such as Cherríe Moraga, Sandra Cisneros, Helena Maria Viramontes, Ana Castillo, and Gloria Anzaldúa, whose work continued and extended the tradition of poetry writing begun by Chicanas in the movement era of the 1970s. Chicana lesbian thought and the internal critique of homophobia in the Chicano community also contributed to the evolution of the movement. From the 1990s through the first decade of the twenty-first century Chicana activists and academics continued their critical examination of the impact of race, class, gender, and sexuality on women's lives and advocated for more just social conditions in the United States and in transnational contexts.

SEE ALSO *Feminism: IV. Western; Nationalism.*

BIBLIOGRAPHY

Arredondo, Gabriela F.; Aida Hurtado; Norma Klahn; Olga Nájera-Ramirez; and Patricia Zavella. 2003. *Chicana Feminisms: A Critical Reader.* Durham, NC: Duke University Press.

Garcia, Alma M. 1997. *Chicana Feminist Thought: The Basic Historical Writings.* New York: Routledge.

Moraga, Cherríe, and Gloria Anzaldúa, eds. 1981. *This Bridge Called My Back: Writings by Radical Women of Color.* Watertown, MA: Persephone Press.

Dionne Espinoza

CHILDCARE

Since the early recorded history of the United States nonfamilial care providers have minded children so that parents could engage in work or other activities (Youcha 1995). In colonial times apprentices were sent to live with masters to learn a trade; this was done to provide vocational training and oversight of a young apprentice. Under slavery, white planters' wives cared for black children while their enslaved parents worked in the fields or in contrast, female slaves served as "mammies" who cared for the plantation owner's children. Urban immigrants in the late nineteenth and early twentieth centuries put children to work in factories and sometimes sent them to charitable day nurseries that were organized to keep children off the streets (Rose 1999). World War II required mothers to work in the defense industry; many of the children of those mothers were placed in federally subsidized day care. In short, people have used care arrangements other than maternal care for children throughout American history.

TRADITIONAL PREFERENCE FOR HOME CARE

Even during the Depression and World War II American social institutions did not widely accept and endorse nonmaternal care for children. The Children's Bureau, a federal agency that propagated a rhetoric of maternalism, advocated the idea that daycare was a necessarily evil that should be secondary to mothers caring for their own offspring (Rose 1999). Americans were ambivalent about children receiving childcare services through the postwar years. During the 1950s notables such as Margaret Mead and Eleanor Maccoby (Michel 1999) made the case that daycare could be benevolent, but many people argued against that view. In a 1958 speech President Dwight Eisenhower encouraged mothers who were prosperous enough not to work outside the home, for "they would have to consider what is the price they are paying in terms of the opportunity that child has been denied," that is, the opportunity to be molded by a mother (quoted in Michel 1999).

CHANGES IN THE POSTWAR ERA

The postwar era saw dramatic changes in women's identities and roles. Labor in the sense of childbirth became more common during the postwar baby boom. Another type of female labor (workforce participation) also increased a trend that continued through the second half of the twentieth century. Concurrently, homes occupied by a mother married to a male breadwinner declined as a proportion of families, whereas female-headed families increased. Women, mothers included, transformed the makeup of the workforce, raising the percentage of women over age sixteen who were working from 33.9 percent in 1950 to 59.8 percent in 1998 (Fullerton 1999). There emerged a systematic, widespread need for childcare. In the absence of uniform national standards for children's care, parents sought affordable local options. Parents entrusted their children to a patchwork of diverse care circumstances, including care by a family member, care in the home of an unrelated provider (family daycare), and the use of a privatized daycare center or nursery school.

CHILDCARE IN THE UNITED STATES IN THE EARLY TWENTY-FIRST CENTURY

Childcare has continued to occupy a very significant place in American life. Across the ages from birth to age five, 60 percent of children and infants (13 million) were in some type of childcare arrangement in the early years of the twenty-first century (Hofferth 1996).

Women's wages have become indispensable to families with single and married mothers alike. For families with young children (under age six) who live on household incomes under $18,000 per year 90 percent of family income on average comes from the mother's earnings. Even in middle-class families earning $36,000 to $60,000 annually the mother's income represents over half (53 percent) (National Association of Child Care Resource and Referral Agencies 2006). In poor family's federal welfare reform in 1996 resulted in pressure on mothers to take jobs and find childcare arrangements.

For the impoverished working poor childcare can deplete meager economic resources because of gaps in funding. For example, Head Start, a nationally funded educational preschool program aimed at the poor, served only 34 percent of three- to five-year-old children living in poverty in that period (Blau 2001).

Despite the broad U.S. childcare landscape, the conditions of childcare have been unsatisfactory in two respects. First, childcare has become unaffordable even for middle-class families. Childcare expenses consume a third or more of the household budget in female-headed families and can be prohibitive for mothers entering the workplace from welfare. Second, the quality of American childcare is inadequate; it generally is agreed among experts that excellent-quality care is exceptional rather than common. The quality issue has dismaying consequences for children and babies who spend substantial time in childcare during a period of profound neurological, cognitive, emotional, and social development. In the late 1990s a study found that 72 percent of infants in childcare entered care by age four months, attending twenty-nine hours a week on average (Vandell 2004).

The impact of childcare on children is complex, partly because there are varied forms of care. American daycare centers, whose use increases with age, account for 27 percent of childcare arrangements for three-year-olds and 51 percent of those arrangements for five-year-olds. Using grandparents as providers declines over the preschool years, falling from 23 percent among three-year-olds to only 14 percent among five-year-olds. Overall, the scattershot ways in which childcare is obtained include parents looking after their own children (15 percent of arrangements at age five) and family daycare (7 percent of care arrangements at age five), among other approaches (Waldfogel 2006).

Center care on average is more expensive than care given by a family daycare provider. Thus, center care disproportionately serves children from families with higher incomes. Further, the highest-quality centers tend to enroll children from more affluent families. (Quality of care is defined by experts to involve care providers trained in child development, a low ratio of teachers to children, a hazard-free and activity-rich setting, activities that are developmentally enriching, and interactions between caregivers and children that are responsive to the children and developmentally appropriate [King and MacKinnon 1998, National Institute of Child Health and Human Development 2003].) Family daycare tends to be of lower quality overall than center care (Crittenden 2001). Partly because they lack information, parents are not necessarily discerning at judging daycare quality (Blau 2001).

In the absence of federal standards, childcare centers are regulated by the individual state. Some states do not require any kind of accreditation, and most do not require that care providers be licensed. One study showed that thirty-two states required no prior training for teachers; in the remaining states, the amount of education required was often minimal. Only twelve states required teachers to have at least a high school diploma (Helburn and Bergman 2002). Family daycare tends to receive less oversight than does center care, with an estimated 82 percent of homes completely unregulated (Crittenden 2001).

The fact that childcare quality falls short in the United States corresponds to the fact that Americans have fewer supports in financing childcare than exist elsewhere in the world. Despite Head Start and other modest subsidies for the poor, the United States has lower levels of public support for childcare than do at least nine European countries (Waldfogel 2001).

Caregivers are central to the quality of care. American caregivers are paid inadequately, resulting in high turnover. In centers only 28 percent of caregiving for infants (age fifteen months) has been rated as positive. This improves only slightly for children three years of age, for whom 34 percent of caregiving is positive (Helburn and Bergmann 2002).

A concern of parents involves the risk of child abuse by care providers. Maltreatment of children in childcare, which was publicized after the 1983 landmark case at the McMartin preschool in California, occurs less frequently than some people suppose. The incidence of sexual abuse in daycare centers (5.5 per 10,000 children) is actually lower than that for children cared for at home (8.9 per 10,000 children). Physical abuse by baby-sitters in private homes most commonly takes the form of overdiscipline (e.g., bruising of buttocks) by caregivers with unrealistic expectations of children or poor comprehension of children's motives (Schumacher and Carlson 1999). The possibility of abuse highlights the importance of both regulatory oversight and caregiver education in regard to normal child behavior. In response to fears of abuse, some say that daycare centers have overreacted by forbidding caretakers to touch children and thus discouraging healthy caregiver affection (Tobin 1997).

POLICY CHALLENGES

Because good care can help children become contributing adult citizens, the public interest is involved in this issue. However, the financial limitations of a privatized system, combined with parents who are inadequately informed, holds back childcare quality.

Proposals to improve childcare have been offered, usually involving a centralized federal role in funding and/or enhancing quality. The economist David Blau, for example, stated that a federal voucher program could attack the cost problem through a market mechanism: childcare vouchers. The aid represented by a voucher would be higher when the voucher was used for higher-quality care (Blau 2001).

Such approaches, if drafted as legislation, could meet with ambivalent reactions. In 1987 the ABC Bill (Act for Better Child Care Services) was introduced to Congress, where it had broad support but failed after vocal opposition by neoconservatives who wished to retain decentralized state control. A major argument against the bill was that its provisions would interfere in families' parenting (Teghtsoonian 1993). Historically, Americans have depended on nonmaternal care of children yet at the same time have exhibited a cultural ethos of maternalism. In some ways modern psychological research has similar underpinnings, pitting nonmaternal care against the mother-child relationship in studies of how childcare affects the mother-child bond (Belsky and Steinberg 1978).

In light of the public decision making that has prevented reform, childcare advocates face a legislative and political challenge. Mobilizing for better care entails wrestling politically with deep-seated cultural beliefs not so much about children as about motherhood (Marchbank 2000). In the future establishing an adequate appreciation of the need for high quality nonmaternal care is likely to be, like childcare itself, a difficult undertaking.

BIBLIOGRAPHY

Belsky, Jay, and Laurence Steinberg. 1978. "The Effects of Day Care: A Critical Review." *Child Development* 49(4): 929–949.

Blau, David M. 2001. *The Child Care Problem: An Economic Analysis*. New York: Russell Sage.

Crittenden, Ann. 2001. *The Price of Motherhood*. New York: Metropolitan.

Fullerton, Howard. 1999. "Labor Force Participation: 75 Years of Change, 1950-1998 and 1998-2025." *Monthly Labor Review* 122(12): 3–12.

Helburn, Suzanne W., and Barbara R. Bergmann. 2002. *America's Child Care Problem: The Way Out*. New York: Palgrave.

Hofferth, Sandra L. 1996. "Child Care in the United States Today." *The Future of Children* 6(2): 41–61.

King, Donna, and Carol MacKinnon. 1988. "Making Difficult Choices Easier: A Review of Research on Day Care and Children's Development." *Family Relations* 37(4): 392–398.

Marchbank, Jennifer. 2000. *Women, Power, and Policy: Comparative Studies of Childcare*. London and New York: Routledge.

Michel, Sonya. 1999. *Children's Interests/Mothers' Rights: The Shaping of America's Child Care Policy*. New Haven, CT: Yale University Press.

National Association of Child Care Resource and Referral Agencies. 2006. *Breaking the Piggy Bank: Parents and the High Price of Child Care*. Toronto: NACCRRA.

National Institute of Child Health and Human Development, Early Child Care Research Network. 2003. "Does Amount of Time Spent in Child Care Predict Socioemotional Adjustment during the Transition to Kindergarten?" *Child Development* 74(4): 976–1005.

Rose, Elizabeth. 1999. *A Mother's Job: The History of Day Care, 1890–1960*. New York: Oxford University Press.

Schumacher, Ruth, and Rebecca Carlson. 1999. "Variables and Risk Factors Associated with Child Abuse in Daycare Settings." *Child Abuse and Neglect* 23(9): 891–898.

Teghtsoonian, Katherine. 1993. "Neo-Conservative Ideology and Opposition to Federal Regulation of Child Care Services in the United States and Canada." *Canadian Journal of Political Science* 26(1): 97–121.

Tobin, Joseph. 1997. *Making a Place for Pleasure in Early Childhood Education*. New Haven, CT: Yale University Press.

Vandell, Deborah Lowe. 2004. "Early Child Care: The Known and the Unknown." *Merrill-Palmer Quarterly* 50(3): 387–414.

Waldfogel, Jane. 2001. "International Policies toward Parental Leave and Child Care." *The Future of Children* 11(1).

Waldfogel, Jane. 2006. *What Children Need*. Cambridge, MA: Harvard University Press.

Youcha, Geraldine. 1995. Minding the Children: Child Care in America from Colonial Times to the Present. New York: Scribner.

Cindy Dell Clark

CHILDHOOD SEXUALITY

Childhood theories on sexuality in the early twenty-first century have been influenced by psychoanalysts Sigmund Freud and Jacques Lacan, object relations theorists, psychologists, and sociologists. Although multiple theorists have written on what kind of childhood experiences influence character, they do not say what the cause of childhood sexuality is or that it lies at the base of adult knowledge and being. Those who treat what causes childhood sexuality, such as feminist authors Dorothy Dinnerstein or psychologist Nancy Chodorow, give a sociological, behavioral interpretation of how sexual difference is created. Physicist and feminist author Evelyn Keller Fox argues for a sociobiological evolution of the genes. Feminist writers on this topic seem to split between believing in an essential woman, as does psychologist Luce Irigaray, and an enslavement of women to heterosexual norms, as do gender theorists Adrienne Rich and Judith Butler. But none tie this sexuality to different ways of knowing or suffering. Object-relations theorists argue for good and bad mothering as the source of behavior, but not of sexuality. Thus psychoanalysts Donald Winnicott, Melanie Klein, Jessica Benjamin, and Heinz Kohut are more concerned with identity than sexuality (Wright 1992).

Indeed contemporary views of childhood sexuality can be traced to Freud's revolutionary find that children are sexual beings. Consideration of childhood sexuality must begin with a review of his groundbreaking book, *Three Essays on Sexuality* (1905), which was written in several parts through 1925.

Freud argued that sexual factors lie at the basis of anxiety neuroses (conditions of acute and unmotivated anxiety) and nervous maladies (the psychoneuroses), and later at the base of character and knowledge itself. Early in his career, Freud argued that erotogenic zones were developed and later repressed after being connected with perversions, which had been widely studied by psychiatrist Richard von Kraft-Ebbing and psychologist Havelock Ellis but never linked to childhood sexuality.

Before viewing children as sexually polymorphous perverse, Freud's initial notion was that sexuality was caused by hysteria developed in childhood and traceable to sexual seduction. In 1897 Freud abandoned his seduction theory and turned to infantile sexuality, which had previously been considered dormant. The catalyst for this change was Freud's discovery of the Oedipus complex in his own analysis, the experience in which both male and female children initially see the mother as a love object. Discontent with this theory as explaining the cause of sexuality, he says the boy chooses his mother and the girl her father, thus making feminine object choice harder for girls since they must relinquish the primordial love object. Lacan makes the adult stage harder for men in that they must choose the partner from which they have had to deviate in order to define themselves as men and differentiate themselves from the primordial symbiosis with the mother. The most important infantile trace retained at puberty is the child's love for his or her parents. In "To Interpret the Cause" (1989) Jacques-Alain Miller argues that Lacan sees the Oedipal structure as an infant's response to the mother's desire. The mother's unconscious desire is an interpretation of the sexual difference, i.e., of the father's name signifier. The function of the mother's desire times the father's name signifiers, means that representations reside in the social other which stands over a quota of libido and makes of the Oedipus (the father's name) the other over jouissance. That is, the reality principle stands over the pleasure principle.

Having decided that sexual impulses operated normatively in the youngest of children, Freud had moved far beyond his theory that sexuality began at puberty, as well as away from the general idea of childhood as innocence and happiness. In the preface to the third edition of *The Standard Edition of the Complete Psychological Works of Sigmund Freud*, Freud stressed that biology did not influence him, but believed psychology shed light on the causality of human behavior and understanding that sexuality is determined by libido or desire (lust). Freud stressed that biology was not an influence on him, but it is psychology that sheds light on the causality of human behavior and knowledge in that sexuality is determined by a non-biological libidinal desire that comes from fantasy and identifications.

In his analyses of infantile sexuality, Freud points to the issue of sexual object which defies the myth of harmonious heterosexual love. Homosexuality also gives lie to that fable. As to perversion, no innate or acquired explanation is right. Rather one must look to an originary bisexuality. He argues against an innate hermaphrodism, pointing out that one partner in a male homosexual relationship will take on feminine characteristics. The key point is that sexual drive is independent of its objects. What is consistent in the sexual aim is the goal of pleasure found, whether the source of that pleasure is the mouth or the anus. There is no normal heterosexual intercourse. Even fetishes can become the aim of libidinal desire. One can include touching and looking. Freud comes up with the notion of passivity as feminine and activity as masculine. Nonetheless he retains a belief in normal versus pathological sexuality.

In *Three Essays on the Theory of Sexuality* (1905), Freud studies the infantile character of sexuality and implies that a certain perversion is common to everyone from infancy on. Later in life adults repress their childhood sexual feelings and experience a kind of amnesia built around disgust, shame, or morality. These memories function unconsciously to the strongest degree. Repression gives the key to a before, because if there is nothing before, what comes forth in analysis could not have been placed there. Indeed sexuality can even be found in the newborn child. The drives, however, are slippery and reaction-formation and sublimation, as well as repression, hide the naked real of the sexual drive. Lacan argued in 1960 that the erotogenic zones are eight Ur-objects that have no alterity, but are constituted in infancy as the cause of desire. The four Freud discovered are the breast, the feces, the urinary flow, and the (imaginary phallus), and Lacan added four others: the gaze, the voice, the phoneme, and the nothing. Later these Ur-objects give rise to four constant drives, the oral, anal, scopic, and invocatory.

Freud argues that primitive manifestations of infantile sexuality appear in sucking, such as thumb sucking, where sucking itself often accompanies the child's rubbing of some sensitive part of his body. Sexual activity is autoerotic. More than nourishment is at stake, the search for pleasure tending to repetition and self-preservation, not to an object. Thus the infant's sexual aim is satisfaction provided by the erotogenic zone itself. Both the labial zone and the anal zone, give themselves up for focus in sexual activity. That toilet functions can arouse sexual excitement is not so unusual. Such stimulations lead to masturbatory functions. In boys the glans part of the penis is in play, in girls, the clitoris. Bathing can also stimulate these sensitive areas.

Freud thus distinguishes three phases of infantile childhood sexuality: early infancy, sexual activity around year four, and the phase of pubertal masturbation. In the fourth year the genital zones become active targets for sexual pleasure until societal pressure suppresses such public displays. The cultural superego is strong enough to induce repression and sublimation. At about the same time that the sexual life of a child reaches its peak between three to five years of age, the child substitutes a craving for knowledge or research. Lacan explained that once sexual difference is discovered by children, even at very early ages, they develop a response to the idea of castration—lack on the part of each sex; he has the penis and she is proof to him that he could lose it. Once this difference—itself a third thing—is discovered, the castration complex develops in boys and penis envy evolves in girls. Lacan translates Freud's terms into the wish to compete in men and the desire to succeed socially in women. Taking us from the infantile to structure, Lacan argues that the experience of lack gives rise to four structures of libidinal being: normative masquerade, the neuroses, the psychoses, and perversion.

Freud further develops the organization of childhood, or pregenital sexual life into the oral and the anal. Later linking these to character types, he sees the neuroses as exemplifications of one or the other fixation. For Lacan the oral and anal drives remain for everyone throughout life. These are structures that make up the drives whose vicissitudes link us to the world and objects in it. The oral, says Freud, is cannibalistic and narcissistic, while the anal is compulsive and sadistic. These drives are active and passive, not yet masculine or feminine, a distinction that Lacan will retain—calling them *fixions,* not fixations—while arguing that neither is sex specific in terms of biological gender..

Having given us a view of childhood sexuality as progressing from the oral stage (narcissistic) to the anal stage (social control), Freud introduces the adult stage of reciprocity where the woman gives up on clitoral pleasure and emphasizes vaginal pleasure. Physician William Masters and psychologist Virginia Johnson, as well as numbers of feminist scholars, and Lacan with his theory of a sexual non-rapport have proved this to be a fictional developmental step. Thus Freud incorrectly departs from his own revolutionary theory. Lacan points out that finding an object is not the adult's goal, but the refinding is a repetition of whatever gave pleasure in childhood.

SEE ALSO *Adolescent Sexuality; Freud, Sigmund; Infantile Sexuality; Lacan, Jacques.*

BIBLIOGRAPHY

Benjamin, Jessica. 1988. *The Bonds of Love.* New York: Pantheon.

Butler, Judith. 1990. *Gender Trouble: Feminism and the Subversion of Identity.* London and New York: Routledge.

Ellis, Havelock. 1905–1942. *Studies in the Psychology of Sex.* New York: Random House.

Freud, Sigmund. 1974. *The Standard Edition of the Complete Psychological Works of Sigmund Freud.* Vols. 1–24, ed. by James Strachey. London: The Hogarth Press and the Institute of Psychoanalysis.

Freud, Sigmund. 1974. "Freud's Correspondence with Fliess." In *The Standard Edition of the Complete Psychological Works of Sigmund Freud.* Vol. 4, ed. James Strachey. London: The Hogarth Press and the Institute of Psychoanalysis. (Orig. pub. 1894.)

Freud, Sigmund. 1974. "On the Grounds for Detaching a Particular Syndrome from Neurasthenia under the Description' Anxiety Neurosis'." In *The Standard Edition of the Complete Psychological Works of Sigmund Freud.* Vol. 3, ed. James Strachey. London: The Hogarth Press and the Institute of Psychoanalysis. (Orig. pub. 1894.)

Freud, Sigmund. 1974. "Three Essays on the Theory of Sexuality." In *The Standard Edition of the Complete Psychological Works of Sigmund Freud.* Vol. 3, ed. James Strachey. London: The Hogarth Press and the Institute of Psychoanalysis. (Orig. pub. 1894.)

Klein, Melanie. 1975. *Love, Guilt, Reparation and Other Works, 1921–1945.* New York: Delta.

Kohut, Heinz. 1978. *The Search for the Self: Selected Writings of Heinz Kohut, 1950-1978,* 2 vols, ed. R. H. Ornstein. New York: International Universities Press.

Krafft-Ebbing Richard 1965. *Psychopathia sexualis,* trans. Harry E. Wedeck. New York: G.P. Putnams's Sons. (Orig. pub.1886.)

Lacan, Jacques. 1966. "The Subversion of the Subject and the Dialectic of Desire in the Freudian Unconscious." *Ecrits,* trans. Bruce Fink. New York: W. W. Norton.

Miller, Jacques-Alain. 1989. "To Interpret the Cause: From Freud to Lacan." *Newsletter of the Freudian Field* 3(1&2): 30-50.

Rich, Adrienne. 1979. *Of Woman Born.* London: Virago.

Winnicott, Donald W. 1971. *Playing and Reality.* London: Tavistock.

Wright, Elizabeth, ed. 1992. *Feminism and Psychoanalysis: A Critical Dictionary.* Oxford: Blackwell Press Ltd.

Ellie Ragland

CHILDREN, GENDER ROLES

SEE *Boys, Construction of; Gender Roles: I. Overview; Girls, Construction of.*

CHINA

This entry contains the following:

I. PRE-MODERN

The area now called China has one of the world's longest and most detailed sexual cultures in the world. For more than 5,000 years of Chinese history, the world's oldest continuous writing system, was almost exclusively the domain of elite men who rarely had contact with the illiterate populous, much less depicted common people. Surviving texts represent emperors and their courts, philosophers, and philosophies. By piecing together clues from these scattered texts, classic books, works of art and archeological artifacts like oracle bones and bronze relics, there is evidence of a generally open early sexual culture during the first three millennia of dynastic history. It was not until after the fall of the Tang Dynasty in 906 CE, when rising literacy and the advent of printing wrought a more balanced historical record, that one can begin to understand how average people performed gender and sexuality. This same period saw the rise of Neo-Confucian dynasties and a corresponding increase of sexual intolerance and disempowerment of women. Significant topics in Chinese sexuality and gender include yin and yang, ancient texts, philosophies of Confucianism and Taoism, gender relations, homosexuality, Neo-Confucianism, family life, prostitution, foot binding, eunuchs, and sex and gender in literature and art.

By the end of the Warring States Period (475?–221 BCE), after more than 1600 years of dynastic historical influence, many philosophical concepts that would influence Chinese gender, society, and sexuality for the next two and a half millennia had already been firmly established. Except for history's occasional female dowager empress, generally male emperors lived behind palace doors teeming with powerful eunuchs, and male and female suitors, all of whom competed for influence at court. Patrilocal and patrilinial families, where women surrendered their former identities and associations to subordinate themselves to a husband and his family, had become the norm. Men could have one wife, but many concubines. Men dominated affairs outside the home, whereas a woman's highest virtue was achieved through duties within. The concepts of inner and outer, light and dark, and the male and female structured these socio-political relations.

By the Zhou Dynasty (1122?–771? BCE), some of these basic elements had complexified into the meaning now associated with the *yin-yang* symbol. Yang, as a pictograph, originally represented the sunny side of a hill, and *yin* the side in shadow. *Yin* evolved to mean everything from cosmic female power, yielding, and interior, to the receptive, deficient, cold, dark, yanic, earth, and moon; *yang* came to mean cosmic male force, initiation, exterior, heat, excess, penetration, light, phallic, heaven, and sun. As during sexual intercourse, the receptive partner receives yet supplies the dominant, so too the penetrating *yang* cannot exist except in relation to receptive *yin*, and vice-versa. As the moon receives and transmits the sun's rays, so do *yin* and *yang* carry on this cosmological dualism throughout time. Thus, gendered elements are seen in the very fabric of the universe.

This *yin-yang* cosmology also forms the metaphysical basis in one of China's oldest and most influential texts, the *Yi Jing* (*I Ching*), or *Book of Changes*. The *I Ching* as a divination system explains worldly action, potential, and ultimately changes itself by quantifying the constant intermingling of heaven and earth as individual male and female elements. These elements are represented as lines, either broken (*yin*) or unbroken (*yang*). Three lines form a trigram; two trigrams form a hexagram.

Because of its complex gender components, the hexagram *ji-ji* is one of the most representative. It goes by many names, including: union, fulfillment, or completion.

Ji-ji is comprised of the trigram *kan* (water, female, broken lines surrounding an unbroken) above *li* (fire, male, unbroken lines around a broken). Between *kan's* broken *yin* lines, one can find the central male *yang* element as an unbroken line. Thus, water rests above the male fire, *li*, which contains the unbroken female line at its heart. Many have noted how these trigrams correspond to sexual coupling. The penetrator, like fire, flares up quickly, but is extinguished by water, an example of satiation by the receptive. The receiving partner, like water, is slow to heat and slow to cool. These complex *yin* and *yang* elements are no accident.

In ancient China, gender was not biological, but instead the outward expression of this cosmology, which informed the model of national and household hierarchy. Over time, female work, such as sewing, was increasingly confined to the "inner" and male work like agriculture to the "outer." These socio-biological norms held currency even after the last decades of the Qing Dynasty (1644–1912), when modern medical terminology began replacing ancient notions.

The *I Ching* is of indeterminate age and origin, and versions of the text have existed for at least four millennia.

Historically received texts with their additions by later scholars differ greatly from earlier versions. These provide fundamental insight into the origins of China's two most influential original philosophical systems, Taoism and Confucianism. Adherents of these social systems competed along with the less popular of the "Four Great Thoughts," Mohism and Legalism, during the Hundred Schools of Thought of the Warring States Period (475?–221 BCE).

Because gender was not seen as coming from the body, its forces could be tapped at will. The importance of assuming characteristically male or female attributes became a hallmark of later Taoist literature. Likewise, Confucius elevated certain aspects of the female because this power exemplified the virtue in being subordinate to ones superiors. Under the Confucian system, everyone, including the emperor, had to submit to the male force or "Will of Heaven." Examining Taoism and Confucianism provides insight into everyday sexuality for ancient Chinese.

EARLY CONFUCIANISM AND THE ROLES OF THE FEMALE

The teachings of Confucius (551–479 BCE), China's wandering Great Sage, are embodied in the Five Classics, which included the *I Ching*, and books of poetry, rites, history, and annals. These include some of the first references to the value of friendship, romantic scenes, and multifarious male and female roles. Confucius's philosophical, religious, moral, and social teachings were interpretation by later thinkers like Mencius (372–289 BCE) and practically obliterated two centuries after his death during the short-lived Qin Dynasty (221–206 BCE), which unified China, enshrined Legalism, and burned scholars and books alike. In the subsequent Han dynasty (206 BCE–220 CE), what survived to be reinterpreted became the official state ideology, and has influenced East Asian life to this day.

Confucianists valued humans above animals because of their capacity for moral cultivation. Under the Confucian tradition, female education in literature, music, or the arts was for low-class performers, concubines, and prostitutes. Confucius believed that a woman's morals were worth cultivating, but her intellect was not. Should a woman gain an opportunity to cultivate her morals through art, letters, and music, she would rank just below a cultivated man.

The Eastern Han (25 BCE–220 CE) was the beginning of official government rhetoric against females. Officials denied women formal education because they were theorized as being dull and unteachable, despite Confucius's belief to the contrary. These early Confucianists taught that non-procreative sex was corrupting and that women's greatest gift was giving a husband a male heir. Of prime importance were roles, familial relations, the moral autonomy of all, and treating others as one would like to be treated. As can be seen in the section "I See on High," in the *Odes*, China's greatest Confucian moral tome, Confucius can be seen as at best favoring men and at worst being misogynistic when he said "Disorder does not descend from Heaven. It is born of women." Contrary to popular belief, Confucius was criticized in his own life for the respect he showed to women.

VITAL LIFE FORCES, TAOISM, AND THE ART OF THE BEDCHAMBER

Taoism, as China's only popular native religion, developed complex and measured sexual prescriptions somewhat incongruous with its more freewheeling social philosophy, which sanctioned drinking, debauchery, and sexuality. Taoists based their cosmology on *yin* and *yang*, the lowly as virtuous, and change as the only constant. Their ultimate goal was oneness with the ultimate and great unnamable *Dao* (*Tao*, or Way), the progenitor of the "ten thousand things." Taoists argued that the "female" force is more capable of blending with the Way because it is yielding, while the "male" goes against the Way because *yang* creates its own change. Practically speaking, Taoism can be cast as a reaction to Confucianism's ritualization.

Taoists also practiced an "inner alchemy," or sexual science, that produced libraries of sex manuals, the first of which are now lost to history. The *Historic Records of the Western Han Dynasty* (221 BCE–220 CE) listed eight such sex manuals under the category *fang zhong*, or "Art of the Bedchamber." This list is apparently only the first record of what already had a long history. Also referred to as the "School of *Yin* and *Yang*" or the "Way of the *Yin*," these first eight texts are all ascribed to ancient sage kings of old or the somewhat mythical founder of Taoism, Lao Zi (Lao Tzu). They seem to have been widely circulated and, at their earliest stages, were concerned with longevity and immortality through sex acts.

By the Sui Dynasty (581–618), these sexology texts were omitted from the historical record. Instead, a new category of sex manuals emerged under "medical books." These handbooks recount the story of the sexual initiation of the legendary Yellow Emperor, a descendant of the fabled sage kings of remote antiquity, who founded China's first dynasty, the Xia, two thousands years BCE. He had three immortal sex education teachers, the Dark Girl, the Plain Girl, and Peng Zu, who initiated him into the entirety of sexual knowledge. These girls instructed later emperors and other males about the "jade stalk," which "rises at her *yin* influence" for penetration of the "jade gate." These secrets, so the story goes, had been transmitted from woman to woman since the Han

Dynasty. These girls taught the Yellow Emperor everything from the reason for different penis sizes to the importance of preserving ones vital essence and collecting the essence of others.

For early Taoists, *yin* and *yang* were only the beginning of their sexual vocabulary. The underlying energy is *qi* (*chi*), which circulates in the body, and is available to the Taoist sexual adept in the refined form, called *jing* (*ching*). In males, *jing* is semen. In females, *jing* is produced as vaginal secretions. Semen was seen as a man's most important possession and was limited. Female *qi*, produced during orgasm, was unlimited. Therefore, these texts go into detail about how to best pleasure female partners and thus collect their life essence. Male masturbation was frowned upon because it led to loss of *yang qi* without being replaced by *yin qi*. Cunnilingus and fellatio were both sanctioned because they left the practitioner with no net gain or loss in *qi*. According to texts, males could die because of loss of *qi*, but both males and females could reach immortality by absorbing the *qi* of their partners.

In early Taoist sex manuals, written by males for the benefit of males, the main goal was the collection of female essence, which was called "plucking *qi*" by the Tang Dynasty's (618–907) influential court physician Sun Simo. *Qi*, like oil in a lamp, he theorized, could be used up. For these practitioners, one girl was not enough. To "cultivate one's nature" (*yang xing*), a man must have sex with as many young girls as possible (preferably eight or more per night, if his harem was sufficient). These young girls should be virgins and ignorant in the sexual arts. For the sake of stamina and because of the preciousness of semen (*jing* essence), ejaculation was to be avoided as long as possible. Sex was a "flowery battle," and "victory" was achieved through exacting methods. The man should first excite her through foreplay "until the [woman's] nose is damp." He should then penetrate hard. After the woman reaches climax, he is to relax inside her and absorb her *jing* essence and allow his semen to return to nourish his brain along the "yellow river" of cerebro-spinal fluid.

Despite the view that Taoists were more "feminist" than Confucianists because they held the "female" in such high esteem, where sex is concerned, women were seen as little more than containers of life essence, available for male pleasure and longevity.

In later dynasties, these sexual manuals would all but disappear from circulation, being replaced by sexual literature and art. When sex manuals were listed as medical texts in later imperial histories, they concerned methods of producing offspring, not immortality.

These Taoist theories influenced the Indian Tantric tradition, which entered China in the eighth century. Along with Tibetan (Mahayana) Buddhism, Tantric practices gained some favor with Mongol emperors of the Yuan Dynasty (1264?–1368). Mahayana Buddhism generally gave few prescriptions for sex, except to avoid sensual indulgences, and the occasional tract against homosexuality, which did nothing to impede the male-male sexual tradition of imperial China.

"SHARING THE PEACH," OR, THE CHINESE MALE HOMOSEXUAL TRADITION

In the early Chinese tradition, as with the Greeks and Romans, same-sex sexual behavior did not essentialize a person as "homosexual." Records of male love exist in the Book of Poetry (*Shi Jing*) and as entries about male favorites in the courts of ten of the eleven Western Han emperors.

References to homosexual male coupling were allusions to historical stories. The earliest such allusion comes from the Zhou Dynasty and concerns the Duke of Ling and his favorite, Mizi Xia. When Mizi Xia sampled an exceptionally sweet peach from the Duke's orchard, he saved half of the peach for Ling. Ling was so moved that he publicly acknowledged his love for Mizi Xia. Thus, male homosexuality became known as "sharing the remaining peach" (*yu tao*). Another reference comes from the Western Han, where the Emperor Ai (6 BCE–1 CE) woke to find his sleeve under his sleeping lover. Rather than wake him, the emperor cut off his sleeve, thus starting a fad of the *duan xiu* or "cut sleeve" at court. The most popular of these references were used well into the Qing Dynasty (1644–1912).

By the Tang and Song Dynasties, there were few references to these imperial male favorites. Love of the "rear chamber" was seen as a threat to marriage obligations and woman's chance of marrying. Like women, male favorites could be a threat to statecraft and could even distract generals from battle. This period also leaves us with the first derogatory references to the male homosexual tradition.

Homosexual marriage was a frequent theme in Ming (1368–1644) and Yuan Dynasty (1264?–1368) fiction. In Fujian Province during the Ming Dynasty, homosexual male marriage was an institution. A young male would usually move in with an older male's family and take on all the attributes of a female wife, and he would be treated as a son-in-law. They eventually could adopt males to raise as sons. These marriages usually ended in heterosexual coupling because of filial obligations to continue the bloodline.

Female homosexuality does not receive the same attention as the male tradition. It is not included in the imperial histories and appeared in no way connected to male homosexuality. Even if a woman were financially and socially independent, which was rare, few escaped marriage or concubinage, except as nuns. The first references to anything resembling modern notions of lesbianism were mostly in the Guangzhou area. These "Golden Orchid Associations" of the Ming Dynasty organized something akin to wedding ceremonies. Couples could adopt female children. One person generally assumed the husband's role and the other the wife's.

The male homosexual tradition, though trampled by the Neo-Confucianists, who demanded familial obligation, survived to the end of the dynastic period. Modern Chinese live largely without knowledge of this history of permissive elite homosexuality.

NEO-CONFUCIANISTS AND THE EVOLUTION OF FAMILY LIFE

Comparatively very little is known about the structure of the Chinese family before the Song Dynasty (960–1279), when printing was invented and written sources became more widespread. It is known that the male was the undisputed official head of the household. Rank, though varying over time and locality, was generally reckoned based on gender and age. The oldest patriarch directed the family's finances. Younger brothers were subservient to older brothers. Mothers could beat their own sons, even in adulthood. Until the Warring States Period, it was legal for a man to kill his own son. Several generations lived together in a single house. Daughters were "married out."

Daughters were generally undesirable because of economic and patrilinial considerations. Only males could carry on the family name and daughters required dowries to attract male suitors—or a suitor's parents, as was usually the case. Unwanted daughters were often killed at birth or sold into slavery at age five or six. These trends strengthened with the rise of Neo-Confucian orthodoxy, starting as early as the Tang dynasty when scholar Han Yu (768–824) beginning calling for restraint in "unbridled passions."

Gaining strength in the Southern (Later) Song dynasty (1127–1279), neo-Confucianists promulgated an extreme form of the ancient philosophy. From references in the classics that men and women should not freely associate, scholars and officials justified gender segregation in all spheres of life. This required them to overlook almost all references to romantic and sexual love in the poetry of the classics.

Under succeeding dynasties, Neo-Confucianism generally gathered cultural currency. Talk of sex became taboo. Foot binding became widespread. Female infanticide became more common. Remarriage became rare as elites erected new monuments to the chaste female and the windowed martyr. Zhu Xi (1130–1200), one of the most influential Neo-Confucian scholars of his day, set the tone of the times in "Reflections on Things at Hand," when he wrote that "a man with passions has no strength, whereas a man of strength has no passions." The Neo-Confucianists departed from earlier schools with their rigid morality and a belief in the innate goodness of humans. Confucius believed goodness must be cultivated. In general, Neo-Confucianists naturalized gender distinctions, providing less opportunity for performative departure from gender roles.

Zhu Xi's teacher, Sima Guang (1019–1086), taught that, at seven years old, boys and girls should no longer eat together. At eight, girls should not leave inner chambers, and should not engage in song and dance. He taught that remarriage was bad for both men and women alike. Girls should learn women's work, which meant cooking, cleaning, and "instruction in compliance and obedience."

Though feminist historians attack Neo-Confucianists as deeply misogynistic, critics like Patricia Buckley Ebrey claim that the Neo-Confucianists' concern with remarriage reflected an extension of preexisting patriarchal concern for female welfare. Remarriage was seen as a threat to the financial stability of the family. These feminists also ascribe too much power to elite philosophers; one of Zhu Xi's disciples actually remarried.

In this complex time, women held roles as slaves, empresses, mothers, wives, merchants, and beggars, but their general sphere was that of the household. According to Neo-Confucianists, chaste and productive women laid the foundation for a nation. Women had their own work, like weaving, which played as important or more important a role in the economy of late imperial China than did much "male" agricultural work.

This Neo-Confucian philosophy, though pervasive, was not omnipresent or totally stifling. In many ways, masculinity was still seen as degrees of femininity. The well-positioned man took on elements of the female to gain favor and show loyalty to his superiors. But a man had the ability to change masters, whereas women were confined to the husbands (and husband's family) they were betrothed to and eventually married.

Men, meanwhile, were still free to sleep with whomever they wanted. During Neo-Confucian times, concubines, who had historically been confined to the households of the most elite, became more affordable for the common man. Concubines who had been trained in singing and literary arts could be rented for the day or the hour, thus blurring the distinctions between concubinage and prostitution.

PROSTITUTION

The origins of the world's oldest profession in China are vague, but by at least the seventh century BCE, there were hundreds of women living and working in palaces and government-owned markets. Prostitution had reached a peak of coordination and sophistication by the Tang and Song Dynasties. Male prostitution was banned during the Song, which hardly curtailed the ordered systems in major cities. During the Ming and Qing Dynasties, private male and female commercial prostitution was widespread, even during periods when the practice was ostensibly outlawed.

FOOT BINDING

One of the most prominent trends in female beauty during the later dynastic period is the practice of foot binding. Though references to beautiful women with small feet are almost as old as written history, foot binding is generally agreed to have emerged in the Northern Song (960–1127) and moved south during the Southern Song (1127–1279). It became widespread during the Ming Dynasty and peaked in the Qing. Even though Chinese literati first railed against this practice in the seventeenth century, it survived well into the Republican period with popular phrases like, "If you love your son, you don't go easy on his studies. If you love your daughter, you don't go easy on her foot binding."

For elite families, these tiny "golden lotus feet" were permanent symbols of their lives of leisure. For lower families, feet lent rank and gentility to a daughter otherwise without chance of raising her social standing. Between the ages of five and seven, girls underwent the painful procedure of having their small toes broken and bent under the foot to the heel and their feet wrapped. For these two years, they were forced into smaller and smaller "golden slippers," dancing and jumping on their feet to get them to the standard three inches or smaller. This impeded their ability to walk and work.

EUNUCHS

Though male foot binding was rare, mutilating the genitals to gain rank and power was not. Eunuchs were some of the few servants who could be trusted to serve palace elite, and even then, the intrigues of eunuchs in state affairs alone require volumes of history. Emperors, princes, wives, and others of high rank each had dozens or hundreds of personal eunuch attendants. Despite attempts by almost every philosophic persuasion in every era to limit eunuch ascendancy, the institution survived until the fall of the Qing Dynasty, when families were still castrating unwanted boys and grown men were undergoing voluntary surgeries for the chance to enter the imperial ranks.

SEX AND GENDER IN LITERATURE AND ART

Chinese art, literature, and other material culture relating to sex are the subject of many vibrant seams in academia. To do justice to this area would require more space than is available here.

Ancient archeological sources show that sexual art, toys, and gendered deities were widespread. One of the earliest female deities in popular religion, *Xiwangmu*, or the Queen Mother of the West, emerged during the Han Dynasty, when other gendered concepts entered art. Dildos of jade, wood, ivory, or plants that swelled when wet have existed for millennia.

Though the one surviving extant text is riddled with errors from an ignorant scribe, the Tang-era "Poetic Essay on the Supreme Joy of the Sexual Union of Yin and Yang and Heaven and Earth" attempted to record the entire range of sexual behavior, including topics of beauty, peasants' sex lives, monastery sex, wedding night tales, puberty, and tales of rape.

By the Ming and Qing Dynasties, literati with unparalleled leisure and erudition dallied in regions near the lower reaches of the Yangtze River in eastern China near Hangzhou and Shanghai. Ming literati centered in Hangzhou created a flourishing trade in erotic woodblock prints, which survived largely in Japanese collections. Erotic novels, women's poems, and widely varying literary works provide the best picture of the lives of everyday lives of Chinese in any dynasty.

With the fall of the Qing Dynasty in 1912, China's conceptions of sexuality and gender underwent significant influence by North American and European scientific thought. Nearly four thousand years of dynastic history had come to a close and with it the end of one of history's most unique, intricate, and isolated sexual cultures.

BIBLIOGRAPHY

Anderson, Mary M. 1990. *Hidden Power: The Palace Eunuchs of Imperial China.* Buffalo, NY: Prometheus.

Dikotter, Frank. 1995. *Sex, Culture and Modernity in China: Medical Science and the Construction of Sexual Identities in the Early Republic Period.* Honolulu: University of Hawaii Press.

Gilmartin, Christina; Gail Hershatter; Lisa Rofel; and Tyrene White, eds. 1994. *Engendering China: Women, Culture and the State.* Cambridge, MA: Harvard University Press.

Ebrey, Patricia Buckley. 2003. *Women and the Family in Chinese History.* New York: Routledge

Goldin, Paul Rakita. 2002. *The Culture of Sex in Ancient China.* Honolulu: University of Hawaii Press.

Goodman, Bryna, and Wend Larson. 2005. *Gender in Motion: Divisions of La bor and Cultural Change in Late Imperial and Modern China.* Lanham, MD: Rowman & Littlefield.

Hinsch, Brett. 1990. *Passions of the Cut Sleeve: The Male Homosexual Tradition in China.* Berkeley: University of California Press.

Hinsch, Brett. 2002. *Women in Early Imperial China.* Lanham, MD: Rowman & Littlefield.

Mann, Susan. 1997. *Precious Records: Women in China's Long Eighteenth Century.* Stanford, CA: Stanford University Press.

Ruan, Fu Fang. 1991. *Sex in China: Studies in Sexology in Chinese Culture.* New York: Plenum Press.

Van Gulik, R. H. 2003. *Sexual Life in Ancient China, a Preliminary Survey of Chinese Sex and Society from Ca. 1500 B.C. till 1644 A.D.* Boston: Brill.

Van Gulik, R. H. 2004. *Erotic Colour Prints of the Ming Period: With an Essay on Chinese Sex Life from the Han to the Ch'ing Dynasty. B.C 2006–A.D. 1644.* Boston: Brill.

Wang, Ping. 2000. *Aching for Beauty: Foot binding in China.* Minneapolis: University of Minnesota Press.

Wilhelm, R., and C. Baynes. 1967. *The* I Ching *or* Book of Changes. Bollingen Series, XIX. Princeton: Princeton University Press.

Joshua Wickerham

II. MODERN

Modern China usually refers to the period starting from the Republic of China. The Republic of China was established in 1911 and marked the end of imperial China's 2,000-year reign. With the beginning of the Republic came new political and economic systems. In practice and theory, inequalities of class were standard in premodern China. The ruling class was superior and gender division was deep rooted. Men outranked women in society, and in marriage husbands had more authority than wives. Women were confined to traditional domestic activities. Did this change in Modern China? This entry will discuss the dramatic changes that occurred regarding gender equality, marriage and divorce, sex education and research, homosexuality, and prostitution.

In Modern China the traditional political inequalities lost their legal force, especially after the establishment of the People's Republic of China (PRC) by the Chinese Communist Party (CCP) in 1949 when the CCP tried to eliminate most legal, social, and economic inequalities. In premodern China, the sexual customs, beliefs, and practices were shaped by medicine, metaphysics, or religious ideas, whereas in Modern China sex and gender has been more influenced by political movements and ideologies.

Chinese communism and ideology are noteworthy for reshaping sexual beliefs and gender roles in Modern China. The general premise of sexuality in socialist China is that an individual's function is to serve a public or social purpose, and like many aspects of individual activities, sexuality falls under political control. Sexuality is considered a worthy element for healthy development of the young. However, there is no clear boundary between public life and private life; all individual behavior (and sex behavior in particular) must be in accordance with the party's principles and ideologies. Correctness of behavior was part of the general structure of the society. Dialectic materialism, the guiding philosophy and principle, teaches that nature is governed by scientific truth and that the human body is a part of nature; therefore it is important for the youth of a nation to know the facts of life, defined by reproduction. The government tries to regulate medical, pedagogical, social, and political aspects of sexuality since it believes orderly, stable, and familiar relationships are essential to political, social, and economic success.

WOMEN CAN HOLD UP HALF THE SKY

The Cultural Revolution (1966–1976), a diminutive for the Great Proletarian Cultural Revolution, was officially launched in 1966 by communist leader Mao Zedong (1893–1976) as a movement that would fundamentally transform the individual and thus society. Denouncing the established ideologies, traditional beliefs, customs, and cultural and political remnants of imperial China as old fashioned, backward, and unscientific, China's new social movement affirmed that the state was for the citizens.

The political changes were expressed by slogans such as "Discard the four Olds; build the four News" and "Women can hold up half the sky," which were privately and publicly recited by school children, political cadres, workers, peasants, and soldiers.

"Women can hold up half the sky," a quotation from an essay by Mao Zedong, summarizes the gender equality he aimed to achieve. Gender inequality was ingrained in the Chinese; men symbolized dominance, superiority, strength, wisdom, and major force, whereas women were considered submissive, inferior, and the passive. This slogan symbolized the efforts of the CCP and the state to address the women's movement as part of its political and ideological mission. Early CCP ideology argued that women's liberation could only be accomplished when all working people were liberated. Only when the proletarians took complete control of political power would women reach full liberation.

March 8th was named Women's Day, a yearly occasion to celebrate women's contributions to the country. Many traditionally male professions and careers, such as the construction work force, military, and natural sciences, began to accept women workers.

In 1940 an editorial in *People's Daily*, the official newspaper of the CCP, stated that modern Chinese women must participate fully in all movements that benefit the state and nation in order to realize their own liberation. In 1949, when the CCP successfully established political control of the entire country, the party mandated that women enter the work force on an equal par with men. A woman's value and liberation were tied to her productivity and contribution to society.

In film, art, literature, opera, and ballet, during the time of the Cultural Revolution, female characters were often portrayed as political activists or military figures who, without exception, were unmarried revolutionaries, determined and devoted to communist ideals. Eight operas were promoted during the ten years of the movement, all of which had female protagonists aged twenty to sixty, and all of whom were presented as political entities rather than individuals. Overt expressions of feminine appearance and conduct were denounced. Women wore the same clothing as men, with only a slight style difference. The Red Guard, the CCP's youth league, expressed its disapproval of anyone who dressed differently; members monitored people in the streets and cut trousers they deemed to be too long. Scholars have used the term *socialist androgyny* to describe the reworking of female gender during this period. Many scholars, in China and elsewhere, consider this approach to women's liberation as a denial of the European and North American concept of feminism, which refers to a gendered analysis of the position and representation of women in society.

SEX EDUCATION AND RESEARCH

Modern China was marked by the introduction of new emerging disciplines such as psychology. In the early 1920s, sex education and sex instruction, sexual advice, and lifestyle choices were widely discussed and covered by newspapers, magazines, and other media as a part of the urban culture; however these advances in thinking never reached rural and other remote areas.

Early proponents of sex education include famous writers and social activists such as Lu Xun, Hu Shi, Zhou Zhuoren, and others. In 1909 Lu Xun, who received his medical education in Japan, introduced sexual anatomy to biology students. In 1919 Hu Shi advocated for women's rights, and Dr. Zhang Yaoxiang, a U.S.-trained psychologist, conducted the first survey on sex and translated a comprehensive lecture series on sex education, complete with a curriculum.

In 1921 Dr. Zhang Jingshen, a scholar educated in France, taught the history of psychology, esthetics and contraception, birth control, eugenics, sex education, sex research, and marriage at Beijing University. He established campus-wide clubs and societies so that he could systematically introduce sexology. Later Zhang Jingshen wrote for a popular newspaper, asking the public to send him their sex histories. Using these submissions, he published, in 1926, the first issues of a periodical called *Sex History*. Later in Shanghai, he published a sex education series, as well as the Chinese translation of English psychologist Havelock Ellis's (1859–1939) works.

In 1936 medical doctor Din Zhan opened a psychological counseling service in Beijing. In 1949 sociologist Fei Xiaotong published a book called *The Reproductive System*, which discussed the roles of both genders in human reproduction.

During the 1920s and 1930s, visitors from Europe and North America spoke to Chinese audiences. These included birth-control leader Margaret Sanger (1883–1966), who spoke at Beijing University, and German physician Magnus Hirschfield (1868–1935), who visited Shanghai and lectured at the Shanghai Women's Club. Another well-known writer, Zhou Zhuoren, introduced Ellis's sex studies and called for better sex education and a new, modern morality. Pan Guangdan completed translating Ellis's *Psychology of Sex* (1933) in 1948.

After 1949 the establishment of the communist regime remapped sex education. A number of political figures including Mao Zedong, Deng Xiaoping, and Zhou Enlai expressed the importance of sex education. Deng Xiaoping backed the Chinese Women's Federation on the absolute necessity and benefit of using contraceptives. Mao Zedong stated that sex education should start at the junior high school level. Zhou Enlai believed that students should be educated about contraception and that understanding issues related to sexual health was important to adolescents. He also pointed out that the most appropriate time for sex education was very early in the development of both boys and girls. A number of pamphlets discussing sex appeared, mostly written by doctors. One, called *Sex Knowledge* (1956), had a first printing of more than 800,000 copies and sold more than 1,400,000 copies in its second year. This progress was hindered by the Cultural Revolution, when sex education was suppressed since it had no role in the political platform. Not surprisingly, a population boom occurred during those years as well.

In 1979 economic reform and open door policies sponsored by the CCP made sex education possible once again. In 1980 China Family Planning Association was officially established. The government's department of education offered population education to high school students as a way of introducing contraception and population control. Also in the early 1980s, symposiums focusing on marriage, family, population control, and sex education were held in many cities. Wu Janping, a U.S.-trained urologist and influential political figure, edited and published the journal *Sexual Medicine* (1983). In southern China, from 1985 to 1994, some local governments sponsored the first lecture series on sex psychology and sexually transmitted disease (STD) control and prevention.

Sex research topics commonly include sex history, sex cultures, STDs, family planning, and adolescence. Since 2000 studies have focused more on sexual behaviors and gender issues, such as transgender and homosexuality, which have high profiles in the media and with the general public but still remain a largely taboo subject. News media covered the first two transsexual surgery cases, one from male to female in 1984, and the other from female to male in 1992. Both operations were performed at Beijing University hospital. Due to increasing wealth of the population, more relaxed social policies, and more individual freedom, the number of sex education and research organizations has increased greatly since the 1980s.

Influential, government-endorsed organizations include the Chinese Sex Education Research Society, founded in 1985 in Shanghai; the Sex Education and Research Society, founded in 1986 in Shanghai; the Sexology of China Association, the Institute for Research in Sexuality and Gender, and the China Family Planning Association, all founded in Beijing in 1990; and the Shanghai Family Planning Association and Shanghai International Center for Population Communication in China, both founded in the 1990s. These organizations function as major research and information centers. In 1984 the Beijing Society for Studies on Marriage and Family conducted one of the first surveys of sex, love, marriage, and family conflict. The Shanghai Sex Sociological Research Center, established and led by Liu Dalin during the 1980s, conducted a survey and published a report called *National Sex Civilization Survey* (1990). The report, which included information from subjects in twenty-seven provinces in China, analyzed 19,559 individual responses to 239 questions concerning sexual and reproductive history. Interestingly the government did not interfere with the report or take any credit for it since the study was financed entirely by private individuals and organizations.

Sex research organizations train sex educators and the general public through workshops and conferences. The First National Workshop on Sex Education was held in Shanghai in 1985. The *Handbook of Sex Knowledge* was published by the Scientific and Technological Publishing House in 1985. In 1988 the first college-level sexology course was taught in China's Peoples University in Beijing. The course was titled *Training Workshop on Sex Science* and included twenty topics. By 1993 about one quarter of all universities and colleges offered courses on human sexuality or sex education. Nationwide conferences on sexology included the annual conference of the Congress of Science of Sex. The first International Conference of Sexology was held in Shanghai, also in 1992. Sex research or education publications included *Sexology* (1992; formerly known *as Sexology of China, Journal of Chinese Sexology*) and *Apollo and Selene*, a bilingual (Chinese/English) magazine that was published by the Asian Federation for Sexology in the same year.

MARRIAGE AND DIVORCE

Arranged marriage and multiple-wife households were characteristic of traditional marriage in China before 1949. Courtship and dating were nonexistent since marriage was arranged by parents or matchmakers, and couples often did not know each other until the wedding day. In fact public displays of affection between woman and man were considered taboo; a woman would be condemned as immoral if she approached a man in public. Social and economic compatibilities were considered important factors for a stable marriage, personality traits or physical attributes less so. In Modern China, young people from urban areas, often well-educated, make deliberate choices to avoid arranged marriages The first law stating that marriage should be based on the free-choice of partners, on monogamy, on equal rights of both sexes, and on the protection of the lawful interests of women and children, was not enacted until 1950. The law prohibited bigamy, concubinage, child betrothal, or any interference with the remarriage of widows, and prohibited giving money or gifts to entice someone into a marriage. These principles were part of the PRC Marriage Law, drafted in the 1980s.

Young people welcomed the freedom to choose marriage partners. However, public courtship was still usually considered a prelude to marriage. Despite the fact that all Chinese had the legal right to freely choose marriage partners, many rural youths simply did not have access to the same social and work networks available to urban dwellers. Clashes between the popular presentation of freedom in the media and the reality of rural life caused some young women to commit suicide when they became the focus of gossip about improper sexual behavior.

In pre-1949 China, when polygamy dominated, the divorce rate was relatively low, but has increased since the end of the 1970s. The most commonly cited reason for divorce had been infidelity of the husband. During most of Chinese history, divorce was considered to be a personal failure or a disgrace to the family. In the early twenty-first century, society more often accepts divorce. Many divorces are initiated by women who will not settle for unhappy marriages since they have economic independence through education and career choices.

First Beijing Wedding Photography Exhibition. *Wedding photography has proved a booming business in China with even the smallest towns offering this service. While white silk dresses are part of the wardrobe in photo studios they are rarely worn at real weddings in China where red is the traditional color for brides.* © ADRIAN BRADSHAW/EPA/CORBIS.

PROSTITUTION

When the CCP took political power in 1949, it abolished prostitution. In 1949 the Beijing municipal government enacted a series of policies designed to close all city brothels and to arrest prostitutes and brothel owners, procurers, and pimps. Other cities, such as Shanghai and Tanjing, followed suit. Thousands of prostitutes were jailed or sent to reform camps. In 1957, during the first National People's Congress, the Rules on the Control of and Punishment Concerning Public Security of the PRC were passed. The new laws effectively banned prostitution. In 1979, again during the National People's Congress, the first criminal law against prostitution was enacted. The penalty for forcing a female to engage in prostitution was a term of imprisonment of three to ten years.

However, despite the law and the severe punishment possible, prostitution persisted. Since the end of the Cultural Revolution, the incidence of prostitution in economically prosperous cities such as Shanghai, Canton, Shenzhen, and Chengdu has risen dramatically. In 1986 the government demanded the eradication of prostitution in an attempt to curtail STDs. According to police reports, in 1987 the average number of prostitution arrests in Canton alone was 11,000.

While brothels were illegal, prostitutes still worked in entertainment and service establishments such as hotels and hair salons. The increasing number of prostitution arrests resulted in the expansion of prison camps. In 1987 sixty-two new prison camps were built in Canton. Many prostitutes in labor camps were reeducated and eventually released, but pimps or human traffickers sometimes received death sentences.

OBSCENITY LAWS

Communist ideology focused on the productivity of people as a social unit, whereas erotic or non-reproductive sexual activity was viewed as morally wrong, socially irresponsible, and a kind of self-indulgence only associated with bourgeois lifestyle—something unacceptable to the Chinese government. CCP reports that no erotic materials were produced in the PRC during the 1950s or 1960s

In 1970, along with the economic reform policy of the CCP, China was flooded with X-rated movies and videos smuggled from Hong Kong and other countries. In time, *yellow*, or pornographic, videos, which had been beyond the financial reach of the average citizen, became much more accessible due to their availability in video stores, hotels, and other venues.

The CCP reacted swiftly to the spread of such materials. Raids on sellers were frequent and materials were confiscated. In 1985 the state promulgated a new anti-pornography law: Underground publishing houses were suppressed. By 1988, during the National People's Congress, lawmakers introduced stiffer penalties for pornography dealers. Dealers could be imprisoned for life if the total value of the pornographic materials was between 150,000 yuan and 500,000 yuan. Ruan's book, *Sex in China* (1991), cited the *International Daily News* (August 24, 1989) as reporting that in 1989 there was an intense effort to eradicate publishing and distribution venues for erotica. More than 11 million books and magazines with explicit sexual content were confiscated and 2,000 distribution centers were raided. In 1990 the highest court in China ruled that courts could impose death sentences on those convicted of human trafficking, including prostitution, and pornography.

HOMOSEXUALITY

In modern China, colonial-era hooliganism statutes, Cultural Revolution campaigns, general sexual taboos, and vestiges of Neo-Confucianism ensured that, for most of the twentieth century, same-sex coupling remained almost completely misunderstood and strictly forbidden. For most Chinese gays, lesbians, and bisexuals, being attracted to the same sex meant a life of denial, punishment, secrecy, and shame. Beginning in the late twentieth century, academic debates and media reports, along with the rise of gay/lesbian bars and social clubs, have combined to give Chinese homosexuals more possibilities to gain legal rights and basic recourse against discrimination.

Though post-1911 campaigns against Confucianism resulted in a successful women's liberation movement, neither nationalist modernization nor communist collectivization of the traditional family could disrupt the Confucian tenets of marriage and childbearing. Most citizens of modern China—regardless of sexual orientation—enter into heterosexual marriages. Chinese are expected to marry by the age of thirty. In 2003 the government of Taiwan promulgated, but never enacted, a law to legalize same-sex marriage. In 2006 same-sex marriage remains illegal in all areas of China.

The catch-all colonial-era hooliganism law enacted by the Republican government made homosexuality and other activities criminal offenses. This statute remained in force after 1949, though the Communists only legally codified this as law in 1979. During the Cultural Revolution, when all aspects of an individual's life could be exposed as potentially *anti-revolutionary*, the government targeted those suspected of deviant sexuality. In 1991 Hong Kong decriminalized consensual sexual activity between two men over twenty-one years of age. The government of the PRC revoked the hooliganism laws in 1997, which tacitly decriminalized private homosexuality, although public displays of any sexual behavior remain illegal in the early twenty-first century. In Taiwan, since the mid 1990s, public political support for homosexuals has been widespread.

Homosexuality received scant attention from the sexual education reform movements in the 1920s and 1930s. Some sexologists and sociologists considered same-sex love (*tong xing lian*) the opposite of so-called natural opposite-sex love (*yi xing lian*). Homosexuality was considered a filthy habit, which could contaminate, infect, and corrupt the social organism. In 1946 Pan Guangdan, a Shanghai sexologist and sociologist, published one of the first modern Chinese essays on the history of Chinese homosexuality, included in his translation of Ellis's *Psychology of Sex*. In 2001 the Chinese Psychology Association removed homosexuality from its list of mental illnesses. Despite the strong political, medical, and social pressure against homosexuality, because of China's long history of homosexual acceptance and lack of religious persecution, Chinese homosexuals have largely avoided the virulent opposition characterized by queer rights struggles in North America and Europe during the second half of the twentieth century.

In the 1980s nonjudgmental studies of homosexuality began to appear. Shanghai University sexologist Liu Dalin's first nationwide sexual survey on homosexuals was published in 1990. In 1991 sociologist Li Yinhe and her husband Wang Xiaobo published *Their World: A Study of the Male Homosexual Community in China*. The book, with its sociological and anthropological dimensions, became a bestseller when it was updated and republished as *The Homosexual Subculture* in 1998. That same year, Qingdao University medical school professor Dr. Zhang Beichuan began publishing *Friend Exchange* (*Pengyou Tongxin*), China's first gay newsletter. Taiwanese writer Pai Hsien-yung published the first modern gay Asian novel, *Crystal Boys* (1983), which is the basis of a number of films and a television series in Taiwan.

In the late 1980s and early 1990s, a few media reports in larger cities like Guangzhou, Shanghai, and Beijing contained gay-themed stories. The subject is still regularly censored and underreported in the PRC.

Comrade (*tongzhi*) is the most common slang term used by Chinese gays. In Cantonese, *Gei* is a popular slang transliteration of gay. In Mandarin Chinese, *Lala* is the most common word for Chinese lesbians.

The first *tongzhi* meeting was held in Hong Kong in 1996. At this meeting the group established a strategy to combat homophobia and secure equal rights for all Chinese sexual minorities.

In China, transgender individuals are generally excluded from the European and North American concept of Gay, Lesbian, Bisexual, Transgender (GLBT) or queer, although transvestitism and drag in gay clubs is not uncommon. Chinese often see transgender people as having a medical condition, whereas homosexuality is more often regarded as a choice or developmental phase.

Activist-scholar and Shanghai Medical University graduate Dr. Wan Yanhai started China's first HIV/AIDS hotline in Shanghai in 1991, which also served the homosexual community. Wan Yanhai also founded one of the first HIV/AIDS concern groups, AIZHI, in Beijing in 1994. Though police monitored and shut down early consultation efforts, every major Chinese city has HIV/AIDS hotlines in the early twenty-first century. The largest cities also have lesbian, homosexual legal rights, and sexual consultation hotlines. In the early 2000s, the PRC began to take the HIV/AIDS crisis seriously, instructing all centers for disease control to work with and educate *tongzhi* groups on the control and prevention of the spread of the virus.

In 2004 Fudan University's medical college, in cooperation with the Chi Heng Foundation, organized the mainland's first class on homosexuality. The graduate health course attracted considerable media attention, despite enrolling only three students. In the fall of 2005, the first undergraduate class—also at Fudan—attracted a full roster of students and even more journalists.

The Republican period saw the emergence of an elite civil society devoted to advancing sexual discourse. Communist appropriation of sexual education and policy to government bodies hampered this debate. Beginning in the 1980s, limited discourse on anti-discrimination, equal rights, and sexual freedom reemerged with a clearer vision of China's long history of homosexuality.

BIBLIOGRAPHY

Cui, Zi'en. 2002. "Filtered Voices: Representing Gay People in Today's China," *IIAS Newsletter* 29: 13.

Dikotter, Frank. 1995. *Sex, Culture and Modernity in China: Medical Science and the Construction of Sexual Identities in the Early Republican Period.* London: Hurst & Company.

Evans, Harriet. 1997. *Women and Sexuality in China: Female Sexuality and Gender Since 1949.* New York, Continuum.

Liu, Dalin. 2005. *Zhongguo Tongxinglian Yanjiu* [Chinese homosexual research]. Shanghai: Zhongguo Shehui Chubanshe.

Pai, Hsien-yung. 1989. *Crystal Boys*, trans. Howard Goldblatt. San Francisco. Gay Sunshine Press.

Ruan, Fang Fu. 1991. *Sex in China: Studies in Sexology in Chinese Culture.* New York: Plenum.

Watson, Rubie S., and Patricia B. Ebrey. 1991. *Marriage and Inequality in Chinese Society.* Berkeley: University of California Press.

Wile, Douglas. 1992. *Art of the Bedchamber: The Chinese Sexual Yoga Classics Including Women's Solo Meditation Texts.* Albany: State University of New York Press.

Joshua Wickerham
Liana Zhou

III. EROTIC ART

The earliest representations of sex in Chinese art date back to 7000 BCE, and sex has been a topic of artistic interest ever since. In prehistoric China, it is likely that people admired natural formations of the female and male sexual organs in caves, ravines, or rocks. Clay vessels with representations of the vulva can be dated to approximately 3000 BCE Rock cuttings dating roughly to 1500 BCE represent sexual organs, and in the Shizhong Temple (Yunnan Province) there is still a large carved stone vagina, which stands in the midst of countless Buddha sculptures.

From the era of the Yellow Emperor (2697–2597 BCE; the founder of Taoism) forward, when the legendary Dark and White Maidens wrote their classics in the art of sex in a question-and-answer format with him, erotic drawings accompanied sex-related texts. Though most of the illustrations are no longer extant, later authors mention that texts such as *Xuan Nü Jing* (Classic of the Dark Maiden) and *Su Nü Jing* (Classic of the White Maiden), which included long lists of sexual exercises, did include pictures. The genre of erotic art known as *spring palace*, or couples having sex in springtime when women went out picking mulberries for silkworms, appeared in the first century CE (eastern Han period) on sculpted bricks and continued in paintings on scrolls and silk.

Medieval erotic art was influenced by courtesan culture and the establishment of the sexual symbolism of bound feet in the tenth century CE Erotic art showed all of the sexual situations, positions, and pairings described in sex-related poems, songs, plays, and stories. These included prostitution, same-sex partners, fellatio, cunnilingus, masturbation, use of dildos, and bestiality. The best-known Ming erotic artists, Tang Yin (1470–1523) and Qiu Ying (b. mid-sixteenth century), painted such scenes on silk scrolls and were among the first to sign their work. Painters and wood-block carvers illustrated sex-related fiction in the late Ming (1368–1644) and early Qing (1644–1912) dynasties, with *Jin Ping Mei*

(1617; The golden lotus) and *Rou Pu Tuan* (1634; The carnal prayer mat) by Li Yu (1611–c. 1680) being among the most popular.

Later Qing erotic artists deviated little from the standards established in the Ming dynasty. They shaped a variety of sexual scenes in bronze and ivory, or painted or enameled porcelain vessels of all sorts in the eighteenth century: chamber pots, perfume burners, goblets, bowls, and snuff bottles. In the nineteenth century, paintings of courtesans on glass and silk-covered boxes with erotic scenes inlaid with carved stone and mother-of-pearl were popular.

By the end of the nineteenth century, refinement and attention to classical themes in Chinese erotic art were disappearing as the ability to mass-produce print and three-dimensional objects increased. It began to show such Western influences as European-style clothes, larger breasts, and longer penises. Much erotic art was destroyed after World War II and in the Cultural Revolution in the late 1960s and early 1970s. As access to the Internet has widely increased, however, Chinese artists and art collectors in the late twentieth and early twenty-first centuries are able to hold virtual shows of drawings, paintings, photographs, and sculptures.

BIBLIOGRAPHY

Beurdeley, Michel; Kristofer Schipper; Chang Fu-Jui; and Jacques Pimpaneau. 1969. *Chinese Erotic Art*, trans. Diana Imber. Rutland, VT: Charles E. Tuttle.

Liu, Dalin. 2000. *Zhongguo Xing Shi Tu Jian* (Illustrated hard book of Chinese sex history). 2 vols. Changchun Shi, China: Shi dai wen yi chu ban she.

Yimen, Rev. 1997. *Dreams of Spring: Erotic Art in China from the Bertholet Collection*. Amsterdam: Pepin Press.

Donna J. Drucker

IV. EROTIC LITERATURE

Erotic literature has a long history in China and it includes all literary forms: poetry, prose, drama, short stories, and novels. Sun Kaiti's *A Catalogue of Chinese Works of Popular Fiction*, published in 1932, is the only known bibliography that included a *pornography* category. Under this heading there were listed forty-two books, some of which were not examined by Sun because of his lack of access to them or because they were simply nonexistent at his time (other reference works documented their prior existence). Story or fiction writing was considered, in Chinese tradition, less prestigious than the writing of formal *classics*. Therefore, Chinese literary authors received no official recognition and in fact would write anonymously. With erotic literature, authors had all the more reason to hide their identities. *Bai Yuan Chuan* (One hundred love stories), *Deng Yue Yuan* (The lamp and moon), and *Hua Ying Jin Zhen* (Fragrant flower) were listed in Sun's catalogue. The most influential works are *Su E Pian* (The lady of the moon), *Jin Ping Mei* (Golden lotus), and *Rou Pu Tuan* (Prayer mats of the flesh); without exception, the authorship of all remain unknown.

Su E Pian was published in 1610 during the Ming dynasty. This rare book contains ninety illustrations that describe forty-three lovemaking positions and the landscape of the lovemaking locations. The preface, by Fang Hu Xian Ke ("The Immortal Square Pot"), mentions the author as being Ye Hua Sheng, another pen name. The novel features Su E, a talented and well-versed young woman, who is one of the concubines of Master Wu. Su E and Wu perform sexual acts in forty-three forms, each of which are poetically named by Su E. The author uses elegant language to describe the outdoor and indoor scenes and how the couple's sexual imagination and practice are inspired and aroused by the natural surroundings. Some sexual positions are given titles, such as Flowers Longing for Butterflies, The Union of Ying and Yang, Boat Widthwise over the Ferry, Lightless on the Palm, and Stopping the Horse to Pull the Saddle. The only complete copy survives at the Kinsey Institute Library in Bloomington, Indiana.

Rou Pu Tuan was written by Li Yu in 1634 and prefaced by the author, who believed that sex acts between a man and a woman benefited one's longevity and that sexual pleasure mitigated the suffering and miseries of daily life. According to Li Yu, eunuchs and Buddhist monks, who lacked such sex acts and pleasure, often had shorter lives as a consequence. The protagonist of Yu's story is a young scholar wanting to enlighten his wife about sexual pleasures. Though he makes many daring and desperate attempts to change her sexual attitudes, he always fails. That is until he purchases an album of erotic paintings. The album, by a well-known artist, contains thirty-six paintings, each of which correspond to a line in the Tang dynasty poem "Spring Reigns in all the Thirty-six Palaces." Using the album as a proper and valid sex education tool ensures the wife's sexual awakenings. The story continues with sexual acts among the husband, his wife, and other sexual partners. In the end, his sexual adventures get him into many troubles, and he retreats to a monastery as a devout Buddhist. There the abbot explains to him that his sexual experience was the necessary path for his salvation, thus, the *prayer mat of the flesh*.

Jin Ping Mei is perhaps the best known Chinese erotic novel and was also published in the Ming dynasty. The novel uses colorful, colloquial language to tell the sexual stories of Ximen Qing and his numerous sexual partners and wives. In it, there are explicit descriptions of oral and anal intercourse as well as details about aphrodisiacs and sexual toys. This novel was the first fictional work to depict sexuality in a graphically explicit manner. It describes in detail the downfall of the Ximen clan during the years 1111–1127, the Southern Song dynasty. *Jin Ping Mei* is named for the three women of Ximen: Pan Jinlian (whose name means "Golden Lotus"), Li Pinger, and Pang Chunmei, a maid who rose to power within the family. A key moment in the novel, the seduction of the lascivious and adulterous Pan Jinlian, occurs early in the book and is taken from an episode in another well-known Chinese novel. After secretly murdering the husband of Pan, Ximen takes her as one of his wives. The story follows the domestic sexual struggles of the women within his clan as they clamor for prestige and influence while the Ximen clan gradually declines in power. *Jin Ping Mei* was reprinted in 1983 with much of its sexually explicit passages purged or modified.

Whereas pieces of erotic literature were often well circulated underground to prevent prosecution, they were among the first novels to be burned or destroyed by government censors throughout Chinese history. Their existence, survival, and destruction were seldom documented or studied. Erotic literature was banned after the People's Republic of China was founded in 1949; rules and regulations associated with public security directly outlawed pornography and obscene material. Individuals responsible for production or distribution of obscene or absurd books, periodicals, or picture books were punishable by detention and a fine. During the early years of the Chinese Communist/Socialist government and the Cultural Revolution, erotic expressions were nonexistent. After the 1970s, along with the market reforms and the open-door policy to the outside world, erotic literature was produced and circulated in the underground world but destroyed under regular surveillance by the government.

BIBLIOGRAPHY

Humana, Charles, and Wang Wu. 1971. *The Ying-Yang: The Chinese Way of Love.* London: Tandem.

Ruan, Fang Fu. 1991. *Sex in China.* New York: Plenum.

Wen Huang

V. WOMEN'S ROLES IN MODERN

The history of female emancipation has had a strong relationship with the history of Chinese modernization since the late nineteenth century. For those engaged in the emancipation struggle, the image of modern woman combined the idea of emancipating the Chinese people from the Qing government with thoughts of liberating women from the extended family and old customs. The hope for a strong China was projected onto the image of the strong female. The growth of feminism in the West contributed to the emergence of Chinese female revolutionaries who represented the ideal form of the Chinese nationalist woman.

The New Culture Movement of 1915 was the first major revival of the issue of women's liberation since the late Qing period. Chinese male intellectuals extended the rebellion against Chinese tradition to embrace female emancipation, grounding it at the same time in Western ideas of individualism and liberal values, and this deepened with the May Fourth Movement in 1919. Women were now part of *New Youth,* and issues of women's rights and women's status in society were raised in the public sphere. The May Fourth Movement also laid the foundation for reform of women's rights in family law, political participation, education, and career during the 1920s and 1930s. For example, in order to improve women's rights in marriage and reduce women's suffering from physical abuse and abandonment, divorce law was reformed in December 1930.

The Chinese Marxist view of women was formed in the wake of the feminist discourses of the May Fourth Movement. Chinese Marxists made a distinction between *nüxing* and *funü,* both terms for women, but with different implications. *Funü* carried the meaning of *kinswomen,* and referred to all Chinese women, but particularly country-dwellers. In contrast, the Marxist *funü* was "the product of revolutionary practice and existed in a future world, after the revolution" (Barlow 1994, pp. 268–269). For the Chinese Marxists, *nüxing,* a neologism from the May Fourth era, belonged to bourgeois ideology.

The concept of the "virtuous wife and good mother" was also central to the process of Chinese modernization, just as it became prevalent in other East Asian countries from the late nineteenth century on. The modern woman's most important role was to be the mother of citizens (Judge 2002, p. 41).

This idea of good mother and virtuous wife then became one of the main themes during the New Life Movement, which was initiated by Chiang Kai-shek and his wife Soong Mei-ling in 1934. Based on Christian ideals, as well as traditional family values, Soong Mei-ling urged women to re-recognize the importance of family and of their new role for the whole society. Home economics was the subject for modern women to study. Soong Mei-ling thought educated women should teach their female neighbors how to write, how to read, and how to educate children.

Women's involvement in the war effort during the Sino-Japanese War from 1937 to 1945 helped consolidate the changes won in previous decades, and the women's movement entered a new chapter after 1949.

BIBLIOGRAPHY

Barlow, Tani E. 1994. "Theorizing Woman: *Funü, Guojia, Jiating*." In *Body, Subject Power in China*, ed. Angela Zito and Tani E. Barlow. Chicago: University of Chicago Press.

Judge, Joan. 2002. "Citizens or Mothers of Citizens? Gender and the Meaning of Modern Chinese Citizenship." In *Changing Meanings of Citizenship in Modern China*, ed. Merle Goldman and Elizabeth J. Perry. Cambridge, MA: Harvard University Press.

Weipin Tsai

CHLAMYDIA

SEE *Sexually Transmitted Diseases.*

CHRIST

The body of Christ was central to late medieval and early modern European culture, not merely as a symbol or an idea but as a physical presence. It hung from crosses in churches and homes and along roadsides, shone from stained-glass windows, and gestured from scaffold and wagon stages. In the form of the Eucharist, Christ's body was not only consumed daily at mass, but also paraded through city streets once per year and reverently displayed in countless chapels for perpetual adoration. It was the object of spiritual meditation and devotion that many now find startlingly physical in focus, and often unexpectedly gendered, or overtly erotic.

CORPUS CHRISTI

The fourth Lateran Council defined the long-held doctrine of transubstantiation in 1215, and devotion to the sacrament soon increased. The doctrine holds that the Eucharistic host or wafer actually becomes the body of Christ upon consecration by the priest at the words of institution, "hoc est corpus meum" (this is my body), while retaining the natural appearance and taste of bread. The Feast of Corpus Christi, first established in Liège in 1246 to celebrate the Real Presence, was formally instituted by Pope Urban IV in 1264, and again by Clement V in 1311; within the next century this midsummer feast became one of the most important events in the church calendar, associated with major processions and theatrical performances. In York, England, a processional cycle of biblical plays produced by trade guilds displaced the ecclesiastical procession of Corpus Christi to the following day; seeing Christ in the flesh, as represented by actors, apparently won out in the popular imagination over seeing Christ in a wafer. Like the procession, however, in which the consecrated host was held high and paraded through the city streets, the plays emphasized the need and desire to see Christ: Characters repeatedly drew attention to his physical presence. The ability to see, touch, or consume the true body of Christ at virtually any time, in the form of the consecrated host, continued to foster devotion, ritual, and superstition. Demand grew to see the moment of transformation, itself associated with the miraculous power to preserve the observer from danger or death, while accounts (and representations) of miraculous bleeding hosts proliferated, often in relation to anti-semitic legends of host desecration.

IMITATIONS OF CHRIST

Many theologians unsurprisingly emphasized faith and good works over visual representation or sensory perception. The still-popular devotional treatise *De imitatione Christi* (The imitation of Christ), published anonymously in 1418 but now attributed to Thomas à Kempis, warns against a critical examination of spiritual mysteries such as transubstantiation, which rely on faith rather than proof or sensory perception. The treatise advocates a life of cheerful, humble devotion and virtue, filled with quiet contemplation and free of passion.

Others took a more visceral approach. The influential Pseudo-Bonaventurean *Meditationes vitae Christi* (Meditations on the life of Christ), composed in the fourteenth century, promoted affective piety through detailed, emotionally stirring meditation on the life of Jesus. Each moment was to be visualized in an imaginative reconstruction of events that might depart significantly from the Gospel accounts. What mattered far more than historical accuracy was a sense of immediacy, of one's personal presence at the event, and an empathetic identification with Christ or with witnesses such as his mother. Horrifying invented details of the Passion narrative such as the scourging of Jesus with knotted or metal-studded whips that repeatedly tore his naked flesh were elaborated in the visions of fourteenth-century mystics such as St. Bridget (Birgitta) of Sweden and Richard Rolle de Hampole and Margery Kempe of England, long before they were filmed for Mel Gibson's *The Passion of the Christ* (2004). The stretching of Jesus's arms on the cross to fit prebored holes for the nails, featured by all the above-mentioned authors, was also represented in the York Crucifixion pageant. Some two dozen actors would have played Jesus in a full production of the York plays, all on different wagon stages, effectively promoting the image of Jesus as Everyman more than as a particular individual. This, too, may have encouraged men and women to imagine Christ's body in a wide variety of highly personal ways.

While an emphasis on his emotional and physical suffering was common, many women in particular also dwelt at length upon more pleasurable ideas, such as the Nativity, or the physical perfection of Christ's body. In the *Revelations* of Bridget of Sweden, immediately after recounting the horrors of the Crucifixion, Jesus's mother describes the physical perfections of her son at the age of twenty, remarking on his hair (dark blond [*crocea brunea*] in the Latin version, auburn in a Middle English translation), pale skin, and red lips, and noting that even his enemies liked to look at him (4:70). Often such visions and meditations coincided with particular events in the church calendar. They were also closely associated with the physical host itself. As Caroline Walker Bynum (1991) states:

> The humanity of Christ with which women joined in the eucharist was the physical Jesus of the manger and of Calvary. Women from all walks of life saw in the host and the chalice Christ the baby, Christ the Bridegroom, Christ the tortured body on the cross ... Most prominent, however, was the Christ of the cross. No religious woman failed to experience Christ as wounded, bleeding, and dying.
>
> *(pp. 130–131)*

Women in particular participated in this suffering, through physical illness and often severe self-mortification.

BRIDES OF CHRIST

Margery Kempe, who like some of her contemporaries suffered frequent uncontrollable fits of weeping at thoughts of Christ, envisioned herself not only as a witness to the Passion, having walked in his steps in Jerusalem on pilgrimage, but also as a servant first to St. Anne, at the birth of Mary, and then to Mary herself, witnessing the births of both John the Baptist and of Jesus. A married woman who bore fourteen children before demanding chastity from her husband, Margery also had visions of a relationship with the adult Jesus that strike the modern reader as remarkably intimate. In one vision she weds Jesus in the presence of his mother and a multitude of saints and angels, after which he tells her:

> thu mayst boldly, whan thu art in thi bed, take me to the as for thi weddyd husbond, as thy derworthy derlyng, and as for thy swete sone, for I wyl be lovyd as a sone schuld be lovyd wyth the modyr and wil that thu love me, dowtyr, as a good wife owyth to love hir husbonde. And therfor thu mayst boldly take me in the armys of thi sowle and kyssen my mowth, myn hed, and my fete as swetly as thow wylt. (Kempe, Chap. 36: you may boldly, when you are in your bed, take me to you as your wedded husband, as your beloved darling, and as your sweet son, for I desire to be loved as a son should be loved by his mother and desire that you love me, daughter, as a good wife ought to love her husband. And therefore you may boldly take me in the arms of your soul and kiss my mouth, my head, and my feet as sweetly as you will.)

Margery takes a literal approach to the *sponsa Christi* motif that was common in poetic and theological writing alike: Standard allegorical interpretation of the biblical Song of Songs, attributed to Solomon, made Christ the mystical bridegroom of the church and of all Christians. In the third of his eighty-six sermons on this highly erotic and poetic text, Bernard of Clairvaux, a twelfth-century Cistercian abbot, expounds upon the opening verse: "Let him kiss me with the kisses of his mouth." Bernard asserts that anyone who has once experienced a mystical kiss from the mouth of Christ will seek it repeatedly, but advises anyone burdened with carnal desire to start humbly at Christ's feet, and then with his hand. In his eighth sermon on this text, alluding to Genesis 2:24, he states that "if marriage according to the flesh constitutes two in one body, why should not a spiritual union be even more efficacious in joining two in one spirit?"

THE SEXUALITY OF CHRIST

Various accounts of spiritual union, by men as well as by women, nonetheless explicitly cite physical sensations and sensual pleasures, many of which seem overtly erotic. When Rupert of Deutz, a twelfth-century Benedictine monk, passionately embraced a crucifix high above an altar, the kissing, according to his account, involved not only lips but also tongues. Richard Rambuss (1998) has demonstrated evidence of "male devotional desire amorously attuned to a male Christ" (p. 238) in the work of major seventeenth-century English writers such as John Donne and Richard Crashaw. Artists and critics alike have in this regard more often taken note of the religious experiences of women. In the ecstatic vision of St. Teresa of Ávila (1515–1582), the subject of Gian Lorenzo Bernini's famous statue in Rome's Cornaro Chapel, not Christ but a handsome angel repeatedly thrust a burning spear through her heart and deep into her entrails, filling her with the fire of God's love. St. Catherine of Siena (1347–1380) not only drank blood directly from the wound in Jesus's side, his gift in recompense for her drinking pus from a woman's infected breast, but was also, like Margery and others, betrothed to Jesus in a vision. As reported by her biographer, Raymond of Capua, the ceremony was presided over by the Virgin Mary and involved a gold ring encrusted with jewels; her own description involves the circumcised foreskin of Jesus.

A cult had grown up around the holy prepuce, a potent symbol of Christ's humanity and physical suffering, and a part of his body thought singularly to have been left on earth after his ascension—a relic claimed by several institutions in the Middle Ages, including abbeys in Charroux and Coulombs in France as well as St. John Lateran in Rome, and by a church in Calcata, Italy, as late as 1983 when it was reported stolen. In *The Sexuality of Christ in Renaissance Art and in Modern Oblivion* (1996), Leo Steinberg has argued that devotion to the foreskin and the Feast of the Circumcision (January 1), like the many fifteenth- and sixteenth-century paintings of Jesus either as an infant or after the Crucifixion that focus the viewer's attention on his penis (the *ostentatio genitalium*), point not merely to Christ's humanity but also to his sexuality. Some sixteenth-century illustrations, most notably a series of paintings of the "Man of Sorrows" by Maerten van Heemskerck, even indicate an erection under the cloth that drapes the loins of the resurrected Christ, his flesh rising not because of lust or any external stimulus but at his will, as Adam's own penis was said by some medieval commentators to have done before the Fall in Eden. Such pictures thus symbolize Christ as the second Adam, reversing the Fall through his resurrection (1 Cor. 15:21–22), and bringing life to all.

JESUS AS MOTHER

In his eighth sermon on the Song of Songs, Bernard discusses the verse "Your breasts are better than wine" (4:10, translating the Vulgate's "pulchriora sunt ubera tua vino," where modern texts have "Your love is better than wine"), which he applies to the bridegroom rather than to the bride as customary, referring to the sweetness and forgiveness that flows from the breast of Jesus. Other writers described Christ in explicitly feminine terms as a nurturing mother. They had biblical precedent: In Matthew 23:37, Jesus compares himself to a hen gathering and protecting her chicks under her wings; he is also conventionally identified with divine Wisdom, personified as a woman in biblical texts such as Proverbs and the book of Wisdom and, like the eternal Word of the first chapter of John's gospel, characterized as participating in the creation of the world. In her book of *Shewings*, an account of revelations she received in 1373, the anchorite and mystic Julian of Norwich writes, "our Lady is our Moder in whome we are all beclosid and of hir borne in Christe, for she that is moder of our Savior, is moder of all that shall be savid in our Savior. And our Savior is our very moder in whom we be endlesly borne and never shall come out of Him" (chap. 57). In the chapters that follow this passage, Julian develops the maternal image at length, noting for instance that "The Moder may geven hir child soken her mylke, but our pretious Moder Jesus, He may fedyn us with Himselfe, and doith full curtesly and full tenderly with the blissid sacrament that is pretious fode of very lif" (chap. 60). As Bynum (1991) states, "Such an identification of Christ's saving role with giving birth as well as feeding is found in a number of fourteenth-century texts" (p. 97), especially by women such as Julian, or Margaret of Oingt (d. 1310), who describes the Crucifixion as Christ giving birth to the world.

DESIRE AND CONTROVERSY

Discussion of ideas such as the femininity of God, the sexuality of Jesus, and the relationship between eroticism and religious devotion by twenty-first-century feminist and queer writers and artists, as well as by theologians, have met with controversy and sometimes outrage. Accusations that such ideas are somehow unchristian indicate a lack of awareness of Christian history. For many, religious devotion remains a matter not just of the soul, but also of the body, and centred on the desirable body of Christ.

SEE ALSO *Catholicism; Christianity, Early and Medieval; Homoeroticism, Female/Male, Concept.*

BIBLIOGRAPHY

Bernard of Clairvaux. 1971–1980. *On the Song of Songs*, trans. Kilian Walsh and Irene Edmonds. 4 vols. Spencer, MA / Kalamazoo, MI: Cistercian Publications.

Bridget of Sweden. 1987. *The Liber Celestis of St. Bridget of Sweden*, ed. Roger Ellis. Vol. 1. Oxford: Oxford University Press, published for the Early English Text Society.

Bynum, Caroline Walker. 1991. *Fragmentation and Redemption: Essays on Gender and the Human Body in Medieval Religion.* New York: Zone Books.

Epp, Garrett. 2001. "Ecce Homo." In *Queering the Middle Ages*, ed. Glenn Burger and Steven F. Kruger. Minneapolis: University of Minnesota Press.

Julian of Norwich. 1993. *The Shewings of Julian of Norwich*, ed. Georgia Ronan Crampton. Kalamazoo, MI: Medieval Institute Publications, Western Michigan University.

Kempe, Margery. 1996. *The Book of Margery Kempe*, ed. Lynn Staley. Kalamazoo, MI: Medieval Institute Publications, Western Michigan University.

Matter, E. Ann. 1990. *The Voice of My Beloved: The Song of Songs in Western Medieval Christianity.* Philadelphia: University of Pennsylvania Press.

The Passion of the Christ. 2004. Directed by Mel Gibson. Equinoxe Films and Newmarket Films.

Rambuss, Richard. 1998. *Closet Devotions.* Durham, NC: Duke University Press.

Steinberg, Leo. 1996. *The Sexuality of Christ in Renaissance Art and in Modern Oblivion.* 2nd edition. Chicago: University of Chicago Press.

Garrett P.J. Epp

CHRISTIANITY, EARLY AND MEDIEVAL

The 1960s and 1970s saw a proliferation of feminist scholarship on European and North American religion. This work served not only to recover a portion of women's history but also to reveal the importance of gender as a tool of analysis in scholarship on religion. The present survey assumes two important caveats made manifest by this feminist work. First, most of the information for these fifteen centuries of Christian history comes from elite Christian men, which means it is partial and ideologically selective. Second, Christianity was never a single, uniform entity but has always been a diverse, multifaceted enterprise. Fierce theological battles over *orthodoxy* and *heresy* led to many ruptures within Christianity. It should be remembered that the distinction between orthodoxy and heresy was often not at all obvious and that it was privileged men who determined which was which.

JESUS, THE MALE SAVIOR

The four New Testament gospels represent Jesus as an unattached Jewish man whose marital status is unspecified. He lived in a peripatetic community of twelve male apostles and sometimes visited the homes of female friends such as Mary and Martha of Bethany (Luke 10:38-42; John 11–12). Although Jesus rarely addresses sexual matters, in Matthew 5:28 he offers a surprising teaching on adultery: "But I say to you that everyone who looks at a woman with lust has already committed adultery with her in his heart" (NRSV translation). Here Jesus equates sexual thought with action while presumably addressing a male audience. In Matthew 5:31–32 and 19:9 Jesus acknowledges that the husband can divorce his wife; however, remarriage is possible only in the case of unchastity (*porneia* in Greek). Mark 10:11–12 and Luke 16:18 forbid remarriage after divorce, which is equivalent to adultery. It is clear in these passages that Jesus is represented as holding conservative views of marriage and rather impossible standards for sexual ideation. This provides a good context for understanding his teaching on celibacy, found only in Matthew 19:10–12: "His disciples said to him, 'If such is the case of a man with his wife, it is better not to marry.' But he said to them, 'Not everyone can accept this teaching, but only those to whom it is given. For there are eunuchs who have been so from birth, and there are eunuchs who have been made eunuchs by others, and there are eunuchs who have made themselves eunuchs for the sake of the kingdom of heaven.'" This passage suggests that Jesus was celibate (a eunuch of sorts) and that celibacy was the superior calling. Origen, a third-century Greek writer, allegedly had himself castrated to avoid the possibility of sexual temptation. Much later, in the Byzantine empire of the twelfth century, eunuchs castrated before puberty were honored as "perfect servants of god" (Ringrose 2003, p 15). That is, they were men biologically but were womanly in appearance, demeanor, and their inability to produce semen.

PAUL AND HIS INTERPRETERS

The apostle Paul understood the physical body as an impediment to spiritual perfection. His view was to become the dominant Christian view through the centuries. Celibacy was the preferred state because the unmarried man and woman were not distracted by family but rather were intensely focused on God. Paul encouraged married couples to have sexual relations often in order to avoid temptation, not to produce offspring. Homosexual practices for men and "unnatural intercourse" for women were condemned (Rom. 1:26–27) because of prevailing attitudes about gender roles. Because the *proper* role of the male was to be active in sexual relations, the homosexual encounter required one male partner to be *passive* or feminine. This gender transgression was condemned, and rigid gender roles were expected. In 1 Corinthians 11:3 Paul explains that women, not men, must cover their heads during worship because "Christ is the head of every man, and the husband is the head of his wife, and God is the head of Christ." Paul constructs a cosmic hierarchy in this passage that requires the woman/wife to be subordinate to her husband. He explains this by implicit reference to Genesis 1:27, although in Genesis 1:27 both woman and man are made in God's image. In 1 Corinthians 11:7 Paul states, "for a man ought not to have his head veiled, since he is the image and reflection of God; but woman is the reflection of man."

In the deutero-Pauline letters (those written by a disciple of Paul) the attitudes toward women become increasingly more restrictive. In Colossians 3:18–4:1 and Ephesians 5:22–6:9 wives are to be obedient to their husbands as to Christ. Husbands are to love their wives and ensure their purity. 1 Timothy 2:11-12 requires women to be submissive and silent and prohibits women from teaching men or having authority over men. A similar passage, now found in 1 Corinthians 14:33–36, was likely added to Paul's letter to echo later misogynist sentiments: "As in all the churches of the saints, women should be silent in the churches. For they are not permitted to speak, but should be subordinate, as the law also says." This fear of woman's voice in part may have its exegetical roots in the Genesis 3 story of Eve, who speaks to the serpent while her male partner stands by silently. The man is later punished by the Lord *because he listened* to the voice of his partner/wife.

WOMEN'S LEADERSHIP IN EARLY CHRISTIANITY

The earliest Jesus movement was composed of apostles, disciples, prophets, and teachers, all of which included both women and men. The most significant woman disciple associated with the earthly ministry of Jesus was Mary Magdalene, who is portrayed in all four gospels as a witness to Jesus's resurrection and is later called the *apostle to the apostles*. In certain apocryphal (nonbiblical) gospels such as the Gospel of Mary, Mary Magdalene, not Peter, is portrayed as the spiritual successor of Jesus, and in the Gospel of Philip, Mary is called Jesus's companion. In the Gospel of Thomas 114, however, Jesus says of Mary, "I myself shall lead her in order to make her male, so that she too may become a living spirit resembling you males. For every woman who will make herself male will enter the kingdom of heaven." The bifurcation of male/masculine as spiritual and female/feminine as physical would become prerequisite for later orthodox teaching. Nonetheless, several women in the New Testament held significant authority. In Romans 16:1 Paul commends Phoebe as a deacon (masculine in Greek) of the church of Cenchreae. The Didascalia Apostolorum (third century) acknowledges the deaconess as the only ordained role permitted to a woman. Her responsibilities were limited to the ministry of women; she does what a deacon cannot do, for the sake of propriety. The Apostolic Constitutions (fourth century) further restricts the role of deaconesses to more menial tasks, until the sixth century in the western church, and as late as the twelfth century in the eastern church, when the role is no longer recognized.

The missionary partners Prisca and Aquila, who are mentioned twice by Paul (1 Corinthians 16:19 and Romans 16:3), are called his "coworkers" and seem to have led house churches in Rome, Ephesus, and Corinth. They are also recognized in Acts 18 (Priscilla and Aquila) as authoritative teachers in the synagogue at Ephesus. Other female heads of house churches include Chloe (1 Corinthians 1:11), Lydia (Acts 16:14–15), and Nympha (Colossians 4:15). In Romans 16:7 Junia is described by Paul as "prominent among the apostles," the only reference to a woman apostle in the New Testament. In Paul's letter to Philemon 2, Apphia "our sister," is one of three people to whom the letter is addressed. Women also exercised prophetic leadership that was recognized by Jesus in Mark 14:3–9 and Matthew 26:6–13 (the anointing woman), and by Paul in 1 Corinthians 11. Acts 21:9 mentions the prophetic leadership of the four virgin (unnamed) daughters of Philip in Caesarea.

In the late second century in Phrygia, the Montanist prophets Priscilla and Maximilla were revered for their divine oracles. The Montanists ordained women bishops, and according to epigraphic evidence other Christian groups did as well, such as the bishop Theodora of Rome (Eisen 2000). One enduring example of women's leadership is found in the apocryphal Acts of Thecla (late second century) where Thecla, an engaged virgin, rejects her fiancé to follow Paul. She escapes execution miraculously, baptizes herself, dresses in men's clothing, and goes off to preach the gospel on her own with Paul's blessing. Finally, both women and men were recognized as martyrs for the faith, sometimes dying gruesome and agonizing deaths. The earliest writing of a Christian woman is the *Martyrdom of Perpetua and Felicitas*, written by Vibia Perpetua in the early third century in North Africa.

EVE, THE CHRISTIAN PANDORA

In the Greek story of Pandora, a woman's inquisitiveness causes her to open a heavenly box from which all human suffering escapes into the world. She is thus solely responsible for all human misery. A clear parallel can be found in the Christian use of Genesis 3, the story of the serpent and the woman in paradise. The woman, who seeks wisdom, takes fruit from the forbidden tree of knowledge and becomes enlightened. The punishments of both the man and woman in Genesis 3 lay the groundwork for later *gender trouble*. The man is told in verse 17, "Because you have listened to the voice of your wife" the ground is cursed. The woman is told in verse 16, "in pain you shall bring forth children yet your desire shall be for your husband and he shall rule over you." This particular passage in Genesis was to become a road map for the relations between the sexes in Christianity. Woman is condemned to be subordinate to her male partner, she is silenced because her voice causes catastrophe and her judgment is impaired, and all sexual encounters will lead to painful childbirth. This is hardly a celebration of romantic love. In 2 Corinthians 11:3 Paul invokes the deception of Eve by the serpent as the metaphor for all false teaching and heresy. Later Christian writers amplified this sentiment. Irenaeus (c. 135–140 to 202–203 CE) paralleled the disobedience of Eve with the obedience of Mary, the mother of Jesus. He describes Eve as "the cause of death for herself and all the human race." Tertullian (c. 160 to 240–250 CE) identifies all women as *Eves*: "You are the devil's gateway." Augustine of Hippo (354–430) similarly comments, "woman was given to man, woman who was of small intelligence and who perhaps still lives more in accordance with the promptings of the inferior flesh than by superior reason." And finally, John Chrysostom (c. 347–407; the archbishop of Constantinople) writes: "God in effect said to Eve, 'I made you equal in honor. You did not use your authority well, so consign yourself to a state of subordination.'" (All translations are from Clark 1990.)

CLERICAL HIERARCHY AND CELIBACY

Ignatius of Antioch, (d. 98–117), confirmed a three-tier model of church hierarchy—bishop, presbyter (later translated priest), and deacon—where the bishop was the sole authority of the community. In book VI.43 of the *Ecclesiastical History*, Eusebius of Caesarea (c. 260–c. 339) reports that the church in Rome in the mid-third century included many additional offices such as subdeacons, acolytes, exorcists, and readers. Also in the third century women and men who had chosen the ascetic or virginal life began to live in monastic communities that were organized under the unquestioned authority of abbesses and abbots, respectively. Nevertheless, women's exclusion from the church hierarchy had already begun to be formulated in the second century. In 476, six decades after the first sack of Rome in 410, the barbarian Odoacer deposed the last Roman emperor, Romulus Augustulus. This date usually marks the beginning of the medieval period, although the eastern Byzantine empire lasted until the fifteenth century. By the sixth century the primacy of the bishop of Rome, as pope, was established. Three centuries later, a learned woman named Joan, who lived as a man, would transgress these growing clerical restrictions by being elected Pope John VIII. Her pontificate allegedly lasted from 856 to 858 before her true identity was discovered. It is also alleged that after her reign, papal candidates were physically examined to confirm their sexual identity.

Beginning in the eleventh century Pope Gregory VII (r. 1073–1085) imposed great ecclesiastical reforms including the mandatory celibacy of all clergy. This meant that married priests were required to leave their families to live in common, sex-segregated communities. The women and children were left to fend for themselves—children were declared *slaves* and deemed to be the property of the church, a fate that would later apply to wives and concubines as well. It is also in this time that the authority of the abbess was supplanted by the authority of the male priest. Whereas clerical celibacy had been addressed as early as the Spanish Council of Elvira (295–302), it was not until the Council of Trullo (692) that bishops were required to separate from their wives and remain celibate upon consecration. This council also prohibited priests and deacons from marrying *after* ordination, which is still the practice of the Eastern Orthodox Church. The Second Lateran Council (1139) prohibited marriage and prescribed celibacy for all ordained men in the Western church.

MEDIEVAL RELIGIOUS ORDERS

The eleventh century saw the proliferation of monastic orders and the reappearance of anchorites, women and men who lived reclusively, sometimes walling themselves up in cells built against church walls with small windows to receive food and to speak with outsiders. In 1098 Robert of Molesme founded the religious order of Citeaux, the Cistercians, which sought to return to strict Benedictine practice. Bernard of Clairvaux (1090–1153) founded over 160 European monasteries, and further developed the Cistercian Order. In the thirteenth century mendicant orders, such as the Franciscans and Dominicans, were founded. Clare of Assisi (1194–1253), a devout follower of Francis of Assisi (1181 or 1182–1226), founded a women's monastery based on the practice of total poverty and was declared abbess in 1216 at the convent of San Damiano. It is estimated that more than 10,000 women looked to her as a spiritual leader.

At the Fourth Lateran Council in 1215, Pope Innocent III (r. 1198–1216) confined women to two life choices, marriage or the cloistered convent. He also prohibited the founding of any new religious orders, male or female, and sought to impose the Benedictine rule on existing orders. Both Francis and Clare had to fight against this ruling and were successful. Other groups, both male and female, rejected this papal decree. One female group was the Beguines, a group of religious women in Belgium, France, Germany, and northern Italy in the early thirteenth century. They were "at the centre of a medieval conflict about the role of women." (Malone 2002, p. 124). These women lived in small groups, professed chastity, and ministered to the sick and poor. They were officially condemned as heretics in 1312, and many were burnt at the stake. The Poor Men of Lyons, or Waldensians, founded about 1173, were another group that practiced poverty and rejected the teaching authority of priests as their members were not ordained. They were eventually condemned as heretics by Pope Lucius III in 1184, and many likely died in the crusade against the Albigensians of 1208.

CONSOLIDATION OF PATRIARCHY

Scholars such as Karen Jo Torjesen associate the enforcement of clerical celibacy with a concurrent "demonization of female sexuality" literally to keep men celibate (Torjesen 1993, p. 224). In 1486 two German inquisitors published the *Malleus maleficarum* [The hammer of witches], which explicitly links women's sexuality with the demonic ability to control sexual acts generally, and the male sex organ specifically. It is estimated that a million women lost their lives to the witch craze that followed. The final event of note for this survey is also from the fifteenth century. Joan of Arc was accused of heresy, blasphemy, and wearing male clothing, and was burned at the stake in Rouen on May 30, 1431. Twenty-five years later she was absolved of all charges against her because of "manifest errors of fact and of law," among other reasons, and was much later canonized a saint by Pope Benedict XV on May 16, 1920. Her experience eerily mirrors the paradox of the inquisitor's techniques concerning women and men condemned as heretics. Exoneration was often possible only through death. As such, this survey has come full circle. The attitudes about sex and gender expressed in the New Testament culminate in the Inquisition, and in the early twenty-first century they continue to dictate Christian attitudes about women's ordination, gay and lesbian unions, and gender. That the canonical gospels preserved Jesus as ostensibly a celibate male continues to have ramifications for both women and men.

BIBLIOGRAPHY

Brown, Peter. 1988. *The Body and Society: Men, Women, and Sexual Renunciation in Early Christianity.* New York: Columbia University Press.

Brubaker, Leslie, and Julia M. H. Smith, eds. 2004. *Gender in the Early Medieval World: East and West, 300–900.* Cambridge, UK: Cambridge University Press.

Bullough, Vern L., and James A. Brundage, eds. 1996. *Handbook of Medieval Sexuality.* New York: Garland Publishing.

Clark, Elizabeth A. 1990. *Women in the Early Church.* Collegeville, MN: Liturgical Press. [Orig. pub. 1983.]

Eisen, Ute E. 2000. *Women Officeholders in Early Christianity: Epigraphical and Literary Studies*, trans. Linda M. Maloney. Collegeville, MN: Liturgical Press.

Elm, Susanna. 1994. *"Virgins of God": The Making of Asceticism in Late Antiquity.* Oxford: Oxford University Press.

Kraemer, Ross Shepard, and Mary Rose D'Angelo, eds. 1999. *Women and Christian Origins.* New York: Oxford University Press.

Kuefler, Mathew. 2001. *The Manly Eunuch: Masculinity, Gender Ambiguity, and Christian Ideology in Late Antiquity.* Chicago: University of Chicago Press.

Malone, Mary T. 2001. *Women and Christianity*, Vol. 1: *The First Thousand Years.* Maryknoll, NY: Orbis Books.

Malone, Mary T. 2002. *Women and Christianity*, Vol. 2: *From 1000 to the Reformation.* Maryknoll, NY: Orbis Books.

Martin, Dale B. 2006. *Sex and the Single Savior: Gender and Sexuality in Biblical Interpretation.* Louisville, KY: Westminster John Knox Press.

Ringrose, Kathryn M. 2003. *The Perfect Servant: Eunuchs and the Social Construction of Gender in Byzantium.* Chicago: University of Chicago Press.

Rousselle, Aline. 1993. *Porneia: On Desire and the Body in Antiquity*, trans. Felicia Pheasant. Cambridge, MA: Blackwell.

Shaw, Teresa M. 1998. *The Burden of the Flesh: Fasting and Sexuality in Early Christianity.* Minneapolis, MN: Fortress Press.

Stafford, Pauline, and Anneke B. Mulder-Bakker, eds. 2001. *Gendering the Middle Ages.* Oxford: Blackwell.

Torjesen, Karen Jo. 1993. *When Women Were Priests: Women's Leadership in the Early Church and the Scandal of Their Subordination in the Rise of Christianity.* San Francisco: HarperSanFrancisco.

Jacqueline Z. Pastis

CHRISTIANITY, REFORMATION TO MODERN

Christianity originated in Palestine in the Middle East and spread within the first century east as far as Persia, into Egypt and North Africa, and across the northern Mediterranean to Spain. During the next three centuries Christianity moved into northern Europe to Britain and Ireland, as well as eastward as far as China. Christianity also progressed north into Central Europe and became the primary religion of the Slavic and Russian peoples. The rise of Islam in the seventh century caused the gradual retreat of Christianity into small enclaves in the Middle East, Central Asia, and North Africa, when many Christians became Muslims. In India and the Far East, Hindu and Buddhist societies limited the spread of Christianity.

The new wave of European expansion and colonization of the world in the sixteenth century brought Christianity, mostly Roman Catholic, to Latin America. Protestants from Britain and Western Europe came to North America, along with Catholic and Orthodox groups from Ireland and southern and eastern Europe. Missionary work, both Roman Catholic and Protestant, spread Christianity in sub-Saharan Africa beginning in the nineteenth century. In the early-twenty-first century there are 2.38 billion Christians throughout the world, a third of the people on earth. The 569 million Christians in Europe are often more nominal than practicing. In Latin America, the 500 million Christians are mostly Roman Catholic, but many practice a folk Catholicism based on pilgrimages and devotion to saints. Evangelical Protestantism is growing in that region. Christianity is expanding fastest in Africa with 377 million adherents in Roman Catholic, Protestant, and indigenous churches. In Asia, there are 322 million Christians but they constitute less than 10 percent of the population. Only the Philippines, colonized by Spain, has a Christian majority. North America has 262.7 million Christians of diverse denominations, 87 percent of the population.

CHRISTIANITY AND SEX AND GENDER ISSUES IN PATRIARCHAL SOCIETIES

Christianity was born into patriarchal societies, both Jewish and Greco-Roman, in which a woman was seen as wife and mother, preferably one who produced male children, but was excluded from political leadership and participation in higher culture. Christianity's main modification of this tradition was the adoption of celibacy as the ideal Christian lifestyle for men and women. Christians were urged to eschew marriage and reproduction to prepare themselves for heaven where they would "neither marry or be given in marriage" (Luke 20:35). This preference for the celibate life, in which men lived in male communities and women in female communities, had an ambivalent effect on the image and aspirations of women. For many celibate women, it meant liberation from enforced patriarchal marriage and serial pregnancies. Female communities also offered the possibility of travel (pilgrimage), the opportunity to study religious texts, and the ability to live a life of religious self-transformation.

Male elites soon dominated the Christian hierarchy, even though women preached and held leadership positions in the in the earliest churches. Celibacy was joined to priesthood for men, while women were excluded from ordained ministry. Male priests and monks looked at all women as dangerously sexual, to be strictly confined to the cloister, for nuns, or to the home. Influential bishops and theologians, such as St. Augustine (354–430), believed that celibacy was the ideal Christian life for men and women. Sex was allowed only within marriage and only for the purpose of reproduction. Any sex for pleasure, even within marriage, was sinful and equivalent to fornication.

Augustine believed that women were created by God to be under male dominion. Women had subverted that dominion in the Garden of Eden by tempting the male to disobey God. Women were the cause of the fall of humanity and entrance of sin into the world. Thus women should be punished by the coercive imposition of male rule in the family and in the church, and should interiorize this subjugation. Only after death would the hierarchy of male over female disappear, and sex roles would be no more. These became the dominant views of the Catholic Church regarding woman and sexuality through the Middle Ages; they continue into the early twenty-first century among traditionalist Christians.

CHRISTIANITY AND THE REFORMATION

These views on women, gender roles, and sexuality were not greatly changed in the Protestant Reformation of the sixteenth century. The main contribution of the Reformation was the abolition of celibacy for both men and women. But the rejection of women's preaching and ordination continued. Married men could now be ordained, but women lost their roles as abbesses, scholars, and teachers within female monastic communities. Protestants continued to believe that women were dangerous temptresses who were responsible for the fall of humanity and must be strictly controlled. Sex was primarily for reproduction, and birth control was not allowed, although there came to be more acceptance of sexual pleasure in marriage. Some Protestants in the sixteenth and seventeenth centuries allowed the possibility of divorce for limited reasons, such as desertion and adultery (but not for wife beating).

The late medieval and Reformation periods also saw the outbreak of witch-hunting, in which hundreds of thousands were killed, mostly women. The persecution of women as witches was fueled by misogynist views of women as irrational, sexually insatiable, and hence prone to consort with the Devil.

In seventeenth century England, Quakers (the Society of Friends) believed that all humans were created equal in the beginning and that Jesus restored this equality. Women were the first witnesses to Jesus' resurrection and were commissioned to announce this *good news* to the male disciples. Thus only by accepting women's preaching and missionary roles do men also receive the good news. Quakers made women *public friends* or missionaries, as well as leaders in their own women's meetings.

These Quaker views of women's equality became more widespread in nineteenth-century United States. Several early Christian feminists were Quakers, including Sarah and Angelina Grimké, Lucretia Mott, and Susan B. Anthony. These Quaker feminists believed that women had been created by God to be man's equal partner, not his subordinate, and that sin and evil came about, not through female temptation, but through men seizing power over others to create systems of unjust domination, such as sexism and slavery. Church and society should be reformed to give women equal rights in society. This included higher education, entrance into professions, property rights, the vote, and legal status as equal citizens. These demands were carried forward by the women's movement into the twentieth century.

CHRISTIAN VIEWS INTO THE TWENTY-FIRST CENTURY

Such views of women's equality, their rights to education, professions, and the vote also spread in Britain, across Europe and into Latin America, Asia, and Africa during the twentieth century. Secular liberalism, rather than progressive Christianity, became the primary vehicle for spreading ideas of women's rights. Many churches resisted equality for woman as contrary to church teaching. Modernization was identified with worldliness and an erosion of traditional religious values. Conservative Christians stereotyped feminism as secular and anti-God.

The nineteenth century was a century of greatly expanded missionary work for Protestant and Catholic churches. Missionaries were sent in large numbers to Africa and Asia to convert pagans to Christianity, while Protestants went to Latin America and the Philippines to make Catholics into Protestants. Catholic women mis-

Nineteenth-century Quaker feminists such as Lucretia Mott (pictured here) represent a first wave of feminist theology.

sionaries were mostly members of religious orders. Protestants also used women as missionaries, most often as missionary wives, but also in their own right.

European and North American women missionaries were seen as necessary to reach other women since many Asian and African cultures did not allow men access to local women. The work of conversion, education, and health initiatives for women had to be carried out by female missionaries. European and North American women missionaries played an ambivalent role in relation to women converts in many Asian and African societies. They were often bearers of Victorian ideas of the role of women. They sought to domesticate women as wives and housekeepers, and restrict the roles that women sometimes played in other societies as farmers, artisans, and merchants. Yet women missionaries also founded hospitals and schools for girls, from primary to college levels. Many Asian and African women converts got their first opportunities for education and entrance into professions in teaching and health care through these missionary-founded schools and hospitals.

Feminist theology represents the major effort within Christianity to reinterpret its traditions to overcome teachings that promote subordination and misogyny. Quaker feminists, such as Sarah Grimké and Lucretia Mott in the nineteenth century, represent a first wave of feminist theology. Such egalitarian views of Christianity were silenced in the late-nineteenth and early-twentieth centuries, but the late 1960s saw a new birth of feminist theologies.

In the early-twenty-first century, feminist theologies spread to diverse groups within North American, African American, Hispanic, and Asian Christian groups, and also to Europe, Latin America, Asia, and Africa. These feminist theologies seek to contextualize their ideas in their distinct cultural and historical contexts, but all believe that women are equal to men in the image of God and that God can be imaged as a female as well as a male. They suggest the true message of Christianity is the liberation of women, and all people, from systems and ideologies of oppression.

Feminist theology has gone hand in hand with the spreading of women's ordination. A few women were ordained in the nineteenth century in liberal denominations, such as the Congregationalists, Unitarians, and Universalists. In the late 1950s to 1970s there was a new surge of women's ordination among Methodists, Presbyterians, Lutherans, and Anglicans in the United States and Europe. In the early-twenty-first century most Protestants ordain women, except for very conservative groups, such as Missouri Synod Lutherans and some Southern Baptists. Roman Catholics and Eastern Orthodox Christians continue to reject women's ordination, although the issue is being debated in both churches.

Reproductive rights are a contentious issue in most Christian churches throughout the world. Birth control and abortion have been rejected by Christianity since its inception. In the 1950s liberal Protestants gradually accepted the use of artificial contraception. In the 1970s some liberal Protestants allowed the possibility of abortion in the early months of gestation in conflict situations where women would experience hardship, economic, psychological, or physical in bearing a child. The Roman Catholic hierarchy continues to strongly reject both abortion and birth control (although the rhythm method of natural family planning is allowed).

Abortion has become a central issue in the *culture wars* in the United States and many other countries, with traditionalist Christians rejecting abortion and some also forbidding artificial contraception, while liberals seek to defend legal access to these rights. Many feminists, secular and religious, see the main issue not as a general valuation of life, but as the desire to control women's sexuality and women's lives. Because there is little cultural or legal interest in supporting lives of children after birth, any extreme emphasis on the absolute value to life in the early stages of insemination, even stem cells, seems largely a question of power and control.

Christianity is not solely misogynist, only teaching women's inferiority and subordination; nor is it primarily liberating to women. Rather, like most religions, it contains a mixture of traditions that can be interpreted in either way. This dichotomy leads to deep conflicts over the definition of women's sexuality and social roles and divides Christians, often in the same churches.

SEE ALSO *Catholicism.*

BIBLIOGRAPHY

Bowden, John, ed. 2005. *Christianity, The Complete Guide.* London: Continuum.

Ruether, Rosemary R. 1998. *Women and Redemption: A Theological History.* St. Paul, MN: Fortress Press.

Rosemary Radford Ruether

CIRCUIT PARTY

A circuit party is a large professionally produced public dance party attended primarily by gay men that lasts all night and into the next day. Beginning in the early 1980s as AIDS benefits and drawing some of their inspiration from rave culture, circuit parties have become progressively more elaborate since their inception—generating affiliated events that sometimes stretch over two or three days, attracting corporate sponsorship, and spawning commercial imitations. Among the oldest and best-known circuit parties are White Party Week in Miami, Gay and Lesbian Mardi Gras in Sydney, the Black and Blue Festival in Montreal, and White Party Palm Springs. These events, along with some two dozen others, form the basis for "The Circuit," a series of parties that spans the globe and continues throughout the year. Gay men who attend several of these events each year often refer to themselves as "circuit boys."

During the mid- to late 1990s, circuit culture began to draw criticism both within and outside the gay community for promoting the use of recreational drugs such as ecstasy and methamphetamine and for contributing to the spread of HIV and other sexually transmitted diseases. Supporters of the phenomenon, however, argue that circuit parties serve a vital function for gay men, providing a sense of community and a celebration of gay identity. Reaching their peak at the end of the 1990s, circuit parties have begun to decline in attendance and popularity since then, possibly because of the increasing cost, the aging of the original generation of circuit boys, and changing tastes among younger gay men.

BIBLIOGRAPHY

"Circuit Noize Interactive." Available from http://www.circuitnoize.com.

Signorile, Michelangelo. 1997. *Life Outside.* New York: HarperCollins.

Dennis Allen

CIRCUMCISION, MALE

Three out of every twenty males throughout the world are circumcised. The operation varies from place to place, but circumcision always involves the removal of some or all of the foreskin of the penis. In one way or another male circumcision is always concerned with the assertion of masculine as opposed to feminine gender. People in different countries, however, may give other reasons for doing it. These may include the celebration or marking of birth, membership of an ethnic or religious group, or mature status in the community. Circumcision may also be a symbolic equivalent to sacrifice, or it may be associated with hygiene or cleanliness.

Sixth dynasty paintings in Egypt indicate that circumcision was performed some 4,500 years ago. The fifth-century BCE Greek historian Herodotus remarks that the Egyptians differed from most other peoples because they performed the operation. Some of Egypt's neighbors, such as the Syrians, had also adopted the practice. Those neighbors presumably included the Hebrews.

Forms of circumcision are (or were) found among contemporary Jews for whom it is prescribed, among Muslims for whom it is strongly preferred, among the majority of males in the United States, among Australian aborigines such as the Aranda, among many but by no means all peoples in sub-Saharan Africa, and in many Asian and Polynesian societies. It is very uncommon among Christians in northern Europe and among native peoples in North and South America.

Some groups in tropical Africa that practice male circumcision also circumcise females by removing part or all of the clitoris, and sometimes by removing part or all of the labia minora. Female genital cutting (as it is now more commonly described) rarely occurs in the absence of male circumcision.

SOCIAL AND TEMPORAL CONTEXT OF MALE CIRCUMCISION

The timing of the operation is variable depending on its function (as a marker of birth or otherwise as a symbol of impending or actual physical and/or social maturity). North Americans might associate circumcision with birth because it is usually performed within a few days thereafter whether by Jewish *mohels* (circumcisers) or by doctors in a hospital. Zoroastrians have it performed by doctors shortly after birth, while the infant is still in the hospital. The Igbo and Yoruba of Nigeria and the Merina of Madagascar also perform circumcision during the first few weeks of the infant's life. Muslims circumcise in childhood, sometimes between the ages of four and seven, but at a later age (about twelve) among groups who insist that a boy learn the Qur'an before circumcision. In all other cases circumcision takes place during adolescence or early manhood. In African societies such as the Ndembu of Zambia a number of youths of varying ages are usually circumcised together every few years because the resources needed to put on a ceremony, including food and drink, may be scarce. Accordingly the description of such ceremonies as "puberty rites" is not entirely accurate.

Victor W. Turner, who did anthropological fieldwork among the Ndembu of Zambia in the 1950s, has provided the most extended account of any circumcision ceremony in the anthropological record (Turner 1962). Ndembu describe the foreskin as the female part of the male, which must be removed by circumcision. Ndembu youths are circumcised by the *mudyi* tree whose white, milky sap symbolizes milk, motherhood, matriliny (Ndembu inherit from their mother or mother's brother), the social order, purity, and virtue. They are symbolically imbued with the qualities of purity, order, and virtue while being literally and metaphorically separated from their former femininity. Their wounds are tended by their fathers and by the young men who are their guardians. They spend six weeks in seclusion with the guardians as their instructors and are visited by the elders in the guise of ancestors. They learn the norms and lore of the community. Women prepare food for them but are not allowed near them. After six weeks, their return to the community as mature men is celebrated. The rite therefore separates boys from the maternal tie, links boys to the male ancestors, teaches them important traditions, and affirms positive social values. It also hardens them by subjecting them to an ordeal—although Turner does not stress this function as much as other writers on initiation rituals.

Among other peoples both in Africa and in other continents where circumcision is performed at birth, ideas of gender separation, gender identity, and fertility may nonetheless be present, but there is obviously less concern with separation from the mother on whom the child will depend for many years.

It is worth noting that although both Jewish and Ndembu circumcision may be described as "rites of passage," a term that presumes religious meaning, circumcision varies in the significance attached to it. The Dogon of Mali and the Merina of Madagascar view the circumcision ritual as important and account for its importance and necessity through origin myths. In some Polynesian communities, however, the approach is more casual. Ritual and mythical elaboration are lacking. In Tahiti, a group of young boys would seek out an operator. There was no grand rite at which the elders presided.

THE ACTUAL OPERATIONS

Circumcision proper (as opposed to superincision and subincision) involves the removal of part or all of the two layers of foreskin or prepuce that cover the glans when the penis is not erect. Jewish circumcision involves the removal of the entire foreskin and the mucus membrane in an operation called *periah*.

Superincision is found in many Polynesian societies such as Tikopia and Tahiti. The dorsal (top) skin of the penis is stretched by insertion of a piece of wood and a cut is made in the foreskin. It is not removed but rather hangs down on either side of the exposed glans.

Subincision involves the slitting of the underside of the penis. The cut may be deep enough to expose the underside of the urethra so that it becomes difficult for the initiate to urinate in a standing position. Australian aboriginal peoples commonly practiced subincision. In the 1890s Baldwin Spencer and F. J. Gillen described the initiation ceremonies of the Aranda of central Australia, which involved both circumcision and subincision. The psychoanalyst Bruno Bettelheim (1954) attributed this rite and other procedures that involve a great deal of bleeding on the part of males to male envy of female menstruation and fertility. In 1967 Philip Singer and Daniel E. Desole developed an ingenious explanation for the custom. The penis of kangaroos is bifid, or split. Male kangaroos have prolonged erections and are icons of fertility; hence men attempt to imitate them. Perhaps the importance of this imaginative theory is that it illuminates how very little is known about why different people adopt different forms of circumcision and why most cultures that do not possess the rite adopt other procedures (or no procedure at all) to mark birth and adolescence.

WHEN CIRCUMCISION IS NOT CARRIED OUT

In cross-cultural terms circumcision is only part of the picture. There are other forms of genital modification, temporary or permanent, that accompany adolescence. These include the wearing of penis wrappers (perhaps following circumcision), sheaths, and gourds. Among some New Guinea peoples the penis may be bled either by applying a thorn to the surface or by inserting something in the urethra. The tongue may also be bled. Ritual nose bleeding and the wearing of nose plugs and bones placed through the nasal septum may accompany initiation.

As these examples illustrate, not all changes accompanying initiation or birth involve genital modification, although some people in Melanesia as well as anthropologists and followers of Sigmund Freud may see the nose as a sexual symbol. The Belgian folklorist Arnold van Gennep, in his 1909 book, *The Rites of Passage*, remarked that it was a pity that the Jews chose to circumcise rather than to perforate the nasal septum. He was inclined to see all changes to the body and its appurtenances as abstract symbols of status change, so that for him removing a finger, shaving hair, and tearing clothing as signs of mourning were rites of a similar type to circumcision. Christians who do not practice infant circumcision do practice baptism. Plains Indian initiation may involve fasting and the arduous vision quest, but there is no circumcision. It should be noted that both male and female circumcision do seem to occur in societies with strongly gendered social systems, but many such societies do not practice circumcision.

JEWISH CIRCUMCISION AND CHRISTIAN REACTIONS TO IT

According to chapter 17 of the book of Genesis, God ordered Abraham to circumcise himself and his son Ishmael and to commence circumcising all male infants after eight days as a sign of the exclusive covenant between God and the Jews. The Jewish philosopher Maimonides (1135–1204) remarked that the custom indeed served as a badge of ethnic distinction. It was commonly believed that circumcision reduced sexual desire and channeled both male and female fertility.

St. Paul and the early Christians felt that membership in God's church need not be inscribed on the body. There could instead be "circumcision of the heart." Christians gradually came to view circumcision as a sign of depravity rather than holiness, and a variety of virulent anti-Semitic myths employed the circumcised penis as a sign of sexual abnormality.

In his 2005 book, *Marked in Your Flesh*, Leonard B. Glick remarks that in the nineteenth century a few Reform Jewish writers, influenced by the Enlightenment, saw circumcision as an irrational act and advocated its replacement and abolition. A minority of Reform Jews ceased to circumcise their male children. Most Jewish scholars, however, continued to defend tradition and also insisted that circumcision was a hygienic practice.

At the same time, a number of gentile doctors in North America began to advocate circumcision. It was thought to prevent infection, because the foreskin produces a lubricant (smegma) that can be a source of infection if proper hygiene is not maintained. Circumcision was said to prevent masturbation, which was thought to be a desirable aim. It was also thought on the basis of dubious evidence to prevent a substantial number of physical and mental diseases. In the first few decades of the twentieth century evidence accumulated that circumcision might prevent cancer of the penis and cancer of the prostate. By the 1960s most male infants in the United States and Canada were circumcised in hospitals. Since 1999 some insurance companies and Medicaid schemes in sixteen U.S. states have withdrawn funding for circumcision because there is uncertainty about its medical benefits.

CONTROVERSIES IN THE EARLY TWENTY-FIRST CENTURY

Since the mid-1970s the practice of female circumcision, which occurs in twenty-eight African countries and more rarely in parts of Indonesia and the Arabian peninsula, has been attacked as a patriarchal human rights violation. There has been less controversy over male circumcision, but its opponents believe that it is every bit as harmful and reprehensible. Scholars opposing circumcision include Ashley Montagu (1995) and the aforementioned Glick, both Jewish anthropologists, and Sami A. Aldeeb Abu-Sahlieh (2006), a Palestinian law professor. They claim that infants suffer great pain at circumcision and are frightened and traumatized. A few hundred die from the operation each year in the United States. Sexual enjoyment and potential are permanently damaged. The medical benefits of the procedure are subject to doubt: Modern hygiene can prevent infections of the foreskin; cancer of the penis is very rare even among the uncircumcised; rates of prostate cancer have nothing to do with circumcision.

It has been noted by some that AIDS rates among the Luo of Kenya who do not practice circumcision appear to be higher than among neighboring groups such as the Kikuyu who circumcise. There has been dispute over claims in a detailed 2005 study by Bertran Auvert and colleagues that circumcision reduced the risk of AIDS infection by 61 percent among three thousand previously uncircumcised heterosexual, young adult males in South Africa. Opponents of circumcision have claimed that the methodology of the study was flawed and noted that circumcision was no substitute for the use of condoms as prophylaxis.

Supporters of circumcision are likely to point to the role supposedly played by the foreskin as a conduit for infection and to use studies such as Auvert's to advance their case. Groups such as the Gilgal Society, which defend circumcision for religious or medical reasons, continue to insist that children do not suffer, may sleep through the surgery if it is performed in early infancy, and do not remember it later on. They insist that no medical harm results. Those who defend circumcision as a religious duty insist that God would not have prescribed a practice that did not benefit humanity.

BIBLIOGRAPHY

Aldeeb Abu-Sahlieh, Sami A. 2006. "Male and Female Circumcision: The Myth of the Difference." In *Female Circumcision: Multicultural Perspectives*, ed. Rogaia Mustafa Abusharaf. Philadelphia: University of Pennsylvania Press.

Auvert, Bertran; Dirk Taljaard; Emmanuel Lagarde; et al. 2005. "Randomized, Controlled Intervention Trial of Male Circumcision for Reduction of HIV Infection Risk: The ANRS 1265 Trial." *PLoS Medicine* 2(11), e298 doi:10.1371/journal.pmed.0020298. Available from http://medicine.plosjournals.org.

Bettelheim, Bruno. 1954. *Symbolic Wounds: Puberty Rites and the Envious Male*. Glencoe, IL: Free Press.

Firth, Raymond. 1983. *We, the Tikopia: A Sociological Study of Kinship in Primitive Polynesia*. 2nd edition. Stanford, CA: Stanford University Press. (Orig. pub. 1957.)

Gennep, Arnold van. 1960. *The Rites of Passage*, trans. Monika B. Vizedom and Gabrielle L. Caffee. London: Routledge and Kegan Paul. (Orig. pub. 1909.)

Glick, Leonard B. 2005. *Marked in Your Flesh: Circumcision from Ancient Judea to Modern America*. Oxford, UK: Oxford University Press.

International Circumcision Information Reference Centre. "Links to Academic and General Sites with More Information." Available from http://www.circinfo.com/links_index.html.

Montagu, Ashley. 1995. "Mutilated Humanity." *Humanist* 55(4): 12–15. Available from http://www.thefreelibrary.com/Mutilated+humanity-a017100243.

Romberg, Rosemary. 1985. *Circumcision: The Painful Dilemma*. South Hadley, MA: Bergin and Garvey.

Singer, Philip, and Daniel E. Desole. 1967. "The Australian Subincision Ceremony Reconsidered: Vaginal Envy or Kangaroo Bifid Penis Envy." *American Anthropologist*, n.s., 69(3/4): 355–358.

Spencer, Baldwin, and F. J. Gillen. 1968. *The Native Tribes of Central Australia*. New York: Dover. (Orig. pub. 1899.)

Thomas, A. 2003. *Circumcision: An Ethnomedical Study*. 4th edition. London: Gilgal Society.

Turner, Victor W. 1962. "Three Symbols of Passage in Ndembu Circumcision Ritual: An Interpretation." In *Essays on the Ritual of Social Relations*, ed. Max Gluckman. Manchester, UK: Manchester University Press.

Andrew P. Lyons
Harriet D. Lyons

CIRCUS AND FAIR

Transgression of gender norms and sexual propriety was practically inherent to the culture of the fair or carnival, and to a lesser extent, strongly present in circus performances. Traveling carnivals originated in European medieval trade fairs, and developed during the early modern period, adding theater performances along public thoroughfares, such as the French *théâtre de la foire* in the seventeenth and eighteenth centuries, and displays of human oddities (Semonin 1996). By the nineteenth century a wide array of shows and single acts constituted programs of public entertainment that traveled to towns and cities, including, by the end of the century, food concessions, rides, games of chance, theaters, fun and horror houses, menageries, and even small circuses (Nickell 2005). In many countries, the fair or carnival became a beloved form of popular public entertainment, gradually losing some of its fascination toward the end of the twentieth century, although it remains alive in the early twenty-first century in county fairs all over the United States and in beach towns like Coney Island in Brooklyn, New York, or Old Orchard Beach in Maine. The circus, which can overlap with the carnival but has a different performance syntax and its own acts, such as clowns or equestrian acrobats, was born in the late eighteenth century in England and in Italy. It became a dominant form of entertainment in the United States, imported in 1793 from Britain as *the rolling show*, and by the late nineteenth century developed into what some scholars refer to as "the culture of the Big Top" (Davis 2002).

BODIES ON DISPLAY

Carnival and circus acts push the body beyond predictable, familiar physical constraints and, through the performance of skill and strength, test the limits of danger. Women performers captured the attention of audiences with daring horse-riding acrobatic acts and perilous exercises on the tightrope or flying trapeze, or by entering the lions' cage and taming ferocious beasts, or by weightlifting and wrestling. Bearded ladies jolted assumptions about the sexed wholeness of the body, normalcy, and the relationship of sex and gender. To compensate for the masculine beard, these women followed a strategy of self-presentation in publicity and photographs that stressed feminine clothing, female needle skills, marriage, and motherhood. For example, bearded ladies Annie Jones (1865–1902), Jane Barnell (aka Lady Olga, 1871–?), Madame Devere (1842–?), Baroness de Barcsy (1866–1925), and Grace Gilbert (1880-1925) all presented themselves in elegant feminine attire (Nickell 2005, Hartzman 2005). Tattooed women were displayed as exotic pictures, their completely decorated body both underlining and concealing nudity in a deeply erotic, but non-normative performance (Mifflin 1997). Male sideshow and trapeze acts could also challenge the boundaries of gender, with ambiguous body contours and gestures, the cultivation of grace and delicacy, or blurred gendered features, complicating sexual binaries.

The marginal, at times even "queer," associations of the carnival and circus were countered by entrepreneurs who stressed gender norms, family life, and a normal business environment. The U.S. circus skillfully manipulated tensions between the attraction power of the bold, risk-taking, new woman, while carefully reinscribing her into conventional feminine sartorial and gestural programs. Nudity was both exploited and hidden—by covering the female performers of *tableaux vivants* (living pictures) with body paint that emphasized contour but hid flesh, carefully controlled to be made "respectable" (Davis 2002). Such contrasts, between strength and daring and the ultrafeminine revealing clothing, were a mainstay of female circus acts.

EROTICISM AT THE FAIR

In turn-of-the-century France, carnivals regularly included Oriental-themed palaces where dancers—presented as avatars of an eponymous "Belle Fatma" or beautiful Fatma, a generic, stereotypical, "Oriental" dancer, usually French-born—regaled spectators with a safe, exotic spectacle of the "Other," through suggestively veiled bodies and sexually charged dances (Çelik and Kinney 1990). This feature of French fairgrounds and amusement parks was ubiquitous, reproduced in music-halls, such as the late-1880s Moulin Rouge in Paris (Oberthür 1994). The Parisian theme, in turn, in the United States, was the source of a whole industry of exotic attractions, and entertainment entrepreneur Frank Bostock (1866–1912) presented his early-twentieth-century exhibits entitled "Gay Paree" or "Moulin Rouge," advertised in brochures as "the sensation of London, the rage of Paris—with Parisian dancing girls and Mirza the queen," that fit into the girl-show genres of the carnival midway. The post–World War II fair in North America maintained an overt sexual component, through revues, shows with chorus girls and strip-tease acts, accompanying state-of-the-art musical performers of black music in particular (Stencell 2002).

In the United States the famous showman P. T. Barnum (1810–1891) created a special kind of museum to exhibit human wonders, along with other departures from natural norms. In France the equivalent was the "Musée Dupuytren" and its ilk, usually located inside the fair or midway. These museums were built on an array of shocking displays, eliciting fear, revulsion, and fascination among viewers, especially through highly visible sexual content. Mummified body parts and bodies in the cases and jars of the *musée anatomique*, provided uncensored glimpses of sexual secrets; the exhibition of a human specimen labeled as foreign or exotic reduced the "Other" to a consumable, helpless product. In the 1920s French poet Pierre MacOrlan (1883–1970) wrote about fairs from the turn of the twentieth century, describing displays of grotesquely deformed female organs made of wax and covered with the marks of syphilis and other sexually transmitted diseases (MacOrlan 1929).

The secreting-away of an exhibit behind heavily drawn curtains could work up viewers' prurient curiosity about the forbidden, promising access to undisclosed sexually illicit displays against an entrance fee of only a few cents extra (Nickell 2005, Stencell 2002). These secrets, once revealed, were simply puns or practical jokes, not remotely resembling the sensational revelations promised.

Fair organizers in turn of the twentieth century Europe were attacked for promoting sleazy sexuality and for favoring actual sex traffic in the alleys and shanties of the fairgrounds. In France, as in Germany (Otterman) moral conservatives periodically led politically motivated campaigns against the fairs and their alleged depravity (Rearick 1985). In 1929 a French journalist attacked the presentation of shows not suitable for children such as "The Mystery of Woman" or "The Well of the Parisian Woman" (Plessis 1929). Others, at the turn of the century, had charged that some erotic fair booths like the "Temple de l'Amour (temple of love), the "Salon de la Belle Amande (beautiful Amanda's salon), and the Palais de Phryné, (the palace of Phrynea—Latin poet Horace's promiscuous lover) were dens of prostitution. These booths were decorated with suggestive photographs and equipped with reflectors and enlarging lenses that allowed spectators to see the reproduction of tableaux from the salons, and they also had adjoining private rooms (Gallici-Rancy [1903?]).

The carnival midway's transgressive connotations continued well into the 1950s, through the presence of sex, eroticism, violent images and emotions, and the social marginality of many of its employees. Queer gender performances were found in North American *half-and-half* shows. These were impersonations of fake hermaphrodites by performers such as Albert-Alberta the man woman (1899–1963), who was actually a man, and maintained the claim to his dual sex—as well as being a native of France—until his death (Hartzman 2005), or the Great Omi, the Zebra man (1892–1969), married to a woman who emulated his zebra tattooing, wore lipstick and nail polish as well during his performances.

After the 1960s, the overtly sexual content of carnivals and fairs may have receded; according to Stencell, "Girl shows were leaving the midway just as go-go clubs, topless bars and hotel lounges with strippers flourished" (2002, p. 244). However, the overall picture seems more complex. English striptease revues, such as "Twisting the Nude," were still operating in the mid-1960s, and standard rides such as the "Skylift" or "The Looping" in Germany, Holland, and France, and even the United States, continued well after that, to exploit images of scantily clad women in suggestive poses on panels and sideboards. Sex shows endured, including the French "*Naturisme*" (nude) show painted by the prolific fairground artist Jacques Courtois, active in the late 1970s. Violent sexual images, inspired by cartoon and horror film motifs, were prevalent from the 1970s on, for instance with a scatological twist on the façade of Coney Island's Dark Maze (Weedon and Ward 2003). In the early twenty-first century, many carnivals and fairgrounds retain the voyeuristic or fetishistic erotic content of the past in the exterior and interior décor of booths and rides. At the same time, since the 1990s women performance artists have blended revue forms and nude or semi-nude dancing with shows infused with their own, less conventional, and less male-driven views of sexuality, for instance at the Coney Island Mermaid Parade (Essig 2005).

BIBLIOGRAPHY

Bone, Howard. 2001. *Side Show: My Life with Geeks, Freaks, and Vagabonds in the Carny Trade.* Northville, MI: Sun Dog Press.

Bostock, Frank C. [1900?] *A Treatise on Street Fairs.* Baltimore, MD: Press of H. L. Washburn

Çelik, Zeinep, and Leila Kinney. 1990. "Ethnography and Exhibitionism at the Expositions Universelles." *Assemblage* 13: 34–59.

Davis, Janet M. 2002. *The Circus Age: Culture & Society Under the American Big Top.* Chapel Hill: University of North Carolina Press.

Essig, Laurie. 2005. "The Mermaid and the Heterosexual Imagination." In *Thinking Straight: The Power, the Promise, and the Paradox of Heterosexuality,* ed. Chrys Ingraham, 151–164. New York: Routledge.

Fretz, Eric. 1996. "P.T. Barnum's Theatrical Selfhood and the Nineteenth-Century Culture of Exhibition." In *Freakery: Cultural Spectacles of the Extraordinary Body,* ed. Rosemarie Garland Thomson, 97–107. New York: New York University Press.

Gallici-Rancy, Henri. [1903?]. *Les Forains peints par eux-mêmes* [Carneys in Their Own Words]. Bordeaux, France: G. Gounouilhou.

Hartzman, Marc. 2005. *American Sideshow. An Encyclopedia of History's Most Wondrous and Curiously Strange Performers.* New York: Jeremy P. Tarcher/Penguin.

MacOrlan, Pierre. 1929. *Fêtes foraines* [Carnivals]. In *Œuvres poétiques complètes* [Complete Poetic Works], ill. Edy Legrand. Paris: Le Capitole.

Mifflin, Margot. 1997. *Bodies of Subversion: A Secret History of Women and Tattoo.* New York: Juno Books.

Nickell, Joe. 2005. *Secrets of the Sideshows.* Lexington: University Press of Kentucky.

Oberthür, Mariel. 1994. *Montmartre en liesse: 1880–1900.* Paris: Musée Carnavalet.

Otterman, Stephan. 2000. "On Display: Tattooed Entertainers in America and Germany." *Written on the Body: The Tattoo in European and American History,* ed. Jane Caplan, 193–211. Princeton, NJ: Princeton University Press.

Plessis, Yves. 1929. "Fêtes foraines et pornographie." *Petit Bleu* (Dossier Bibliothèque de L'Arsenal, Paris, #RO 16589).

Rearick, Charles. 1985. *Pleasures of the Belle Epoque: Entertainment and Festivity in Turn-of-the-Century France.* New Haven, CT: Yale University Press.

Semonin, Paul. 1996. "Monsters in the Marketplace: The Exhibition of Human Oddities in Early Modern England." In *Freakery: Cultural Spectacles of the Extraordinary Body,* ed. Rosemarie Garland Thomson, 69–81. New York: New York University Press.

Stencell, A. W. 2002. *Seeing is Believing: America's Sideshows.* Toronto: ECW Press.

Thomsom, Rosemarie Garland, ed. 1996. *Freakery: Cultural Spectacles of the Extraordinary Body.* New York: New York University Press.

Weedon, Geoff, and Richard Ward. 1981; 2003. *Fairground Art.* London: New Cavendish Books.

Francesca Canadé Sautman

CIVIL WARS

SEE *War.*

CLEOPATRA

68 BCE–30 CE

Cleopatra VII Thea Philopator was a member of the Ptolemaic dynasty and the last pharaonic ruler of Egypt. The Ptolemies, descendents of the Macedonian general Ptolemy I (c. 366–283 BCE), had ruled Egypt for more than two centuries by the time of Cleopatra's birth. Cleopatra, an astute politician, attempted to resist the growing might of Rome by forming an eastern alliance with Mark Antony (c. 82–30 BCE). But her plans failed, and her death saw Egypt absorbed into the Roman Empire.

CLEOPATRA AND JULIUS CAESAR

Ptolemy XIII and his sister-wife Cleopatra VII came to the throne in 51 BCE. The relationship between the two quickly deteriorated, and in summer 48 BCE, Rome was forced to intervene to prevent civil war. Julius Caesar (r. 58–44 BCE) summoned Ptolemy and Cleopatra to Alexandria and, angered by Ptolemy's involvement in the murder of the Roman statesman Pompey (106–48 BCE), declared Rome's support for the queen. Cleopatra and Caesar spent the winter besieged in Alexandria. By the time Roman reinforcements arrived the following spring, the two were lovers. Defeated, Ptolemy XIII fled and drowned in the Nile.

Cleopatra, Queen of Egypt. © BETTMANN/CORBIS.

Cleopatra, now married to her eleven-year-old brother Ptolemy XIV, was restored to her throne. In June 47 BCE, she gave birth to Caesar's son, Ptolemy Caesar (Caesarion, 47–30 BCE). Cleopatra and Ptolemy followed Caesar to Rome, returning to Egypt after Caesar's assassination in 44 BCE. Ptolemy died soon after and the three-year-old Caesarion became Ptolemy XV.

CLEOPATRA AND MARK ANTONY

Two men ruled the Roman World at that time: Octavian (later called Augustus, 63–14 BCE) controlled the western empire and Mark Antony controlled the east. Cleopatra allied herself with Antony and the two became lovers. In 40 BCE, Cleopatra gave birth to twins. But back in Rome, Antony was preparing to marry Octavian's sister, Octavia.

In 37 BCE Antony left Rome for Syria, where he sent for Cleopatra. Together they planned an alliance that would restore the Egyptian empire. Initially all went well, and Egypt regained some of its lost eastern territories. But the 36 BCE Parthian campaign was a disaster, and in 31 BCE, Octavian defeated Antony and Cleopatra at the battle of Actium. Cleopatra retreated to Alexandria and, as Antony set off for battle, locked herself in her mausoleum. Incorrectly informed that Cleopatra had committed suicide, Antony fell on his sword. He was taken back to Alexandria and died in Cleopatra's arms. Cleopatra committed suicide by either snakebite or by poisons on August 12, 30 BCE.

A FEMME FATALE?

Cleopatra's story was recorded by contemporary historians primarily interested in the lives of the Roman rulers. Plutarch's *Parallel Lives* served as the inspiration behind William Shakespeare's *Antony and Cleopatra*. Cleopatra's appearances on stage, page, and screen have led to her acceptance as the archetypal femme fatale. Contemporary images of Cleopatra, however, suggest that she was not an outstanding beauty. Her portraits may be split into two distinct groups: Whereas the Egyptian-style images show a traditional Egyptian queen, her classical portraiture shows Cleopatra in Roman dress and hairstyle. Perhaps most lifelike of all, her coins show a woman with a prominent nose and chin who looks determined rather than seductive.

SEE ALSO *Egypt, Pharaonic.*

BIBLIOGRAPHY

Hughes-Hallett, Lucy. 1990. *Cleopatra: Histories, Dreams, and Distortions.* London: Bloomsbury.

Walker, Susan, and Sally-Ann Ashton, eds. 2003. *Cleopatra Reassessed.* London: British Museum.

Joyce A. Tyldesley

CLITORIDECTOMY

SEE *Female Genital Mutilation.*

CLITORIS

The clitoris is a smooth round knob of tissue located just above the urethra at the opening of the vagina and is the major site of female sexual stimulation. The word *clitoris* comes from the Greek *kleitoris*, meaning "little hill" or "slope," or possibly *klei-eo*, meaning "to shut." It is sometimes referred to as "clit" in slang, a term that is also used derogatorily to describe a contemptible female. The French call the clitoris a *bijou*, meaning "jewel," the Russians call it a *pokhotnic*, meaning "lust," and the Tuamotuan people of Polynesia have at least ten different words for this sexual organ.

PHYSIOLOGY OF THE CLITORIS

Embryologically, the clitoris derives from the same tissue as the penis. The presence of the male hormone testosterone during early fetal development causes this tissue to differentiate into a penis, and the absence of the hormone causes the tissue to develop into a clitoris. Though both organs function to transmit and receive sexual sensation, the penis also contains the urethra, which provides the means for expelling sperm and urine from the body. As the sex researchers William H. Masters and Virginia E. Johnson (1966) point out, the clitoris's only known function is to give sexual pleasure to the woman.

The body of the clitoris consists of a shaft with a glans located at its distal end. Though the average clitoris is approximately 1 inch long and 1/4 inch wide, there is considerable variability in the size among women. There is no connection between the size of the organ and its sensitivity to sexual stimulation. The clitoris contains a rich network of nerve endings and is highly sensitive to both direct and indirect stimulation. Accordingly, during sexual activity, women often prefer indirect stimulation of the organ by stroking the clitoral hood or the mons, the fatty tissue above the clitoral area. Lubrication from the vagina, saliva, or personal lubricant products also helps to improve sensation on the glans by eliminating discomfort caused by direct friction on the sensitive tissue. Like its homologue the penis, the clitoris is composed of erectile tissue consisting of the corpora cavernosa, two spongy masses of tissue filled with numerous tiny blood vessels that become engorged with blood during sexual stimulation and cause the organ to enlarge. Physiologically, the process is similar to that of a penile erection in that the clitoris emerges away from the body, but because of its smaller size, this movement is not always obvious.

The clitoris is covered by a prepuce or clitoral hood (analogous to the male foreskin) that is a continuation of the skin of the upper portion of the labia minora. The clitoral glans (the visible and most sensitive aspect of the organ) may be revealed by parting the labia minora and retracting the hood (it is usually the prepuce that is pierced in what is often mistakenly called a clitoral piercing). Smegma, from the Greek word meaning "that which is wiped off," is a cheeselike secretion that often accumulates under the clitoral hood or around the clitoris and is formed by the deposit of local secretions and sloughed-off skin. It has no known physiological purpose and can sometimes become infected by microscopic organisms that form lumps under the prepuce, and these lumps can make sexual activity painful. This can easily be avoided by retracting the hood during bathing to wash off any accumulated material.

FUNCTION OF THE CLITORIS

During sexual stimulation (through direct genital contact or erotic psychological factors), the clitoris and its surrounding genital tissue experience myotonia (muscular tension or rigidity) and vasocongestion (the pooling of blood in the corpora cavernosa). The accumulation of blood causes the clitoris to swell and the nearby labia to flatten and spread, exposing the clitoris to stimulation. Masters and Johnson describe this early phase of sexual response as the excitement stage. As stimulation continues, the woman enters a plateau stage, an advanced state of arousal that immediately precedes orgasm and is characterized by further vasocongestion and swelling of the clitoris and other external genital organs. As a result, the clitoris shortens and withdraws beneath the clitoral hood. This is sometimes mistaken as a sign of diminished arousal, but in fact it is a physiological manifestation that the woman's sexual response is increasing. Orgasm, the next stage, follows soon after and provides a release of sexual tension. Climax is marked, on average, by three to fifteen contractions or pulsations that occur at close intervals. During the final or resolution stage, the orgasm triggers the release of the pooled blood in the clitoris and other engorged areas. Within five to ten seconds following sexual climax, the clitoris returns to its normal, unaroused state. Though the clitoris may remain sensitive to further stimulation immediately following this resolution, women, unlike men, do not experience a refractory period when they are incapable of experiencing another orgasm. As a result, if sexual stimulation continues, women can become aroused again and achieve multiple orgasms. When orgasm does not occur after arousal, sexual tension gradually diminishes as pooled blood slowly leaves the clitoris and other genital areas.

HISTORICAL AND CULTURAL BELIEFS ABOUT THE CLITORIS

Freudian psychoanalytic theory describes two types of female orgasm: the clitoral and the vaginal. Clitoral orgasms were believed to result from direct clitoral stimulation (such as with masturbation) and were symptomatic of childhood fixation. Vaginal orgasms, achieved through coitus, were thought to signal the passage of the woman to a mature sexuality. Masters and Johnson, who monitored women's sexual response, later refuted this theory. Their findings suggested that female orgasm involves the same physiological events whether the stimulation is clitoral or vaginal. They did note, however, that orgasms achieved through masturbation (especially of the clitoris) were frequently more intense than those reached through coitus alone. This may be the result of the indirect stimulation of the clitoris during coitus (as the thrusting of the penis causes the clitoral hood to move back and forth over the clitoris). Other researchers suggest that there may be three categories of female orgasm—vulval, uterine, and blended—and that the source of stimulation (whether clitoral or vaginal) is not a determining factor in the type of climax.

In the early nineteenth century, physicians used to treat hysteria, a condition named for the Greek word for uterus, *hystera*, by manually stimulating the clitoris until the woman reached a cathartic release. One enterprising doctor devised a mechanical vibrator to give his fingers a rest and to speed up the time necessary for treatments. Clitorectomies, the surgical removal of the clitoris, were performed in the United States in the nineteenth and early twentieth centuries to cure chronic masturbation or promiscuity in women. Clitorectomies and clitoralplasties (surgical reduction of the clitoris) continue to be performed even into the early twenty-first century in cases in which an infant girl is born with a prominent clitoris, even when there is no other indication other than aesthetic.

In many African and Middle Eastern cultures, especially in Muslim countries including Indonesia, young girls undergo a circumcision that may involve the nontherapeutic surgical removal of portions or all of the external genitalia, including the clitoris, the clitoral hood, and labia (a procedure that would correspond to the removal of the penis as well as other external genitalia in males). Female circumcision also may involve sewing the opening to the vagina closed, leaving only a very small hole for urine and menses to exit the body. Though the practice may have originated in ancient efforts to improve genital hygiene (perhaps by eliminating or reducing the amount of accumulated smegma under the prepuce), there is no medical indication for female circumcision. Nevertheless, the procedure is widely practiced, with roughly 100 to 140 million women having undergone the procedure and an additional two million females circumcised each year. Various groups, including Amnesty International and the World Health Organization, condemn the practice as female genital mutilation (FGM), the most common form being the excision of the clitoris and the labia minora.

Proponents of female circumcision defend the practice, citing the following as deeply held beliefs:

1. It is a traditional rite of passage for young girls into womanhood;
2. It maintains culturally mandated chastity and fidelity by suppressing sexual desire in women;
3. It improves a woman's fertility and survival of the fetus (despite medical evidence that it can interfere with both);
4. The practice is required by the Islamic faith (though female circumcisions were practiced prior to Islam).

While most female circumcisions (80%) are performed on young girls or infants, adult women voluntarily submit to the procedure because of societal beliefs that women with intact genitals are impure. Female genital mutilation may lead to medical consequences including shock, pain, hemorrhage, urine retention, and scarring. In addition, damage may result in urinary incontinence, sexual dysfunction, complications in childbirth, and psychological anxiety and depression.

By the twenty-first century, the clitoris has become a figure in the struggle for women's rights. One of the major focuses of this fight is the eradication of the practice of FGM, a controversial position that has generated counterclaims that efforts to ban female circumcision represents a Western condescension of traditional Islamic beliefs. Women's advocacy groups also assert that the clitoris has been neglected and misunderstood even by Western cultures for centuries, noting that the most important organ for female sexual sensation rarely receives more than a brief paragraph in anatomy or physiology textbooks. Further, they claim that young girls are culturally conditioned to deny their clitorises by well-meaning parents who teach their daughters that they have vaginas but omit the presence of the clitoris even though it is part of the external and visible genitalia. In addition, young girls are commonly taught to wear underpants at night, a practice that subliminally sends the message that the female genitalia is unclean and should not be touched.

SEE ALSO *Orgasm.*

BIBLIOGRAPHY

Chalker, Rebecca. 2000. *The Clitoral Truth: The Secret World at Your Fingertips.* New York: Seven Stories Press.

Masters, William H., and Virginia E. Johnson. 1966. *Human Sexual Response.* Boston: Little, Brown.

Rathus, Spencer A.; Jeffrey S. Nevid; and Lois Fichner-Rathus. 2005. *Human Sexuality in a World of Diversity.* 6th edition. Boston: Pearson Allyn and Bacon.

Diane Sue Saylor

CLOSETS

Derived from the French *closet,* itself from the Latin word *clausum* (shut), the English word closet, meaning a private room, appeared first in the fourteenth century. Starting in about 1400, the meaning was extended to include any secret place, real or metaphorical (i.e., the closet of the conscience). A storage room, the common North American meaning, arose in the late-sixteenth and seventeenth centuries, as did other specialized meanings, such as a room used for private devotion or a bathroom (water-closet). The phrase *closet-sins* can be found in seventeenth-century texts, while the phrase *skeleton in the closet* (a dark secret) did not appear until the mid-nineteenth century. The idea that a forbidden sexuality is the secret in the closet first appeared in the mid- and late-twentieth century, in phrases such as *to be in the closet* and *come out of the closet, closet queen*, and *closet case* (though probably the colloquial use of such phrases predates their use in written form). George Chauncey, in *Gay New York: Gender, Urban Culture, and the Making of the Gay Male World, 1890–1940* (1994), suggests that the social experience of closeting is largely a post-World War II phenomenon.

The closet was crucial to twentieth-century gay/lesbian politics, with coming out of the closet into visibility constituting the major strategy of gay liberation. While sociologist Steven Seidman argues in *Beyond the Closet* (2002), a study focused largely on the United States, that the closet no longer remains constitutive of lesbian/gay experience, almost all queer lives still begin within the closet of nuclear families (especially in Europe and North America) that assume the heterosexuality of their children, and coming out remains an integral part of most gay/lesbian/bi/trans lives.

The closet is central to queer theory, largely because of the work of critical theorist Eve Kosofsky Sedgwick in *Epistemology of the Closet* (1990). Sedgwick analyzes the ways in which a late-nineteenth and early-twentieth century Euro-American sexuality emerged and was shaped into the binarism of homo/heterosexuality. She shows how sexuality was (and remains) especially charged around questions of knowledge and ignorance, secrets and their disclosure. The closet is, for Sedgwick, a "curious space that is both internal and marginal to the culture: centrally representative of its motivating passions and contradictions, even while marginalized by its orthodoxies" (1990, p. 56). Related to Sedgwick's work is literary critic D.A. Miller's analysis in *The Novel and the Police* (1988) of the open secret, a secret generally known but unspoken.

While Sedgwick focuses on the late-nineteenth and twentieth centuries, she acknowledges that the specific attachment of epistemological questions to homosexuality is the culmination of a long Western association of sexuality with secrets and unspeakability. Saint Paul admonishes, "But fornication, and all uncleanness, or covetousness, let it not be once named among you" (Ephesians 5:3), and later Christian writers reiterate and elaborate this taboo. In the Middle Ages unnamability was closely attached to sodomy, as professor of religion Mark Jordan shows in *The Invention of Sodomy in Christian Theology* (1997). A good deal of medieval and early modern scholarship—e.g., Karma Lochrie's *Covert Operations* (1998) and Richard Rambuss's *Closet Devotions* (1998)—has focused its attention on the construction of erotically charged closets.

BIBLIOGRAPHY

Chauncey, George. 1994. *Gay New York: Gender, Urban Culture, and the Makings of the Gay Male World, 1890-1940.* New York: Basic Books.

Lochrie, Karma. 1998. *Covert Operations: The Medieval Uses of Secrecy*. Philadelphia: University of Pennsylvania Press.

Miller, D.A. 1988. *The Novel and The Police.* University of California Press.

Rambuss, Richard. 1998. *Closet Devotions.* Durham, NC: Duke University Press.

Sedgwick, Eve Kosofsky. 1990. *Epistemology of the Closet.* Berkeley: University of California Press.

Seidman, Steven. 2002. *Beyond the Closet: The Transformation of Gay and Lesbian Life.* New York: Routledge.

Steven F. Kruger

CLOTHING

Fashion is the primary framework through which human beings read and understand the concept of gender. Whereas the term *fashion* can be understood to mean clothing styles that change in swift succession (Johnson 2003), it is often used synonymously with the word *dress* to refer to an assemblage of modifications and supplements to the body, including such things as coiffed hair, painted skin, tattoos, garments, jewelry, and accessories (Roach-Higgins 1992) arrayed in a formal arrangement that "expresses the aesthetics and customs of a cultural period" (Schreier 1989, p. 2). According to Renaissance scholar Stephen Greenblatt (b. 1943) quoted in Christopher Breward's *The Culture of Fashion*, ties between the ideas of fashion and identity parallel "etymological changes in the word *fashion* itself: 'As a term for the action or process of making, for particular features or appearance, for a distinct style or pattern, the word had long been in use, but it is in the sixteenth century that the word *fashion* seems to come into wide currency as a way of redesigning the forming of a self" (Breward 1995, p. 69).

SEX AND GENDER

The primary genders framed in fashionable dress in most of European and North American culture are masculine (heterosexual implied) and feminine (heterosexual implied). Scholars such as Marit K. Munson define other sexual identities, such as homosexual-male (gay), homosexual-female (lesbian), transsexual (either male to female or female to male), transvestites, drag queens, cross-dressers, and ceremonial assumption by men or women of symbols of the other as alternative genders (e.g., Munson 2000). Several of these categories are defined by their use of fashion as an expression of gender choice, as discussed by Cressida Heyes, who includes as transgender "gays, lesbians and straights who exhibit any kind of dress and/or behavior interpreted as 'transgressing' gender roles" (Heyes 2003, p. 1107). This article addresses mainly European and North American society and primarily with masculine and feminine differentiation.

GENDER AND FASHION STUDIES

The study of gender through dress has been concentrated within the historical and art–historical approaches, where it is often associated with developing feminist analysis of historical materials (Jones 2004, Grossinger 1997). Within the anthropological and sociological disciplines, the study of gender and dress often refers to *traditional* or indigenous and ceremonial wear and its meanings within that culture (Taylor 2002, Eicher 2001), but it also encompasses approaches combining the elements of multiple discourses, contradictions, and active production of meaning. Literary criticism also addresses issues of gender identification, as does women's studies. Finally, within the burgeoning field of fashion studies, the study of gender is often associated with how humans define themselves as *masculine* or *feminine* through the medium of clothing (Holliday 2001).

GENDER AS CHANGING SOCIAL CONSTRUCTION

Throughout known human history men and women have distinguished themselves from one another using clothing and related forms of adornment. In each time and place and social structure, the complete appearance that constitutes masculine or feminine has been different—a social construct in its own right. These nuances of appearance are not always apparent to subsequent observers of these trends. For example, a twenty-first-century viewer might interpret the pink silk suit worn by a perfumed and made-up French courtier (male) of 1760 as effeminate or very feminine. Within the context of the eighteenth-century French court, however, such an outfit was an expression of masculinity, skillful understanding of court negotiation, and power. Whereas the color pink became associated with femininity sometime in the nineteenth century, a few vestiges of the earlier masculine association remain. One example is the pink polo shirt still commonly sold by men's clothiers such as LaCoste and Polo.

GENDER, DRESS, AND OCCASION

In her essay "Appearance and Identity," Valerie Steele points out that women tend to wear more clothing than men do on an everyday basis, expressing cultural ideals of modesty, but this paradigm shifts for ceremonial occasions, such as rites of passage, religious ceremonies, and warfare (Steele 1989a). In her work with the Kalabiri tribe of Nigeria, Joanne B. Eicher studies this idea in greater depth, comparing tribal practice for both daily and ceremonial wear with European and North American bridal practice (as expressed in *Brides* magazine). Her findings seem to support a general idea that ceremonial dress for women tends to focus on their sexual attributes (waist, breasts, back, and arms) whereas masculine ceremonial dress tends to emphasize power and wealth (employing more clothing and jewelry, not less) on such occasions (Eicher 2001).

THE PROGRESSION OF FASHION

Fashion as people think of it, with varied options, styles, and cyclical changes of features worn by members of the upper classes (with less expensive versions that trickle down to lower classes) began somewhere between the twelfth and fourteenth centuries in Europe. During the twelfth century both men and women wore floor-length robes with very similar cut and decoration. Noblemen could be distinguished by their long hair and beards. The contemporary ecclesiastical chronicler Vitalis described this style: "They parted their hair from the crown of the head to the forehead, grew long and luxurious locks like women, and loved to deck themselves in long, overtight shirts and tunics … scarcely any knight appears in public with his head uncovered and decently shorn …" (Tortora 1994, p. 93). Skirts might be slit front and back for riding horseback, and they often carried swords.

In contrast, women frequently would wear veils or caps. This theme of feminine head coverings continues through many eras. A further division in female status was often made between married and unmarried women. Generally, an unmarried woman might show some of her hair, whereas a married woman wore veils or caps. Untidiness or inappropriately loose hair on a married woman might be associated with immodest behavior, as demonstrated in this instruction by Menagier de Paris, an older man writing to his young wife in the late fourteenth century: "Take care first that the collar of your shift [underdress], and of your … cotte [dress], and surcoat, do not hang out one over the other as happens with certain drunken, foolish or witless women, who have no care for their honor, nor for the honesty of their estate or of their husbands, and who walk with roving eyes and heads horribly reared up like a lion, their hair straggling out of their wimples [pieces of veil worn under the chin] …" (Tortora 1994, p. 110).

A major shift in fashion silhouette and construction took place beginning in France and spread to the rest of Europe and England after 1340. Men and women left the long, loose garments of the twelfth and thirteenth centuries behind and began to wear more tightly fit and carefully shaped clothing. For younger men this included garments in new, shorter popular lengths ranging from the knee to just below the crotch. Literature of the time marked the shape of a man's leg as a style point. For women concurrent styles remained long, but suddenly exposed neck, shoulders, and bosom. This trend for fitted garments may have developed from men's quilted armor padding, and required padding and elaborate fitting to produce the desirable barrel-chested shape of the era. Women's garments likewise were worn tight, and emphasized the waist and an expanded chest area. Garments for both men and women were fitted and shaped in ways that affected and created a new posture.

In the fifteenth century both men and women added voluminous robes over the fitted garments or cotes. Here again, women's clothes continued to be long, but shorter garments remained an option for men. Women's headdresses took a leap toward the fantastical; they are depicted as quite tall, often bifurcated, and frequently elaborately decorated, whereas men's remained somewhat simpler. Advice offered to the Lover in the contemporary *Roman de la Rose* (a popular poem of the time quoted in Breward's *The Culture of Fashion*) instructs a man to "dress well and wear good footwear, as your pocketbook permits. You should have a good tailor who knows how to sew fine stitches and make your sleeves well fitting. Wear fresh, new shoes quite frequently, so closely fitting that lower-class people will wonder how you got into them and how you will take them off. When you go out, carry gloves, a silk purse, and wear an attractive belt ... Wash your hands, polish your teeth, and have no sign of dirt on your fingernails. Sew on your sleeves, comb your hair, but do not make use of any face makeup, which is for women only, or for sodomites" (Breward 1995, p. 23).

Note that these descriptions emphasizes appropriate attire for the station of both male and female, but with different traits celebrated in masculine (have a good tailor) and feminine (honesty of estate or of their husbands.) The same type of chivalric romance describing dress for the lover above is quoted describing the object of his passion thus: "She had blond hair finely curled. The eyes were gay and laughing, the face shapely, the nose high and well-placed. The lips were more red than a cherry or a rose [perhaps the impetus for the cosmetic enhancement eschewed for the Lover] ... and her teeth were white and fine. She had breasts, hard, which lifted up her gown just as if they were nuts, she was slender about the waist so that one could enclose it in two hands. The daisies lying under the instep of her feet ... were outright black compared to her feet and legs, so very white was the little girl" (Breward 1995, p. 32).

The middle of the fifteenth century saw the introduction of one of the most notoriously anatomical fashion accessories in the history of European and North American fashion. The codpiece began as a triangular piece of cloth fastened over the opening at the top of men's hose. It continued to develop, however. By the first decade of the sixteenth century, it had expanded into an oval or tubular protrusion over the wearer's crotch, often standing out from underneath men's short doublet skirts. As the sixteenth century progressed, it developed in size and prominence. It was usually decorated to coordinate with men's elaborate trunkhose, or the top part of men's leg coverings that were frequently paned, embroidered, and stuffed. Codpieces made of rich fabrics pulled though slashes in the base fabric for a multitextured effect are depicted frequently in portraiture in the second half of the sixteenth century. To put the codpiece in context with the rest of fashion, this era saw unprecedented artifice and shaping in clothing for both sexes. Men's clothes early in the century included tightly fitted lower hose, a skirted doublet fit tightly over the chest, and a gown with exaggerated broad sleeves, and evolved into a series of attenuated and artificially produced cone shapes by the century's end.

Women's clothes demonstrated similar artifice. Sometime in the early sixteenth century the corset, perhaps the most conspicuously fetishized female garment in European and North American fashion, developed from earlier fitted and shaped bodice styles. By the end of the sixteenth century women's clothes were even more extremely shaped than men's, with long rigid bodice fronts enforced by corsetry, low décolletage and long skirts padded to an extreme drumlike width at the hip.

Certain common characteristics between men and women's clothes, such as elongated bodice/doublet points, wide neck ruffs, and the wearing of tall, *masculine-styled* hats created a cultural anxiety about appropriate gender display. This was expressed by Puritan pamphleteer and poet Phillip Stubbes (1550?–1593?), writing in England in the mid-1580s: "Our apparell was given us as a signe distinctive to discern betwixt sex and sex, & therfore one to weare the Aparel of another sex, is to participate with the same, and to adulturate the veritie of his own kinde" (Breward 1995, p. 93).

In the seventeenth century both men's and women's clothes had simplified, in both silhouette and embellishment. But the luxurious court of French king Louis XIV (1638–1715) at Versailles brought the return of rigidly shaped, elaborate styles for women and heavily embellished clothes for men. It also introduced more modern men's clothing in the form of jacket, vest, and loose short pants. It is from these pieces that men's iconic power garment, the three-piece suit, developed into a recognizable outfit. English King Charles II (1630–1685) brought this combination of vest and long coat with him when he returned to take the throne in England in 1666. The diarist Samuel Pepys (1633–1703) observed this change in fashion: "This day the King begins to put on his vest, and I did see several persons of the House of Lords and Commons too, great courtiers, who are in it; being a long cassock close to the body, of black cloth and pinked [cut] with white silk under it, and a coat over it, and the legs ruffled with a black riband like a pigeon's leg' and upon the whole I wish the King may keep it, for it is a very find and handsome garment" (Tortora 1994, p. 185).

As the seventeenth century progressed, greater association between women and fashion and frivolity developed. This trend began with further differentiation between the lives of men and women concurrent with the rise of urban environments (Breward 1995). Extending into the eighteenth century this trend fueled changes both for the workers in fashion industries, as well as the ideals of what men and women should wear. Breward discusses the sexual connotations of urban female fashion "ritualized and bound up in the follies of fashion, gratuitous consumption and entertainment" (Breward 1995, p. 102). By the eighteenth century the urban fashion business had evolved partly based on the evolving assumptions that women were essentially more interested than men in fashion and that fashion itself was inherently frivolous (Jones 2004). Fashion's very production began to bifurcate along gender lines, "shaped by rivalries between seamstresses, linen drapers, ladies' hairdressers and fashion merchants" (Jones 2004, p. 5). This shift represented a battle on the part of female seamstresses in Paris to make a livelihood independent from the male-run tailor's guild. The seamstresses used as a principle argument that "female seamstresses should make clothing for women and children because ... it was consonant with female modesty to be dressed ... by a woman" (Jones 2004, p. 82).

At the beginning of the eighteenth century, both men's and women's clothing was elaborate, colorful, and multilayered. In the middle of the century, at its most extreme, well-to-do women wore corsets with elaborate hoops that extended their skirts many feet to the sides. Men's clothing retained the form of breeches, fitted vest, and long coat, while the breeches and vest moved from loose to formfitting. Both men and women of the upper classes wore pale colors, dramatic woven silks, and elaborate trimmings, as illustrated by an observer named Mary Granville in 1739: "The Duchess of Bedford's petticoat was green padusoy [sic], embroidered very richly with gold and silver and a few colours; ... there was an abundance of embroidery, and many people in gowns and petticoats of different colours. The men were as fine as the ladies ... My Lord Baltimore was in light brown and silver, his coat lined quite throughout with ermine" (Tortora 1994, p. 243).

Nineteenth-Century Costume Print of Two Women Strolling. *This image emphasizes the exaggerated trains that were popular in nineteenth-century dress.* © HISTORICAL PICTURE ARCHIVE/CORBIS.

"THE GREAT MASCULINE RENUNCIATION"

By the end of the eighteenth century this similarity in color and embellishment between the dress of men and women had largely evaporated. Whereas men's dress of the early nineteenth century still appears quite colorful by late twentieth-century standards, it had simplified dramatically from the apparel worn by Lord Baltimore as described above. Speculation about causes for this shift has occupied many fashion theorists, most famously the psychologist J. C. Flugel (1884–1955). In his 1930 work *The Psychology of Clothes*, Flugel referred to the transformation of men's clothing between 1760 and 1795 from the colorful silks of the French Ancien régime(the social and political systems in place before the Revolution of 1789) to the soberer attire worn by men since the French Revolution as "The Great Masculine Renunciation." He described this event thus: "Men gave up their right to all the brighter, gayer, more elaborate, and more varied forms of ornamentation, leaving these entirely to the use of women, and thereby making their own tailoring the most austere and ascetic of the arts." He goes on to explain several reasons for this change in fashion, including, "[Men] henceforth aimed at being only useful. So far as clothes remained of importance to him, his utmost endeavors could lie only in the direction of being 'correctly' attired, not of being elegantly or elaborately attired" (Purdy 2004, p. 103). He ascribes the background of this change to the new social order dictated by the French Revolution, which demanded "a greater uniformity of dress, a uniformity achieved particularly by the abolition of those distinctions which had formerly divided the wealthy from the poor. … [The] change in question implied at the same time a greater simplification of dress, by a general approximation to more plebeian standards that were possible to all. This tendency to greater simplification was powerfully reinforced by a second aspect of the general change of ideals which the Revolution implied by the fact that the ideal of work had now become respectable. … [With the Revolutionary ideals] a man's most important activities were passed, not in the drawing-room, but in the workshop, the counting-house, the office-places which had, by long tradition, been associated with relatively simple costume" (Purdy 2004, p. 104).

Flugel's primary argument, that men no longer cared about being fashionably dressed, has been attacked in recent work by Breward, who uses examples from nineteenth-century trade publications to describe modish clothing for gentlemen at the turn of the twentieth century: "Far from conforming to the constraining dictates of renunciation, [fashionable dress] traced the demands of the social calendar as closely as the female wardrobe" (Breward 2001, p. 165). Both Steele and Breward explain this shift in fashion as a shift in fashionable definitions of masculinity: setting aside the ideal of an aristocratic courtier, not to a bank clerk, but to the ideal of an English country gentleman (Steele 1989b, p. 16). This shift away from French formality reflects English pastoral ideals and the development of North American culture, with its underlying antielitist themes. Within this evolving context masculine ideals shift focus to physical vigor enforced by the emerging technology of tailoring. Breward illustrates this new ideal by describing how the tape measure, a new garment construction tool, allowed tailors to "construct a unique cloth carapace … [using] published rules which presented systems of proportion as universal law [and] lent tailors the ability to fit a generalized pattern to anyone who desired it" (Breward 2001, p. 166).

Tailors themselves identified this new mechanical ability with humanistic ideals of art and philosophy. Dr. Henry Wampen, a German mathematician whose books on tailoring made a large impact on nineteenth-century tailoring methods, expressed it thus: "I took a great interest in art and philosophy, and a question was then much discussed whether the Grecian ideal of beauty was simply ideal or founded on a scientific basis. … I was induced to measure certain statues, and I came to the conclusion that the Grecian sculptors worked on a scientific basis …" (Breward 2001). Lest this seem far from the discourse of fashion, consider the text of a series of *Punch* cartoons of 1882, titled "Lost Illusions." These showed a male subject wearing sporting and formal wear commented on by an audience of potential female suitors. In the plate showing athletic wear, the gentleman "looked like a young Greek god, fresh from Olympus." In the formal wear plate, the same man dressed in a morning suit "looked for all the world like a commonplace young clerk." Later, the same subject models for an intellectual, who perceives that he looks "like a Greek god even in his every-day clothes!" (Breward 2001, pp. 173–174).

In fact, despite an increasing availability of goods and services, the rise of the department store (a public space designed particularly as a place for women to purchase clothing and accessories) and increasing differentiation between social roles for men and women, silhouettes worn by men and women in the 1840s and 1850s had some similarities. "Health and beauty in both sexes require that the chest should be thrown well forward, the shoulders carried back, the carriage erect, free and unconstrained," admonished a self-improvement book of 1845 (Kidwell 1989a, p. 127). The method by which men's and women's clothing achieved this silhouette was different, however. Women's sloping shoulders and narrow waists were achieved by corsets, petticoats, and strategically placed linens. Gentlemen's shapes were more often built in by tailors using careful cut and padding (Kidwell 1989a.) Whereas both men and women might wear fashionably narrow waistlines, descriptions of their bodies in contemporary literature focused on different aspects. The lacing in a man's trousers, which created that narrow waist, might instead be described as enhancing his breadth of shoulder, whereas any description of the fullness of a woman's skirts, in contrast to her corseted waistline, might be seen as showing off her small waist (Kidwell 1989a).

THE FRAGMENTATION OF FASHION

In the twentieth and twenty-first centuries, media culture has decentralized fashion categories, providing many more ways for individuals to express identity. The introduction of movies and then television have brought images of cultural icons to every small town that could put up a screen or receive a television signal. As the twentieth century progressed, these media came into use by more and more specific interest groups as marketers identified more differentiated target markets. Popular cable television shows, such as *Queer as Folks*, would have been unthinkable in the 1950s when media outlets tended to emphasize white heterosexual and family-oriented norms. This show maintained a healthy, if specific interest, market share in 2000.

Medical advancements allowing men and women to alter their gender status have continued to add categories to the gender continuum, and the World Wide Web has augmented this by providing infinite scope for discussion of the process. Scholarly observation and discussion has made the topic of gender expression somewhat self-conscious in practice: "Gender expression is thus not only an aesthetic choice about cosmetics or hairstyle, skirts or suits. It is also implicated in politically fraught behaviors, economic marginalization and exploitation and political consciousness" (Heyes 2003, p. 1111). Despite this complexity, fashion and dress practices are tightly bound into gender definitions and expressions and provide endless scope for further study.

BIBLIOGRAPHY

Barnes, Ruth, and Joanne B. Eicher, eds. 1992. *Dress and Gender, Making and Meaning in Cultural Contexts.* Providence, RI: Berg.

Breward, Christopher. 1995. *The Culture of Fashion.* Manchester: University of Manchester Press.

Breward, Christopher. 1999. *The Hidden Consumer: Masculinities, Fashion and City Life, 1860–1914.* Manchester: Manchester University Press.

Breward, Christopher. 2001. "Manliness, Modernity and the Shaping of Male Clothing." In *Body Dressing,* ed. Joanne Entwistle and Elizabeth Wilson. Oxford: Berg.

Breward, Christopher. 2004. *Fashioning London, Clothing and the Modern Metropolis.* Oxford: Berg.

Cordwell, Justine M., and Ronald A. Schwarz, eds. 1979. *The Fabrics of Culture: The Anthropology of Clothing and Adornment.* Paris: Mouton.

Crane, Diana. 2000. *Fashion and Its Social Agendas: Class, Gender and Identity in Clothing.* Chicago: University of Chicago Press.

Davis, Fred. 1992. *Fashion, Culture and Identity.* Chicago: University of Chicago Press.

Eicher, Joanne B. 2001. "Dress, Gender and the Public Display of Skin." In *Body Dressing,* ed. Joanne Entwistle and Elizabeth Wilson. Oxford: Berg.

Entwistle, Joanne, and Elizabeth Wilson, eds. 2001a. *Body Dressing.* Oxford: Berg.

Entwistle, Joanne. 2001b. "The Dressed Body." In *Body Dressing,* ed. Joanne Entwistle and Elizabeth Wilson. Oxford: Berg.

Frick, Carole Collier. 2002. *Dressing Renaissance Florence: Families, Fortunes and Fine Clothing.* Baltimore: Johns Hopkins University Press.

Grossinger, Christa. 1997. *Picturing Women in Late Medieval and Renaissance Art.* Manchester: Manchester University Press.

Heyes, Cressida. 2003. "Feminist Solidarity after Queer Theory: The Case of Transgender." *Signs: Journal of Women in Culture and Society.* 28(4): 1093–1120.

Holliday, Ruth. 2001. "Fashioning the Queer Self." In *Body Dressing,* ed. Joanne Entwistle and Elizabeth Wilson. Oxford: Berg.

Johnson, Kim K. P.; Susan Torntore; and Joanne B. Eicher, eds. 2003. *Fashion Foundations, Early Writings on Fashion and Dress.* Oxford: Berg.

Jones, Jennifer M. 2004. *Sexing La Mode: Gender, Fashion and Commercial Culture in Old Regime France.* Oxford: Berg.

Kidwell, Claudia Brush. 1989a. "Gender Symbols or Fashionable Details?" In *Men and Women, Dressing the Part,* ed. Claudia Brush Kidwell and Valerie Steele. Washington, DC: Smithsonian Institution Press.

Kidwell, Claudia Brush, and Valerie Steele, eds. 1989b. *Men and Women, Dressing the Part.* Washington, DC: Smithsonian Institution Press.

Landini, Roberta Orsi, and Mary Westerman Bulgarella. 2001. "Costume in Fifteenth-Century Portraits of Women." In *Virtue and Beauty,* ed. David Alan Brown. Princeton, NJ: Princeton University Press.

Martin, Richard, and Harold Koda. 1989. *Jocks and Nerds: Men's Style in the Twentieth Century.* New York: Rizzoli.

Munson, Marit K. 2000. "Sex, Gender and Status: Human Images from the Classic Mimbres." *American Antiquity* 65(1): 127–143.

Purdy, Daniel Leonard, ed. 2004. *The Rise of Fashion, a Reader.* Minneapolis, MN: University of Minnesota Press.

Ribeiro, Aileen. 2005. *Fashion and Fiction, Dress in Art and Literature in Stuart England.* New Haven, CT: Yale University Press.

Roach, Mary Ellen, and Joanne B. Eicher. 1965. *Dress, Adornment, and the Social Order.* New York: John Wiley and Sons.

Roach, Mary Ellen, and Joanne B. Eicher. 1973. *The Visible Self: Perspectives on Dress.* Englewood Cliffs, NJ: Prentice-Hall.

Roach-Higgins, Mary Ellen; Joanne B. Eicher; and Kim K. P. Johnson, eds. 1995. *Dress and Identity.* New York: Fairchild Publications.

Rothstein, Natalie, ed. 1992. *Four Hundred Years of Fashion.* London: Victoria & Albert Museum.

Schreier, Barbara A. 1989. "Introduction." In *Men and Women, Dressing the Part,* ed. Claudia Brush Kidwell and Valerie Steele. Washington, DC: Smithsonian Institution Press.

Steele, Valerie. 1985. *Fashion and Eroticism: Ideals of Feminine Beauty from the Victorian Era to the Jazz Age.* Oxford: Oxford University Press.

Steele, Valerie. 1989a. "Appearance and Identity." In *Men and Women, Dressing the Part,* ed. Claudia Brush Kidwell and Valerie Steele. Washington, DC: Smithsonian Institution Press.

Steele, Valerie. 1989b. "Clothing and Sexuality." In *Men and Women, Dressing the Part,* ed. Claudia Brush Kidwell and Valerie Steele. Washington, DC: Smithsonian Institution Press.

Taylor, Lou. 2002. *The Study of Dress History.* Manchester: Manchester University Press.

Taylor, Lou. 2004. *Establishing Dress History.* Manchester: Manchester University Press.

Tortora, Phyllis, and Keith Eubank. 1994. *Survey of Historic Costume.* 2nd edition. New York: Fairchild Publications.

Tseelon, Efrat. 1995. *The Masque of Femininity: The Presentation of Woman in Everyday Life.* London: Sage.

Tseelon, Efrat, ed. 2001. *Masquerade and Identities: Essays on Gender, Sexuality and Marginality.* London: Routledge.
Weiner, Annette. B., and Jane Schneider. 1989. *Cloth and the Human Experience.* Washington DC: Smithsonian Institution Press.

Elizabeth McMahon

COCK RING

SEE *Sex Aids.*

CODPIECE

A codpiece is a piece of fabric fashioned into a pouch used to cover and hold a man's genitals. The term is derived from the Middle English *cod,* meaning "bag" or "scrotum." Originally nothing more than a triangular piece of cloth tied at the three corners, the codpiece developed into an impressive, self-sustaining sartorial construction that soon shed its original utilitarian function to become an unabashed statement of masculinity and male ego.

The codpiece first appeared in Europe in the mid-fourteenth century when the hemline of men's tunics reached midthigh, placing the unprotected genitals at risk of exposure or discomfort. By the mid-fifteenth century, when hemlines reached the top of the thighs, the codpiece became both obligatory and swank. Codpieces were often constructed with fabric of contrasting color, elaborately embellished with bows, jeweled pins, and embroidery, or stuffed and slashed as fashion might dictate, all to draw attention to the male genitals. They could also serve as pouches for coins, kerchiefs, pins, and other paraphernalia. Codpieces also served as venues for male boasting and exhibitionism, and this naturally attracted the wrath of preachers and the derision of literary wits.

After its heyday in the 1530s and 1540s, when it was often sizable, loaf shaped, and protruding, the codpiece in the 1550s and 1560s began to wane in size and splendor, becoming smaller, more oval shaped, and set closer to the body, though it was still erect. By the 1570s to 1580s the codpiece disappeared completely behind the ample folds of the new male fashion for voluminous trunk hose, a victim of a changing political and cultural climate conditioned by the spread of the various religious reform movements, as well as by the presence on the throne—or immediately behind it—of powerful female figures such as Elizabeth I of England and Catherine de Médicis, which made such unabashed statements of virility and male sexuality rather unadvisable.

SEE ALSO *Clothing; Masculinity: I. Overview.*

BIBLIOGRAPHY

Eisenbichler, Konrad. 1988. "Bronzino's Portrait of Guidobaldo II Della Rovere." *Renaissance and Reformation* 24(1): 21–33.
Persels, Jeffery C. 1997. "Bragueta Humanística, or Humanism's Codpiece." *Sixteenth Century Journal* 28(1): 79–99.
Simons, Patricia. 1994. "Alert and Erect: Masculinity in Some Italian Renaissance Portraits of Fathers and Sons." In *Gender Rhetorics: Postures of Dominance and Submission in History,* ed. Richard C. Trexler. Binghamton, NY: Medieval and Renaissance Texts and Studies.

Konrad Eisenbichler

COITUS

Derived from the past participle of the Latin verb *coire,* meaning "to go" or "to come together," the term *coitus* indicates a specific act of sexual intercourse that also is known as coition or copulation. This "coming together" generally is understood in heteronormative terms as the penetration of a woman's vagina by a man's penis in a way that joins their bodies via their genitalia.

NATURE AND TYPES OF COITUS

During coitus the man and woman insert the erect penis into the vagina and then begin to move their hips repetitively in back-and-forth thrusting or rocking motions to create friction as the penis moves within the vaginal canal, thrusting until orgasm and/or penile ejaculation occurs. Penile-vaginal penetration and the joining of two bodies are the principal physical characteristics of coitus, distinguishing it from sexual acts such as genital petting, masturbation, and other nonpenetrative or solitary sex acts.

The term *coitus* may be modified to signify specific kinds of sexual intercourse other than penile-vaginal intercourse, such as coitus interfemoris, or femoral coitus, the thrusting of a penis between the closed thighs of a partner; intermammary coitus, the thrusting of a penis between the breasts of a partner; anal coitus, the penile penetration of a partner's rectum; and oral coitus, the stimulation of the genitalia by the mouth and/or tongue. Each of these modifications avoids the possibility of pregnancy as an outcome of sexual intercourse; this indicates that another standard characteristic of coitus has been an emphasis on human reproduction.

Coitus remains the primary means of human reproduction, yet men and women often engage in coitus for purposes of recreation, pleasure, and social, spiritual, or religious imperatives that may not include reproduction as the end goal of sexual intercourse. Because coitus is

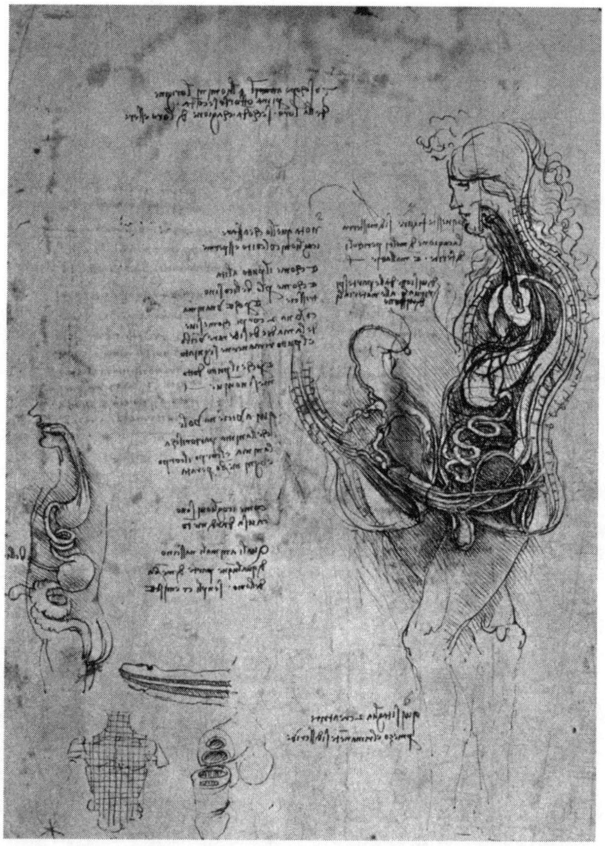

Drawing of the Human Sexual Organs by Leonardo Da Vinci. THE GRANGER COLLECTION, NEW YORK.

engaged in for nonreproductive purposes, birth control is a regular consideration and possible concern for sexually active men and women. Historically, the most common methods of birth control have been coitus interruptus (the withdrawing of the penis before ejaculation) and coitus reservatus (the delaying or suppressing of ejaculation), although coitus reservatus also is associated with male and female sexual pleasure; for example, it is endorsed in Tantric teachings as a method of increasing a man's psychosexual energy. Coitus interruptus and coitus reservatus may be supplemented by birth control devices such as condoms and female birth control methods. Because coitus is linked to both procreation and pleasure, it has been regulated, controlled, and shaped through sociocultural customs and codes that dictate acceptable contexts and even positions for intercourse.

POSITIONS

According to Vatsyayana's ancient Indian manual for love-making the *Kama Sutra* (c. fourth century CE), there are more than sixty possible positions for sexual intercourse and more than five hundred variations of those positions. Yashodhara's number, however, includes minuscule differences in limb placement and even in the sounds made during coitus. Muhammad ibn Muhammad al-Nafzawi's Arabic sex manual *The Perfumed Garden* (c. 1410 CE) draws from the *Kama Sutra* but reduces the number of possible sexual positions to twenty-seven. According to the anthropologist Edgar Gregersen (1983), the range of positions may be understood as combinations of the following coital characteristics: four general postures of partners—lying, sitting, squatting, and standing; two general orientations between partners—face-to-face and rear entry; and three general positions of "dominance"—man on top, woman on top, and side by side (Gregersen 1983). Although no single position is more "normal" or "natural" than another, Gregersen states that cultural differences indicate a general preference for a particular position. For instance, the most popular position in European and North American societies has tended to be the "missionary position," whereas many African societies have demonstrated a preference for side-by-side intercourse. The four most common coital positions can be described as follows.

Lying Face to Face, Man on Top Also known as the missionary position in Western English-speaking nations, this was considered the proper sexual position by Christian missionaries who attempted to spread its practice in consonance with Saint Paul's religious teachings that "women should be subject to their husbands" and that husbands must demonstrate their dominance in copulation (Gregersen 1983, p. 58). In this position the man and woman face each other with the woman lying on her back and the man poised or lying atop of her.

According to the sexologists Joann DeLora and Carol Warren (1977), the position may be varied to adjust stimulation and even power differentials. For example, "the woman may place her legs together, between those of the man, allowing less vaginal penetration, or she may draw her knees up toward her chest with the man between her legs, thus facilitating deeper penetration. The man may lie with his body resting on the woman's, with much body contact, or he may use his arms and legs to keep his weight off her body, permitting her to move freely and be a more active partner. Also he may sit back on his heels and lift her buttocks to rest on his thighs, allowing either of them to stimulate her clitoris manually if she desires it" (DeLora and Warren 1977, p. 68).

Lying or Sitting, Face to Face, Woman on Top The earliest representations of the woman on top position can be found in the art of ancient Mesopotamia (c. 3000 BCE). The man reclines or sits, and the woman straddles him, either resting most of her body against his or sitting atop him with her torso upright. This position allows the woman greater movement and ease for self-stimulation of her breasts and/or clitoris, and it may be varied by the woman choosing to face away from her partner or placing her legs between his legs for less penetration. DeLora and Warren note that some of the benefits of this position are that the "woman has more freedom of movement than the man and the position is more tiring for her than for him. However, most males have more ejaculatory control in this position than in some others where they must take a more active role" (DeLora and Warren 1977, p. 68).

Lying Face to Face, Side by Side Considered the least tiring position for both partners, this position may be the preferred posture "when one (or both) of the partners is tired, sick or old. It can also be used during the last months of pregnancy" because it limits the depth of penetration and the physical energy expended to engage in intercourse (Gregersen 1983, p. 60). The partners lie on their sides facing each other, and the woman may wrap her top leg over the man's hip or lift her leg to varying heights to allow a greater or lesser depth of penetration. The leg placements of both partners may vary according to their personal preferences. As in most face-to-face positions, lying side by side "allows for freedom in sex play and displays of affection" (DeLora and Warren 1977, p. 68).

Rear-Entry Position This position also is known as *coitus in retro* (entry from behind). Christians who believed the missionary position to be the "civilized" or devout position associated rear-entry coitus with bestiality. Interestingly, animal themes have been used across cultures to describe rear-entry sexual intercourse. For instance, in Western English-speaking countries such as the United States "doggy style" has been a popular label; in Middle Eastern Arabic-speaking cultures it has been known as "after the fashion of the bull;" in China variations of rear-entry sex have been described as the "Leaping Tiger"; and the *Kama sutra* titles numerous variations of rear-entry coitus as "congress of a cow," "congress of a goat," "forcible mounting of an ass," and the like.

Although there are many postures of rear-entry coitus, determined, for instance, by the partners' choice to stand, lie, or kneel, all require that the man enter the woman from behind. According to DeLora and Warren, most rear-entry positions "allow for deep penetration" (except when a woman lies flat on her stomach) and "provide opportunity for manual clitoral stimulation" (DeLora and Warren 1977, p. 71).

Each of these descriptions of coital positions uses the heternormative vocabulary common in the discipline of sexology and in sex manuals. However, each position can be executed by males engaged in anal coitus or women engaged in mutual genital stimulation.

SOCIOCULTURAL AND HISTORICAL CONTEXTS

An examination of how coitus has been performed, understood, and depicted across cultures and historical periods shows great deviations in sexual beliefs and practices. Even within a particular culture sexual customs and beliefs may differ considerably. For instance, Aleksandr V. Gura (2005) in his study of coitus in Slavic folk culture noted that although Slavic Christians believed sexual intercourse to be "unclean" and even spiritually dangerous, regional customs associated with that common belief varied significantly. Russians and other Orthodox Slavs tended to cover religious icons or turn their faces to the wall and remove the pectoral cross during coitus. However, in northern Russia newlyweds could not receive communion or confess their sins for a year after consummating their marriage because of their contamination. Other Slavs thought that an "imprint of impurity quite often remained on the young wife until giving birth to a child," and Bulgarians thought that premarital sex or adultery might cause drought or hail (Gura 2005, p. 30). Gura's study demonstrates the motivation of social groups to interpret and regulate sexuality according to religious and/or medical beliefs, a motivation that is common to most cultures. Gura's work also indicates that the social and religious mores about coitus easily shift and change with regional differences and sociohistorical contexts.

The ways in which sexually active partners understand coitus and choose to engage in sexual intercourse are shaped most often by the religious, medical, and civil discourses of their historical context. Because coitus is linked directly to human reproduction, most societies have created religious and/or civil institutions such as marriage to regulate reproduction. The two most common sexual regulators across cultures and historical periods have been religious and civil codes that attempt to restrict sexual intercourse to marriage and the prohibition of sexual intercourse with a close relative, also known as incest. Because coitus is necessary for human reproduction, few cultures or societies prohibit it entirely. There are, however, often strict prohibitions for select groups, including members of religious orders such as Roman Catholic priests and Buddhist lamas, for whom sexual acts are prohibited almost entirely as part of spiritual training and religious protocols.

Many historians and cultural critics who have charted the changing beliefs and codes that inform sexual practices indicate that there is no normal or singularly natural way to engage in coitus. Rather, such scholarship has tended to show that sex is socially constructed and that coital practices may be infinitely varied. However, culturally based studies of human sexuality often depict the general trends or dominant beliefs that govern sexual practices so that it is possible to understand how sexual norms shift according to cultures and historical eras.

The sociologist Gail Hawkes in *Sex and Pleasure in Western Culture* (2004) traces ideas about sex in European and North American societies from ancient Greece through the twentieth century. According to Hawkes, most philosophers and physicians in ancient Greece considered sexual desire and pleasure crucial to both men's and women's physical and spiritual health so long as intercourse was practiced in moderation and for rational purposes. Sexual desire and pleasure therefore were not considered sinful but were associated with a reasoned connection to the divine. Hippocratic (medical) practitioners advocated coitus, which could include male intercourse with other males, as essential for a person's general health: "Sexual activity aids sleep, encourages strong masculine growth, 'predisposes the soul to tranquility' and 'dampens immoderate ardour'" (Hawkes 2004, p. 38).

Such beliefs were not shared by the Stoics (300–50 BCE), who renounced physical pleasure as a means of participating in divine reason. Their teachings were drawn upon by the Gnostics (100–200 CE), who "supplied a more uncompromising basis for the early Christian" sexual beliefs (Hawkes 2004, p. 45). Gnostic teachings went so far as to categorize marriages as either "pure" or "defiled" on the basis of the couple's engagement in sexual intercourse. "A defiled marriage was one in which sexual intercourse takes place. A pure union demanded sexual abstinence as a necessary route to perfection—the means by which the body can be controlled and transformed" (Hawkes 2004, pp. 45–46). The Gnostic association of sexuality with bestiality had a powerful influence on the development of the view of the body in Western Christianity.

It was not until the seventeenth and eighteenth centuries that European and North American societies began to regulate through civil law sexual activities between men and women, men and men, and men and animals. Hawkes states that although "sex between men and women had always been valued more highly as the norm, homoerotic encounters between men, especially in the upper classes, were [previously] tolerated" (Hawkes 2004, p. 100). During that time surgeons and physicians, increasingly working outside a religious framework, began both promoting "the physical emotional and social advantages" of sex and focusing on issues of female sexuality. Those medical authorities specifically promoted the necessity of sexual arousal in the woman, giving detailed accounts of foreplay, methods to enhance sexual pleasure, and the value of vaginal orgasm (achieved via coitus) for a woman's health.

Western cultures have demonstrated ambivalence in regard to religious, scientific, and civil understandings of sexuality. Michel Foucault (1980) described how sex and sexuality emerged as key political concerns of Western societies in their attempts to order and manage the lives of individuals. Much of this social control, according to Foucault, takes place via discourses of power or authority such as those emerging out of religious, state, or medical institutions that both regulate and shape the ways in which individuals view their sex and sexuality.

In the twentieth century the discourses and codes regulating sexual intercourse became increasingly secularized or medicalized in most Western or westernizing nations. Social movements such as the women's liberation movement of the 1960s and 1970s in the United States promoted sexual liberation in part through a woman's control of her reproduction through the use of female contraceptives such as the birth control pill and the loosening of socioreligious endorsements of marriage as a prerequisite to sexual intercourse. Men and women participate in the normalizing of sexuality and their sexual practices to the extent that they are subjected to and become invested in the categories, classifications, and norms propagated by scientific and administrative discourses.

THE STUDY OF SEX AND THE COITAL IMPERATIVE

Sexual science at the turn of the twentieth century began undermining eighteenth- and nineteenth-century notions that reproductive heterosexuality is a natural given. Sigmund Freud, for instance, argued that social forces define and redefine sexual mores and taboos. Sexual instinct rooted in the desire for sexual pleasure, according to Freud, had become "subordinate to the purposes of reproduction," and therefore, any sexual activity that "aims solely at pleasure is given the uncomplimentary name of 'perverse' and as such is proscribed" (Hawkes 2004, p. 150). If the regulation of sexual behavior based on reproductive imperatives was shown to limit human sexual practices, the recognition that neither coitus nor sexual pleasure in general must be equated with reproduction suggests there is no single truth about sexuality.

The cultural critic Angus McLaren (1999) posits that sexuality is too complex and diverse for there to be truths about it. However, the equation of sexual pleasure with heterosexual reproductive coitus has proved to be a resilient notion for interpreting and understanding human sexuality. "Most people," McLaren stated, disregard or "lament the notion that nature no longer provides a solid basis upon which the organization of sexuality can be built" (McLaren 1999, p. 223). Both in popular conceptions of human sexuality and in later-twentieth-century scientific studies of sexuality, heterosexual coitus remained the idealized sexual activity and the perceived inevitable outcome of most sexual activities, including petting and masturbation.

This continued elevation of coitus as the ultimate or ideal sexual act is what Margaret Jackson (2002) termed "the coital imperative," establishing heterosexual coitus as the normative sexual practice against which all other sexual activities are measured. Even Alfred Kinsey's mid-twentieth-century findings on the prevalence of tabooed sexual behaviors such as bestiality, homosexuality, and masturbation among Americans employed coitus as the standard by which sexual practices were determined. Practices such as "pre-marital petting and masturbation were regarded as important merely as a means to an end—the avoidance of sexual 'maladjustment in marriage,' defined as the failure of women to achieve orgasm from coitus" (Jackson 2002, p. 85).

Significantly, the modern emphasis on coitus as the preferred means for a woman to achieve orgasm both implies that a penis is necessary to female sexual pleasure and ignores data suggesting that the majority of women achieve orgasm through clitoral stimulation or masturbation, not through penile-vaginal intercourse. Similarly, the work of William Masters and Virginia Johnson tended to emphasize the penis as "indispensable to the release of female sexual tension" (Jackson 2002, p. 86). In general, the insistence among scientists on a biological model of sexuality (with an emphasis on reproductive sex) and on the importance of penile-vaginal penetration as the end goal of sexual activity inevitably privileges the penis as the primary agent of sexual intercourse and pleasure. "Such an analysis" Jackson stated, "automatically rules out the possibility that our fore-mothers engaged in sexual practices with other women, or in non-coital sexual expression with men, and practiced coitus only for the purposes of reproduction" (Jackson 2002, p. 87). Scientific discourse can inscribe prevalent gender biases through the privileging of coitus as the primary goal of any other sexual activity.

The coital imperative is in part a product of scientific models and programs that emerged in the early twentieth century that promoted the "training of heterosexuality" (Hawkes 2004, p 155). According to such programs, "First the sexual instinct must be channeled towards penetrative sex. Second, the couple must be trained in achieving mutual orgasm." Third, women must be encouraged to prefer the vaginal orgasm of coitus over clitoral orgasms associated with masturbation and other nonpenetrative sexual activities (Hawkes 2004, p. 156). Promoted by sexologists and physicians who took on the "regime" of training heterosexuality, coitus became the ultimate and most "natural" sexual act. The continued prevalence of such values may help explain why terms such as *sex* and *sexual intercourse* continued to be synonymous with coitus in the early twenty-first-century.

BIBLIOGRAPHY

Burton, Richard Francis. 2004. *The Kama Sutra of Vatsyayana*. New York: Penguin Group.

Chester, Robert, and Christopher Walker. 1980. "Sexual Experience and Attitudes of British Women." In *Changing Patterns of Sexual Behaviour: Proceedings of the Fifteenth Annual Symposium of the Eugenics Society*, ed. W.H.G. Armytage, R. Chester, and John Peel. London and New York: Academic Press.

Delora, Joann S., and Carol A. B. Warren. 1977. *Understanding Sexual Interaction*. Boston: Houghton Mifflin.

Foote, Nelson N. 2002. "Sex as Play." In *Sexualities: Critical Concepts in Sociology*. Vol. 1, ed. Ken Plummer. London and New York: Routledge.

Foucault, Michel. 1980. *History of Sexuality: An Introduction*. New York: Vintage.

Gebherd, Paul H. 1980. "Sexuality in the Post-Kinsey Era." In *Changing Patterns of Sexual Behaviour: Proceedings of the Fifteenth Annual Symposium of the Eugenics Society*, ed. W.H.G. Armytage, R. Chester, and John Peel. London and New York: Academic Press.

Gregersen, Edgar. 1983. *Sexual Practices: The Story of Human Sexuality*. New York: F. Watts.

Gura, Aleksandr V. 2005. "Coitus in the Symbolic Language of Slavic Culture." *Folklore* 30: 135–144.

Hawkes, Gail. 2004. *Sex and Pleasure in Western Culture*. Cambridge, UK, and Malden, MA: Polity Press.

Jackson, Margaret. 2002. "Sex Research and the Construction of Sexuality." In *Sexualities: Critical Concepts in Sociology*. Vol. 1, ed. Ken Plummer. London and New York: Routledge.

McLaren, Angus. 1999. *Twentieth-Century Sexuality: A History*. Oxford and Malden, MA: Blackwell.

Simon, William, and John H. Gagnon. 2002. "On Pyschosexual Development." In *Sexualities: Critical Concepts in Sociology*. Vol 1, ed. Ken Plummer. London and New York: Routledge.

Skinner, Marilyn B. 2005. *Sexuality in Greek and Roman Culture*. Malden, MA: Blackwell.

Kristina Banister Quynn

COLETTE, SIDONIE-GABRIELLE
1873–1954

One of the most celebrated women writers in France, Colette, born Sidonie-Gabrielle Colette on January 28, 1873 in the French village of Saint-Sauveur-en Puisaye, wrote novels and short stories focused on women, passion, sexuality, and love. First famous for her series of novels about the romantic and sexual education of the school girl, Claudine, Colette made publicly evident the much broader range of sexual knowledge and experience enjoyed by adolescents. Claudine, a lover of both women and

Sidonie-Gabrielle Colette. **PUBLIC DOMAIN.**

men, became a popular figure in early twentieth-century French culture, inspiring a blouse collar (the Claudine collar) and a line of cosmetics. Colette also wrote about the relations between mother and daughter, and produced more than twenty-two novels and short story collections during her long career including *The Vagabond* (1911), *Cheri* (1920), *My Mother's House* (1922), *The Pure and the Impure* (1941), and *Gigi* (1945).

Colette's father was a retired army captain and amputee who collected taxes. Her mother, known as Sido, was a colorful, unconventional woman who valued gardens and animals above social respectability. When she was twenty, Colette married Henri Gauthier-Villars, a writer and critic fifteen years her elder. Gauthier-Villars encouraged Colette to write and, according to one legend, locked Colette in her room until she had completed her daily quota of pages. The four novels featuring the character Claudine were initially published between 1900 and 1903 under Gauthier-Villars' pen name, Willy, leading some to conclude that the novels' accounts were the inventions of a middle-aged man instead of the artistry of a young woman.

Colette divorced Gauthier-Villars in 1906 and became an inventive and daring music hall performer. Working as an acrobat and sketch artist, Colette bared one breast during a performance and later simulated intercourse, a bit that caused a riot at the Moulin Rouge. During this time, she had a lesbian relationship with the Marquise de Belboeuf (Missy), who for a time managed her career and public image. She also figured prominently in the Parisian Left Bank culture of expatriate lesbian writers such as heiress Natalie Barney.

Returning to her career as an author, Colette married Henri de Jouvenal des Ursins, a newspaper editor, and began a long and fruitful career as a fiction writer. She gave birth to one child, also named Colette. During World War I, she converted her husband's estate into a hospital for wounded soldiers, which earned her the accolade of being a Chevalier of the Legion of Honor, the first of many laurels she would acquire. From 1920 until her death in 1954, Colette produced more than fifteen novels and story collections, known for their sensitive and insightful treatment of characters who occupied the margins of polite society. Focusing on gigolos, courtesans, bisexuals, and gay and lesbian characters, many of Colette's novels and stories explore the conflicts among desire, sensuality, identity, passion, and independence. *Cheri*, for example, tells the story of the relation between a younger, spoiled gigolo and his older lover. *The Pure and the Impure* recounts the relationships of four lesbian couples. *My Mother's House* and *Sido* (1930) recall the joys of Colette's childhood and the eccentric virtues of her mother. In all of her work, Colette treats sexuality and passion openly and as integral forces in people's lives that compel choices and compromises, enable freedom and fulfillment, and end often in sadness and nostalgia.

By the 1920s, Colette was France's most renowned woman writer. In Paris she associated with artist Jean Cocteau and members of his circle who constituted part of the literary avant-garde of the time. She was the first woman elected to the Academie Goncourt and the Belgian Royal Academy, both indicia of respect for her writing. She divorced Henry de Jouvenal in 1924, and in 1935 married the Jewish jeweler Maurice Goudaket, whom she hid during the Nazi occupation of France in World War II. In her later years, Colette suffered from debilitating arthritis, but continued to write until her death in Paris on August 3.

Colette's sensitive and open treatment of issues of love and sexuality helped to foster public consideration of sexuality as a necessary part of the human experience. By humanizing marginal figures and showing how such admirable characters as Claudine experienced a variety of desires, Colette not only demonstrated that passion and desire were more varied and universal than had been previously acknowledged, but that homosexual and heterosexual desires coexist as part of a larger human drama.

SEE ALSO *Adolescent Sexuality; Puberty.*

BIBLIOGRAPHY

Colette, Sidonie-Gabrielle. 1941. *The Pure and the Impure*, trans. Herma Briffault. New York: New York Review of Books, 2000.

Phelps, Robert, ed. 1978. *Belles Saisons: A Colette Scrapbook.* New York: Farrar, Straus and Giroux.

Thurman, Judith. 2000. *Secrets of the Flesh: A Life of Colette.* New York: Ballantine Books.

Judith Roof

COLONIALISM

In the opening chapter of *Empire and Sexuality*, the historian Ronald Hyam makes the claim that the growth of the British Empire was fueled by the "export of surplus sexual energy" (Hyam 1990). Although this may appear strange to those who think that imperial growth was fueled by the export of surplus capital, it makes an important connection between colonial empires, gender, and sexuality. At a certain level the space of other cultures, of the Other (as theorized by Edward Said in *Orientalism* [1978]), was always the space of a sexuality denied, fantasized, or projected by European culture. Thus, although the empire is the space of sex, especially the unspeakable sexual practices of the Other, the mechanisms of projection, denial, and fantasy both predate and outlive the period of formal colonialism.

THE EXPORTATION OF SEXUAL ENERGY

What these two areas (the export of surplus sexual energy and its production and projection) share is their gendered nature: The energy being exported is unquestionably male (in the nineteenth century the idea that women had any sexual energy, let alone an internationally exportable surplus, would have been shocking), as are the sexual fantasies and projections. The imposition of an essentially male imagination can be seen through the gendering and sexualizing of geography. Examples range from the early engraving by artist Jan van der Straet (1523–1605) of explorer Amerigo Vespucci (1454–1512) confronting America in the shape of a naked indigenous woman to Said's categorization of the discourse of Orientalism as encouraging "a peculiarly (not to say invidiously) male conception of the world" that included the Orient's "feminine penetrability" and in which "women are usually the creatures of the male power-fantasy. They express unlimited sensuality, they are more or less stupid, and above all they are willing" (Said 1978, pp. 206–207).

THE DOMESTIC AND INTERNATIONAL REGULATION OF SEXUALITY

Although gender, sexuality, and sexual preferences and practices are intimately and variously related to colonialism, it can be very difficult in the context of a range of European empires to offer satisfactory generalizations because of the variety of attitudes and behaviors both within and across the different empires during their 400-year history. One thing that is generalizable is the fact that the major period of growth of the colonial empires from the late eighteenth century onward coincided with other developments in European society that had important effects on issues of gender and sexuality in those empires. The elaboration of colonialism as a transnational system of power and control was partnered by and in certain ways depended on a different approach to power and control domestically. As Michel Foucault (1979) argued, this period saw the European states increasingly develop strategies of *bio-power* as a framework for the regulation of the body, both that of the individual and the collective body of the general population. If the regulation of bodies and behaviors was central to good government at home, it was even more so in the colonies, where the populations were inherently more problematic. In Foucault's work, however, power does not function only in a repressive or controlling manner; it is also *productive*, inciting or encouraging preferred forms of behavior. That is true for both the colonizers and the colonized, though frequently in very different ways.

Although Hyam would counterpose domestic regulation to a realm of colonial *freedom*, it is clear that the regulation of male behavior, perhaps even more than female behavior, became more formalized and constraining as the British Empire itself became more formalized. For example, when the British East India Company ruled India, its employees, especially in the military, were encouraged to marry Indian women. In that period even high-ranking officers, bureaucrats, and wealthy merchants openly took Indian wives or mistresses. After the Indian mutiny of 1857 and the assumption of direct control by the British government, however, an altered moral and ideological climate as well as greater government surveillance and regulation produced a reversal of attitude toward India, with its crucial ideological role as the jewel in the imperial crown.

The higher the position one occupied, the greater the regulation and penalties, and cross-cultural relationships became punishable by social ostracism, loss of one's job, or possibly worse: Rudyard Kipling's short story "Beyond the Pale" (1890) ends with the highly symbolic near castration of a British official who ignores the rules and loves an Indian girl. The punishment for the girl is brutal mutilation, and the fact that that act is carried out by an

Indian reinforces the supposed universality of the opening statement of the narrative: "A man should, whatever happens, keep to his own caste, race and breed. Let the White go to the White, and the Black to the Black" (Kipling 1890, p.159). A tragic result of the policy of encouraging and then discouraging cross-cultural sexual relationships was the creation of dual-heritage Anglo Indians whose hybrid nature was not acceptable to either of the *pure* races from which they sprang.

FEAR OF MISCEGENATION

At the same time the moral climate in India grew more difficult, in other parts of the British Empire, such as Africa and Malaya, attitudes continued to be tolerant toward white men who had relationships with black women. The converse—white women and black men—was never acceptable anywhere in the empire. As far as the colonial regulation of female behavior was concerned, the primal fear of Europeans was racial mixing or dilution of their whiteness, and miscegenation became the great colonial taboo.

All white women in the colonies or in contact with black men at home in the metropolis therefore carried an enormously ideologically value-laden responsibility for the future of the race. Although all societies have controlled access to their female members, especially by male outsiders, that became a very highly charged issue in the racialized power politics of colonialism. As science and pseudoscience contributed to that process in the second half of the nineteenth century, the growth of the eugenics movement intensified the political climate, as everything from the maintenance of social order and hierarchy to the ability to field an army of strong, healthy soldiers was linked to the question of breeding. Proper sexual reproduction allowed proper social reproduction, and that was as true for the colonial empire as it was for the mother country.

If unauthorized access to white women was the greatest transgression colonized subjects could perpetrate, rape represented its most graphic instance, an ever-present menace. The very idea of the rape of white women by colonized subjects could reduce white men to murderous fury. In the Indian mutiny, for example, the possibility that Englishwomen captured at Cawnpore might have suffered *a fate worse than death* (as well as actual death) was sufficient to make *Remember Cawnpore!* the battle cry for the English as they carried out a brutal retribution. (A similar spirit of murderous irrationality grounded in unsubstantiated fantasy characterized the period of lynching in the United States.) The fact that rapes did not occur regularly or perhaps at all did not alleviate the obsessive fear that white women were in a permanent state of danger. The central event, or nonevent, of E. M. Forster's novel *A Passage to India* (1924) is an alleged attempted sexual assault on a white woman by an Indian doctor.

The other side of this ever-present but never-realized threat is the fact that rapes were carried out by white men. That history runs at least from the routine sexual abuse of female slaves by plantation owners in the Americas, through the rape and murder of Indian women by British soldiers in India in the 1930s, to the rape of Kenyan women by British soldiers and colonial functionaries during and after the Mau Mau insurgency of the 1950s. In Kenya rapes by the British were echoed by their African Home Guard subordinates, but Caroline Elkins (2005) argues that failure to emulate the British left one open to the charge of being a Mau Mau sympathizer.

COLONIAL VERSUS COLONIZED MASCULINITY

At the other extreme from this kind of male behavior was the idealized form that colonial power in its productive mode aimed to incite. That was the imperial hero: brave, honorable, truthful, loyal, and restrained, the embodiment of Christian virtue, as analyzed by Graham Dawson (1994). The remodeling of upper-class English masculinity in the nineteenth century, which was carried out in part by the public school system, found its apogee in this figure, which was relayed to the youth of the empire through hundreds of fictional and factual narratives.

The ideological antithesis of this figure lay in various representations of colonized masculinity. Those representations included the Oriental male as effeminate (and therefore no match for his manly English counterpart), as sexually voracious (unlike the civilized and restrained Englishman), and, in Katherine Mayo's *Mother India* (1927), as the unrepentant brutalizer of pitiful child brides too young for marriage or intercourse. As is frequently the case with ideology, no consistency was required of those negative images so long as they allowed the colonizer to be seen in a good light. As Said argued, "Orientalism depends for its strategy on this flexible *positional* superiority, which puts the Westerner in a whole series of possible relationships with Orient, without ever losing him the relative upper hand" (Said 1978, p. 7). In this way the process of identity formation on the part of the colonizers, whether in terms of gender, sexuality, or nationality, should proceed smoothly, though there is always the possibility of coming up against uncomfortable reality.

POSTCOLONIAL ISSUES

Despite its apparent strength and durability, colonialism was only a phase in the larger global project of imperialism, and the international, transcultural, and imperial politics of sex and gender did not end with the period of decolonization in the mid-twentieth century. Although some practices and policies are specific to and enabled by the possession of colonial empires, they do not necessarily end with the formal ending of those empires, and two topics from the colonial period have a great deal of current relevance.

Female Genital Mutilation In Kenya in the late 1920s the missionary society of the Church of Scotland set out to ban female genital mutilation. That campaign inevitably evokes comparisons with the British outlawing of *sati*, in which a Hindu woman cremates herself on her husband's funeral pyre, in early nineteenth-century India and carries the same ideological image Gayatri Spivak sees as epitomizing the whole colonial enterprise: "Imperialism's image as the establisher of the good society is marked by the espousal of the woman as object of protection from her own kind"; this also can be stated as, "White men are saving brown women from brown men" (Spivak 1994, pp. 94 and 92). Although they were actively involved in modernizing and Christianizing male circumcision in Kenya, the missionaries refused to approve of female clitoridectomy and instead tried to stamp it out. Gikuyu people reacted to the perceived attack on their cultural and spiritual identity because along with breaking the profound individual and collective link to the earth created by the ritual shedding of blood, the ban created a group of women who could not be considered clean, disciplined, responsible, or marriageable and thus were nonpersons in Gikuyu terms. Conceptions of what it meant to be a proper man and woman in Africa were deeply opposed, but not simply along racial lines, as Gikuyu converts to Christianity often sided with the missionaries. Gikuyu resistance to the ban fed on and fed back into a more general resistance to British colonial rule and a generation later culminated in the Mau Mau insurgency.

The reemergence of the issue in a wider context in the 1980s and 1990s both in Africa and in diaspora communities in the Europe and North America often was seen in terms of white Europeans attempting to impose their cultural values on others. The fact that the matter is more complex, however, is demonstrated by the film *Warrior Marks* (1993), which was made by two prominent nonwhite feminists: the African-American novelist Alice Walker (b. 1944) and the British-Asian director Pratibha Parmar. Its vigorous championing of the right of African women not to undergo genital mutilation—supported by moving testimony from African women—was criticized as an example of latter-day colonialist mentality. (Conversely and in some ways ironically, a film on the same subject by the Senegalese male director Ousmane Sembene (b. 1923), *Mooladé* [2004], was well received.) Although the practice lacks any evident justification other than its asserted traditional nature, it is clung to tenaciously and stands as one kind of limit to a would-be universal discourse of rights.

The Veil Both in Muslim countries and in Islamic communities in non-Muslim states, the wearing of a veil has been an issue from the colonial period into the postcolonial period. The politics of veiling and unveiling under colonialism were examined by Frantz Fanon (1965) in the context of the Algerian war of liberation from the French. Although the colonizers saw the removal of the veil as part of the necessary liberatory modernizing of their Muslim colonies, for Fanon a darker process was at work: The veil constituted an obstacle to the power of the colonizers to look at whatever they wished, and so "the rape of the Algerian woman in the dream of a European is always preceded by a rending of the veil" (Fanon 1965, p. 45).

In the context of the liberation struggle, however, Algerian women came to use the veil in ways that were directly political and even revolutionary and had profound implications for their gender and sexual identities. Unveiled, women could move in the European part of town unnoticed, carrying messages or bombs in their handbags, as portrayed in Gillo Pontecorvo's (1919–2006) film *Battle of Algiers* (1963). Veiled, women could hide documents and weapons in their voluminous clothing. Unveiling forced them to experience their bodies in new and disconcerting ways, but the conscious political use of the veil, Fanon felt, stripped it of any repressive traditional power. Even if he was overoptimistic on that point, thinking about the veil could never be the same after his analysis.

In an extensive discussion of colonial and postcolonial veiling in *Colonial Fantasies*, Meyda Yeğenoğlu concludes, "The veil is a dress, but a dress which we might consider as articulating the very identity of Muslim women" (Yeğenoğlu 1998, p. 119). However, this can be true only in terms of a deliberately constructed identity rather than the essentialist one suggested by the quote in light of the way in which the growth of systematically Arabized or Islamicized societies across the Muslim world, particularly in the postcolonial period, has involved the adoption of the veil by women whose identities previously had not been articulated by it.

Some of the most contentious examples of the politics of postcolonial veiling and unveiling have occurred in Europe, as in the case of *l'affaire des foulards* in France in the 1990s in which schoolgirls were forbidden to wear Islamic headscarves in the name of state secularism, and the 2006 case of a British Muslim teaching assistant who lost her job for refusing to remove her full-face veil while teaching. In addition to the ongoing politics of the veil, the global panic in the wake of the attack on the Twin

Towers in New York on September 11, 2001, has meant that any unapologetic display of Muslim identity carries a price.

Colonialism wielded the power of life and death over its subjects, but not usually through their sexual behavior. The government of U.S. President George W. Bush (b. 1946), however, has made medical aid to African countries devastated by the AIDS pandemic conditional on their promotion of a policy of sexual abstinence rather than sex education and the use of condoms; indeed, condom use constitutes grounds for the withdrawal of funding. The absence of any political or economic benefit for the United States makes this look like colonialism at its most messianic: the embodiment of a supposedly God-given right to control the lives of anyone whom colonial power can reach.

BIBLIOGRAPHY

Ballhatchet, Kenneth. 1980. *Race, Sex and Class under the Raj: Imperial Attitudes and Their Critics, 1793–1905.* London: Weidenfeld and Nicholson.

Dawson, Graham. 1994. *Soldier Heroes: British Adventure, Empire, and the Imagining of Masculinity.* London: Routledge.

Elkins, Caroline. 2005. *Imperial Reckoning: The Untold Story of Britain's Gulag in Kenya.* New York: Henry Holt.

Fanon, Frantz. 1965. "Algeria Unveiled." In *Studies in a Dying Colonialism*, trans. Adolfo Willy. New York: Monthly Review Press.

Foucault, Michel. 1979. *The History of Sexuality.* Vol. 1. Harmondsworth, UK: Penguin.

Gill, Anton. 1995. *Ruling Passions: Sex, Race and Empire.* London: BBC Books.

Hyam, Ronald. 1990. *Empire and Sexuality: The British Experience.* Manchester, UK: Manchester University Press.

Kipling, Rudyard. 1890. "Beyond the Pale." In *Plain Tales from the Hills.* New York: F. F. Lovell.

Mayo, Katherine. 1927. *Mother India.* London: Jonathan Cape.

Said, Edward W. 1978. *Orientalism.* New York: Pantheon.

Spivak, Gayatri Chakravorty. 1994. "Can the Subaltern Speak?" In *Colonial Discourse and Post-Colonial Theory: A Reader*, ed. Patrick Williams and Laura Chrisman. New York: Columbia University Press.

Yeğenoğlu, Meyda. 1998. *Colonial Fantasies: Towards a Feminist Reading of Orientalism.* Cambridge, UK, and New York: Cambridge University Press.

Patrick Williams

COMICS CODE

Comics codes originated as a result of a post-World War II expectation in the rise of juvenile delinquency, attributable to the absence of mothers from homes during the war as they replaced their soldier husbands in the workplace. The fears were whipped into a frenzy by parents, teachers, religious figures, and some politicians, in public meetings, radio broadcasts, and periodical articles. In their eyes, comic books were the source of all types of youth problems, ranging from poor English and reading skills to juvenile delinquency.

The main concerns about comics pertained to their portrayals of crime and horror, although gender and sex figured prominently in the deliberations leading up to the writing of the codes. For example, the noted New York psychiatrist Fredric Wertham and other writers in the 1940s called attention to scantily clad women as undesirable elements of comic books.

When the first Comics Code was written by the Association of Comics Magazine Publishers in 1948, the first of six briefly stated points was that "sex, wanton comics should not be published" and that no female should be "indecently or unduly exposed" and "in no event more nude than in a bathing suit commonly worn in the United States of America." Furthermore, divorce was not to be shown in a "humorous," "glamorous," or "alluring" way.

Gender and sex were major discussion points in the pivotal year 1954, when comics came under investigation in U.S. Senate hearings, Wertham's influential book *Seduction of the Innocent* was published, and the Comics Magazine Association of America Comics Code was put into effect, administered by the Comics Code Authority.

In his book, Wertham scrutinized gender depictions, saying gender was linked to violence in comics as women were generally portrayed as victims or villains. Wertham thought comic books showing women as objects to be abused or used as decoys in crime settings resonated with young male readers' viewpoints. When women were comic book villains, the subtext, according to Wertham, was that men had to unite against such women. The book also covered romance comics, pointing out that they usually showed women in humiliating or inadequate roles.

The Comic Code of 1954 was one of the most stringent media codes of all time. Under sections on costume and marriage and sex, it banned nudity in any form, suggestive posture, illicit sex relations (hinted or actual), and sex perversion, and called for females to be drawn in proper dress "reasonably acceptable to society" and "realistically without exaggeration of any physical qualities." Love and romance were to be treated in a manner to protect the sanctity of marriage and the value of the home.

The code was revised twice, in 1971 and 1989, adapting to society's more liberal stance on sex. The 1971 code stated that illicit sex acts and seduction could be hinted at, while the 1989 version allowed adult relationships to be shown with good taste and sensitivity and acceptable to a mass audience. Costumes are acceptable if they "fall within the scope of contemporary styles and fashions"; not allowed are "primary, human sexual characteristics" and "graphic sexual activity."

Still in effect, the Comics Code covers only the mainstream comic book industry. Independent and alternative companies, more prone to explicit and nonconformist portrayals of sex and gender, do not belong to the Comics Code Authority.

BIBLIOGRAPHY

Beaty, Bart. 2005. *Fredric Wertham and the Critique of Mass Culture.* Jackson: University Press of Mississippi.

Lent, John A., ed. 1999. *Pulp Demons: International Dimensions of the Postwar Anti-comics Campaign.* Madison, NJ: Fairleigh Dickinson University Press.

Nyberg, Amy Kiste. 1998. *Seal of Approval: The History of the Comics Code.* Jackson: University Press of Mississippi.

John A. Lent

COMICS/COMIC STRIPS

Gender and sexuality have figured prominently in the development of comic books and comic strips, and women cartoonists—though relatively rare at times and in places—have been active from the earliest days of cartooning. In fact, one of the earliest strips in the world, Britain's *Ally Sloper*, was drawn by Marie Duval in the 1870s.

DEVELOPMENT OF COMICS IN THE UNITED STATES

In the United States, women drew newspaper funnies within six years after the appearance of *The Yellow Kid* (1895), generally recognized as the first American comic strip. The works of these early "queens of cute" usually portrayed pet animals, cherubic children in nineteenth-century clothing, or women decked out in curls, ruffles, and lace. Among these comics were Rose O'Neill's *Kewpies* (1909), after which the famous and lucrative doll was named; Louise Quarles's *Bun's Puns*, Grace Kasson's *Tin Tan Tales for Children*, and Agnes Repplier III's "The PhilaBusters" (all 1901); and Kate Carew's *The Angel Child* (1902). Other pioneering women cartoonists included Grace Gebbie Drayton, Fanny Y. Cory, Jean Mohr, Marjorie Organ, and Nell Brinkley.

Women's cartooning skills were not isolated to newspaper funny pages; they were also visible in many of the advertisements and fashion designs of the day. One of Drayton's accomplishments, for example, was the creation of the Campbell Kids (for Campbell Soup) advertising icons, and Brinkley's elegant women characters set fashion trends in real life. Curlers and hair wavers were named after her, and in Broadway's Ziegfeld Follies, a Brinkley Girl was featured. Cartoonists' style renditions often hit a chord with women, Charles Dana Gibson's "Gibson Girl" hairdos being a prime example. For decades, a number of comic strips drawn by women carried cut-out paper dolls that readers could dress.

The heyday of women's strips coincided with, or more likely resulted from, the fast, free-wheeling jazz era, a period when women won the right to vote and entered the workforce, chiefly as office workers, and the flapper epitomized one of the early sexual revolutions.

The earliest working girl comic strip was A. E. Hayward's *Somebody's Stenog*, which appeared in 1916 and featured Cam O'Flage, who worked for a nuts and bolts company. Other working girl characters were Martin Branner's *Winnie Winkle the Breadwinner* (1920), Russell Branover's *Tillie the Toiler* (1921), and Larry Whitington's *Fritzi Ritz* (1922), a flapper turned working girl. All three were drawn by men, as were most of the flapper strips, whose female characters only had men and good times on their minds. Among the early ones, all generated by men, were *The Affairs of Jane* (1921), *Beautiful Bab* (1922), *Dumb Dora* (1924), *Boots and Her Buddies* (1924), *Etta Kett* (1925), *Merely Margy* (1929), and *Blondie* (1930). The flapper strip also coaxed more women into the profession. Virginia Huget did several flapper strips, including *Molly the Manicure Girl* (1929), *Campus Capers* (1928), and *Gentlemen Prefer Blondes,* a 1926 adaptation of Anita Loos's bestseller. A more successful woman cartoonist was Ethel Hayes with *Flapper Fanny Says.* Hayes passed her character on to Gladys Parker, known later for the long-lasting *Mopsy.* Another feature, *Duley, the Beautiful Dumb-bell,* set in Hollywood, had its continuity credited to actress Constance Talmadge. The flapper strip faded in the 1930s, when the grimness of the Depression put high fashion, flappers, playboys, and a frivolous lifestyle out of reach. They were replaced by unglamorous characters dealing with real problems, such as poor, big-hearted *Apple Mary* (1932) by Martha Orr, and the cheerful orphan girls, *Little Orphan Annie* (1924), *Little Annie Rooney* (1927), and *Little Miss Muffet* (1935).

Women cartoonists began to trespass on male terrain in the 1930s and early 1940s, when they began drawing dramatic continuity strips (*Apple Mary* was the first) and featuring female heroes. In the newspaper funnies, Dahlia Messick adopted the male name Dale and in 1940 created *Brenda Starr*, an attractive red-headed girl reporter, and in the new genre of comic books, Tarpe Mills and Paddock Munson drew heroines for *Adventure Comics* and *Amazing Mystery Funnies.* Mills' costumed Miss Fury preceded William Moulton Marston's enduring Wonder Woman by a few months in 1941 as a comic book superheroine. Mills and Munson assumed sexually ambiguous names, as did other women (C. M. Sexton, Odin Burvik, and others) who drew action characters.

WORLD WAR II AND POST-WORLD WAR II

When American men went to war in 1942, the number of women doing comic books tripled and stayed at that level until the end of the 1940s. Some drew male superheroes, others wartime heroine characters such as Ann Brewster's *Yankee Girl* or Jill Elgin's *Girl Commandos*. Most exemplary in its positive treatment of women at the time was Fiction House, which had the largest female staff, many of whom were also given writing assignments. Female characters in Fiction House stories were different in that they were in charge and not just decoration or foils for heroes to admire or rescue.

After World War II, women cartoonists moved into the burgeoning fields of teen girl strips and romance comic books. Teen comics usually portrayed young girls in family and school environments and in their perpetual quests for boyfriends; they also exhibited their artists' keen awareness of fashion and, on occasion, touched upon the gender inequality issue. Popular teen strips were Ruth Atkinson's *Patsy Walker* (1944), Hilda Terry's *Teena* (1941), Linda Walter's *Susie Q. Smith* (1945), and Marty Links's *Bobby Soxer* (1944). Characters in the workforce were cast in traditional jobs, such as *Tessie the Typist* (1944) or *Nellie the Nurse* (1945). Romance comic books, which often portrayed women desperately seeking romance or being humiliated and jilted in love affairs totally controlled by men, were very popular in the 1940s and 1950s; Valerie Barclay and Ruth Atkinson created many of them.

In short supply during the first half-century of U.S. comic art were black women cartoonists and female editorial cartoonists. Jackie Ormes was the first black woman cartoonist (and one of only four black cartoonists total) with her strip *Torchy Brown* (1937), carried in fifteen African-American newspapers. Until much later, Edwina Dumm was the only woman editorial cartoonist, beginning in 1916 on the *Columbus* (Ohio) *Monitor*.

With the drop in the comics market in the 1950s, (because of claims the books were harmful to children) and the return of women to fulltime household duties after the war, the number of women in the field dropped considerably. By the mid-1960s, when the major companies were reduced to Marvel and DC, and both concentrated on superheroes that appealed to young boys, only Marie Severin and Ramona Fradon remained in mainstream comics. In some cases, women artists would not compromise their style to draw the violent action that superhero comics demanded.

FEMINISM AND COMICS

The underground press movement of the late 1960s and 1970s brought women back to comics, although not directly. At first, women were excluded from underground comics, which sparked them to start their own books, the first of which was *It Ain't Me, Babe* in 1970. The Wimmen's Comix Collective was set up, and in 1972, *Wimmen's Comix* and *Tits 'n' Clits* were published, the latter as a reaction to the sexism women saw in male-created underground comics. Much of the women's anger was directed at Robert Crumb, whose oversized black character Angelfood McSpade was subjected to all types of unimaginable indignities.

During the last quarter of the century, women continued to draw their own stories in comic books, strips, or graphic novels. Some were very personal memoirs discussing normally taboo subjects such as menstruation, lesbianism, rape, and incest and other sexual abuse. Others expressed women's anger toward men, even showing scenes of castration, or detailed the mundaneness of daily life. Prominent artists among these types were Roberta Gregory, Aline Kominsky-Crumb, Alison Bechtel, Diane DiMassa, and Canadian-born Julie Doucet. Titles of some of their works, such as *Dirty Plotte*, *Dykes To Watch Out For*, *Hothead Paisan: Homicidal Lesbian Terrorist*, and *Bitchy Bitch: World's Angriest Dyke!*, left no doubt about these women's emotions.

In the 1970s, Women's Liberation reached mainstream comics with a new batch of superheroines such as Valkyrie, the Cat, Ms. Marvel, and Spider-Woman, but women's readership of superhero/superheroine comics never reached appreciable heights. For example, a 1994 DC Comics survey lists only 5.9 percent female readership compared to 92.9 percent male. During the last quarter of the twentieth century, many superheroines were male-hating protagonists, professional assassins, or hypersexed, bloodthirsty killers. Many contemporary women comics creators opted to draw for small press publishers, such as Fantagraphics, Drawn and Quarterly, Last Gasp, and Rip Off Press, but some also draw for the mainstream. Among the latter are June Brigman, a mainstay penciler and cover artist for Marvel for more than twenty-five years; Jan Duursema, lead artist of *Star Wars* since 2000; Barbara Kesel, a writer, letterer, and editor since 1981; Devin Grayson, who consistently appears in top comics writers' lists as a contract writer for DC; Gail Simone, writer for DC's *Birds of Prey*, mainstream comics' longest-running female-led comic book after *Wonder Woman*, and other veterans such as Ann Nocenti, Marie Severin, Colleen Doran, Amanda Conner, and Louise Simonson.

Daily newspapers and syndicates continued to have a few popular strips with women as dominant characters into the twenty-first century, notably, *For Better or For Worse* (1979) by Canadian Lynn Johnston, and *Cathy* by Cathy Guisewite (1976), both of whom have won the National Cartoonists Society's Reuben Award. Because of

Cathy Guiswite. *Cartoonist Cathy Guiswite, working on her popular* Cathy *comic strip.* AP IMAGES.

the limits of mainstream syndication, some women self-syndicate with weekly newspapers, such as Lynda Barry and Nicole Hollander, or with the few comics tabloids, such as Alison Bechtel with her lesbian-focused strip.

Women's comics in the United States have gained in stature in recent decades, not just in terms of numbers of artists, but also by the fact that women have held top executive positions (Jenette Kahn as president of DC; Diana Schutz as one of the heads of Dark Horse). The genre now has a website, Sequential Tart (www.sequentialtart.com), started in 1998; an association, Friends of Lulu, begun in 1995 by Trina Robbins; and its own historian (Trina Robbins, who prefers to be called an herstorian).

OUTSIDE THE UNITED STATES

In other parts of the world, women and comics are bound together, although for the most part, the profession is predominantly a male domain. Nearly every country of Europe has female comics creators. Claire Bretécher of France has drawn very popular satirical works, especially the strip *Le destin de Monique*, started in 1983; and her countrywoman Chantal Montellier is famous for her album *Blues* (1979), a critical analysis of society. In Sweden, Cecilia Torudd became an important cartoonist with her strip *Ensamma Mamman* (The single parent mother) recounting her own parenting experiences in the 1970s, and Lena Ackebo is noted for her satirical comics.

Women often have been the major subjects of European comics. In England, girls and teen comic books flourished in the late 1960s and early 1970s, with as many as thirty weekly and monthly titles appearing simultaneously. By 2000, only *Bunty* (founded 1958) survived. Individual female characters stood out over the years, such as Jacques Tardi's *Adèle Blanc-Sec* (1976), a French daily strip and graphic novel depicting a freelance writer, a character who served as a stepping stone to very real women characters later; Guido Crepax's *Valentina* (1968) in Italy, a young alluring photographer modeled after American actress Louise Brooks; and England's *Modesty Blaise* and *Jane* strips.

Latin American comics have yielded some important female characters, perhaps the most well-known of whom is Mônica, a precocious little girl created by Brazil's Mauricio de Sousa, who established a comics empire around her. Other characters dealt with gender politics, such as *Aleida*, a frivolous, petty female created by Venezuela's Vladimir Flórez (Vladdo), and raw sexuality, such as Argentina's *Flopi Bach* (created by Carlos Trillo, Eduardo Maicas, and Garcia Seijas) who presents a disturbing portrayal of women.

In few places in the world has gender been as prominent in comics as in Asia. Women assume roles both stereotypical and equitably modern. In the Philippines, for instance, traditional love stories with pining lasses and happy endings are the bestselling *komiks*; Sri Lankan sixteen-page "comics papers" and the newspaper funnies also dote on romance, sometimes with rather daring portrayals of the dress and actions of female characters. As in many instances worldwide, women are pictured in the hackneyed either/or set of good mothers/wives or dirty prostitutes/vamps.

The *Amar Chitra Katha* comic books of India, known for their portrayals of Indian historical and mythological stories, took many hard knocks for their portrayals of women; the national university women's group of India reported the series emphasized for women a "home syndrome," self-sacrifice, obedience to men, and a high fertility rate. Generally, the criticism has been that *Amar Chitra Katha*'s depictions were based on the ancient Hindu code of *manu* that stated "good" women were mothers and wives ready to sacrifice their all for their men; "evil" women were bold and arrogant adventuresses, all of whom came to a deserved end. Indian comics can be categorized as portraying women as goddess, demon, warrior, victim, and companion.

Thai comics treat mothers and wives as non-sexual beings and men as desirous of multiple sexual encounters. A favorite topic of Thai comic books is domestic violence, a major problem in Thailand, but the abuse is committed by strong, sometimes enormous, women wielding *sak*s (pestles) as they beat or threaten weak, emasculated husbands. In Thai, sak and *khrok* (mortar) represent male and female sex organs, respectively; thus, a woman with a pestle suggests a phallus-wielding female. Also, wives are portrayed as short, stocky, unattractive women with big mouths; unmarried women have hourglass figures and gentle personalities. Gender problems are common topics of Indonesian comics (especially newspaper strips), because they and social hierarchy issues are safer topics than politics.

In Japan and Korea, comics are bisected by gender, to the extent that there is even one Seoul comics store exclusively for women. Girl's comics, called *shoujo manga* in Japan and *soonjung manhwa* in Korea, also treat romance and sexuality, but are concerned with much more, including every type of human relationship, as well as areas such as sports, everyday life, history, horror, and science fiction. Shoujo manga have more freedom than soonjung manhwa to deal with sexual taboos such as rape, sadomasochism, and the Lolita complex (sex associated with young girls). In Japan, comics for women and girls are prevalent enough to be subdivided into shoujo, *redikomi* (ladies'), and young ladies, or simply, those dealing with before marriage, after marriage, and before and after marriage, respectively, although the boundaries between the three are vague. Redikomi manga, which are increasing in number, appeal to the increasing number of career women, presenting women's desires when they are no longer girls and offering them alternate role models. They differ from shoujo in that they give a realist perspective on women's lives, for example, by visualizing the theme of sexuality using adult women's bodies and sometimes dealing with social issues. Young ladies' comic books, catering to women in the age group of late teens through twenties, came about in the late 1980s and 1990s. A favorite topic of these comics is the various types of love affairs a woman might have.

Shoujo and soonjung manhwa also are different from Western comic books in a number of ways, especially in that they are produced and consumed by women, some of whom have gained much respect and financial reward. Korea's Kim Hyerin won the prestigious cartoonist of the year award in 2003; Rumiko Takahashi, who has sold more than 100 million copies of her manga, including *Maison Ikkoku* (1986) and *Ranma ½* (1989), may be the richest woman in Japan.

In both Japan and South Korea, women make up a large part of the comics' audience. A 2000 survey in Japan found that 42 percent of women surveyed between the ages of twenty and forty-nine and 81 percent of teenage girls read manga regularly. More than 100 manga titles target the female audience; the largest, *Ribbon*, has a monthly paid circulation of more than one million. Popular are manga with homosexual content. A survey of 2,005 Koreans conducted in 2003 reported women were more experienced manhwa purchasers than men, that soonjung was the most preferred genre (21.6 percent), and that Korean authors (49.5 percent) were more popular than Japanese (46.4 percent). The figures show that still there is a considerable affinity for Japanese manga, which is understandable since Korean girls comics began with imitative copies or pirated reprints of shoujo.

The keen interest Japanese and Korean females have taken in comics has spread to girls and women in other parts of Asia—where, until recently, comics reading was mainly a male activity—and abroad, where girls, all but abandoned by U.S. comics publishers, have become voracious readers of Japanese (and now, Korean) girls' comics.

Images of women in cartooning are expected to change considerably as more women enter the field. The number in Asia is slowly increasing, with many in Japan and Korea (women make up 40 percent of the Korean comic artists pool); until recently, fewer than a dozen in China, although the number is increasing as the manga wave crests; and others who have gained prominence in Malaysia (Cabai, who has a magazine namesake), Pakistan (Nigar Nazar), and elsewhere. The three most productive *komiks* (comic books) writers in the Philippines for years have been women—Elena Patron, Nerissa Cabral, and Gilda Olvidado.

Generally, the role of women in comics worldwide has not been a dominant one. Men usually have written and drawn the comics and have managed the corporations that produce them; they have also been the ones who created the often stereotyped female images. But there have been exceptions, such as in post-1970 United States, in Japan and South Korea, and elsewhere, where women cartoonists have created their own types of comics and characters and have attempted to give a more realistic perspective of the female psyche.

BIBLIOGRAPHY

Franzen, Monika, and Nancy Ethiel. 1988. *Make Way! 200 Years of American Women in Cartoons*. Chicago: Chicago Review Press.

Horn, Maurice. 2001. *Women in the Comics*, revised edition. Philadelphia: Chelsea House.

Lent, John A. 2005. *Cartooning in Latin America*. Cresskill, NJ: Hampton Press.

Robbins, Trina. 1993. *A Century of Women Cartoonists*. Northampton, MA: Kitchen Sink Press.

Robbins, Trina. 1996. *The Great Women Superheroes*. Northampton, MA: Kitchen Sink Press.

Robbins, Trina. 1999. *From Girls to Grrrlz: A History of Comics from Teens to Zines*. San Francisco: Chronicle Books.

Robbins, Trina, and Catherine Yronwode. 1985. *Women and the Comics*. London: Eclipse Books.

John A. Lent

COMING OUT

Coming out is an expression used to describe the process of revealing one's nonnormative sexuality. It is most commonly used in reference to homosexuals, but is also applicable to bisexual, transsexual, and transgendered individuals. The term is a shortened form of the phrase *coming out of the closet,* in which the closet refers to the anonymity of hidden sexual practice or desire. Individuals who have not publicly identified their homosexuality are referred to as being *in the closet.* An alternate form of coming out is *outing,* which is an involuntary disclosure of one's homosexuality or other nonnormativity by another person. Outing can also refer to any inadvertent revelation of one's sexuality, whether by another or by oneself. Coming out generally has a positive connotation and is seen by many (but not all) as the foundation of a healthy relationship to one's sexuality, while outing is generally a more negatively valued practice and is seen as harmful and invasive to the individual, and only marginally useful to the larger homosexual community.

Coming out has also traditionally described the moment when a young woman enters formal society, her debut. In this circumstance, the term signifies the end of adolescence (which is a transitional, and thus a nonnormative, period of sexual development) and the emergence into normative heterosexuality, eventually leading to marriage. There is no evidence that the term as it is applied to homosexuality is linked to or derived from its use in formal society, but their complete opposition in meaning is noteworthy.

THE COMING OUT PROCESS

Coming out functions metaphorically as a moment in time, when the closet door opens and its inhabitant emerges. In practice, it is more often a process over time than a single moment, as a closeted individual usually comes out repeatedly to different audiences and under different circumstances. Even more fundamentally, however, coming out is generally understood as having two primary parts, one internal and one external.

Coming out to oneself involves recognizing one's own desires and choosing to acknowledge them. This phase of the coming out process often happens during adolescence, which is often seen as the primary moment of sexual identity formation, although it can happen at any point in life. This can be an extremely complicated step, primarily because the general expectation of heterosexuality is so strong that nonnormative sexualities are rarely acknowledged to or discussed favorably with children and adolescents, thus providing few, if any, homosexual role models. Youths who question their sexuality, therefore, may not fully understand the nature of their situation or how they might deal with it. People often describe this stage of questioning as a sensation of *feeling different* without being fully able to specify the difference they feel.

Once this awareness of difference has been achieved, it is possible to come out to others. Although a complicated and multipart process, it is usually referred to somewhat singularly as *coming out.* When coming out is a voluntary process, individuals often begin by coming out to one or more people who they consider most likely to be accepting of their homosexuality—frequently a friend or a group of friends. From there, they may choose to come out to people whose response they are less sure of, or even to those they feel sure will be unaccepting. Many individuals choose not to come out to everyone, and often make those choices based on the type of relationship they have with each person. For instance, coming out at work might be risky if harassment or discrimination is likely to result, and thus one might choose to remain closeted at work. Conversely, some choose to remain closeted at work not out of fear, but out of a belief that one's sexuality, whatever it might be, is irrelevant to the workplace and thus not a topic for discussion in that venue. Similarly, people generally make highly individual choices about coming out in religious groups they may belong to, as well as in other ideologically based organizations.

Coming out to family seems to be the largest or riskiest step in the coming out process for many, as the consequences are often greatest. To a certain extent, employment, religious affiliation, and friendships are all things that can be discarded and exchanged if necessary after coming out, but family involves a more permanent kind of connection. Many are thus unwilling to risk rejection by their families and remain closeted to them, or at least to certain family members.

The acceptance by friends and family is, like coming out itself, often a process over time, although some relationships are permanently severed as a result. Many people, however, have found their relationships either unchanged or even strengthened over time as a result of coming out. Several organizations such as PFLAG (Parents, Families and Friends of Lesbians and Gays) have arisen as a visible support system for individuals coming out as well as for those they come out to.

COMING OUT AS EMPOWERMENT

It is often claimed that sexuality is unique among human characteristics in that it is not visible in the way that sex, race, social class, and other categories are. Therefore, one's sexual desires and practices cannot be known to the larger community unless one comes out. While this understanding of the invisibility of sexuality versus other characteristics has substantial flaws, it does have a degree of relevance. In fact, all categories to which an individual belongs have certain expectations, and violating those expectations always carries some social risk. Rather than claiming that sexuality is a different kind of characteristic than others, it is perhaps more appropriate to say that it carries more value, that the expectations associated with it are seen as more absolute, and that violating them carries greater risk. It is also for this reason that coming out is seen as a primary means of empowerment in the homosexual community. Announcing one's homosexuality publicly is seen as a means of claiming ownership of it. In this way, homosexuality figures less as an affliction, as it has often been formulated, and more as a right or even a privilege. The fact that the risks associated with coming out can be so great makes the act substantially more powerful and socially meaningful.

Beginning with the shocking, even violent coming out moments such as the Stonewall riots of 1969, the power of publicly coming out has been realized and capitalized upon. Much of the subsequent gay rights movement has held the necessity of coming out as a central tenet; this has led to both the "silence = death" response to the AIDS epidemic in the 1980s and the growth of outing an individual (almost always a figure of power or a celebrity) involuntarily, thus revealing the ubiquity of homosexuality in contemporary culture.

COMING OUT AS RITE OF PASSAGE

Coming out is viewed as a rite of passage within the homosexual community. It is first and foremost seen as an acceptance of oneself and one's own sexuality. Because coming out potentially involves rejection, it is symbolically important as a kind of exchange of one community for another. The homosexual community largely imagines itself as an alternate, automatically accepting set of relationships that an individual can substitute for family, friends, and colleagues from whom they might be estranged. This is furthered by the self-identification of the homosexual community as a *family* or as a *tribe*, indicating both relationships among members and responsibility within the group for each other. This imaginary family is more often like a conventional one, however, in that it has factions, divisions, and internal struggles, all contained within a loose collective.

COMING OUT STORIES

The coming out experience is seen as central to identity formation, both in the individual and of the homosexual community. For this reason, coming out stories are one of the most common modes of bonding in the community. It is not unusual for people to share their experience of coming out with others as a means of establishing some kind of relationship with them. Because coming out is seen as a process unique to and definitive of homosexuality, there is an expectation that every member does have a coming out story. It is the exchange of these stories that many see as foundational to the idea of community and that creates pressure on individuals to share their stories. These stories are also seen as a source of both individual and group strength, particularly when they involve a painful rejection that is then survived by the individual. Gay and lesbian literature and film are dominated by coming out stories.

The stories most often told, of course, are the more spectacular and painful ones, usually those positioning the homosexual as the consummate victim (rejected by their family and often injured or killed) or as an epic hero overcoming obstacles (who then usually abandons at least part of his or her family and forms a new community). The extremity of either of these models has helped maintain the belief that coming out is a risky process, although there are many who believe that it may be less traumatic in most cases than is popularly believed.

There have been attempts to institutionalize or ritualize coming out in some ways, in an effort to maintain the importance of coming out while also making it seem a less risky and monumental experience. One example is National Coming Out Day, which is sponsored annually by the Human Rights Campaign.

SEE ALSO *Homosexuality, Contemporary: I. Overview.*

BIBLIOGRAPHY

Califia, Pat. 2000. *Public Sex: The Culture of Radical Sex.* 2nd edition. San Francisco: Cleis Press.

Chekola, Mark. 1994. "Outing, Truth-Telling, and the Shame of the Closet." In *Gay Ethics: Controversies in Outing, Civil Rights, and Sexual Science*, ed. Timothy F. Murphy. New York: Haworth Press.

"Coming Out." Human Rights Campaign. Available from http://www.hrc.org.

D'Emilio, John, and Estelle B. Freedman. 1997. *Intimate Matters: A History of Homosexuality in America.* 2nd edition. Chicago: University of Chicago Press.

Johnson, Bret K. 1997. *Coming Out Every Day: A Gay, Bisexual, and Questioning Man's Guide.* Oakland, CA: New Harbinger Publications.

Signorile, Michelangelo. 2003. *Queer in America: Sex, the Media, and the Closets of Power.* Rev. edition. Madison: University of Wisconsin Press.

Brian D. Holcomb

COMMUNISM AND MARXISM

Karl Marx's (1818–1883) writings are most closely associated with the economic and social domination associated with class, with little attention to the inequalities associated with gender. Marx had little to say directly about the system of gender domination prevalent in his own time, and he was not publicly associated with the contemporary movement for the emancipation of women—contrast his silence with the writings of John Stuart Mill (1806–1873) in *The Subjection of Women* (1869), for example. Nonetheless, the foundations of Marx's critique of bourgeois society provide a foundation for a socialist feminism, and these themes had great influence on communist political programs and societies in the twentieth century.

In the *Communist Manifesto*, Marx and Frederick Engels (1820–1895) offered scathing polemical criticisms of the bourgeois family and the exploitation of women: "[The bourgeois] has not even a suspicion that the real point aimed at is to do away with the status of women as mere instruments of production" (Marx and Engels 1848, pp. 57). However, the critique displays little insight into the ways that gender relations and the social institutions of the family affect the life situations of women, and it fails to identify the structural ways in which women were denied access to political positions, economic opportunity, or basic components of health assurance. Engels devoted more extensive attention to issues surrounding sex, gender, and the family in his anthropological book *The Origin of the Family, Private Property, and the State* (1884). Based largely on the work of the early ethnographer Lewis Henry Morgan (1818–1881), Engels argues that there is great historical variety in the sexual and reproductive practices of primates and human groups. And he offers a historical hypothesis for the emergence of the paired-couple family: the emergence of private property and slavery. Neither Marx nor Engels offered a coherent statement of socialist feminism, and neither offered specific commentary or criticism of the political, social, and economic disadvantages experienced by women in nineteenth-century Europe.

However, the fundamental themes of social criticism that Marx puts forward—alienation, domination, inequality, and exploitation and a critique of the social relations that give rise to these conditions—have clear implications for a theory of gender equality and emancipation. First, Marx's theory of alienation is premised on assumptions about the nature of the human being, involving the ideas of freedom, self-expression, creativity, and sociality (Marx [1844]). The situations of everyday life in which patriarchy and sexism obtain—the situations in which existing social relations of power, authority, and dominance are assigned on the basis of gender and sex, including marriage, the family, and the workplace—create a situation of alienation and domination for women. Second, Marx's theory of exploitation (expressed primarily in *Capital* [1867]) extends very naturally to the social relations of patriarchy. Patriarchy and the bourgeois family system embody exploitation of women, within the household and within the workplace. Finally, Marx's strong moral commitment to the overriding importance of social equality is directly relevant to a socialist feminist critique of contemporary society. The unequal status and treatment of women is an affront to the value of human equality. Thus Marx's principles lay the ground for a formulation of a socialist feminism.

Socialist and communist theorists of the decades between the death of Marx and World War I (1914–1918) gave specific prominence to issues of women's equality. Vladimir Lenin (1870–1924) gave attention to the problem of sexual inequality in bourgeois society in his journalism and in a widely read interview with the German feminist Clara Zetkin (1857–1953). Other leading communist thinkers of the decades between 1880 and 1920 also placed issues of female emancipation and women's equality at the center of the socialist agenda (e.g., Rosa Luxemburg [1870–1919], Nikolai Bukharin [1888–1938], Zetkin, Leon Trotsky [1879–1940], and Alexandra Kollontai [1872–1952]). These developments had important consequences for the policy priorities of communist governments once they seized power in Russia, China, and Cuba.

The communisms of the Soviet Union, China, and Cuba placed sexual equality at the top of the agenda for social transformation. Bolshevik political rhetoric emphasized the equality of women as a central communist goal before and during the revolution. In the 1920s the government of the Union of Soviet Socialist Republics (USSR) undertook to establish a legal framework guaranteeing legal equality for women, including full citizenship, equal pay, and the right of divorce. A particularly important figure in Soviet efforts to create sexual equality in the new communist society was Kollontai, author of *The Social Bases of the Woman Question* (1908). A crucial legal document with the goal of establishing gender equality was the Code on Marriage, the Family, and Guardianship (1918). The USSR demonstrated a higher level of equality in employment and education opportunities for women than most European countries during the period (Jancar-Webster 1978).

The most militant advocacy for women's rights occurred in the early years of Soviet power. Joseph Stalin's (1879–1953) conquest of state power in 1924 brought a primary focus on the power of the Communist Party and a retreat from the leftist values of prerevolu-

Influential Socialist Clara Zetkin. ROGER VIOLLETT/GETTY IMAGES.

tionary communism—including the earlier communist advocacy for radical emancipation of women. Kollontai's strong advocacy for women's issues and her advocacy for sexual freedom for women led to her removal as a significant government voice in the 1920s. Based on a pronatalist national economic policy, Soviet policy discouraged contraception, resulting in very high rates of abortion in the 1950s through the 1970s (12 to 16 per 100 women between the ages 15 to 49 compared with U.S. rates in the range of 2 to 3 per 100 women in that same age group), and these rates only began to fall significantly in the 1990s. One should not overstate the degree of women's equality regarding politics in the USSR and China; though female participation in political organizations and offices generally exceeded that of most European and North American democracies at any given time, it fell far short of parity at any level of political activity.

The Chinese Communist Party (CCP) likewise placed the emancipation of women as one of its leading revolutionary goals, and CCP commanders made specific efforts to mobilize women in the base areas in the 1930s and 1940s (Chen 1986). Profeminist themes found resonance among Chinese women because there was a tradition of feminist thought in Chinese politics extending back to the May Fourth Movement (a revolutionary movement that began with student demonstrations in Beijing on May 4, 1919). A central target of Chinese efforts for establishing women's equality was the traditional family and marriage system. Arranged marriage, domination by the mother-in-law, and subordination of the wife to the authority of the husband were long-established features of Chinese society, and Chinese communists were determined to end these practices (Hinton 1966). After seizing power in 1949 the communist state undertook a series of fundamental legal reforms to establish the equality of women, including the areas of family and marriage (the Marriage Law of the People's Republic of China [PRC] was instituted in 1950), literacy and female education, electoral rights (the Electoral Law of the PRC went into effect in 1952), equality of treatment during the period of land reform, and guarantee of the right to labor outside of the household. There was also a specific and long-term effort within the CCP to develop and advance women into positions of leadership within the party, both before and after the revolution. It is generally agreed that the status of women in China has improved markedly since 1949 in terms of education, political participation, marital freedom, and economic independence (Tao, Zheng, and Mow 2004).

The Cuban revolution likewise brought systemic change for the situation of Cuban women, and Cuba became a model for the developing world in its success in ending the oppression of women. More fully even than the USSR or the PRC, Cuba succeeded both in incorporating legal equality for women into its constitution and fundamental legal system and in changing the actual outcomes for the broad population of Cuban women in virtually all segments of society. The percentages of female legislators, lawyers, doctors, scientists, and managers are among the highest in any country. Women represent a majority of Cubans in higher education—often a large majority. Female health indicators likewise show an internationally distinctive high level of attainment, with high female life expectancy and low infant mortality. Nicola Murray provides a detailed accounting of the role and status of women in postrevolution Cuba (1979).

Socialist and communist ideas thus had a large effect on progress toward greater gender equality in the twentieth century. For a mix of reasons, both ideological and political, women leaders and the issue of the equal treatment of women have had substantial influence on policies and outcomes in the Soviet Union, Eastern Europe, China, and Cuba. This progress has occurred in multiple spheres in the areas of legal and constitutional declarations of equality of treatment; in the transformation of some of the basic institutions governing family, marriage, and childrearing; and in the successful provisioning of basic social goods (education, healthcare, access to economic opportunities) in a way that comes closer to establishing equality of outcomes for men and women.

BIBLIOGRAPHY

Chen, Yung-fa. 1986. *Making Revolution: The Communist Movement in Eastern and Central China, 1937–1945.* Berkeley: University of California Press.

Engels, Frederick. 1977 [1884]. *The Origin of the Family, Private Property, and the State: In the Light of the Researches of Lewis H. Morgan*, ed. E. B. Leacock. London: Lawrence & Wishart.

Hinton, William. 1966. *Fanshen: A Documentary of Revolution in a Chinese Village.* New York: Vintage.

Jancar-Webster, Barbara. 1978. *Women under Communism.* Baltimore, MD: Johns Hopkins University Press.

Marx, Karl. 1964 [1844]. *Economic and Philosophic Manuscripts of 1844*, ed. D. J. Struik. New York: International Publishers.

Marx, Karl. 1977 [1867]. *Capital*, Vol. 1. New York: Vintage.

Marx, Karl, and Frederick Engels. 1998 [1848]. *The Communist Manifesto: A Modern Edition*, ed. E. J. Hobsbawm. London: Verso.

Mill, John Stuart. 1970 [1869]. *The Subjection of Women.* New York: Source Book Press.

Morgan, Lewis Henry. 2000 [1877]. *Ancient Society.* New Brunswick, NJ: Transaction Publishers.

Murray, Nicola. 1979. "Socialism and Feminism: Women and the Cuban Revolution, Part One." *Feminist Review* 2: 57–73.

Murray, Nicola. 1979. "Socialism and Feminism: Women and the Cuban Revolution, Part Two." *Feminist Review* 3: 99–108.

Tao, Jie; Bijun Zheng; and Shirley L. Mow, eds. 2004. *Holding up Half the Sky: Chinese Women Past, Present, and Future.* New York: Feminist Press at the City University of New York.

Zetkin, Clara. 1920. "Interview with Lenin on 'The Women's Question.'" In *The Lenin Anthology*, ed. R. C. Tucker. New York: Norton.

Daniel Little

COMPUTERS

> When I first got my BP6 I put it in a case, but then I realized cases were gay so I took it out of the case. I have some modular shelf/racks I got from Lowe's and it sits on there. The power supply is strapped underneath with a bungee cord. No need for case fans. You will be a better person and more of a man or woman if you take it out of the case. I threw mine in the dumpster. . . . Cases are for fags.

The words above belong to an unregistered user at the Ars Technica open forum posted on April 15, 2000, at 19:05. The (re)actions of this (homophobic?) computer user and builder actually illustrate well the significance and complexities of human–computer interaction at the object level. When the same user continues his criticism, it becomes clear that he despises the design and looks of some of the computers in Apple's iMac line, just introduced at that time, and associates them with his homophobic definitions of "gay" identity and iconography: "Of course if you don't have a case you forgo the opportunity to select a gay blue imac ripoff case or more likely paint your case pink and stencil, 'I'm so Gay' on it."

Indeed, this user was not alone in his reaction to the iMac's design and colors, and similar reactions arose to the many "iMac-wanna-be" PC imitations. Numerous PC users and "I Hate Macs" sites constituted a virtual Internet campaign against Apple's revolutionary designs and the "sexualization process" of computer cases.

Starting in 1998, the colorful and "juicy" iMac computers became best-sellers in their class. The iMac colors and transparent designs took over the entire all-in-one sector of the computer market, and thousands of everyday consumer products such as coffee makers, toasters, pens, toys, and irons began hitting the market with similar colors and designs. The iMac look became an object design cult in popular culture.

Outraged by such an invasion, a user in France came up with a now-defunct "I Hate Macs" web site, where he or she posted numerous anti-Mac images mocking the design fetishisms of Steve Jobs, the cofounder and CEO of Apple Computer, and the sexualization and genderization of computer cases and other plastic objects.

In fact, the company itself sought to impose a "She" identity upon its early iMacs. Apple's famous TV commercial "She Comes in Colors" successfully established this gender association with the personal computer. With the five different iMacs positioned in a circle, monitors facing out, the Rolling Stones's 1967 psychedelic rock ballad "She's a Rainbow" accompanies the twirling rainbow of feminized machines, this time in a postmodern setting:

> She comes in colors everywhere
> She combs her hair
> She's like a rainbow
> Coming, colors in the air
> Oh, everywhere
> She comes in colors

In February 2001 Jobs introduced the new and improved iMac SE, and, according to the web site apple-history.com, two new patterns "were molded into the case using a technique which took Apple 18 months to perfect." One wonders if Apple's CEO and his designers wanted to capitalize more on the already established public conception of the previous iMacs' gender connotations. On March 3, 2001, Jack Maher, writing on the MacFixIt web site, related the following about his family's flower design iMac SE:

> Our family just received a Flower Power iMac SE from the Apple Store. The site said to expect a seven day wait, we got it in three. My wife and daughter think the Flower Power design is beautiful. The coloration is subtle and not as garish as it may appear from the photos on the Apple site. The colors are pastels and translucent. The machine sits on my wife's desk, alongside a window. When the sun passes through the case, it creates a very pleasant appearance. Definitely NOT your standard Beige Box.

The user's comments about the plastic enclosure of the computer are fascinating. Indeed, his and his family's interaction with their new object is not a classical human–computer interaction. He does not talk about how fast their new computer is, what it is capable of doing, and so on. He focuses solely on the flowery plastic, thus equating the plastic clothing with the machine's body itself. Perhaps more than any other hardware company, Apple invests heavily in researching human psychology and consumer interactions with objects. For potential "male" users, the iMac SE's see-through graphite design is quite revealing and seems to be based on the voyeuristic tendencies of the male gaze.

Computer magazines dedicated to the Mac platform seemed to be delighted that the minority status of the MAC OS (operating system) could be changed with the success and popularity of the iMac line. The Macintosh "geek" culture was happy that the iMac runs only Mac OS and not Windows. A cartoon published in the May 2000 issue of *Mac Addict* magazine not only expressed Apple's "victory" over Microsoft but also provided further testimony of the accepted gender status of the iMac: "Sorry. . . . I don't do windows!"

Following the gender success of the iMac, many small companies saw the business potential in producing iMac peripherals (quite similar to the multitude of later products that claimed to add more functionality to the iPod line). Many of these peripheral companies focused on the sex and gender associations of their iMac products in hopes of rapid sales boosts. One of the most successful such companies was Contour Design, which, among many other peripherals, developed and produced "nice legs" for the already beautiful female iMac.

The portable partner of the fruit-colored iMacs (Jobs being a vegetarian) were the iBooks. On July 29, 1999, on his TechTV show "Silicon Spin," John Dvorak described Jobs's new laptop computer:

> The only thing missing from the Apple iBook is the Barbie logo. The system, which looks like a makeup case, promises to be a disaster once people come to their senses. . . . [T]his system is an embarrassment. . . . I can only describe it as a 'girly' machine. You expect to see lipstick, rouge, and a tray of eye shadow inside when you open it. You don't expect to see a 12-inch LCD; you expect to see a 12-inch mirror. No man in his right mind will be seen in public with this notebook.

Dvorak's angry, and somehow sexist, reaction to the new Apple laptop was not the only one. In an interview with *Business Week* published online on January 18, 2002, Jeff Raskin, who joined Apple's Cupertino headquarters in 1978 and shortly after that became the manager of the "Macintosh Project," sounded as straightforward as possible in his criticism of Jobs's attachment to the form fetish:

> What Steve Jobs did was decree that the Apple II was to have an aesthetic enclosure. He said we have to put this in a pretty box. We can't sell a naked board. He was absolutely right. But what he has been doing ever since is repeat that formula. They keep the hardware up to or slightly above the standard set by PCs, but they can't think outside the pretty box.

No matter how much the new revolutionary designs of Apple's enclosures were criticized by some leading analysts and computer experts, millions of consumers embraced the unusual form fetish found in these machines, from iBooks to Power Macs. It came as no surprise that the October 2000 issue of *Playboy* magazine featured a playmate on its front cover, posing with an Apple iBook. The color of the playmate's shorts and the curves of her body were photographed in unison with an iBook in an effort to make her look like the computer and the computer look like her. Just like the reified model, an object of the male gaze, the computer itself is transformed into an aesthetically pleasing plastic object by focusing only on its colorful shell. Neither of the two models, the human or the machine, manifests any other sign of their being beyond their enclosures.

At the MacWorld Expo in January 2001, Jobs introduced his high-end notebook computer for "professionals," the PowerBook G4 Titanium, which featured a 15.2-inch "megawide" LCD display, a slot-loading DVD drive, and a 400 MHz PowerPC CPU, all housed in an enclosure made of titanium. Quite a luxury at the time, the titanium look and power was a departure from the flashy plastic color designs. As argued above, the lower-end iMacs and iBooks had "sex appeal." Jobs made it clear at the expo that the new PowerBook G4 was not only powerful but also sexy: "We think it has the power and the sex."

The Wired News web site used the headline "Titanium titillation" for its article on the new computer:

> [It] is very small and sleek and has just about everything you'd need to replace a desktop machine. And when you look at it up close, you realize just how amazing the attention to detail is. . . . At the Apple booth, a bunch of guys (they're always guys) [were] admiring one of the new PowerBooks on a revolving pedestal. . . . They started dancing and clapping with glee.

Apple certainly is not alone in assigning sex and gender identity to computer products. Regardless of their operating systems, many companies have tried to sell their products (from small peripherals to computers) through a clever manipulation and, in many cases, exploitation, of sex and gender values and perceptions. Research on this subject suggests that the weaker the quality of the product is (including of course the entire iMac line), the greater the need for the usage of sex and gender in marketing it. The buyers of high-end machines (from workstations to highly expensive servers and other specialized computers) do not need to be manipulated through sex- and gender-obsessed advertisements. Indeed such a business strategy would backfire. Generally speaking, these buyers are highly educated and possess a great deal of technological knowledge, and their attraction to the product is based on the technology itself, not the color and "sex appeal" of the enclosure. Compaq, known for its run-of-the-mill budget PCs, had once placed great emphasis on the "gender qualities" of its Presario desktops and notebooks in its advertisements and attempted to provide its potential male and female buyers with an "iMac taste" based on the buyers' sexual "chemistry" and their presumed gender/color associations (see *PC World*, September 2000, p. 61, and *Maximum PC*, September 2000, p. 1).

Personal computer companies' feminization of their budget machines is neither country nor culture specific. This is more or less an international marketing phenomenon. An ad published in the Turkish version of *Chip* magazine targets the potential male buyer with a sex-centered interpretation of an all-in-one PC ("The Best Model of the World," *Chip*, August 2000, p. 41). The woman in the ad is "en ince" (the slimmest), "en şık" (the most stylish), "en modern" (the most modern), and "en kullanışlı" (the most utilitarian). The camera's focus is on the model. The machine itself is just a pretty background prop hoping to be sold in the chaos of a cognitive confusion.

The models featured in the ads for VAIO FJ computers continue Sony Corporation's determination to establish the "female" identity of its FJ series notebooks. VAIO FJs are known to be middle-of-the-road computers designed for middle-of-the-road computing tasks. In general, Sony's VAIO desktops and notebooks have a reputation for their high-end parts and impeccable attention to detail. Only for the FJs, however, is this much emphasis placed on sex and gender. The FJ's advertisers (like those of the early iMacs) have been paying special attention to the feminization of the machine by showing the "special" and "sweet" color enclosures being carried by professional models with black, blond, and red hair. Especially through the FJ, VAIO engineers, designers, and advertisers seem to be attempting to create a new level of human–computer interaction, an interaction that goes above and beyond the user's traditional computing needs and habits. The FJ and its ads seem to center around the establishment of new postmodern lifestyles that are colorful, polished, flirtatious, and daring.

BIBLIOGRAPHY

"Can Jobs 'Think Outside the Pretty Box'?" 2002. *Business Week*, January 18. Available from http://www.businessweek.com/technology/content/jan2002/tc20020118_5216.htm.

"iMac (Early 2001)." Apple-history.com. Available from http://www.apple-history.com.

Kahney, Leander. 2001. "Jobs Tells It Like It Is." Wired News, January 13. Available from http://www.wired.com/news/technology/0,1282,41160,00.html.

"Nice Legs." 2000. *Mac Addict*, May, 103.

Kemal Silay

CONCUBINAGE

The term *concubinage* from the Latin expression *concubīna*, which derives from *con* (with) and *cubare* (to lie), refers to the state of a man and woman cohabiting as married persons without the full sanctions of legal marriage. A woman who enters this kind of relationship is known as a concubine. Concubinage may be of long—even lifelong—duration and sexually exclusive. But because this relationship is usually without legal protection for the woman and her children, it can also be terminated with relative ease. In contrast to a wife, a concubine has limited rights of support. Although her children might obtain acknowledgement as the man's offspring, their entitlement to property was usually restricted, especially if the father had progeny by his legal wife. In general, the practice of concubinage has endured in many different civilizations and until the early twenty-first century, because it was (and is) a means of protecting inheritance without denying men sexual pleasure. In some societies, such as imperial China, concubinage also became a demonstration of conspicuous consumption, awarding prestige to those men able to afford it.

Concubinage has been practiced since ancient times. Anthropologists have argued that most societies have made a distinction between legally sanctioned unions and the cohabitation of unmarried couples (concubinage) or casual sexual relations. Written evidence from ancient Mesopotamia demonstrates there was differentiation between legitimate marriage and concubinage. In ancient Israelite society, men were free to have sexual relations with concubines (and slaves or servants) along with their wives. There are several dramatic stories in the Old Testament involving concubines. *Judges 19* narrates the sad fate of a concubine thrust outside of her house, then gang-raped for an entire night, and finally murdered by her own master. In *2 Samuel 5:13* one learns of King David taking concubines, and in *2 Samuel 15:16*, his leaving ten concubines behind when he fled Jerusalem in the face of Absalom's coup. By contrast, in the case of ancient Egypt, where women of all social classes had the same legal rights as men, and marriage was monogamous, there is doubt whether concubinage did in fact exist.

In classical Greece the concubine occupied the status between the wife and mistress or courtesan. The well-known passage from Apollodorus's speech *Against Neaira* differentiates three categories of women in Athens: "For we have courtesans (*hetairai*) for pleasure, and concubines (*pallaki*) for daily service of our bodies, (and) wives (*gunaikes*) for the production of legitimate offspring and to have a reliable guardian of our household property" (Davidson 1997, p. 73). One of the effects of Pericles's (495–429 BCE) citizenship law of 451 BCE was to limit the ability of concubines' children to inherit. They inherited only when a man had no children by his recognized wife.

In ancient Rome, concubinage had a somewhat different status. There it could be considered a lasting sexual union, the resort of those who could not legally marry such as legionary soldiers, or persons of different social status such as a senator and a freed woman. The second and third centuries CE saw a proliferation of laws on concubines, which made clearer what constituted legal marriage and what legal status concubinage held. Unlike marriage where the giving of a dowry was the norm, long-term concubinage did not involve such property exchange. A dowry (being understood as the property a wife brought to the marriage) was not legally necessary for either Roman or Greek marriage, but there was a strong moral duty for this institution. A marriage without a dowry created the impression of concubinage. Thus, in ancient Rome, concubinage was not a union adjunct to marriage, but, rather, proved an alternative, especially for widower men. Several Roman emperors—Vespasian (9–79 CE), Marcus Aurelius (121–180 CE), and Antoninus Pius (86–161 CE) among them—lived with concubines after the death of their wives. As all these rulers had already designated heirs to their throne, and did not marry the women with whom they lived, they avoided the squabbles between heirs descended from different wives, which had occurred in Hellenistic monarchies.

With the decline and fall of the Roman Empire, the distinction between marriage and concubinage blurred because of the attitudes of the Christian church. As early Christian ideas on marriage stressed consent above dowry to be the constituent element of legal marriage, it became difficult to distinguish concubinage from clandestine marriage where consent had been given, but no dowry. Although ecclesiastical pressure against concubinage among the clergy and the laity did exist throughout the Middle Ages, canon law in fact adopted an ambivalent attitude toward this practice. Saint Augustine's (354–430) ideals of lifelong monogamy for royalty and celibacy for servants of the church notwithstanding, the records for the Carolignian and Merovingian dynasties demonstrate concubinage persisted among sovereigns and their descendants, as well as the clergy and the laity. Even the medieval canon lawyer's (Franciscus Gratian [d. 1159]) attempts to wrestle with the problems of clerical concubinage did not offer a satisfactory solution, and for the next several hundred years the vagaries associated with concubinage circumscribed the status of sexual relations among the married and unmarried of whatever social class. It would take the church's Tridentine reforms (held from 1545–1563) to abolish the legality of concubinage and clandestine marriage. From then onward, both the Catholic and Protestant churches subjected sexual activity to regulation in official documentation.

Such regulatory attitudes also guided the mindset of the first Europeans who explored and colonized the New World. In pre-Hispanic MesoAmerica and the Andes, where polygamy was common practice, the imposition of Christian models of behavior prompted the Indian native population to substitute concubinage and forms of slavery in response to their overlords. Concubinage with Spaniards also served as a means for natives, and later black slaves, to enter colonial society, which also contributed to the transfer of landed property to the Spanish and half-castes. In Dutch Asia the keeping of concubines was at first widespread among Dutch East India Company officials as well as ordinary crew, but in 1622 the company authorities issued an edict forbidding the practice. Thereafter, marriage between Dutch (Calvinist) men and local (converted Christian) women was encouraged.

In other regions outside Western Europe concubinage was a vehicle for dynastic reproduction. Indian rajas, khans, and sultans kept large harems with concubines, a practice that persisted even under the British Raj in the princely states. Iranian monarchs and noblemen from the sixth century BCE until the nineteenth century CE

Fifth-Century Fresco Painting of Two Concubines. © JEREMY HORNER/CORBIS.

(i.e., first Zoroastrian and subsequently Sunni and Shi'ite elites) maintained large harems with numerous concubines. Among the ruling elite of the Ottomans, it was the custom for nearly 200 years before the reign of Suliman the Magnificent (1520–1566) to take concubines rather than wives to avoid interdynastic strife. Suliman's restructuring of the Ottoman political system used marriage as the vehicle for dynastic reproduction and primogeniture as a principle of succession. Thereafter, women, as members of the royal family, also began to exercise social and political power. The quarters where these royal women and their children lodged was the harem, that part of the imperial enclosure forbidden to male strangers. By the seventeenth century the harem became a site of European fantasy and obsession. As evidenced by their many paintings, Europeans thought the harem to be a location of sexual license, symbolic of Oriental despotism, and the weakness of the Turkish sultanate. But, in fact, the harem was an important government agency for the supervision of Ottoman statecraft. One may compare it to the Keno Palace in Nigeria where for over 500 years its concubines supervised the Hausa state's grain and indigo operations.

Harem is also the usual rendition of the Chinese language term *hougong*, literally meaning "the palaces behind." These were large-size quarters in the imperial palace for the emperor's consorts and concubines, as well as their servants. Ordinary Chinese people also possessed concubines who commonly came from an impoverished background, but men could have only one wife. A man who still had no heir at the age of forty was encouraged to take a concubine, but often rich men acquired a series of concubines to mark their status. Whereas the sons of concubines were equal to those of the wife in matters of inheritance, the status of their mothers was usually no more than a servant or maid. Moreover, a concubine was expected to obey her master's wife. Until the Qing dynasty (1644–1911), it was illegal for a man to promote his concubine to wife, even if his wife had died. The low-class status of concubines continued well into the twentieth century.

Now in the early twenty-first century, as increasing numbers of men and women in Euro-America choose to live together without marrying, the word *concubinage* has taken on new legal, social, and cultural meanings. In France *concubinage* is the official term for the cohabitation of heterosexual and (since 1998) homosexual couples. But concubinage in other societies outside Euro-America probably continues to carry a social stigma.

SEE ALSO *Harems.*

BIBLIOGRAPHY

Bernand, Carmen, and Serge Gruzinki. 1996. "Children of the Apocalyse: The Family in MesoAmerica and the Andes." In *A History of the Family.* Vol. 1, *Distant Worlds, Ancient Worlds.* Vol. 2, *The Impact of Modernity*, ed. André Burguière, Christine Klapisch-Zuber, Martine Segalen, and Françoise Zonabend. Oxford, UK: Polity Press.

Bohmbach, Karla. G. 1999. "Conventions/Contraventions: The Meanings of Public and Private for the Judges 19 Concubine." *Journal for the Study of the Old Testament* 83:83-98.

Bray, Francesca. 1997. *Technology and Gender: Fabrics of Power in Late Imperial China.* Berkeley: University of California Press.

Brundage, James A. 1975. "Concubinage and Marriage in Medieval Canon Law." *Journal of Medieval History* 1(1): 1–17.

Burguière, André, and François Lebrun. 1996. "Priest, Prince, and Family." In *A History of the Family.* Vol. 1, *Distant Worlds, Ancient Worlds.* Vol. 2, *The Impact of Modernity*, ed. André Burguière, Christiane Klapisch-Zuber, Martine Segalen, and Françoise Zonabend. Oxford, UK: Polity Press.

Davidson, James. 1997. *Courtesans and Fishcakes: The Consuming Passions of Classical Athens.* London: Harper Collins.

Demosthenes. 1964. *Demothenes VI: Private Orations L-LVIII*, trans. A. T. Murray. Cambridge, MA: Loeb Classical Library.

Ebrey, Patricia. 1986. "Concubines in Sung China." *Journal of Family History* 11(1):1–24.

Eisenbach, Emlyn. 2004. *Husbands, Wives, and Concubines: Marriage, Family, and Social Order in Sixteenth Century Verona.* Kirksville, MO: Truman State University Press.

Goody, Jack. 1990. *The Oriental, the Ancient, and the Primitive: Systems of Marriage and the Family in the Pre-Industrial Societies of Eurasia.* Cambridge, UK: Cambridge University Press.

Isom-Verhaaren, Christine. 2006. "Royal French Women in the Ottoman Sultans' Harem: The Political Uses of Fabricated Accounts from the Sixteenth to the Twenty-first Century." *Journal of World History* 17 (2):159–196.

Nast, Heidi. 2005. *Concubines and Power: Five Hundred Years in a Northern Nigerian Palace.* Minneapolis: University of Minnesota Press.

Peirce, Leslie. 1993. *The Imperial Harem: Women and Sovereignty in the Ottoman Empire.* New York: Oxford University Press.

Pomeroy, Sarah B. 1975. *Goddesses, Whores, Wives, and Slaves: Women in Classical Antiquity.* New York: Schoken Books.

Robins, Gay. 1993. *Women in Ancient Egypt.* London: British Museum Press.

Rousselle, Aline. 1996. "The Family under the Roman Empire: Signs and Gestures." In *A History of the Family.* Vol. 1, *Distant Worlds, Ancient Worlds*, Vol. 2, *The Impact of Modernity*, ed. André Burguière, Christiane Klapisch-Zuber, Martine Segalen, and Françoise Zonabend. Oxford, UK: Polity Press.

Stafford, Pauline. 1998. *Queens, Concubines and Dowagers: The King's Wife in the Early Middle Ages.* London: Leicester University Press.

Watson, Alan. 1967. *The Law of Persons in the Later Roman Republic.* Oxford, UK: Clarendon Press.

Zonabend, Françoise. 1996. "An Anthropological Perspective on Kinship and the Family." In *A History of the Family.* Vol. 1, *Distant Worlds, Ancient Worlds.* Vol. 2, *The Impact of Modernity*, ed. André Burguière, Christiane Klapisch-Zuber, Martine Segalen, and Françoise Zonabend. Oxford, UK: Polity Press.

Harriet T. Zurndorfer

CONDOM

SEE *Contraception: IV. Relation of to Sexual Practices and Gender Roles.*

CONDUCT BOOKS

As didactic literature, conduct books did not adhere to a particular form or subject matter. They were written for a specific but usually anonymous audience, which could be male or female, aristocratic or, especially in the late Middle Ages, bourgeois. Determining the actual audience for the books is complicated since the texts were appropriated by readers of status other than those intended. People of lower social status read conduct books of the upper class precisely with the aim of learning aristocratic behavior and, ultimately, attaining elite status. Subtypes of conduct literature include the Mirrors for Princes, the estates poem, and the courtesy book. Historians also consider many other texts that do not conform to any of these subtypes to be conduct literature.

MIRRORS FOR PRINCES

The Mirrors for Princes were written for an aristocratic, male audience. While they are hardly representative of conduct literature generally, since in some cases either the author or the patron could be identified, these texts were among the first conduct books to be edited and studied. The *Policraticus* (early 1160s) by English ecclesiastic John of Salisbury (1115–1120), dedicated to Thomas Becket but written with Henry II in mind, is fairly typical of the genre, with its blending of moral, political, and legal concerns. The author shows little interest in sexual matters, but the Prince is enjoined to exercise moderation in all areas of his public and personal life and to shun bodily pleasure so as not to become, like Julius Caesar, "ensnared in the bonds of Venus by a shameless woman" (John of Salisbury 1990, p. 35).

An *Enseignement des Princes* (Instruction of Princes) figures among the didactic works of the thirteenth-centurycourtly poet Robert de Blois, as does a companion text, the *Chastoiement des dames* (Correction of Ladies). Contrastive reading of these texts provides insight on how courtly society in northern France constructed the masculine and feminine spheres. While the *Enseignement* focuses on the Prince's social interactions in the public arena of the court, the *Chastoiement* emphasizes feminine honor and *mesure* in an exposition in which the fetishized female body becomes the locus of male anxiety (Krueger 1990). In a somewhat similar way, the *Miroir des bonnes femmes* (Mirror of Good Women, c. 1300) describes, for the urban elite of Burgundy in the fourteenth and fifteenth centuries, female honor as the "ideological locus of social prestige upon which the whole family builds its new status" (Ashley 2001, p. 102).

ESTATES POEMS

Usually written by clerics and advocating respect of the Church's prerogatives and teachings, estates poems either idealize or satirize the various estates of Christian society. The earliest example in the vernacular is the *Livres des manières* by Etienne de Fougères, chaplain to Henry II, in which the author seeks to define the proper relationship among the estates after the murder in 1170 of his colleague, Thomas Becket. Etienne is preoccupied with female sexuality, making women one of his six estates of society. He expresses no interest in peasant women but lambastes the bourgeoises (females of the class) who think themselves "courtly" (*courtoises*) if they take a lover or who may seek to settle a debt by having sex with their creditors. He is most ferocious in dealing with the ladies of the court, whom he accuses of adultery, homicide, infanticide, and, in a lengthy tirade, lesbianism. The satirical tone of this passage and others in the poem belies a deep-seated anxiety over female sexuality, particularly the thought that women might escape the control of men.

COURTESY BOOKS

Late-medieval courtesy books were written either for noble or bourgeois readers and circulated widely in urban communities, especially after the appearance of printed versions, such as *Caxton's Book of Curtesye* (c. 1477). Typically focusing on behavior in the household and at table and more generally on issues of economy and consumption, courtesy books tend to be highly attentive also to issues of social standing and gender. For instance, *What the Goodwife Taught Her Daughter*, which circulated in the mid-fourteenth to the late-fifteenth centuries, focuses specifically on female behavior in and outside the household. Although ostensibly a book of advice for bourgeois daughters, medievalist Felicity Riddy argues that it more likely served as a guide for women managing bourgeois households and female servants from either lower social backgrounds or the countryside. In this text unregulated female sexuality is presented as potentially disruptive to relations within the household and damaging to its good standing in the social fabric of the broader community.

One of the most striking features of conduct books, especially more developed ones like the *Mesnagier de Paris* (written in 1394 by a Parisian householder for his young wife) or the *Livre du Chevalier de la Tour Landry pour l'enseignement de ses filles* (written in 1371–1372 by a provincial nobleman for his daughters), but also shorter texts like Jean Gerson's *Sur l'excellence de la virginité* (1395–1398), is the way in which their patriarchal discourse seeks to harmonize conflicting concerns (social, familial, sexual, spiritual) and construct a script for living for a subject. As such, they are more prescriptive than descriptive, but they offer many insights into social and sexual dynamics in the medieval and early modern periods.

BIBLIOGRAPHY

Amer, Sahar. 2001. "Lesbian Sex and the Military: From the Medieval Arabic Tradition to French Literature." In *Same Sex Love and Desire among Women in the Middle Ages*, eds. Francesca Canadé Sautman and Pamela Sheingorn. New York: Palgrave.

Ashley, Kathleen. 2001. "The *Miroir des bonnes femmes*: Not for Women Only?" In *Medieval Conduct*, ed. Kathleen Ashley and Robert L. A. Clark. Minneapolis: University of Minnesota Press.

Ashley, Kathleen, and Robert L. A. Clark, eds. 2001. *Medieval Conduct*. Minneapolis: University of Minnesota Press.

Bornstein, Diane. 1983. *The Lady in the Tower: Medieval Courtesy Literature for Women*. Hamden, CT: Archon Books.

Clark, Robert L. A. 2001. "Jousting without a Lance: The Condemnation of Female Homoeroticism in the *Livre des manières*." In *Same Sex Love and Desire among Women in the Middle Ages*, ed. Francesca Canadé Sautman and Pamela Sheingorn. New York: Palgrave.

John of Salisbury. 1990. *Policraticus*, trans. Cary J. Nederman. Cambridge, UK: Cambridge University Press.

Krueger, Roberta L. 1990. "Constructing Sexual Identities in the High Middle Ages: The Didactic Poetry of Robert de Blois." *Paragraph* 13(2): 105–131.

Nicholls, Jonathan. 1985. *The Matter of Courtesy: Medieval Courtesy Books and the Gawain-Poet*. Woodbridge, UK: D. S. Brewer.

Riddy, Felicity. 1996. "Mother Knows Best: Reading Social Change in a Courtesy Text." *Speculum* 71(1): 66–86.

Robert L. A. Clark

CONFUCIANISM

Confucius is the Latinized honorific name for K'ung Ch'iu (551–479 BCE), acknowledged founder of the tradition. His goal was to produce *junzi* (noble sons), morally perfected and ritually sophisticated gentlemen who would give their lives to the service of the state. Chinese women of the time did not hold public positions of political power, and thus Confucius had no female students. Indeed, tradition maintains that the master had little to say about women at all. In the *Lunyu*, the brief collection of Confucius's teachings known in English as the *Analects*, women are described merely as difficult to deal with.

The prominent early Confucian interpreter Mencius, or Mengzi, (371–289 BCE) accepted the notion that women were socially subordinate. He also made clear that the worst form of unfiliality was to have no sons, thereby lending implicit support for a system of secondary wives and concubinage that valued women solely for their reproductive capacity. Yet Mencius never suggested that women were intellectually inferior or in greater need of moral education than men. Women, like men, were understood to possess innately the seeds of justice, propriety, wisdom, and humaneness that, if nurtured properly, would grow into true humanity. Nothing in the earliest texts of the tradition denied women the capacity or possibility of becoming a *gentleman* despite the gendered terminology.

After centuries of interstate warfare, the Han dynasty (second century BCE through the second century CE) ushered in a time of relative peace and stability. A Confucian academy was founded, and its tenets were established as state orthodoxy. The ritual texts compiled during this time, such as the *Liji* [Book of rites], dictated that the sexes be differentiated and kept distinct and distant from the age of seven onward. Men and women were to be separated within the home, even to the degree that their clothes should not be hung on the same peg. Although few beyond the wealthy upper class ever followed the myriad sex-segregation rules laid out in the ritual texts, a general notion of maintaining distinctions and distance between males and females was widely observed.

The Han Confucian scholar Dong Zhongshu (179–104 BCE) is credited with melding indigenous cosmologies, in particular the yin and yang theory, with Confucian political and moral ideologies to demonstrate the centrality of the ruler in upholding cosmic order. He constructed a comprehensive model of rulership that associated the ruler with yang (characterized by strength, growth, light, and the promotion of life) and asserted the primacy of yang over yin (characterized by passivity, weakness, darkness, and destructive tendencies). This correlation of the ruler with yang and the ruled with yin confirmed the necessary dominance of yang. All people manifest yang and yin qualities, and as people fulfill different sides of their core relationships, they shift between yang and yin status. However, the binary hierarchy of Han cosmology fueled the tendency to diminish the estimation of yin-associated individuals, which included eunuchs and homosexuals as well as women. *Woman* was essentially the embodiment of yin, and a growing ambivalence toward them ensued.

Despite this growing ambivalence, a new literary genre—biographies of virtuous women—appeared in the Han. Archivist Liu Xiang (77–6 BCE) compiled the *Lienü zhuan* [Biographies of exemplary women], sketching the lives of notable women, including those whom he found wise and able in reasoning. These traits were not praised independently but were valorized insofar as they were manifest in the service of family or state needs. Maternal virtue was prized most highly, and the most famous exemplar was Mencius's widowed mother. She moved their residence three times in search of an environment conducive to her son's moral upbringing, and she once shocked her son by destroying her weaving—their source of income—in response to his lack of diligence in his studies. Thoughtful, wise, and bold in her initiatives, she illustrates the Han acceptance of womanly virtue in still-surprising and public ways.

The second gendered literary genre to emerge during this time was books of instruction for women, the first of which was written by Ban Zhao (d. 116 CE), an educated woman associated with the imperial court. Her work, the first explicitly didactic text for women, *Nüjie* [Instructions for women], clearly illustrates both the emergent ambivalence toward women during the Han and the Confucian tradition's privileging of the male gaze. She was a champion of girls' education—but only so that they might better fulfill their ritual responsibilities, support their husbands, and educate their own children. Drawing on images found in newly canonized texts such as the *Shijing* [Odes] and *Liji*, Ban Zhao promoted the subordination of women by urging them to cultivate humility and the four virtues of chaste and demure conduct, upright bearing, propriety in speech, and efficiency in work.

Ban Zhao's work proved singularly influential. It was copied and imitated over the centuries, but with each new generation of instructional texts, the estimation of female abilities diminished. The realm of female influence was increasingly limited to the domestic sphere: men go out, women stay in. For women of the upper classes, this ultimately meant virtual confinement to the nonpublic rooms and courtyards of the home; for women of lower economic classes, the need for their labor in the fields, in the market, with the herds, in the production of silk, or in the manufacturing of household items meant that such notions were often given little more than lip service in the face of practical necessity.

All women, however, were governed by the doctrine of *thrice following*. The original context for thrice following in the *Liji* was that females were to follow the social rank of the male head of their household (in style of dress or ritual processional order); later reinterpretations incorporated a sense of submission to authority so that the term came to be understood as the *three obediences*. In this way women labored under a considerable burden: In addition to their economic contributions, they were expected to be good wives and virtuous mothers whose universal vocation was to establish a harmonious domestic environment so that the men who dominated their lives could more successfully pursue their public endeavors.

Legal protections for women were few but significant. A woman's property, including her dowry, was her own, even after marriage. And although a man could divorce his wife for any of seven conditions (failure to produce a son or to serve his parents, or for promiscuity, theft, disease, loquacity, or jealousy), a woman had three possible lines of defense. First, if her husband's parents had died and she had mourned them, she was understood to be linked to the family permanently and could not be cut off. Second, if divorcing a woman would render her homeless and destitute, she could not be abandoned. The third condition is both poignant and telling: If the woman had been the wife of youth and poverty, enabling the man to rise to his current status, she could not be dismissed. A woman could divorce her husband for a variety of reasons, but she risked poverty, social isolation, forced remarriage, and the certain loss of any minor children to the father's family. A woman of the upper economic echelons might be taken back into her natal family and supported, but for the overwhelming majority of women, remaining with one's husband, however bad or brutal, might well be the better choice.

Confucian sex and gender ideals were not confined to China. Beyond its shifting borders, the historical interplay between native identity and Chinese influence dramatically affected gender identities and the range of acceptable social roles for men and women. Both Korea and Vietnam were subordinated to Chinese rule for centuries. As outpost colonies, or commanderies, their native elite populations often embraced Confucianism for its principles of orderly government and for the literacy and literary culture that accompanied it.

Korea's peninsular location formed a natural bridge between China and Japan, and merchants, missionaries, and travelers traversed its territory; cultural imports competed with indigenous traditions. However, although Korea's political, educational, and aesthetic sensibilities were influenced greatly by China, the country was far from major Chinese cultural centers and thus could maintain a degree of cultural autonomy. The preservation of Korean cultural identity was aided by its language, an Altaic tongue closer to Japanese than Chinese, and by a strong female shamanic tradition focused on maintenance of close ties with ancestral and spirit worlds.

By the fourth century China's hold on its far-flung colonies weakened. Korea's disparate clans united into three kingdoms, all of which embraced Mahayana Buddhism. Historical works suggest that even in the northernmost kingdom of Koguryo, relations between the sexes were quite free. Chinese observers noted with discomfort that companionate marriages were valued in every social stratum and remarriage was widely accepted. Liberal relations between the sexes continued from the late seventh through the tenth centuries under the Silla dynasty. In the succeeding Koryo period (918–1392), despite the increasing influence of a revitalizing Confucianism from Song dynasty China (960–1279), men and women continued to enjoy a great degree of freedom in public as well as private matters. Women could be acknowledged heads of households and had equal inheritance rights with men. Shocked Chinese ambassadors sent reports of nude bathers of both sexes swimming together. Gradually, however, the ideals of gender segregation and silence, submission, and chastity for women gained currency once Confucianism was adopted as state ideology in the early Choson dynasty (1392–1910).

With the development of Neo-Confucian schools during the Song dynasty, ambivalence toward women was unprecedented, as women were identified as the locus of male distraction—an attitude that led not only to increased regulation of women but served also to deepen their erotic attraction. Silk and textile production was increasingly commercialized and offered the possibility of significant wealth for women, who still retained personal property rights. The booming economy, however, produced conditions in which the commodification of women and the trade in them increased; as an emergent merchant class grew, a lively market developed for concubines, courtesans, prostitutes, maidservants, and slaves. Footbinding, initially a practice of the courtesan class, spread beyond that social group and was practiced, to varying degrees, by women of all but the lowest socioeconomic groups, for whom the crippling of half the labor force could not be tolerated.

During the Song dynasty, manuals of family instruction proliferated. In them, appreciation for womanly talents in the domestic realm vie with the advocacy of confining concepts, such as chastity for both the unmarried and the widowed. The Confucian scholar Yuan Cai (late twelfth century) made note of wise and worthy women with stupid, unworthy, or inept husbands who nonetheless somehow managed the family on their own, keeping the accounts and not allowing others to take advantage of them. Similarly, the great architect of Neo-Confucianism, Zhu Xi (1130–1200), emphasized functional distinctions between men and women but affirmed that unless a woman was educated and cultivated, she could not perform her crucial function within the home.

The conflation of sex and gender, the reduction of women's roles to that of wife and mother, and the resultant tight controls over women's sexuality and autonomy, reached their apex when Neo-Confucianism was established as state orthodoxy in the later Yuan (1280–1368) and Ming dynasties (1368–1644). Functional literacy rates were rising and the printing of cheap illustrated morality books produced a shared culture in which the Neo-Confucian obsessions with chastity for women and filiality for men predominated. The lives of upper-class men were dominated by the drive for public success, whether through education and advancement in the civil service examination system or through commercial endeavors. Upper-class women, again confined to the upper quarters, might be educated and cultivated, but their social value was derivative; by the Ming-Qing dynastic transition (mid-seventeenth century), the ideal wife was described as one who complemented her husband *like a shadow or an echo.*

Not all Confucian scholars held such diminished views of women; records indicate many over the centuries, acquiescing to their daughters' pleas to be educated or not to have their feet bound or not to be married to a man of lesser abilities. Famously, K'ang Yuwei (1858–1927) persuaded the emperor to institute what was later called the Hundred Days' Reform. K'ang's Confucian vision radically advocated peace and equality for all people, including women. He felt that men and women should be free to choose their marriage partners and to move equally in the public sphere. His reform program, as its name indicates, was short-lived, undone by the empress dowager.

In Korea, Neo-Confucianism was promoted by the founders of the Yi and Choson dynasty (1392–1910) to justify their control and to better regulate their state. Following the Chinese system, examination in Confucian texts now determined the selection of officials, who—heavily influenced by Neo-Confucian's suspicion of women and by the yin and yang theory—inaugurated a process that gradually eroded women's rights and privileges. Ancient practices of matrilocality were abandoned in favor of patrilocal residence and orientation; also, the legal status of wives and mothers was reduced, inheritance laws changed from equal distribution among all siblings to sole inheritance by the eldest son, and widow chastity was strictly enforced. Exemplary biographies of virtuous women, didactic texts for women, and books of family instruction proliferated and promoted the most restrictive Confucian vision of women—a vision that could have severe consequences for men as well. Even the most accomplished man might find his upward mobility within the *yangban* system (stratified civil bureaucracy) stymied by the discovery of an unchaste woman in his family line. It is arguable that Korean implementation of Confucian sex and gender rules surpassed even the most rigid laws in China. By the early twentieth century Confucianism permeated every aspect of Korean society and its ideals of quiet, obedient, chaste, and industrious women who were completely nativized.

Unlike Korea and Vietnam, Japan never suffered occupation by the Chinese. Geographic and social isolation fostered a strong consciousness of native identity, fostered by an indigenous religious tradition, Shinto, that imbued the land and its people with a distinctive sacredness. Chinese influences were consequently slower in coming and were adopted selectively. Nonetheless, Confucian influence gradually increased during the mid- to late Heian era (ninth to twelfth centuries), and women in the upper classes were increasingly relegated to the domestic realm and to auxiliary ritual roles. Some turned to literary pursuits, as the development of the kana syllabaries facilitated literacy; Heian court ladies wrote volumes of elegant literary works (in contrast to their male contemporaries, whose Chinese-language works are less distinguished). Women in the Kamakura period (1185–1333) still commanded a degree of respect, evidenced by the retention of historical rights to inherit property and titles. In a new appreciation of the concept of thrice following, women of the samurai and upper classes were expected to manifest the same ideals of courage, loyalty, sacrifice, and stoicism as their fathers, husbands, and sons.

Once the Tokugawa rulers (1603–1868) espoused Neo-Confucianism as the ideological basis for their rule, male domination became the norm; the estimation of women as little more than heir providers gradually filtered down through Japanese society. The Meiji Restoration (1868) did little to restore women's earlier status. Men were awarded rights and privileges but women were accorded duties and obligations. When rights for women were granted, as in the 1872 mandate for women's education, the rationale provided was in complete accord with Confucian norms: Women should be educated so that they might become *ryusai kembo*, or good wives and mothers.

In Vietnam Confucian influence was as varied over time as it was geographically, waxing and waning with the rise and fall of the Ly and Tran (1054–1400) and Le and

Nguyen (1428–1802) dynasties. In general, Confucian social values and mores were espoused more than enforced, and their adoption was often a byproduct of a desire to take on attitudes and rituals conducive to maintaining a close and supportive family network. For this reason Zhu Xi's *Jiali* [Family instructions] was as honored as any classic Confucian philosophical work. However, as in China, textile production afforded women their own means of livelihood and a modicum of social power, as did opportunities to avoid or abandon restrictive family obligations by renouncing the world and entering a Buddhist nunnery.

Throughout the Confucian-influenced cultures of East and Southeast Asia, the twentieth century witnessed the collapse of dynastic systems of rule, followed by successive waves of republicanism, communism, and capitalism. In China early twentieth-century social reformers called for the abolition of feudal Confucian attitudes and practices typified by the subordination of women and manifest in high rates of female infanticide and low rates of literacy, earnings, and autonomy. The early Chinese Communist Party institutionalized the vilification of Confucianism and declared that as *women hold up half the sky*, they should be put to equal use in building the new society. In practice female Communist Party members have been employed typically in supporting organizational roles or in bureaus that focus on domestic or women's affairs.

Marriage, divorce, and inheritance laws have redressed certain historical wrongs, but changes have been slow in coming. The People's Republic of China (PRC) altered its marriage laws in 1950, but popular resistance proved widespread, with the greatest resistance often coming from women who feared the loss of what authority they had as mothers and mothers-in-law. The PRC government also attempted to alter traditional norms out of a desperate need to curb rampant population growth. In the early 1970s a draconian one-child policy was imposed. Despite a campaign in 1974 (as part of an anti-Confucius campaign) to encourage the valuing of girls, a shift to matrilocal marriage, and a reinvention of filiality to encompass care for both parents and parents-in-law, the identification of heir with son remained little changed. Moreover, the traditional view that women are responsible for reproduction is largely unchallenged. Male contraceptive use is generally low and thus women have borne the brunt of coercion (forced intrauterine device insertion, abortion, and sterilization) for failures to comply with the policy, regardless of familial pressure for additional pregnancies in hopes of having a son. One consequence of the one-child policy has been a rise in female infanticide; a second has been the commodification of abandoned female babies for the foreign adoption market.

Since the late 1970s and early 1980s, reappraisals of Confucian tradition have been ongoing. Concern over a perceived moral decline that has accompanied the rise of capitalism has been one cause; another is the appreciation of Confucianism's role in the success of other East Asian economies. The result is a shifting mix of resurgent traditional values complicated by rapid economic change. In urban areas and among the more educated, sex roles are more flexible than ever before, but in general, as women move out of the domestic sphere and take up outside employment, they tend to shoulder a double burden. Men go out and women may now also go out, but the latter also spend long hours staying in. Domestic chores and child-rearing responsibilities continue to fall disproportionately on women. Under the multiple stresses of tradition and modernity, it is not surprising, therefore, that as many as 25 percent of all rural women attempt suicide, according to one recent estimate.

Technological advances have combined with continuing son-preference to a devastating effect on the sex ratio of male to female babies. A normal ratio would be 105 to 106 boys born for every 100, reflecting a natural imbalance that compensates for higher male mortality rates. In 2000, the ratio was 110 to 100, and in 2005, 118 to 100. In that same year in the southern province of Hainan, the ratio reached as high as 135 to 100. As alarming as these figures may be, it is worth noting that the modern imbalance is charted at birth and is attributed to sex-selective abortions following ultrasound scanning. Prior to these technologies female infanticide was widely practiced and extant census records indicate similar sex ratio imbalances among the adult general population in certain rural provinces in the nineteenth century. Worrisome consequences of the present phenomenon of *lost girls* are its future effect on both men and women: It is estimated that by 2020, there will be a surplus of 30 million men of marriageable age in China, the majority of them seeking heterosexual partners. Already in some rural areas, girls and women are once again being sold into marriage and realize few, if any, of the rights the law affords them.

In the other Confucian cultures of East Asia, the postwar years of the twentieth and early twenty-first centuries have witnessed the dismantling of aspects of the Confucian sex–gender system, albeit slowly and sometimes fitfully. In the Republic of China (Taiwan) the nationalist government eagerly employed factory women in the 1950s and 1960s as part of a plan to build a powerful economy; once economic success was assured in the 1970s, women were urged to retreat to traditional roles as wives, mothers, and part-time volunteers. By the early twenty-first century, under the influence of feminist and gay-rights movements, traditional relationships and gender roles are challenged daily. So-called *New Confucian* thinkers such as Tu Weiming (b. 1940), along with scholars from both Confucian and non-Confucian backgrounds, seek to recover a more balanced view of historical roles for women and men and to question assumptions about the gendered division of labor within Confucianism's five relationships. Sociologist Li Kuo-Ting (b. 1910) has called for a new sixth relationship (of an individual to a group) to reflect the needs of a modern civil society.

In Japan the Confucian legacy is also clear yet complex. Parliament in 1986 passed the Equal Employment Opportunity Law for Men and Women, which, despite its name, did not prohibit the differential treatment of women in the workplace; the law requires only that employers *endeavor* to prevent discrimination. Women are expected to leave their job or career in favor of marriage and motherhood, although resistance is observable in that the average marriage age for women has been rising steadily since the 1980s. A well-publicized example of the conflict between career and marriage was played out in 2006 when Crown Princess Masako (b. 1963), a former career diplomat whose marriage to the crown prince had only produced a daughter, came under intense public scrutiny for her failure to produce an heir. Although the biological facts of fetal sex-determination were well understood, there was significant public sentiment that the princess had simply waited too long to marry and begin having children and thus had put the line of succession in jeopardy. The feared crisis was averted when Princess Kiko (b. 1966), wife of the emperor's younger son and widely perceived as a traditional Japanese woman, bore her third child—a son.

That a Japanese woman's career is secondary to her reproductive function is evidenced in the understanding of women's earnings being seen as supplemental rather than essential to their family's maintenance. The majority of women continue to earn far less than their male counterparts and are typically bypassed for promotions in favor of their male counterparts. Secondary status in the workplace, however, should not be interpreted as entirely negative for women. Reluctant to interrupt their career, however slowly it may progress, or to leave the outside world permanently, increasing numbers of women are delaying marriage significantly or deciding to forego it altogether; others are returning to the casual workforce after their children are grown. The numbers of single women who continue to live in their natal home and amass significant personal savings, and the increasing numbers of middle-aged women with both money and leisure time, has translated into an adult female population with greater autonomy than ever before—and with varied means of exercising it through consumerism, continuing education, and travel. Conversely, the burden of familial (and filial) responsibility continues to weigh on men, often trapping them in lifelong corporate careers that offer little mobility or challenge.

In the Republic of Korea the 1948 constitution mandated equality for men and women, but it was not until 1987 that laws were strengthened by the revised constitution and not until 1991 that new family laws abolished differential inheritance for sons and daughters. Women labor under the familiar dual burden of working outside the home only to return and assume domestic responsibilities as well. Although Korean women, as with women in Japan, are often highly educated, they remain barred from the highest levels of the corporate and academic worlds; most Korean women labor in low-wage production jobs. Child care facilities remain inadequate to the demand, forcing women out of the workplace for years at a time.

Throughout Confucian Asia the early twenty-first century is bringing moves to reevaluate tradition as these cultures struggle to combine economic success with the challenges of becoming modern industrial and technologically sophisticated societies. For Confucians new social configurations form the greatest challenge to the vitality of the tradition. Confucians now debate the role of same-sex partnerships; homosexuality was historically tolerated if it did not interfere with the marital bond (i.e., the requirement to produce a legitimate heir), but can such partnerships be construed as families in any traditional sense? Likewise, the increasing shift from patrilocality to neolocal patterns of residence for young adult couples has altered the meaning and practice of filial responsibilities for sons as well as daughters, as has the sex-ratio imbalance resulting from population limitation measures. Indigenous feminist movements continue to challenge Confucian patriarchal structures and in the process to change conditions of education, employment, and social relations for men and women alike.

These same reevaluations are occurring in diasporic communities in Europe and North America. Statistically underreported as a worldwide religious tradition, Confucianism beyond East Asia is a somewhat invisible but deeply rooted cultural system that continues to direct the lives of Chinese, Japanese, Korean, and Vietnamese emigrants. How Confucian emphases on familial responsibilities (including parental participation in choice of marriage partners and pressure to produce an heir), filial obligations (particularly heavy on sons in terms of educational attainment and marriage expectation), and the gendered nature of labor will alter in the global environment of the twenty-first century remains to be seen, but given the longevity and tenacity of the tradition, it is a sure bet that it will be a lively struggle.

BIBLIOGRAPHY

Birge, Bettine. 1989. "Chu Hsi and Women's Education." In *Neo-Confucian Education: The Formative Stage*, ed. Wm. Theodore de Bary and John W. Chaffee. Berkely: University of California Press.

Carlitz, Katherine. 1994. "Desire, Danger, and the Body: Stories of Women's Virtue in Late Ming China." In *Engendering China: Women, Culture, and the State*, ed. Christina Gilmartin. Cambridge, MA: Harvard University Press.

Deuchler, Martina. 1992. *The Confucian Transformation of Korea: A Study of Society and Ideology*. Cambridge, MA: Harvard University Press.

Furth, Charlotte. 1990. "The Patriarch's Legacy: Household Instructions and the Transmission of Orthodox Values." In *Orthodoxy in Late Imperial China*, ed. Kwang-ching Liu. Berkeley: University of California Press.

Gelb, Joyce, and Marian Lief Palley, eds. 1994. *Women of Japan and Korea: Continuity and Change*. Philadelphia: Temple University Press.

Hinsch, Bret. 1990. *Passions of the Cut Sleeve: The Male Homosexual Tradition in China*. Berkeley: University of California Press.

Hinsch, Bret. 2002. *Women in Early Imperial China*. Lanham, MD: Rowman and Littlefield.

Iwao, Sumiko. 1994. *The Japanese Woman: Traditional Image and Changing Reality*. Cambridge, MA: Harvard University Press.

Kelleher, Theresa. 1987. "Confucianism." In *Women in World Religions*, ed. Arvind K. Sharma. Albany: State University of New York Press.

Nyitray, Vivian-Lee. 2000. "The Real Trouble with Confucianism." In *Love, Sex, and Gender in the World Religions*, ed. Joseph Runzo and Nancy M. Martin. Oxford, UK: Oneworld.

Nyitray, Vivian-Lee. 2007. "Confucianism." In *Fundamentalism and the Position of Women in World Religions*, ed. Arvind K. Sharma. New York: Crossroads/Continuum.

Raphals, Lisa Ann. 1998. *Sharing the Light: Representations of Women and Virtue in Early China*. Albany: State University of New York Press.

Vivian-Lee Nyitray

CONTRACEPTION

This entry contains the following:

I. OVERVIEW

Contraception is the prevention of conception or impregnation. This is in contrast to birth control, which is control of the number of children born. Conception is the process of becoming pregnant, whereas impregnation is fertilization (the union of two gametes; in the case of humans, a sperm and an egg).

The World Health Organization (WHO) categorizes current contraceptive devices and methods into eight classes:

1. Hormonal (includes oral, injectable, transdermal, and cervical delivery of contraceptive hormones; also includes emergency contraception [morning-after] pills)
2. Implants
3. Intrauterine devices (IUDs, including emergency contraception IUDs)
4. Barrier methods (includes male and female condoms, methods of spermicide delivery, diaphragms, and cervical caps)
5. Fertility awareness-based methods (the avoidance of conception/impregnation during fertile periods)
6. Lactational amenorrhea (lack of fertility caused by the hormonal changes of lactation)
7. Coitus interruptus (withdrawal of the penis from the vagina before ejaculation)
8. Surgical sterilization (male and female)

Effectiveness rates vary in the United States, ranging from 99.5 percent for sterilization, to 24 percent for cervical cap use in women who have previously given birth, to 15 percent for random chance alone (World Health Organization 2004, p. 6). The effectiveness of many forms of contraception is also affected by the technique of the person using it; for instance an improperly applied condom or improperly inserted diaphragm will increase the probability of conception.

It is likely that contraception has been practiced since the inception of humanity. First designed by trial and error and imbued with sacred, mystical, and political implications common to the period in which they were practiced, contraceptive methods became increasingly effective as a result of rational design arising from greater understanding of male and female reproductive anatomy in the 1850s.

Although religious and political factors impact the acceptance and utilization of contraception in the early twenty-first century, the medical, social, and political need for rational contraception is generally accepted.

SEE ALSO *Chastity Belt.*

BIBLIOGRAPHY

World Health Organization, Department of Reproductive Health and Research. 2004. "Medical Eligibility Criteria for Contraceptive Use." In *Medical Eligibility Criteria for Contraceptive Use*, 3rd edition. Geneva: Author.

Christine R. Rainey

II. BELIEFS AND MYTHS

Myths and beliefs about conception and contraception reflect the beliefs and mores of the culture of the society and the level of knowledge regarding reproductive anatomy. Anatomists and biologist supplanted the early influence of priests, shamans, and seers as reproductive anatomy was better defined.

Most early theories of male and female roles in contraception are linked to the existence and influence of outside entities; for instance one ancient belief held that a woman could become pregnant by bathing in a stream populated with eels. Similarly others believed that a male child entered its mother in the shape of a serpent, while a female child entered as a snail. Others believed that a *wandering womb child,* in the shape of a small frog, would leave the mother's body at night in search of food and water. If the woman closed her mouth and the womb child was unable to return, the woman remained childless.

Belief in the spirit world often influenced opinions about conception and contraception. Ancient Nordic texts describe spirit children who resided in bodies of water or trees. A woman who swam or bathed in water or consumed fruit from a tree containing a spirit child would become pregnant.

Similarly other myths regarding conception were centered on then-current understanding of the uterus. Ancient Egyptians considered the uterus an independent animal capable of performing different types of movement within the woman's body. Greco-Romans, notably Hippocrates, believed that if the uterus were not fed sufficient sperm it became feral within the woman's body, wreaking havoc on other internal organs and unable to produce children.

Myths and beliefs surrounding contraception in the early twenty-first century, in many instances, continue to demonstrate a misunderstanding or lack of knowledge of the human reproductive system and functions.

Some common untrue myths and exaggerations about contraception include:

- Breastfeeding is 100 percent effective for contraception
- A woman cannot become pregnant without experiencing an orgasm
- A man cannot impregnate a woman if he does not experience an orgasm
- A woman cannot become pregnant the first time she has sex with a man
- A woman has one fertile day monthly; sex on the other days is safe
- Sex standing up, or sex with the woman on top, is effective for contraception
- Plastic wrap or balloons are excellent substitutes for male condoms
- Pregnancy will not occur if the man ejaculates outside the vagina
- Douching after sex prevents pregnancy
- A woman who showers, bathes, or urinates immediately after sex will not become pregnant
- Oral contraceptives are immediately effective
- Oral contraceptives can be used only for a short portion of the woman's reproductive life
- Oral contraceptives always cause weight gain
- Oral contraceptives cause high blood pressure
- Oral contraceptives cause fibroid tumors in women
- Oral contraceptives are a treatment for endometriosis
- Oral contraceptives cause acne
- Intrauterine devices (IUDs) cause sterility or infertility

Other untrue myths and exaggerations include:

- Women cannot become pregnant on a boat
- Women cannot become pregnant if they consume large amounts of milk
- Ingestion of folic acid increases the chance of becoming pregnant
- A male is fertile only when his testicles feel cold to the touch
- A male can decrease his sperm count by drinking large amounts of alcohol immediately before sex
- Pregnancy occurs only if sex occurs daily
- Cola soda douches are effective contraceptives

BIBLIOGRAPHY

Connell, Elizabeth B. 2002. "The History of Contraception." In *The Contraception Sourcebook.* New York: Contemporary Books.

Rathus, Spencer A.; Jeffrey S. Nevid; and Lois Fichner-Rathus. 2005. "Contraception and Abortion." In *Human Sexuality In a World of Diversity.* 6th edition, ed. Spencer A. Rathus; Jeffrey S. Nevid; and Lois Fichner-Rathus. Boston: Allyn & Bacon.

Christine R. Rainey

III. METHODS

The modern birth control movement began in 1912 when Margaret Sanger (1883–1966), a public health nurse, became concerned about the adverse health effects of frequent childbirth, miscarriages, and abortion. Challenging laws prohibiting distribution of information about (and access to) contraception, she opened the first family planning clinic in Brooklyn, New York, in 1916. The American Birth Control League, a precursor of the Planned Parenthood Federation, was founded in 1916 with the stated purpose, "To enlighten and educate all sections of the American public in the various aspects of the dangers of uncontrolled procreation and the imperative necessity of a world programme of birth control" (Sanger 2003).

Further legal actions during the 1920s and 1930s made contraceptive information and methods more accessible. In 1942 the American Birth Control League was reorganized and renamed the Planned Parenthood Federation of America. In 1960 the United States Food and Drug Administration (FDA) approved the first oral contraceptive, and the U.S. Supreme Court declared state laws banning contraceptive use by married couples unconstitutional (Griswald v. Connecticut, 381 U.S. 479 [1965]), clearing the way for further legal challenges and creating an environment that encouraged development of new birth control methods.

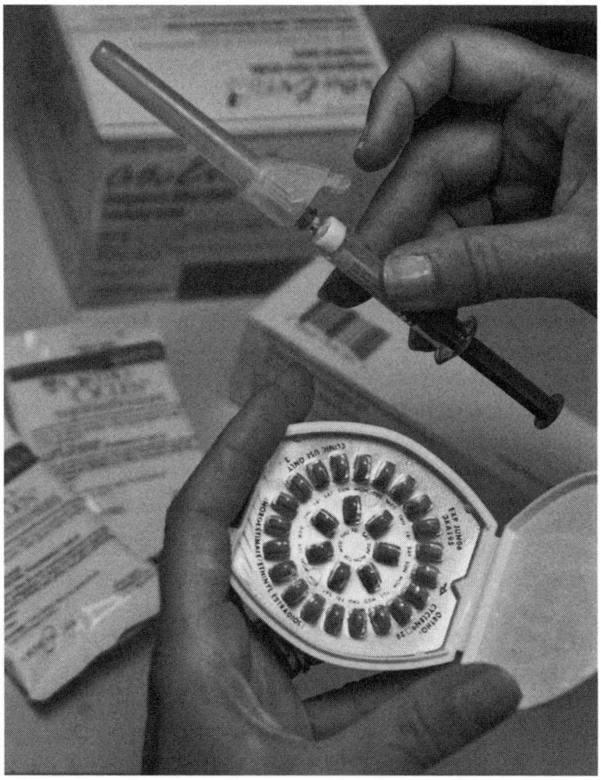

Injectable and Oral Contraceptives. *An injectable hormonal contraceptive (top) and a traditional oral contraceptive pill.* AP IMAGES.

METHODS OF CONTRACEPTION

There are several mechanisms of birth control: hormonal manipulation, hormonal implants, intrauterine devices, emergency modes of preventing pregnancy, barrier methods, fertilization awareness methods, and surgical sterilization.

Hormonal (includes oral, injectable, transdermal, and cervical delivery of contraceptive hormones; also includes emergency contraception [morning-after] pills) The reproductive cycle and fertility of a woman is under intricate hormonal control and can be manipulated by administration of estrogens, progestins, or a combination of both to modulate menstrual cycles and prevent ovulation. Oral contraceptives (birth control pills) are the most common method of female hormonal contraception. Following animal research in the 1930s and 1940s, a precursor of progesterone (a progestin) was discovered in Mexican yams. This discovery of a readily available, abundant source of progesterone precursor heralded the commercial development of progesterone tablets, which were initially approved by the FDA in 1957 for the treatment of gynecologic disorders. In 1960 the FDA approved the first preparations for contraceptive use.

Commercial development of a multitude of combination progestin/estrogen, progestin-only, and estrogen-only tablets, with varying formulas, strength combinations, and packaging, soon followed. All had in common two aspects: a cycle of twenty-one days of active hormonal ingredient(s), and the need for daily oral administration. Other regimens, including eighty-four days or twenty-four days of active hormone ingredient(s), have become available since 2000.

Contraceptive hormones can also be administered by long acting (depot) injection administered every three months, transdermally by use of a patch applied to the skin (typically weekly), or by the use of a hormone-infused flexible ring inserted around the edges of the cervix and left in place for one month.

Implants Contraceptive implants were approved by the FDA for human use in 1990. Flexible, closed plastic capsules containing active hormones, they are inserted under the skin, eliminating the need for daily oral dosing. The composition and total number of capsules inserted vary by product; most capsules are between thirty and forty four millimeters long and are designed to provide contraception for a maximum of five years. Other capsules designed to provide up to three years of contraception are in development. All implants require insertion and removal by a healthcare provider in a minor surgical procedure. Biodegradable implants that will not require surgical removal also are in development.

Intrauterine Devices (IUDs, including emergency contraception IUDs) IUDs are small objects inserted into the uterus. Although the exact mechanism for their effectiveness is not well understood, it is hypothesized that the IUD creates an inflammatory foreign body reaction in the uterus, creating a hostile environment for implantation of a fertilized ovum.

Development of modern IUDs began in the early 1900s but faltered due to political and social pressures. The German physician Ernst Gräfenberg reported the clinical performance of an IUD in 1929; however reports of pelvic inflammatory disease (PID), combined with political pressures exerted by the Nazi party, stifled further research. Development continued until the 1950s, with researchers utilizing a variety of materials and conformations. In 1958 Lazar Margulies developed a plastic coil IUD, the Margulies coil, but this device was soon supplanted by the Lippes Loop, created by another American physician, Jack Lippes. The Lippes Loop became the most widely prescribed IUD in the United States during the 1970s.

Further refinements have since included design of the T-shape IUD and the addition of copper or progesterone to the device itself. The copper IUD is T-shaped, wound with fine copper wire, and can remain in place for ten years. The progesterone IUD is also T-shaped and contains a reservoir of progesterone for delayed release; it may be left in place for one year. The most common side effects include cramping, bleeding, and accidental expulsion of the IUD.

Emergency Contraception Emergency contraception (EC) can be accomplished via the administration of EC pills (ECPs or morning after pills) or the insertion of a copper IUD. The term morning after pill is a misnomer. ECPs may be administered immediately after unprotected intercourse, or up to 120 hours after. Effectiveness is highest when taken as soon as possible. Two types of ECPs are available—progestin-only and a progestin-estrogen combination (oral contraceptives). The high-dose progestin-only pill has largely replaced the progestin-estrogen combination pills; it works by preventing the release of an ovum from the ovary and may prevent the fertilization of an ovum or attachment of the fertilized ovum to the uterus wall. The progestin-only pill will not affect a fertilized egg already attached to the uterus.

Copper-bearing IUDs may be inserted up to five to seven days after ovulation to prevent implantation of the fertilized ovum in the uterine wall. However difficulties in determining the exact time of ovulation make this method less dependable.

Barrier Methods Barrier methods are those that physically prevent the union of egg and sperm. Methods include male and female condoms, spermicide (which also kills sperm), diaphragms, and cervical caps.

Male condoms are tubular sheaths applied over the penis to capture and store sperm during intercourse. They must be removed from the vagina intact and cannot be reused. Although condoms made of thin animal intestine were popular before the early 1980s, the possibility of AIDS transmission greatly diminished popularity. Latex has since become the most popular material for condoms. Men and women should use only water-based lubricants if necessary; oil-based lubricants degrade the integrity of the condom. Female condoms, much less common than male condoms, form a tubular corridor between the opening of the vagina and the cervical cap to prevent penetration of sperm into the cervix.

Spermicides are available as jellies, creams, ointments, and foams. In addition to presenting a physical barrier to the passage of sperm into the cervix, they contain chemicals designed to kill sperm.

Diaphragms are shallow latex domes or cups designed to fit snugly over the entire tip of the cervix. The outer ring is flexible to facilitate insertion through the vagina. Women should use diaphragms with spermicides to enhance effectiveness. They can be inserted up to two hours before sexual intercourse, and remain in place for at least six hours after.

Cervical caps resemble diaphragms but are smaller and designed to fit over the cervical opening (os) itself. The cap is filled approximately one-third full with spermicide before insertion through the vagina. The cap is inserted immediately before intercourse and must be left in place for at least eight hours.

Fertility Awareness-based Methods Fertility awareness-based methods (the avoidance of conception/impregnation during fertile periods) are also known as rhythm methods. Fertile periods can be gauged by tracking menstrual cycles on a calendar; measurement of the woman's basal body temperature; changes in viscosity of cervical mucus; or ovulation prediction kits.

In a woman with a regular twenty-eight-day menstrual cycle, ovulation occurs fourteen days prior to menstruation. By tracking menstrual cycles on a calendar couples can determine a woman's fertile periods and avoid unprotected intercourse during that time.

A woman's body temperature rises slightly (between 0.4 and 0.8 degrees Fahrenheit) immediately before, during, and after ovulation. Similarly the quantity of vaginal mucus increases and viscosity thins before ovulation. Ovulation prediction kits measure the quantity of leutenizing hormone (LH) in the woman's urine. LH levels surge twelve to twenty-four hours before ovulation. Thus the couple is able to monitor the period during which fertilization is most likely.

Lactational amenorrhea (lack of fertility caused by the hormonal changes of lactation) is a contraceptive method based on the infertility of a woman who is fully breastfeeding. Prolactin released during suckling of the infant suppresses ovulation, thus preventing pregnancy.

Coitus interruptus is withdrawal of the penis from the vagina before ejaculation, preventing the deposition of semen in the vagina.

Surgical Sterilization (male and female) Vasectomy is the most common method of male surgical sterilization. In a minor surgical procedure, the vas deferens is cut, a small section is removed, and the ends are tied off or cauterized. Sperm do not reach the urethra and are resorbed by the body. Vasectomy does not affect the male sex drive or sexual performance.

Tubal sterilization (tubal ligation or having one's tubes tied) is the most common form of female sterilization. The fallopian tubes are tied off or clamped to prevent the union of sperm and ova. This is accomplished through a small incision in the abdomen in which the surgeon secures the fallopian tubes by hand or by use of a laparoscope. Tubal ligation does not affect sex drive or performance. Alternatively hysterectomy (a major surgical procedure in which the uterus is removed) renders a woman sterile. However, due to removal of the hormones manufactured by the uterus, hysterectomy can affect female sexual response and arousal.

BIBLIOGRAPHY

Baird, David T., and Anna F. Glaser. 1999. "Science, Medicine and the Future: Contraception." *British Medical Journal* 319: 969–972.

Blackwell, Richard E. 2005. "Nonhormonal Contraception." In *Essential Reproductive Medicine*, ed. Bruce R. Carr, Richard E. Blackwell, and Riccardo Azziz. New York: McGraw-Hill, Medical Publishing Division.

Sanger, Margaret. 2003. *The Pivot of Civilization*. Introduction by H. G. Wells. Forward by Peter C. Engelman. Classics in Womens' Studies. Humanity Books 2003. Amherst, NY.

World Health Organization, Department of Reproductive Health and Research. 2004. "Medical Eligibility Criteria for Contraceptive Use." In *Medical Eligibility Criteria for Contraceptive Use*. 3rd edition. Geneva: World Health Organization.

Christine R. Rainey

IV. RELATION TO SEXUAL PRACTICES AND GENDER ROLES

While the primary use for contraception is to prevent pregnancy, it also has many other applications. In particular, both condoms and birth control pills have non-contraceptive therapeutic uses.

CONDOMS

Though the surest way to avoid contracting or spreading sexually transmitted diseases (STDs) is to practice abstinence or limit sex to a monogamous, long-term relationship; when that is not practical, condoms provide an important form of defense. Consistent and proper use of latex condoms helps prevent the spread of diseases such as chlamydia, gonorrhea, trichomoniasis, and human immunodeficiency virus (HIV) but provide only limited protection against other diseases such as human papillomarvirus (HPV or genital warts), syphilis, and genital herpes because infective tissue or lesions may occur outside the area normally covered by a condom. Condoms should be used with water-based lubricant since oil or petroleum-based products can cause the latex to break down. Condoms with nonoxynol-9 (a spermicide) should be avoided since they may actually increase the chance of transmitting HIV between partners. In non-monogamous relationships, condom usage is advised even with sexual practices unlikely to result in pregnancy, including oral sex (fellatio, cunnilingus, or anilingus). To avoid spreading disease during oral sex, it is important to keep both semen and vaginal fluids out of the mouth. The use of an unlubricated, non-spermicidal condom will help prevent the transmission of disease in men. Flavored condoms, which help dispel the latex taste, are available. A dental dam (a square of latex or silicone) or a condom that has been cut into a square serves as a barrier between the mouth and the vagina or anus. Premade dental dams have the advantage of being larger and thus covering more surface area. Female condoms (a latex tube fitted with two rings at each end, which is inserted into the vagina—one ring fitting snuggly against the cervix and the other remaining outside and covering the vulva) are also helpful in preventing disease. The use of condoms in anal sex helps prevent urethritis (an infection of the urethra) by shielding the penis from exposure to residual fecal matter in the rectum. Condoms are the only form of contraception that offers protection against the spread of infection.

In addition, condom use is sometimes prescribed to treat cervical mucous incompatibility with the sperm, a condition where the woman manufactures antibodies to her partner's sperm resulting in unwanted infertility in couples trying to conceive. In this case, condoms are not used to prevent conception but rather to facilitate it. After three to six months of condom usage during intercourse, the woman creates fewer antibodies thus allowing the sperm to pass through the cervix where it can then fertilize the egg.

ORAL CONTRACEPTIVES

Birth control pills have other therapeutic applications beyond pregnancy prevention. Oral contraceptives are frequently prescribed for medical conditions, especially those dealing with menstruation. They are helpful in the treatment of irregular menstrual cycles (oligo-ovulation), dysmenorrhea (lower abdominal pain and cramping associated with menstrual periods), and dysfunctional uterine bleeding (such as spotting between periods) by controlling the hormonal balance. Birth control pills also provide hormonal therapy for patients with endometriosis, a common and painful condition where endometrial cells from the inner lining of the uterus are regurgitated through the fallopian tubes during menstruation and implant in the abdominal or pelvic cavity. The main treatment is hormonal suppression with or without surgical excision of the ectopic (outside of the uterus) tissue. Because of the increased rate of cancer of endometrial tissue in women suffering from this condition, hormonal therapy with birth control pills (with both progesterone and estrogen) is often prescribed.

Certain cases of hirsutism (a condition noted by excessive facial and body hair caused by the over-production of male hormones or androgens) may benefit from the administration of oral contraceptives. The condition is often associated with anovulatory ovaries and the cessation of menstrual cycles. In severe cases, the clitoris enlarges, the voice deepens, and balding can occur. Because most cases involve excess androgen production, treatment is directed toward interfering with the hormonal imbalance. Oral contraceptives may work by inhibiting the hormones that stimulate the secretion of the androgens. In addition, birth control pills are useful in treating acne associated with hirsutism (as well as non-androgen related outbreaks).

RELATION OF CONTRACEPTION TO GENDER ROLES

As soon as people made the connection between sexual intercourse and pregnancy, undoubtedly, the search began for the safest and most reliable way to prevent it. Early methods of birth control were behavioral, such as abstinence, which needed to be practiced equally between male and female partners. The Bible mentions the sin of Onan or *spilling the seed*, which includes the withdrawal method of birth control (coitus interruptus) in which the man avoids ejaculation until after he withdraws his penis from the vagina.

Old folk remedies generally centered on the woman's role in contraception. It is not surprising that women, who bore the risks of pregnancy and the subsequent care of the children, were eager to experiment through trial and error to find a way of controlling conception. Early Egyptian women douched with a wine and garlic mixture or inserted a plug of crocodile dung and sour milk into the vagina as an early barrier or spermicide (or merely to discourage sex through the presence of the concoction itself). Early Greeks and Romans placed absorbent material in the vagina to soak up the semen. Though penis sheaths were documented back to ancient Egypt, they were mainly decorative. Later linen versions were used (very often unsuccessfully) to prevent conception, an attempt at shared responsibility for pregnancy prevention between the sexes.

By the 1900s, contraceptive methods included vaginal sponges, douching, withdrawal, abstinence, and notably (owing to the invention of vulcanized rubber in 1842) the rubber condom. However these options became increasingly inaccessible to women as attitudes about contraception changed. Abortions were banned, owing in part to the danger they posed to women in pre-antibiotic days, but the subsequent prohibition on birth control or information about contraceptive methods (even for married women) was due to a certain degree of sexual politics since women had no say in legislation. Women's access to birth control was severely limited in the United States in the late 1800s by the Comstock Act (1873), which made it illegal to distribute birth control information through the mail on the grounds that it was obscene. States passed other laws making it illegal for individuals to give information to each other, including physicians to their patients.

During this time, doctors (predominantly male) began to replace midwives in the management of pregnancy and birth, removing yet another possible avenue through which women could receive birth control specifics. A married woman (for it was illegal to dispense contraception to unmarried women) needed documented proof that pregnancy would endanger her life to acquire legal and medical permission for access to contraceptive advice or materials. Activists like Margaret Sanger (1883–1966) in the early twentieth century challenged the contraception laws, but it was not until 1965 that birth control was finally legally accessible to all adults.

In 1960 the first oral contraceptive for women was marketed, and the U.S. Supreme Court decision in *Roe v. Wade* (1973) made abortion legal during the first trimester of pregnancy. For the first time women had the means and the power to control their own fertility without relying on the compliance of their male partners. Nevertheless patriarchal institutions, such as the Catholic Church, continued to oppose the use of artificial contraception.

CONTEMPORARY VIEWS ON CONTRACEPTION

In the early twenty-first century, the responsibility for birth control still lies predominately with women. Types of contraception for women far outnumber those for men. Except for the addition of vasectomy, the methods available to men have remained largely unchanged since the nineteenth century. Women's options though have greatly improved in efficacy and convenience: IUDs, diaphragms, sponges, female condoms, vaginal spermicides, and, significantly, birth control pills. The introduction of birth control pills ushered in a revolution that included sexual freedom for women, though with a cost: Female methods of birth control come with a higher risk for potential health issues for the woman. Though researchers have worked on developing a male oral contraceptive, none exists, due in part to potential side-effects (including dizziness, drowsiness, constipation, impotence, and permanent infertility) and the reluctance of women to accept a form of birth control that relies exclusively on male compliance.

Worldwide, women assume a disproportionate share of the responsibility for the prevention of pregnancy compared to men. According to a 1998 United Nations study, 40 percent of couples rely on female-based contraceptive methods and only 8 percent on male-based methods (United Nations 1998, p. 175). Figures for elective sterilization follow a similar pattern. Though vasectomy is a quick, simple surgery that may be performed in a doctor's office, more women undergo tubal ligation, which is more complicated and costly. Many insurance companies will pay for a woman's elective sterilization but not for a man's. Researchers suggest a variety of reasons for the imbalance between the genders in responsibility for birth control. One is the attitude that a women's position is partially defined by her role as child bearer, and as such she must control her fertility. Also many women prefer a form of contraception that puts them in control. Ultimately the most convenient, reliable, nonsurgical methods of birth control are those used by women.

BIBLIOGRAPHY

Cisler, Lucinda. 1970. "Unfinished Business: Birth Control and Women's Liberation." In *Sisterhood is Powerful: An Anthology of Writings from the Women's Liberation Movement*, ed. Robin Morgan. New York: Random House.

Cook, Rebecca J.; Bernard M. Dickens; and Mahmoud F. Fathalla. 2003. *Reproductive Health and Human Rights: Integrating Medicine, Ethics, and Law*. Oxford, UK: Clarendon Press.

Speroff, Leon; Robert H. Glass; and Nathan G. Kase. 1994. *Clinical Gynecologic Endocrinology and Infertility*. 5th edition. Baltimore, MD: Williams & Wilkins.

Tannahill, Reay. 1980. *Sex in History*. New York: Stein and Day.

United Nations. "World Contraceptive Use 1998." Available from http://www.un.org/esa/population/pubsarchive/wcu/wcutoc.htm.

Diane Sue Saylor

V. POLICIES AND EFFECTS

Contraception serves to control the reproductive outcome of sexual intercourse between a fertile male and a fertile female. As modern methods of contraception were being developed in the mid-twentieth century, many institutions began to formulate policies attempting to govern the use of "artificial" contraception, often linked with policies about abortion. These institutions included governments and government agencies, religious groups, and medical and professional organizations.

GOVERNMENTAL POLICIES

Governmental policies typically view contraception in the context of population increase or decrease, variously prohibiting, encouraging, or requiring the use of contraception to serve differing demographic, economic, political, and social agendas. Governments employ a variety of methods, including moral propaganda, economic incentives and disincentives, legal and administrative policies, and public-service advertising. Several examples from the late twentieth and early twenty-first centuries illustrate the variety of governmental policies, both in intended impact on fertility and in whether they were directed primarily at women or men.

India In the mid-twentieth century population growth rates, especially in Asia, were perceived as skyrocketing in this region, contraceptive policy has been directed at curbing population growth. India's initial population-control effort of 1964–1965 provides an example of a governmental contraception policy intended to decrease population growth rates by employing methods directed primarily at men. This program focused on vasectomy, using incentives for "adopters" (the notorious transistor radio for men who would submit to a vasectomy on the spot); "canvassers," or recruiters paid to deliver vasectomy prospects to clinics (Repetto 1968); and penalties for men with more than a specified number of children. In some areas, vasectomy was forcibly imposed. This wildly unpopular program lasted only slightly over a year and contributed to the downfall of Indira Gandhi's government. It is believed to have had little direct impact on population growth rates in India. A later statement of

Indian government policy—promulgated April 16, 1976, and intended (as the statement put it) to secure the future of the nation, remove poverty, and counter a "population explosion of crisis dimensions" (Singh 1976, p. 309) that would dilute the country's economic progress and continued to offer monetary compensation for sterilization (of both males and females) but also proposed other methods of promoting family planning.

China A governmental policy intended to limit population growth by employing contraceptive methods focused primarily on women is to be found in China's one-child policy, introduced in 1979 and, although eroding, is still officially in force. Aware that it had a quarter of the world's population but only 7 percent of its arable land, China limited urban dwellers to only one child; rural residents in some areas were permitted a second child if the first has a disability or is a girl. China's population-containment policy has made use of circumstantial controls as well as virtually universal access to modern contraception and abortion to limit fertility: The age of marriage was increased, spouses were sometimes assigned to work in different cities, women's menstrual cycles were publicly monitored, and the use of contraception was encouraged or mandated. Penalties, including fines, loss of employment, and loss of housing and benefits, were imposed for excess births. The use of an intrauterine device (IUD) after the birth of a first child was required, and sterilization was required after a second; these two long-term methods have accounted for 90 percent of contraceptive methods used since the 1980s and have kept abortion rates to almost half that in the United States (Hesketh, Li, and Zhu 2005), although some choice in types of contraceptives is now permitted.

The one-child policy, maintained for more than two decades—the approximate duration of a generation—has had a dramatic impact on China's growth rate. Growth rates had begun to decline before the one-child policy was put in place, but with its sustained imposition, growth rates dropped from a 1969 high of almost 6 children per woman to 1.7, below replacement rate, in 2004. The social impact of this policy is referred to as the "4:2:1" phenomenon (Hesketh, Li, and Zhu 2005), describing the obligations of responsibility given the proportion of grandparents and parents for each child.

Romania In the wake of World War II, population growth rates in Eastern Europe dropped to the lowest in the world, and many Eastern European governments developed pronatalist policies governing contraception and abortion. Nicolae Ceausescu's Romania, which in 1966 strictly limited abortion, provides an example of a governmental policy intended to increase a state's population (and hence its workforce). Women were expected, indeed required, to have at least four children: This was "every healthy Romanian woman's patriotic duty" (Legge and Alford 1986, p. 725). As in many other Eastern European countries (for example, Russia, Poland, and Yugoslavia, and to a lesser extent the German Democratic Republic, Hungary, and Czechoslovakia), artificial birth control and modern forms of contraception were not readily available or of very low quality. The impact of Romania's 1966 abortion prohibition is well documented: The birthrate peaked sharply within a year, but the principal long-term effect was a dramatic rise in illegal abortion and maternal mortality. As in much of Eastern Europe, reliance on withdrawal and abortion has remained the primary means of fertility control.

Global Family Planning Family planning programs have been instituted in the majority of the world's nations. Although the early programs strongly emphasized contraception and population control, since the 4th International Conference on Population and Development in Cairo in 1994, greater emphasis has been placed on economic development, women's education, employment for women, women's access to health care, reduced infant and child mortality, and other noncoercive means of social change associated with reducing population growth rates. Modern contraception has been made widely available in many areas of the developing world, largely financed by foreign-aid programs, and enhanced methods of promoting knowledge, access, and practice are in place. The term *birth control* has been largely replaced by *family planning*. In the 1960s fewer than 10 percent of married women were using contraception; by 2003 the proportion was 60 percent (Cleland et al. 2006).

Despite these trends, population reduction programs in some nations, particularly China and India, have been sharply criticized where pressures to decrease family size combined with a strong preference for sons, result in "missing girls"—a sharp imbalance in gender ratios at birth. More focused contraception programs are sometimes also criticized for bias. For example, governmental programs that provide special access to contraception for specific population subgroups—inner-city adolescent girls, for example—are sometimes said to be racially biased. Some attack the use of contraceptive technology, such as that used in family-planning programs, as "a destructive and even deadly weapon in the war on population" (Hartmann 1995, pp. 173–174). In addition, government programs and even the open-market availability of contraception have also faced criticism: A Christian pregnancy-counseling organization, A Woman's Concern, labels the distribution of contraceptives as "demeaning to women."

Population Decline and Fertility Encouragement Population decline, or perceived decline, is also of concern in many European and Asian countries, to some degree offsetting the attention paid to contraception. Governmental programs in some countries where fertility rates have been falling, such as Germany, provide special benefits for childbearing, including financial payments, maternity/paternity leave, home loans, and child care, although these countries continue to provide access to modern methods of contraception. Concern with high AIDS mortality rates in sub-Saharan Africa has deflected attention from family planning, and although condoms used for disease prevention also have a contraceptive effect, birthrates remain high: 5.9 children per woman in west Africa, 5.7 in east Africa, and 6.3 in middle Africa (Glasier et al. 2006), although these high birthrates may be accompanied by high death rates and particularly high rates of infant mortality. In some countries, high birthrates are encouraged by dissident or subordinate population subgroups, which are led to mistrust or reject contraception, or by groups that have been subject to population-reducing disasters such as ethnic massacres, wars and civil wars, refugee dislocations, epidemics of infectious disease, and natural disasters, including earthquakes and tsunamis.

Nevertheless, there remains a substantial "unmet need" for contraception, encompassing an estimated 120,000 couples in 2006, most but not all in developing countries. The fecund married women in these couples wish to avoid further childrearing or to postpone their next child for at least two years but are faced with an absence of contraception. Even in the developed world, including countries such as the United Kingdom where contraception is available free of charge, most pregnancies that end in abortion are conceived either without any contraception, with incorrect or inconsistent use, or with the use of less-effective methods (Glasier et al. 2006).

RELIGIOUS GROUPS

The policies of religious groups concerning contraception range from condemnation to celebration. Among Protestant groups, the Episcopal Church, the Presbyterian Church (U.S.A.), the United Methodist Church, and the Unitarian Universalist Church support the use of contraception as a component of responsible family planning, variously emphasizing the importance of strong and stable families, healthy and wanted children, and the sexual expression of love between married couples. Some also accept the use of contraception in relationships outside marriage. Southern Baptists and Evangelical Lutherans accept the use of contraception by married couples. Many other Protestant groups encourage individual decision-making about contraception.

Judaism's three principal branches differ in attitudes about contraception. Orthodox Judaism discourages contraception, permitting abstinence only, except for health reasons, and indeed the Orthodox practice of restraint from intercourse for a specified number of days after the menses serves to encourage intercourse at the time of ovulation, ensuring maximum fertility. Reform Judaism's view is much like that of the liberal Protestant groups, supporting contraception for responsible family planning and other reasons. Islam also exhibits a wide variety of views: Some traditions insist that all family planning methods are prohibited; others point out that male withdrawal is clearly permitted in the Koran; and others accept contraception in general, especially to protect the health of the woman or the well-being of the family. Islam encourages procreation; so do Hinduism, Catholicism, evangelical Christianity, and Mormonism.

The Roman Catholic Church holds one of the most strongly prohibitive teachings concerning contraception. As articulated in Pope Paul VI's 1968 encyclical letter, *Humanae Vitae*, Catholicism condemns the use of all forms of artificial contraception and all sterilization "permanent or temporary," or "any act specifically intended to prevent procreation," insisting that the sexual act of a married couple must be capable of being both "unitive" and "procreative." Catholicism does accept the use of "natural" family planning based on rhythm methods. Adherence to the teaching varies. In the United States, Catholic women (of non-Hispanic ethnicity) use artificial contraception at the same rate as do Protestants and Jews.

While religious teaching concerning contraception is usually presented as a matter of individual spiritual commitment, some critics insist that the rejection of contraception by specific religious groups (such as Catholicism and Islam) is a pronatalist policy in disguise—a matter of sectarian arithmetic intended to increase the number of that group's adherents.

MEDICAL AND SOCIAL POLICIES

Medical and social policies have often focused on the role of contraception in promoting individual and community health. Traditional medical policy in the United States was highly paternalistic, holding that a woman's request for fertility control by means of sterilization could be honored only if her age, multiplied by the number of living children she already had, reached an adequate figure. This rule is no longer invoked, but physicians remain reluctant to use irreversible sterilization procedures for young adults without children. Contemporary medical policy has focused on the importance of effective contraception in preventing unwanted pregnancy, on making a wide range of types of contraception available to women, and on encouraging informed, reliable use.

Noting that in the developing world, unsafe sex is the second most important risk factor for disability and death and the ninth most important in the developing world (Glasier et al. 2006), calls have been issued for universal, reliable access to modern methods to prevent both unintended pregnancy and sexually transmitted diseases.

Political friction has surrounded several forms of contraception. Controversial events have included the manufacturer's concealment in the early 1970s of the safety risks of the Dalkon Shield IUD (Hartmann 1995), friction over suggestions for nonvoluntary implantation of Norplant in women receiving welfare (Moskowitz and Jennings 1996), disputes over abstinence-only programs as politically motivated in both domestic and international contexts (Fathalla et al. 2006), disagreement over whether health insurance policies should be required to cover contraception for women, and disputes over the refusal of some pharmacists to dispense the so-called morning-after pill and/or contraception in general. Data bearing on some disputes has been assembled: For example, in the United States 77 percent of the drop in pregnancy rates among younger teens, ages fifteen to seventeen, is due to improved contraceptive use and 23 percent to abstinence; in eighteen- and nineteen-year-olds, better contraceptive use is responsible for 100 percent of the decline (Santelli et al. 2007). In general, medical and global-health organizations stress the importance of the revitalization of political commitment to improving sexual and reproductive health for all, including access to safe and reliable contraception.

THE FUTURE

Governmental policies, religious teachings, and medical and institutional policies variously cover female and male natural family planning, withdrawal, condom use, male and female sterilization, and "artificial" or technologically advanced female contraception. But few governmental, religious, or medical entities have developed policies concerning new technologies for long-term male contraception. It remains to be seen whether such technologies will be successfully developed and if so, whether governmental, religious, and medical and policies will generally track policies concerning "artificial" female contraception.

BIBLIOGRAPHY

Cleland, John; Stan Bernstein; Alex Ezeh, et al. 2006. "Family Planning: The Unfinished Agenda." *Lancet* 368(9549): 1810–1827.

Cohen, Joel E. 1995. *How Many People Can the Earth Support?* New York: Norton.

Fathalla, Mahmoud F.; Steven W. Sinding; Allan Rosenfield; and Mohammed M. F. Fathalla. 2006. "Sexual and Reproductive Health for All: A Call for Action." *Lancet* 368(9552): 2095–2100.

Glasier, Anna; A. Metin Gülmezoglu; George P. Schmid; et al. 2006. "Sexual and Reproductive Health: A Matter of Life and Death." *Lancet* 368(9547): 1595–1607.

Hartmann, Betsy. 1995. *Reproductive Rights and Wrongs: The Global Politics of Population Control.* Rev. edition. Boston: South End Press.

Hatcher, Robert A.; James Trussell; Felicia Stewart; et al. 2004. *Contraceptive Technology.* 18th edition. New York: Ardent Media.

Hesketh, Therese; Li Lu; and Zhu Wei Xing. 2005. "The Effect of China's One-Child Family Policy after 25 Years." *New England Journal of Medicine* 353(11): 1171–1176.

Legge, Jerome S., Jr., and John R. Alford. 1986. "Can Government Regulate Fertility? An Assessment of Pronatalist Policy in Eastern Europe." *Western Political Quarterly* 39(4): 709–728.

Moskowitz, Ellen H., and Bruce Jennings, eds. 1996. *Coerced Contraception? Moral and Policy Challenges of Long-Acting Birth Control.* Washington, DC: Georgetown University Press.

Paul VI. 1968. Encyclical Letter *Humanae Vitae* (July 25, 1968). Vatican City: Vatican.

Repetto, Robert. 1968. "India: A Case Study of the Madras Vasectomy Program." *Studies in Family Planning* 1(31): 8–16.

Santelli, John S.; Laura Duberstein Lindberg; Lawrence B. Finer; and Susheela Singh. 2007. "Explaining Recent Declines in Adolescent Pregnancy in the United States: The Contribution of Abstinence and Improved Contraceptive Use." *American Journal of Public Health* 97(1): 150–156.

Singh, Karan. 1976. "National Population Policy: A Statement of the Government of India." *Population and Development Review* 2(2): 309–312.

Margaret P. Battin

COPROPHILIA

Coprophilia is the condition of desire for sexual gratification and sexual arousal derived from the smell, taste, or sight of feces or from the act of defecation. It commonly is referred to by the slang term *scat.* Although ostensibly a somewhat limited practice, it figures prominently in the foundations of the science of psychology. Sigmund Freud outlined a stage of psychosexual development called the anal stage that involves the child's obsession with the anus as an erogenous zone. The process of toilet training sets up a conflict between the child's pleasure in defecation and pressures exerted on the child to control his or her bodily functions. The way children resolve this conflict is seen as a primary means of establishing the way they later will deal with authority and issues of possession.

DEFINITIONS OF COPROPHILIA

Coprophilia is related to this psychosexual conflict but is not a developmental stage. It is a condition that occurs in adults and represents the small number of individuals who reject social pressure to control elimination and instead find the act of defecation pleasurable and erotic. Because of the relationship of coprophilia to eroticism and anality, for much of the twentieth century it was considered by psychologists to be related almost exclusively to homosexuality (Karpman 1948). After frank analyses of actual sexual behavior such as that of Alfred Kinsey and other studies in the post–sexual revolution era, the ascription of coprophilia solely to homosexuals has been shown to be false. In fact, so few data exist that there appears to be no consensus about the connection between coprophilia and the choice of sexual partners.

The term *coprophilia* also has a more general definition as an affinity that can become an erotic fascination with filth and uncleanliness. Among the very few case studies that address coprophilia, several use the term in this sense. A 1955 study of a woman named Evangeline, for instance, describes the pleasure she took in maintaining a filthy home. Although a great deal of the filth consisted of her feces and that of her pets, most was of a generalized nature (rotting food, dust, animal hair, etc.). She expressed no particular interest in the act of defecation but took delight in its product as well as the presence of other types of waste material (Xavier 1955).

REACTIONS TO COPROPHILIA

Coprophilia generally is regarded as the most taboo consensual sexual activity and commonly is reviled as much as or more than violent or nonconsensual acts such as rape and pedophilia. It is considered so transgressive that unlike other fetishistic or paraphilic sexual practices, there is very little published literature on the topic. Not only is there a dearth of popular material, but even academic literature seems to shy away from the topic. A very few medical and psychological studies have been conducted, but even among those disciplines little research exists. The *Diagnostic and Statistical Manual of Mental Disorders* (DSM-IV) of the American Psychiatric Association (1994) classifies coprophilia as a paraphilia, or atypical sexual interest. It falls under the category of "Paraphilia Not Otherwise Specified," which is a blanket designation used to describe conditions that occur in such small segments of the population that they do not warrant individual headings. This is not an accurate measure of the prevalence of the practice, however, for the DSM-IV is primarily a diagnostic tool for conditions that are to some degree debilitating. If sexual activity involving feces is incorporated into an individual's sexual practice with no apparent effect on other aspects of that person's life, it will not necessarily figure into the statistics in the DSM-IV.

A nonscientific measure of the discourse on coprophilia would be the pornography industry. Although the adult entertainment industry is quick to capitalize on most sexual practices, including rape, pedophilia, sex with animals, and other fringe practices, very few magazines, web sites, or films feature coprophilia. A limited number exist, although there is no concrete information about their popularity. The majority of noncommercial web sites that address the topic seem to be constructed by practitioners of coprophilia, making their information biased at best.

THE PRACTICE OF COPROPHILIA

Coprophilia usually is considered an unsafe sexual practice because of the possibility of infection from contact with the waste products of the human body. Contact with one's own feces is generally safer than contact with that of a partner, but both carry risk, particularly of bacterial infection. Hepatitis is a particular danger to coprophiliacs, although many other infections are also possible. Coprophilia can be practiced relatively safely if there is no direct contact with the feces. If it is practiced alone, this would include smelling or looking at the feces after defecation; using mirrors, video technology, or photography to watch oneself defecate; or taking extreme pleasure in the sensation of defecation. These acts are less safe when practiced with a partner, but if the arousal and gratification arise primarily from viewing the act of defecation or from smelling the feces, the risk of infection is minimal.

Several variations on these practices exist, along with a proliferation of slang terms that seem to belie the ostensibly small population of individuals who practice coprophilia. The term *glass-bottom boat* is used to describe defecation onto a piece of glass, clear plastic wrap, or another transparent material while a partner watches from below. Thus, there is a feeling of being defecated on without actual contact with the feces. Direct defecation onto a partner's body without a barrier is described by the slang terms *steamer* and *Cleveland steamer*. This is a far riskier behavior, but as long as the feces do not come into contact with broken skin or a body opening, the risk of infection is minimal.

The most taboo form of coprophilia is the eating of feces, or coprophagia. It is thought to be practiced by an exceptionally small number of people and is one of the most risky sexual behaviors. Some species of animals, such as rabbits, routinely practice coprophagia as a part of their digestive process, and others, such as dogs, engage in the practice without any obvious physiological need. In humans, however, it is a rare occurrence.

One case study indicates that the consumption of feces can be a means of disposal of feces used for other sexual acts; the erotic sensation may be confined to coprophilia, whereas coprophagia serves essentially to destroy the evidence of coprophilic practice (Hingsburger 1989). True coprophagia, in which pleasure is taken in the act, seems to be confined to the realm of mental illness; even popular references to coprophilia almost never extend to coprophagia. There are at least partial exceptions to this, however. In water sports or urolagnia, the consumption of the body's waste products is somewhat common. This practice is limited to urine, however, and does not include solid waste. Also, there is a somewhat common sexual practice called anilingus (referred to by the slang terms *rimming* and *tossing salad*) in which the anus is licked by a sexual partner. In almost all cases, however, cleanliness of the anus is desired by the person performing anilingus. Although the practice is related to taking pleasure from an ostensibly taboo act, the fascination is with the anus itself, not with defecation or feces.

Even rarer are instances of humans consuming the feces of other species, although such cases have been documented. One instance was captured on film: In the 1972 movie *Pink Flamingos* the director John Waters filmed his star, the drag queen Divine, picking up the feces of a dog and eating them. The intent of the scene was to establish the complete perversion of the character as Divine campaigned for the title "the world's filthiest person." Even among the variety of sexual practices depicted in the film, the scene showing coprophagia is by far the best known and most notorious.

BIBLIOGRAPHY

American Psychiatric Association. 1994. *Diagnostic and Statistical Manual of Mental Disorders: DSM-IV.* 4th edition. Washington, DC: Author.

Freud, Sigmund. 1953 (1900). *The Interpretation of Dreams*, trans. James Strachey. London: Hogarth Press.

Hingsburger, Dave. 1989. "Motives for Coprophilia: Working with Individuals Who Had Been Institutionalized with Developmental Handicaps." *Journal of Sex Research* 26(1): 139–140.

Karpman, Ben. 1948. "Coprophilia: A Collective Review." *Psychoanalytic Review* 35(3): 253–272.

Rosebury, Theodor. 1969. *Life on Man.* New York: Viking Press.

Xavier, Cedric M. 1955. "Coprophilia—A Clinical Study." *British Journal of Medical Psychology* 28: 188–190.

Brian D. Holcomb

COURTESANS

Courtesans are at the high end of the sexual traffic in women. Although some achieved great wealth, most began as poor girls who were sold or driven into the sex trade as their only means to a better life. Etymologically the word courtesan refers to a woman attached to a royal court, a female courtier. Most often she was elegantly dressed and coiffed, beautiful, mannerly, a talented singer, dancer, or musician, and a great wit or conversationalist. She was a woman trained to attract attention and to please men. In contrast to prostitutes who have many clients and whose incomes range from bare subsistence to comfort, courtesans usually had a single patron who paid all their extravagant expenses. James Davidson (1998) notes the distinction to be made between the gift-exchange practice of the ancient Greek *hetaeras* that established a relationship of patronage and friendship, and the commodity-exchange practice of the prostitute that did not. While some *hetaeras* took cash as well as relationship-establishing gifts in exchange for their company, during which sex was a distinct possibility, prostitutes were explicitly paid cash for sex. This distinction between presents and payments is useful for ancient and medieval India as well, especially in the case of the *devadāsīs* who were supported by their temples and by kings. In later periods of European history courtesans were associated with royal courts that had the money, leisure, and interest to enjoy their various talents, such as the courts of Renaissance Italy and of eighteenth- and nineteenth-century France and England, although almost any man possessed of great wealth was welcomed by them. Courtesans were often in direct competition with male courtiers for the acquisition of patronage, wealth, and political influence, and the acrimony of courtiers is apparent in the male-dominated voice of history (Rosenthal 1992).

While men used courtesans for pleasure, religions used them for didactic purposes. The religions of the world abound with stories about repentant courtesans, such as legends of the Magdalene, or about their venality and dangerous powers of seduction, which they used to jeopardize male religious practice. This is equally true in South Asia, with the additional belief that they were powerful sources of fecundity on many levels.

INDIA

Courtesans have long been a staple of South Asian myth, literature, drama, and ritual life. Plays featuring courtesans were frequently performed during spring fertility festivals to help promote the fruitfulness of humans, animals, and crops. In keeping with this connection between courtesans and fecundity, there are many tales in which a king can only end a drought by sending a courtesan to seduce a celibate sage. This theme was enacted in an annual ritual by *devadāsīs*, the sacred courtesans at the temple of Jagannātha in Puri, in order to hasten the monsoon rains. The connections between semen and rain have a long history in the ancient world, and both are also connected to fecundity and thus to power. It was believed that by withholding his semen a sage could blight the land, unless the king had a greater command over the powers of fertility, or unless he could command the auspicious powers of a beautiful and fertile woman. In similar scenarios, the god Indra sends divine courtesans (*apsaras*) to seduce celibate sages whose spiritual power threatens his own.

There are also many Buddhist and Hindu stories in which courtesans fail in their attempts at seduction, which serve several purposes: Whereas they highlight an ascetic's control of his sexuality, they also serve as a warning about the dangers of sexuality to spiritual power and they define women as sexual temptresses.

Courtesans in India, and in Japan as well, lived in their own section of town, a red-light district of sorts, but one in which the arts flourished. Many were accomplished singers, musicians, dancers, poets, and wits, and they knew the arts of costume, cosmetics, and setting. The courtesan district was imagined to be separate from the mundane world, to be a place of art and refinement, populated by beautiful, sexually available women. In Japan, this is known as the "Floating World." The entrance fee, of course, could be high; plays and stories frequently tell of men who met financial ruin in their pursuit of the many pleasures offered by these skillful women.

Devadāsīs present the most complex picture of South Asian women who have been classified as courtesans. This complexity is connected to the sacredness of their temple office, and thus to their relationship with divine beings, and to kings, who in India, as in many parts of the world, were considered divine. Indeed, *devadāsīs* brought together the courtesan and the sacred by often classifying themselves as *apsaras*, divine courtesans.

One became a *devadāsī* either by inheriting the office, for instance being the daughter of a *devadāsī*'s brother, or being adopted by a *devadāsī*, as *devadāsīs* were not supposed to give birth to children. Instead, their stored-up procreative powers were heightened by their sexual activity, which they passed on to the brides and infants they blessed, and to the entire kingdom through their ritual functions. They were ceremonially dedicated to the temple before they reached puberty (a tradition that was outlawed in 1947 by the Devadasi Act), and from that moment they were considered married to the ruling deity of the temple. Since the king was considered to be the living incarnation of the god Jagganātha (Viṣṇu in his incarnation as Kriṣṇa), a tradition existed that the king consummated the marriage. If she wanted, a *devadāsī* could then establish a liaison, but only with an upper caste man who lived in the area served by the temple.

The most famous Buddhist courtesan was the beautiful and rich Amrapālī, known throughout India for her intelligence and accomplishments. In her story the ascetic and the courtesan receive a new twist: It is the ascetic, the Buddha, who seduced the courtesan into abandoning worldly life, for Amrapālī became a Buddhist nun and achieved enlightenment. Buddhist authors also used courtesans to dramatize teachings about impermanence, especially of the body. For instance, in a poem attributed to Amrapālī after she had become a Buddhist nun and grown old, she says:

> Once my body was lovely as polished gold;
> now in old age it is covered all over with tiny
> wrinkles. . . .

In the *Saundarānanda*, a popular literary work by the first-century Buddhist monk Aśvaghoṣa, the Buddha takes his half-brother to see the beautiful *apsaras* of heaven in order to get him to abandon his beautiful wife and become a monk.

JAPAN

The complexity of Japanese prostitution is demonstrated by the hundreds of words that can refer to prostitutes, who participated in a hierarchical world based on rank, artistic accomplishment, and beauty. Since even noble families could fall on hard times, girls from all levels of society were sold into prostitution, as were samurai wives caught in adultery. The highest ranked were the *tayu*, who were proficient in dancing, singing, playing musical instruments, composing poetry, serving tea, and other arts. The distinctive and magnificent clothing of courtesans included almost foot-high black-lacquered wooden clogs. Geishas did not arrive on the scene until the late eighteenth century. The word *geisha* means artist, indicating that they were entertainers, mainly musicians and dancers. Their roles changed time and again as Japanese society changed, but their main function was and is to entertain and amuse men at banquets. Any involvement with the sex trade is hard to pin down. While they had different licenses than prostitutes, some clearly engaged in sexual activity with their customers. Traditionally, the transition from apprentice to geisha involved a one-time sexual encounter with a patron.

Both courtesans and geishas were often the subject of Kabuki plays that end in the double suicide of the woman and her lover due to thwarted love (Shively 1978). Kabuki began with the performance of a woman called Okuni in 1603; she mimed and danced the role of a dandy visiting a brothel, which became another enduring theme in Kabuki. Theatrical performers and prostitutes have long been associated in many parts of the world; in

Courtesans. *Illustration of Japanese courtesans in a brothel.* © ASIAN ART & ARCHAEOLOGY, INC./CORBIS.

Japan, courtesans and actors were both represented in popular prints, some of which were sexually explicit.

ANCIENT GREECE

In ancient Greece, courtesans are usually thought of as hetaeras, such as the well-known Aspasia, made famous by her relationship with Pericles (c. 495–429 BCE) and admired by Socrates. But *hetaera* is a slippery term that was also used for more common prostitutes, including those who were slaves. The best-known hetaeras are from the late fifth to the third centuries BCE. Generally, they were hired for an evening or longer as escorts. Sometimes men formed alternative households with them. Rarely, they had their own households. Those who did were called *megalomisthoi*, or "big fee" hetaeras; these courtesans were written about in plays, mainly comedies, and posed for artists. Phryne, a fourth-century BCE courtesan, modeled for the first Classical female nude by Praxiteles. According to Callistratus (*On Hetaeras*), Phryne became so rich that, after the destruction of Thebes by the Macedonians, she offered to have the city wall rebuilt if they would put up the inscription: "Alexander may have knocked it down, but Phryne the hetaera got it back up again."

Hetaeras were taken to festivals and drinking parties all over Greece, but especially to elaborate dinner parties known as symposia, which also usually included female sex-workers of other categories. Like geishas, hetaeras were cultivated and charming, and they made these banquets more pleasurable for men, often pretending to enjoy men's off-color jokes and telling some of their own.

MODERN EUROPE

In the nineteenth century prostitution was widespread throughout the major capitals of the world, but nowhere else was it as highly regulated as in Paris with its registry of prostitutes and the dreaded bimonthly medical checks for venereal disease. Yet there were many ways around registering, which was voluntary until enforced after an arrest. Procuresses prevented actual police scrutiny of prostitutes, while underpaid girls working in shops or laundries supplemented their incomes through an older lover. Further up the social scale, women who had slipped a notch or two were able to maintain independent establishments where they entertained men. At the top were the celebrated courtesans whose extravagant lifestyle was a testament to the wealth of their patrons. This was actually a financially impractical situation, since the courtesan spent almost all she was given on display without being able to secure anything for her future. It also made her the focus of widespread criticism when hard times hit.

This is the era of Blanche de Païva, a Russian émigré whose excessive but beautiful home still stands on the Champs Elysées; Marie Duplessis, who was the inspiration for Alexandre Dumas's *La Dame aux camélias*; and Apollonie Sabatier, who was immortalized in the poems of Charles Baudelaire.

During La Belle Époque (c. 1890–1914), some of the best-known courtesans were dancers who performed at the Folies Bergères, which provided them with a very public opportunity to display their charms and which continued the long-standing associations between prostitutes and performers. Among these, Caroline Otero, frequently called "the last great courtesan," stands out. She was born the illegitimate daughter of a Gypsy mother and a Greek army officer in 1868. Like her mother, she began earning her living as a dancer while still a child. By 1890 she was a major star on the Paris stage, courted and feted by a slew of wealthy and aristocratic lovers who made her jewel collection the talk of Europe. Unfortunately, she lost her entire fortune through her passion for gambling and a series of bad investments. She died, destitute, in 1965.

The world-renowned Mata Hari also met a bad end. Born in provincial Holland in 1876, she was named Margaretha Geertruida Zelle. She escaped the narrow life awaiting her by answering a newspaper ad seeking a wife for a colonial military officer stationed in the Dutch East Indies. After several years and two children, she began performing native dances at the officers' club. When her marriage failed, at age twenty-seven she went to Paris to begin a career as a highly erotic oriental dancer and a courtesan with innumerable lovers. Her greatest success was between 1905 and 1920, but her talent as a dancer was limited and she grew fat, petulant, and poor. In the middle of World War I she fell passionately in love with a much younger Russian officer serving with the French. In her wild pursuit of him from one military post to another, she used forged papers to cross national borders, which led to the accusation that she was a spy for Germany. She was found guilty and executed by a firing squad in 1917.

CONCLUSION

In a wide variety of patriarchal societies, royal and rich men created a market for talented, beautiful, and sexually available women who were able to mingle socially with powerful men in ways virtuous women were not. Most languages have a rich vocabulary of terms to place women in various sexual categories (Davidson 1998, Young 2003). For example, in Sanskrit there is the distinction between the *kula-strī* (a wife, a woman from a good family) and *vāra-strī* (a courtesan, a restraining woman). This distinction between the good wife and the bad courtesan is particularly brought out by the contrast in sixteenth-century Venice: between the courtesan's social mobility, public role, and relative freedom of movement and the restrictions imposed on the movements and public role of aristocratic women. In literature and art they were both denigrated as venal and overly sexed women or romanticized as women with noble feelings, courage, and loyalty. In all this may be seen that courtesans were products of male longing for a bad girl who could be controlled and who would love the controlling man for his domination.

Economically, this categorization into good and bad breaks down even further. Courtesans were bad because they drained men of money, but they were also lauded as the treasures of Venice because they fulfilled the need for sexually available women in a prosperous mercantile city-state, and they attracted rich tourists. Sex tours have long existed. Similarly, in the Tamil epic *Manimekhalaï* (Shatton 1989), a young courtesan is initially thwarted in her desire to become a Buddhist nun by the leaders of her city who see her as a major attraction of wealth to their city.

Because they are bad (and have money), courtesans appear to have a freedom of movement and expression unknown to other women but, like their extravagant costumes and jewels, their freedom was part of a performance piece that reflected glory on their male protectors. The courtesan could, and often was, brought down hard and fast because she was always under legal constraint and thus even more vulnerable to male whim than "good" women.

BIBLIOGRAPHY

Apffel Marglin, Frédérique. 1985. *Wives of the God-King.* Delhi: Oxford University Press.

Aśvaghoṣa. 1932. *The Saundarananda, or Nanda the Fair*, trans. E. H. Johnston. London: Oxford University Press.

Dalby, Liza Crihfield. 1998. *Geisha*. Berkeley: University of California Press.

Davidson, James. 1998. *Courtesans & Fishcakes: The Consuming Passions of Classical Athens.* New York: St. Martin's.

Mogador, Céleste. 2001. *Memoirs of a Courtesan in Nineteenth-Century Paris*, trans. Monique Fleury Nagem. Lincoln: University of Nebraska Press.

Rosenthal, Margaret F. 1992. *The Honest Courtesan: Veronica Franco, Citizen and Writer in Sixteenth-Century Venice.* Chicago: University of Chicago Press.

Rounding, Virginia. 2003. *Grandes Horizontales: The Lives and Legends of Four Nineteenth-Century Courtesans.* New York: Bloomsbury.

Shattan, Merchant-Prince. 1989. *Manimekhalaï: The Dancer with the Magic Bowl*, trans. Alain Daniélou. New York: New Directions Books.

Shively, Donald H. 1978. "The Social Environment of Tokugawa Kabuki." In *Studies in Kabuki: Its Acting, Music, and Historical Context*, ed. James R. Brandon, et al. Honolulu: University Press of Hawaii.

Young, Serinity. 2003. *Courtesans and Tantric Consorts: Buddhist Sexualities in Narrative, Iconography, and Ritual.* London: Routledge.

Serinity Young

COURTLY LOVE

The term *courtly love* (*amour courtois, amore cortese, fin' amor*) was coined by the literary critic and philologist Gaston Paris in 1883 in an essay on Chretien de Troyes's *Conte de la Charrette* to define the chivalric love bond between Lancelot and Guinevere. Paris described it as an illicit and adulterous form of love accompanied by an almost sacred and obsessive devotion to the lady (*domna)* or lord (*midons*, from *meus dominus*). The socially inferior lover aspires to obtain the favor of the loved one to whom he or she pledges obedience, humility, and faithfulness and become worthy of that person through virtuous deeds, courtesy, and noble acts. The lover-troubadour is at the mercy of the lady and must comply with whatever she demands; the verb *servir* comes to be defined as "to love." Feudalism, kingship, and religious fervor, especially in the form of the Marian cult, were major contributors to the genesis and practice of courtly love, and the lady would be not only a sovereign but a *typus Mariae*, a type of the Virgin Mary.

DEFINITION OF COURTLY LOVE

Courtly love is a religion of love that contradicts Christian theology and its social conventions, for it transgresses the boundaries of Christian marriage and proposes a love relationship between socially unequal persons. Elements such as the lady's married status, jealousy, the suspense of waiting, physical distance, clandestine meetings, the excitement of the possible encounter, the envy of others, and the role of nature in arousing expectations were contributing factors to the cult. Courtly love would become the inspiration and practice of male poets, or trobadours, from *troubars* (from the late Latin *tropare,* meaning to compose music in tropes) and female poets (*troubatriz)* in the courts of Provence in southern France and nearby territories, using the *langue d'oc* in contrast to the *langue d'oïl* of the north, where poets were called *trouvères*. The poems were to be transmitted orally with musical accompaniment, as in the tradition of the Galician-Portuguese *Cantigas*.

Gaston Paris defined the major components of this idealistic, passionate, and spiritual love that was influenced by Ovid's *Ars Amatoria*, the sociopolitical conditions of twelfth-century courts, and the flourishing of Provencal love lyrics. It consisted of a code or set of rules of love that could be practiced in the refined and sophisticated courts of southern France, northern and southern Italy, Catalonia, and northern Spain. That part of Spain had absorbed an Arabic civilization that might have contributed poetic forms such as the *pastourelle* and a code of behavior, the *senhal,* that prohibited the identification of the loved one, as demanded by social etiquette.

Paris located *amour courtois* at the court of Marie de Champagne, the daughter of Eleanore of Aquitaine, where the poet Chretiens de Troyes and the theorist Chaplain Andreas Capellanus, who codified the rules of courtly love in the treatise *De arte honeste amandi*, were active. Capellanus's treatise prescribed the rules for courts frequented by wandering minstrels, ladies, and suitors engaged in contests of amorous entertainment that included *questions galantes questioni d'amore*, a sort of riddle game resolved by the mistress or the *midons*. Some of the prescriptions advocated by Capellanus are that marriage should not be an impediment to true love; that a lover cannot be bound by one love; that no one who is loved can refuse anything to love and nobody can love if he or she is not driven by the power of love ("Amor ch'a nullo amato amar perdona," says Francesca da Rimini [Dante's *Inferno*, canto 5, line 103]); and that the literary convention of *fole amor* (mad love) obscures the lover's reason.

The idea of a hidden love whose revelation can be damaging and fateful is contained in the *senhal*, the hidden identity. The *midon*'s love enhances the nobility, dignity, and valor of the lover. The assumed social position of the loved one and the lover in these poems, akin to that of the feudal lady or lord and vassal, and the obsessive idolatry of the loved one became a poetic practice that spread quickly to other regions and countries and persists today. It had a particular influence on vernacular love poetry in Italy, on the Sicilian School at the court of Frederick II in Palermo, and later on the poets of Tuscany and Bologna, including Guido Guinizelli, the founder of the Sweet New Style (*Dolce stil novo*).

DANTE'S DEFINITION OF COURTLY LOVE

The first critical exposition of this form of poetry is recorded by Dante in *Vita Nuova,* where he gives a concise chronology of the development of vernacular lyric poetry in the countries of *Romania* and states that poets wanted to make their verse intelligible to ladies. In *Purgatorio*, canto 26, Dante attributes to Guinizelli the highest achievement of the Italian vernacular, but Guinizelli gives that honor to Arnaut Daniel, the Provençal love lyricist and craftsman of the most audacious techniques, such as the *sestina*. To honor the poet Dante makes him speak in Provençal in *Purgatorio*, stressing how the learned Tuscan poet wrote in that expressive and refined language of love. Dante might have been influenced by the troubadours, but primarily in terms of language and technique; in his conception, *gentilezza* and *cortesia*, as expressed in the fourth book of the *Convivio*, are innate virtues that are not related to the courts. Although he states that the word *cortese* derives from *corte*, he believes that *virtu'* (virtue) and good manners or customs *bei costumi* are no longer present in the courts. Thus, his *canzone* and philosophical exposition in *Convivio* IV challenge the belief that nobility is derived from inheritance and champion the presence of individual virtue and merit at every social level. The audience for the *Convivio* is in fact diverse and democratic and includes women.

POETIC FORMS AND TECHNIQUES

The historical existence of courtly love and the issue of whether it was the product of critics' imagination have been subject to debate. However, this form of poetry has a concrete textual reality with rules and governing poetic images in which nature and society play a leading role, especially in terms of language, prosody, and rhetoric. Subsequent poets found these poems worthy of imitation, from Dante and Petrarch, to the poets of the late Italian Renaissance, to those of the Pleiade, to Spenser, to the European romantics and postromantics, and to modern poets such as Eliot and Pound, Adrienne Rich, and Muriel Rukeyser, among others.

MODERN ANALYSES

C. S. Lewis (1958) wrote that this form of poetry was revolutionary and everlasting: "Even our code of etiquette, with its rule that women always have precedence, is a legacy from courtly love, and is felt to be far from natural in modern India or Japan. … French poets, in the eleventh century, discovered or invented, or were the first to express, that romantic species of passion which English poets were still writing about in the nineteenth. They affected a change which left no corner of our ethics, our imagination, or our daily life untouched, and they erected impassable barriers between us and the classical past or the Oriental presence. Compared with this revolution the renaissance is a mere ripple on the surface of literature" (pp. 3–4). In contrast to that statement, Peter Dronke (1968) attempts to demonstrate that *amour courtois* is not necessarily a new conception of love: "For I would like to suggest that the feelings and conceptions of *amour courtois* are universally possible, possible in any time or place and on any level of society. They occur in popular a well as in learned or aristocratic love poetry. … The unity of popular and courtly love poetry is manifest in the courtly experience, which finds expression in both" (pp. 2–3).

Martin de Riqueur (1948) proposes a fourfold thesis of origins: folkloric, Arabic, Medio-Latin, and liturgical. Modern criticism holds to the view that structural and stylistic elements of Provencal poetry were derived from Arabic predecessors in El Andalus, the center of Arab civilization in Spain, such as the *Book of Flowers* by Ibn Dawoud and the *Dove Neck's Ring* of Ibn Hazam, as well as Avicenna's *Treatise on Love,* which deals with human and divine love. The Mozarabic *Khardjas* and the lyricism found in the *muwwashah* or *canso* definitely were assimilated into the *chanson de toile*, the *canso*, and the *pastourelle.* The Arabic influence also may be present in the Sicilian School because of the Arab presence in that island for more than one hundred fifty years.

MAJOR POETS IN THE TRADITION OF COURTLY LOVE

Some of the exponents of courtly love operated in the castles and courts of Occitania, which became the target of the Albigensian crusade initiated by Innocent III in 1209 against the Cathars, who professed a mixture of Gnosticism and Manichaeism. The fall of the fortress of Montsegur in 1244 resulted in the de facto eradication of the practice of courtly love that had begun with William of Aquitane (d. 1127), who wrote eleven *canzos* (songs) in the language of Limousin that were filled with desire and verdant backgrounds and who was influenced by Robert D'Abrissel (1050–1117), who founded the monastery of Fons Ebraus, which attracted many aristocratic ladies, and soon was to be an enemy of the Church.

Those who honored this poetry and its tradition include Bernard de Ventadour (1148–1194), Marcabru (c. 1135–1158), Jaufré Rudel (who set the theme of *enamourment* from afar), Peire Vidal (1180–1210), Peire Cardenal, Bertrand de Born (died 1210), Girault de Borneilh (1165–1200), and Arnaut Daniel (1180–1210). Among the many women *troubairitz*, the Countess of Dia from Die, born circa 1140 and married to the Lord of Die, who explicitly said, "*Ben volria mon cavalier tener un ser en mos bratz nut*" [How I wish just one night I could caress/ that chevalier with my bare arms] was the first and most renowned (Bogin 1980, p. 88). Others include Almuc de Castelnau and Iseut de Capio (c. 1140); Azalais de Poicarrages (c. 1140); Maria de Ventadorn (born circa 1165), who in a *tenson* with Guy d'Ussel said that she should never honor the lover as a lord, but as a friend; Alamanda whose *vida* Giraut wrote and who exchanged a *tenson* with him (a discussion on courtly behaviour between two people or an exchange through verbal invective); Garsenda (born circa 1170); Isabella (c. 1180), who says: "Elias Cairel, I want to know/ the truth about the love we once had; so tell me, please/ why you have given it to someone else" (Bogin 1980, p. 111); Lombarda, who writes in *trobar clus*, (dfficult or hermetic style, in contrast to *trobar leu,* easy style) Clara D' Anduza; Castelloza, perhaps the finest woman *troubatriz*; and Guillelma de Rosers, whose *vida* was authored by Lanfranc Cigala, a Genoese lawyer and poet (Bogin 1980). Those poets used forms such as the *canso, tenso, sirvente, alba,* and *pastourelle*, and their stanzas were called *coblas* and the *envoi* and *tornada.*

These women and men created a conception of love poetry that inaugurated a new era in Western European literature that was characterized by the aspiration to gain access to a loved one in body or in spirit. In this system every married lord or lady had an admirer who understood true love; this explains the travails, jealousies, laments, *planhs*, waiting, and disappointments that make up these erotic experiences. The desired *midons* of the troubadours and *troubatriz* become the subject of psychological and poetic turbulence, of hallucinations, fantasy games, and phantasms. The ultimate goal is partial fulfillment or partial joy, for total satisfaction is prohibited by the inequality of the lovers' status. *Fin' amor* is present in the courts of Occitania and its civilization, where the reality of love oscillates between the platonic, the religious, the spiritual, the erotic, and the adulterous.

The condition of women in the lower classes was that of a domestic servant exposed to the caprices of the lord or that of a *femna* or *molher* in the middle strata subject to the husband or the father. A lady (*domna*) in the higher class was subject to her lord; thus, the troubadour and *troubatriz* found the solution in the poetic practice of *fin' amor,* breaking the social barrier through adulterous love, even if only in spirit

The peculiarity of *fin'amor* is that the concept of the lady is paradoxically opposed to the traditional portrayal by moralists, theologians, and Church Fathers: that she is subject to the weakness of the flesh. In *fin'amor* she in effect uses her intellect and superior position, her distance and coldness, to entice her lover.

Arnaut Daniel would say: "*Tot iorn meilleur et esmeri/ Car la gensor serve e coli/ Del mon, so.us dic en apert*" [Every day I am a better man and purer/ for I serve the noblest lady in the world,/ and I worship her,/ I tell you this in the open]. Giraut de Borneihl (1165–1200) wrote: "*Si la belle cui sui profers me vol onrar D'aitan que m denhe soufertar/ qu'eu sia sos fis entendens/ sobre totz sui rics e manens*" [If the beautiful lady I want to belong to/ wants to honor me just so much that she agrees to let/ me be her faithful lover/ I am might and rich above all men]. The Countess of Dia advocates openness, frankness, and sincerity regarding her loved one: "*Dompna que en bon pretz s'enten deu ben pausars'entendensas/ en un pro cavalier valen/ pois qu'ill conois sa valenssa, que l'aus amar a presenssa;/que dompna, pois am'a presen,/ ja pois li pro ni li valen/ no.n dirant mas avinenssa.*" [The lady who knows about valor/should place her affection/ in a corteous and worthy knight/ as soon as she has seen his worth,/ and she should dare to love him face to face; for corteous and worthy men/ can only speak with great esteem/ of a lady who loves openly]. In the poem "A chantar m'er de so qu'ieu non volria," [Of things I'd rather keep in silence I mus sing:] the envoy states: "Mas aitan plus vuoill li digas, messatges,/ qu'en trop d'orguoill ant gran dan maintans gens."But above all, messenger/ make him comprehend, that too much pride has undone many men." Tibors (born circa 1130), perhaps the earliest of the *troubaritzs*, says with spontaneity: "*bel dous amics, ben vos posc on ver dir/ que anc non fo qu'ieu estes sin desir*"[Sweet handsome friend, I can tell you truly/ that I have never been without desire] (Bogin, 1980, p. 80). Bleiris de Romans, about whom very little is known, wrote a chanson addressed to another woman, Lady Maria. Scholars have denied that this might be an amorous song to another woman, but its sincere tone and content betray such erotic love. The poems of Alais, Iselda, and Carenza surely contain allegorical elements (Bogin 1980).

DIFFERENCES BETWEEN MALE AND FEMALE TROUBADOURS

Women troubadours have traits distinctive from those of their male counterparts, and as Bogin (1980) points out, they were not slaves to tradition but were "free of formulas" and genuine in revealing their feelings. The key is that they were "writing for personal not professional reasons" (p. 68). This can be seen in all their poems, and they use a much more concrete language that reveals the true individual in a form of "feminine writing" (*écriture feminine*).

Male troubadours appear to employ much more artificial, conventional language and use constructed images as if they were part of a system. The women, though well versed in courtly rhetoric, seem to employ a language of the soul and of the heart, not necessarily advocating a physical relationship but instead the recognition of their individuality and worth, the nobility of their feelings and frustrations. Although the women troubadours may not surpass the men in their technique, they improve the poetry in terms of themes and realism, sincere sentiments and language.

BIBLIOGRAPHY

Bogin, Meg. 1980. *The Women Troubadours*. New York and London: Norton.

De Rougement, Denis. 1983. *Love in the Western World*, trans. Montgomery Belgion. Princeton, NJ: Princeton University Press.

Dronke Peter. 1968. *Medieval Latin and the Rise of European Love Lyric*. 2nd edition. Oxford: Clarendon Press.

Goldin, Frederick. 1963. *Lyrics of the Troubadours and Trouvères: An Anthology and a History*. Garden City, NY: Anchor.

Goldin, Frederick, comp. 1967. *The Mirror of Narcissus in the Courtly Love Lyric*. Ithaca, NY: Cornell University Press.

Huizinga, Johan. 1954. *The Waning of the Middle Ages: A Study of the Forms of Life, Thought, and Art in the XIVth and XVth Centuries*. Garden City, NY: Anchor.

Lewis, C. S. 1958. *Allegory of Love: A Study of Medieval Tradition*. New York: Oxford University Press.

Newman, F. X., ed. 1969. *The Meaning of Courtly Love*. Albany: State University of New York Press.

Paris, Gaston. 1883. "Le Conte de la Charrette." *Romania* XII.: 459 ff.

Riqueur, Martin de. 1948. *Resumen de Literatura Provenzal Trobadoresca*. Barcelona, Spain: Editorial Seix Barral.

Zumthor, Paul. 1992. *Toward a Medieval Poetics*, trans. Philip Bennet. Minneapolis: University of Minnesota Press.

Giuseppe Di Scipio

CREATION STORIES

While some scholars point to the positive role of creation stories as the sources of moral values that encourage cohesiveness of the society (Malinowski 1962), feminist thinkers argue that creation myths have carried a negative influence on the life of women. Because most creation stories mirror the patriarchal structures of their culture, they often encourage women's subordination and passivity.

INDO-EUROPEAN MYTH

The Rig-Veda, the Vedic creation hymn, shares much with many other Indo-European myths (Greek, Zoroastrian, Celtic, central and western European, etc.) such as polytheism and its veneration of nature. Chapter 10 of the Rig-Veda (c. 1500–1300 BCE) describes a creative process as the sacrifice of the thousand-headed, thousand-footed primal man Parusa. When the gods perform the sacrifice of Parusa, there emerges a clear hierarchy as the upper parts of his body are employed for creation of higher states of existence and the lower for the more common. Out of Parusa's head emerges the sky, while his feet become the earth.

Parusa is a man, which signifies that all reality, even the divine, has its origin from a male body. While recognizing male primacy, the Vedic hymn describes a reciprocal engendering that is taking place between the female and the male energies. The female creative energy arises out of Parusa, but this female energy is also a source of Parusa, an energy that is necessary for the fashioning all of reality. This female energy will appear in future Hindu mythology as Sakit, the creative energy of the principal male Hindu gods.

HINDUISM

In contrast to the oldest, Vedic account of creation, in later tradition (200 BCE), creation comes from Brahma (the masculine expression of Brahman), who creates through his thought ("out of nothing"). While in principle Brahman is beyond gender, the expressions of the divine responsible for creation are often portrayed in masculine images. In addition to Brahma, Shiva (the destroyer, god of procreation) is also masculine. During the fifth century CE, Hindu scriptures introduced a single Great Goddess (Devi, Shakta) who is the material cause of creation (tantric and Shakta traditions). Within the tantric tradition, various female incarnations of the Great Goddess provide the masculine Gods with their creative abilities. Thus, the masculine creators (Brahma or Shiva) rely on their female divine cohorts (Lakshmi or Kali) for their creative abilities. While the male gods are still performing their creative acts, they are impotent without the creative energy (shakti) provided by their female consorts.

Kali testifies to the power of the female goddess (one of many incarnations of Devi) because she defines the fierce divine. Carrying a sword, Kali wears a girdle of severed heads and a necklace of skulls. Fitting for a consort of Shiva, she symbolizes the power of destruction, but this mode of operation leads to a creative process of transformation. As Kali destroys the impediments to realizing the truth, she frees the followers to follow the truth. While the tantric followers of Kali see her as a cherishing mother, others see her as a stereotype of female chaotic presence, which is blamed for bringing destruction on others. Still others believe that Kali provides a needed counterbalance to the stereotypical concepts of femininity.

BUDDHISM

From a Buddhist perspective, this universe is not the only one that exists, but rather there is a cycle of "creations" and destructions that follow one another. At the same time, Buddhist teaching rejects the idea of a creator of the universe. Instead, the universe is maintained by the cycle of causal conditioning called dependent origination. This concept centers around a radical interdependence between all aspects of reality. Everything that exists, exists because it depends on the existence of everything else. That is, nothing can exist without specific causes that bring it about; however, these causes, depend on other causes or conditions. As a result, it is impossible to single out one specific cause for the whole matrix.

The concept of God as creator or as savior is rejected in Buddhism. Because human salvation is a matter of self-realization reached through enlightenment, it is this form of human creativity that is stressed by Buddhists. In the Mahayana tradition, Buddhas and bodhisattvas assist human efforts along the path of enlightenment. These are celestial or earthly beings who have reached enlightenment but were once ordinary human beings. Kuan-yin, a female bodhisattva of compassion, postpones her nirvana (state of bliss, release from the cycle of reincarnation) in order to assist others in their efforts toward enlightenment. Another important female Buddha is Tara found in Vajrayana Buddhism. She appears in two forms—Green Tara and Red Tara—the former specializing in compassionate action, and the latter in removing obstacles to enlightenment. Red Tara wears a garland of severed heads and carries a hooked knife and in many ways resembles the Hindu Kali.

ZOROASTRIANISM

The Zoroastrian creation story describes creation out of chaos by Mazda Ahura, an omnipotent and omniscient god creator. If Mazda Ahura represents the beneficent, high deity, the other lesser deity, Angra Mainyu, represents the evil spirit that brings chaos and disorder. Already within this original dualism there is a gender distinction because Mazda Ahura is referred to as the "father or of order" and the wise lord, whereas the source of disorder (embodied in Angra Mainyu) is personified as feminine. Mazda Ahura and Angra Mainyu produce, respectively, beneficent spiritual beings and as well as demonesses. Whereas beneficent beings include both passive feminine and active masculine beings, demonesses are exclusively feminine.

The first human pair, Mashya (male) and Mashayana Mashyana (female), had their common origin from the semen of the first human, an androgyne named Gayo-Maretan. Initially they sinned together and shared mutual responsibility for the sin. This original equality is soon replaced, however, when Mashyana commits an irreligious ritual act of worshipping the demonic spirits. As a result, woman is seen as susceptible to temptation and evil and as the source of spiritual chaos.

ANCIENT GREEK

Only in the late eighth century BCE do we find the fully developed The Greek creation myth appears fully developed only in the late eighth century BCE in the work of the poet Hesiod. In the beginning there is an absence of form, the absence itself called Chaos. Out of Chaos arises Gaea (the earth), Tartarus (deep pit), and Eros (love). Gaea gives birth by herself to Uranus (the sky) on whom she bestows equal partnership and who becomes her mate. Uranus engages in a continual sexual encounter with Gaea in order to avert keep the offspring from emerging into the world and thus engendering. In order to free herself, Gaea arms her son Kronos, who castrates Uranus of his power over Gaea. The earth and the sky are thus forever separated.

Gaea appears as a powerful goddess, who eliminates the schemes of her cohort by employing her son. Out of Uranus's severed genitals, Gaea creates the female Furies, who are responsible for assuring retributive justice in the world. Gaea is a prototype for other strong female Goddesses goddesses in the Greek pantheon (such as Rhea, Demeter, and Athena) who manipulate their destiny through intricate plotting, enlisting the help of their children, withholding fertility, or giving birth.

Humanity is fashioned by a divine artisan, Hephaestus, or the mediator Prometheus (according to Hesiod). There is a separate account of the origin of a woman. When Prometheus steals fire for the human race, Zeus punishes humanity by creating an evil called woman. The first woman, the mother of all women, is both beautiful and evil and receives the name Pandora. She is the very goddess who, according to the patriarchal rendering of Hesiod, by opening her box releases all woes that afflict humankind.

BABYLONIAN

The Babylonian myth of Enuma Elish (1100 BCE) depicts the primal force as water, which that from the beginning takes on male and female characteristics. That is, there is a commingling between the male Apsu, the primordial freshwater ocean, and Tiamat, the female saltwater. Out of this pairing emerge several generations of gods. The Strife ensues, in which newer generations of male gods revolt against the original pair. Younger gods kill Apsu, which, in turn, results in the an all-out battle between Tiamat and the rest of the gods. The gods finally conquer Tiamat and create the world out of her dismembered body. The gruesome detail of the cutting of Tiamat's body communicates the pleasure over the conquest of the goddess. The story suggests that the primordial female goddess not only introduced chaos into the universe but also received a deserved punishment.

The vanquished body of Tiamat gives rise to the new hierarchy, i.e., that of heaven over earth, male power over female power. The female passion (or chaos) is subdued by the male rational order.

JUDAISM AND CHRISTIANITY

Hebrew and Christian tradition derive their creation story from the book of Genesis, where God is described as creating the universe out of nothing by the power of divine words. There are two creation stories describing the creation of the first human couple, Adam and Eve, in Genesis 1:1–2:3 and Genesis 2:4–3:24. The first account (c. sixth century BCE) stresses the equality of both the sexes as it speaks of both as being created in the image of God. In the second narrative (c. tenth century BCE), Eve is created out of Adam's rib and is the one who leads Adam to disobey the divine commandment. Traditionally this second story was understood as a sign of women's subordination to men because Eve was created after Adam, from Adam, and for Adam. Furthermore, her disobedience was taken as evidence of her vicious nature, which brings evil into the world. Eve and all women were thus seen as the weaker, inferior sex. Contemporary scholars either reject completely the second story as intrinsically patriarchal or reinterpret the myth. New interpretations point to the fact that creation from Adam symbolizes the mutual need for companionship while the eating of the fruit by Adam and Eve pictures the joint disobedience of the first couple. Eve's initiative to consume the fruit could also be interpreted in a positive light as an expression of her more independent nature.

Jewish apocryphal tradition relates a story about another first woman, Lilith, who according to rabbinic tradition was a night demon who seduced men and killed children. Jewish feminists agree with the tradition that Lilith asserted equality with Adam, but reject the demonic portrayal. Instead, they suggest that such a negative rendition of Lilith reflects a patriarchal fear of a strong female presence.

ISLAM

In Islam, as in Judaism and Christianity, God creates the universe out of nothing in six days. Adam and Eve—the first human beings—appear in the Muslim scenario as well, but there are significant differences between the Muslim and the Hebrew accounts. Overall, the Muslim creation story of the first couple affirms the equality of Adam and Eve. According to the Qur'an, Adam and Eve are created from one genderless source (*nafs*); they have one point of origin that comes from one living entity. In contrast to Genesis, Eve is not formed out of Adam, but both Eve and Adam are formed from a previously existing, genderless being. After creation out of *nafs*, Adam and Eve are irrevocably linked to each other in providing comfort, companionship, and support. Satan tempts both Adam and Eve, and both disobey by eating from the tree. The Qur'an leaves no possibility to infer that Eve is a secondary and inferior form of creation, nor that she is more responsible for the Fall fall of humanity. Eve is not singled out as the initiator or temptress of evil, and instead Adam and Eve share the same culpability for their deeds.

SEE ALSO *Adam and Eve.*

BIBLIOGRAPHY

Adams Leeming, David, and Margaret Adams Leeming. 1995. *A Dictionary of Creation Myths*. New York: Oxford University Press.

Bonnefoy, Yves, and Wendy Doniger, eds. 1991. *Mythologies*. Chicago: University of Chicago Press.

Choksy, Jamsheed K. 2002. *Evil, Good, and Gender: Facets of the Feminine in Zoroastrian Religious History*. New York: Peter Lang .

Gross, Rita M. 2000. *Soaring and Settling: Buddhist Perspectives on Contemporary Social and Religious Issues*. New York: Continuum.

Hiltebeitel, Alf, and Kathleen M. Erndl, eds. 2000. *Is the Goddess a Feminist? The Politics of South Asian Goddesses*. New York: New York University Press.

Holm, Jean, and John Bowker, eds. 1994. *Women in Religion*. London: Pinter Publishers.

Malinowski, Bronislaw. 1962. *Sex, Culture, and Myth*. New York: Harcourt, Brace and World.

Plaskow, Judith, and Carol P. Christ. 1989. *Weaving the Visions: New Patterns in Feminist Spirituality*. San Francisco: Harper and Row.

Sharma, Arvind, ed. 1994. *Religion and Women*. Albany: State University of New York Press.

Wadud, Amina. 1999. *Qur'an and Woman: Rereading the Sacred Text from a Woman's Perspective*. 2nd edition. New York: Oxford University Press.

Wioleta Polinska

CRIME

SEE *Sex Crimes.*

CROSS-DRESSING

SEE *Transvestism.*

CRUISING

Cruising refers to the act—and the art—of soliciting a type of sexual activity that is anonymous, impersonal, and often promiscuous. Commonly associated with gay male sexual cultures, cruising references the search for public sex in bars, bathhouses, backrooms, clubs, discos, gyms, beaches, parks, dumpsters, public restrooms (tearooms in the United States or, in the United Kingdom, cottage houses), highway rest stops, piers, churches, and, most recently, on the Internet. When one individual cruises another individual to *get off* or to *hook-up*, such interactions are usually prompted by exchanges that involve mutual and sometimes silent recognition of the search for sexual gratification—a smile, a nod, a hand gesture towards the crotch, a light from a cigarette—that may or may not result in sexual contact. Cruising thus references the activities that occur prior to sexual contact between two or more individuals.

While cruising is considered to be an act that occurs between anonymous persons, it has also been integral to the formation of gay male sexual cultures. Historians and cultural critics of sexual history have shown that the visual, verbal, and non-verbal codes constituting cruising have been central components to the development of urban gay male subcultures since at least the late nineteenth century. Through their cruising, early twentieth-century gay men transformed public spaces such as the Young Men's Christian Association (YMCA), the bathhouse, the cafeteria, and the street into erotic zones that permitted the mutual recognition and enactment of same-sex desire. Later generations of gay men—particularly those in the late 1960s and early to mid-1970s—would make cruising an integral aspect of modern urban gay life, so much so that it has stereotypically come to define gay male sexual activity in the decades prior to the acquired immune deficiency syndrome (AIDS) crisis. Though often impersonal, cruising facilitates the development of a collective gay male group identity. Numerous self-identified gay male authors such as Samuel R. Delany, David Wojnarowicz, Edmund White, and Michel Foucault have commented on the communitarian possibilities latent within this anonymous act.

While it enables the mutual recognition of gay desire, cruising is not entirely the domain of gay men. Even though cruising permits gay men a space of identity recognition, it is not always reliant on the recognition of a shared sexual identity. Historian George Chauncey argued that gay men would frequently cruise *trade*—men who did not self-identify as gay—in public parks in the 1920s and 1930s. And as sociologist Laud Humphreys demonstrated in his influential sociological evaluations of public restrooms in the United States, cruising in the 1960s was an act by which many men who did not self-identity as gay often participated in their search for sexual gratification. Moreover cruising can also occur between opposite-sex individuals, as well as women who self-identify as lesbians. Indeed many erotic encounters that do not have monogamous coupling as their end results could be considered versions of cruising.

Precisely because cruising has been associated with anonymous, impersonal public sex, it has also been a point of controversy both inside and outside the gay community. Critiques of cruising as an erotic practice that promotes promiscuity appear in the documents of homophile organizations such as the Mattachine Society as well as those of radical gay organizations such as Gay Liberation, have been voiced during the numerous local and national sex panics that emerged as a result of the ongoing AIDS crisis, are subtext in films such as William Friedkin's homophobic *Cruising* (1970), and are even raised in debates over gay marriage in the United States and elsewhere. Such critiques are commonly accompanied by an increased policing of public spaces where cruising occurs as well as attempts to close bars and clubs that permit individuals to cruise each other.

While cruising in public spaces such as bars, piers, and parks has come under fire in the early twenty-first century, a renaissance of cruising has occurred on the Internet. Places available for anonymous, impersonal sexual exchange are cataloged on websites, some according to town, city, state, as well as university. Other sites permit individuals to post data about themselves for a possible hook-up. Likewise chat rooms on the Internet facilitate sexual contacts between individuals or groups. These mediated social spaces adopt functions similar to those of public spaces in the early-twentieth century, suggesting that cruising will remain central to late modern erotic life.

SEE ALSO *Frottage.*

BIBLIOGRAPHY

Chauncey, George. 1995. *Gay New York: Gender, Urban Culture, and the Making of the Gay Male World.* New York: Basic Books.

Humphreys, Laud. 1970. *Tearoom Trade: Impersonal Sex in Public Spaces.* Chicago: Aldine Publishing.

Scott Herring

CUNNILINGUS

SEE *Oral Sex; Sexual Practices.*

CUPID

SEE *Eros, Cupid.*